THE

100 BEST

STOCKS

YOU CAN BUY

2002

John Slatter

Adams Media Corporation
Avon, Massachusetts

Dedication

In the past, I have dedicated my books to my wife and other family members. This time, I would like to depart from that pattern and honor two veteran stock brokers who have given me a great deal of help in writing this book—and both have done it with alacrity. If you need a good broker, one who knows what he's talking about and will give you the ultimate in service, call Bob Link in Cincinnati or George Morris in Cleveland.

George Morris, First Union Securities (800) 537-4105
Bob Link, Prudential Securities (800) 635-5191

Acknowledgments

Writing a book is far easier than finding a publisher. My first book, *Safe Investing*, didn't find a home until I latched on to my dutiful agent, Edythea Ginis Selman. Edy knows how to find a publisher, and she knows how to convince the editor that I am worth paying a living wage.

My publisher, Adams Media, has treated me like a king. That could be because the editor is Claire Gerus, an easy person to do business with.

Published by
Adams Media Corporation
57 Littlefield Street, Avon, MA 02322
www.adamsmedia.com

ISBN: 1-58062-536-3

Printed in Canada.

J I H G F E D C B

This book is not designed or intended to provide or replace professional investment advice. Readers should invest with care, including seeking specific professional advice, since investments by nature involve significant risk and can result in financial losses. The past performance of the investments reported in this book does not guarantee or predict future performance.

Cover design by Mike Stromberg.

This book is available at quantity discounts for bulk purchases.
For information, call 1-800-872-5627

Visit our exciting small business website: www.businesstown.com

Table of Contents

Part I
The Art and Science of Investing in Stocks

Part II
100 Best Stocks You Can Buy

Part I
The Art and Science of Investing in Stocks

When to Buy, When to Sell

One question I am often asked is: When should you sell? It's not an easy question to answer. However, I believe that I have come up with an answer that works 80 percent of the time. It could have a major impact on your investment strategy. I realize that's a rather dramatic statement, but I am sure you will agree when you finish reading this chapter.

What it amounts to is very simple: Own stocks during the six cold months. Avoid stocks during the six balmy months. Go fishing and enjoy yourself. I came across the idea when I read an article by Mark Hulbert, editor of *The Hulbert Financial Digest*. He is also a freelance writer whose column—one that I never fail to read—appears every other Sunday in *The New York Times*.

The idea was originally created by Sven Bouman, a portfolio manager at Aegon, an insurer based in the Netherlands, and Ben Jacobsen, an associate professor of finance at Erasmus University Rotterdam. These two researchers found that the pattern existed between 1970 and 1998 in thirty-six of thirty-seven developed and emerging markets countries. In the British stock market, moreover, the strategy worked all the way back to 1694. No, that's not a typographical error.

According to Mark Hulbert, the reason this idea works is because "investors tend to reduce their equity holdings before their summer vacations, which in turn lowers the stock market's returns."

Looking around the world, the following list outlines how investors have fared in the six cold months (between January 1970 through August of 1998), versus the six warm months. For instance, in Hong Kong, stocks advanced 11.0 percent during the cold months, compared with 5.9 percent in warm months. In other countries, the pattern was similar:

Denmark: 7.6 vs. 5.6
The United States: 8.5 vs. 3.0
Canada: 8.4 vs. 1.6
The United Kingdom: 13.1 vs. 0.9
Spain: 12.0 vs. 0.7
Germany: 8.8 vs. 0.5
Japan: 8.8 vs. -0.3
France: 13.1 vs. -0.8
Italy: 13.6 vs. -2.6

In order to satisfy my own curiosity, I decided to do some research of my own. I first tackled the Dow Jones Industrial Average, wondering whether it tended to perform better in the November-though-April period than through the May-through-October stretch. In order to make my study, I went to Wall Street

City (*www.wallstreetcity.com*). It's a great site for doing historical research on thousands of stocks, as well as several indexes, such as the Dow Jones Industrial or the S&P 500. Unfortunately, I was unable to go back beyond late 1988. Even so, I was satisfied with my results, since it confirmed the studies of Bouman and Jacobsen.

The first period I checked was from October 31, 1988 to April 30, 1989. In that cool six-month period, the Dow 30 advanced from 2148.65 to 2418.80, a gain of 12.57 percent. However, in the next six warm months, the Dow advanced to 2603.48, a gain of only 7.64 percent, thus lending credence to the strategy. Similarly, this is how it worked in the years that followed:

Performance Oct. 31, 1988 to April 30, 2001

	Winter (10-31 to 4-30)	Summer (4-30 to 10-31)
1988–89	+12.57%	+7.64%
1989–90	-3.50	-8.07
1990–9	+18.24	+6.28
1991–92	+9.45	-3.95
1992–93	+6.24	+7.38
1993–94	+0.03	+6.15
1994–95	+10.57	+10.05
1995–96	+17.11	+8.27
1996–97	+16.25	+6.18
1997–98	+21.79	-5.20
1998–99	+25.57	-0.55
1999–20	+0.04	+2.21
2000–01	-2.15	—
Averages	+10.17%	+3.03%

To summarize the table, the average performance of the Dow Jones 30 in the winter periods was a plus 10.17 percent, compared with only 3.03 percent during the summer periods.

At this point in my research, I was beginning to become a believer. Even so, I was not content to stop there. Next, I looked at the Standard & Poor's 500 to see if the same thing was happening there. Here's what it looked like.

Performance Oct. 31, 1988 to April 30, 2001

	Winter (10-31 to 4-30)	Summer (4-30 to 10-31)
1988–89	+10.79%	+9.94%
1989–90	-2.81	-8.10
1990–91	+23.47	+4.56
1991–92	+5.73	+0.90
1992–93	+5.14	+6.28
1993–94	-3.62	+4.75
1994–95	+8.97	+13.32
1995–96	+12.50	+7.81
1996–97	+13.62	+14.14
1997–98	+21.56	1.18
1998–99	+21.53	+2.08
1999–2000	+6.57	-1.59
2000–2001	-12.34	—
Averages	+8.55%	+4.41%

At this point, I was convinced that Mark Hulbert was indeed onto something. But I was still not sure how I could use this information. After all, investors usually buy individual stocks, not indexes. I wondered whether it would work on the thirty stocks that make up the Dow Jones Industrial Average. To find out, I went back to the Internet to obtain the help of Wall Street City. The first stock I printed out was General Electric. My printout included the monthly closing prices on the stock from October 31, 1988 to April 30, 2001.

General Electric
Performance Oct. 31, 1988 to April 30, 2001

	Winter (10-31 to 4-30)	Summer (4-30 to 10-31)
1988–89	+12.06%	+13.26%
1989–90	+15.61	-18.74
1990–91	+36.01	-2.44
1991–92	+11.06	+0.14
1992–93	+18.11	+7.03
1993–94	-1.82	+2.61
1994–95	+14.59	+12.96
1995–96	+22.15	+25.24
1996–97	+14.74	+16.45
1997–98	+31.81	+2.72
1998–99	+20.44	+28.59
1999–2000	+16.05	+4.58
2000–2001	-8.20	—
Averages	+15.59%	+7.70%

Once again, the strategy had worked. However, GE, after all, is a super growth stock. How about one like International Paper that is a cyclical stock, with plenty of ups and downs, rather than steady growth.

International Paper
Performance Oct. 31, 1988 to April 30, 2001

	Winter (10-31 to 4-30)	Summer (4-30 to 10-31)
1988–89	+7.37%	+1.27%
1989–90	-0.25	-6.30
1990–91	+35.21	+20.88
1991–92	-1.97	-13.09
1992–93	+1.54	-9.51
1993–94	+9.66	+14.18
1994–95	+3.36	-3.90
1995–96	+7.77	+6.90
1996–97	-0.88	+6.51
1997–98	+15.97	-11.02
1998–99	+14.81	-1.29
1999–2000	-30.17	-0.95
2000–200	+ 6.32	—
Averages	+5.29%	+0.32%

As you might expect, International Paper is not a get-rich type of stock. Even so, it performs better in winter than in the warmer months. Without going through each of the thirty Dow stocks individually, here is a table that summarizes the results of each stock.

All 30 Dow Stocks
Performance Oct. 31, 1988 to April 30, 2001

	Winter (10-31 to 4-30)	Summer (4-30 to 10-31)
Alcoa	+16.11%	+0.75%
American Express	+14.47	+4.80
AT&T	+5.64	+2.50
Boeing	+7.84	+7.10
Caterpilla	+6.42	-2.62
Citigroup	+21.41	+4.53
Coca-Cola	+8.66	+12.19
DuPont	+10.96	+1.05
Disney, Walt	+20.01	-1.80
Eastman Kodak	+1.62	+1.59
ExxonMobil	+8.25	+3.60
General Electric	+15.59	+7.70
General Motors	+16.29	-8.98
Home Depot	+20.14	+15.67
Honeywell	+14.69	+0.81
Hewlett-Packard	+28.07	-6.91
IBM	+10.70	+2.93
Intel	+25.09	+12.69
International Paper	+5.29	+0.32
JP Morgan Chase	+16.68	+3.15
Johnson & J.	+9.95	+10.18
McDonald's	+14.32	-0.14
Merck	+7.21	+12.77
Microsoft	+25.13	+19.15
Minnesota Mining	+8.71	+3.12
Philip Morris	+6.00	+15.40
Procter & Gamble	+4.86	+12.50
SBC Communications	+3.05	+10.55
United Technologies	16.68	+1.90
Wal-Mart	+14.58	+9.45
Averages	+13.15%	+5.20%

Of course, no mechanical approach to investing is a sure thing. In this instance, six stocks failed to conform to the strategy: Coca-Cola, Johnson & Johnson, Merck, Philip Morris, Procter & Gamble, and SBC Communications. *Even so, 80 percent of the thirty blue chip Dow stocks performed better in cold weather than during warm weather.* That's an amazing statistic.

If you are still a skeptic, you might wonder if this strategy works with Dow Jones stocks only. How about the stocks in this book? I checked it out by examining the first thirty stocks in *The 100 Best Stocks You Can Buy 2001.* The same pattern persisted, although the number that performed better in the winter than in the summer was only 73.3 percent, not 80 percent. The average performance during these chilly months was 10.89 percent, or well ahead of the 6.56 percent in the sunny months.

A More Random List

Still not satisfied that I had stumbled on to something worthwhile, I made a final test by selecting thirty stocks from those designated as part of the Standard & Poor's 500. It is not a random list as defined by statisticians, however. I simply opened the S&P Stock Guide at a random place, in this instance at the letter E. I worked my way through the book by picking all stocks that were not public utilities and had a history back to October 31, 1988. The reason I skipped regulated companies is because my study shows they do not conform to this pattern. They usually perform better during the summer than during the winter. The same holds true for most health care stocks, but there were none in my list of thirty.

In any event, my results matched almost perfectly with the thirty Dow stocks and the stocks from my book. An impressive 80 percent performed better during the cold months than during the warm ones. The average performance during cold periods was a plus 13.31 percent, compared with only 5.69 percent during warm periods. In the table below are the thirty stocks. I have used an asterisk to denote which group performed better.

30 S&P Stocks
Performance Oct. 31, 1988 to April 30, 2001

	Winter (10-31 to 4-30)	Summer (4-30 to 10-31)
Dow Jones & Co.	+9.12*%	-3.08%
Dow Chemical	+10.13*	-6.27
Dover	+11.57*	+4.09
Donnelley, R. R.	+7.46*	-1.75
Dollar General	+18.91*	+9.50
Equifax	+7.76	+8.39*
Engelhard	+13.34*	+2.04
Emerson Electric	+7.81*	+5.36
EMC	+33.07*	+32.53
Electronic Data	+16.24*	+1.23
Ecolab	+11.21*	+5.40
Eaton	+16.34*	-5.65
Fifth Third Bank	+10.37	+14.65*
FedEx	+13.90*	+2.43
Federal Nat'l Mort.	+12.15	+17.08*
First Union	+9.81*	+1.92
Fiserv	+18.41*	+10.98
First Boston	+19.78*	-3.03
FMC	+7.20*	+3.72

	Winter (10-31 to 4-30)	Summer (4-30 to 10-31)
Ford Motor	+17.80*	-4.45
Forest Labs	+16.86*	+14.13
Franklin Resources	+13.38	+14.13*
Gannett	+12.61*	-0.40
GAP	+26.86*	+8.91
General Dynamics	+8.62	+15.34*
General Mills	+2.18	+9.73*
Genuine Parts	+8.10*	-3.62
Georgia Pacific	+16.30*	-4.82
Gillette	+9.37*	+8.41
Golden West	+12.50*	+12.25
Averages	+13.31%	+5.69%

Conclusion and Summary

With this evidence in mind, how can it be employed to improve your portfolio's performance? If you are a conservative investor and want to reduce your risk, it might be a good idea to sell some of your stocks at the end of April each year and leave the proceeds in a money-market fund.

You might also consider buying new stocks at the end of October, not during the summer. If you have stocks that you want to dump, wait until the end of April. Keep them during the more favorable winter months before you cast them aside. The ones to hold onto are utilities and medical stocks, since they uniformly do fine during the warm months.

If you have most of your stocks in an IRA or some other tax-deferred account, you might want to sell everything at the end of April, leaving the proceeds in a money-market account to earn 5 percent interest. After all, the Dow stocks in this study had an average return in a typical cold-weather period of 13.15 percent. Add in another 2.5 percent and you have a total annual return of 15.65 percent. What's wrong with that—particularly when you consider the vastly reduced risk?

Why Invest in Stocks?

Investing is a complex business. But, then, so is medicine, engineering, chemistry, geology, law, philosophy, photography, history, accounting—you name it. In fact, investing is so intimidating that many intelligent individuals avoid it. Instead, they stash their money in certificates of deposit (CDs), annuities, bonds, or mutual funds. Apparently they can't face buying common stocks. This is too bad, because that's precisely where the money is made. You don't make money every day, every week, or even every year. But over the long term, you will make the most out of your investment dollars.

Look at the Facts

One persuasive study contends that common stocks will make money for you in most years. This study, done by the brokerage firm Smith Barney, looked at the thirty-five one-year periods between 1960 and 1995.

The study computed total return, which adds capital gains and dividends. Over that span, stocks (as represented by the Standard & Poor's 500 index) performed unsatisfactorily in only eight of those thirty-five years. In other words, you would have been better off in money-market funds during those eight years. Common stocks would have been more successful in twenty-seven of those thirty-five years.

Investing for the Long Term

Investing, however, is not a one-year endeavor. Most investors start their programs in their forties and fifties, which means they could be investing over a twenty-, thirty-, or forty-year period.

If we look at the relative returns of different investments over five-year periods—rather than one-year periods—the results are even more encouraging. During the years from 1960 through 1994, there were thirty-one such periods. In only two of those five-year periods did the total return of the Standard & Poor's-based portfolio become negative.

Let's move ahead to all ten-year holding periods. There were twenty-six in that span. Exactly 100 percent worked out profitably. Equally important, the returns to the investor were impressive in all of these one-, five-, and ten-year periods. The one-year periods, for instance, gave you an average annual total return of 11.1 percent; for five-year periods, it was 10.5 percent, and for ten-year periods, it was 10.2 percent.

Based on this study, we can say with confidence that over a lifetime of investing, an investor will reap a total annual return of 10 percent or more. If you compare this with the amount you could earn by owning CDs, annuities, government bonds, or any other conservative investment, the difference is considerable.

Some Profitable Comparisons

Let's see how that difference adds up. Suppose you invested $25,000 in a list of common stocks at the age of forty, and your portfolio built up at a 10 percent compound annual rate. By the time you reached sixty-five, your common stock nest egg would be worth $270,868.

Now, let's say you had invested your money in government bonds, yielding 6 percent. The same $25,000 would be worth only $107,297, which is a difference of $163,571. Neither of these calculations has accounted for income taxes or brokerage commissions.

Now, let's look at the timid soul who invested $25,000 in CDs at age forty and averaged a return of 4 percent. By age sixty-five, that investment would be worth a paltry $66,646.

Why Doesn't Everyone Buy Common Stocks?

That's a good question, and I'm not sure I can provide you with a satisfactory answer. Part of the reason may be ignorance. Not everyone is willing to investigate the field of common stocks. These noninvestors may be too preoccupied with their jobs, sports, reading, gardening, travel, or whatever. Then there are those who are heavily influenced by family members who have told them that stocks are too speculative and better left to millionaires. (Of course, that's how many of these millionaires became millionaires.)

Even if you are convinced that I may be right about the potential of stocks, you are probably wondering how anyone can possibly figure out which stocks to buy, since there are tens of thousands to choose from. That, in essence, is the purpose of this book.

A Real-Life Example

If you are a newcomer to investing, you may still doubt that you are capable of building a portfolio of stocks that will make you rich. Not all stocks are going to live up to their early promise, no matter how much time you devote to making a selection. On the other hand, even if you pick your stocks blindfolded, you will have some winners. Let's suppose that you want to invest $100,000 in 20 stocks, or $5,000 in each. Some will work out and some won't.

Hypothetically, it does not seem unreasonable to project that 10 of these stocks will just plug along, making you neither rich nor poor. Suppose we assume that these 10 stocks will appreciate (rise in value) an average of only 7 percent per year over the next 10 or 20 years. Toss in a 2 percent annual dividend and the total return adds up to 9 percent per year. That is not exactly

riches, since stocks over the last 75 years have averaged about 11 percent.

At any rate, here is what your $50,000 will be worth at the end of 10 years and 20 years:

$118,368 $280,221

Next, let's look at the three stocks that performed above your wildest dreams. They appreciated an average of 15 percent per year. Add in a modest annual dividend of only 1 percent, and you have a total return of 16 percent.

Assuming you invest $5,000 in each of these three stocks, here is how that $15,000 climbs over the next 10- and 20-year periods:

$66,172 $291,911

So far, so good. Now, for the bad news. Two of your stocks hit the skids and never recovered. Total results for the $10,000 invested in these losers is: zero.

$00,000 $00,000

Finally, five of your 20 stocks do about average. They appreciate an average of 9 percent per year and have an average yearly dividend of 2 percent. That's a total return of 11 percent. Since you have five stocks in this category, your total investment is $25,000. Here is what you end up with 10 and 20 years from now:

$70,986 $201,558

If we add up these various results, the final figures make you look reasonably rich:

$255,525 $773,690

By contrast, had you acted in a cowardly manner and invested exclusively in CDs, you would have only the following at the end of the two periods:

$162,889 $265,330

One final note. If you figure in taxes, you look even better, since the capital gains (on your stocks) are taxed at a much lower rate than ordinary income (which applies to CDs). And, you wouldn't even have to worry about capital gains on your stocks if you elected not to sell them.

For Busy Investors, a Strategy That Rarely Fails

As far as I know, I'm one of the few writers who gives readers the opportunity to call if they have any questions. That's why my telephone number is on the page opposite the inside back cover of this book. When you consider the tens of thousands of investors who read my books, very few actually call. And when they do, they are startled and surprised that I usually answer the phone myself—no secretary to screen out malcontents, deadbeats, and cranks.

One of the readers who called a few weeks ago was Horst Graben, a CPA from Wyoming.

"I liked your book, Mr. Slatter, and I read every word. In fact, I actually read it twice, since there are a lot of succulent morsels to digest."

"In other words," I said, "You are *not* calling to complain."

"Well, yes and no," he said. "With 100 stocks to pick from, I am having trouble deciding which ones to buy—and when to sell them if they falter."

I thought for a moment and then said, "Most investors find buying a lot easier than selling. Too often, they let a stock sag down week after week, and suddenly they realize it's down 40 percent, and they grit their teeth, hoping it will start back up again. Usually, it doesn't."

"So what should I do?" Horst Graben asked.

"If you are going to manage your own portfolio, you have to be prepared to keep track of your stocks. That means you have to read quarterly and annual reports. It also means reading such publications as the *Wall Street Journal*, the *New York Times*, *Forbes*, *Barron's*, *Business Week*, *Fortune*, and *Better Investing*."

"I was afraid you would say that," he said. "The only problem I have is time. I'm particularly busy during tax season; I work seven days a week. And even during the rest of the year I have journals to read and other business commitments. As you might have guessed, I'm a CPA with a busy practice. Reading all that investment stuff is out of the question."

"I can understand your plight, Mr. Graben. Most successful people are busy. That's why they're successful. They spend fifty or sixty hours a week making sure they stay successful."

"Are you telling me to forget about stocks and put my money in mutual funds or certificates of deposit?"

"Absolutely not," I assured him. "I have a systematic approach to stock selection that is made to order for people like you. However, I am reluctant to divulge this strategy unless you promise not to tell a soul about it—not even your wife. Are you prepared to do this?"

"Well, let me think. If you tell me how I can manage my investments without having to do a lot of research and study, you are insisting that I keep the strategy a secret. No one is to know. Okay, I agree."

"Now that I know I can trust you, here goes," I said. "It involves investing exclusively in the thirty stocks that make up the Dow Jones Industrial Average." Then I read him the current components of the index, including their ticker symbols:

Alcoa (AA)
American Express (AXP)
AT&T (T)
Boeing (BA)

Caterpillar (CAT)
Citigroup (C)
Coca-Cola (KO)
Disney, Walt (DIS)
DuPont (DD)
Eastman Kodak (EK)
ExxonMobil (XOM)
General Motors (GM)
General Electric (GE)
Hewlett- Packard (HWP)
Home Depot (HD)
Honeywell (HON)
Intel (INTC)
International Business Machines (IBM)
International Paper (IP)
Johnson & Johnson (JNJ)
McDonald's (MCD)
Merck (MRK)
Microsoft (MSFT)
Minnesota Mining (MMM)
Morgan, J. P. (JPM)
Philip Morris (MO)
Procter & Gamble (PG)
SBC Communications (SBC)
United Technologies (UTX)
Wal-Mart (WMT)

"That sounds like a great list," he said. "In other words, I concentrate on these thirty stocks, instead of the 100 in your book. Is that what you are saying?"

"Right. These are some of the world's greatest blue-chip stocks. Not all of them will be winners, but enough of them will so you will end up a millionaire." Then, I went on to outline how to implement the Dow 30 strategy.

The reason the strategy rarely fails is because it entails investing exclusively in the thirty stocks that make up the Dow Jones Industrial Average. Most investors judge their results by this average. It follows that if you invest in all thirty stocks, your performance will approximate that of this well-known index.

Incidentally, if you forget the names of these thirty stocks, you can refresh your memory by consulting the *Wall Street Journal* any day of the week. Look in the third section (*Money and Investing*) on page 3.

Are You Ready to Be Mediocre?

Buying these thirty stocks may seem like a simplistic and cowardly approach to investing, since you are guaranteed that you will be merely average, or mediocre. And who wants to be mediocre? Most mutual funds would be delighted to be. Only a small percentage have been average in the past. The vast majority have been below average.

Nothing Is Perfect

To be sure, this method of managing a portfolio has some shortcomings:

• You will miss out on such growth stocks and high-flyers as Yahoo!, America OnLine, Harley-Davidson, Pfizer, Illinois Tool Works, Interpublic, Cisco Systems, Dell, and Lucent.

• You may end up owning a few lackluster performers such as Texaco, Eastman Kodak, Bethlehem Steel, Woolworth, and International Paper. Three of those stocks, incidentally, are no longer in the index: Texaco, Bethlehem Steel, and Woolworth. Nor are Chevron or Westinghouse (now CBS). They were replaced in 1997 by Hewlett-Packard, Johnson & Johnson, Wal-Mart, and Travelers (now Citigroup). This move markedly improved the quality of the Dow Jones Industrial Average—it added four super growth stocks to the index. In 1999, moreover, four new stocks were added: Microsoft, SBC Communications, Home Depot, and Intel, which improved the growth prospects of the index.

• You could achieve the same objective by investing in an index fund.

In Defense of My Strategy

In my view, the reasons why this strategy has merit can be summed up as follows:

On the face of it, investing seems incredibly complex because of the thousands of alternatives. In the realm of mutual funds, for instance, there are more than 10,000 to choose from. What's more, there is no strategy that leads you to the best ones. Nor are lists gleaned from financial magazines particularly helpful.

If you elect to invest in stocks, the field is even more crowded. Among the stocks listed on the New York Exchange are some 3,000 stocks. If you venture into the over-the-counter market (or Nasdaq), the choices are vast, at least 5,000. And we haven't even mentioned the immense field of foreign equities.

That's why it makes sense to find a simple—yet effective—way to invest in common stocks. The thirty stocks in the Dow Jones Average give you a playing field that is not nearly as overwhelming or complex as the above alternatives. And these companies are well-managed and unlikely to disappear. To be sure, they don't always thrive, but they have the size and financial strength to make a comeback. They can afford to cast aside inept CEOs and replace them with executives with proven track records.

Best of all, thirty stocks is a number that you can keep track of. They are not obscure and are well-covered by Wall Street analysts and the *Wall Street Journal*, as well as by such periodicals as *Barron's*, *Forbes*, and *Fortune*. If you concentrate your attention on these stocks, you can bypass the other 3,000 stocks. It makes sense that most investors can become familiar with these thirty stocks and be able to determine which ones are best, based on the ample information available from the media, brokerage houses, investment manuals, and annual reports.

An important reason to concentrate on these thirty companies relates to their size. Most of them are very large companies. If you like small companies, however, this list is not for you. On the other hand, I am not convinced that small companies are the way to go. At least one authority presents solid evidence that you are usually better off with large companies. Of course, there are years in which the reverse is true.

The authority I am citing is Kenneth L. Fisher, founder, chairman, and CEO of Fisher Investment, Inc. For the past fifteen years, he has been a regular contributor to *Forbes* magazine. In an article in one of my favorite publications, *Better Investing* (June 2000), Mr. Fisher says: "On average, small stocks beat big stocks by 1.18 percent annually from 1926 through 1999. But this is highly deceptive. That entire advantage disappears completely if you eliminate two very similar years, 1933 and 1944—the very first years of the twentieth century's two biggest bull markets. Otherwise, big and small cap have done exactly the same."

Mr. Fisher goes on to say, "Eliminate three multiyear runs at the start of the century's three biggest bull markets (1933–34, 1942–45, and 1975–76) and in the rest of history big cap beat small cap by 2.2 percent per year—quite opposite to popular belief."

Finally, he goes on to say, "Early in bull markets, small stocks do best. Other times and throughout bear markets, big stocks lead."

You'll be happy to learn that most of the thirty Dow stocks are discussed in the 2002 edition of *The 100 Best Stocks You Can Buy*.

Not every investor, of course, has sufficient funds to buy all thirty stocks. On the other hand, good diversification can be achieved by owning fifteen or twenty. In any event, there is no need to buy the entire portfolio on day one. If you set aside $5,000 a year and start at age forty, you can buy one stock each year. By the time you reach sixty-five, you will own twenty-five stocks. From then on, sit back and live off the dividends. In many instances, the dividends will increase every year, helping you keep pace with inflation.

The thirty stocks in the Dow are not always the same. In 1999, for instance, four new stocks were added and four were deleted. On average, about one stock is replaced each year. This is your cue to sell the stock that is tossed out, replacing it with new blood. Because of the low turnover, your taxes on capital gains are minimal, as are your brokerage charges.

Buying an index fund has become popular in recent years, as investors have observed that managed mutual funds don't often do as well. However, not everyone is satisfied to be average. If you invest in the thirty Dow stocks, you can use your ingenuity to pick the fifteen or twenty with the best prospects, casting aside the ones that don't impress you.

A $100,000 Package to Consider

If you want to play a more active part in selecting your stocks, here is an approach that might appeal to you. Let's say you have $100,000 to invest. Set aside $10,000 in a money market fund. Invest the rest as follows:

Pick out the ten stocks that you think are going to be big winners and invest $4,000 in each one, for a total of $40,000. Next, pick the ten that you think may also do better than average. Invest $3,000 in each, for a total of $30,000. Finally, invest $2,000 in the ten stocks that you think will be also-rans. That brings your overall total to $90,000 in stocks and $10,000 in cash.

This Strategy Saves You Money

Picking stocks can also save you money, as compared with mutual funds. The average fund charges 1.5 percent a year. By managing your own portfolio, you can avoid this expense ratio.

Many of the Dow stocks, incidentally, will permit you to buy stock directly from the company, thus sidestepping a commissionbroker. Once you own a few shares of such stocks as Exxon Mobil or Procter & Gamble, you can purchase more by merely mailing in $500 or $1,000, which will be invested without a commission.

The DRIP (dividend reinvestment plan) has some shortcomings. For one thing, you can never be sure what price you will pay, since your check may not be invested for a week or more after you mail it in. The same is true when you decide to cash in some shares.

Even more troublesome are the tax consequences when you sell your shares. To calculate your cost basis, you have to tabulate the price paid with each dividend and for each payment mailed in. If you haven't kept meticulous records, the chore might be daunting, to say the least.

In a Nutshell

When I finished explaining my Dow 30 idea to Horst Graben, he said, "It sounds like an interesting idea. Let me try to summarize what you have said. As I see it, the idea of buying these thirty stocks is to make it easier for me to keep track of the stocks I plan to buy.

"It also assures me that I will be investing in many of the nation's leading companies, such as GE, ExxonMobil, Merck, Procter & Gamble, and IBM. In other words, no speculating. Since I am busy taking care of clients, it gives me more time to devote to their welfare, and thus makes them happy with my services. Anything else?"

"I think you have the picture, Horst. And don't forget the tax implications. Since the stocks in the Dow stay pretty much the same year after year, you probably won't have to sell more than one or two stocks a year—and they're usually ones that haven't done well, so the tax bite won't be onerous.

"One final word. Remember your solemn promise not to mention this ingenious scheme to anyone!"

"You have my word as a CPA."

Nine Mistakes That Investors Make

Every time I take my spiffy chariot in for a grease job or repairs I have to sit in the waiting room watching a TV program that someone else likes and I don't. For that reason, I always take along a good book. The trouble is that the cacophony on the TV interferes with my concentration.

The last time I found myself suffering in the waiting room I came up with the answer: talk to one of the other customers who are also enduring the mindless drivel. Of course, I wouldn't want my wife to find out who I was talking with, so please don't let her find out about Valira del Nord.

The reason that Mrs. del Nord (a tall, middle-aged, and well-dressed woman) was willing to break the ice was because I had displayed prominently on the floor next to my chair a copy of my latest book, *The 100 Best Stocks You Can Buy*. I never venture out of the office without a copy because you never know who might bite and buy one.

She spotted the title and said, "I see you like reading about the stock market. My husband and I used to invest, but lately we are a bit fed up with what's been happening. We're ready to switch back to certificates of deposit—I think they're called CDs."

"That's a shame," I said. "I always tell my clients that common stocks are the best place to put your money—not CDs."

"Your clients?"

"Yes, I manage people's accounts when I'm not writing books on the stock market."

"Apparently you get your ideas from books like the one by your chair. Isn't that plagiarism?"

"You're right. If you steal something from another author, you can get in trouble. But this book happens to be one I wrote, so there should be no problem."

"Wow!" she said. "Maybe I should buy an autographed copy of your book, and then I'll find out what we're doing wrong? My name is Valira del Nord. I assume you're John Slater."

"Not exactly, it's Slatter, but I'll forgive you if you buy a copy of the book—no checks please! As far as what you're doing wrong, my latest book doesn't go into that in any great detail, but I do have some ideas on the subject. If you have the time, I'll give you the latest scoop."

"I think I have the time," said Mrs. del Nord. "It seems to take an eternity to get something done here. I really dread having to get the car fixed, but my husband says it's my job. He's too busy. Maybe I should buy the book for him and make him do the waiting the next time."

"Assuming I get around to writing a new chapter," I said. "I think I'll call it "The Ten Big Blunders That Investors Make." How does that sound?"

"That might be a bit strong, but I think you're on the right track. What's blunder number one?"

"*Failure to diversify*. Nearly everyone gets fixated on one or two sectors of the market, such as banks, utilities, oil stocks, or technology. There are over seventy different industries to choose from—at least according to Value Line, but no one seems to care."

"Maybe that's what happened to us, Mr. Slattery. We had about a dozen technology stocks, plus three or four mutual funds. We made it big in 1999, but 2000 was a disaster."

I thought of telling her that my name was not Slattery, but I decided it probably didn't matter. After all, some people really go off the deep end and call me Snyder or Slaughter. Whatever. As long as they buy the book, I'm happy.

"When I worked for a brokerage house in Cleveland," I said, "one of my duties was to analyze portfolios for the firm's customers, those who had assets of $100,000 or more. In nearly all instances, these people thought they were well diversified, since they often owned twenty or more stocks. However, those twenty stocks typically included half a dozen utilities and a similar number of banks and oil companies. What's even worse, a few of those investors had nearly all their money tied up in one stock. Such inattention to diversification merely invites disaster."

"In other words," Mrs. del Nord said, "if something happens to one of those sectors, you can end up bleeding at the mouth."

"How aptly put," I said. "I like that. I think I'll put it in my next book."

"My husband and I have been bleeding at the mouth and have not been sure what to do about it. Do you have the answer?"

"Of course. That's why I write books, since investors expect that I know everything about everything. If they ever find out the truth, book sales will plummet. Meanwhile, let me outline the best way to achieve adequate diversification."

"I assume you will force me to buy a book if you give me all this free advice."

"I think 'force' is a bit strong— 'coerce' might be a better word. Well, here goes. For starters, I think twenty stocks is a good number to shoot for. Some experts would disagree. Their thinking is that you dilute your results by owning that many stocks. They say you should work like a beaver to find five or ten great stocks and put all your money in them. By contrast, if you own twenty stocks, the second ten will be much less attractive and will pull down your results."

"I can see that you don't agree."

"Exactly. I agree, however, that you should make a concerted effort to pick good stocks by doing your homework— reading such publications as *Value Line*, the *Wall Street Journal*, *BusinessWeek*, *Fortune* magazine, *Better Investing*, company annual reports, and Standard & Poor's tear sheets."

"That sounds like a lot of work. There must be an easier way."

"If you were going to buy a home, would you make an effort to look at couple dozen before you settled on the right one?"

"I see what you mean. If we want to be millionaires, we have to pay the price. It makes me tired to think about it."

"Maybe the service manager will pop out of his hole and announce that your car is ready. Then, you won't have to listen to me any more."

"Good thought, but he's not due for at least an hour. Listening to you is at least better than watching the idiot box."

"Now that we have covered diversification, let's move on," I said. "The next blunder that people make is *paying too much for a stock*."

"What's too much?" Mrs. del Nord asked.

"A good way to determine if a stock is overpriced is to calculate the P/E ratio. Technology stocks are a good example. Many of them are growing at a fast clip, perhaps 20 or 30 percent a year. But the price tag may be 50, 75, or even 100 times earnings. That's fine as long as growth doesn't start to slow down—as it eventually does. Let's say that earnings per share have been climbing at 30 percent a year and suddenly fall to only 20 percent a year. Inevitably, the price of the stock will plunge. In 2000, any number of hot stocks fell precipitously."

"I think you just struck a raw nerve," said Valira del Nord.

"Most of our stocks that unraveled were those with a high P/E. By the way, exactly how do you calculate the P/E?"

"That's a good question. Unfortunately, there is no good answer. Most analysts divide the current price of the stock by the earnings per share (EPS) that they expect in the next twelve months. For instance, if the stock is trading at $89 and the estimated earnings per share are $2.75, you divide that into $89 and your P/E is 32.4, which is a bit on the high side. Many pharmaceutical stocks have multiples in that range."

"I thought you said there was no good way to calculate the P/E ratio," said Mrs. del Nord, with a quizzical look on her face.

"Exactly. My method of calculating the price-earnings multiple is to use the *actual* earnings—not the estimated earnings. According to academics who do research on such things, the estimates made by analysts are often very wide of the mark. What's even worse, they tend to be far too high—rarely are they too low."

"So you use actual earnings. Right?"

"I prefer to use earnings recorded for the most recent twelve months," I said. "They're readily available—either in the Standard & Poor's *Stock Guide* or in *Value Line*. Let's say that the company in the above example actually earned only $2.25, rather than $2.75. If you divide $2.25 into $89, you get a P/E ratio of 39.6—that's a lot higher than 32.4, the one calculated by the analyst."

"I'm still a bit confused," said Mrs. del Nord. "What is your upper limit on P/E?"

"In most instances you should compare the price-earning multiple to the market, such as the Dow Jones Average or the Standard & Poor's Average. If stocks are selling for twenty-two times earnings,

for instance, I might be willing to pay thirty, but I would balk at a P/E of 40, 50, or 75—no matter how fantastic the company might seem."

"Would you pardon me a minute, Mr. Slattery, while I go into the shop and see if they have started to work on my car?"

When she came back, I said, "From the look on your face, I can assume that the mechanic is still out to lunch. Maybe you had better get a cup of coffee and listen to the rest of my ten blunders. Here's number three."

She took my advice and started on her coffee. "Wow, this container is hot! I wish someone would come up with a plastic cup that didn't put you in the hospital. Sorry, Mr. Slaughter. Go ahead. I have plenty of time for lesson three. The service manager told me they don't have the part my car needs, so he has to put out an all-points bulletin to see if anyone in Vermont can rescue me."

"Maybe they can rescue me at the same time," I said. "Back to blunder number three: *Don't buy a stock with a high payout ratio.* In other words, examine what percentage of earnings per share are paid out in dividends. For instance, if the company earns $4 a share and pays out $3, that's too much. I would much prefer a company that paid out less than 50 percent—30 or 40 percent would be even better."

"I don't think that applies to us. Most of the tech stocks we own don't pay a dividend at all."

"I'm not sure that's the best answer either," I said. "Companies that don't pay a dividend are often very speculative. They can be extremely volatile. I think you have already found that out," I said.

"Don't remind me!"

"Next, let's look at blunder number four—*too much trading.* Many investors get impatient and sell their stock after a modest increase in price. When a stock goes from $30 to $45, they think it's time to take a profit—before it falls back to $30. They reason that you can't lose money by taking a profit."

"That makes sense to me," said Valira del Nord.

"I suppose it might work out in some instances, but it is usually a better strategy to let your profits run and cut short your losses. That way your big winners will be able to help you offset your small losers."

At that moment the service manager emerged and accosted Mrs. del Nord. "Sorry for the long delay, but your car is ready."

"It looks like you won't be able to find out about the other blunders," I said. "Maybe you better buy my book so that you can hone your skills in picking stocks."

"But you said you wouldn't take a check," she said, picking up her purse and heading for the cashier's window.

"I've just changed my policy," I blurted out. "After all, what are friends for?" It was too late; she left me with another unsold book.

I guess that means that I have to continue enumerating my ten blunders for my faithful readers. Mistake number five is *don't fail to read the company's quarterly and annual reports*. The CEO and other officers don't always tell you the whole truth about the company, but they are not likely to distort the truth. If they do, you had better sell the stock. By reading the company's reports you can determine if you still want to remain a shareholder.

Blunder number six is *failing to subscribe to periodicals* that may shed light on what's going on with the companies in your portfolio. Reading the *Wall Street Journal*, *Forbes*, *Barron's*, and *BusinessWeek* will keep you up to date on recent developments, such as new products, changes in management, acquisitions, and analysts' opinions.

You Can't Predict the Market

Still another shortcoming (blunder number seven) to avoid is *failing to invest in stocks after a long decline*. There is no way to predict how long a bear market will last. It could be a few months, as it was in 1987, or it could be two years, as it was in 1973 and 1974. If you are still building a portfolio, you should be investing new money on a regular basis, such as every six months or once a year. If you are setting aside 10 percent of your income, don't suddenly decide to make it 5 percent because you are convinced that the market is headed for a dismal year. You aren't that smart—nor am I. A good rule to follow is to invest when you have the money, not when someone on *Wall Street Week* says, "Next year will be a good one for stocks."

This brings us to mistake number eight—*failure to develop an appropriate asset allocation strategy*. This is covered in considerable detail in a separate chapter, so I will not repeat myself here.

Recordkeeping

The final blunder is *failure to keep adequate records*. You should have a filing cabinet that holds a folder for each stock. The first thing you should put in that file is the confirmation slip for the purchase of the stock, which should have been sent to you by your broker. Then, when you sell the stock, you will know what you paid for it so that you can tell your accountant. He in turn will tell the IRS, and you won't have to go to jail.

However, if you do end up in the slammer, I hope you will still keep buying the new editions of my book. And one last thing, if you run into Valira del Nord, would you put in a good word for me? Maybe you can convince her that she should buy the book. She really needs it.

Some Thoughts on Analyzing Stocks

Ideally, a stock you plan to purchase should have all of the following characteristics:

- A rising trend of earnings, dividends, and book value per share.
- A balance sheet with less debt than other companies in its particular industry.
- An S&P rating of B+ or better.
- A P/E ratio no higher than average.
- A dividend yield that suits your particular needs.
- A stock that insiders are not selling in significant quantities.
- A below-average dividend payout ratio.
- A history of earnings and dividends not pockmarked by erratic ups and downs.
- Companies whose return on equity is 15 or better.
- A ratio of price to cash flow that is not too high when compared to other stocks in the same industry.

Where to Get Information

If you are going to concentrate your efforts on the 30 Dow stocks, you must do some reading. Most people don't want to own all 30 stocks. In addition, you will probably find some stocks not to your liking. Let's say you are opposed to tobacco—then you may want to omit Philip Morris from your portfolio. Or, you may think that traditional retailers, such as Sears & Roebuck, are not going to do well against such companies as Wal-Mart; Bed, Bath & Beyond; or Home Depot. Similarly, a cyclical company like International Paper might appear too stodgy for an aggressive investor.

Because the Dow stocks are large and prominent, there is no shortage of information about them. In any given day, the *Wall Street Journal* will have a story about one or two Dow stocks. The same might be said for the *New York Times*. If you are serious about doing your homework, it would be wise to clip out these articles and file them away for future reference. You will also see articles on these companies in such publications as *Barron's*, *Better Investing*, *Forbes*, *Business Week*, and *Fortune*.

There are two well-known advisory services that you won't want to ignore: Standard & Poor's publishes "tear sheets" on thousands of companies. Of course, your only interest will be in the thirty Dow stocks. These tear sheets are available in public libraries and brokerage houses.

And don't forget to check *Value Line Survey*. It reviews 1,700 companies on a regular basis. Every thirteen weeks, your Dow Stocks are updated. This service costs over $500 a year, but is readily available in brokerage offices and libraries.

In this modern age, you may also be tempted to seek out information on the Internet. Here is a sampling of what you can check:

- *www.briefing.com* reports upgrades and downgrades on stocks by full-service brokers and gives a detailed report on the market three times daily. It also offers in-depth comments on several stocks during the day.
- *www.hoovers.com* provides profiles of thousands of companies, as well as financial data and links to company home pages.
- *www.investorama.com* provides more than 8,000 links to other investment Web sites.
- *www.zacks.com* provides consensus earnings predictions for the coming quarter, current year, and next year. It also shows whether company insiders are buying or selling.

The Four Essentials of Successful Investing

If you want to be rich at sixty-five, here are the factors to bear in mind.

First, start young. Many people wait until age fifty before they realize what has happened. Let's assume you want to have $1 million by age sixty-five. That may not be enough, but it's a lot more than most people have when they decide to retire from the world of commerce and frustration.

If you start at age thirty-five and can realize an annual return of 10 percent compounded, you will have to put aside $6,079 each year. If you delay until you are forty-five, it will mean you have to set aside $17,460 each year. If you start at age fifty-five, the amount gets a little steep—$62,746!

Invest Mostly in Stocks, not Bonds

It takes commitment, even if you start early, to save for the future. But if you buy bonds, CDs, or a money market fund, the task is even tougher. Let's try the different ages again, but this time assuming a compound annual return of 6, instead of 10, percent.

If you start at thirty-five and want to have a million bucks at sixty-five, it will mean plunking $12,649 into a CD each year—that's a lot more than the first illustration, which required an annual payment of $6,079. If you start at age forty-five, the annual contribution will have to be $27,185. Finally, those who start their programs at age fifty-five and pick fixed-income vehicles will be forced to set aside $75,868 each year.

Don't Be a Spendthrift

An important ingredient of successful investing is discipline. Of course, it pays to earn an above-average salary. If you make $30,000 a year and have four children, you are not likely to end up rich. Sorry about that.

On the other hand, there are plenty of people who make great incomes and still don't own any stocks. The reason: They can always find things to buy.

Successful investors not only make a good income, but they are thrifty shoppers. For instance, do you *need* a new car every two years? I happen to be rich, and I buy used cars. Not rusted out jalopies—normally, I buy Buicks that are three years old.

If you want to find out how people get rich, you should get *The Millionaire Next Door* by Thomas J. Stanley and William D. Danko. Typically, millionaires are extremely careful how they spend their money, and they invest in good-quality common stocks with very infrequent trading.

Picking the Right Investments

The final factor is picking the right stocks or mutual funds. Surprisingly, this is the *least* important factor. That's because no one knows how to do it consistently. There are mutual funds with good records, but those managers are rarely able to duplicate their performance year after year. However, that shouldn't deter you from trying. You will pick your share of winners if you do your homework and exercise patience. Finally, make sure you don't make any big bets. I prefer to own twenty or more stocks, with no more than 10 percent in any one industry.

In brief, here are the four rules:
- Start early in life to invest.
- Invest in common stocks.
- Invest enough to make it worthwhile, such as 10 percent of your income. You can only do this if you are thrifty.
- Study this book and do enough reading to ensure you pick stocks that have the potential to make you rich.

Basic Terminology

If you are new to the investment arena, you may have difficulty understanding parts of this book. To get you over the rough spots, I have listed some common expressions that appear frequently in books on investing. You will also encounter them in the *Wall Street Journal*, *Forbes*, *Business Week*, *Barron's*, and other periodicals devoted to investing.

This is not a glossary but merely a brief list of terms that are essential for understanding this book. If you would like a more complete glossary, refer to either of my previous books: *Safe Investing* (Simon & Schuster, 1991) or *Straight Talk About Stock Investing* (McGraw-Hill, 1995).

Analyst

In nearly every one of the one hundred articles, you will note that I refer to "analysts" and what they think about the prospects for a particular stock. Analysts are individuals who have special training in analyzing stocks. Typically, they have such advanced degrees as M.B.A.s or C.F.A.s. Many of them work for brokerage houses, but they may also be employed by banks, insurance companies, mutual funds, pension plans, or other institutions. Most analysts specialize in one or two industries. A good analyst can tell you nearly everything there is to know about a particular stock or the industry it's part of.

However, analysts can be dead wrong about the future action of a stock. The reason is surprises. Companies are constantly changing, which means they are acquiring, divesting, developing new products, restructuring, buying back their shares, and so forth. When they make a change and announce this change to Wall Street, the surprise can change the course of the stock. In short, analysts can be helpful, but don't bet the store on what they tell you.

As you can see, analysts are usually intelligent, hard working, and conscientious. Even so, they don't always succeed in guiding you to riches. Perhaps the biggest beef most people have is the tie that analysts have to the companies they follow. They know these people well and may be reluctant to say anything negative.

One reason for this is economic. Most brokerage firms make a ton of money from their investment banking division. If the analyst antagonizes the company, that company may give its investment banking business to a firm that says nice things rather than pointing out warts and all.

This reluctance to see no evil and speak no evil can be seen when you examine the number of times that analysts advise investors to sell. According the research firm First Call, more than 70 percent of the 27,000 recommendations outstanding in November 2000 were strong buys or buys. Fewer than 1 percent were sells or strong sells. To recap: of the 27,000 recommendations, 26.6 percent were holds, 36.8 percent were buys, and 35.7 percent were strong buys, and a mere 0.9 percent were sells or strong sells. I rest my case.

Annual Report

If you own a common stock, you can be certain that you will receive a fancy annual report a couple of months after the close of the year. If the year ends December 31, look for your annual report in March or April. If the fiscal year ends some other time of the year, such as September 30, the annual report will appear in your mailbox two or three months later.

Not all investors read annual reports, but they might be better off if they did. Although most companies will not list their problems, you can usually get a pretty good idea how things are going. In particular, read the report by the president or CEO. It's usually one, two, or three pages long and is written in language you can understand.

If you want detailed information on the company's various businesses, the annual report will often overwhelm you with details that may be difficult to fathom. If you are really curious about what they are trying to say, feel free to call the investor contact. I have provided the name of this person in all one hundred stocks listed. Have a list of questions ready, and call during the person's lunch hour, leaving your name and phone number. This sneaky little strategy means the cost of the call back will be paid by the company, not you. By the way, don't assume you will be intimidated by the investor contact. Investor contacts are usually quite personable and helpful.

Asset Allocation

This is not the same as diversification. Rather, it refers to the strategy of allocating your investment funds among different types of investments, such as stocks, bonds, or money-market funds. In the long run, you will be better off with all of your assets concentrated in common stocks. In the short run, this may not be true, since the market occasionally has a sinking spell. A severe one, such as that of 1973–74, can cause your holdings to decline in value 20 percent or more. To protect against this, most investors spread their money around. They may, for instance, allocate 50 percent to stocks, 40 percent to bonds, and 10 percent to a money-market fund. A more realistic breakdown might be 70 percent in stocks, 25 percent in bonds, and 5 percent in a money-market fund.

Balance Sheet

All corporations issue at least two financial statements: the balance sheet and the income statement. Both are important. The balance sheet is a financial picture of the company on a specific date, such as December 31 or at the end of a quarter.

On the left side of the balance sheet are the company's assets, such as cash, current assets, inventories, accounts receivable, and buildings. On the right side are its liabilities, including accounts payable and long-term debt. Also on the right side is shareholders' equity. The right side of the balance sheet adds up to the same value as the left side, which is why it is called a balance sheet.

In most instances, corporations give you figures for the current year and the prior year. By examining the changes, you can get an idea of whether the company's finances are improving or deteriorating.

Bonds

Entire books have been written on the various kinds of bonds. A bond, unlike a stock, is not a form of ownership. A bond is a contractual agreement that means you have loaned money to some entity, and that entity has agreed to pay you a certain sum of money (interest) every six months until that bond matures. At that time, you will also get back the money you originally invested—no more, no less. Most bonds are issued in $1,000 denominations. The safest bonds are those issued by the U.S. government. Not since the War of 1812 has there been a default on government bonds. The two advantages of bonds are safety and income. If you wait until the maturity date, you will be assured of getting the face value of the bond. In the meantime, however, the bond will fluctuate, because of changes in interest rates or the credit-worthiness of the corporation. Long-term bonds, moreover, fluctuate far more than short-term bonds. But enough about bonds. This book is about stocks.

Capital Gains

When you buy common stocks, you expect to make money in two ways: capital gains and dividends. Over an extended period of time, about half of your total return will come from each sector. If the stock rises in value and you sell it above your cost, you are enjoying a capital gain. The tax on long-term capital gains is less than it is on dividends—a maximum of 20 percent if the stock is held for 12 months.

Closed-End Investment Company

A managed investment portfolio, similar to a mutual fund, which is generally traded on a stock exchange. The price fluctuates with supply and demand, not because of changes in the assets within the trust. An open-end investment trust, or mutual fund, changes in size as investors buy new shares or surrender their shares for cash. A closed-end trust, by contrast, does not permit new money to be invested, nor can shares be redeemed by the company. Thus the number of shares remains the same once the trust begins trading. One feature of the closed-end trust is worth mentioning: they often sell at a discount to their asset value. An open-end trust always sells at precisely its asset value.

Common Stocks

We might as well define what a common stock is, since this whole book is devoted to them. All publicly owned companies—those that trade their shares outside of a small group of executives or the founding family—are based on common stocks. A common stock is evidence of partial ownership in a corporation. Most of the stocks described in this book have millions of

shares of their stock outstanding, and the really large ones may have in excess of 100 million shares. When you own common stock, there are no guarantees. If the company is successful, it will probably pay a dividend four times a year. These dividends may be raised periodically, perhaps once a year. If, however, the company has problems, it may cut or eliminate its dividend. This can happen even to a major company, such as IBM, Goodyear, or General Motors. As I said, there are no guarantees.

Investors who own common stock can sell their shares at any time. All you do is call your broker, and the trade is executed a few minutes later at the prevailing price—which fluctuates nearly every day, sometimes by a few cents or sometimes two or three points.

Current Ratio

The current ratio is calculated by dividing current assets by current liabilities. Current assets include any assets that will become cash within one year, including cash itself. Current liabilities are those that will be paid off within a year. A current ratio of 2 is considered ideal. Most companies these days have a current ratio of less than 2.

Diversification

Since investments are inherently risky, it pays to spread the risk by diversifying. If you don't, you may be too heavily invested in a stock or bond that turns sour. Even well-known stocks such as Alcoa, International Paper, Eastman Kodak, and American Express can experience occasional sinking spells.

To be on the safe side, don't invest more than 5 percent of your portfolio in any one stock. In addition, don't invest too heavily in any one sector of the economy. A good strategy is to divide stocks among twelve sectors: basic industries, capital goods/technology, capital goods, consumer growth, consumer cyclical, consumer staples, credit cyclical, financial, energy, transportation, utilities, and conglomerates.

Here's a rule of thumb that will keep you out of trouble: Invest at least 4 percent in each sector but not more than 12 percent. That means that you should own at least twelve stocks so that you have representation in all twelve sectors.

Dividends

Unlike bonds, common stocks may pay a dividend. Bonds pay interest. Most dividends are paid quarterly, but there is no set date that all corporations use. Some, for instance, may pay January 1, March 1, July 1, and September 1. Another company may pay February 10, May 10, August 10, and November 10. If you want to receive checks every month, you will have to make sure you buy stocks that pay dividends at different times of the year. The Standard & Poor's *Stock Guide* is a source for this information, as is the *Value Line Survey*. Most companies like to pay the same dividend every quarter until they can afford to increase it. Above all, they don't like to cut their dividends, since investors who depend on this income will sell their shares, and the stock will decline in price. If you use good judgment in selecting your stocks, you can expect that your companies will increase their dividends nearly every year.

Dividend Payout Ratio

If a company earns $4 per share in a given year and pays out $3 to its shareholders, it has a payout ratio of 75 percent. If it pays out only $1, the payout ratio is 25 percent. A low payout ratio is preferred, since it means that the company is plowing back its profits into future growth.

The Dividend Reinvestment Plan

Unless you are retired, you might like to reinvest your dividends in more shares. Many companies have a dividend reinvestment plan (also known as a DRIP) that will allow you to do this, and the charge for this service is often minimal. Most of these companies also allow you to mail in additional cash, which will be used to purchase new shares, again at minimal cost.

In recent years, a few companies have created "direct" dividend reinvestment plans. Unlike most plans, direct plans enable you to buy your initial shares directly from the company. To alert you to which companies have direct plans, I have inserted the word *direct*. Companies having such plans include ExxonMobil, McDonald's, Procter & Gamble, Merck, and Lilly. Incidentally, you can rarely buy just one share. Many companies have a minimum, such as $500.

This may sound like a good way to avoid paying brokerage commissions, but there are some drawbacks to bear in mind. For one thing, you can't time your purchases, since it may be a week or more before your purchase is made.

Even worse is calculating your cost basis for tax purposes. By the time you sell, you may have made scores of small investments in the same stock, each with a different cost basis. Make sure you keep a file for each company so that you can make these calculations when the time comes. Or, better still, don't sell.

Dollar Cost Averaging

Dollar cost averaging is a systematic way to invest money over a long period, such as 10, 15, or 20 years. It entails investing the same amount of money regularly, such as each month or each quarter. If you do this faithfully, you will be buying more stock when the price is lower, and less stock when the price is higher. This tends to smooth out the gyrations of the market. Dollar cost averaging is often used with a mutual fund, but it can just as easily be done with a company that has a dividend reinvestment plan (DRIP).

Income Statement

Most investors are more interested in the income statement than they are the balance sheet. They are particularly interested in the progress (or lack of it) in earnings per share (EPS). The income statement lists such items as net sales, cost of sales, interest expense, and gross profit. As with the balance sheet, it makes sense to compare this year's numbers with those of the prior year.

Inflation-Indexed Treasury Bonds

Conventional bonds—those that pay a fixed rate of return, such as 5 percent—have one big drawback: They are vulnerable to rising interest rates. For example, if you buy a bond that promises to pay you 5 percent for the next fifteen or twenty years, you will lose principal if interest rates climb to 7 percent. The reason is that new bonds being issued give investors a much better return. Thus, those that pay only 5 percent will sag in price until they hit a level that equates them to the new bonds that pay 7 percent. The loss of principal, moreover, is much greater with long-term bonds, such as those due in 15, 20, or 30 years.

By contrast, short-term bonds, those coming in due in three or four years, are much less volatile because you can often hold the bonds until the maturity date. Thus, you are certain to receive the full face value. Of course, you can do the same thing with a twenty-year bond, but twenty years is a long time.

The way to beat this disadvantage is to buy the relatively new bonds being issued by the U.S. government, since they are indexed to inflation. For this reason, you are unlikely to lose principal. To be sure, they pay less initially, currently 3.8 percent. But the ultimate return may be much better if inflation continues to impact the economy.

Suppose you invested $1,000 in inflation bonds at the current yield of 3.8 percent. If consumer prices rose 2.5 percent over the next year, your principal would climb to $1,025, and you would earn interest equal to 3.8 percent on this growing sum. Thus, if you spent the interest but didn't cash in any bonds, you would enjoy a rising stream of income while keeping your principal's spending power intact.

One thing to bear in mind: With inflation-indexed Treasury bonds, you have to pay federal income taxes each year on both the interest you earn and also the increase in the bonds' principal value. One way to take the sting out of this tax is to use these bonds in a tax-deferred account, such as an IRA.

Despite the tax implications, inflation bonds may be useful outside an IRA. Because these bonds don't perform as erratically as conventional bonds, they can be a good place to park money you may need if something unexpected comes along, such as a medical bill not fully covered by insurance. If inflation-indexed bonds ring a bell, ask the teller at your bank to get you started. She won't charge you a fee, and there is no red tape.

Investment Advisor

Investors who do not have the time or inclination to manage their own portfolios may elect to employ an investment advisor. Most advisors charge 1 percent a year. Thus, if you own stocks worth $300,000, your annual fee would be $3,000. Advisors differ from brokers, since they do not profit from changes. Brokers, by contrast, charge a commission on each transaction, which means they profit from changes in your portfolio. Advisors profit only when the value of your holdings increases. For instance, if the value of your portfolio increases to $500,000, the annual fee will be $5,000. You, of course, will be $200,000 richer.

Moving Average

Some investors use the moving average to time the market. The strategy is to buy a stock when it is selling above its moving average and selling when it falls below. A popular moving average is the 200-day version. A dotted line is drawn, taking the average price of the stock over the previous 200 days. The actual price of the stock is plotted on the same graph. Studies show that this method of timing the market does not work on a consistent basis.

PEG Ratio

The PEG ratio is supposed to be helpful in determining if a stock is too expensive. It is calculated by dividing the price-earnings ratio by the expected earnings growth rate. Let's say the P/E ratio of American International Group is 34.39, which is calculated by dividing the price ($98) by the expected EPS in 2001 of $2.85. Meanwhile, the earnings per share in the 1989–99 period expanded from $.67 to $2.18, a compound annual growth rate of 12.52 percent. When you divide 34.39 by 12.52, the PEG ratio is 2.75. According to Michael Sivy, a writer for *Money* magazine, "Stocks with a PEG ratio of 1.5 or less are often the best buys."

By that rule, you would avoid American International Group. Curiously, Mr. Sivy includes AIG on his list of "100 Stocks for Long-Term Investors," published in January 2001. By his calculation, AIG had a PEG ratio at that time of 2.5.

Once again, I am a doubting Thomas. Who is to say what a company's future growth rate will be? You can easily determine what it has been in the past. And that may give you some indication of the future, but it is far from reliable. The P/E ratio is also a slippery number, since you are expected to base it on the EPS for the year ahead. I prefer to base it on the most recent twelve months, since that is a figure that does not depend on a crystal ball.

Preferred Stock

The name sounds impressive. In actual practice, owning preferred stocks is about as exciting as watching your cat take a bath. A preferred stock is much like a bond. It pays the same dividend year in and year out. The yield is usually higher than a common stock. If the company issuing the preferred stock does well, you do not benefit. If it does poorly, however, you may suffer, since the dividend could be cut or eliminated. My advice is: Never, never buy a preferred stock.

Price–Earnings Ratio (P/E)

This is a term that is extremely important. Don't make the mistake of overlooking it. Whole books have been written on the importance of the P/E ratio, which is sometimes referred to as "the P/E" or "the multiple."

The P/E ratio tells you whether a stock is cheap or expensive. It is calculated by dividing the price of the stock by the company's earnings per share over the most recent 12 months. For instance, if you refer to the *Stock Guide*, you will see that Leggett and Platt had earnings of $2.23. At the time, the stock was selling for $52. Divide that figure by $2.23 and you get a P/E of 23.32.

In most instances, a low P/E indicates a stock that Wall Street is not too excited about. If they like a stock, they will bid it up to the point where its P/E is quite high, let's say 25 or 30. Coca-Cola is such a stock. In this same *Stock Guide*, Coca-Cola had annual earnings per share of $1.59. Based on the price of the stock at that time (it was $75), that works out to a P/E ratio of 47.17. Of course, Coca-Cola is extremely well regarded by investors and is expected to do well in the future—but is it really worth 47 times earnings?

Stock Split

Corporations know that investors like to invest in lower-priced stocks. Thus, when the price of the stock gets to a certain level, which varies with the company, they will split the stock. For instance, if the stock is $75, they might split it three-for-one. Your original 100 shares now become 300 shares. Unfortunately, your 300 shares are worth exactly the same as your original 100 shares. What it amounts to is this: Splits please small investors, but they don't make them any richer. One company, Berkshire Hathaway, has never been split. It is now worth a huge amount per share: over $60,000. It also pays no dividend. The company is run by the legendary Warren Buffett. He has made a lot of people very wealthy without a stock split or dividend.

Technician

There are two basic ways to analyze stocks. One is *fundamental*; the other is *technical*.

Fundamental analysts examine a stock's management, sales and earnings potential, research capabilities, new products, competitive strength, balance sheet strength, dividend growth, political developments, and industry conditions.

Technicians, by contrast, rarely consider any of these fundamental factors. They rely on charts and graphs and a host of other arcane statistical factors, such as point-and-figure charts, breadth indicators, head-and-shoulders formations, relative strength ratings, and the 200-day-moving average. This technical jargon is often difficult to fathom for the average investor. Among professional portfolio managers, the fundamental approach predominates, although some institutions may also employ a technician.

The question is: Do technicians have the key to stock picking or predicting the trend of the market? Frankly, I am a skeptic, as are most academic analysts. Among the nonbelievers is Kenneth L. Fisher, the longtime columnist for *Forbes* magazine who I mentioned earlier. His columns are among my favorites. Here is what Mr. Fisher says about technicians. "One of the questions I hear most often is, 'Can charts really predict stock prices?' Naturally, there is only one answer: a flat 'No.'"

Mr. Fisher goes on to say: "There is virtually nothing in theory or empiricism to indicated anyone can predict stock prices based solely on prior stock price action. Nevertheless, a big world of chartists continues to exist, amplified by recent Internet day trading. Yet the world of investors with long-lasting success is devoid of them."

Such eminently successful portfolio managers as Peter Lynch and Warren Buffett, for instance, don't resort to charts and other technical mumbo jumbo.

Yield

If your company pays a dividend, you can relate this dividend to the price of the stock in order to calculate the yield. A $50 stock that pays a $2 annual dividend (which amounts to 50 cents per quarter) will have a yield of 4 percent. You arrive at this figure by dividing $2 by $50. Actually, you don't have to make this calculation, since the yield is given to you in the stock tables of the *Wall Street Journal*. Here are some typical yields from mid-2001. Coca-Cola, 1.5 percent; ExxonMobil, 2.0 percent; General Electric, 1.3 percent; Illinois Tool Works, 1.2 percent; Kimberly-Clark, 1.8 percent; and Minnesota Mining and Manufacturing, 2.0 percent. Although the yield is of some importance, you should not judge a stock by its yield without looking at many other factors.

Some Simple Formulas for Asset Allocation

Serious investors spend a lot of time deciding which stocks or mutual funds to buy. I can't quarrel with that. If you are going to invest $10,000 in Merck, Illinois Tool Works, Praxair, Leggett & Platt, or United Technologies, you shouldn't do it without some research and thought.

On the other hand, some financial gurus maintain that it is far more important to make an effort to achieve an effective approach to asset allocation. They believe that you should place your emphasis on how much of your portfolio is invested in such sectors as:

Government bonds
Corporate bonds
Municipal bonds
Convertible bonds
Preferred stocks
Large-capitalization domestic stocks
Small-capitalization domestic stocks
Foreign stocks
Foreign bonds
Certificates of deposit
Annuities
Money-market funds

There are probably a few other categories you could include in your portfolio, but I think that examining this list gives you an idea of what is meant by asset allocation.

To illustrate the importance of asset allocation, look at 1998. You may recall that the long bull market temporarily aborted in mid-July of that year. Prior to that time, the big blue chip stocks had been making heady progress. Beneath the surface, however, the small and medium-size stocks were already in their own bear

market. Thus, if you had avoided these smaller companies in the first six months of 1998, you would have sidestepped the devastation that was taking place in this sector.

After mid-July, however, the big stocks—particularly the financial stocks such as J. P. Morgan, Travelers (now Citigroup), and American Express—took a real tumble. The best place to be during this period was in U.S. government bonds. Once again, we are talking about asset allocation and how it can help or hurt you.

My Approach to Asset Allocation

From the comments made so far, you can see that asset allocation, like everything else in the world of finance, can get rather complex and confusing. It is no wonder that many people don't delve into this arcane realm. That's where John Slatter comes to the rescue. My idea of investing is to make it simple. After all, there are just so many hours in the day. If you are still gainfully employed, you probably work eight hours a day making a living. In the evenings, you may spend a few hours a week reading journals and other material so that you don't get fired. Obviously, that doesn't leave much time for studying the stock market.

For my part, I don't invest in many small-cap stocks, foreign stocks, bonds, convertibles, preferred stocks, or most of the other stuff on my list. I prefer to invest mostly in big-cap stocks (such as ExxonMobil, GE, Merck, IBM, Procter & Gamble, and Johnson & Johnson) and money-market funds (a safe alternative to cash).

This reduces my categories to two, not a dozen. All you have to do is decide what percentage of your portfolio is in stocks. The rest is in a money-market fund. Of course, the *percentage* is vitally important.

A Few Alternatives to Consider

Some people may be shocked that I am not concerned about foreign stocks. One firm I once worked for insisted that we strive to invest 20 percent of each investor's portfolio in foreign stocks, such as Schlumberger, Repsol, Royal Dutch Petroleum, British Telecommunications, or Elf Aquitaine.

I have no objection to such stocks, but I see no urgency to adhere to a rigid percentage. For one thing, foreign stocks are more difficult to research. Their annual reports are far less revealing than those put out by corporations here at home. They also have different and less informative accounting.

In any event, the United States has hundreds of great companies. We are the envy of the world when it comes to business. The Japanese—at least for a decade or two—tried to convince people otherwise. But they have spent that last several years wallowing in a serious recession.

As far as bonds are concerned, they don't have a particularly impressive record. Except for a year here or there, common stocks have always been a better place to be. What's more, the return on bonds today is not much better than the rate you can get on a money-market fund.

One more thing: Bonds, even U.S. Treasuries, have an element of risk; they decline in value when interest rates go up. Long-term bonds, moreover, slide precipitously when rates shoot up.

I don't want to spend too much time discussing the shortcomings of the rest of the list. I would prefer to point out the virtues of major stocks, such as McDonald's, Wal-Mart, Hewlett-Packard, J. P. Morgan, AT&T, Chevron, Alcoa, Eli Lilly, Minnesota Mining, and Walt Disney.

Blue chip companies are not likely to go bankrupt. To be sure, they have their troubles, but they are big enough to hire a CEO who can bring them back to life. Among the thirty companies in the Dow Jones Industrial Average, for instance, such companies as IBM, Eastman Kodak, AT&T, Sears, Roebuck, United Technologies, and AlliedSignal were restructured in recent years by a few dynamic executives.

Major corporations are also found in most institutional portfolios such as mutual funds, pension plans, bank trust departments, and insurance companies. One reason they like these big-capitalization stocks is liquidity. Since institutions have huge amounts of cash to invest, they feel comfortable with these stocks. The reason: The number of shares outstanding is huge, which means they won't disturb the market when they buy or sell. By contrast, if a major institution tries to invest a million dollars in a tiny Nasdaq company, the stock will shoot up several points before they complete their investing. It could be just as disruptive when they try to get out. As a consequence, major companies are in demand and are not left to drift. On the other hand, there are thousands of small companies that no one ever heard of. The only investors who can push them up are individuals—not institutions.

Another reason I like big companies is because they can afford to hire top-notch executives and they have the resources to allocate to research and marketing. In addition, their new products, acquisitions, management changes, and strategies are discussed frequently in such publications as the *Wall Street Journal,* the *New York Times, Barron's, Fortune, Forbes,* and *BusinessWeek,* all of which I subscribe to.

How Much Should You Invest in Stocks?

When it comes to deciding on the percentage you should devote to common stocks, there are several alternatives that should be considered. All have some merit, and none are perfect.

In fact, there is no such thing as a perfect formula for asset allocation. It depends on such factors as your age and your temperament. It might also depend on what you think the market is going to do. If it's about to soar, you would want to be fully invested. But if you think stocks are poised to fall off a cliff, you might prefer to seek the safety of a money-market fund.

Forget About Everything Else and Buy Only Stocks

Believe it or not, there are some investors who are convinced that common stocks—and common stocks alone—are the royal road to riches. A good friend of mine has never bought anything but stocks, and he's been doing it for many years. He even went through the severe bear market of 1973–74, when stocks plunged over 40 percent. He wasn't exactly happy to see his stocks being ground to a pulp, but he hung on. Today, he is a millionaire many times over. He's now sixty years old, still a comparatively young investor. His name is David A. Seidenfeld, a businessman in Cleveland.

Dave got his start by listening to the late S. Allen Nathanson, a savvy investor who wrote a series of magazine articles on why common stocks are the best way to achieve great wealth. Dave Seidenfeld recently collected these essays and published them as a hardcover book, *Bullishly Speaking*, which is available in bookstores.

If you start investing early, such as in your forties, this method can work. If you systematically invest, setting aside ten or fifteen percent of your earnings each year and doing it through thick and thin, you won't need any bonds, money-market funds, or any of the other alternatives that financial magazines seem to think you must have. You will arrive at retirement with a large portfolio that will enable you to live off the dividends.

However, if you arrived late to the investment party—let's say in your late fifties or early sixties—you may not be able to sleep too well if you rely entirely on common stocks. After all, stocks have their shortcomings too. They tend to bounce around a lot, and they can cut their dividends when things turn bleak.

Some Options to Consider

If you are an ultraconservative investor, I suggest you invest only 55 percent of your portfolio in common stocks. To be sure, when the stock market is marching ahead, as it has in recent years, you won't be able to keep pace. But if it falters and heads south for a year or two, your cautious approach will keep you out of the clutches of insomnia. Frankly, I don't think such a timid approach is the best way to approach asset allocation. However, I worked for a firm a few years ago that used this formula on nearly everyone. As far as I know, there weren't too many people complaining.

A better way to handle the uncertainty is to invest 70 percent in stocks, with the rest in a money-market fund. Once you decide on a particular percentage, stick with it. Don't change it every time someone makes a market forecast. These market forecasts don't work often enough to pay any attention to them. To my knowledge, no professional investor has a consistent record in forecasting. Every once in a while, one of these pundits makes a correct call at a crucial turning point, and from that day on, every one listens intently to the pronouncements of this person—until the day the pronouncement is totally wrong. That day always comes.

My Favorite Formula for Asset Allocation

I think age is the key to asset allocation. The older you are, the less you should have in common stocks. If you are age 65, you should have 65 percent in common stocks, with the rest in a money-market fund. If you are younger than 65, add 1 percent per year to your common stock sector. As an example, if you are 60 years old, you will have 70 percent in stocks.

If you are older than 65, deduct 1 percent a year. Thus, if you are age 70, you will have only 60 percent in stock. When you reach 80, you will be 50–50. And if you are much younger than 65, let's say 45, you will have 85 percent in stocks.

If you are not sure what this all means, here is a table breaking down the two percentages by age:

Age	Stocks	Money-Market Funds
40	90%	10%
45	85	15
50	80	20
55	75	25
60	70	30
65	65	35
70	60	40
75	55	45
80	50	50
85	45	55

Part II

100 Best Stocks You Can Buy

The following table lists the 100 stocks discussed in this book. A brief description of the stock appears here.

In the table, "Industry" refers to one of the company's main businesses. This is not always easy to express in one or two words.

For instance, United Technologies is involved in such industries as aircraft engines, elevators, and air conditioning equipment. To describe the company succinctly, I arbitrarily picked the designation "aircraft engines."

Similarly, General Electric presents an even more daunting problem since is owns NBC and makes appliances, aircraft engines, medical devices, and a host of other things.

The "Sector" designation indicates the broad economic industry group that

the company operates in, such as transportation, capital goods, energy, consumer cyclicals, and so forth. Experts will tell you that a properly diversified portfolio should include at least one stock in each of the twelve sectors. However, I see no problem in having stocks in nine or ten sectors.

"Category" refers to one of the following: (1) income (Income), (2) growth and income (Gro Inc), (3) conservative growth (Con Grow), or (4) aggressive growth (Aggr Gro). For diversification, it might make sense to have some representation in each category even though you may have a strong preference for only one.

I have not included the page numbers because of space limitations. In any event, it is easy enough to find a particular stock since they appear alphabetically in the book.

Company	Symbol	Industry	Sector	Category
—A—				
Abbott Laboratories	ABT	Med Supplies	Cons Staples	Con Grow
Air Products	APD	Chemical	Basic Ind	Con Grow
Alberto-Culver*	ACV	Cosmetics	Cons Staples	Con Grow
Alcoa	AA	Metals	Basic Ind	Aggr Gro
American Express	AXP	Credit Card	Financial	Aggr Gro
American Water Works	AWK	Water Util.	Utilities	Gro Inc
American Home Prod.	AHP	Drugs	Cons Staples	Con Gro
Amer. Int'l Group*	AIG	Insurance	Financial	Aggr Gro
Avery Dennison	AVY	Adhesives	Basic Ind.	Con Grow
—B—				
Baldor Electric	BEZ	Elect. Equip	Capital Goods	Gro Inc
Bank of New York*	BK	Bank	Financial	Con Grow
Baxter Int'l	BAX	Med Supplies	Cons Staples	Aggr Gro
Boeing	BA	Aerospace	Capital Goods	Aggr Gro
Boston Properties*	BXP	REIT	Cons Cyclical	Income
BP p.l.c.	BP	Oil	Energy	Grow Inc
Bristol-Myers Squibb	BMY	Drugs	Cons Staples	Con Grow
—C—				
Cardinal Health*	CAH	Healthcare	Cons Staples	Aggr Gro
Caterpillar	CAT	Machinery	Capital Goods	Gro Inc
Cedar Fair	FUN	Entertain.	Cons Staples	Income

Chevron	CHV	Oil	Energy	Grow Inc
Chubb	CB	Insurance	Financial	Con Grow
Citigroup	C	Bank, Ins.	Financial	Con Grow
Clayton Homes	CMH	Housing	Credit Cyclic	Aggr Gro
Clorox	CLX	Household Pd	Cons Staples	Gro Inc
Coca-Cola	KO	Beverages	Cons Staples	Con Grow
Colgate-Palmolive	CL	Household Pd	Cons Staples	Con Grow
ConAgra*	CAG	Food	Cons Staples	Income
Costco Wholesale	COST	Wholesale	Cons Cyclical	Aggr Gro

—D—

Delphi Automotive	DPH	Automotive	Cons Cyclical	Con Grow
Disney, Walt	DIS	Entertain.	Cons Staples	Aggr Gro
Dominion Resources*	D	G&E Utility	Utilities	Income
Dover	DOV	Machinery	Capital Goods	Con Grow
Duke Energy	DUK	Energy	Utilities	Grow Inc
DuPont	DD	Chemicals	Basic Ind.	Grow Inc

—E—

Emerson	EMR	Elect Equip	Capital Goods	Con Grow
Energen*	EGN	Natural Gas	Utilities	Grow Inc
Ethan Allen	ETH	Furniture	Credit Cycl	Aggr Gro
Equity Office Prop.*	EOP	REIT	Cons Services	Income
ExxonMobil	XON	Oil	Energy	Grow Inc

—F—

FedEx Corporation	FDX	Air Freight	Transportation	Aggr Gro

—G—

Gannett	GCI	Publishing	Cons Services	Con Grow
General Dynamics*	GD	Defense	Cap Goods-Tech	Aggr Gro
General Electric	GE	Elect Equip	Capital Goods	Con Grow
General Motors	GM	Automobile	Cons. Cyclical	Grow Inc
Gentex*	GNTX	Automotive	Cons. Cyclical	Aggr Gro

—H—

Harley-Davidson	HDI	Recreation	Cons Staples	Aggr Gro
Hershey Foods*	HSY	Food	Cons Staples	Con Grow
Hewlett-Packard	HWP	Computers	Cap Goods-Tech	Aggr Gro

—I—

Illinois Tool Works	ITW	Machinery	Capital Goods	Con Grow
Intel	INTC	Computers	Cap Goods-Tech	Aggr Gro
Int'l Business Mach	IBM	Computer	Cap Goods-Tech	Aggr Gro
International Paper	IP	Paper	Basic Ind	Gro Inc
Interpublic*	IPG	Advertising	Cons Cyclical	Con Grow

—J—

Jefferson-Pilot	JP	Insurance	Financial	Gro Inc
Johnson Controls*	JCI	Elect Equip	Capital Goods	Con Grow
Johnson & Johnson	JNJ	Med. Supplies	Cons Staples	Con Grow

—K—

Kimberly-Clark	KMB	Tissues	Basic Ind	Gro Inc
Kimco Realty	KIM	REIT	Cons Services	Income

—L—

Leggett & Platt	LEG	Furn Compon	Credit Cycl	Con Grow
Lilly, Eli	LLY	Drugs	Cons Staples	Aggr Gro
Lowe's Companies*	LOW	Retail	Credit Cycl	Con Grow
Lubrizol	LZ	Oil Additives	Basic Ind.	Income

—M— *2003*

McDonald's *out*	MCD	Restaurant	Cons Services	Con Grow
McCormick & Co.	MCCRK	Spices	Cons Staples	Con Grow
McGraw-Hill	MHP	Publishing	Cons Services	Con Grow
Medtronic *n*	MDT	Med. Devices	Cap Goods Tech	Aggr Gro
MDU Resources	MDU	G&E Utility	Utilities	Income
Merck	MRK	Drugs	Cons Staples	Con Grow
Microsoft	MSFT	Comp. Soft.	Cap Goods-Tech	Aggr Gro
Minnesota Mining *out*	MMM	Diversified	Cap Goods-Tech	Gro Inc
Morgan, J. P., Chase JPM *n*	Bank	Financial	Grow Inc	

—N—

National City	NCC	Bank	Financial	Income
New York Times* *n out*	NYT	Publishing	Cons Services	Con Grow
Nordson	NDSN	Machinery	Capital Goods	Cons Gro

—O—

Orthodontic Centers* OCA *n out*	Dental	Cons Services	Aggr Gro	

—P—

PepsiCo* *n*	PEP	Beverages	Cons Staples	Con Grow
Pfizer	PFE	Drugs	Cons Staples	Aggr Gro
Philip Morris	MO	Tobacco	Cons Staples	Income
Piedmont Nat'l Gas *n*	PNY	Nat'l Gas	Utilities	Income
Pitney Bowes	PBI	Postage Mtrs	Cap Goods-Tech	Gro Inc
Praxair	PX	Indust Gases	Basic Ind	Con Grow
Procter & Gamble	PG	Household Pd	Cons Staples	Con Grow

—R—

Royal Dutch Petrol. *n out*	RD	Petroleum	Energy	Gro Inc

—S—

SBC Communications *n*	SBC	Telephone	Utilities	Gro Inc
Stryker *n*	SYK	Medical Sup	Cons Staples	Aggr Gro
Sysco Corporation	SYY	Food Distrib.	Cons. Staples	Con Grow

—T—

Texas Instruments *n out*	TXN	Computers	Cap Goods-Tech	Aggr Gro

—U—

United Parcel *n out*	UPS	Package del.	Transportation	Aggr Gro
United Technologies	UTX	Aircraft Eng	Cap Goods-Tech	Con Grow

—V—

Varian Medical *n*	VAR	Med. Devices	Cap Goods-Tech	Con Grow
Vectren* *n*	VVC	Gas & Elect.	Utilities	Gro Inc
Verizon* *n*	VZ	Telephone	Utilities	Gro Inc
Vulcan Materials *out*	VMC	Const Materi	Credit Cyclic	Gro Inc

—W—

Wachovia	WB	Bank	Financial	Gro Inc
Walgreen*	WAG	Drug Stores	Cons Staples	Aggr Gro
WGL Holdings	WGL	Natural Gas	Utilities	Income
Washington Mutual* *n out*	WM	Thrifts	Financial	Aggr Gro
Washington Real Est.	WRE	REIT	Cons Cyclical	Income
Weyerhaeuser *out*	WY	Forest Prod	Basic Ind	Gro Inc

—Z—

Zebra Technologies* *n out*	ZBRA	Printing	Cap Goods-Tech	Aggr Gro

---

* New in this edition.

CONSERVATIVE GROWTH

Abbott Laboratories

100 Abbott Park Road □ Abbott Park, Illinois 60064-6000 □ Investor contact: John Thomas (847) 938-2655 □ Dividend reinvestment plan is available: (847) 937-7300 □ Web site: www.abbott.com □ Ticker symbol: ABT □ S&P rating: A+ □ Value Line financial strength rating: A++

In its biggest acquisition to date, Abbott Laboratories bought the drug business of the German chemicals giant BASF AG for $6.9 billion early in 2001.

BASF's Knoll Pharmaceuticals has developed a promising rheumatoid arthritis treatment, a drug referred to as D2E7. Analysts believe it could be a blockbuster, with annual sales of $1 billion or more. The drug is expected to be commercially available in 2003.

Prior to the purchase of Knoll, Abbott had come under fire from analysts for not having a major blockbuster drug either in the works or on the market. Its top-selling drug has been Depakote, which treats bipolar disorder and generates $700 million a year in annual sales. Abbott's joint venture with Takeda Chemical Industries benefits from more than $2 billion in annual sales of Prevacid, but Abbott splits those profits with its Japanese partner.

Prior to the Abbott deal, many companies were seeking the rights to the D2E7, a drug that acts against Tumor Necrosis Factor (TNF), an activator of various inflammatory cells. In immune-system diseases such as rheumatoid arthritis, inflammation and pain go on a rampage in joints and other connective tissues. D2E7, however, prevents TNF from attaching to tiny receptors on human inflammatory cells.

Most analysts view the purchase of Knoll as being driven by Abbott's desire to bolster its pipeline of drugs under development. In this regard, Knoll has impressive credentials. Apart from D2E7, Knoll has intriguing compounds in the works for advanced pain, psychosis, heart disease,

asthma, lupus and a range of other so-called autoimmune ailments in which a patient's body, in essence, attacks its own tissue.

Under Abbott's CEO, Miles White, the company has been bent on augmenting research and development expenditures. With the Knoll acquisition, Abbott's pharmaceutical R & D spending is likely to expand by 50 percent to about $1 billion a year. What's more, the company's annual drug sales will increase by Knoll's $2.1 billion, adding significantly to Abbott's $2.6 billion.

Company Profile

Abbott Laboratories is one of the largest diversified health care manufacturers in the world, with 2000 revenues of $13.7 billion. The company's products are sold in more than 130 countries, with about 40 percent of sales derived from international operations. ABT has paid consecutive quarterly dividends since 1924.

Abbott's major business segments include Pharmaceuticals & Nutritionals (prescription drugs, medical nutritionals, and infant formulas) and Hospital & Laboratory Products (intravenous solutions, administrative sets, drug-delivery devices, and diagnostic equipment and reagents).

At the end of 2000, the company's leading brands were:

- AxSym systems and reagents (immunodiagnostics)
- Biaxin/Biaxin XL/Klalcid/Klaricid (macrolide antibiotic)
- Depakote (bipolar disorder; epilepsy; migraine prevention)
- Depakote ER (migraine prevention)

- Ensure (adult nutritionals)
- Isomil (soy-based infant formula)
- MediSense glucose monitoring products
- Similac (infant formula)
- Ultane/Sevorane (anesthetic)

Although revenue growth in Abbott's infant formula and diagnostics businesses has slowed in recent years, new drugs (such as the antibiotic clarithromycin), new indications (including the BPH claim for Hytrin), the launch of disease-specific medical nutritionals, and cost cutting (diagnostics and hospital supplies) continue to boost the company's profits.

Shortcomings to Bear in Mind

- Not everyone is convinced that Abbott's acquisition of Knoll Pharmaceuticals was a wise move. According to Mark Tatge, writing for *Forbes* magazine, "[D]oes the $6.9-billion deal really make it a better company? It almost quintuples Abbott's debt and adds only $400 million to operating income."

  Still another analyst, Carol Levenson, research director at Gimme Credit in Chicago, said, "If ever we've seen a defensive acquisition, surely this must be it. Presumably a company with $7.5 billion in debt looks less appetizing than one with $1.6 billion."

Reasons to Buy

- In the fall of 2000, the Food and Drug Administration (FDA) gave approval to Kaletra, a new Abbott drug for the treatment of HIV, the virus that causes AIDS. Kaletra belongs to a class of drugs known as protease inhibitors, which block the protease enzyme that helps prevent the virus from replicating or infecting new cells. As in many AIDS drugs, Kaletra is meant to be taken in conjunction with other medications. Results from an Abbott study show that Kaletra reduced levels of HIV to undetectable levels in 79

percent of patients who hadn't previously been treated. By contrast, the forty-week study said that Pfizer's Viracept (the top-selling domestic protease inhibitor) reduced levels of the AIDS virus in 64 percent of patients.

  What's more, Kaletra is proving to be effective in patients who have failed other treatments. Equally significant, Kaletra rarely causes side effects such as headache, nausea, or vomiting. Side effects—if severe—frequently keep patients from following the doctor's orders in using drugs consistently and correctly. With such an impressive side-effect profile and potency, researchers are beginning to think doctors using Kaletra will eventually figure out a way to keep the virus suppressed indefinitely.

  Abbott also sells an AIDS drug known as Norvir. Kaletra is formulated with a small dose of Norvir. As you might expect, Kaletra could cut into Norvir sales, which were about $100 million in 2000, but the gain from Kaletra will easily outweigh any potential sales "cannibalization."

  Analysts expect Kaletra to generate about $500 million in worldwide annual sales three years after the 2000 approval date.

- The cornerstone of Abbott's neuroscience business is Depakote, a versatile agent for the treatment of epilepsy and bipolar disorder as well as the prevention of migraine headaches. In 1998, Depakote surpassed lithium, the long-standing market leader, to become the agent most prescribed by psychiatrists for treating patients who experience manic episodes associated with bipolar disorder (also known as manic depression).

- Abbott is focusing on global opportunities for its pediatric nutritional products, particularly the newly reformulated Similac infant formula. This product has been launched in more than twenty countries, including the United States.

The reformulation has made Similac closer than ever to breast milk. The new formulation is marketed as Improved Similac in the United States and as Similac Advance and other Similac trademarks in the rest of the world. It is the only infant formula with added nucleotide levels patterned after the potentially available nucleotides from breast milk. Nucleotides, the building blocks of DNA and RNA, are compounds found naturally in all cells and in breast milk. The new formula is the product of a seven-year research effort—the largest such program ever conducted by Abbott's nutritional research scientists.

- Abbott is the leader in rapid testing, in both hospitals and doctors' offices, with tests for strep, pregnancy, and a microbe that causes ulcers. The company's Determine line of tests are self-contained, low cost, and easy to use. Since its acquisition of MediSense, Inc. in 1996, the company's blood glucose monitoring systems have been well received by diabetic patients.

- Many people with diabetes must test themselves frequently, drawing their own blood by sticking their fingertips, applying the blood to test strips, and correctly operating meters to read their blood glucose levels.

Abbott's MediSense Products organization spent four years designing a meter to make self-monitoring painless, minimally invasive, and easy to perform. In December 2000, MediSense launched the result of its engineering—the Sof-Tact meter (or Soft-Sense, as it is called in Europe). To make the testing regimen virtually painless, Abbott engineers and scientists designed a device that would draw blood from less sensitive parts of the body, such as the forearm or upper arm, which have fewer nerve endings than fingertips. With a single press of a button, the device provides the user with an accurate reading in thirty seconds or less, using only 2 microliters of blood rather than the 10 microliters required of other meters.

- Anesthesia is a cornerstone of Abbott's hospital pharmaceutical strategy. The company's worldwide leadership in anesthesia is providing the catalyst for growth in other hospital business segments, particularly outside the United States

Abbott's inhalation anesthetic, sevoflurane (marketed as Ultane in the United States and Sevorane in other countries), had the most successful new hospital product launch in Abbott history. Anesthesiologists in fifty-six countries now use this versatile agent. Sevoflurane has broad applicability for both induction and maintenance of anesthesia in pediatric and adult patients. And because it allows patients to emerge from anesthesia rapidly and smoothly, it has helped the company penetrate the growing market for outpatient surgery. Sevoflurane has experienced steady growth since its introduction in 1994. It is the induction agent of choice for anesthesiologists who have administered it.

- Abbott acquired Perclose, Inc. late in 1999. Since its founding in 1992, Perclose has been dedicated to one mission—creating a new standard for vascular care following catheterization procedures. To treat patients' cardiovascular conditions, interventional cardiologists and radiologists use angioplasty, stents, and other catheterization procedures, which involve opening the femoral artery in the thigh. After the procedures, doctors must close the access site.

Traditionally, doctors have used various forms of compression to close the opening to the artery, including direct pressure, sand bags, or mechanical clamps. Compression techniques, however, require a longer healing process for patients, causing discomfort and adding to their hospital stays. In the 1990s, Perclose pioneered suture-mediated arterial closure technology. The Closer, Perclose's next-generation device, allows doctors to close access wounds faster and easier by swiftly deploying a ready-made suture. Unlike compression or the use of collagen plugs, both of which rely on the

body's clotting process, The Closer allows patients to get up almost immediately after their procedures, which means going home sooner than was possible in the past. In addition, it gives physicians the option of using anticoagulants or blood thinners before, during, and after coronary procedures—a choice they never had prior to suture-mediated devices such as the Closer. In Abbott's first year of owning Perclose, sales mushroomed by more than 60 percent.

Total assets: $15,283 million
Current ratio: 1.72
Common shares outstanding: 1,547 million
Return on 2000 shareholders' equity: 32.5%

		2000	1999	1998	1997	1996	1995	1994	1993
Revenues (millions)		13746	13178	12513	11889	11018	10012	9156	8408
Net income (millions)		2786	2446	2334	2079	1874	1689	1517	1399
Earnings per share		1.78	1.57	1.50	1.32	1.18	1.06	.94	.85
Dividends per share		.76	.68	.60	.54	.48	.42	.38	.34
Price	High	56.2	53.3	50.1	34.9	28.7	22.4	16.9	15.4
	Low	29.4	27.9	32.5	24.9	19.1	15.4	12.7	11.3

CONSERVATIVE GROWTH

Air Products and Chemicals, Inc.

7201 Hamilton Boulevard ▫ Allentown, Pennsylvania 18195-1501 ▫ Investor contact: Alexander W. Masetti (610) 481-5775 ▫ Dividend reinvestment plan is available: (888) 694-9458 ▫ Web site: www.airproducts.com ▫ Fiscal year ends September 30 ▫ Listed: NYSE ▫ Ticker symbol: APD ▫ S&P rating: A- ▫ Value Line financial strength rating: B++

Air Products got its start in helium in the 1950s when the federal government hired the company to extract this "noble gas" from natural gas deposits in the Midwestern United States—currently the world's main source of helium. Nearly fifty years later, Air Products is the world's leading helium producer.

Helium has the lowest melting and boiling points of any element. It is colorless, odorless, and nonflammable. Helium is used in light-air balloons and to make artificial "air" (with oxygen) for deep-sea

divers. It is also used in welding, semiconductors, and lasers. In addition, liquid helium is used in cryogenics, a branch of physics that studies materials and effects at temperatures approaching absolute zero.

In fiscal 2000 (ended September 30, 2000), the company tripled its processing capacity at its Liberal, Kansas facility to more than one billion standard cubic feet per year.

The helium market is expected to expand by at least 6 percent per year, a rate that suggests another expansion in the

Kansas complex will be needed about every two years. And by supplying helium to high-growth markets such as laser welding, semiconductor manufacturing, and fiber optics manufacturing, Air Products is growing faster than the market. The company's KeepCOLD Cryogen Fill Services Program supplies more than 4,500 MRI customer sites around the world. Finally, Air Products owns Gardner Cryogenics, a world leader in manufacturing liquid helium and liquid hydrogen distribution and storage equipment.

Company Profile

Air Products and Chemicals, Inc. is a leading supplier of industrial gases and related equipment, specialty and intermediate chemicals, as well as environmental and energy systems. It has operations in thirty countries and had revenues of $5.5 billion in fiscal 2000.

Air Products's industrial gas and chemical products are used by a diverse base of customers in manufacturing, process, and service industries.

In the environmental and energy businesses, Air Products and its affiliates own and operate facilities to reduce air and water pollution, dispose of solid waste, and generate electric power.

Industrial Gases
- APD is a world leader.
- Its products are essential in many manufacturing processes.
- Gases are produced by cryogenic, adsorption, and membrane technologies.
- They are supplied by tankers, on-site plants, pipelines, and cylinders.
- International sales, including the company's share of joint ventures, represent more than half of Air Products' gas revenues.

The markets served by Industrial Gases include chemical processing, metals, oil and gas production, electronics, research, food, glass, health care, and pulp and paper. Principal products are industrial gases, such as nitrogen, oxygen, hydrogen, argon, and helium, and various specialty, cutting, and welding gases.

Chemicals
- APD has a leadership position in over 80 percent of the markets served.
- Markets include a wide range of attractive, diversified end uses that reduce overall exposure to economic cycles.
- World-scale, state-of-the-art production facilities and process technology skills ensure consistent, low-cost products while enhancing long-term customer relationships.
- International sales, including exports to over 100 countries, represent almost 40 percent of APD's business.

The markets served by the Chemicals operation include adhesives, agriculture, furniture, automotive products, paints and coatings, textiles, paper, and building products. Its principal products are emulsions, polyvinyl alcohol, polyurethane and epoxy additives, surfactants, amines, and polyurethane intermediaries.

Environmental and Energy Systems
- Facilities, owned and operated with partners, dispose of solid waste, reduce air pollution, and generate electrical power.
- Strong positions are built by extending core skills developed in the industrial gas business.
- Forces driving this market are environmental regulations, demand for efficient sources of electrical power, utility deregulation, and privatization. Principal products are waste-to-energy plants, electric power services, and air pollution control systems.

The markets served by Environmental and Energy Systems include solid waste disposal, electrical power generation, and air pollution reduction.

Equipment and Services

• Cryogenic and noncryogenic equipment is designed and manufactured for various gas-processing applications.

• Equipment is sold worldwide or manufactured for Air Products's industrial gas business and its international network of joint ventures.

The markets served by Equipment and Services include chemicals, steel, oil and gas recovery, and power generation.

Highlights of 2000

■ Achieved record sales and record net income, excluding special items.

■ Achieved outstanding operating leverage; 9 percent revenue growth resulted in 18 percent earnings growth.

■ Improved operating return on net assets to 11.1 percent.

■ Reduced absolute capital spending by 12 percent compared with the prior year.

■ Reduced selling, general, and administration costs, excluding acquisitions, compared with 1999.

■ Divested the polyvinyl alcohol business.

■ Acquired the remaining 51 percent of Korea Industrial Gases.

■ Increased its dividend for the eighteenth consecutive year.

Shortcomings to Bear in Mind

■ Air Products has a rather leveraged balance sheet. Its common stock represents only half of capitalization. My preference is for common stock to represent 75 percent of capitalization.

■ Air Products had to record a $300-million after-tax charge in the second quarter of 2000 as a result of its failed joint attempt to acquire rival BOC Group, p.l.c. Its partner in the deal was Air Liquide SA of France. The two companies said they would withdraw their bid of $11 billion because they couldn't meet the May 12 deadline on which their offer expired.

Reasons to Buy

■ Demand for industrial gas has been strong. This high demand is more than a cyclical phenomenon and is being fueled by new applications and new industrial gas production technology.

■ Beyond its leadership in tonnage hydrogen, Air Products also has a substantial liquid hydrogen business. The National Aeronautics and Space Administration (NASA) is the world's largest customer of liquid hydrogen. The company has been serving NASA since the 1960s, when APD first began supplying hydrogen for the Apollo space program. Over the last twenty years, Air Products has safely and reliably provided hydrogen for NASA's space shuttle engine-testing program and all eighty-five shuttle launches.

■ Today, some 60,000 customers in North America—once served by eighty different locations—are now managed from the company's Single-Point-Of-Contact Center using state-of-the-art information technology systems. The number of error-free deliveries is improving, customer runouts are significantly lower, and APD's customers are increasingly positive about the changes made.

■ Air Products's reputation for reliability and innovation has made the company a preferred supplier to the electronics industry. As the market leader in North America and Europe and a strong competitor in Asia through joint ventures, APD's global infrastructure assures its electronics customers that they can count on receiving the same high-quality products and services regardless of where they are.

■ Air Products continues to be among the lowest-cost, highest-quality manufacturers in the chemicals industry.

■ Earnings and dividends have been advancing at a healthy clip. EPS climbed from 98 cents in 1990 to $2.46 in 2000, a compound annual growth rate of 9.6 percent. In the same ten-year stretch, dividends expanded from 35 cents to 74 cents, a growth rate of 7.8 percent.

■ Because of APD's technical leadership, operating expertise, and established franchises, the company is the world's number one supplier of HYCO (hydrogen, carbon monoxide, and syngas, a mix of hydrogen and carbon monoxide) products. Government regulations for cleaner fuels will double worldwide HYCO demand in the next eight years, creating an opportunity for Air Products to make disciplined investments that will deliver strong revenue and profit growth.

■ Sales of the company's electronics division were up about 30 percent in 2000 compared with the prior year. What's more, Harold A. Wagner, the com-pany's outgoing CEO, says APD "will continue to achieve solid double-digit growth. By capitalizing on our technical expertise in fluorine chemistry and working closely with our customers, we positioned nitrogen trifluoride as the chamber-cleaning agent of choice. As a result, by the spring of 2002, we will have tripled our capacity, in order to meet growing global demand."

■ In 2000 the company received more than thirty awards from major customers. For instance, Lucent Technologies's Microelectronics Group gave APD its Pinnacle Award, rating the company the best of its gases and chemical suppliers. Sumitomo Sitix Silicon, Inc. named Air Products Supplier of the Year based on the company's superior supply capability and customer service.

Total assets: $8,270 million
Current ratio: 1.31
Common shares outstanding: 209 million
Return on 2000 shareholders' equity: 18.6%

		2000	1999	1998	1997	1996	1995	1994	1993
Revenues (millions)		5467	5020	4919	4638	4008	3865	3485	3328
Net income (millions)		533	451	489	429	416	368	264	268
Earnings per share		2.46	2.09	2.22	1.95	1.69	1.62	1.03	1.16
Dividends per share		.74	.70	.64	.58	.54	.51	.48	.44
Price	High	42.2	49.3	45.3	44.8	35.3	29.8	25.2	24.3
	Low	23.0	25.7	33.2	25.2	21.9	19.4	18.8	18.2

CONSERVATIVE GROWTH

Alberto-Culver Company

2525 Armitage Avenue ▢ Melrose Park, Illinois 60160 ▢ Investor contact: Wesley C. Davidson (708) 450-3145 ▢ Web site: www.alberto.com ▢ Dividend reinvestment plan is not available ▢ Fiscal year ends September 30 ▢ Listed: NYSE ▢ Ticker symbols: ACV and ACV.A ▢ S&P rating: A+ ▢ Value Line financial strength rating: B++

For almost forty years, the Alberto-Culver Company, a pioneer on the global package goods stage, has carried the flag from country to country, continent to continent. Today, the company sells its products, such as Alberto VO5 and St. Ives Swiss Formula, in 120 countries, with manufacturing facilities in Sweden, the United Kingdom, Australia, Argentina, Mexico, Puerto Rico, and Canada, as well as here at home.

Following the acquisitions in Argentina and Chile in 1999, Alberto-Culver added to its lineup in fiscal 2000 when its Swedish subsidiary, Cederroth International, acquired Soraya in Poland, including its factory, sales organization, and popular skin-care line. In addition to a base in Poland, Soraya gives the company an additional resource for expanding its business throughout Eastern Europe, which it sees as an excellent future growth platform for its products.

Company Profile

Alberto-Culver is a leading developer and manufacturer of personal care products, primarily for hair care, retail food products, household items, and health and hygiene products. Alberto-Culver is comprised of three strong businesses built around potent brands and trademarks:

• Alberto-Culver USA develops innovative brand-name products for the retail, professional beauty, and institutional markets. Personal-use products include hair fixatives, shampoos, hair dressings, and conditioners sold under such trademarks as Alberto VO5, Bold Hold, Alberto, Alberto Balsam, Consort, TRESemme, and FDS (feminine deodorant spray).

• Retail food product labels include SugarTwin, Mrs. Dash, Molly McButter, Baker's Joy, and Village Saucerie.

• Household products include Static Guard (antistatic spray) and Kleen Guard (furniture polish).

• Alberto-Culver International has carried the Alberto VO5 flag into more than 120 countries and from that solid base has built products, new brands, and businesses focused on the needs of each market.

• Sally Beauty Company is the engine that drives Alberto-Culver. With over 2,000 outlets in the United States, the United Kingdom, Canada, Puerto Rico, Japan, and Germany, Sally is the largest cash-and-carry supplier of professional beauty products in the world. It is the market leader by a wide margin. Sally capitalizes on its dominance in that niche, which gives beauty professionals the opportunity to purchase products from a wide selection of vendors at wholesale prices without having to manage and carry inventory in their stores. Sally is the largest distributor of professional beauty supplies in the world.

Alberto-Culver's products do not have a common origin. They have come to the company in diverse ways. For instance, the original Alberto VO5 Hairdressing was a small regional brand that the company acquired because it felt it had national sales potential.

In another instance, the FDS products and its mousse products had counterparts in the marketplace in Europe. Consequently, ACV brought the ideas to the United States and introduced its products to an American audience.

In another realm, Mrs. Dash, Static Guard, and Consort were all developed internally by the company's research and development team because its customers identified a need that these products met.

In yet another instance, SugarTwin and TRESemme were acquired by the company as tiny brands and grown to the strong positions they hold today.

Perhaps the company's most important acquisition—after the original purchase of Alberto VO5 Conditioning Hairdressing—was the purchase of the Sally Beauty Company, originally a chain of twelve stores, many of which were franchised.

Today the chain has over 2,000 company-owned stores, including units in Great Britain, Germany, and Japan. The typical Sally Beauty store averages 1,800 square feet and is situated in a strip shopping center. It carries more than 3,000 items.

About three-quarters of Sally Beauty's sales are to the salon and barber professional who finds at Sally an unmatched selection of professional beauty supplies available at discount prices. In addition to the supplies they need, these professionals find in Sally a valuable source of information about trends and products that they can take back to their customers.

One of the keys to Sally's success is the ability to quickly get product from warehouse to shelf. This process starts with proprietary point-of-sale registers in each Sally store that record and report each sale. Sally is now investing millions of dollars to add a second POS register to each store to enhance its ability to serve customers.

Shortcomings to Bear in Mind

■ Over the past forty-five years, the company has experienced steady growth. However, it can't match the stylish image of some competitors. Indeed, retailers often relegate their bargain-basement products to the bottom shelf—eye level, of course, would be a better place to catch the consumer's attention. And professional hair stylists turn their noses up at its old standbys such as Alberto VO5, TRE-Semme, and St. Ives Swiss Formula.

"They've got good products, but they are not linked with the current expression of high style," said Brian Hurley, president of Fairman, Schmidt & Hurley, an advertising agency that is familiar with hair-care advertising.

These pejorative comments don't seem to faze CEO Howard Bernick. "We have stood the test of time. We've been hearing predictions of our demise from so-called financial experts, but we keep going from record year to record year."

■ Sally Beauty Company experiences domestic and international competition from a wide range of retail outlets, including mass merchandisers, drug stores, and supermarkets, carrying a full line of health and beauty products. In addition, Sally Beauty competes with thousands of local and regional beauty supply stores and full-service dealers selling directly to salons through both professional and distributor sales consultants as well as cash-and-carry outlets open only to salon professionals. Sally also faces competition from certain manufacturers that employ their own sales forces to distribute professional beauty products directly to salons.

Reasons to Buy

■ Alberto-Culver has survived—and grown—by staying true to its low-cost niche. In the past couple years, the company freshened up the forty-five-year-old brand, Alberto VO5, with new herbal shampoos that sell for as little as $.99 a bottle. By contrast, Clairol's Herbal Essences sell for six times as much. The new herbal shampoos helped propel sales of Alberto VO5 shampoos up 39 percent in calendar year 2000.

The company also introduced facial creams for St. Ives, such as one that includes retinol, an antiwrinkle ingredient. In early 2001, moreover, the company expanded its TRESemme line of hair-care products with a new shampoo and conditioner designed to hold more moisture in the hair.

■ Despite what its critics say, the company had a stellar year in 2000. In the words of Mr. Bernick, "Our Alberto-Culver North American consumer products business had a spectacular year, with a sales increase of 18.4 percent and a profit increase of 25 percent. Our Alberto VO5 shampoos and conditioners are selling to consumers at a stronger pace than at any time in our history."

■ The company's Sally Beauty Company—the largest and most successful distributor of professional beauty supplies in the world—also fared well in 2000 and continued its consistent top- and bottom-line growth. It achieved a 16 percent sales increase to over $1.25 billion. The traditional Sally store chain expanded in 2000, adding fifty-seven new stores in the United States to reach 1,901 by fiscal year end 2000.

- Alberto VO5 Conditioning Hairdressing remains by far the number one brand in its category and the best-selling hairdressing in the world. VO5 is among the market leaders in the United States, Great Britain, Scandinavia, Canada, Mexico, Australia, and Japan.
- In over 120 countries, Alberto-Culver International markets or manufactures many of the consumer brands that it markets in the United States, including Alberto VO5 and St. Ives Swiss Formula brands.

In addition, some of the company's international units offer products unique to their markets. In the Scandinavian countries, for example, it is the market leader in a wide range of toiletries and household products. In the United Kingdom, the company is a market leader in hair-styling products. What's more, it has introduced several items in the hair-coloring segment. Finally, in Canada, Alberto-Culver produces the top-selling Alberto-European styling line, and its SugarTwin artificial sweetener is number one in its category.

- In the past ten years (1990–2000), the company's earnings per share advanced from $.65 to $1.72, a compound annual growth rate of 10.2 percent. In that period, EPS experienced only one down year, when earnings dipped from $.65 to $.53 in 1991. In the same ten-year stretch, annual dividends per share climbed from $.10 to $.30, a compound growth rate of 11.6 percent.

Total assets: $1,390 million
Current ratio: 2.17
Common shares outstanding: 56 million
Return on 2000 shareholders' equity: 17.1%

	2000	1999	1998	1997	1996	1995	1994	1993
Revenues (millions)	2247	1976	1835	1775	1590	1358	1216	1148
Net income (millions)	97.2	86.3	83.1	75.6	62.7	52.7	44.1	41.3
Earnings per share	1.72	1.51	1.37	1.25	1.06	.94	.79	.72
Dividends per share	.30	.26	.24	.20	.18	.16	.14	.14
Price High	43.5	27.9	32.4	32.6	25.0	18.3	13.7	14.1
Low	19.4	21.6	19.8	23.6	16.3	12.9	9.7	10.1

AGGRESSIVE GROWTH

Alcoa, Inc.

201 Isabella Street at 7th Street Bridge □ Pittsburgh, Pennsylvania 15212-5858 □ Investor contact: Charles D. McLane (212) 836-2674 □ Dividend reinvestment plan is available: (800) 317-4445 □ Web site: www.alcoa.com □ Listed: NYSE □ Ticker symbol: AA □ S&P rating: B+ □ Value Line financial strength rating: A

An advanced aluminum alloy developed by Alcoa is creating a major stir in the plastics industry. Called QE-7, the new material is the hardest, strongest, and longest lasting aluminum alloy available to make molds for injection molding of plastic parts.

QE-7 aluminum's thermal conductivity is 4.5 times higher than that of steel. This feature gives molding customers shorter cooling times, reduced cycle time, higher productivity, and improved finished-part stability.

In the first year of production using QE-7 tooling to mold polypropylene, a major domestic toy maker showed productivity gains of 30 percent compared with molds made of P20 steel, the industry standard until now. Studies by Purdue University and trials at GE Plastics also demonstrated cycle-time savings in the 20 to 30 percent range using a variety of polymers. A major introduction program for QE-7 began in 2001.

Highlights of 2000

Alcoa had another solid year in 2000, with net income the highest in the company's 112-year history. The acquisitions of Reynolds Metals Company and Cordant Technologies Inc. were completed in 2000 and began adding to earnings in the fourth quarter. These acquisitions are not a new strategy for Alcoa. Over the past five years, the company has completed thirty-two acquisitions on four continents.

- Net income of $1,484 million, a 41 percent increase over 1999.
- Revenues of $22,936 million, also a 41 percent increase.
- Return on average shareholders' equity of 16.8 percent.
- Achievement of the $1.1-billion cost-reduction target.
- Aluminum shipments of 5,398 million metric tons, a gain of 21 percent over the prior year.

Improved financial results for 2000 were the result of higher volumes, aided by the Reynolds and Cordant acquisitions, coupled with an increase in aluminum prices and continued operating improvements.

Company Profile

Alcoa (formerly Aluminum Company of America), founded in 1888, is the world's leading integrated producer of aluminum products. These products are used worldwide by packaging, transportation, building, and industrial customers. In addition to components and finished products, Alcoa produces alumina, alumina-based chemicals, as well as primary aluminum for a multitude of applications.

Alcoa's operations are broken down into the following segments:

The alumina and chemicals segment includes the production and sale of bauxite, alumina and alumina chemicals.

Aluminum processing comprises the manufacturing and marketing of molten metal, ingot, and aluminum products that are flat-rolled, engineered, or finished.

The nonaluminum products segment includes the production and sale of electrical, ceramic, plastic and composite materials products, manufacturing equipment, gold, separations systems, magnesium products, as well as steel and titanium forgings.

Since aluminum is expensive and has difficulty competing against steel—even though it has some admirable qualities—it might appear to be a rare element. Not so.

Aluminum is an abundant metal and, in fact, is the most abundant metal in the earth's crust. Of all the elements, only oxygen and silicon are more plentiful. Aluminum makes up 8 percent of the crust. It is found in the minerals of bauxite, mica, and cryolite, as well as in clay.

Until about a hundred years ago, aluminum was virtually a precious metal. Despite its abundance it was very rare as a pure metal. The reason: it was so difficult to extract from its ore.

This is because aluminum is a reactive metal, and it cannot be extracted by smelting with carbon.

To solve the enigma, displacement reactions were tried, but metals such as sodium or potassium had to be used, making the cost prohibitive.

Electrolysis of the molten ore was tried, but the most plentiful ore, bauxite, contains aluminum oxide, which does not melt until it reaches 2050°C.

The solution to the problem of extracting aluminum from its ore was discovered by Charles Hall in the United States and by Paul Heroult in France—both working independently. The method now used to extract aluminum from its ore is called the Hall-Heroult process.

I won't bore you with the steps taken to effect this process. The important fact to remember is that it is far from cheap. Even so, it can be done economically enough to make aluminum the second most widely used metal. However, it is not likely to replace iron and steel any time soon. Iron makes up more than 90 percent of the metals used in the world.

The main cost in the Hall-Heroult process is electricity. So much energy is required that aluminum smelters have to be situated near a cheap source of power, normally hydroelectric.

The price of entry into the business is so high that it discourages most upstarts from taking the plunge.

On the other hand, this frustrating effort to produce commercial aluminum is worth the cost because the white metal has a number of valuable attributes: it has a low density; it is highly resistant to corrosion; it is light-weight—one-third the weight of steel; it is an excellent reflector of heat and light; it is nonmagnetic; it is easy to assemble; it is nontoxic; it can be made strong with alloys; it can be easily rolled into thin sheets; it has good electrical conductivity; it has good thermal conductivity; and it doesn't rust.

Shortcomings to Bear in Mind

- Partially offsetting the positive factors in 2000 were higher energy prices, a higher effective tax rate, and softening in the transportation, building, construction, and distribution markets.
- In early 2001, Alcoa said it would cut production at two smelters in the Northwest, where power shortages are especially acute. On the other hand, Alcoa might actually benefit from higher energy costs. According to analysts, it appears that the aluminum market is now as tight as it has been since 1988, and prices could double or even triple during 2001 as plants cut production.

Reasons to Buy

- In 2000, Alcoa invested $2.3 billion to buy Cordant Technologies in a move to further diversify beyond its aluminum-making business. With the purchase of Cordant, based in Ogden, Utah, Alcoa is moving into the growing and profitable aerospace and industrial markets. It is the goal of Alain J. P. Belda, Alcoa's president and CEO, to have Alcoa expand into a $40-billion company by 2004, from $16.3 billion in 1999. Cordant's largest market is industrial gas turbines that generate power. The company's other businesses consist of rocket-propulsion systems, fasteners, and super-alloy and titanium components used in jets.
- During periods when the aluminum industry suffers through a protracted slump in aluminum prices, Alcoa has seen its profits rise. Part of that is due to the effects of recent acquisitions. But much of the improvement can be traced to a new corporate philosophy called the "Alcoa Business System." Essentially, it calls for plants to produce more, faster, and not let it sit on

the docks for too long. The new production processes are "deceptively simple and seemingly obvious," says one analyst. But on top of other cost-cutting efforts already in the works, they are helping Alcoa weather what otherwise might be a dismal year. As aluminum prices recover—either because of growing demand or because excess capacity is shuttered—Alcoa stands to see earnings jump dramatically. Analysts say that each penny increase in the LME price of aluminum boosts Alcoa's per-share earnings by about 12 cents. LME refers to the spot price of aluminum ingots on the London Metals Exchange. Normally, the prevailing world price of aluminum is an important determinant of aluminum companies' profits. From 1982 through 1995, Alcoa's earnings and the LME price moved in lock step. Since then, however, the LME price has dropped while Alcoa's earnings have held steady or drifted up. According to the company's chief financial officer, Richard Kelson, "We are breaking away from the LME pricing."

■ Efforts to develop low-cost, high-performance aluminum casting methods for the automotive industry are progressing on several fronts. In 2000, Alcoa acquired Alloy Technologies Ltd., which manufactures aluminum castings using patented technology.

Alcoa is working with Lingotes Especiales, S.A., of Spain to expand the commercial application of this process—called automated green sand casting (AGSC)—for automotive components. AGSC is a low-cost, high-volume, flexible process that is already producing parts for several European carmakers. Alcoa Automotive's British Casting Center in Leyland, England is currently the focal point of AGSC development.

■ The Mercedes-Benz S-Class is the newest production model from the German automaker to feature aluminum in body structure applications. Introduced at the 1999 Geneva Auto Show, the car went into full production in early 2000. Alcoa Automotive's Casting and Extrusion Finishing plant in Soest, Germany is producing several components for this path-breaking Mercedes, including an Alcoa Vacuum Die Cast sidewall component as well as extrusions for the front and rear roof frames and supporting cross members for the passenger compartment.

■ New products are the lifeblood of any consumer products company. In 2000, Alcoa Consumer Products fired up one new product introduction after another. Here are a few examples:

● Reynolds Extra Wide Plastic Wrap, with a width of 18 inches, is 50 percent wider than other plastic wraps for easy covering of larger food items, platters, and containers.

● Reynolds Grill Buddies Foil Sheets are extra heavy-duty sheets of aluminum foil that lay over the grill to provide a clean cooking surface and prevent delicate food from dropping through. Precut slots allow the special flavors of grilling to come through.

● Presto Sure-Seal Disposable Containers come in two convenient sizes—soup and salad, and entree. They can be used for storing, freezing, and microwaving food, and they are dishwasher safe.

■ Several new products, moreover, are slated for introduction in the next year or two. Alcoa's purchase of Reynolds is adding significantly to this effort with new technologies, improved processes, and a strong R&D commitment.

Total assets: $31,691 million
Current ratio: .95
Common shares outstanding: 814 million
Return on 2000 shareholders' equity: 16.8%

	2000	1999	1998	1997	1996	1995	1994	1993
Revenues (millions)	22936	16323	15340	13319	13061	12500	9904	9056
Net income (millions)	1484	1054	859	759	555	796	193	67
Earnings per share	1.80	1.41	1.22	1.09	.79	1.11	.27	.10
Dividends per share	.50	.40	.38	.25	.33	.23	.20	.20
Price High	43.6	41.7	20.3	22.4	16.6	15.1	11.3	9.8
Low	23.1	18.0	14.5	16.1	12.3	9.2	8.0	7.4

AGGRESSIVE GROWTH

American Express Company

World Financial Center □ 200 Vesey Street □ New York, New York 10285 □ Investor contact: Susan Korchak (212) 640-4953 □ Dividend reinvestment plan is available: (800) 842-7629 □ Web site: www.americanexpress.com □ Listed: NYSE □ Ticker symbol: AXP □ S&P rating: A- □ Value Line financial strength rating: A

The American Express of today is a far cry from the American Express of even five years ago. After a long period of stagnation and decline, the number of Amex cards in circulation has been climbing. What's more, the company—known for its signature green charge cards and travelers checks—seems to be learning to play the credit card game, which requires a different set of skills than the traditional charge card business.

Because of its recent success under the able leadership of former CEO Harvey Golub, the stock of AXP over the past decade has outperformed not only its peers among the S&P 500 but the rambunctious Nasdaq as well.

One factor to bear in mind is the emergence of Kenneth Chenault, who took the reins as the company's CEO at the beginning of 2001.

"When Ken joined American Express twenty years ago, no one would have taken odds that he would be CEO," said John O. Utendahl, one of Chenault's closest friends and the owner of Wall Street's biggest minority-controlled firm, Utendahl Capital. "But as crazy as this may sound, Ken would

have taken that bet. The playing field for minorities may not be level, but when Ken plays, he plays to win."

Prior to his elevation to the corner office overlooking the New York harbor, Ken Chenault had spent about four years as the number two man under the indomitable Harvey Golub. In that role, Chenault spearheaded Golub's effort to boost the company's financial performance and reinvigorate both its core card business and its corporate culture.

As the economy showed signs of weakening in 2001, Ken Chenault, the new man at the helm of American Express, had his work cut out for him. In 2000, the company did well, with a rise in revenues of 13 percent and a gain in net income of 14 percent.

Company Profile

American Express is best known for its flagship charge card and travelers check products. It also offers travel-related services, financial advisory services, and international banking services. The company is the world's largest travel agency (tied with Japan Travel) and issuer of traveler's checks.

Continuing the reconfiguration it began with the spinoff of stockbroker Lehman Brothers, the company is focusing on its corporate travel and credit card businesses and has launched an online bank.

The company's growth strategy focuses on three principal themes:

• Expanding its international presence.

• Strengthening the charge card network.

• Broadening its financial services offerings.

Travel-Related Services

Travel-Related Services (TRS) markets travelers checks and the American Express Card, including the Gold Card, the Platinum Card, the Corporate Card, and the Optima Card. TRS also offers business-expense management products and services, corporate and consumer travel products, tax preparation and business-planning services, magazine publishing, and merchant transaction processing. In 2000, TRS reported a net income of $1.93 billion, up 14 percent from the prior year.

American Express Financial Advisors

Financial Advisors provides financial products, including financial planning and advice, insurance and annuities, investment products such as mutual funds, limited partnerships, investment advisory services, trust and employee plan administration services, personal auto and homeowner's insurance, and retail securities brokerage services. In 2000, American Express Financial Advisors reported a net income of $1.03 billion, a gain of 10 percent over 1999.

American Express Bank Ltd.

American Express Bank Ltd. offers products designed to meet the financial services needs of corporations, financial institutions, affluent individuals, and retail customers. Primary business lines are corporate banking and finance, correspondent banking, private banking, personal financial services, and global trading. The unit also operates the Travelers Check business. In 2000, American Express Bank reported net income of $29 million, compared with $22 million the prior year.

Shortcomings to Bear in Mind

■ Analysts are concerned over American Express's revenue, which began decelerating in mid-2000. They point out that the company is more susceptible than the average card issuer to a slowdown in revenue growth as a result of a slowing economy (notably because a greater proportion of its revenue stream is derived from charge volume). As one analyst pointed out, "Although American Express enjoys one of the premier brand names among financial services companies, peers enjoy revenue growth that is faster."

■ In the past ten years (1990–2000) American Express had a solid record of earnings increases, from $.71 in 1990 to $2.07 in 2000, for a compound annual growth rate of 11.3 percent. However, its record of dividend increases is essentially flat. In the same ten-year stretch, dividends per share inched ahead from $.31 to $.32. On the other hand, the dividend payout ratio is extremely growth-oriented because the company pays out less than 16 percent of its earnings, preferring to reinvest the rest in company expansion.

Reasons to Buy

■ In a world where thieves and bandits are lurking around every corner—not to mention those who are prowling around the Internet—it's not surprising that credit card holders are sometimes reluctant to order merchandise over the Web, fearing that one of those miscreants will latch on to the number and use it to buy a new Bentley.

American Express to the rescue. In late 2000, the company was a pioneer in the development of a credit card without a number. Instead, the new card lets you make a purchase with a random number. This number is valid for one transaction only. The primary goal, American Express said, is to convert an untold number of potential shoppers who troll through the Web sites but don't shop because they are reluctant to send their private credit card data. American Express hopes to tap into the mounting pressure on online ventures to turn Web traffic into actual sales and profits. Although the new technology will lower fraud risk, the company does not plan to change the rates charged to merchants.

- Over the past decade American Express has acquired about seventy accounting firms, including the largest independent accounting firms in Chicago and New York. American Express officials say the company is aiming to become "a national accounting practice."

With fifty offices in eighteen states, including all the biggest markets, it has already made a giant step toward that goal.

American Express Tax and Business Services is now the ninth-largest accounting firm in the United States according to Bowman's *Accounting Report*. In 1998 AXP bought Altschuler, Melvoin and Glasser, the largest non–Big Five accounting firm in Chicago. Before that, it acquired Goldstein Golub Kessler & Company, a New York-based accounting firm that was the nation's largest single-office CPA firm.

According to a company spokesman, "We have a goal to become one of the biggest tax advice firms in the United States. Our cardholders have been asking for tax services."

- American Express's Blue credit card has been a huge success. Demand for the card, which contains a computer chip to make buying products on the Internet easier, has been more than twice the expected rate. The card also offers such perks as no annual fee, a low fixed-interest rate, and a link to the company's Web site for online bill payment and other money-management software. What's more, the company launched a rewards program for Blue similar to the programs currently offered with its other cards.

- Like most of corporate America, AXP is determined to get its share of Internet business. According to Ruediger Adolf, American Express senior vice president, Strategy and Business Development, "Our strategy for winning on the Internet consists of four basic elements:
  1. Becoming and remaining a leader in online payments;
  2. Making American Express the preferred destination for financial services, lifestyle, and travel;
  3. Establishing comprehensive online servicing that achieves the same high level of service for which American Express is already known;
  4. Reengineering our business activities to significantly increase our value to our customers, our employees and our shareholders."

Mr. Adolf goes on to say, "The assets that have made American Express one of the leading global financial services companies are highly relevant on the Internet:

- We have one of the most recognized and respected brands in the world, representing security, integrity, and trust. In fact, in a recent survey Interbrand rates American Express as one of the top twenty world's most valuable brands.
- We have deep relationships across a variety of different customer sets. For

example, we have a large and affluent cardmember base with over 49 million cards in force worldwide. We own, manage, or administer nearly $300 billion of assets for our 2.3 million financial services customers. And we transact with millions of merchants in over 200 countries and territories.

- We have a broad and diverse product set catering to the financial and travel-related needs of our consumer, small business, and corporate customers. Globally, we have over 500 different card products in over 25 markets."

Total assets: $154,423 million
Common shares outstanding: 1,355 million
Return on 2000 shareholders' equity: 25.3%

	2000	1999	1998	1997	1996	1995	1994	1993
Revenues (millions)	22085	21279	19026	17760	16237	15841	14282	14173
Net income (millions)	2810	2475	2201	1991	1739	1564	1380	1172
Earnings per share	2.07	1.81	1.59	1.38	1.30	1.04	.89	.77
Dividends per share	.32	.30	.30	.30	.30	.30	.30	.33
Price High	63.0	56.3	39.5	30.5	20.1	15.0	11.0	12.2
Low	39.8	31.6	22.3	17.9	12.9	9.7	8.4	7.5

CONSERVATIVE GROWTH

American Home Products Corporation

Five Giralda Farms ▢ Madison, New Jersey 07940 ▢ Listed: NYSE ▢ Investor contact: Thomas G. Cavanagh (973) 660-5000 ▢ Dividend reinvestment plan is available: (800) 565-2067 ▢ Web site: www.ahp.com ▢ Ticker symbol: AHP ▢ S&P rating: B ▢ Value Line financial strength rating: A+

"Biotechnology played a key role in the development of PTP-112, a novel treatment for type 2 diabetes," said Kurt Steiner, Ph.D., Senior Director, Biological Research, Wyeth-Ayerst Research, the pharmaceutical arm of American Home Products Corporation.

"In type 2 patients—who constitute the vast majority of diabetics—the pancreas continues to produce insulin, but the tissues in the body that normally react to insulin don't respond properly or efficiently. As a result of this 'insulin resistance' blood sugar levels rise, and vital processes in the body that usually are triggered by insulin don't respond appropriately, creating serious health problems such as kidney failure, nerve damage, and blindness."

According to Dr. Steiner, "We wanted to get at the root of the problem and find a way to overcome insulin resistance. Our search for potential therapeutic targets focused on the PTPase family of enzymes because they are directly involved in the process of 'turning off' insulin receptors.

"With the help of biotechnology, we validated one specific target enzyme, PTP-1B. We then created a humanized, recombinant version of the protein to use with a high-throughput screen, rapidly testing tens of thousands of compounds to find one that would inhibit the action of the enzyme. Upon finding a promising candidate, we refined it using technologies such as X-ray crystallography and molecular modeling, along with creative medicinal chemistry to enhance the structure of the compound for greater efficacy. The result of that work was PTP-112, a small molecule with a novel therapeutic action that keeps the insulin receptor 'turned on' and prolongs the body's responses to insulin. PTP-112 is scheduled to begin Phase II clinical trials in 2001."

Company Profile

American Home Products Corporation is a global leader in pharmaceuticals, consumer health care products, and animal health products. Its products are sold in more than 150 countries. AHP's worldwide resources encompass more than 48,000 employees, manufacturing facilities on five continents, and one of the industry's broadest R & D programs, representing all three major discovery and development platforms—small molecules, proteins, and vaccines.

AHP's broad, growing lines of prescription drugs, vaccines, nutritionals, over-the-counter medications, and medical devices benefit health care worldwide. Among the company's leading products are such names as Triphasal, Norplant, Premarin, Cordarone, Naprelan, Orudis, Advil, Anacin, Dimetap, Robitussin, Preparation H, Centrum vitamins, Primatene, SMA, Lodine, and Effexor.

Shortcomings to Bear in Mind

- The company agreed to pay the federal government $30 million as part of a settlement with the Food and Drug Administration (FDA) over alleged manufacturing problems at company plants in Pearl River, New York and Marietta, Pennsylvania. The FDA action, taken in late 2000, came after a series of inspections earlier in the year uncovered quality-control issues at the plants. The FDA said it did not find contaminated products and was not aware of any illnesses. Even so, it called the manufacturing problems serious violations of rules meant to ensure that drugs and vaccines are sterile and of high quality.

"We were putting in place improvements in order to meet FDA and our own expectations," said Bruce Burlington, senior vice president for regulatory affairs and compliance at Wyeth-Ayerst, a subsidiary. "FDA concluded that we were not moving as fast as they expected us to."

"It's a non-event," said Neil B. Sweig, a drug-industry analyst at Ryan Beck Southeast Research. Mr. Sweig said the financial impact to the company is negligible.

Reasons to Buy

- American Home Products's revenue growth in 2000 underscores the strength of its global pharmaceutical business. Today, more than 81 percent of net revenues are from pharmaceuticals—up from 51 percent just ten years ago.
- AHP's performance in new product introductions is among the most impressive in the industry. Wyeth-Ayerst, the company's ethical pharmaceutical division, received regulatory approval for seven major pharmaceutical and vaccine products from June 1999 to May 2000, the best product approval record in the industry during that time span.
- The company took aggressive action during 2000 to move toward resolution of the diet drug (Redux and Pondimin) litigation involving AHP. In August 2000, the company received trial court approval of the negotiated nationwide, class action settlement of the litigation, which covers the vast majority of the individuals who used the company's diet drugs. Among patients who opted

out of the settlement, about 80 percent of claims now have been settled or are subject to settlement agreements. In the fourth quarter of 2000, the company recorded an additional charge of $7.5 billion related to the litigation, bringing the total charges to $12.25 billion. American Home Products believes "that no further charges will be required."

■ The strong growth of the company's human pharmaceutical business in 2000 reflected the impact of new product launches as well as the continuing strength of AHP's cornerstone global products.

Sales of the Premarin family of hormone replacement therapy products approached $1.9 billion for the year. Worldwide sales of the Effexor family of antidepressants reached nearly $1.2 billion in 2000—a 48 percent increase over 1999. Enbrel (to treat congestive heart failure) achieved $690 million in global sales. Wyeth-Ayerst continued to expand these key product lines in 2000 with new claims, indications, and dosages: Effexor XR was approved in the United States for the long-term treatment of generalized anxiety disorder; Enbrel received FDA approval for inhibiting the progression of structural damage in the joints of early stage rheumatoid arthritis (RA) patients; and regulatory submissions were filed for new, lower dose formulations of Premarin and Premarin/MPA products.

■ The company's new products also produced significant results in 2000. Meningitec, a meningococcal Group C conjugate vaccine, reached the market in the United Kingdom in October 1999, enabling the U.K. Department of Health to initiate a vaccination program before the 1999–2000 winter season. Meningococcal disease is one of the most common causes of death in children and young people under the age of twenty in the United Kingdom. In January 2001, the U.K. Department of Health reported a 90 percent reduction in the number of meningococcal Group C cases in the age group at highest risk—attributed to the inception of the vaccination program.

■ Prevnar, the first vaccine to help prevent invasive pneumococcal disease in infants and young children, has been well-received in both the private and public health sectors following its recommendation for infant immunization. After FDA approval in early 2000, Wyeth-Ayerst shipped more than 9 million doses of Prevnar for a total of $461 million in sales in 2000. The European Union approved the vaccine in February 2001.

■ In February 2000, the FDA approved Protonix for short-term treatment in the healing and symptomatic relief of erosive esophagitis. Following a May 2000 launch, Protonix had a successful first year with sales of $145 million in 2000.

■ AHP has a strong presence in the osteoarthritis treatment market with Synvisc, the leading viscosupplementation product in the United States. Synvisc is injected into the knee to restore lubrication and cushioning to the joint. Synvisc, jointly developed with Genzyme Biosurgery, increased sales in 2000 by 44 percent to $179 million.

■ Whitehall-Robins Healthcare (which produces products sold over the counter rather than by prescription) continues to be a leader in the global consumer health care market. Total sales in 2000 were nearly $2.5 billion, driven by increased sales in the company's three largest consumer health care categories—analgesics, cough/cold/allergy products, and vitamins/nutritional supplements. Ten of the division's products rank number one or two in their category in the United

States. What's more, two global consumer health care brands—Advil and Centrum—are among the top ten selling consumer health care brands in the world.

■ AHP's Fort Dodge is a global leader in the animal health industry. Fort Dodge sales in 2000 reached nearly $800 million, an increase of 20 percent over the prior year. Fort Dodge has expanded recently through innovative product development supplemented by a series of strategic acquisitions. Product introductions during the year included the launch in Australia of ProHeart SR12, a groundbreaking, once-a-year injectable for the prevention of heartworms in dogs. ProHeart SR12 entered the U.S. market in 2001.

■ American Home Products formed a biotechnology research alliance with Elan Corporation p.l.c. in the spring of 2000 to develop an Alzheimer's vaccine. The alliance will allow AHP and the Irish firm to collaborate in research, development, and marketing of an experimental therapy called AN-1792 to treat mild to moderate Alzheimer's and possibly prevent the onset of the affliction. Elan's preclinical research has shown that the therapy reduces and prevents the development of amyloid plaque, a substance associated with Alzheimer's.

■ Premarin and its family of products are the most prescribed medications in the United States. Considering that Premarin has been on the market for nearly sixty years, this leadership position is particularly noteworthy. And now there are new opportunities to use Premarin as a springboard to expand the company's women's health care franchise.

Research provides increasing evidence of the potential consequences of estrogen deficiency on bone mineral density, cardiovascular health, and cognitive functioning. Wyeth-Ayerst, through its Women's Health Research Institute, is at the forefront of research in hormone replacement and estrogens. Currently, the company is pursuing Phase III studies of lower doses of Prempro to determine its benefits on bone and on menopausal symptoms.

Trimegestone, a new progestin for hormone replacement and contraception, is undergoing evaluations in combination with Premarin, as well as with 17 B-estradiol for hormone replacement and with ethinyl estradiol for contraception.

Total assets: $21,092 million
Current ratio: 1.64
Common shares outstanding: 1,310 million
Return on 2000 shareholders equity: NM

	2000	1999	1998	1997	1996	1995	1994	1993
Revenues (millions)	13263	11881	13463	14196	14088	13376	8966	8305
Net income (millions)	2514	2133	2474	2160	1883	1338	1528	1469
Earnings per share	1.90	1.61	1.85	1.67	1.48	1.10	1.24	1.18
Dividends per share	.92	.91	.87	.86	.79	.76	.74	.72
Price High	65.3	70.3	58.8	42.4	33.3	25.0	16.8	17.3
Low	39.4	36.5	37.8	28.5	23.5	15.4	13.8	13.9

American International Group, Inc.

70 Pine Street □ New York, New York 10270 □ Investor contact: Charlene M. Hamrah (212) 770-6293 □
Dividend reinvestment plan is not available □ Web site: www.aig.com □ Listed: NYSE □ Ticker symbol: AIG □
S&P rating: A+ □ Value Line financial strength rating: A+

Several factors set American International Group (AIG) apart from other insurance and financial services organizations:

Extensive worldwide network. More than half of AIG's pretax income has traditionally come from overseas sources. AIG's global network traces its roots to insurance operations established in China and Southeast Asia over eighty years ago, and today that network spreads around the world.

Disciplined underwriting and strict expense controls. These bedrock principles guide AIG's operations and result in a general insurance combined loss expense ratio that regularly runs up to ten points better than the industry average.

Financial strength. AIG holds the highest ratings from the principal rating services and ranks first in net profits by a wide margin among all U.S.-based insurance operations and seventeenth among all U.S. public corporations.

Company Profile

American International Group is the leading domestic international insurance organization and the largest underwriter of commercial and industrial insurance in the United States. Its member companies write property, casualty, marine, life, and financial lines insurance in some 130 countries and jurisdictions. The company is also engaged in a range of financial services and investment management businesses.

AIG's global businesses also include financial services and asset management, including aircraft leasing, financial products, trading and market making, consumer finance, institutional, retail and direct investment fund asset management,

real estate investment management, and retirement savings products.

Core Businesses
- The largest U.S. commercial property-casualty insurance operation.
- A growing U.S. personal lines business.
- The most extensive international life and general insurance businesses of any insurance organization.
- A portfolio of highly targeted financial services businesses.
- A growing global asset management business.
- Retirement savings product through SunAmerica.

Business Overview
Domestic General Brokerage Group (DBG) markets property-casualty insurance products and services through brokers to corporate America and other commercial customers. The DBG companies write most classes of insurance and are leaders in many specialty classes, including directors and officers, professional, and management liability.

Domestic Personal Lines markets personal insurance products, principally automobile insurance, in the United States using multiple distribution channels. The Mass Marketing Division, providing coverage for preferred and standard auto risks, has expanded its direct-to-consumer programs to forty-six states. The Specialty Auto Division features nonstandard auto programs, produced by independent agents, with operations in thirty states.

Foreign General Group comprises AIG's international property-casualty operations, encompassing Asia, the Pacific Rim, the Americas, Europe, Africa, and the Middle East. Operating through American International Underwriters (AIU), the group markets a full range of property-casualty products to both consumer and commercial clients.

Life Insurance operations, located largely overseas, comprise the most extensive worldwide network of any life insurer. American International Assurance Company, Ltd. (AIA) is the leading life insurer in Southeast Asia. Nan Shan Life Insurance Company is one of the largest life insurance companies in Taiwan. American Life Insurance Company (ALICO) operates in about fifty countries in the Far East, Europe, the Middle East, South Asia, Latin America, and the Caribbean.

Domestically, based on assets, the SunAmerica life companies collectively rank in the top two percent of all U.S. life insurers. AIG Life Companies (U.S.) are among the fastest-growing issuers of life insurance in the United States and, with the support of AIG, hold the highest ratings from both Moody's and Standard & Poor's.

Financial Services Group consists of International Lease Finance Corporation, the global market leader in leasing and remarketing of advanced technology commercial jet aircraft to airlines around the world; AIG Financial Products Corp., which specializes in a wide variety of standard and customized interest rate, currency, equity, and credit products; AIG Trading Group Inc., which engages in hedged trading and market making in foreign exchange, interest rates, and base and precious metals; and AIG Consumer Finance Group, Inc., which is engaged in developing a multiproduct consumer finance business with an emphasis on emerging markets.

The Asset Management Group consists of AIG's growing investment management businesses. AIG Global Investment Group, Inc. subsidiaries and various other investment management operations of AIG manage nearly $34 billion of third-party institutional, retail, and private equity assets on a global basis.

John McStay Investment Counsel, L.P. provides money-management services, specializing in smaller and mid-capitalization growth equities and real estate securities, and manages the Brazos family of mutual funds. SunAmerica Asset Management Corp. manages a family of twenty-five U.S. retail mutual funds and serves as an investment advisor for SunAmerica's variable annuities.

AIG Asset Management International, Inc. develops, distributes, and manages retail mutual funds worldwide; with 9,000 affiliated representatives, the SunAmerica Financial Network is the primary distribution channel for SunAmerica's retirement savings products and services. Other asset management businesses include private banking and real estate investment management.

Shortcomings to Bear in Mind

■ Looming over AIG is the issue of succession, although some believe that Maurice "Hank" Greenberg, the company's CEO, is irreplaceable. "Who can succeed him? Nobody," insists one industry insider. "The company should probably be broken up following Greenberg's departure because no one else has the granular control of all of AIG's disparate operations. Everything fits together because Hank makes it fit together."

One thing working in Greenberg's favor is a strain of longevity in his family. To be sure, he is past normal retirement age—he turned seventy-six in May of 2001. However, his mother lived beyond ninety. Another relative lived to be over 100, according to Evan Greenberg. "That probably means that

Dad will be around aggravating all of us for at least another twenty-five years," he observes, only partly in jest.

- After building the most powerful insurance company in America, Hank Greenberg wanted to leave one of his sons in charge when he retired or died. But that dream seemed to evaporate in the fall of 2000 with the abrupt announcement that Evan Greenberg, his forty-six-year-old son, was leaving American International Group. Mr. Greenberg had designated Evan, the president and chief operating officer, as the crown prince and had repeatedly defended him as the best choice for the job.

    Evan Greenberg said he was leaving because "it is time for a change, and I'd like to do something different."

    "I'm not the guy to run AIG," he told subordinates when he disclosed his resignation decision. According to one source, Evan Greenberg decided to depart because "he found himself working to the bone" and second-guessed about his performance.

Reasons to Buy

- In a major move, American International Group acquired American General Corporation in May of 2001 for $23 billion in stock. Based in Houston, Texas, American General has 1,350 offices in forty states and employs 16,000. This deal scuttled an earlier pact for Britain's Prudential p.l.c. to buy American General.

    When Mr. Greenberg disclosed that the company had bid for American General in April of 2001, he pointed to its fast-growing variable annuity business as a major attraction, one that he could combine with AIG's SunAmerica unit. The deal also makes American International Group one of the nation's largest life insurers. Prior to the takeover, the bulk of the AIG life insurance business was overseas.

- According to analysts at Credit Suisse First Boston Corporation, American International Group is unusually well positioned for future growth, based on such factors as:
  - Its scope and profitability worldwide.
  - The capability of its management.
  - Innovative product development to satisfy specific market needs.
  - A high level of pricing and underwriting discipline.
  - The ability to reinsure any risk underwritten (thereby reducing exposure to earnings and capital from large claims).
  - The largest foreign market position of any U.S.-based insurer.
  - The scope of AIG's worldwide operations allows capital to be allocated to faster-growing, less-competitive, more attractive markets.
  - The breadth of the company's operations and its disciplined underwriting have contributed to a superb operating record.
  - AIG's domestic general insurance operations have one of the lowest expense ratios of any property-casualty-related insurer. This favorable expense ratio is an important competitive advantage.

- In a move to broaden its property and casualty business and expand abroad, AIG bought HSB Group Inc. in mid-2000 for $1.2 billion. HSB is the parent company of Hartford Steam Boiler Inspection and Insurance Company. The largest domestic insurer of machinery and against equipment breakdown, HSB Group has provided specialty property coverage since 1866. "It seems to me a smart transaction," said Alain Karaoglan, an analyst with Donaldson Lufkin & Jenrette. "HSB has some unique expertise that complements AIG. They can take that expertise and export it internationally and be very successful."

Total assets: $307 billion
Common shares outstanding: 2,343 million
Return on 2000 shareholders' equity: 15.6%

	2000	1999	1998	1997	1996	1995	1994	1993
Premiums earned (millions)	17407	15544	14498	12692	11855	11406	1028	79567
Net income (millions)	5737	5055	3766	3332	2897	2510	2176	1939
Earnings per share	2.45	2.13	1.91	1.69	1.46	1.26	1.09	.95
Dividends per share	.15	.13	.12	.10	.09	.08	.07	.06
Price High	103.8	75.3	54.7	40.0	27.6	22.6	15.9	15.8
Low	52.4	49.4	34.6	25.2	20.9	15.2	12.9	11.6

GROWTH AND INCOME

American Water Works Company

1025 Laurel Oak Road □ P. O. Box 1770 □ Voorhees, New Jersey 08043 □ Investor contact: James E. Harrison (856) 346-8200 □ Dividend reinvestment program is available: (877) 987-9757 □ Web site: www.amwater.com □ Ticker symbol: AWK □ S&P rating: A □ Value Line financial strength rating: A

American Water Works Company announced at the end of 2000 that it had joined forces with DuPont Qualicon to introduce an easier and lower-cost method of detecting Cryptosporidium parvum in drinking water.

Cryptosporidium is a waterborne parasite that is found in drinking water in the United Kingdom and the United States. This deadly organism can cause diarrhea, abdominal cramps, vomiting, and fever and can be fatal to people with damaged immune systems, such as those with AIDS or leukemia. Conventional filtration and chlorine disinfection are not effective at removing the parasite.

The new test—called the BAX System—is a breakthrough screening method that applies genetics-based testing to water samples for fast, accurate results. Through the use of polymerase chain reaction, the BAX system provides yes-no answers within four hours after sampling, without the need for confirmation or expert interpretation results.

"The water industry has been monitoring Cryptosporidium for the past decade," said Mark LeChevallier, Ph.D., Director of Research for American Water

Works. "Ever since the first recognized waterborne outbreaks of Cryptosporidium parvum in the 1980s, researchers have been working to better understand the occurrence and control of the organism. Until now, the test used to detect the organism in water was complicated, time-consuming, expensive, and did not detect all of the organisms in a sample. As it becomes more widely used, this new test will help to prevent future outbreaks of this potentially deadly organism."

The American Water Works Company has been at the forefront of Cryptosporidium research for the past decade. It developed the combined Giardia, Cryptosporidium antibody test that has become the standard method of testing used throughout the water industry.

Company Profile

In addition to being the most capital intensive of all utilities, the water business in the United States is highly fragmented. Ninety percent of the country's estimated 60,000 separate water systems serve fewer than 3,000 people each and are finding it increasingly difficult to provide the capital required to remain profitable and to provide adequate service. Thus, regional approaches are emerging as the preferred solution to the nation's water service challenges.

For its part, American Water Works Company, Inc. is a holding company of water utilities. Together with its twenty-three wholly owned water service companies, it represents the largest regulated water utility business in the United States.

Subsidiaries serve a population of about ten million people in more than 1,300 communities in twenty-three states, from Pennsylvania and Tennessee in the East and Southeast to Indiana and California in the Midwest and West. AWK serves a total of 2.5 million customers.

American Water Works gets most of its water from lakes, rivers, and streams, but also taps wells and other utilities to produce more than 250 billion gallons of water each year.

The American Water Works Service Company, a subsidiary, provides professional services to affiliated companies. These services include accounting, administration, communication, corporate secretarial, engineering, financial, human resources, information systems, operations, rates and review, risk management, and water quality. This arrangement, which provides these services at cost, affords affiliated companies professional and technical talent otherwise unavailable economically or on a timely basis.

Shortcomings to Bear in Mind

■ The weather plays an important part in the fortunes of a typical water company. They do best during hot, dry summers, since this stimulates the use of water for showers, lawns, and gardens. However, if the weather is excessively dry, the government may step in and ration the use of water for car washing, gardens, and lawns.

On the other hand, if the region is deluged with rain, there is far less reason for customers to water their lawns and gardens. They may even take fewer showers if the temperature is cool.

American Water Works, for its part, is not as seriously hurt by a dry summer in one or two of its territories, assuming the weather is not severe in its other jurisdictions. Smaller water companies, by contrast, usually serve parts of a single state or city and are more vulnerable to droughts or other vagaries in the weather.

■ A water utility—like all public utilities—is closely regulated by a state commission. Each state has its own commission, some of which are more politically motivated than others. They tend to settle rate cases by favoring the consumer rather than the company.

■ Public utilities fret about interest rates. There are two reasons: For one thing, they borrow a lot of money, and high interest rates boost their costs. Secondly, they offer investors a good source of income. However, when interest rates rise, some investors may sell their utility shares and go elsewhere to take advantage of the higher interest rates. When this happens, the shares of the utility decline.

Reasons to Buy

■ Revenues increased 7 percent in 2000 to $1.35 billion. Contract management revenues from American Water Works Services accounted for about 45 percent of this revenue increase. The remainder resulted from rate increases and the addition of about 200,000 people to the population served by the company. These growth factors served to offset the sales volume losses caused by abnormal summer weather conditions.

■ The water utility industry is extremely fragmented, but it is becoming less so as takeovers reduce their ranks. Even so, there are still more than 60,000 independent water systems. Most are owned by financially constrained local municipalities or private investors. The attraction of many of these smaller utilities to the larger water companies is the risk reduction they could provide through geographic diversification.

The smaller entities have another serious problem: Water utilities have had to spend large sums of money in recent years in order to bring their plant and equipment up to the standards mandated by the Safe Drinking Water Act, the Clean Air Act, and other regulations. In this realm, the larger investor-owned utilities are much better suited to tap the financial markets in order to raise the needed cash to solve regulatory mandates.

To meet today's standards of quality, reliability, and affordability requires ever-increasing technical expertise, financial resources, and operational efficiencies. In this environment, size and financial strength become essential elements in satisfying the water service needs of customers. Yet, 90 percent of the water systems in the nation serve fewer than 3,300 people each, and 97 percent serve fewer than 10,000.

■ American Water Works has been active on the acquisition front. In 2000 the company completed ten acquisitions. What's more, applications for fifteen acquisitions were awaiting regulatory approval at the end of the year. Since 1990, American Water Works has completed more than 100 acquisitions, adding more than 3.5 million people and 700 communities to the company's service territory.

In February 2001, AWK announced that its Pennsylvania subsidiary had received approval from the Pennsylvania Public Utility Commission to purchase the water and wastewater assets of the City of Coatesville Authority (CCA). At the time, the company's CEO, J. James Barr, said, "The Coatesville system currently serves 8,600 water customers and 6,500 wastewater customers, making this purchase of municipally owned assets the largest privatization project of its kind in the nation." Privatization in the water industry is not new. However, most of the nation's large privatization projects to date have involved only transfer of operating responsibility, not asset ownership.

■ One of the key characteristics of the consolidation of the water utility business is the demand for high water quality. Unlike any other utility service, water companies must protect the safety of their product because people drink it. Pollution of water sources, better testing technology, and government regulation are requiring additional water filtration, chemical treatment, and extensive water monitoring.

For many water systems, that means skyrocketing costs and greater technical expertise in the operation and monitoring of water treatment facilities. Assuring water quality today requires an ongoing investment in research, construction, testing, and monitoring.

A leader in the water business, American Water Works and its subsidiaries have long committed the capital and employee resources needed to maintain a high level of water quality across the twenty-three-state system of water utilities.

Recently, new regulations and public concern have centered on naturally occurring parasite contaminants such as giardia and cryptosporidium. American Water Works has reacted in anticipation of these regulations with the incorporation of particle-count monitoring, improved disinfection, and upgraded filtration. In addition, with regulation targeting more stringent control of byproducts from the use of chlorine and other chemicals, process modification and alternative disinfectants are being introduced into existing facilities.

Another potential future treatment requirement is the removal of radon from some well water sources. American Water Works has tested every source of well water in its operations and is prepared to introduce either aeration or granular activated carbon filtration when needed.

■ The water utility business is less competitive than other utility businesses. For one thing, it is not threatened by the competitive pressures weighing down the electric and telephone utility businesses.

Water is a relatively inexpensive commodity to obtain but a difficult one to transport, which makes competition in the industry less likely. Barriers to entry include the immense cost of infrastructure development and necessary proximity to a water supply.

Total assets: 6,135 million
Current ratio: 0.45
Common shares outstanding: 98 million
Return on 2000 Shareholders' equity: 9.6%

	2000	1999	1998	1997	1996	1995	1994	1993
Revenues (millions)	1351	1261	1017	954	895	803	770	718
Net income (millions)	157	148	127	115	102	92	74	79
Earnings per share	1.61	1.53	1.54	1.45	1.31	1.26	1.17	1.15
Dividends per share	.90	.86	.82	.78	.70	.64	.54	.50
Price High	29.4	34.8	33.8	29.7	22.0	19.6	16.1	16.1
Low	18.9	20.5	25.3	19.9	17.8	13.4	12.6	12.3

CONSERVATIVE GROWTH

Avery Dennison Corporation

150 North Orange Grove Boulevard □ Pasadena, California 91103-3596 □ Investor contact: Cynthia S. Guenther (626)-304-2204 □ Dividend reinvestment plan is available: (800) 756-8200 □ Web site: www.averydennison.com □ Listed: NYSE □ Ticker symbol: AVY □ S&P rating: A+ □ Value Line financial strength rating: A

Avery Dennison Corporation announced in early 2001 that it had established Avery Dennison Medical, a new business unit in the company's Worldwide Specialty Tape Division.

Avery Dennison Medical will operate as a full-line supplier, building on its core competencies in manufacturing, converting, and research and development to create specialized adhesives and proprietary technologies for the wound-care, surgical, ostomy, electro-medical, and diagnostic markets.

"Our specialty tapes are already used by some of the largest medical product innovators in the industry," said Philip M. Neal, chief executive officer of Avery Dennison. "The health care industry is constantly looking for new products that will reduce costs and improve patient outcomes."

"Highly specialized wound-care products that reduce the time required for care or improve the quality of patient comfort will win," added Mr. Neal. "Advances in medical technology have resulted in new, minimally invasive surgical procedures that have created increased demand for advanced, over-the-counter health care products as patient care shifts from the hospital to the home environment."

The demand for advanced health care management products is projected to expand annually at double-digit rates. Key factors driving growth include longer life spans and new medical technologies that reduce mortality and morbidity as well as enhance quality of life.

Company Profile

Avery Dennison is a global specialty chemical, industrial, and consumer-products company. Its pioneering pressure-sensitive technology is an integral part of products found in virtually every major industry. The company was formed in 1990 with the merger of Avery International Corporation and Dennison Manufacturing Corporation.

The company's primary businesses are organized into two sectors under a decentralized management structure.

The Pressure-Sensitive Adhesives and Materials Sector manufactures adhesives and base materials for industrial and commercial applications. In 2000, this unit made up 53 percent of sales and 42 percent of operating profits.

The Consumer and Converted Products Sector manufactures self-adhesive products for the office and home—including desktop printer labels and cards, markers, and organization and presentation products—and a variety of self-adhesive industrial labels, fastening devices, self-adhesive industrial labels, fastening devices, self-adhesive postage stamps, battery tester labels, and other specialized label products for global markets. This unit was responsible for 47 percent of sales in 2000 and 58 percent of operating profits.

The company employs more than 17,400 people in 200 manufacturing and sales facilities that produce and sell Avery Dennison products in eighty-nine countries.

The company is best known for its Avery-brand office products, Fasson-brand self-adhesive base materials, peel-and-stick postage stamps, industrial and security labels, retail tag and labeling systems, self-adhesive tapes, and specialty chemicals. Well-known products include the United States Postal Service's self-adhesive stamps and Duracell's battery-testing labels.

Under the Avery Dennison and Fasson brands, the company makes papers, films, and foils coated with adhesive and sold in rolls to printers. The company also makes school and office products (Avery, Marks-A-Lot, Hi-LITER), such as notebooks, three-ring binders, markers, fasteners, business forms, tickets, tags, and imprinting equipment.

Shortcomings to Bear in Mind

- Value Line Survey, a leading statistical and advisory service, is not convinced that now is the time to buy shares in Avery. "We think Avery Dennison may have a tough time generating more than marginal revenue gains in 2001. First, the slowing economy will probably hurt volumes, particularly for pressure-sensitive materials, in which Avery holds approximately 40 percent market share domestically."

- In a report issued in early 2001, Credit Suisse First Boston Corporation said, "In addition to weakening economic trends, near-term trends among office products superstore customers are generally poor, with retail store closings and inventory reductions likely to crimp near-term demand for Avery's office products."

Reasons to Buy

- "Avery Dennison acquired Dunsirn Industries Inc. in early 2001. Dunsirn is a leading provider of nonpressure-sensitive materials to the narrow web printing industry. Dunsirn, based in Neenah, Wisconsin, also provides high-quality, contract slitting and distribution services for paper, film, textile, non-woven, and specialty roll materials.

"Avery Dennison's roll materials capabilities will expand overnight with the additional technical expertise, sales channel, and distribution infrastructure that Dunsirn brings to us," said Mr. Neal. "Our global reach will enable us to grow the business by introducing Dunsirn products to international markets, while our Fasson customers will benefit from the convenience of purchasing roll materials, both pressure-sensitive and nonpressure-sensitive, from a single source."

- The dividend has been increased for twenty-five consecutive years. In the last ten years, dividends advanced from $.32 to $1.11, a compound annual growth rate of 13.2 percent. In the same period, earnings per share expanded from $.58 to $2.85, a growth rate of 17.3 percent.

- Self-adhesive labels imprinted with bar codes have greatly increased the speed and accuracy of baggage sorting—as well as a multitude of other tasks. For instance, they're used for inventory control, product tracking, distribution, and logistics management. What's more, you'll find them everywhere, from airports to hospitals to warehouses to retail stores to packages ordered on the Internet.

- The company's Fasson-brand materials set the industry standard for variable information printing applications. They ensure superior barcoding, which translates into accurate scanning. Also, they stay stuck to a wide variety of surfaces, even in harsh environments.

- In another sector, Avery Dennison automotive products decorate, seal, identify, and secure items throughout millions of automobiles. The automotive industry uses the company's specialty self-adhesive tapes instead of nuts, bolts, and other fasteners. What's more, that industry uses Avery's labels to carry all kinds of important information—from part numbers to safety warnings—on components like air bags and radiator covers.

These products can also enhance a car's appearance, inside and out, with attractive exterior graphics, including decorative striping, and interior laminates, such as wood-grain films. In addition, Avery Dennison Avloy Dry Paint film is changing the way the automotive industry thinks about finishing plastic-based car parts. Major manufacturers are using the company's performance films more and more as an alternative to spray-painting—on everything from side moldings to spoilers. And with good reason. Avery Dennison Avloy film looks great and is durable, cost-effective, and friendly to the environment.

- Although Avery Dennison is well-known for its office products, the company is now expanding beyond the office with useful, creative, and fun products for making personalized items right at home. These include greeting cards, banners, posters, flyers, and T-shirts.

- Even the wine industry is being attracted to Avery products. For wine label designers, the possibilities are endless. According to management, "Wineries love the production efficiencies—hundreds of domestic wineries are using pressure-sensitive labels already—and Avery Dennison is leading the way worldwide."

Avery Dennison's Decorating Technologies Division worked with E&J Gallo Winery to create a new Avery Dennison Clear ADvantage heat-transfer label for a new line of wines known as Wild Vines. Gallo selected the Avery Dennison labeling process because of its unique capability in achieving a frosted-bottle look.

- Nor has the company ignored the Internet. The Avery Web site enhanced consumer awareness and demand for Avery-brand products. The site, which drew several million hits in 2000, provides free Avery Wizard and Avery LabelPro software, which can be downloaded to create an instant base of new customers.

- The company now has a European Films Center in Gotha, Germany, the largest label film facility outside North America, to meet rapidly growing demand for Fasson pressure-sensitive label materials throughout Europe.

- The company's Fasson Roll Specialty business has achieved double-digit growth, creating innovative, customized solutions—such as dissolvable labels, holographic films, and unique wall covering materials—that incorporate pressure-sensitive adhesive technology.

- South of the border, Avery has been aggressively pursuing its Latin American growth strategy—including the acquisition of a prominent pressure-sensitive materials business in Colombia and substantial majority ownership in its label materials operation in Argentina—significantly strengthening the company's market presence of its roll materials business in this expanding region.

- Across the Pacific, despite economic turmoil in some Asian nations, the company's label materials operation in Asia Pacific continues to grow, reflecting the rapid growth of consumer products markets in the region. Sales of the company's pressure-sensitive materials have been growing in China at a double-digit pace.

- In April 2001, Polaroid Corporation and Avery Dennison introduced an instant photo identification badge kit that contains everything needed to produce cut-and-paste photo ID badges. Included in the kit is a Polaroid Pocket ID instant camera as well as easy-to-print-and-format name badges provided by Avery.

Total assets: $2,699 million
Current ratio: 1.23
Common shares outstanding: 110 million
Return on 2000 shareholders' equity: 34.6%

	2000	1999	1998	1997	1996	1995	1994	1993
Revenues (millions)	3894	3768	3460	3346	3222	3114	2857	2609
Net income (millions)	284	215	223	205	174	143	109	83
Earnings per share	2.85	2.55	2.15	1.94	1.61	1.34	.99	.72
Dividends per share	1.11	1.13	.87	.72	.62	.56	.50	.45
Price High	78.5	73.0	62.1	45.8	36.5	25.1	18.0	15.8
Low	41.1	39.4	39.4	33.4	23.8	16.6	13.3	12.6

GROWTH AND INCOME

Baldor Electric Company

5711 R. S. Boreham Jr. Street □ Fort Smith, Arkansas 72901 □ Investor contact: John A. McFarland (501) 646-4711 □ Dividend reinvestment plan is available: (800) 509-5586 □ Web site: www.baldor.com □ Listed: NYSE □ Ticker symbol: BEZ □ S&P rating: A □ Value Line financial strength rating: B++

With annual sales of just over $600 million, Baldor Electric Company is a pygmy among giants. What sets Baldor apart, analysts believe, is its innovative approach to business. For one thing, Baldor offers a broad selection of motors. What's more, it produces motors in small lot sizes that only fit the needs of a small group of customers. About one-third of what it sells are custom products.

Second, the company is a domestic manufacturer. Even so, Baldor's margins are about the same as most of its competitors. Some of these rivals, moreover, also include higher-margined mechanical transmissions linkage products. What's more,

Baldor has the highest margins of any domestic industrial motor manufacturer. Analysts think part of the explanation relates to Baldor's fragmented customer base—it has over 8,000 customers. Additionally, the company sells only a modest volume into the consumer market where the customers are large and can exercise significant pricing leverage.

Third, Baldor doesn't have its own sales force. Instead, it relies on independent sales representatives who are paid on commission. Each of these agents has an exclusive territory and sells all of Baldor's products in that region. In addition, the mix of Baldor's business is more heavily weighted to distributor sales—50 percent of sales, compared with 33 percent for the industry. This is a plus factor because distributors tend to concentrate on the replacement market—it's more recession-resistant than the original-equipment realm.

Company Profile

Baldor makes electric motors that power pumps, fans, conveyor belts, and all the other automated components that keep modern factories humming. It competes successfully against much larger firms such as Emerson Electric and General Electric. But what Baldor lacks in size, it more than makes up for in flexibility and profitability.

Baldor Electric designs and manufactures a broad product line to serve its customers' diverse needs. Industrial AC and DC electric motors, ranging from 1/50 through 800 horsepower, are the mainstay of the company's products.

Baldor's line of Standard-E motors are designed to meet the efficiency requirements of the Energy Policy Act. Baldor's premium efficient Super-E motors are widely recognized as offering some of the highest efficiencies. These higher efficiencies translate into lower operating costs to the motor end-user.

Baldor also offers customers a wide range of "definite-purpose" motors. Examples include Baldor's Washdown Duty, motors which are ideal for food processing and other wet environments. Baldor's Chemical Processing line of cast-iron motors are built for the harsh environment of mills and processing plants. Baldor Farm Duty motors meet the rugged outdoor requirements in the agricultural market. Also included are broad lines of brakemotors, explosion-proof, C-Face pump motors and gearmotors.

The fastest growing segment of Baldor's product line is adjustable-speed drives. The company offers DC SCR controls, AC inverters and vector control, and a wide range of servo and positioning products. Baldor markets Matched Performance by offering customers matched motor and control packages with lab-tested performance.

Baldor recently introduced the Baldor SmartMotor, an integrated motor and adjustable-speed control. Now available from 1 to 10 horsepower, this breakthrough new product is easy to install and offers many performance advantages.

Shortcomings to Bear in Mind

■ Like a lot of other companies, Baldor took its lumps in the early part of 2001. According to the Standard & Poor's tear sheet, "Net sales in the 13 weeks ended March 31, 2001, declined 5 percent, year to year, reflecting a broad-based decrease in orders and restructuring costs in Europe. Despite well controlled SG&A expenses, operating profit dropped 37 percent."

Reasons to Buy

■ Baldor Electric spends thousands of hours every year talking with customers to see how the company is perceived. Baldor consistently receives high grades. In recent surveys, for instance, 82 percent of those interviewed named Baldor first when asked, "What motor line do you prefer?"

- Management's philosophy toward inventories is not typical. Although many efficiency experts argue that manufacturers should strive for just-in-time operations, Baldor has a mind of its own. Baldor believes that, given the nature of its customers, the benefits of having inventories on hand outweigh the costs. Quick delivery times are very important to Baldor's customers, especially the distributors. Therefore, having available products and being able to deliver nearly any motor in less than twenty-four hours helps the company to obtain sales. What's more, the margins on short-lead-time sales are also higher.

- Information is an important competitive advantage for Baldor. The company's CD-ROM electronic catalog, first introduced in 1994, is now in its fifth edition. It is used by over 30,000 customers. BEZ's Web site, moreover, is visited daily by users around the world. In 1998, Baldor added 285 new motors and drives to its catalog. The company now offers more than 5,000 different products—far and away the industry's broadest line of stock motors and drives.

- In 2000 Baldor was first to introduce a new technology grease developed by Exxon especially for electric motor bearings. This new grease has a lubrication life up to four times longer than other greases in temperatures as high as 350°F. It also exhibits greater durability to mechanical shearing forces and has superior resistance to washout, rust, and corrosion.

- The long-awaited move to factory automation is gaining momentum, which is good news for Baldor. Such core industries as pulp and paper, mining, and petrochemical, for instance, are devising new, more efficient methods of operation. These include

applications perfect for Baldor's extensive line of high-performance drives, from logging and sawmilling to textiles and plastics.

- Electric motors and drives are used in virtually all industries. Take, for example, the high-precision robotic positioning needs of medical equipment and semiconductor manufacturers. These represent new and fast growing markets for Baldor servos, especially the company's new palm-size BSM 50 brushless servo motor.

- Baldor engineers have been working for several years on a line of commercial-duty motors. These motors are designed for use in commercial applications such as ventilation blowers used in shopping malls and fast-food restaurants where industrial motors are too much for the job. Baldor has also developed special flange-mount pump commercial motors. The company estimates the domestic market for these commercial motors to be as much as $400 million.

- Today, the industrial drives business is growing much faster than the motor business. In fact, within a couple of years, the company believes it will be as big as the entire industrial motor business. This nearly doubles BEZ's opportunities for growth domestically and abroad.

  Baldor high-performance drives are now being used in applications previously handled by fixed-speed motors. The result is far greater productivity, flexibility, and reduced operating costs.

- More than half of the company's capital equipment has been replaced during the past five years. Its work force is nonunion. The company relies on a vertically integrated manufacturing strategy to achieve solid quality control, producing most of the component parts that go into its motors, such as laminations, endplates, rotors, and conduit boxes.

■ Somewhat surprisingly, motor manufacturing is still a rather labor-intensive endeavor (final assembly is still done largely by hand). However, Baldor has invested heavily in modernizing its factories, using a concept called flexible-flow manufacturing. The essence of flexible flow, compared with the prior-batch system is this: In the past, the company might have produced hundreds and perhaps thousands of a particular motor model before switching production to another, thereby generating a potentially large (and unnecessary) finished goods inventory of each model. With flexible flow, production runs are much shorter—perhaps even tailored to a single order. Each worker puts together a complete motor from a tray of parts. The tray is tagged with a computer printout directing the assembler what kind of motor to build, how to assemble the parts, and how to test the complete motor. As a result of the Baldor approach, lead times for custom motors have been dramatically reduced and are running at about one-half of the competition.

■ The popularity of Baldor's Web site, *www.baldor.com*, continues to grow, with over 20,000 separate visits per month. *Plant Services* magazine named the company's Web site as one of the best at serving the needs of plant engineers. Baldor recently added a feature to give its distributors the ability to check inventory availability on any of the company's more than 5,000 stock products, such as motor efficiency data, dimension drawings, and Matched Performance curves. What's more, new products are highlighted as well as information on the company's training classes, trade shows, sales offices, and service centers. In addition, Baldor made it easy for someone to quickly locate nearby Baldor stocking distributors by simply entering a zip code.

■ In the first quarter of 2001, Baldor introduced some 500 new stock products, including commercial motors in fractional horsepower sizes, an expanded line of premium efficient motors, larger explosion-proof motors commonly used in the oil and gas industry, and portable generators from Pow'R Gard Generator Corporation, acquired late in 2000. This purchase should fit nicely into Baldor's existing motor and drives business, since generators represent another cost-efficient method for customers to meet their energy needs. Analysts look for Pow'R Gard, which should add $25 million to revenues in 2001, to enhance earnings in 2001.

Total assets: $465 million
Current ratio: 2.98
Common shares outstanding: 34 million
Return on 2000 shareholders' equity: 17.5%

	2000	1999	1998	1997	1996	1995	1994	1993
Revenues (millions)	621	577	589	558	503	473	418	357
Net income (millions)	46	44	45	40	35	32	26	19
Earnings per share	1.34	1.19	1.17	1.09	.97	.84	.70	.52
Dividends per share	.49	.43	.40	.35	.29	.26	.21	.16
Price High	22.5	21.7	27.2	23.8	18.8	19.9	13.6	12.3
Low	14.9	17.0	10.1	18.2	13.9	12.9	10.6	8.1

The Bank of New York Company, Inc.

One Wall Street □ New York, New York 10286 □ Investor contact: Rick Stanley (212) 635-1854 □ Dividend reinvestment plan is available: (800) 432-0140 □ Web site: www.bankofny.com □ Listed: NYSE □ Ticker symbol: BK □ S&P rating: A □ Value Line financial strength rating: A

Focused acquisitions, which add both new customers and new products, continue to play an important role in Bank of New York's overall growth strategy. The company announced ten acquisitions in 2000. In the Corporate/Master Trust servicing area, the company acquired four books of business, with Harris Trust being the most significant.

In another sector, the company enhanced its global trade execution and clearing operations with four key acquisitions: SG Cowen Securities, Schroder & Company, BHF Securities, and GENA. Finally, the Bank of New York expanded its BNY Asset Management and Private Client Services group through the addition of Ivy Asset Management, a leading alternative investment fund of funds manager, and Bank of America's Advisory Custody activity for high-net-worth clients.

Company Profile

Bank of New York does not dominate the New York landscape. Even so, the bank is thriving after several years of shuffling its businesses and swallowing a string of small, niche-oriented acquisitions.

While largely sitting out the recent merger wave that is reshaping the banking group, Bank of New York has carved out a growing and highly profitable role as one of the nation's major processors of basic securities transactions. In fact, analysts say it resembles a processor more than a bank, especially considering its relatively modest consumer banking operation.

According to one analyst, "BK can probably be most accurately described as a

leading global trust bank, rather than a traditional lending institution."

The Bank of New York is one of the largest bank holding companies in the United States, with total assets of more than $77 billion at the end of 2000.

The company provides a complete range of banking and other financial services to corporations and individuals worldwide through its core businesses. These services include: securities and other processing, corporate banking, retail banking, trust, investment management, and private banking and financial market services.

The company's principal subsidiary, the Bank of New York, is one of the largest commercial banks in the United States. It was founded in 1784 by Alexander Hamilton and is the nation's oldest bank operating under its original name.

The bank is an important lender to major domestic and multinational corporations and to midsize companies nationally. It is the leading retail bank in suburban New York. The bank is also the largest provider of securities-processing services to the market and a respected trust and investment manager. It also provides cash-management services to corporations located primarily in the Mid-Atlantic region.

In the realm of Securities Servicing and Global Payment Services, Bank of New York is the world's premier asset servicer and global payments provider. What's more, the bank ranks as the number one or two provider in most of the markets it serves. Growth across business lines accelerated in 2000, produced by strong sales momentum, revenues from strategic acquisitions, and expansion of global financial markets. Aggressive investment in leading-edge technology helped the company to capitalize on a rapidly changing global market. Fee revenues in 2000 climbed to $1.91 billion, a 26 percent increase.

In the Retail Banking sector, BK operates a network of 349 full-service branches, establishing the bank as a leader in the suburban metropolitan New York market. These branches offer a combination of traditional banking and alternative banking services, including financial planning and insurance products to about three-quarters of a million individual households and businesses.

With over $14 billion in core deposits, retail banking continues to provide a stable, low-cost funding source that supports lending activities throughout the bank. Results in 2000 were exceptional, with mutual funds swept balances and total noninterest income increasing by 27 percent and 15 percent, respectively.

Corporate banking is responsible for the worldwide management of commercial and institutional relationships. Experienced relationship managers oversee the delivery of the full range of the bank's credit and noncredit products and focus on cross-selling the bank's fee-based services.

Bank of New York is focused on maintaining strong asset quality and balancing the risks and profitability of every client relationship. An important result of this strategy is that the bank's credit-only exposures have declined from 45 percent of the portfolio in 1994 to only 8 percent in 2000 as the bank's risk portfolio improved.

BNY Asset Management and Private Client Services provide a comprehensive range of investment products and capabilities designed to meet the current and emerging needs of institutions and high-net-worth individuals worldwide.

BNY Financial Corporation is the second largest factoring operation in the United States and the largest in Canada. (Factoring takes place when borrowers sell their accounts receivable to a lender at some discounted value.) For over fifty years, the company has served the factoring needs of leading designers and manufacturers of apparel, as well as the textile, carpet, service, furniture, electronics, and toy industries among many others.

In 2000, superior long-term investment performance, aggressive new business development, expanded investment capabilities, and favorable growth trends resulted in record fee revenue of $296 million, up 21 percent over 1999.

Global Markets encompasses the bank's foreign exchange and interest-rate risk management businesses, including BK's global trading and sales activities. Successful cross-selling of the bank's growing global securities servicing client base, combined with the sale of new products and solutions, led to record revenues of $261 million in 2000.

Shortcomings to Bear in Mind

- Bank of New York has many admirable features and tends to sell at a premium P/E ratio. Whether the price is too high is debatable. Here is what Standard & Poor's *Stock Reports* said in a 2001 report: "With a 38 percent rise in 2000, the shares easily out-performed the broader market and regional bank peers. We believe this reflected investor realization of the company's unique business mix, which is much less interest-rate-sensitive than that of other regional banks, and its ability to maintain healthy earnings growth in a variety of interest-rate environments.

  "In light of the high percentage of income that the company derives from noninterest-income activities, we continue to view BK's revenue base as more valuable than that of its regional bank competitors, and as justifying a premium P/E multiple for its shares."

Reasons to Buy

■ The Bank of New York is a revenue-growth story, characterized by high-quality earnings that result from the successful execution of the bank's consistent long-term strategy. That strategy is to promote securities servicing, global payment, and fiduciary services to the bank's clients worldwide.

In 2000, securities servicing fees expanded by 33 percent, reaching $1.7 billion. BNY Asset Management and Private Client Services fees rose by 21 percent, reaching $296 million, primarily due to strong investment performance and new business. The company's non-U.S. revenues continued to expand to almost one-third of total revenues at the end of 2000, compared with only 12 percent five years ago. A distinguishing characteristic of the bank's high-quality revenues stream is that 62 percent of it was comprised of noninterest income, compared to 41 percent in 1995.

■ The bank is a premier provider of interest rate and currency derivatives, including currency and interest-rate options. The bank's derivatives business is client driven and complemented by sophisticated risk-management systems. Broader product capabilities and focused relationship management were key drivers of revenue growth in 2000, as business increased by 30 percent.

■ BNY Asset Management is a premier investment manager, offering client-specific solutions and exceptional results. Bank of New York is one of the largest investment managers in the United States, with over $66 billion in assets under management, and growth in 2000 included the addition of another $6 billion.

■ American depositary receipts (ADRs) enable U.S. investors to invest in dollar-denominated equity and debt securities of foreign companies and government agencies, and provide the issuers of these securities access to the U.S. capital markets.

Growth in this business has been very strong, driven by the increased globalization of the capital markets. The company had another record year in 2000 in this operation, with trading volume reaching a high of 29 billion shares valued at $1.2 trillion. Continuing BK's leadership, the bank achieved a 64 percent share of all new public-sponsored programs by adding 114 new clients from thirty-three countries, including fifty programs that listed on a U.S. exchange for the first time. Among the new listings were Pearson, BASF, VSNL, and China Unicom. In addition, seventeen clients named the Bank of New York as successor depositary, including Zurich Financial Services and Compania Anonima Nacional Telefonos de Venezuela. Bank of New York is the world leader, with a market share of 65 percent of all ADR programs, with more than 1,400 clients from sixty-nine countries. ADR revenue grew in 2000 largely because of an increase in crossborder mergers, acquisitions, and trading activity.

■ As one of the world's largest stock-transfer agents, the Bank of New York provides a full range of technology-enhanced services, such as record-keeping, dividend payment and reinvestment, proxy tabulation, and exchange agent services to over 14.5 million shareholders, representing 550 issuers. In 2000, the bank's shareholder accounts grew by more than 25 percent, testament to the company's reputation for quality, service, and new business efforts.

■ The Bank of New York has consistently invested in the technology necessary to improve its processing efficiency and accommodate incremental volume. As an example, BK designed a personal computer-based information delivery system called Workstation. It enables the bank's processing customers to access a range of securities-related data captured by the bank from their own office. Software the bank has developed, moreover, has allowed the bank to adapt this technology for use in virtually all of its securities-processing businesses.

Total assets: $77,241 million
Return on average assets: 1.85%
Common shares outstanding: 740 million
Return on 2000 shareholders' equity: 26.08%

	2000	1999	1998	1997	1996	1995	1994	1993
Loans (millions)	39262	38881	38340	36577	36105	36931	32291	28562
Net income (millions)	1429	1282	1192	1104	1020	914	749	559
Earnings per share	1.92	1.67	1.53	1.36	1.21	1.08	.93	.68
Dividends per share	.66	.58	.54	.49	.42	.34	.28	.21
Price High	59.4	45.2	40.6	29.3	18.1	12.3	8.3	7.8
Low	29.8	31.8	24.0	16.4	10.9	7.1	6.2	6.3

AGGRESSIVE GROWTH

Baxter International, Incorporated

One Baxter Parkway □ Deerfield, Illinois 60015 □ Investor contact: Robert Cox (847)-948-4554 □ Dividend reinvestment program is available: (800) 446-2617 □ Web site: www.baxter.com □ Listed: NYSE □ Ticker symbol: BAX □ S&P rating: B □ Value Line financial strength rating: A+

Fifty years ago, people with end-stage renal disease (ESRD), or kidney failure, faced certain death. There was no treatment that could replicate the function of the kidneys—to remove toxins, waste, and excess water from the bloodstream. Nor were transplants an option a half century ago. There is still no cure for end-stage renal disease. Without either dialysis or a kidney transplant, a person with ESRD will die. In 1956, Baxter introduced the first commercial hemodialysis (HD) machine, making life-saving dialysis therapy possible for thousands of people suffering from kidney failure.

Today, there are some one million dialysis patients worldwide. About 86 percent of them use HD as their primary therapy. The other 14 percent use peritoneal dialysis (PD), a newer, home-based therapy pioneered by Baxter in the late 1970s. Today, Baxter is a world leader in providing products and services to people with ESRD, serving patients in more than 100 countries.

Dialysis treatment rates are expected to grow significantly in developing countries in the years ahead, if economic growth continues. In Latin America, for instance, dialysis treatment rates are expected to double over the next several years. That's because of an aging population, increasing health care coverage, and better diagnosis of kidney disease.

"We see the company's highly profitable renal business gaining ground in 2001, as it continues to buy dialysis centers overseas, strengthens its hemodialysis business, and expands the U.S. renal management systems business," according to a report issued by the brokerage house, Morgan Stanley Dean Witter in 2001.

Company Profile

Baxter dates back to 1931, when it was the first producer of commercially prepared intravenous solutions. The company is now a leading producer of medical products and equipment with an emphasis on products and technologies associated with the blood and circulatory system. Sales abroad accounted for more than 50 percent of revenues in 2000.

In 2000, the company spun off its CardioVascular business as a separate publicly traded company. As now constituted, Baxter operates three divisions:

Medication Delivery

2000 Sales: $2.7 billion

Manufactures a range of products used to deliver fluids and drugs to patients. These products provide fluid replacement, nutrition therapy, pain management, antibiotic therapy, chemotherapy, and other therapies.

The company provides intravenous (IV) and irrigating solutions in flexible plastic containers; premixed liquid and frozen drugs for IV delivery; IV access systems and tubing sets; electronic IV infusion pumps; solutions, containers, and automated compounding systems for IV nutrition; IV anesthesia devices and inhalation agents; and ambulatory infusion systems.

In 2000 Baxter upgraded its Colleague electronic infusion pump for global use and added multiple languages for certain key markets. Worldwide placements of the Colleague pump continue to rise, with 50,000 new channels placed in 2000. Also in 2000 the company introduced a new pump for post-operative pain management, the lpump Pain Management System, in the United States. Programmed in multiple languages and designed for

global use, Baxter launched the lpump in Europe and Canada in 2001. In addition, the company brought out several new premixed IV drugs in 2000, including the first global premixed drug, Aggrastat, a cardiac compound developed by Merck.

BioScience

2000 Sales: $2.4 billion

This segment produces therapeutic proteins from plasma and through recombinant methods to treat hemophilia, immune deficiencies, and other blood-related disorders. These include coagulation factors, immune globulins, albumin, wound-management products, and vaccines. Baxter also has a stake in blood-collection containers and automated blood-cell separation and collection systems. These products are used by hospitals, blood banks, and plasma-collection centers to collect and process blood components for therapeutic use or for processing into therapeutic products such as albumin. Therapeutic blood components are used to treat patients undergoing surgery, cancer therapy, and other critical therapies.

In 2000, Baxter received approval in the United Kingdom for NeisVac-C, a new meningococcemia vaccine. The company also received approval from the U.S. Food and Drug Administration (FDA) for a new application device for its Tisseel fibrin sealant. In 2001 or early 2002, Baxter expects European approval for a new therapeutic protein for protein C deficiency and pathogen-inactivation technology for platelets. Other products in development include a next-generation recombinant Factor VIII using a totally protein-free manufacturing process; a cell culture-derived vaccine for influenza; a new tetanus, diphtheria, and acellular pertussis vaccine; a European vaccine for Lyme disease; pathogen-inactivation technology for plasma and red cells; and a recombinant form of hemoglobin that may be used instead of blood to carry oxygen to vital organs.

Renal

2000 Sales: $1.8 billion

The Renal segment provides a range of renal dialysis products and services to support people with kidney failure. The company is the world's leading manufacturer of products for peritoneal dialysis (PD), a home dialysis therapy. These products include PD solutions, container systems, and automated machines that cleanse patients' blood overnight while they sleep. Baxter also manufactures dialyzers and instrumentation for hemodialysis (HD). Baxter's Renal Therapy Services (RTS) operates dialysis clinics in twelve countries outside the United States, while Renal Management Strategies Inc. (RMS) works with U.S. nephrologists to provide a kidney-disease management program to health care payers.

Baxter continues to develop new PD solutions to better manage specific patient needs. One example is Extraneal, which improves the removal of excess fluids and toxins from patients with end-stage renal disease. Introduced in Europe in 1997 and approved in twenty-eight countries, Extraneal today is being used by more than 6,000 European patients—more than a third of Baxter's European PD population—and is currently under regulatory review in the United States.

In the spring of 2000, Baxter completed its acquisition of Althin Medical AB, a leading manufacturer of HD products based in Ronneby, Sweden. The acquisition greatly expands Baxter's product offering for HD and strengthens its position in the global HD market.

Another solution, Physioneal, was introduced in Europe and began clinical trials in Japan in 2000. Also in 2000, as a result of Baxter's acquisition of Althin Medical, the company began selling an HD machine globally called the Tina. Baxter also introduced a new HD machine called Meridian in the United States. Future products include several new HD dialyzers and the Aurora home HD machine.

Shortcomings to Bear in Mind

■ Growth in earnings per share is rather pedestrian. In the 1990–2000 period, earnings per share increased from $.82 to $1.53, a compound annual growth rate of only 6.4 percent. In the same ten-year span, dividends edged up from $.32 to $.58, a growth rate of 6.1 percent. What's more, the $.58 dividend has been paid in each of the past three years.

Reasons to Buy

■ As its name suggests, Baxter International is a global enterprise, and more than half of sales come from overseas. CEO Harry M. Jansen Kraemer Jr. contends he has the Rx to improve all of its global operations. "Big companies are most efficient when they're most focused on what they do well," he says, listing research and development, manufacturing skills, and worldwide distribution as Baxter's strengths.

■ As we enter the twenty-first century, the growing, aging population is creating unprecedented, explosive growth in medical conditions that occur more frequently and grow more acute with age. Baxter manufactures and markets products and services that are used to treat patients with many of these conditions, including cancer, trauma, hemophilia, immune deficiencies, infectious diseases, kidney disease, and other disorders.

The company also makes products that are used in the treatment of patients undergoing most surgical procedures. All of these conditions can cause severe physical, emotional, and financial burdens to patients and their families. Baxter's role is to help alleviate these burdens by developing innovative technologies that improve the patient's quality of life and medical outcome, and lower the overall cost of patient care. The majority of Baxter's businesses are pioneers in their field, with more than 70 percent of sales coming from products with leading market positions.

- Injury or trauma is the leading cause of death for people under age forty-four. Many trauma victims receive Baxter products—IV solutions, plasma-volume expanders, blood-transfusion products, and other products for fluid replenishment and blood-volume stabilization.

- Infectious diseases continue to cause illness and death around the world. While some infectious diseases have been conquered in some regions through modern advances in antibiotics and vaccines, new diseases are constantly emerging. Lyme disease, AIDS, and new strains of influenza are all diseases that have emerged within the last twenty years. Baxter makes the leading vaccine for tick-borne encephalitis (TBE), a potentially fatal disease common in portions of Europe and Asia. The company recently introduced its next-generation TBE vaccine, Ticovac. Baxter also is developing vaccines for influenza and Lyme disease.

- In 2000 Baxter completed the acquisition of North American Vaccine Inc., based in Columbia, Maryland, broadening its position in the global vaccines market. The company also established an equity position in British vaccine developer Acambis, which will better position each company to develop and commercialize their respective vaccine pipelines.

- Baxter products are used in a variety of surgical applications. Most people undergoing surgery require IV access for solutions and medicines. Precise infusion requires sophisticated electronic infusion pumps to regulate flow. Baxter provides a broad range of anesthetic agents and delivery devices for general anesthesia. The company makes fibrin sealant to facilitate blood clotting and wound healing in surgery.

- Baxter is using the Internet to improve operating efficiencies by utilizing business-to-business (B2B) arrangements. For instance, the company is working with Ariba (a leading provider of Internet-based B2B electronic commerce network solutions) to find ways to improve procurement and supply-chain management. In 2000 Baxter saved $30 million from strategic outsourcing. This number could expand to $75 million in 2001.

Total assets: $8,733 million
Current ratio: 1.08
Common shares outstanding: 588 million
Return on 2000 shareholders' equity: 27.8%

	2000	1999	1998	1997	1996	1995	1994	1993
Revenues (millions)	6896	6380	6599	6138	5438	5048	9324	8879
Net income (millions)	915	779	731	652	575	485	596	539
Earnings per share	1.53	1.32	1.27	1.16	1.06	.88	1.07	.98
Dividends per share	.58	.58	.58	.57	.59	.56	.52	.50
Price High	45.2	38.0	33.0	30.2	24.1	22.4	14.5	16.4
Low	25.9	28.4	24.3	20.0	19.9	13.4	10.8	10.0

The Boeing Company

100 North Riverside Plaza □ **Chicago, Illinois** □ **Listed: NYSE** □ **Investor contact: Paul Kinscherff (206) 655-2608** □ **Dividend reinvestment plan is available: (888) 777-0923** □ **Web site: www.boeing.com** □ **Ticker symbol: BA** □ **S&P rating: B** □ **Value Line financial strength rating: A**

Nearly four years after winning a shot at designing what could become the Pentagon's all-purpose fighter jet, Boeing sent aloft its Joint Strike Fighter (JSF) in the fall of 2000. Except for a minor leak of hydraulic fluid, the X-32A flew flawlessly.

Shortly thereafter, however, its rival, a model built by Lockheed, also began test flights. The event marked the start of a series of test flights that culminated in the summer of 2001 with the Pentagon's choice of a winner.

The JSF will be the first fighter jet built for service by the Air Force, the Navy, and the Marine Corps. With anticipated orders of more than 3,000 jets by the U.S. military and more from allies, the new Joint Strike Fighter is expected to be the biggest Pentagon contract ever and the last U.S. fighter jet built for a generation. The X-32A is the Air Force and Navy version of the plane. Another Boeing model of similar design, the X-32B, has short-takeoff and vertical-landing capability and was tested early in 2001. That model is destined for the U.S. Marines and the British Royal Navy and Air Force. The winner of the competition will have a contact for $300 billion over nearly two decades.

Affordability will be the key to landing the JSF contact. Unlike past budget-busting military jet programs, the Pentagon has put a premium on keeping JSF prices affordable. The basic Air Force version of the plane is supposed to carry a sticker price of about $30 million—far below the comparable cost of about $84 million apiece for the more sophisticated F-22.

The massive program's impact on the defense industry is expected to be so profound that the Pentagon has debated picking a design and then awarding the actual work to both Lockheed and Boeing, partly out of concern that the loser could go out of the military contract business.

Company Profile

Founded eighty-five years ago by William E. Boeing, the Boeing Company is the leading aerospace company in the world, as measured by total revenues. The holder of 5,075 patents, Boeing is the world's largest manufacturer of commercial jetliners and military aircraft and provides related services worldwide.

Boeing is also NASA's largest contractor. The company's capabilities and related services include helicopters, electronic and defense systems, missiles, rocket engines, launch systems, and advanced information and communications systems. Boeing has customers in 145 countries.

Boeing's military aircraft include the F/A-18 Hornet strike fighter, the F-15E Eagle fighter-bomber, the C-17 Globemaster III transport, and the AH-64D Apache Longbow helicopter.

Boeing's space operations include communications satellites, Delta rockets, and the space shuttle (with Lockheed Martin). Finally, the company is also prime contractor for the International Space Station.

Boeing's defense and space operations (about one-third of revenues) primarily makes the F-18 fighter jet for the U.S. Navy, the E-3 Airborne Warning and Control System (AWACS), the 767-based AWACS, and CH-47 helicopter. The company also has important development programs: the Joint Strike Fighter, the Airborne Laser, the F-22 fighter, and the expendable launch vehicle. Finally, the unit also makes Delta rockets, primarily used to carry commercial and military satellites.

Highlights of 2000

- Achieved operating margins of 7.4 percent, a 25 percent increase over the prior year, resulting in net earnings of $2.5 billion, or $2.88 per share, excluding nonrecurring items.
- Produced strong free cash flow of $4.9 billion.
- Completed 146-million-share repurchase program and authorized a new 10 percent share repurchase program.
- Increased the dividend by 21 percent.
- Completed strategic acquisitions, including Hughes's space and communication businesses and Jeppesen. (See details below.)
- Delivered 489 commercial jetliners; commercial backlog rose strongly, to $89.8 billion; launched longer-range 777, 747-400, and 767-400ER aircraft.
- Received an $8.9-billion multiyear contract for 222 F/A-18E/F Super Hornet aircraft; JSF X-32A concept demonstrator entered test flight.
- Received $6 billion follow-on order to National Missile Defense contract.
- In March 2001, Boeing shocked the city of Seattle—its home for the past eighty-five years—by announcing that it would move its headquarters to one of three cities: Chicago, Denver, or Dallas-Fort Worth. The company said that only 500 of its headquarters staff of 1,000 would move to the new city, which turned out to be Chicago.

Boeing became Illinois's biggest company in terms of sales, surpassing Sears, Roebuck & Co., McDonald's, and Motorola. The new headquarters gave Boeing global access, a central location, cultural diversity, and a strong education system. Boeing's CEO commented that still another key reason why Chicago was the site chosen was, "the ability to get anywhere in the world" from O'Hare International Airport.

Shortcomings to Bear in Mind

- Despite an all-out effort by Boeing to sell its huge 747-X to Singapore Airlines in the fall of 2000, it failed to fend off the feisty European plane maker, Airbus Industrie. Singapore Airlines placed an $8.6-billion order for twenty-five of the proposed Airbus Industrie's A3XX super-jumbo planes. The average price of the twenty-five planes works out to $344 million, including spare parts. Boeing, by contrast, offered to reduce the 747-X price to as low as $142 million. The deal is the single largest order for the A3XX and is perhaps the first to give the stamp of market approval for the super-jumbo plane. Singapore chose the A3XX because the plane would hold fifty-five more seats than the new enlarged 747 that Boeing is working on. Singapore's order marked the first high-profile defeat for Boeing's proposed 747-X. Some analysts pointed out that Singapore's role as an influential carrier may be a bit overblown. Not all of Singapore's airplane purchases have fared well. The airline also was an early buyer of the Douglas MD-11—a slow-selling, gas-guzzling wide-body jet that not many other airlines elected to buy.

Airbus said the $225-million double-decker A3XX, which is scheduled for first deliveries in 2006, will cost $10.7 billion to develop. Many analysts think the figure could go higher—to $16 billion or more. Even at a lower price tag of $14 billion, Airbus would have to sell 528 of the planes over the next twenty years to break even and 665 for it to be a financial boon, projects Lehman Brothers, Inc. There's the rub: Boeing argues that the entire market for such gigantic planes could number fewer than 350, of which it expects to grab 50 percent with its enhanced 747s. "We absolutely believe that there's a need for larger planes, but the size of the market is the issue," said Alan R. Mulally, president of Boeing's Commercial Airplanes Group. For its part, Airbus contends the potential is much larger, 1,500 units. By choosing to invest $4 billion to extend the 747 rather than churning out a whole new plane, Boeing is banking on the lower estimate.

The next few years will bring a pitched battle for sales of new super jumbo jets. Without doubt, there will be risks involved for both companies. Airbus could suffer financially if it fails to sell enough of its planes to justify development costs of $10.7 billion. Boeing, meanwhile, risks losing its dominance of a most-profitable market share if the new Airbus craft turns out to be a big success.

Reasons to Buy

■ Boeing took control of Hughes Electronics Corp.'s space and communications unit in the fall of 2000, completing a transaction that made Boeing a dominant player in the satellite communications industry. Prior to the acquisition, Hughes was the world's leading satellite maker. Hughes's expertise is expected to enable Boeing to develop new businesses, such as providing broadband Internet and global positioning services for military and civilian aircraft. With the deal the company picked up Hughes' backlog of more than forty satellite orders valued at about $5 billion. Boeing said that the Hughes acquisition will bolster revenues from its Space and Communications division by about 35 percent, to nearly $10 billion in 2001.

■ Boeing intends to play a prominent role in the new economy. In late 2000, the company created three new operations to accomplish this objective.

● Connexion by Boeing provides high-speed Internet and entertainment services to commercial airlines and business jets.

● Air Traffic Management is geared up to overhaul and improve the technology for air-traffic control and airport operations.

● Boeing Capital Corporation is the company's burgeoning financial-services business.

This move expanded the company's operating units to six and put the new economy ventures on equal footing with its core businesses: Commercial Airplanes, Military Aircraft and Missiles, and Space and Communications.

■ Boeing was unpleasantly jolted when it lost the order for Singapore Airlines (see above), but it bounced back in October 2000 with a major deal with Air France for as many as 20 of its 777 wide-body planes. The decision solidified Air France's allegiance to the 777-300. The twenty-plane deal could be worth as much as $4 billion.

The transaction was significant because Boeing made it with a carrier in the back yard of its European rival, Airbus Industrie. Air France is 62 percent state-owned. The French government also owns a piece of Airbus through its stake in the new European Aeronautic Defense and Space (EADS).

- About 85 percent of the world's jetliners are built by Boeing, and an estimated $74 billion a year is spent to keep them flying. However, up until recently Boeing was giving away its engineering drawings to third-party service providers. No longer. It is now making an across-the-board push into maintenance, modifications, financing, air-traffic control, even pilot training. "This could be big stuff," said Cai von Rumohr, an aerospace analyst with SG Cowen. Already, more than 20 percent of Boeing's military revenues emanate from activities such as maintaining air force bases, and its Web site for spare parts generated revenues of $400 million a year. In a sign of how far the services push might go, Boeing agreed to buy thirty-four used 757s from British Airways, convert them into freighters, and lease them to carrier DHL with a fixed hourly maintenance fee.

- In 2000, Boeing purchased Jeppesen Sanderson, a flight-information provider, for $1.5 billion in cash. Jeppesen, based in Denver, provides print and electronic flight-information services, including navigation data, computerized flight planning, and aviation software products. The company generated $235 million in sales in 1999 and had a handsome profit margin of 25 percent. The deal should help Boeing's charge into the vast market for aviation services, considered crucial to boosting revenues and profits and offsetting the cyclical peaks and valleys in Boeing's core commercial airplane business.

"Jeppesen is the world's number one source for flight information services, so it's a perfect fit for our aviation services portfolio," said Boeing's Phil Condit. "If you're a pilot almost anywhere in the world, you know Jeppesen."

- Boeing's commercial airplanes group has been focusing on making its assembly lines more efficient and nailing down costs. "There was a time when they really didn't know how much a plane cost when it went out the door," said Heidi Wood, an aerospace analyst with Morgan Stanley Dean Witter. "Now they know exactly how much it costs and how much to charge for it to turn a profit."

Total assets: $42,018 million
Current ratio: 0.83
Common shares outstanding: 888 million
Return on 2000 shareholders' equity: 22.8%

	2000	1999	1998	1997	1996	1995	1994	1993
Revenues (millions)	51321	57993	56154	45800	22681	19515	21924	25438
Net income (millions)	2513	2309	1120	632	976	393	856	1244
Earnings per share	2.44	2.49	1.15	.63	1.42	.58	1.26	1.83
Dividends per share	.59	.56	.56	.56	.55	.50	.50	.50
Price High	70.9	48.5	56.3	60.5	53.8	40.0	25.1	22.4
Low	32.0	31.6	29.0	43.0	37.1	22.2	21.1	16.7

Boston Properties, Incorporated

800 Boylston Street ◻ Boston, Massachusetts 02199-8001 ◻ Listed: NYSE ◻ Investor contact: Elaine Quinlan (617) 236-3463 ◻ Dividend reinvestment plan is available: (888) 485-2389 ◻ Web site: www.bostonproperties.com ◻ Ticker symbol: BXP ◻ S&P rating: Not rated ◻ Value Line financial strength rating: Not rated

Boston Properties, a leading real estate investment trust (REIT) based in Boston, purchased the site for the future Times Square Tower from the Prudential Insurance Company at the end of 2000 for $164 million.

The forty-seven-floor, 1.2 million-square-foot Class A office building will be built by Boston Properties on the south side of 42nd Street between Broadway and Seventh Avenue in New York City. Construction started in the second quarter of 2001, with initial occupancy expected in the fourth quarter of 2003. Times Square Tower was designed by the world-renowned architect David M. Childs of the firm Skidmore, Owings & Merrill, LLP. Among the initial tenants in the new Times Square Tower will be the accounting firm of Arthur Andersen, which will occupy 524,000 square feet of space.

Company Profile

Boston Properties is one of the premier office real estate companies with Class A office buildings situated in markets that are difficult to enter, such as Boston, New York, Washington, and San Francisco. Erecting new office buildings is difficult because of the physical constraints of these particular cities coupled with stringent approval processes and the complexity of the building process. Yet the demand for office space continues unabated, causing rents to climb.

At the end of 2000 the company's properties were highly concentrated in these four cities with 28 percent in Boston, 22 percent in Washington, D.C., 21 percent in San Francisco, and 16 percent in New York City, with 13 percent listed under "other." Distribution by property category was as follows: 64 percent in urban office, 30 percent in suburban office, and 6 percent "other."

These thriving centers of commerce, government, education, and science are consistently ranked among the top office markets in the country. Historically, office space in these cities has commanded higher rental rates and had lower vacancy rates than virtually all other markets in the United States.

Among the company's largest properties are the Embarcadero Center in San Francisco, with 3,931,381 net rentable square feet; the Prudential Center in Boston, with 2,140,832 square feet; and Carnegie Center in Princeton, New Jersey, with 1,856,018 square feet.

At the other extreme are such smaller properties as Three Cambridge Center in Cambridge, Massachusetts, with 107,484 net rentable square feet; the Arboretum in Reston, Virginia, with 95,584 square feet; 17 Hartwell Avenue in Lexington, Massachusetts, with 30,000 square feet; and 560 Forbes Boulevard, with 40,000 square feet.

Boston Properties, Inc. is a self-administered and self-managed real estate investment trust (REIT) that develops, redevelops, acquires, manages, operates, and owns a diverse portfolio of Class A office, industrial, and hotel properties.

Class A office buildings are generally considered those that have excellent locations and access, attract high-quality tenants, are well-maintained, and professionally managed.

The company is one of the largest owners, acquirers, and developers of Class A office properties in the United States.

Founded in 1970, the company's primary focus is office space. However, its property portfolio also includes hotels and industrial buildings.

Since becoming a public company in June 1997, Boston Properties has experienced rapid growth by acquisitions in excess of $4 billion of office properties in existing and complementary markets. The company's expanding asset base is comprised of 144 properties, totaling 37.1 million square feet. To support continued growth, Boston Properties raised over $800 million of equity through a secondary stock offering in January 1998, $140 million in May 1999, and $634 million in October 2000.

What Is an Equity REIT?

Equity REITs make their money by owning properties, as opposed to mortgage REITs, which lend money to property owners. Equity REITs allow you to invest in a diversified collection of apartment buildings, hospitals, shopping centers, hotels, warehouses, and office buildings.

Like mutual funds, REITs are not taxed themselves, providing they pay out at least 95 percent of their taxable income. That translates into fat dividends for shareholders, as REITs pass along the rents and other income they collect. Dividend yields are typically 6 percent or more. "Put it all together, and you are looking at a double-digit total return. Over the long haul, the return should be lower than traditional stocks, but higher than bonds," says Chris Mayer, a real estate professor at the University of Pennsylvania's Wharton School.

Kevin Bernzott, an investment adviser in Camarillo, California, views REITs as a stock-bond hybrid. "If you select quality REITs, they kick off a highly predictable stream of income, and eventually you may get some price appreciation. We plug them into the bond portion of the portfolio. They're almost like a bond with an equity kicker."

Shortcomings to Bear in Mind

- Although Boston Properties is an outstanding REIT, it is not the cheapest. Its P/E ratio is well above average for the group.
- Some investors might be concerned that Boston Properties is not well diversified because most of its properties are situated in only four cities. Also, the company's holdings are essentially concentrated in office buildings to the exclusion of such sectors as retail shopping centers, apartment buildings, and industrial parks.

Reasons to Buy

- The company's management believes prospects for internal growth are strong in light of the REIT's high-quality portfolio and the fact that its properties are situated in desirable locations in markets that are experiencing rising rents, low vacancy rates, and increasing demand for office and industrial space.

  Internal growth prospects are also bolstered by the fact that the company's properties are usually in markets in which supply is limited by the lack of available sites and by the difficulty in obtaining the necessary approvals for developing vacant land. These high barriers to entry argue for the trust's ability to obtain strong increases in rental revenue in the years ahead.
- In 2000, rental rates in Class A office buildings in San Francisco, Midtown Manhattan, Washington, D.C., and Boston climbed by 20 percent to more than 50 percent. This gave the company the opportunity to release a number of properties. A total of 3.8 million square feet of space was leased for an average

of 47 percent above the rates of expiring leases.

- Boston Properties has always followed a conservative strategy of entering into long-term leases with tenants of strong financial standing so that in any given year the turnover with its existing portfolio is moderate. More specifically, leases on only 7.5 percent of the space in existing buildings will terminate in 2001 and only 8.3 percent in 2002.
- Another key indication of the company's strength it the occupancy rate. In 2000, 98.9 percent of space was under lease. The prior year the figure was 98.4 percent. And in 1998 the occupancy rate was also very high at 97.1 percent.
- Boston Properties has long been recognized for its ability to create value through the development of its own properties, as opposed to purchase. While notable acquisitions have been an important part of its impressive growth, the company has also demonstrated that high returns can be achieved by employing its team of skilled professionals to create projects from the ground up. Boston Properties has fully staffed development and construction operations in each of its markets. The company, moreover, has more development project in the works today than at any other office REIT.

In early 2001, Boston Properties had sixteen projects under development totaling 5.7 million square feet. It also owned or controlled additional sites that could support the development of another 9.6 million square feet. None of these projects will proceed without adequate market support, however. Of the 5.7 million square feet already under construction, more than 72 percent of the space has been committed to companies with strong balance sheets and good operating histories.

- Boston Properties employs the latest advances in technology and Internet-based services to enhance the quality and profitability of all of its operations in order to improve the work environment of its tenants. During 2000 the company deployed new tenant amenities to enhance the competitive position of the company's properties, expanding the number of telecommunications and broadband service options available to tenants and installing flat panel displays delivering news, information, and targeted advertising in building elevators.

Throughout the company an advanced networked infrastructure provides streamlined internal communications, operation, and control. A powerful set of databases and integrated systems, significantly augmented during 2000, delivers real-time information to both employees and tenants and serves as a platform for improving services, with more and more business with tenants, suppliers, and service providers now conducted over the Internet.

- Rapid advances and innovations in technology and communications are fundamentally restructuring the domestic economy. Boston Properties is well positioned to benefit from these changes by catering to such "knowledge-based" businesses as accounting, law, financial services, consulting, and technology—enterprises that are expanding faster than many other sectors of the economy. Firms in these sectors currently account for about 68 percent of BXP's tenants and are a key focus for the future.

Demand for office space by these companies were especially strong in 2000. Of the 3.5 million square feet already leased in the company's new development projects now underway, over 90 percent is leased to these types of tenants. These are primarily established companies committing to long-term leases who make significant communications and information technology investments in their space to improve productivity and efficiency. And because they have a higher concentration of income-generating professional staff and fewer support staff, these tenants compete aggressively for the best space available and can support the higher rents necessary for this.

By concentrating on providing office space to established companies, Boston Properties participates in the rapid growth of the knowledge-based sector of the nation's economy while limiting its exposure to the uncertainties of newly formed enterprises.

Total assets: $ 6,226 million
Current ratio: NA
Return on 2000 equity: 8.9%
Common shares outstanding: 71.4 million

	2000	1999	1998	1997	1996	1995	1994	1993
Revenues (millions)	879	787	514	140*				
Net income (millions)	146	114	93	35.2				
Earnings per share	2.05	1.72	1.53	.70				
Funds from operations	3.31	2.89	2.50	1.96				
Dividends per share	2.04	1.75	1.66	1.62				
Price High	44.9	40.8	41.6	36.2				
Low	29.0	30.9	33.4	30.3				

*Statistical information only available since the company went public in 1997.

GROWTH AND INCOME

BP p.l.c.

Britannic House, 1 Finsbury Circus □ London EC2M 7BA, □ United Kingdom □ Investor contact: Terry LaMore (212) 451-8034 □ Dividend reinvestment program is not available □ Web site: www.bp.com □ Listed: NYSE □ Ticker symbol: BP □ S&P rating: Not rated □ Value Line financial strength rating: A++

BP p.l.c. unveiled a whole new gasoline pump experience in 2000, one in which drivers will stand in the glow of the gas station's solar canopy, check the weather forecast on the touch-sensitive screen on the pump, then punch a few buttons to order a fresh chicken sandwich from the station's minimart.

The concept gas station, dubbed PP Connect, was developed under cloak-and-dagger conditions in an unmarked warehouse in McDonough, Georgia, thirty miles south of Atlanta. The reasons for pumping up the gas experience are no secret. According to company officials, the jazzed-up station may increase convenience-store sales, which are more profitable than gasoline sales. Companies are under heavy pressure to do so, said Daniel J. Yergin, the head of Cambridge Energy Research Associates. "Gasoline retailing is an incredibly competitive business where you live and die on the basis of pennies. People are very sensitive about gasoline prices, but they don't give a second thought about running into a convenience store to pick up a six-pack of soft drinks or Hostess Twinkies."

Since 1977, the percentage of gasoline stations that are also convenience stores has gone from 5 percent to 45 percent.

Company Profile

Formed from the merger of British Petroleum and Amoco (year-end 1998), BP p.l.c. is the holding company of the world's third largest petroleum company. Its main activities are exploration and production of crude oil and natural gas and refining. It also has a stake in petrochemicals, natural gas, and solar power generation.

BP produces oil in nineteen countries and has proved reserves of 12.7 billion barrels of oil equivalent, including large reserves in Alaska and the North Sea. BP has well-established operations in Europe, North and South America, Australia, and Africa. The company is the largest U.S. oil and gas producer and one of the two top gas producers in Canada. The company owns more than 28,000 service stations throughout the world.

BP is second only to Royal Dutch in terms of total oil and gas production and reserves. The company is a major producer of petrochemicals, selling products to bulk, wholesale, and retail customers in more than sixty countries. Products include acetic acid, acrylonitrile, and polyethylene.

Shortcomings to Bear in Mind

- In the past ten years (1990–2000), earnings per share were far from impressive, rising from $1.66 to $3.49, a compound annual growth rate of only 7.7 percent. In the same ten-year span, dividends per share edged up from $1.06 to $1.35, a modest growth rate of 2.4 percent.
- Two of Alaska's most controversial offshore oil ventures are the target of fervent environmental criticism because they are the first U.S. offshore production projects to use undersea pipelines. Situated in BP's Arctic Ocean Northstar fields, which hold between 140 million and 150 million barrels of crude oil each, these fields could eventually help steady Alaska's falling production and ease a long decline in U.S. domestic output.

The projects should add more than 120,000 barrels per day to Alaska's output, which has fallen nearly 10 percent over the last year to below 920,000 barrels per day, its lowest level since 1950. In its defense, a company spokesman said, "We designed a pipeline that, if operated properly, should never leak." On the other hand, critics who oppose the dominance of oil over the environment in the region believe that undersea pipelines in the Arctic's Beaufort Sea are vulnerable to seasonal ice floes known to scour the ocean floor.

- Demand for BP's chemicals was firm in the first half of 2000, but weakened in the final two quarters, as the global economy began to sputter. Annual production, however, rose 1 percent to 22.1 million tons, despite operational difficulties at Grangemouth, Scotland. Several initiatives to promote cost and capital efficiency helped offset pressure on margins that were close to cyclical lows, as high oil and gas prices boosted feedstock costs. Then, too, the weakness of the euro added pressure on margins in the company's European operations.
- Over the past few years, BP has plowed most of its Russia investment into a 10 percent stake in Sidanko, a onetime oil conglomerate that formerly owned some of the most valuable energy assets in Russia, notably the Chernogorneft field in Siberia. More recently, production subsidiaries of Sidanko were pushed into bankruptcy and sold off under controversial circumstances, essentially leaving the parent company as an empty shell. A Russian company, Tyumen, bought Chernogorneft at a fraction of its value. BP and others have accused Tyumen, which is nearly half owned by the Russian government, of tampering with the courts to influence the bankruptcy proceedings and liquidation sales.

Reasons to Buy

- In late 2000 BP announced that it would boost its capital spending by 13 percent through 2003. By the end of the period, annual capital spending will reach the $13.5-billion level. The augmented spending will be used to accelerate high-return projects, notably oil production from deep-water fields in the Gulf of Mexico and gas production in Trinidad. BP's decision came at a time when supplies were tight amid strong worldwide demand for oil and gas. Analysts say that BP's reputation as a trendsetter would spur other oil companies to follow suit.

- BP holds extensive leases in the federal waters of the Gulf of Mexico. It is one of the three largest acreage holders in the Gulf and the leading acreage holder in the Gulf's deep-water portion. Onshore, the company operates some 470 natural gas wells and 330 oil wells.

  The Houston region's offshore production currently totals about 240,000 barrels of oil equivalent a day. Production onshore in the region is more than 365,000 barrels of oil equivalent a day. These figures will rise sharply as off-shore projects under development come on stream.

- The company's refining and marketing operation had an outstanding year in 2000 with record results and a highly competitive 22 percent return on fixed assets. Refining benefited from significantly higher margins and strong growth in convenience-store sales coupled with a strong oil trading performance and cost reductions.

- The acquisition of Atlantic Richfield (ARCO) gives BP a very lucrative refining and marketing position on the West Coast. In addition, the company will benefit from ARCO's huge natural gas reserves in Southeast Asia. What's more, BP is on track to harvest about $3.5 billion a year in cost savings as a result of well-defined synergies that are beginning to materialize.

- The recent acquisition (for $4.7 billion in cash) of the London-based oil refining company, Burmah Castrol (whose best-selling product is the well-known Castrol motor oil), transformed BP's lubricants presence. Castrol will become BP's leading lubricants brand with its products made available both through BP's 28,000 retail sites as well as to the company's automotive, industrial, and marine customers around the world. Even though the company paid what an Argus Research analyst says was "a rather hefty premium for Burmah Castrol, the benefits of bringing into the fold a popular brand with particular strength in Asia is expected to increase BP's refining and marketing revenues significantly. In addition, the cost-cutting opportunities are huge, as well as the existing potential for the sale of almost $800 million in non-core and redundant Burmah Castrol assets."

- In emerging markets, fuel sales rose by 22 percent, and the company opened seventy-five new retail sites in Latin America, Poland, Russia, and Africa. Growth in aviation fuels was strong in 2000. Finally, BP purchased Exxon-Mobil's 30 percent interest in the European fuels joint venture for $1.5 billion.

- During 2001 many new products are expected to come on stream, including six major oil and gas fields in the Gulf of Mexico, Alaska, Angola, Egypt, and Norway. Deep-water production in the Gulf of Mexico is set to more than double by 2004. More than 300 BP Connect convenience retail sites sporting the new helios brand mark are planned to open worldwide as part of a longer-term re-imaging plan. The company also plans to have the new brand in place on more than 5,000 sites by the end of 2001.

Petrochemicals capacity is to be increased at Grangemouth and Hull in the United Kingdom. In Canada, production of linear alpha-olefins is scheduled to begin at a new world-scale facility, while in Alaska BP will start construction of a revolutionary gas-to-liquids test facility at Nikiski.

■ The company's stake in solar energy performed well in 2000. Production and shipments surged 31 percent compared with the prior year as BP sold a total of 42 megawatts of solar panel generating capacity. High-profile projects included the United States's largest solar housing project in Los Angeles, as well as the installation of solar panels to power apartments in the athletes village at the Sydney Olympic games. In 2000 the company also completed the conversion of 200 service stations worldwide to solar power.

■ In the realm of technology, BP sharpened its performance. The company applied new fiber-optic sensors in many wells to monitor pumps, pressures, and flow rates, thus reducing operating costs and boosting production capabilities. What's more, the company added capability to its seismic imaging tools, allowing it to discern the shape of hydrocarbon reservoirs more clearly. The company also worked with suppliers to develop a high-strength steel that reduced the cost of gas pipelines. In chemicals, BP introduced new PTA technology that lowers the costs of units and reduces most emissions by two-thirds.

■ In 2000 BP became the first oil and gas company to purchase LNG (liquid natural gas) vessels not tied to a single gas source or customer. The company also commercialized a novel process to remove sulphur from gasoline and diesel at low cost—with no loss of octane. This is helping to advance the rate at which BP can introduce new clean fuels. By the end of 2000, cleaner fuels had gone on sale in fifty-six cities worldwide, compared with a goal of forty.

Total assets: $89,561 million
Current ratio: 1.08
Common shares outstanding: 22,529 million
Return on 2000 shareholders' equity: 17.1%

	2000	1999	1998	1997	1996	1995	1994	1993
Revenues (millions)	148062	83566	68304	71274	76490	57047	50667	52425
Net income (millions)	12555	6204	4468	4628	4114	2070	2001	1062
Earnings per share	3.49	1.92	1.39	2.44	2.18	1.13	1.08	.59
Dividends per share	1.35	1.31	1.45	1.32	1.08	.83	.52	.48
Price High	60.6	62.6	8.7	46.5	35.9	26.0	21.3	16.3
Low	43.1	40.2	36.5	32.4	23.6	18.9	14.6	10.5

CONSERVATIVE GROWTH

Bristol-Myers Squibb Company

345 Park Avenue □ New York, New York 10154-0037 □ Listed: NYSE □ Investor contact: Tim Cost (212) 546-4103 □ Dividend reinvestment plan is available: (800) 356-2026 □ Web site: www.bms.com □ Ticker symbol: BMY □ S&P rating: A □ Value Line financial strength rating: A++

Peter R. Dolan, age forty-five, often regarded at the next CEO of Bristol-Myers Squibb, took that post in May 2001, replacing Charles A. Heimbold, age sixty-seven, who retired. Mr. Dolan joined the company in 1988 and became president in early 2000.

Peter Dolan first achieved recognition by convincing consumers to buy more Jello when he was with General Foods (now part of Philip Morris). Mr. Dolan said his consumer marketing expertise will serve him well now that drug companies can no longer rely primarily on selling their drugs by having their salespeople hand out samples and leave product literature with the medical profession. These days, pharmaceutical companies are reaching out to consumers through advertising as well. Nor are they neglecting to use their blandishments on the governments and the managed care companies that pay for most drugs.

Mr. Dolan has shown that his marketing talents can create higher sales in the pharmaceutical realm. As president of Mead Johnson Nutritional Group of Bristol-Myers in 1995, he boosted Enfamil to the number one infant formula in the United States by advertising it to mothers, in addition to promoting it to pediatricians.

Analysts are convinced that the new CEO has exceptional credentials. "What Peter Dolan brings to the table is his global view, his strength of being a strategic thinker and planner," said Richard Lawrence, pharmaceutical analyst for Parker Hunter Inc. "He's an aggressive, young CEO who wants to leave his mark—his own mark—and he's going to want to do it early on and get some momentum behind the company in the next few years."

Company Profile

Bristol-Myers is a global leader in chemotherapy drugs and ranks near the top in cardiovascular drugs and antibiotics. Heart drugs include Pravachol, a cholesterol-reducing agent, and Capoten/Capozide and Monopril, which are antihypertensive preparations. Through a joint venture with Sanofi, SA, BMY produces Plavix, a platelet aggregation inhibitor for the prevention of stroke, heart attack, and vascular diseases; and Avapro, an angiotensin II receptor blocker

that treats hypertension. Principal anticancer drugs consist of Taxol, Paraplatin, VePesid, and Platinol.

The company features a wide variety of anti-infective drugs, including Duricef/Ultracef, Cefzil, and Maxipime antibiotics, and Videx and Zerit AIDS therapeutics.

The company's nutritionals encompass infant formulas such as Enfamil and ProSobee, vitamins, and nutritional supplements.

Shortcomings to Bear in Mind

- Bristol-Myers has been going through a difficult period. Early in 2000 the company was forced to reapply to the Food and Drug Administration to market its experimental cancer drug, Orzel, which will delay the drug's release. The company also postponed its FDA application for its promising blood-pressure drug, Vanlev, after some patients developed severe facial swelling. BMY is in the midst of enrolling patients in a huge and expensive 25,000-person trial to prove the drug's safety.

  The company's biggest-selling drug, Pravachol, is fast losing market share to rival cholesterol-lowering pills sold by Pfizer and Merck. And early in 2001 the company lost its exclusive rights to sell Glucophage, a diabetes drug that had sales of $1.7 billion in 2000.

- A federal judge dealt a sharp setback to the company in the fall of 2000. The ruling may open the way for an immediate introduction of generic competition to BMY's blockbuster drug, Taxol. As a result of the ruling, which was appealed, Ivax Corporation, a generic drug maker, will soon be able to sell its version of paclitaxel, the chemical name for Taxol. The FDA gave tentative approval to Ivax's generic version of Taxol the month before the ruling.

  Taxol, BMY's important cancer drug, is obtained from the bark of yew trees found mainly in old-growth forests. It derives its ability—unique among cancer drugs—to block a cancer cell from dividing and growing. It does so by way of a clever defense mechanism that fir-like yew trees use to fend off fungal infections and other disease-causing germs.

Like everything else, Taxol does not always act like a wonder drug. Some fast-dividing cancer cells can mutate into forms resistant to the drug. In some instances, patients with advanced cancer who initially benefit from Taxol cease to respond after several cycles of treatment because their cells become resistant, too. Despite conducting dozens of trials over the years, Bristol-Myers has been frustrated in its efforts to expand Taxol's effectiveness beyond certain breast, ovarian, and lung cancers.

- In the spring of 2001, a federal judge handed the company a stinging defeat when he ruled that generic drug maker Mylan Laboratories must be permitted to sell a cheap copy of BMY's highly profitable anti-anxiety drug, BuSpar. In 2000, sales of that drug totaled $709 million, making it the company's fifth-largest seller.

Reasons to Buy

- In mid-2001, BMY bought DuPont's drug business in a $7.8-billion cash purchase. DuPont's bestselling drug is Sustiva, a widely used part of the drugs combined in a "cocktail" to treat AIDS. It had sales of $386 million in 2000. The new drug will enhance Bristol-Myers's AIDS products, which include Zerit and Videx. At the time of the purchase, DuPont had three additional AIDS compounds under development. For its part, Bristol-Myers is also working on new AIDS preparations. Commenting on the deal, CEO Peter Dolan said several promising drugs under development by DuPont have "blockbuster potential."
- Drug companies often fret about generic competition. Once the patent on a popular drug expires, generic versions sweep

into the market and prices of the original version plummet.

But the news was not all bad. A few weeks before the company lost patent protection on Glucophage, it received approval from the U.S. Food and Drug Administration (FDA) to market Glucovance for patients with Type 2 diabetes, which typically afflicts middle-age adults. About 15 million Americans suffer from Type 2 diabetes. Maintaining tight blood-sugar control is crucial for such patients. Patients who fail to heed this advice may develop such serious complications as blindness, kidney failure, nerve damage, strokes, and heart attacks.

The new drug combines two widely used pills into one and thus provides patients with the potential of attacking the two main causes of diabetes with one medication. According to a study reported at a meeting of the American Diabetes Association in June 2000, the combination pill enabled many patients to achieve better control over blood-sugar levels than when they took either of the two drugs alone. The two medicines are metformin, which BMY markets under the brand name Glucophage, and glyburide, a generic drug.

The approval of Glucovance gives Bristol-Myers a new product to help protect its Glucophage franchise. Glucovance won't have to worry about generics for three years. This is an important development because Glucophage is the leading drug for the treatment of diabetes. Annual revenues from the company's diabetes product have been at blockbuster levels—on the order of $2 billion.

- BMY announced that it would sell, swap, or spin off its Clairol beauty care business and another unit that sells medical equipment so that it could focus more on the highly profitable business of prescription drugs. In a meeting held with analysts and investors in the fall of 2000, CEO Charles A. Heimbold Jr. said that after selling these two businesses, prescription drugs would make up 85 percent of the company's sales and 90 percent of its profits. Bristol-Myers has long resisted pressure from investors to sell Clairol, which had $2.4 billion in sales in 1999, or about 13 percent of the company's total. They employ 7,000 of BMY's 54,000 employees. In late May 2001, a deal to sell Clairol was finally struck with Procter & Gamble for $4.25 billion. The medical equipment business, which is known as Zimmer Inc., sells hip replacements and other supplies. In 2001 the company announced that Zimmer would be spun off to shareholders as a tax-free distribution by the end of the third quarter. The company's decision to concentrate on its pharmaceutical business was cheered by analysts, who valued the two businesses together at between $5 billion and $7 billion.

- In August 2000, Bristol-Myers said it listed with the FDA a new patent related to Taxol that had been issued to American BioScience, a small generic drug maker in Santa Monica, California. Earlier in that month Bristol-Myers came away second best after trading legal barbs with American BioScience. When the courtroom tussle subsided, a federal court judge issued a temporary restraining order demanding that the giant pharmaceutical firm list the new patent, which covers single-dosage forms of paclitaxel, the chemical name for Taxol.

    However, Bristol-Myers, following the development with the FDA, had the upper hand. At least for now, any generic drug maker that attempts to introduce a cheap copy of Taxol will have to clear new patent hurdles. Taxol generated $1.6 billion in sales for Bristol-Myers in 2000. As a result of the latest development, Taxol may be able to retain its patent for as much as thirty months longer than previously expected.

"Branded companies are getting more and more sophisticated in using regulatory and legal tactics to thwart generic competition," said Carl Seiden, a pharmaceutical analyst with J. P. Morgan.

- Bristol-Myers Squibb has paid a dividend to its shareholders for an unbroken sixty-eight years—since becoming a public company in 1933. What's more, the company has increased the dividend each year since 1972. Earnings per share, moreover, have also done well, climbing from $.83 in 1990 to $2.36 in 2000, for a compound annual growth rate of 11 percent.

- Sustagen, a nutritious flavored milk substitute for preschool and school-age children and pregnant or lactating mothers, is particularly popular in Latin America and Asia. As Mead Johnson seeks to standardize the product's formulation, Sustagen has become a cornerstone of the division's efforts to globalize its business.

- In a new strategy designed to exploit the fast-moving advances in human gene science, Bristol-Myers, the world's number one maker of cancer drugs, is gearing up a major research initiative to usher in a new era of cancer care. The company's goal is to enhance the effectiveness of its existing drugs, as well as those under development. This would be accomplished by tailoring all future treatment to an individual's unique genetic personality.

    To accomplish this, BMY has a major agreement with one of the premier gene-hunting companies, Millennium Pharmaceuticals, Inc. of Cambridge, Mass., to determine the unique genetic makeup of tumors. Bristol-Myers plans to use Millennium's "molecular fingerprinting" to help identify which patients will respond best to which drugs. The new gene-based approach is being aggressively promoted by the National Cancer Institute and embraced by major cancer treatment centers and other drug makers.

- The company's research and development expenditures in 2000 increased by 10 percent over the prior year and totaled $2 billion, or 9.5 percent of revenues. What's more, Bristol-Myers Squibb has more than fifty drugs in development, including treatment for cancer, hypertension, diabetes, obesity, heart failure, coronary thrombosis, stroke, hepatitis, infectious diseases, migraine, inflammation, pain, and skin disorders.

- BMY had seventeen products with sales in excess of $100 million in 2000. Among the leaders were Pravachol, up 7 percent to $1.8 billion; Glucophage, up 32 percent to $1.7 billion; Taxol, up 7 percent to $1.6 billion; Plavix, up 65 percent to $903 million; Buspar, up 17 percent to $709 million; Paraplatin, up 15 percent to $690 million; Knees, up 10 percent to $416 million; and Avapro, up 49 percent to $381 million.

Total assets: $17,578 million
Current ratio: 1.74
Return on 2000 equity: 44.6%
Common shares outstanding: 1,955 million

	2000	1999	1998	1997	1996	1995	1994	1993
Revenues (millions)	21331	20222	18284	16701	15065	13767	11984	11413
Net income (millions)	4711	4167	3630	3205	2850	2600	2331	2269
Earnings per share	2.36	2.06	1.80	1.61	1.42	1.28	1.15	1.10
Dividends per share	.98	.86	.78	.76	.75	.74	.73	.72
Price High	74.9	79.3	67.6	49.1	29.1	21.8	15.3	16.8
Low	42.4	57.3	44.2	26.6	19.5	14.4	12.5	12.7

AGGRESSIVE GROWTH

Cardinal Health, Incorporated

7000 Cardinal Place ◻ Dublin, Ohio 43017 ◻ Investor contact: Jennifer A. Fillman (614) 757-5592 ◻ Dividend reinvestment plan is not available ◻ Web site: www.cardinal.com ◻ Fiscal year ends June 30 ◻ Listed: NYSE ◻ Ticker symbol: CAH ◻ S&P rating: A- ◻ Value Line financial strength rating: B++

Cardinal Health's record of outstanding performance has given the company its preeminence in health care supply procurement and distribution. Each Cardinal business consistently outperforms its competitors because of its leadership position and superior resources available under the Cardinal Health umbrella.

What's more, Cardinal boasts strong management, superior service levels, industry information sharing, greater operating leverage, and a lower cost of capital.

Cardinal has long delivered strong revenue and operating income growth while maintaining a solid balance sheet. By leveraging its infrastructure to operate more efficiently, operating earnings growth consistently outpaces revenue growth.

Analysts at Deutsche Banc Alex. Brown, moreover, "expect this trend to continue, as the company further integrates its acquisitions. Indeed, both return on sales and return on committed capital reached record levels" in fiscal 2000.

The Deutsche Banc Alex. Brown report went on to say, "In our view, Cardinal distinguishes itself from its competition by providing consistently superior service to its customers. Significantly, Cardinal is also an innovator, continually adding incremental services and instituting more efficient ways of conducting business."

Company Profile

Cardinal Health provides innovative products and services to tens of thousands of customers in the health care industry. The company maintains market-leading positions in pharmaceutical formulation, manufacturing, packaging, and distribution; medical-surgical product manufacturing and distribution; and automation and information services by working with its customers to address challenges they face in the quickly changing health care environment. Cardinal is a *Fortune* 60 company, with annual revenues of more than $25 billion produced by 42,000 employees on five continents.

Cardinal operates a family of businesses, offering many complementary products and services to its health care manufacturer and provider customers. The company segregates its operations into four primary business segments that reflect the products they provide and the customers they serve:

• Pharmaceutical Distribution and Provider Services (45 percent of fiscal 2000 operating earnings) offers pharmaceutical and specialty product distribution, repackaging, retail pharmacy franchising, hospital pharmacy management, and other services to health care providers.

• Medical-Surgical Products and Services (28 percent of operating earnings) manufactures and distributes a comprehensive array of medical-surgical and lab products used by hospitals, surgery centers, physicians' offices, and long-term care facilities.

• Pharmaceutical Technologies and Services (16 percent of fiscal operating earnings) provides comprehensive services to pharmaceutical manufacturers and biotechnology companies, including proprietary drug delivery technologies and contract manufacturing processes, integrated packaging services, as well as sales and marketing.

• Automation and Information Services (11 percent of operating earnings) develops automated systems for dispensing pharmaceuticals and medical-surgical supplies and a variety of information systems used by health care providers and manufacturers.

Highlights of Fiscal 2000

■ Solid growth, as revenues climbed 17 percent to $25.2 billion.

■ Net earnings expanded even more impressively, up 24 percent to $730 million. This marked the thirteenth consecutive year in which earnings exceeded the company's goal of achieving 20 percent growth.

■ Diluted earnings per share advanced 25 percent to $1.71, excluding the impact of special one-time charges.

■ Return on shareholders' equity reached 19.3 percent, a new high.

Shortcomings to Bear in Mind

■ The health care industry is subject to constant change as a result of product innovation, cost pressures, competitive pressures, and new legislation.

■ Because Cardinal has been so consistently successful, it is a difficult stock to buy at a reasonable price. Typically, it sells at a P/E of 30 or more.

Reasons to Buy

■ For the past ten fiscal years (ending June 30, 2000), total return to shareholders has compounded at an annual pace of 29 percent, or well in excess of the Standard & Poor's 500.

■ Health care is an enormous industry, representing about 13 percent of the gross domestic product. With an aging population, there is a solid long-term demand for everything that Cardinal does. For example, during the next five years, more than $34 billion of branded pharmaceuticals face patent expiration. Cardinal's Pharmaceutical Distribution and Provider Services businesses should benefit from this trend because sales of generic products tend to be more profitable for the company than sales of equivalent branded products.

At the other end of the spectrum, Cardinal's Pharmaceutical Technologies and Services businesses are well positioned to assist branded manufacturers in the development of new or reformulated pharmaceutical products to help replace sales of products losing patent protection. In addition, the government appears poised to pass some form of Medicare drug benefit for seniors that should encourage greater consumption of pharmaceuticals, especially generics.

■ Cardinal Health provides manufacturers with highly efficient and economical distribution services essential for its products. Cardinal handles all of the logistics, inventory and receivables management, and administrative activities involved in delivering pharmaceutical products to more than 26,000 pharmacy locations every day.

For its pharmacy customers, Cardinal consolidates orders for products, potentially from hundreds of manufacturers, into pharmacy-specific deliveries of the right products to the right place at the right time.

■ Cardinal's operations include full-line drug distribution as well as several specialty pharmaceutical distribution businesses that address specific customer or manufacturer requirements. These businesses include the nation's leading pharmaceutical repackaging operation (currently used by six of the ten largest retail chains in the country); a leading blood plasma and specialty drug distributor; and a company that provides full-service, third-party logistics to manufacturers.

This group includes three additional businesses, complementary to distribution, for pharmacy providers:

• Medicine Shoppe International is the country's leading franchiser of independent retail pharmacies with nearly 1,300 of these apothecary-style pharmacies in the United States and nine other countries. Medicine Shoppe offers a successful, alternative business format to retail pharmacists who prefer to own their own store.

• For hospitals, Owen Healthcare offers pharmacy and materials-management services that help customers control costs while enhancing the quality of patient care.

• The recently formed Cardinal Health Staffing Network assists Cardinal retail and hospital pharmacy customers with their staffing needs as they face a growing shortage of pharmacy professionals. Through these businesses, Cardinal Health has become one of the largest employers of pharmacists in the nation with more than 2,200 pharmacists on its staff.

■ The company is a favorite of brokerage-house analysts. For instance, here is what Andrew L. Speller, an analyst with A. G. Edwards says, "We view CAH as one of the better positioned companies to reap the benefits from the ever-changing health care environment. The company's strategy has created a unique platform in the industry, in which we view as the GE of Health Care."

The company's goal is to build a leading presence in health care distribution with high value, complementary products, and services that enable its customers to improve operational efficiency and quality for the patient. Cardinal has the largest breadth, depth, and scale of product offerings across the entire health care continuum, as 99 percent of its operating earnings are derived from businesses that have the number one or number two positions.

"In fact, several of CAH's subsidiaries are dominant in their respective fields as Pyxis (the leading provider of automated pharmaceutical and medical-supply dispensing systems to hospitals and other sites of care) has in excess of 85 percent market share in automated dispensing technology; R. P. Scherer has more than 90 percent share in pharmaceutical softgel capsules; Owen has a 70-percent-plus market share in outsourced pharmacy services; and Allegiance custom sterile kits have more than a 50 percent market share. It is very hard to find any one company that offers the breadth or depth of CAH's product offerings or the operational expertise that the company has in all of its businesses."

■ In fiscal 2000, Pharmaceutical Technologies and Services achieved a number of major accomplishments:

• The segment achieved record revenues (up 15 percent) and operating earning (up 25 percent).

• It broadened its service portfolio with several important acquisitions.

• It expanded capacity at ten plants, including a major expansion of Scherer's softgel operation in Tampa, a high-rise packaging warehouse in Philadelphia, and a new label and insert facility in New Jersey.

• Pharmaceutical Technologies helped manufacturers develop and launch important new or reformulated drugs, including Abbott's Norvir, Glaxo Wellcome's Agenerase, and Lilly's Zyprexa in Zydis form.

Total assets: 10,265 million
Current ratio: 1.72
Common shares outstanding: 414 million
Return on 2000 shareholders' equity: 19.3%

	2000	1999	1998	1997	1996	1995	1994	1993
Revenues (millions)	25247	21481	12927	10968	8862	7806	5790	1967
Net income (millions)	730	574	283	221	160	85	63	31
Earnings per share	1.71	1.37	1.13	.90	.73	.59	.47	.36
Dividends per share	.07	.07	.05	.04	.03	.03	.03	.02
Price High	69.9	55.5	50.9	35.0	26.0	17.2	14.3	11.5
Low	24.7	24.7	31.0	22.9	15.5	12.3	9.9	5.8

GROWTH AND INCOME

Caterpillar Incorporated

100 N. E. Adams Street ❑ Peoria, Illinois 61629-7310 ❑ Investor contact: James W. Anderson (309) 675-4549 ❑ Dividend reinvestment plan is available: (800) 446-2617 ❑ Web site: www.cat.com ❑ Listed: NYSE ❑ Ticker symbol: CAT ❑ S&P rating: B+ ❑ Value Line financial strength rating: B++

Caterpillar and DaimlerChrysler teamed up to form a global alliance in late 2000 to make vehicle parts, including medium-size truck engines, fuel systems, and other powertrain parts. The companies said they would produce 300,000 medium-size engines between them each year. The 50-50 alliance is expected to immediately add to Caterpillar's earnings and will have a considerable impact on earnings in the years ahead.

About two-thirds of the engines go into such vehicles as delivery trucks and school buses. A third are used in off-road vehicles such as construction or mining equipment, a market in which Caterpillar is the leader. Both companies said they expect the deal will result in large savings in research and development costs as they design engines to comply with strengthening regulations on engine noise and emissions.

A significant aspect of the arrangement comes from fuel systems, which inject fuel in pulses into piston chambers of the engines. Within five years the companies expect sales of fuel systems will triple from its current combined level of $600 million. Unlike gasoline-powered engines, which rely on spark plugs for their combustion, diesel engines ignite their fuel by compression. With increasing concerns about emissions control, fuel systems are increasingly seen as an important way to make diesel engines more fuel efficient.

Alexander Blanton, an analyst with Ingalls & Snyder, said the most attractive part of the alliance is that "each company can benefit from what the other has already done. They won't have to reinvent the wheel." Under the agreement the companies will continue to compete against each other in the manufacture and sale of heavy-duty engines, but DaimlerChrysler's Freightliner brand of heavy trucks will buy its engines from Caterpillar.

Company Profile

Headquartered in Peoria, Illinois, Caterpillar is the world's largest manufacturer of construction and mining equipment, diesel and natural gas engines, and industrial gas turbines. It is a *Fortune* 50 industrial company with more than $26 billion in assets.

Caterpillar's broad product line ranges from the company's new line of compact construction equipment to hydraulic excavators, backhoe loaders, track-type tractors, forest products, off-highway trucks, agricultural tractors, diesel and natural gas engines, and industrial gas turbines. Cat products are used in the construction, road-building, mining, forestry, energy, transportation, and material-handling industries.

Over the years, Caterpillar has earned a reputation for rugged machines that set industry standards for performance, durability, quality, and value. The company's goal is to remain the technological leader

in its product lines. Today, thanks to accelerated design and testing, computer-based diagnostics and operations, and greatly improved materials, the company can deliver to customers new and better products sooner.

Caterpillar products are sold in nearly 200 countries. The company delivers superior service through it extensive worldwide network of 195 dealers, composed of 64 dealers in the United States and 131 abroad. Many of these dealers have relationships with their customers that have spanned at least two generations. More than 80 percent of Cat's sales are to repeat customers.

Caterpillar products and components are manufactured in forty-one plants in the United States and forty-three plants in Australia, Brazil, Canada, England, France, Germany, Hungary, India, Indonesia, Italy, Japan, Mexico, the Netherlands, Northern Ireland, China, Poland, Russia, South Africa, and Sweden.

Caterpillar's commitment to customer service is demonstrated by the fastest parts delivery system in its industry. Caterpillar's customers can obtain replacement parts from their dealers usually upon request. If not, Caterpillar ships them anywhere in the world within twelve hours, often much sooner.

Caterpillar offers its customers an easy means of buying Cat equipment through its financial products subsidiary, Caterpillar Financial Services Corporation, a global enterprise with an $11.6-billion managed portfolio.

Highlights of 2000

Caterpillar reported revenues of $20.18 billion in 2000, 2 percent higher than the prior year. However, a 3 percent increase in physical volume and a 10 percent increase in Financial Products revenues were partially offset by the unfavorable impact of the stronger U.S. dollar on sales abroad, primarily on the euro.

Profit of $1.05 billion, or $3.02 per share, was $107 million more than in 1999. The increase was helped primarily by higher physical volume, improved prices (excluding currency), manufacturing efficiencies, and a favorable income tax adjustment.

Shortcomings to Bear in Mind

- Caterpillar has an extremely leveraged balance sheet—only 33 percent of its capitalization is in common equity. I prefer 75 percent. What's more, coverage of bond interest is a low 2.9 times. I prefer 6 times.

Reasons to Buy

- While best known for its construction, mining, and earth-moving implements, Caterpillar is also a leading manufacturer of power-generating equipment. Of late, orders for generators are pouring in from around the world. Electric power "is Caterpillar's largest growth opportunity," said Douglas Oberhelman, vice president in charge of Caterpillar's engine products division.

  Utility deregulation and the growth of the Internet are creating solid demand for generating equipment here at home. What's more, in third-world countries local power generation is a popular alternative to dams and centralized power plants.

  Generator-equipment revenues in 2000, moreover, reached the $2.6 level—up a healthy 40 percent over the prior year. Caterpillar officials are looking for this burgeoning business to climb to $6 billion, or 20 percent of the company's total revenue by the year 2006—up from the 10 percent level as recently as 1999.

- In 2001 the company purchased Pioneer Machinery, Inc., a distributor of forestry equipment. Pioneer has twenty-nine stores and about 450 employees in six states: West Virginia, Virginia, Georgia, North Carolina, South Carolina, and Florida.

- Growth. That single word better than any other explains Caterpillar. In recent years Caterpillar has dramatically increased its global presence through expanded facility locations. According to Mr. Barton, "We have furthered our industry leadership through major growth initiatives, including joint ventures, acquisitions, new and improved products, and the addition of innumerable services."

- A growing family of diverse service organizations complements the company's global leadership in machines and engines and will help fuel growth.

  - Caterpillar Financial Services has twenty offices in fourteen countries to support the sale of Cat equipment around the world. Plans are to expand into Asia Pacific, Brazil, Poland, and the Czech Republic.

  - A new subsidiary, Caterpillar Redistribution Services, helps Cat dealers sell used Cat equipment while providing customers with Caterpillar's unmatched product support.

  - Caterpillar Logistics Services provides logistics services, including managing inventories and distribution for other companies' products. Sales have grown 70 percent since 1994, with promising growth still ahead.

- As opportunities abound, the company anticipates that sales will exceed $30 billion before the end of the new decade. The growth will come two primary areas: new products and expansion into new markets. Increasingly, the company uses acquisitions and joint ventures as a means to grow in both areas. Since 1991, Caterpillar has entered into thirty-eight acquisitions or joint ventures that range from partial to 100 percent ownership.

■ In the realm of new products, here is a summary of its progress:

- *Engines:* To meet the world's growing demand for new ways to provide power, Caterpillar's engine business is expanding its capabilities in electric power generation, fuel systems, and distributed power. New initiatives include acquisition of German engine manufacturer MaK and formation of a joint venture with the United Kingdom's F. G. Wilson, a world leader in generator set packaging. Sales of electric power generation products and systems could triple in the next few years, the company believes.

- *Agriculture:* As farms grow larger and the agriculture industry becomes more high tech, Caterpillar strengthened its commitment to farmers. As a result of the company's more aggressive agriculture strategy, Caterpillar formed a joint venture with Claas, a German combine/harvester manufacturer, and is broadening its ag tractor product line.

- *Forestry:* The growing forestry industry is looking for more productive machines that also respect the environment. Caterpillar's renewed commitment to the forestry industry has seen the acquisition of a Swedish forest products group along with investment in the first Caterpillar facility dedicated solely to the manufacture of forest products.

- *Compact machines:* The $3.6-billion compact machines industry is growing at an 11 percent clip and represents a significant opportunity for Caterpillar to expand its customer base. In this realm a number of new product families show promise: mini hydraulic excavators, compact wheel loaders, skid steer loaders, and a comprehensive range of nearly sixty work tools designed to enhance versatility.

■ According the company, more than 80 percent of the people in the world live in developing countries. In these regions there is limited access to water, electricity, and transportation. Currently, sales of Caterpillar products into these regions account for only about 23 percent of total company sales. That percent will grow as Asia, Central Europe, and the Commonwealth of Independent States, in particular, continue to invest in developing highways, bridges, and waterways necessary to sustain economic growth.

Total assets: $26,635 million
Current ratio: 1.46
Common shares outstanding: 344 million
Return on 2000 shareholders' equity: 18.8%

	2000	1999	1998	1997	1996	1995	1994	1993
Revenues (millions)	20175	19702	20977	18925	16522	16072	14328	11615
Net income (millions)	1051	946	1513	1665	1361	1136	955	681
Earnings per share	3.02	2.63	4.11	4.37	3.54	2.86	2.35	1.68
Dividends per share	1.33	1.25	1.15	.95	.78	.60	.32	.15
Price High	55.1	66.4	60.8	61.6	40.5	37.6	30.3	23.3
Low	29.6	42.0	39.1	36.3	27.0	24.1	22.2	13.5

Cedar Fair, L. P.

One Cedar Point Drive ◻ Sandusky, Ohio 44870-5259 ◻ Investor contact: Brain C. Witherow (419) 627-2233 ◻ Dividend reinvestment plan is available: (800) 278-4352 ◻ Web site: www.cedarfair.com ◻ Listed: NYSE ◻ Ticker symbol: FUN ◻ S&P rating: Not rated ◻ Value Line financial strength rating: B+

In 2000 Cedar Point unveiled yet another roller coaster, the Millennium Force, which is higher than a football field is long—310 feet. If you care to ride this monster, you will drop at an 80 degree angle and career down the tracks at 92 miles per hour.

Millennium Force generated unprecedented media coverage. And people came from all over the world to ride it, from rock stars, movie stars, and famous athletes to coaster enthusiasts from Colorado, Florida, England, and Germany to families from Cleveland, Detroit, Columbus, Lansing, Toledo, and other Midwestern cities that make up Cedar Point's primary market.

Company Profile

Cedar Fair, L. P. owns and operates five amusement parks, two major water parks, three resort hotels, several year-round restaurants, a marina, and an RV campground. The company's parks attract more than 10 million visitors a year.

Cedar Fair prides itself on the growth of its roller coasters. Cedar Point alone boasts fourteen—more than any other park in the world. All told, Cedar Fair parks have thirty-eight roller coasters, including some of the tallest, steepest, and highest-rated coasters ever built.

Cedar Fair's Five Parks

Cedar Point, which is located on Lake Erie between Cleveland and Toledo, is one of the largest amusement parks in the United States; it serves a total market area of 22 million people.

Valleyfair, located near Minneapolis/St. Paul, draws from a total population of 8 million people in a multistate market area.

Dorney Park & Wildwater Kingdom is located near Allentown, Pennsylvania; it serves a total market area of 35 million people in the Northeast.

Worlds of Fun/Oceans of Fun, in Kansas City, Missouri, draws from a total market area of 7 million people.

Knott's Berry Farm, near Los Angeles, is one of several major year-round theme parks in southern California. It serves a total market area of 20 million people and a large national and international tourist population.

How They Operate

The parks are family oriented, providing clean and attractive environments with exciting rides and entertainment. Except for Knott's Berry Farm (which is open all year), the operating season is generally from May through September.

The parks charge a basic daily admission price that provides unlimited use of virtually all rides and attractions. Admissions accounted for 50 percent of revenues in 2000, with food, merchandise, and games contributing 41 percent and accommodations the other 9 percent.

Tax Considerations

Cedar Fair is a publicly traded master limited partnership (MLP). The MLP structure is an attractive business form because it allows the partnership to pay out the majority of its earnings to its owners without first paying significant federal and state income taxes at the entity level, avoiding what is known as the corporate form as double taxation of earnings.

Ownership of Cedar Fair, L. P. units is different from an investment in corporate stock. Cash distributions made by the partnership are treated as a reduction of basis and are generally not taxable. Instead, unitholders must pay tax only on their pro rata share of the partnership's taxable income, which is generally lower. The partnership provides the tax information necessary for filing each unitholder's federal, state, and local tax returns on I.R.S. Schedule K-1 in mid-March each year.

The tax consequences to a particular unitholder will depend on the circumstances of that unitholder; however, income from the partnership may not be offset by passive tax losses from other investments. Prospective unitholders should consult their tax or financial advisors to determine the federal, state, and local tax consequences of ownership for these limited partnership units.

Ownership of limited partnership units may not be advisable for IRAs, pension, and profit-sharing plans and other tax-exempt organizations, nonresident aliens, foreign corporations and other foreign persons, and regulated investment companies.

Highlights of 2000

- Great new rides made the difference for Cedar Fair, as the company's parks entertained a record number of guests. Overall, combined attendance at the nine properties totaled a record 11.7 million people, or 4 percent above the prior year's 11.2 million and 2 percent above the previous record set in 1998.

- The successful debuts of Millennium Force at Cedar Point and Power Tower at Valleyfair made strong contributions to 2000. Cedar Point posted a 4 percent increase in attendance, finishing the year at 3.4 million

guests, and Valleyfair attendance was up 6 percent to 1.2 million.

- However, Dorney Park in Allentown, Pennsylvania suffered an 11 percent decrease in attendance, to 1.3 million guests, due to extremely poor weather. The Northeast and Mid-Atlantic states had one of the coolest and wettest summers on record, and this significantly hurt attendance. Overall, Dorney Park had forty-six rain days during the season compared with only twelve in 1999, and only twenty-eight days of 80 degrees-plus weather in 2000 compared to sixty in 1999.

- On a more positive note, combined in-park per capita spending across the nine properties continued to rise, increasing 3 percent to a record $34.75.

Shortcomings to Bear in Mind

- About two-thirds of the company's revenue is derived from the Midwest and Mid-Atlantic regions. Adverse economic conditions in these regions could hurt attendance at Cedar Fair parks. On the other hand, the acquisition of Knott's Berry Farm lessens this risk somewhat.

- When you file your income tax, you may find that Cedar Fair has failed to send you the usual paperwork. In 2001 I didn't get mine till March 20. I had already given my CPA the rest, and he had completed my return before I realized my blunder. Unfortunately, it was back to square one—at my expense. One other thing: Since Cedar Fair operates in several states, you may find you have to pay a few of them some tax money. Otherwise, it is a great stock.

- Each of the company's parks faces some direct competition from other parks. For instance, Dorney Park competes with Hershey Park in central Pennsylvania and Six Flags Great Adventure in the New York and New Jersey metropolitan area.

Out West, the newly acquired Knott's Berry Farm has to tussle with six parks, all within fifty miles. They include Adventure City, Castle Amusement Park, Disneyland, Six Flags Magic Mountain, Scandia Family Fun Center, and Pacific Park. Cedar Point, the company's biggest park, competes with three nearby parks: Paramount Kings Island in southern Ohio and Sea World and Geauga Lake, both near Cleveland. Valleyfair faces the least competition: Adventureland, 250 miles away in Des Moines, and Camp Snoopy, an indoor park at the Mall of America fifteen miles away, now owned by Cedar Fair. Worlds of Fun's competition consists of Silver Dollar City in Branson, Missouri, and Six Flags Over Mid America outside St. Louis.

Reasons to Buy

- In 2001, Knott's Berry Farm will get a full year's benefit from Perilous Plunge, the world's highest and steepest water ride, which was scheduled to open in the summer of 2000 but did not debut until late in the season. At 121 feet high with an amazing 75-degree drop, Perilous Plunge is the water version of Millennium Force. The company is "confident it will be a strong draw for Knott's Berry Farm."
- Both Cedar Fair and Knott's Berry Farm are recent recipients of the Applause Award, the industry's highest honor for "foresight, originality, and sound business development." And for the third consecutive year Cedar Fair received the prestigious Golden Ticket Award, which goes to the best amusement park in the world in an international survey conducted by Amusement Today, a newspaper that ranks the "best of the best" in the amusement industry.

The company's parks also placed four coasters in the Top Roller Coaster ranking: Magnum, number one; Millennium Force, number two, and Raptor, number five. Dorney Park's Wildwater Kingdom, moreover, ranked as the number three water park in the Amusement Today survey.

- Cedar Fair's parks are well-run and boast profit margins that are the highest in the industry.
- The company invested $38 million in capital expenditures across its nine properties in 2001.
- In 2001, Dorney Park introduced Talon, a world-class suspended coaster with a 135-foot-tall first hill and a terrifying 58 mph first drop. Talon is Dorney's sixth roller coaster. According to CEO Richard L. Kinzel, "We are confident this great new ride, combined with a more normal weather pattern, will drive increased attendance and profits in 2001."
- At Cedar Point, more than a third of the park's visitors, the highest ever, spent the night as part of their visit to the park. To build this momentum, said Mr. Kinzel, "We are adding an upscale camping complex, called Lighthouse Point, to our popular Camper Village RV campground. Lighthouse Point will feature upscale cabins, cottages, and RV campsites, as well as a swimming pool, fishing pier, and other amenities."
- According to one analyst, Cedar Fair's management team "exhibits both strength and depth." The general managers at the five parks have an average tenure of nearly twenty-five years with the company.
- Cedar Fair operates in an industry with high barriers to entry, with scant likelihood of new competition. The absence of direct competition gives the parks pricing power in their regions, bolstering profit margins.

Total assets: $764 million
Current ratio: 0.32
Partnership units: 51 million
Return on 2000 partners' capital: 23.5%

	2000	1999	1998	1997	1996	1995	1994	1993
Revenues (millions)	473	438	420	264	250	218	198	179
Net income (millions)	78	86	84	68	74	66	61	50
Earnings per share	1.66	1.63	1.58	1.47	1.59	1.45	1.37	1.13
Dividends per share	1.50	1.40	1.29	1.26	1.20	1.14	1.06	.95
Price High	20.9	26.1	30.1	28.3	19.5	18.6	18.3	18.3
Low	17.4	18.4	21.8	17.7	16.1	14.1	13.4	13.5

GROWTH AND INCOME

Chevron Corporation
(soon to be ChevronTexaco Corporation)

575 Market Street □ San Francisco, California 94105-2856 □ Investor contact: Pierre Breber (415) 894-9376 □ Dividend reinvestment plan is available: (800) 842-7629 □ Web site: www.chevron.com □ Listed: NYSE □ Ticker symbol: CHV □ S&P rating: B+ □ Value Line financial strength rating: A++

Continuing the trend toward consolidation in the oil patch, Chevron acquired Texaco in a $43-billion transaction in the fall of 2000. Once the merger is completed (in the second half of 2001), the company will be the world's fourth largest, behind ExxonMobil, Royal Dutch, and BP. This move came on the heals of earlier mammoth mergers, including Mobil with Exxon and BP Amoco with Atlantic Richfield.

This was not the first attempt by the two companies to fashion a deal. In June 1999 talks collapsed following a disagreement over price and which company would control the board of the merged group. However, the retirement in January 2000 of Kenneth Derr from the posts of chairman and CEO of Chevron cleared the way for the two companies to reopen negotiations.

The new company, now called Chevron Texaco Corporation, expects to see savings that come from the elimination of some 4,000 jobs. In addition, savings will be realized from jettisoning of less-profitable units and streamlining some operations, a process that oil experts say has been going on throughout the industry since 1980. An early estimate of these savings is $1.2 billion per year. "The hidden value in mergers," according to Larry Goldstein, president of the Petroleum Industry Research Foundation, "is that you cut people and inventory. Companies have realized that they may not have control over the price of crude oil, but they do have control over costs."

Those cuts, in turn, have profoundly changed the main business of oil companies. The market giants now focus much more heavily on exploration and production rather than refining and selling gasoline, which they do primarily through joint ventures.

Company Profile

Chevron is a worldwide petroleum company with important interests in chemicals and minerals. It is a leading domestic producer of crude oil and natural gas and a marketer of refined products, and it is active in foreign exploration and production and overseas refining and marketing. Chevron operates several segments:

Exploration and Production

Chevron explores for and produces crude oil and natural gas in the United States and twenty-five other countries. The company is the third largest domestic natural gas producer.

Major producing regions include the Gulf of Mexico, California, the Rocky Mountains, Texas, China, Canada, the North Sea, Australia, Indonesia, Angola, Nigeria, Kazakhstan, Alaska, Republic of Congo, Papua New Guinea, Colombia, Peru, and Ireland. Exploration areas include the above, as well as Alaska, Azerbaijan, Bahrain, and Qatar.

Refining

CHV converts crude oil into a variety of refined products, including motor gasoline, diesel and aviation fuels, lubricants, asphalt, chemicals, and other products. Chevron is one of the largest refiners in the United States.

The company's principal U.S. locations are El Segundo and Richmond, California, Pascagoula, Mississippi, Salt Lake City, Utah, El Paso, Texas, and Honolulu, Hawaii. The company also refines in Canada (through its Caltex affiliate) Asia, Africa, Australia, and New Zealand.

Marketing

Chevron is one of the leading domestic marketers of refined products, including motor gasoline, diesel and aviation fuels, lubricants, and other products. Retail outlets number 7,900 in the United States and 200 in Canada; Caltex supplies about 9,000 retail outlets worldwide.

Supply and Distribution

The company purchases, sells, trades, and transports—by pipeline, tanker, and barge—crude oil, liquefied natural gas liquids (such as propane and butane), chemicals, and refined products.

Chevron has trading offices in Houston, Walnut Creek, California, London, Singapore, Mexico City, and Moscow. What's more, the company has interests in pipelines throughout the United States and in Africa, Australia, Indonesia, Papua New Guinea, Europe, and the Middle East. Chevron has tanker operations worldwide.

Chemicals

The company's main products are benzene, styrene, polystyrene, paraxylene, ethylene, polyethylenem and normal alpha olefins. Chevron also produces a variety of additives used for fuels and lubricants.

Chevron operates plants in nine states and in France, Brazil, Mexico, Singapore, and Japan. Through affiliates and subsidiaries, the company operates or markets in more than eighty countries.

Highlights of 2000

- Through new discoveries, acquisitions, and other additions, Chevron replaced more than 150 percent of the oil and gas it produced in 2000—the eighth consecutive year the company was able to add more reserves than it produced.
- Chevron reduced its debt ratio to 24 percent, the lowest level since the company's 1984 merger with Gulf.
- The company implemented a $6-billion capital and exploratory spending plan for 2001, which was focused on Chevron's strategic priority to profitably expand its upstream (exploration and production) business.
- Chevron repurchased $1.4 billion of common shares through a stock buyback program. Buying back shares increases earnings per share.
- Chevron strengthened its chemicals business by forming a world-class joint venture with Phillips Petroleum Company.

Shortcomings to Bear in Mind

- The outlook for the company's chemicals business remains uncertain because of fluctuating feedstock costs, depressed demand, and excess capacity conditions for commodity chemicals. While results early in 2000 benefited from price increases for certain products, the industry experienced a weakening of margins in the second half of the year. Chevron expects these conditions to persist in 2001.
- Chevron's record of growth is not impressive. In the 1990–99 period, earnings per share inched ahead from $3.01 to $3.14. However, in 2000 the company had an extraordinary year as it benefited from higher oil prices, and EPS jumped to $7.97. In 2000 the average spot price for a barrel of West Texas Intermediate, a benchmark crude oil, was $30.34 compared with $19.30 in 1999. It seems probable that $30 crude oil may not continue indefinitely.

  In the same ten-year span, dividends advanced from $1.48 to $2.60, a compound annual pace of 5.8 percent. Although this is an excellent company in many ways, it does not look like a growth company. That's why I have labeled Chevron a growth and income stock.

Reasons to Buy

- When the merger with Texaco is complete, ChevronTexaco Corporation will have:
  - Top-tier upstream positions, with reserves of 11.2 billion barrels of oil equivalent.
  - Production of 2.7 million barrels per day and excellent exploration opportunities.
  - An integrated, worldwide refining and marketing business.
  - A global chemicals business and significant growth platforms in natural gas and power.
  - Industry-leading skills in technology innovation.

  According to CEO Dave O'Reilly, "The merger will bring together two leading energy companies to form a global enterprise that, working from $78 billion in assets, is highly competitive across all energy sectors, is projected to achieve at least $1.2 billion in annual cost savings, and is well positioned for growth."

- In 1950 world crude oil reserves were estimated at 76 billion barrels, which was about a twenty-year supply at the rate of consumption at that time. In the fifty years since, the world has used 600 billion barrels, and there's an estimated 1 trillion barrels in proved reserves. The world's oil supply now is greater than it has ever been; if we didn't find another drop of oil, we would still have a fifty-year supply left.

- Gross crude oil production form the Tengiz Field in Kazakhstan averaged 229,000 barrels a day in 2000, up from an average of 214,000 in 1999. As a result of a plant expansion, production is expected to average 260,000 barrels a day in 2001. Tengiz is operated by the Tengizchevroil (TCO) joint venture, in which Chevron's equity interest expanded to 50 percent from 45 percent upon completing an acquisition in early 2001.

  Construction of the Caspian Pipeline from the Tengiz Field to the Russian Black Sea port of Novorossiysk is on schedule. Start-up of the $2.6-billion project is expected in mid-2001, with initial capacity of 600,000 barrels a day. Chevron holds a 15 percent interest in the Caspian Pipeline Consortium.

- In 2000 Chevron and Phillips Petroleum agreed to combine their chemical operations into one of the world's largest petrochemical companies. The combined business will have revenues of about $5 billion and will generate $150 million in annual cost savings by the end of 2001.

- A flurry of publications noted Chevron's technology savvy in 2000. In naming Chevron one of America's fifty best companies at using and understanding the Internet, *Smart Business* said the company "has become both an incubator of Web-based businesses and a technology venture capitalist." *PC Week* included Chevron among its Fast Track 100 of Internet innovators, and *Business 2.0* and *Red Herring* lauded Chevron's high-tech leadership.

- Industrywide, 70 percent of oil remains locked in reservoirs unrecovered by conventional technologies. Late in 2000, Chevron and Schlumberger, the oil field services firm, launched a multiyear research project to provide the next-generation tools to increase recovery rates

from existing reservoirs. The joint effort, says technology vice president Don Paul, "will allow us to develop a superior set of next-generation software products and modeling capabilities that neither would be able to accomplish individually."

- Converting natural gas into clean, powerful liquid fuels promises to expand energy supplies and conserve nonrenewable resources. Chevron combined forces with Sasol Limited, the world's largest synthetic fuels producer, to create a global joint venture. The first major project is targeting development of a world-class GTL (gas-to-liquids) facility in Nigeria. Now, with other research and government partners— including the U.S. Department of Energy—Chevron is making GTL even more practical.

Total assets: 41,264 million
Current ratio: 1.07
Common shares outstanding: 654 million
Return on 2000 shareholders' equity: 27.5%

	2000	1999	1998	1997	1996	1995	1994	1993
Revenues (millions)	50592	35448	30557	35009	36874	31322	30340	32123
Net income (millions)	5185	2070	1339	3180	2651	1962	1693	1819
Earnings per share	7.97	3.14	2.04	4.83	4.06	3.01	2.60	2.80
Dividends per share	2.60	2.48	2.44	2.28	2.08	1.93	1.85	1.75
Price High	94.9	113.9	90.2	89.2	68.4	53.6	47.3	49.4
Low	69.9	73.1	67.8	61.8	51.0	43.4	39.9	33.8

CONSERVATIVE GROWTH

The Chubb Corporation

15 Mountain View Road ◻ Post Office Box 1615 ◻ Warren, New Jersey 07061-1615 ◻ Investor contact: Gail E. Devlin (908) 903-3245 ◻ Dividend reinvestment plan is available: (800) 317-4445 ◻ Web site: www.chubb.com ◻ Listed: NYSE ◻ Ticker symbol: CB ◻ S&P rating: B+ ◻ Value Line financial strength rating: A

Chubb has always been known for its appetite for risk and its innovative approaches to satisfying customers' needs. These traits have enabled the company to grow and prosper over the decades. However, Chubb is also known

for financial strength and fairness and speed of paying claims—qualities that are very important to its customers. CEO Dean R. O'Hare points out, "We are committed to protecting this financial strength by accepting only prudent risks and leaving the reckless gambles to our competitors."

This reputation was reinforced in an article in a *New York Times* article published on October 15, 2000. "Many brokers can provide examples of how Chubb has gone the extra mile on claims," said the *Times* reporter. A Chubb agent told the *Times*, "I sleep well when I know my customers are going to be treated right."

Chubb is famous for its expertise in insuring the possessions of the affluent. According to Mr. O'Hare, "We know how to value—and repair or replace if necessary—the custom features and workmanship that characterize upscale homes. We know upscale cars and yachts. And we know jewelry, art, antiques, and collectibles as no other insurer knows them. In our litigious society, we also know they need large amounts of excess liability coverage, and we have the capacity and financial strength to provide it."

Company Profile

In 1882 Thomas Caldecot Chubb and his son Percy opened a marine underwriting business in the seaport district of New York City. The Chubbs were adept at turning risk into success, often by helping policyholders prevent disasters before they occurred. As the twentieth century got underway, Chubb had established strong relationships with the insurance agents and brokers who placed their clients' business with Chubb underwriters.

The Chubb Corporation was formed in 1967 and was listed on the New York Stock Exchange in 1984. Today, Chubb stands among the largest insurers in the United States and the World. Chubb's 12,000 property and casualty employees serve customers from 135 offices throughout North America, Europe, South America, and the Pacific Rim.

Chubb has an excellent reputation for designing specialty property-casualty insurance products and providing high-quality service to its agents and policyholders. In an industry where product and service differentiation is limited, Chubb's specialty lines of property-casualty businesses are a significant franchise. Chubb's strengths include a worldwide branch structure; innovative and targeted product development; a high level of pricing, underwriting, and reserving discipline; and a fair approach to settling claims.

Shortcomings to Bear in Mind

- According to a 2001 report written by Credit Suisse First Boston Corporation, "Chubb's standard commercial lines insurance operations remain a serious concern. Chubb is pursuing corrective programs for this book, including raising rates, canceling risks, and re-underwriting."

- In the past ten years (1990–2000), earnings per share advanced at a snail's pace, rising from $2.90 to $4.01, a compound annual growth rate of only 3.3 percent. In the same period, dividends expanded from $.66 to $1.32, a growth rate of 7.2 percent.

- Value Line Survey, a leading statistical and advisory service, has a negative comment: "Although Chubb's privileged place in the high-end personal lines market doesn't appear to be at risk, we believe it will come up against increasingly tougher competition. AIG, for one, is rolling out some products, we believe. It is a formidable competitor, known to be aggressive, and generally stands out as a low-cost producer." (American International Group [AIG] is also recommended in this book.)

Reasons to Buy

- Chubb made solid progress in 2000. For instance, net written premiums advanced 11 percent to $6.3 billion, nearly three times the 4 percent growth the year before. Operating income increased an impressive 20 percent to $681 million, a big improvement over 1999 when operating income declined 8 percent.

Operating income per share in 2000 increased 15 percent to $3.82. Aided by lower catastrophe losses, the company's net underwriting loss narrowed to $24 million, a major improvement over the prior year when the loss was $179 million. This improved the combined loss-and-expense ratio to 100.4 percent, compared with 102.8 percent in 1999. Property and casualty after-tax investment income expanded by 6 percent to $735 million, and net income climbed 15 percent to $715 million.

- The big news of 2000 was the end of price cutting. In the words of CEO Dean R. O'Hare, "I think we can take credit, because we finally convinced investors that the long, devastating price war in standard commercial lines was coming to an end, as evidenced by rates that were rising and sticking.

"Chubb was the trailblazer in raising rates, and during 2000 we implemented our second annual round of rate increases. Over the two years of 1999 and 2000, cumulative renewal rate increase in the U.S. totaled seventeen points.

"Because of continued subpar underwriting results in standard commercial lines, there is general acknowledgment in the industry that rates are still inadequate, as one might expect after twelve years of declining rates and only two years of rate increases—and just one year of increases in the case of many insurers. There's a lot more catching up to be done."

- In January 2000, *Fortune* magazine named Chubb to its list of The 100 Best Companies to Work for in America.
- The repeal of the Glass-Steagall Act is a positive development for the industry. It puts all sectors of the financial services industry on a level playing field, and it enables companies to form alliances with other financial institutions and extend market reach through joint ventures. For example, it enables two institutions to complement the product expertise of one with the distribution network of another.

- One of Chubb's specialties in personal lines is valuable articles coverage, which insures jewelry, antiques, fine arts, and other collectibles. Increased purchases of jewelry and fine arts resulting from the strong economy in the United States have made valuable articles insurance a growing market for Chubb. Here, too, the company's branded policies offer superior coverage and claim service, and Mr. O'Hare says, "We believe we are the largest underwriter in this profitable market."

- Chubb is among a select segment of insurers with a large stake in overseas business. In the past, foreign property-casualty insurance markets have grown at a faster pace than those in the United States.

In 2000 Chubb made progress in its globalization efforts as the company reached a major milestone: the opening of its office in Shanghai. Mr. O'Hare said, "We worked long and hard to get started in the potentially vast Chinese market, and we look forward to building our business there.

"Our largest presence in the Asia-Pacific region is in Australia, followed by Hong Kong, Japan, Singapore, and Korea. Our largest market in Europe is the United Kingdom, followed by Germany, France, the Netherlands, and Belgium. In Latin America, our largest markets are in Brazil, Argentina, Colombia, and Mexico. All told, we have 135 offices in thirty-one countries, and our goal is to increase the percentage of our non–U.S. business from 17 percent to 33 percent by 2005."

- Chubb has an excellent reputation for designing specialty property-casualty insurance products and providing high-quality service to its agents and policy-holders, according to Credit Suisse First Boston Corporation. "In an industry in which product and service differentiation is limited, Chubb's specialty lines of property-casualty insurance are a significant franchise. Chubb's strengths include a worldwide branch structure; innovative and targeted product development; a high level of pricing, under-writing, and reserving discipline; and a fair approach to settling claims."

- Over the years Chubb has received many awards and top rankings from agents, brokers, rating agencies, and the media. The year 2000 was typical. The company collected awards ranging from "general insurer of the year" in Aus-tralia to "personal lines insurer of the year" in the United Kingdom to "pre-ferred provider of accident insurance" in Germany. In the words of CEO O'Hare, "Chubb continues to be regarded around the world as a leader when it comes to offering innovative products, outstanding customer service, and a great place to work."

Total assets: $25,027 million
Common shares outstanding: 175 million
Return on 2000 shareholders' equity: 9.8%

		2000	1999	1998	1997	1996	1995	1994	1993
Premiums earned (millions)		6145	5652	5304	5157	4569	4147	3776	3505
Net income (millions)		681	621	707	770	486	697	528	344
Earnings per share		4.01	3.66	4.19	4.39	2.76	3.93	2.98	1.96
Dividends per share		1.32	1.28	1.24	1.16	1.08	.98	.92	.85
Price	High	90.3	76.4	88.8	78.5	56.3	50.3	41.6	48.2
	Low	43.3	44.0	55.4	51.1	40.9	38.1	34.3	38.0

CONSERVATIVE GROWTH

Citigroup, Incorporated

153 East 53rd Street □ New York, New York 10043 □ Investor contact: Sheri Ptashek (212) 559-4658 □ Dividend reinvestment plan not available □ Web site: www.citigroup.com □ Listed: NYSE □ Ticker symbol: C □ S&P rating: A □ Value Line financial strength rating: A

Citigroup is by far the world's largest credit card company, with 97 million cards in force worldwide. Cards are the hub of the consumer sector. A credit card is usually among the client's first services purchased from Citigroup, and therefore it becomes the basis for introducing clients to products from the company's other divisions.

Cards are often the first product the consumer business introduces when it enters a new country, as was the case in 1999 with Egypt. In newer Citigroup consumer markets, such as Hungary, Poland, and Turkey, the card business supplies the company's growth and its broadest appeal to customers.

Company Profile

In one of the largest corporate mergers in history, Citigroup was formed in late 1998 with the combination of Citicorp (a large bank) and Travelers Group (a major insur-ance company). Citigroup is now the nation's largest financial services firm.

Melding traditional banking and insurance businesses together on a scale never attempted, the company's goal is to serve the financial needs of the widest possible audience on a global scale. Operations break down as follows:

The Global Consumer Segment

This includes branch and electronic banking, consumer lending services, credit card and charge card services, personalized wealth-management services for high-net-worth clients, and life, auto, and home-owners insurance.

Several specialized units include mortgage banking, which creates mortgages and student loans across North America and cards, which offers products such as Master-Card, VISA, Diners Club, and private-label credit cards. It has some 53 million card-member accounts; consumer finance services, which maintains 980 loan offices in forty-five states; and insurance, which offers annuities and various life and long-term-care insurance to individuals and small businesses.

In 2000, total Global Consumer net income amounted to $5.3 billion, a gain of 22 percent over the prior year.

The Global Corporate and Investment Bank Segment

This segment provides investment advice, financial planning and retail brokerage services, banking and other financial services, and commercial insurance products throughout the United States and in ninety-eight foreign countries.

The segment includes Salomon Smith Barney, which offers investment banking services such as underwriting of fixed-income and equity securities. Specialized units include emerging markets, which offers cash management, short-term loans, trade services, project finance, and fixed-income issuance and trading to countries outside North America, Western Europe, and Japan; global relationship banking, which offers cash management, foreign exchange, securities custody, and structured products to multinational companies; and commercial lines, which provides property and casualty insurance through brokers and independent agencies throughout the United States.

In 2000, this group of operations produced a net income of $6.4 billion, a gain of 28 percent over 1999.

Global Investment Management and Private Banking

Global Investment Management and Private Banking includes asset management services provided to mutual funds, institutional, and individual investors, and personalized wealth management services for high-net-worth clients. This group is comprised of the SSB Citi Asset Management Group and the Citibank Private Bank.

The SSB Citi Asset Management Group includes Salomon Brothers Asset Management, Smith Barney Asset Management, and Citibank Global Asset Management. These businesses offer a broad range of asset management products and services from global investment centers around the world, including mutual funds, closed-end funds, managed accounts, unit investment trusts, variable annuities, and personalized wealth management services to institutional, high-net-worth, and retail clients.

In 2000, this segment of the company had income of $685 million, a gain of 15 percent over the prior year.

Shortcomings to Bear in Mind

- Citigroup's acquisition of Associates First Capital Corp. in 2000 has caused some critical comments. According to one analyst, the Dallas company, which makes loans to consumers and companies with poor credit, faces a host of potential problems. Changes in Japan's regulatory climate, a downturn for the U.S. trucking industry (where it's a major lender), a Federal Trade Commission review, and a jump in credit-card losses could all signal lower profits for Associates.

Associates, which Ford Motor Company spun off three years ago, makes high-interest-rate loans to predominantly low- and middle-income consumers through nearly 2,800 branches in the United States and thirteen other countries. According to one observer, "More than one highflier has stumbled in recent years after buying a company such as Associates that lends to borrowers who can't qualify for bank loans."

- Who will run the company when its two top executives are no longer at the helm? Already, the company's cochairman, John Reed, has left the company. And Sanford I. (Sandy) Weill, the company's CEO, is showing signs that he may be relinquishing his post in the next few years. Citigroup is a huge and complex company that needs a talented leader. Will that CEO come from inside, or will the board look elsewhere?

- Citigroup's Salomon Smith Barney investment bank and its Citibank commercial bank in Europe have been lagging behind their principal Wall Street competitors: Goldman Sachs Group, Morgan Stanley Dean Witter, and Merrill Lynch. The acquisition of Schroders PLC of the United Kingdom is aimed at closing this gap.

However, analysts are not all convinced that the Schroders deal is a panacea for all of Citigroup's concerns in Europe. To be sure, Schroders is strong in corporate finance in Eastern Europe, France, Italy, and the United Kingdom. On the other hand, Schroders ranked only sixteenth in European mergers and acquisitions in 1999.

What's more, some analysts point out that the acquisition may not be easy for Citigroup to digest. Foreign purchases of British investment banks have been notoriously difficult to pull off because the cultures of well-established British banks

have been hard for outsiders to penetrate. In fact, Citigroup has had its own travails in merging with Salomon Smith Barney, a former Traveler's unit.

Reasons to Buy

- The acquisition, involving $31.1 billion in Citigroup stock, of financial services group Associates First Capital Corporation is a move that strengthens Citigroup's international business. "In one step, we catapult our international earnings in these rapidly growing segments by more than 40 percent," said Sandy Weill. "We are particularly excited about the Associates' strong presence in Japan, where it is the fifth largest finance company, and in Europe, where it has more than 700,000 customers."

The deal gave Citigroup control of the largest publicly traded finance company in the United States. The acquisition of Associates, which was closed at the end of 2000, is expected to add at least $.10 a share to Citigroup's earnings in the first year of the combined operation. The two companies have considerable overlap in their consumer finance units, which means duplicated services can be eliminated at a savings to the combined company.

- In still another major move, Citigroup announced in May 2001 that it would buy Mexico's second-largest bank, Group Financiero Banamex-Accival SA, for $12.5 billion in cash and stock. The largest takeover in Mexican history further consolidated Mexico's banking system, which has been recovering after the chaos of the mid-1990s banking crisis that culminated in a $100-billion bailout.

The deal makes Citigroup the largest bank in a country that remains severely lacking in financial services for the average citizen. The acquisition provides a major boost to Citigroup's aspirations in emerging markets, which chairman

Sandy Weill believes will be a major drive of the company's growth and profitability in the next five years.

Mr. Weill said that the Mexican economy is "underbanked," with lending accounting for only 15 percent of gross domestic product, compared with 29 percent in Brazil and 72 percent in the United States. "So you can get a feel for what we think the opportunities for growth are going to be in the next five years."

According to Jason Mollin, an analyst at Bear Stearns in New York, "We can safely say that the worsening impact of the Mexican crisis is behind us. Only remnants are left, and these will become less and less important as times goes on."

■ Although Citigroup is a global giant in the financial services sector, it now wants to expand its horizons by becoming a one-stop outlet for business and consumer financial products. To achieve these goals, the company plans to make acquisitions and cross-sell more services now that Congress has repealed banking restrictions that date back to the 1930s. Until the law was changed in the fall of 1999, banks were not allowed to own insurance companies and brokerage houses.

■ In 2000 the company purchased the investment banking operations of Schroders PLC—the last independent investment bank in London—for $2.2 billion. The deal aims to bring Schroders's mergers and acquisitions expertise and European client relationships together with Citigroup's sizable European fixed-income business. The acquisition of Schroders will double the size of Salomon Smith Barney's investment banking and stock business in Europe. "It puts us two or three years ahead of where we might have been had we not done this," said Weill.

Citigroup agreed to pay about $220 million in incentives to retain hundreds of the most important Schroders employees, said Michael Carpenter, chairman and CEO of Salomon Smith Barney. Most of those employees did not own significant amounts of stock in Schroders—the founding family owned 45 percent of its stock.

■ In 2001 the company acquired European American Bank (EAB) from ABN AMRO Bank N.V. for $1.6 billion, plus the assumption of $350 million in preferred stock. Headquartered in Uniondale, Long Island, EAB is one of Long Island's largest banks. It has $11.5 billion in deposits, $15.4 billion in assets, and ninety-seven branches, including sixty-seven in Long Island's Nassau and Suffolk counties and thirty in the five boroughs of New York City.

■ Citigroup has established teams of executives worldwide, including six in Japan alone, who are dedicated to finding new purchases in conjunction with the executives in charge of individual businesses there. Further streamlining in Citigroup's regional management structure is also being considered, a move that may make the acquisitions process smoother.

■ The Internet will play a significant role in the growth of the cards business. Citibank cards are among those most frequently used for Internet purchases today, and the company's goal is to be the payment vehicle of choice for online shoppers. Citigroup already offers online account management, an Internet-only credit account, an online shopping mall that provides savings exclusively to Citibank cardholders, and CitiWallet for convenient and secure Internet shopping. As consumers grow more comfortable shopping and paying over the Internet, they will be more inclined to use the company's online financial services, such as banking and brokerage.

Total assets: $902,210 million
Common shares outstanding: 5,351 million
Return on 2000 shareholders' equity: 20.4%

	2000	1999	1998	1997	1996	1995	1994	1993
Revenues (millions)	76887	57237	48936	47782	*			
Net income (millions)	1352	9947	6342	7751				
Earnings per share	2.74	2.19	1.77	2.12				
Dividends per share	.52	.41	.12					
Price High	59.1	58.3	35.5					
Low	35.3	32.7	19.0					

*Because of the merger with Travelers in 1998, no other statistics are available for prior years.

AGGRESSIVE GROWTH

Clayton Homes, Inc.

Post Office Box 15169 □ Knoxville, Tennessee 37901 □ Investor contact: Carl O. Koella, III (865) 380-3206 □ Web site: www.clayton.net □ Dividend reinvestment plan is available: (800) 937-5449 □ Fiscal year ends June 30 □ Listed: NYSE □ Ticker symbol: CMH □ S&P rating: A- □ Value Line financial strength: B++

Among the eight members of the company's board of directors, three have the last name of Clayton. James L. Clayton is chairman of the board; Kevin T. Clayton is CEO; and B. Joe Clayton is CEO of Clayton Automotive Group. Each is an owner of company stock. For his part, James L. Clayton owns 27.9 percent of Clayton Homes common stock.

This concentration of power in the hands of the Clayton clan may smack of nepotism, but I prefer to think that the family's large stake in the business will keep them hustling to make Clayton Homes a success—as it certainly has been in the past.

Company Profile

Clayton Homes, Inc. is a vertically integrated manufactured housing company headquartered in Knoxville, Tennessee. Employing more than 7,400 people and operating in thirty-three states, the company builds, sells, finances, and insures manufactured homes. It also owns and operates residential manufactured housing communities.

The company makes a wide variety of single- and multisection manufactured homes. They are factory built, completely finished, constructed to be transported by trucks, and designed as permanent, primary residences when sited.

The company's homes range in price from $10,000 to $75,000. They vary in size from 500 to 2,400 square feet.

The Manufacturing group is a leading producer of manufactured homes, with twenty plants supplying homes to 1,101 independent and company-owned retail centers.

The Retail group sells, installs, and services factory-built homes. At the end of fiscal 2000 there were 318 company-owned retail centers in twenty-three states.

Financial Services provides financing and insurance for homebuyers of company-owned and selected independent retail sales centers through Vanderbilt Mortgage and Finance, a wholly owned subsidiary.

The Communities group owns and operates seventy-six manufactured housing communities with 20,168 home sites in twelve states.

Highlights of 2000

• The company was awarded 2000 Manufacturer of the Year by the Manufactured Housing Institute.

● Clayton Homes opened its twentieth manufacturing plant (in Hodgenville, Kentucky).

● The company expanded Vanderbilt's loan servicing to $4 billion.

● It increased the number of company-owned stores to 318.

● It raised independent retailer locations to 707.

● The company purchased $205 million in portfolios.

● It upgraded the Clayton Homes Web site at *www.clayton.net*.

● Clayton Homes developed 460 new community sites.

● It introduced its proprietary Internet LINK system to 330 company-owned locations.

● The company securitized $1.3 billion in manufactured housing mortgages.

● It reduced its over-thirty-day delinquency to 1.67 percent, a key performance measure.

Shortcomings to Bear in Mind

■ In fiscal 2000 the industry was faced with increased competition and bloated inventory levels. In one two-month period, for instance, nineteen industry plants were closed, and retailers began closing satellite locations. On the other hand, such industry problems have historically helped Clayton, presenting the company with opportunities to acquire talent, operating facilities, and loan portfolios.

■ The company does not expect good tidings in fiscal 2001. CEO Kevin T. Clayton says, "The coming year will be difficult for all industry participants. More stores and manufacturing plants will close, financing will continue to tighten, and housing stocks will likely remain out of favor."

Mr. Clayton says, however, that "the company has historically survived and prospered in similar business cycles. Clayton's loan portfolio performs well and provides an annuity type income—as do the Communities and insurance operations. The company has a strong balance sheet and one of the most seasoned management teams in the industry." He concludes that "CMH has been profitable for 26 consecutive years, and 2001 will be no exception."

Reasons to Buy

■ During 2000, Clayton Homes opened twenty-six retail centers and closed fourteen underperforming units. The company continually evaluates specific markets and opens, acquires or closes retail centers as conditions warrant. Of the twenty-six new openings, ten were acquired and sixteen were greenfield start-ups.

■ In the same period, net sales of the Communities group increased 28 percent to $45 million, as 25 percent more homes were sold while the average home selling price increased 3 percent. The company added 460 sites during 2000, bringing the total to 20,168.

■ In 2000 Clayton's plants produced and sold 26,348 homes, representing 39,355 floors. Product mix was divided 49 percent multisection versus 51 percent single-section homes. Manufacturing sales revenues fell by 4.6 percent to $624 million due to the industry's excessive capacity and bloated retail inventories—closing one of every seven industry plants. On the other hand, all Clayton plants continued to operate and were profitable except for the new Hodgenville, Kentucky plant that opened in April 2000.

■ The Hodgenville facility expanded the company's presence in the Midwest and is well positioned to serve the prime manufactured housing states of Michigan, Indiana, Ohio, Illinois, and Pennsylvania. Historically, 50,000 manufactured homes are shipped into the Midwest each year. Prior to the Hodgenville plant opening, Clayton was underrepresented in the region.

■ Growth among the company's four groups has varied from quarter to quarter and year to year, but the synergies involved in this very-difficult-to-execute concept have enabled the company to consistently achieve records. While one group is undergoing a period of slower growth, another group is enjoying high growth. The challenge of balancing and maintaining the model should not be underestimated, especially since other industry leaders have taken multiple charges to restate their securitization models. On the other hand, Clayton Homes has taken a conservative approach to growth and risk management.

■ Despite a modest dip in earnings in fiscal 2000, the company has an impressive record of growth. In the most recent ten-year period (1990–2000), earnings per share advanced from $.18 to $1.03, a compound annual growth rate of 19.1 percent.

■ The Community group capitalizes on every aspect of profitable vertical integration. Residents may choose a quality home from the company's Manufacturing group, select an attractive home site in the community, and secure their mortgage and insurance from the Clayton Financial Services group.

■ In fiscal 2000 Clayton Homes purchased $95 million in manufactured housing loans originated by Chase Bank. The company expects the transaction to bolster earnings in fiscal 2001, which began July 1, 2000. "This portfolio represents another strategic purchase for Clayton Homes," said Kevin Clayton, president and CEO. "The loans overlay well with our current retail and marketing activities. The company

will earn three levels of profit from the transaction, as the loans will be insured, re-sold, and servicing retained."

■ The Communities group best exemplifies the company's unique brand of vertical integration. When the group sells a home, profit is realized from five different components of the transaction, including manufacturing, retailing, financing, insuring, and leasing the home site.

In fiscal 2000 the Communities group expanded its portfolio to seventy-six properties with 20,168 home sites. Clayton Crossing in East Tennessee held its grand opening in June, with seventy-six sites developed and a total build out of 271 sites. Clayton Crossing offers amenities, including larger sites for multisection homes, off-street parking, garages, and attractive landscaping.

■ Clayton's finance subsidiary, Vanderbilt Mortgage and Finance, enjoys a sterling reputation. As one competitor commented, "It's a class act." Clayton's retail managers—unlike most salespeople—make money not simply by selling home but also by sharing in the profit and losses on the associated loans. If a loan goes bad, the sales manager "eats 40 percent to 50 percent of the loss," according to a company spokesman.

■ The Financial Services group successfully navigated an extremely challenging year. During fiscal 2000 Vanderbilt Mortgage and Finance originated and securitized more than $980 million in mortgages, raising the total serviced portfolio to $4 billion, up 13 percent for the year.

■ CMH Insurance achieved its strategic growth plan in 2000. Net insurance premiums written totaled a record $63.5 million for the year, up 4 percent. It utilized such insurance products as homeowners, family protection, and the homebuyer protection plan, an extended warranty product.

Total assets: $1,506 million
Current ratio: 6.81
Common shares outstanding: 138 million
Return on 2000 shareholders' equity: 14.5%

	2000	1999	1998	1997	1996	1995	1994	1993
Revenues (millions)	1293	1344	1128	1022	929	758	628	476
Net income (millions)	144	155	138	120	107	87	69	54
Earnings per share	1.03	1.06	.92	.80	.72	.59	.47	.37
Dividends per share	.06	.06	.06	.06	.05	.03	Nil	Nil
Price High	13.1	15.4	18.1	15.6	14.5	15.0	11.5	10.6
Low	7.7	8.3	10.7	10.1	9.9	6.8	6.6	7.1

GROWTH AND INCOME

The Clorox Company

1221 Broadway □ Oakland, California 94612 □ Investor contact: Steve Austenfeld (510) 271-7270 □ Web site: www.clorox.com □ Dividend reinvestment plan is available: (888) 259-6973 □ Fiscal year ends June 30 □ Listed: NYSE □ Ticker symbol: CLX □ S&P rating: A □ Value Line financial strength rating: A+

Over the years the name Clorox has become synonymous with household bleach. No wonder. Since the company introduced its first pint of Clorox bleach in the 1920s, the Clorox Company has come to dominate the domestic bleach market with nearly a 70 percent share.

Today, Clorox has evolved into a diversified consumer-products company whose domestic retail products include many of the best-known brands of laundry additives, home cleaning and automotive-appearance products, cat litters, insecticides, charcoal briquettes, salad dressings, sauces, and water-filtration systems. The great majority of the company's brands are either number one or number two in their categories. Included in Clorox products are such well-known names as Formula 409, Liquid-Plumr, Pine-Sol, Soft Scrub, S.O.S., Tilex, Armor All, Kingsford charcoal, Match Light, Black Flag insecticides, Fresh Step cat litter, Hidden Valley salad dressing, and Kitchen Bouquet.

Company Profile

In 1913 a group of Oakland businessmen founded the Electro-Alkaline Company, a forerunner of the Clorox Company. The company originally produced an industrial-strength liquid bleach. It was sold in five-gallon crockery jugs to industrial customers in the San Francisco Bay area.

A household version of Clorox liquid bleach was developed in 1916 and subsequently was distributed in sample pint bottles. Demand for the product grew, and its distribution was gradually expanded nationally until it became the country's best-selling liquid bleach.

Clorox was a one-product company for its first fifty-six years, including the eleven years from 1957 through 1968 when it was operated as a division of the Procter & Gamble Company. Following its divestiture from Procter & Gamble in 1969, the company has broadened and diversified its product line and expanded geographically. Today, Clorox manufactures a wide range of products that are marketed to consumers in the United States and internationally. It is also a supplier of products to food service and institutional customers and the janitorial trades. Although the company's growth in the first few years after divestiture came largely through the acquisition of other companies and products, strong emphasis is now being given to the internal development of new products.

Clorox's Professional Products unit is focused on extending many of the company's successful retail equities in cleaning and food products to new channels of distribution, such as institutional and professional markets and the food service industry.

Internationally, Clorox markets laundry additives, home cleaning products, and insecticides, primarily in developing countries. What's more, Clorox is investing heavily to expand this part of its business. Overall, Clorox products are sold in more than seventy countries and are manufactured in thirty-five plants at locations in the United States, Puerto Rico, and abroad.

Shortcomings to Bear in Mind

- At least one analyst is negative on the outlook for Clorox. Harry Milling, an analyst with Morningstar, says the "culprit is lower sales because of declining market share, as Clorox focused on its ailing Glad bag business while ignoring its core housecleaning product business." Mr. Milling goes on to say that "Clorox plans heavy promotional activity, such as price cuts. This will cause major margin erosion." He puts the blame on CEO G. Craig Sullivan who is "responsible for ballooning the company's number of product segments with his expensive decision to buy First Brands for $2 billion." In one final blast, Mr. Milling says, "He got Clorox into this mess, and it's time the board replaced him."

Reasons to Buy

- In eight years, Clorox's business outside the United States has blossomed from 7 percent of sales to 19 percent, or $771 million in fiscal 2000. The company invests in countries that offer the best potential for sales growth and profitability in its core product categories.

In Latin America, Clorox's primary focus, the company has acquired leading regional brands, placed experienced management teams on the ground, and introduced global brands such as Clorox liquid bleach with great success. What's more, according to Sullivan, "We have an excellent platform for continued international top-line and profit growth in the years ahead."

- The company has been active on the acquisition front. But integrating these new products takes time and effort. In the company's 2000 annual report Mr. Sullivan said, "During the last 18 months, our people successfully integrated and began revitalizing the principal product lines we gained from First Brands Corporation in January 1999: Glad bags and wraps, STP automotive products, and the Scoop Away and Jonny Cat brands of cat litter. We eliminated inefficient pricing and promotion practices and redirected the savings into sustainable brand-building programs such as advertising. We eliminated more than 1,500 low-margin items; and we brought in-house the manufacture of Armor All product and Fresh Step Scoop cat litter to capitalize on newly acquired production facilities. Finally, we launched strategic sourcing initiatives that leverage our greater size and purchasing power to reduce our costs."

- In fiscal 2001 Clorox introduced its response to the needs of the modern driver with the launch of STP 6,000 Mile Oil Extender, a new premium oil additive that enables users to drive up to 6,000 miles between oil changes. The introduction of the new additive comes on the heels of extensive qualitative research showing the number one undelivered benefit consumers seek from an oil additive is extending their oil change interval. In addition, a recent survey shows that nearly 55 percent of Americans worry more about changing their oil on a regular basis than other routine car maintenance tasks.

STP 6,000 Mile Oil Extender became available in stores nationwide late in 2000; it carries a price tag of $6.99 for the fifteen-ounce bottle. According to the company, "The major benefit that this product brings to users is that Oil Extender maintains the viscosity of the motor oil while boosting the level of the oil's performance additives. By boosting these ingredients, STP 6,000 Oil Extender provides an extra level of protection in your motor oil."

- You might wonder why anyone would want to be the nation's number one maker of cat litter. Apparently Clorox likes the idea. The CEO of the company says he wants Clorox to be number two or better in every category in which it competes. In fiscal 1999 Clorox acquired the First Brands Corporation, a firm that makes Glad trash bags, STP car care products, as well as three kinds of cat litter. First Brands gave Clorox a leading share of the market in all three categories. Not least, the cat litter business has very high margins.

  The deal added STP to the company's Armor-All, the car protectant maker it bought a year earlier. Not only is Clorox now number one in car care products, but it now has a 30 percent stake in plastic bags and plastic wrap with the addition of the Glad lines.

- The company's Brita water filtration systems business completed another year of record shipments and profits, as well as clear category leadership. Growth in this business was propelled by continued household penetration by Brita systems coupled with strong growth in the sales of replacement filters.

  In fiscal 2001 the company announced an agreement with Brita GmbH of Germany to acquire full control of Brita water filtration products in North and South America, including the exclusive use of the Brita trademark, full

rights to develop and market new products under the Brita name, and all business assets in the region.

"The buyout of the joint venture will enhance the ability of Brita Products to pursue new business opportunities, and improve its operating efficiency in the Americas," according to Scott Weiss, Clorox's general manager for Brita Products. He added that the two Brita entities will continue to share marketing, research, and development information.

- Clorox continues to expand where the company sees an opportunity to enter a market with a competitive advantage. Once Clorox acquires a business, it expands it by modernizing plants. What's more, the company builds mass through line extensions and strategic acquisitions.

  Clorox also upgrades packaging and leverage marketing expertise gained in the United States by putting it to use in a new country with the company's just-acquired brands. In sum, that's how Clorox built leadership positions in the majority of its worldwide markets.

  For example, in Argentina the company's liquid bleach brand, Ayudin, holds a 70 percent share in the market. Arco Iris and Ayudin Ropa Color, Clorox's brands of color-safe bleach, dominate the competition. The company's two brands in the stain-remover category, Arco Iris and Trenet, have a combined share of over 90 percent, and the company's sponge business, Mortimer, holds nearly one-half of the market.

  There are similar success stories in Brazil, Chile, the Republic of Korea, and Malaysia. And, in close step with the company's domestic business, the bulk of its international sales volume is represented by Clorox Company brands that are either number one or number two in their respective categories.

Total assets: $4,353 million
Current ratio: .94
Common shares outstanding: 235 million
Return on 2000 shareholders' equity: 23.4%

	2000	1999	1998	1997	1996	1995	1994	1993
Revenues (millions)	4083	4003	2741	2533	2218	1984	1837	1634
Net income (millions)	420	391	298	249	222	201	180	168
Earnings per share	1.75	1.63	1.41	1.21	1.07	.95	.84	.77
Dividends per share	.80	.72	.64	.58	.53	.48	.47	.43
Price High	56.4	66.5	58.8	40.2	27.6	19.8	14.9	13.8
Low	28.4	37.5	37.2	24.3	17.5	13.8	11.8	11.0

CONSERVATIVE GROWTH

The Coca-Cola Company

One Coca-Cola Plaza ▫ P. O. Drawer 1734 ▫ Atlanta, Georgia 30301 ▫ Investor contact: Larry M. Mark (404) 676-8054 ▫ Dividend reinvestment plan is available: (888) 265-3747 ▫ Web site: www.thecoca-colacompany.com ▫ Listed: NYSE ▫ Ticker symbol: KO ▫ S&P rating: A- ▫ Value Line financial strength rating: A++

Coca-Cola is no longer merely a soft drink company. In its plans, for instance, is the introduction of a milk-based product. At first the company declined to reveal many details about "Project Mother," its initiative to develop dairy-based products. All it said was that it would be testing at least five milk drinks in 2001.

Soft-drink companies "have a compulsion to grow," said Tom Pirko, president of BevMark Inc., a beverage-industry consultant. "The question is, where do you get it? You don't get if from banging the drum on the same old products."

Coke has been talking with nutritionists and pediatricians—as well as moms and kids—to find the perfect beverage blend. Although the company is mum on details of its milk initiative, Victoria Reid, who heads the company's innovation efforts directed at youngsters, said any milk-based product made by Coca-Cola would have to have two key features: taste and nutrition.

Coffee or Tea, Anyone?

Meanwhile, the company made another move in the direction of diversifying beyond its traditional products with a foray into the coffee realm, where Pepsi and Starbucks are also carving out profits with Frappuccino. In early 2001 Coke acquired the maker of Planet Java coffee in a move to expand its portfolio of noncarbonated drinks, a fast-growing area in which archrival PepsiCo has also been making aggressive efforts of late. Coke plans to take the brand nationwide through its bottler network, as well as to expand flavors.

Planet Java sells for $1.29 to $1.39 in 9.5-ounce bottles and has been distributed since August 2000 by Coke's largest bottler, Coca-Cola Enterprises, Inc. It comes in three brands: Tremble, with added caffeine; Javachino; and Milky Wave, which combines coffee, chocolate, and caramel flavors.

In a related move, the company formed a joint venture with the Swiss food group, Nestle SA, in order to speed up their efforts to tap into the booming "new beverages" market. A spokesman for Nestle said a joint venture company of the two biggest names in the food and drinks industry would launch new so-called health beverages and enter new markets. Such drinks include tea-based drinks. Iced-coffee, already a success in Japan, can also be introduced in other markets, he said.

Coke Teams Up with Procter & Gamble

In still another major move in 2001, the company joined forces with giant Procter & Gamble. This new company will benefit from the breadth of Coke's global distribution network and P&G's research and development skills. The new company, with about forty brands, 6,000 employees, and fifteen manufacturing plants, will have annual sales of about $4.2 billion. Coke's contribution to the new entity is the Minute Maid juice division, which includes Hi-C and Five-Alive beverages, plus its Fruitopia drink. Procter & Gamble will bring to the venture Pringles chips and Sunny Delight juice drinks.

Douglas Daft, Coke's CEO, hopes the new company will be able to rev up long-neglected Minute Maid and accelerate efforts already under way to develop and bring to market new "health and wellness" beverages such as BeginIt, a breakfast-on-the-go drink.

Company Profile

The Coca-Cola Company is the world's largest producer and distributor of soft-drink syrups and concentrates. Company products are sold through bottlers, fountain wholesalers, and distributors in nearly 200 countries. The company's products represent about 48 percent of total soft-drink unit-case volume consumer worldwide. (A unit-case is equal to twenty-four eight-ounce servings.)

Trademark Coca-Cola accounts for about 68 percent of the company's worldwide gallon shipments of beverage products (excluding those distributed by the Minute Maid Company).

The company's allied brands account for the remaining 32 percent of gallon sales. These brands are Sprite, diet Sprite, TAB, Fanta, Fresca, Mr. Pibb, Hi-C, Mello Yello, Barq's, POWERADE, Fruitopia, and specialty overseas brands.

The company's operations are managed in five operating groups and the Minute Maid Company. Excluding those products distributed by the Minute Maid Company, the company's unit-case volume by region is as follows: North America Group, 31 percent; Latin America Group, 25 percent; Greater Europe Group, 21 percent; Middle and Far East Group, 19 percent; and Africa Group, 4 percent.

The Minute Maid Company, headquartered in Houston, Texas, is the world's largest marketer of juice and juice-drink products.

Major products of the Minute Maid Company include the following:

- Minute Maid chilled ready-to-serve and frozen concentrated citrus and variety juices, lemonades, and fruit punches
- Hi-C brand ready-to-serve fruit drinks
- Bright & Early breakfast beverages
- Bacardi tropical fruit mixes

Shortcomings to Bear in Mind

- Coca-Cola and PepsiCo each saw no change in their shares of the domestic soft-drink industry in 2000, with Coke at 44.1 percent and Pepsi at 31.4 percent. What's more, sales growth for both companies didn't enjoy much fizz.

  Some analysts blamed soft-drink price increases as the main reason that sales slumped during the 1999–2000 period. However, that may not be the only reason that the industry has reason to fret. For instance, Beverage Marketing Corp., an industry consultant, pointed to an aging population and increased competition from noncarbonated beverages such as bottled water and juices. The company also said that per capita consumption of carbonated soft drinks fell in 2000 for the second year in a row following several decades of growth; it was 55.7 gallons per person in 2000 compared with 55.9 gallons the prior year.

- Coke is the ultimate global company, selling $20 billion worth of beverages in nearly 200 countries. Its mission seems simple—sell more drinks to more people in more countries. But the execution can be difficult. The soda market here at home, by far the company's largest, is stagnant. Overseas markets, and especially the developing ones that Coke depends on for growth, are volatile.

And the theory that everyone, everywhere, will someday be drinking as much of the company's sodas as Americans do now—425 cups per person per year—doesn't seem to hold water. Coke also has been slow to recognize consumers' shift away from soda and toward an array of juices, sports drinks, teas, coffees, and bottled waters.

- In mid-2000, bowing to regulatory scrutiny, Coca-Cola abandoned its plans to acquire Cadbury Schweppes PLC's beverage brands in Mexico and Canada. Coke CEO Douglas Daft said the company "is committed to playing by the house rules wherever we do business."

In Canada, PepsiCo and its Canadian bottlers of Cadbury's products there had objected to the Coke deal, and government regulators delayed ruling on the acquisition. In Mexico, regulators recommended against the deal with Cadbury a year earlier, and Coke's appeal of the recommendation was effectively denied in July 2000, according to Coke.

The company first announced the agreement to acquire Cadbury's soft-drink brands outside the United States in late 1998, but it was unable to win approval from regulators for the European Union and several other countries. They feared the brands would give Coke too much market share. As a result, the companies scaled back the accord, removing much of Western Europe and certain other countries from the deal. On a more positive note, Coke said it has thus far successfully acquired Cadbury brands in about 160 countries for about $1 billion.

- In a tussle with its leading competitor, Coke lost out when PepsiCo acquired

South Beach Beverage Company (SoBe) in the fall of 2000. SoBe has come to personify the trendy category of herb and vitamin-fortified beverages. These New Age drinks include juice blends and teas that contain nutrients like gingko, guarana, and kava with names such as Zen Blend and Lizard Fuel. The deal also strengthened Pepsi's position in noncarbonated beverages, which are growing fifteen times faster than carbonated soft drinks. SoBe became a particularly attractive acquisition target when Cadbury Schweppes PLC acquired Snapple, another major noncarbonated beverage brand, from Triarc Companies a month earlier. Unfortunately, this development put two powerful noncarbonated brands—Snapple and SoBe—in the hands of Coke's competitors.

Reasons to Buy

- The CEO of Coca-Cola, Douglas Daft, has drawn on the lessons he learned in his previous post as head of the company's Asian operations. His mantra is "Think local, act local." Daft wants to sell more products suited to local tastes under existing U.S. brands (Minute Maid juices, POWERADE sports drinks, Dasani water) or new ones tailored to local markets (such as a drink in Japan called Tea Water Leafs).

This strategy is based on two facts about the global market. One is that Coke already controls 51 percent of carbonated drink sales around the world but only 18 percent of the total non-alcoholic beverage market. On that basis alone there's simply much more room for Coke to expand in noncarbonated drinks. Second, outside the United States, noncola drinks are far more popular than colas.

- Mr. Daft is decentralizing management. To get closer to local markets he is reassigning hundreds of headquarters people to far-flung outposts. And, rolling back the overambitious expansion plans of previous CEO M. Douglas Ivester, he is biting the bullet on poorly performing ventures in the Baltics and Japan, which will cost $813 million in writedowns.

The speed at which Coke's CEO is moving to bring change to Coke is winning him plaudits from observers, analysts, and influential investors in the company. The changes, those around him say, have been needed for years and are only the beginning. "I'm very impressed thus far not only with the quality of the management shifts, but the implications they have for the organization and the message it sends," said one analyst.

■ Coke placed the Interpublic Group of companies in charge of the advertising of its flagship product. The decision, made at the end of 2000, reinforced a relationship that dates back decades but had weakened during the 1990s as the company formed alliances with dozens of agencies not owned by Interpublic. Under the new arrangement, Interpublic (the third largest advertising group in the world) is to use a new advisory council to develop a variety of strategic and creative marketing communications concepts.

"One of the things that Coca-Cola needs to get brand Coke growing again at a healthy rate is focused, cohesive, creative advertising," said John D. Sicher, editor of *Beverage Digest*, an industry newsletter. "This could be a wonderful move."

Total assets: $20,834 million
Current ratio: .72
Common shares outstanding: 2,487 million
Return on 2000 shareholders' equity: 21.3%

	2000	1999	1998	1997	1996	1995	1994	1993
Revenues (millions)	20458	19805	18813	18868	18546	18018	16172	13967
Net income (millions)	2177	2431	3533	4130	3492	2986	2554	2188
Earnings per share	.88	.98	1.42	1.64	1.40	1.19	.99	.84
Dividends per share	.68	.64	.60	.56	.50	.44	.39	.34
Price High	66.9	70.9	88.9	72.6	54.3	40.2	26.7	22.5
Low	42.9	47.3	53.6	50.0	36.1	24.4	19.4	18.8

CONSERVATIVE GROWTH

Colgate-Palmolive Company

300 Park Avenue ▢ New York, New York 10022-7499 ▢ Listed: NYSE ▢ Investor contact: Bina Thompson (212) 310-3072 ▢ Dividend reinvestment plan is available: (800) 756-8700 ▢ Web site: www.colgate.com ▢ Ticker symbol: CL ▢ S&P rating: A ▢ Value Line financial strength rating: A++

The U.S. Surgeon General recently cited oral disease as a "silent epidemic," of which the primary victims are inner-city children. Initially designed to improve the oral health of urban youngsters in the United States, Colgate's Bright Smiles, Bright Futures program has expanded to address oral care needs in eighty countries.

In the midst of expanding the company's reach, Colgate dental vans are stopping in cities across the country. New York, Houston, Atlanta, Chicago, and Los Angeles are examples of the many cities where children benefit from the expertise of volunteer dental professionals. Colgate's partnership with retail giants such as Wal-Mart and Kmart reaches children and their families outside stores across the United States. Each year, this campaign reaches five million children in the United States as well as another 49 million around the world.

Company Profile

Colgate-Palmolive is a leading global consumer products company, marketing its products in over 200 countries and territories under such internationally recognized brand names as Colgate toothpaste and brushes, Palmolive, Mennen Speed Stick deodorants, Ajax, Murphy Oil Soap, Fab, and Soupline/Suavitel, as well as Hill's Science Diet and Hill's Prescription Diet.

With 70 percent of its sales and earnings coming from abroad, Colgate is making its greatest gains in overseas markets. Travelers, for instance, can find Colgate brands in a host of countries:

● They'll find Total toothpaste, with its proprietary antibacterial formula that fights plaque, tarter, and cavities, in more than seventy countries.

● The Care brand of baby products is popular in Asia.

● Colgate Plax makes Colgate number one in mouth rinse outside the United States.

● The Colgate Zig Zag toothbrush, popular in all major world regions outside the United States, helps make Colgate the number one toothbrush company in the world.

● Axion is an economical dishwashing paste popular in Asia, Africa, and Latin America.

Highlights of 2000

■ Sales increased 7 percent, fueled by such innovative new products as the Colgate Actibrush battery-powered toothbrush, Colgate Fresh Confidence toothpaste, Colgate Herbal toothpaste, Palmolive Naturals soap and shower gel, Colgate Sparkling White toothpaste, and Hill's Science Diet Feline Hairball Control.

■ In North America, Colgate boosted its market share in nine of its twelve major product categories, scoring impressive gains in toothpaste, toothbrushes, dishwashing

liquid, and body cleaning. Oral care was the company's fastest-growing category, with gains from Colgate 2-in-1 toothpaste and mouthwash, the Colgate Actibrush battery-powered toothbrush, Colgate Sparkling White toothpaste, and new Colgate Total Plus Whitening, which began to ship at the end of December 2000.

Notably, Colgate further increased its leadership in the U.S. toothpaste market, reaching 32.6 percent share in the final quarter of 2000, topping any quarter in recent history. Higher market shares for both bar and liquid soap reflected success of Irish Spring aloe, Softsoap Fruit Essentials body wash and hand soap, and Softsoap 2-in-1 with moisturizing lotion.

■ The Colgate Actibrush battery-powered toothbrush and Colgate Fresh Confidence toothpaste helped drive strong Oral Care growth across Europe in 2000. Colgate has moved up to or strengthened its number one positions in the United Kingdom, Ireland, Portugal, and France, where it doubled its market share in manual and battery-powered toothbrushes. The success of new Colgate Herbal toothpaste helped drive strong growth in Central Europe and Russia. New varieties of Palmolive shower gel fueled Personal Care growth, especially Palmolive Vitamins with Vitamin E Complex for long-lasting skin protection.

■ Colgate's market leadership in toothpaste continues to expand in China where national market share stood at nearly 26 percent at the end of 2000. During that year Colgate widened distribution to 498 cities, successfully launched Colgate herbal toothpaste, and formed a joint venture with Sanxiao, China's leading toothbrush maker.

Shortcomings to Bear in Mind

■ This stock has two concerns that should be considered: Because of Colgate's excellent record, the stock sells for a high P/E. Secondly, the balance sheet doesn't quite suit me. Common equity is below 50 percent of capitalization.

Reasons to Buy

- Colgate concentrates research expenditures on priority segments that have been identified for maximum growth and profitability. For example, the fast-growing liquid body-cleansing category has benefited from continuous innovation. The result: European sales of Palmolive shower gel have nearly tripled during the past four years. The latest innovation, Palmolive Vitamins, uses unique technology to deliver two types of Vitamin E to the skin, thus providing both immediate and long-lasting protection.

  In another sector, focused R & D at Colgate's Hills subsidiary has resulted in a superior antioxidant formula that helps protect pets from oxidative damage, including damage to the immune system. This discovery led to a significant nutritional advance of Hill's Science Diet dry pet foods, introduced in the United States in the summer of 2000. The product has gained excellent reception from vets, retailers, and their customers, aided by national media advertising. Hill's scientists have also developed a new Prescription Diet brand formulation that nutritionally helps avoid food-related allergies.

- Adding to region-specific initiatives is the company's vast consumer intelligence. Colgate interviews over 500,000 consumers in more than thirty countries annually to learn more about their habits and usage of the company's product.

- Colgate's global reach lets the company conduct consumer research in countries with diverse economies and cultures to create product ideas with global appeal. The new product development process begins with the company's Global Technology and Business Development groups analyzing consumer insights from various countries to create products that can be sold in the greatest possible number of countries. Creating "universal" products saves time and money by maximizing the return on R & D, manufacturing, and purchasing. To assure the widest possible global appeal, potential new products are test-marketed in lead countries that represent both developing and mature economies.

- A global leader in pet nutrition, Hill's continues to strengthen its ties to veterinarians. Record levels of advertising supported a U.S. campaign for Science Diet, themed, "What Vets Feed Their Pets." New Science Diet products include dry varieties for cats, new canned varieties in chunk and gravy form for cats, and dry varieties for dogs.

- To best serve its geographic markets, Colgate has set up regional new product innovation centers. From these centers, in-market insight from thousands of consumer contacts is married with R & D, technology, and marketing expertise to capitalize on the best opportunities. Early on, the consumer appeal, size, and profitability of each opportunity are assessed. Once a new product concept is identified, it is simultaneously tested in different countries to assure acceptance across areas. Then, commercialization on a global scale takes place rapidly.

  A prime example is Colgate Fresh Confidence, a translucent gel toothpaste aimed at young people seeking the social benefits of fresh breath and oral health reassurance. The process from product concept to product introduction in Venezuela took only one year. Within another six months, Colgate Fresh Confidence had been expanded throughout Latin America and began entering Asia and Europe. Today, less than a year after its first sale, Colgate Fresh Confidence is available in thirty-nine countries and is gaining new Colgate users among the targeted age group. Colgate Fresh Confidence, moreover, has expanded even faster than Colgate Total, the most successful toothpaste introduction ever.

Total assets: $7,252 million
Current ratio: 1.24
Common shares outstanding: 572 million
Return on 2000 shareholders' equity: 72.5%

		2000	1999	1998	1997	1996	1995	1994	1993
Revenues (millions)		9358	9118	8972	9057	8749	8358	7588	7141
Net income (millions)		1064	937	849	740	635	541	580	548
Earnings per share		1.70	1.47	1.31	1.14	1.05	.90	.96	.85
Dividends per share		.63	.59	.55	.53	.47	.44	.39	.34
Price	High	66.8	58.9	49.4	39.3	24.1	19.3	16.3	16.8
	Low	40.5	36.6	32.5	22.5	17.2	14.5	12.4	11.7

INCOME

ConAgra Foods, Incorporated

One ConAgra Drive □ Omaha, Nebraska 68102-5001 □ Investor contact: Chris Klinefelter (402) 595-4154 □ Dividend reinvestment plan is available: (800) 214-0349 □ Web site: www.conagra.com □ Fiscal year ends last Sunday in May □ Listed: NYSE □ Ticker symbol: CAG □ S&P rating: A □ Value Line financial strength rating: A

ConAgra Foods acquired International Home Foods Corporation in fiscal 2001 for about $2.9 billion, including $1.3 billion in debt. This move enhanced the company's diversification by adding such products as Chef Boyardee pasta products, PAM cooking spray, Gulden's mustard, Bumble Bee Tuna, and other well-known shelf-stable products. International Home Foods's product portfolio is a good fit for ConAgra and should create immediate value for the company.

Twenty years ago, ConAgra had minimal presence in value-added foods and a limited number of recognizable brands. Today, ConAgra is known for household branded foods such as Healthy Choice, Butterball, Banquet, Hunt's, Orville Redenbacher's, Reddi-wipe, Slim Jim, and Armour. ConAgra has twenty-seven brands with retail sales in excess of $100 million each.

Company Profile

ConAgra Foods, Inc. (he name was changed from ConAgra, Inc. in the fall of 2000) is one of the world's most successful food companies. As North America's largest foodservice manufacturer and second largest retail food supplier, ConAgra is a leader in several segments of the food business.

ConAgra has uniquely positioned its assets to take advantage of meals prepared at home as well as in such foodservice institutions as schools, hospitals, and restaurants. Food products generate more than $20 billion in sales and $1.5 billion in operating profit. As a result of a constantly improving business mix, more than 75 percent of the company's profits are generated from sales of branded and value-added products. Less than 25 percent of the company's food profits come from commodity operations.

ConAgra's operations broke down as follows in fiscal 2000 (in millions of dollars):

Sales	Operating	Profit
Packaged Foods	$7,713.5	$1,087.9
Refrigerated Foods	12,522.2	490.7
Total Food Business	20,235.7	1,578.6
Agricultural Products	5,150.1	331.1
Business Segment Total	25,385.8	1,909.7

Packaged Foods

In this segment, shelf-stable foods include a host of major brands, including Hunt's, Healthy Choice, Wesson, Orville Redenbacher's, Slim Jim, Act II, Peter

Pan, Van Camp's Beanee Weenee, Manwich, Hunt's Snack Pack, Swiss Miss, Knott's Berry Farm, Chun King, La Choy, Rosarita, Gebhardt, Wolf Brand, Pemmican, Penrose, and Andy Capp's.

Under foodservice products are such major brands as Lamb Weston, Fernando's, Casa de Oro, Holly Ridge and Rosarita.

In the frozen food sector are such major brands as Healthy Choice, Banquet, Marie Callender's, Kid Cuisine, MaMa Rosa's, Papa G's, Gilardi's, The Max, Morton, Patio, Chun King, and La Choy.

Finally, Packaged Foods also has a substantial stake in dairy case products such as Parkay, Blue Bonnet, Fleischmann's, Move Over Butter, Egg Beaters, Healthy Choice, County Line, Reddi-wip, and Treasure Cave.

Refrigerated Foods

In this sector, the company is involved in the production and marketing of fresh and branded processed meats, beef and pork products, and chicken and turkey products for grocery, foodservice, institutional, and special market customers.

Major brands include Butterball, Healthy Choice, Armour, Eckrich, Swift Premium, Decker, Ready Crisp, Cook's, Hebrew National, Monfort, Country Pride, To-Ricos, Texas BBQ, Brown 'N Serve, Golden Star, and National Deli.

Agricultural Products

This segment includes basic grain processing, food ingredients, and the value-added business of crop inputs and yield-enhancement services. The Food Ingredients group and its flour milling company are the processing and milling components of the agricultural segment. Major businesses include flour milling, specialty food ingredients manufacturing, oat and corn milling, dry edible bean processing and merchandising, and barley malting.

In the United Agri Products segment, principal activities include the distribution of crop input (seeds, fertilizer products, crop protection chemicals, and information systems) in the United States, Argentina, Bolivia, Canada, Chile, Ecuador, France, Mexico, Peru, South Africa, Taiwan, the United Kingdom, and Zimbabwe.

In the Trade Group segment, the company's principal activities are marketing bulk agricultural commodities throughout the world. Major businesses are grain procurement and merchandising, food-related commodity trading, and commodity services.

Shortcomings to Bear in Mind

- ConAgra's balance sheet contains more debt than I would like. Capitalization is about 48 percent common equity, well below the 75 percent that I would prefer. However, coverage of debt interest is adequate, at better than six times.

Reasons to Buy

- The implementation of ConAgra's Operation Overdrive (in May of 1999) restructuring plan hurt earnings in the short term, with a total of about $775 million in pretax charges by the end of fiscal 2000. The remaining $100 million was taken in the following year. The restructuring led to the closing of thirteen manufacturing plants, seventeen smaller facilities, the sale of nine noncore businesses, and the reduction of headcount by 5,200 people, or 7 percent of the work force. The goal of the restructuring is expected to save $600 million per year and to boost pretax profit margins to 6.5 percent, from 4.3 percent prior to Operation Overdrive. As a result of the restructuring, actual earnings per share fell from $1.36 in 1988 to $.75 the following year and $.86 in 2000. However, the table at the end of this article does not reflect these one-time charges.

- ConAgra is the most diversified food company in the world with more than seventy brands, along with meat processing, grain milling, and trading operations across major sectors.

- The Packaged Foods segment experienced growth in both sales and operating profit in 2000 as a result of the public's ever increasing desire for convenient meals and ConAgra Foods's emphasis on building brands.

  A significant portion of the 4 percent growth in Packaged Foods' sales can be credited to gains in French fries, specialty meat operations, shelf-stable grocery snack products—such as Slim Jim, Orville Redenbacher's, Act II, and Hunt's Snack Pack—as well as major frozen food brands Banquet and Marie Callender's.

  Operating profit rose 11 percent to $1.1 billion, as strategic investments in advertising and promotion stimulated sales and profits for many of ConAgra Foods's best-known frozen food and shelf-stable brands. In addition, new products, such as Act II Corn on the Cob Microwave Popcorn and Marie Callender's French Bread Pizza, augmented sales and margins.

- The company's Refrigerated Foods had an exceptional year in 2000. Strong consumer demand for fresh red meat products, coupled with manufacturing improvements, pushed operating profits up 33 percent to $491 million and increased sales by 8 percent to $12.5 billion.

  Butterball, Armour, Eckrich, Cook's, and Hebrew National, the best-performing brands in the company's processed meat operations, benefited in a big way from ConAgra's emphasis on creating and marketing value-added and branded products.

- One way to judge a company is to examine its return on shareholders' equity. In this regard, ConAgra gets high marks. In the most recent five years, return on equity has averaged an impressive 27.8 percent and was 29.6 percent in fiscal 2000.

- ConAgra has an excellent balance between its two food businesses. In the words of Bruce Rohde, the company's CEO, "Given that roughly half of our $20-plus-billion of food sales are to the retail channel and the other half go to serve restaurants and institutions in the foodservice channel, we are aligning our resources to parallel the way people eat. We buy, make, and sell our products with these channels, and their customers, in mind."

  Mr. Rohde went on to say, "We are positioned to create substantial value for our shareholders as eating away from home continues its rapid growth. At the same time, we are increasing our emphasis on new product development. We are focusing on value-added and higher-margin opportunities in both of these channels because that is what benefits our shareholders, customers, and consumers."

- ConAgra has increased earnings per share for twenty consecutive years at a compound annual growth rate of 14.6 percent. During the same period, dividends per share increased annually at an average rate of 15.3 percent. On a more negative note, during the most recent ten-year period the growth rate of earnings per share was only 10.6 percent, mainly due to single-digit growth in 1992, 1993, 1998, and 1999. During the same ten years, however, dividends per share increased at an average rate of 15.1 percent, including increases of 16.9 percent in 1992, 15.4 percent in 1993, 14.7 percent in 1998, and 14.3 percent in 1999.

Total assets: $12,296 million
Current ratio: 1.06
Common shares outstanding: 519 million
Return on 2000 shareholders' equity: 29.6%

	2000	1999	1998	1997	1996	1995	1994	1993
Revenues (millions)	25386	24594	23841	24002	24822	24109	23512	21519
Net income (millions)	801	696	628	615	545	496	437	392
Earnings per share	1.67	1.46	1.36	1.34	1.17	1.03	.91	.79
Dividends per share	.79	.69	.61	.53	.46	.42	.35	.32
Price High	24.4	34.4	33.6	38.8	27.4	20.9	16.6	16.8
Low	15.1	20.6	22.6	24.5	18.8	14.9	12.8	11.4

AGGRESSIVE GROWTH

Costco Wholesale Corporation

999 Lake Drive □ Issaquah, Washington 98027 □ Investor relations: (425) 313-6699 □ Dividend reinvestment plan is not available □ Web site: www.costco.com □ Listed: Nasdaq □ Fiscal year ends Sunday nearest August 31 □ Ticker symbol: COST □ S&P rating: B □ Value Line financial strength rating: B++

Costco's strategy of retailing has grown in popularity among consumers and small-business owners in recent years. As a consequence, it has taken market share from such traditional retailers as supermarkets and drugstores. As the leader in its field, Costco should be able to strengthen its position further by broadening its line of products and services, coupled with further penetration into new markets both at home and abroad.

A reputation for merchandising excellence and quality are a hallmark of Costco's operations. These attributes have not gone unnoticed. The American Customer Satisfaction Index survey conducted by the University of Michigan Business School in November 2000 showed that Costco had the highest customer satisfaction rating of any domestic traditional national retailer.

Company Profile

Costco is the largest wholesale club operator in the United States (ahead of Wal-Mart's Sam's Club). Costco operates a chain of membership warehouses that sell high-quality, nationally branded and select private label merchandise at low prices to businesses purchasing for commercial use, personal use, or resale. The company also sells to individuals who are members of select employee groups.

Costco's business is based on achieving high sales volumes and rapid inventory turnover by offering a limited assortment of merchandise in a wide variety of product categories at very competitive prices.

As of December 2000, the company operated a chain of 349 warehouses in thirty-two states (251 locations), nine Canadian provinces (fifty-nine locations), the United Kingdom (eleven locations, through an 80-percent-owned subsidiary), Korea (four locations), Taiwan (three locations, through a 55-percent-owned subsidiary) and Japan (two locations). The company also operates nineteen warehouses in Mexico through a 50-percent joint venture partner.

Costco units offer discount prices on nearly 4,000 products, ranging from alcoholic beverages and computer software to pharmaceuticals, meat, vegetables, books, clothing, and tires. Food and sundries account for 60 percent of sales. Certain club memberships also offer products and services, such as car and home insurance, mortgage services, and small-business loans.

A typical warehouse format averages about 127,000 square feet. Floor plans are designed for economy and efficiency in the use of selling space, in the handling of merchandise, and in the control of inventory. Merchandise is generally stored on racks above the sales floor and is displayed on pallets containing large quantities of each item, reducing labor required for handling and stocking.

Specific items in each product line are limited to fast-selling models, sizes and colors. Costco carries only an average of about 3,500 to 4,500 stock keeping units (SKUs) per warehouse. Typically, a discount retailer or supermarket stocks 40,000 to 60,000 SKUs. Many products are offered for sale in case, carton, or multiple-pack quantities only.

Low prices on a limited selection of national brand merchandise and select private-label products in a wide range of merchandise categories produce high sales volume and rapid inventory turnover. Rapid inventory turnover, combined with operating efficiencies achieved by volume purchasing in a no-frills self-service warehouse facility, enables the company to operate profitably at significantly lower gross margins than traditional retailers, discounters, or supermarkets.

The company buys virtually all of its merchandise from manufacturers for shipment either directly to the warehouse clubs or to a consolidation point (depot) where shipments are combined so as to minimize freight and handling costs.

Highlights of 2000

- Sales exceeding $31.6 billion, reflecting a 17 percent increase over fiscal 1999.
- Comparable sales increases of 11 percent for warehouses open for more than one year.

- Average sales of $101 million per warehouse.
- Net income of $631 million, compared with $545 million the prior year.
- 32.8 million Costco cardholders worldwide.
- The company entered new markets such as Texas and the Midwest states, as well as several new states in the Southeast.
- During 2000, Costco opened twenty-one new warehouses, compared with only fourteen in 1999.
- New markets opened in 2000 included Memphis, Cincinnati, Fort Meyers, and Naples in the United States, as well as several overseas including Aberdeen, Scotland, Haydock, England, and Xalapa, Mexico.

Shortcomings to Bear in Mind

- Costco's Standard & Poor's financial strength rating is below average, at B. However, Value Line gives the company an average B++ rating.
- The wholesale club industry could be vulnerable to an economic slowdown, even though it sells basics, because of its business-membership exposure. What's more, the company's competition has stepped up its presence and is modeling itself more closely to the Costco strategy.
- Not everyone agrees that Costco is going to continue its winning ways. According to one analyst, "Costco is settling into a period of slower top-line growth. Over the past several years, Costco has consistently been able to generate double-digit comparable-store sales gains. However, given the slowdown in the pace of economic activity and the level of consumer spending, we are not surprised to see this streak snap."
- In fiscal 2001, earnings will be under pressure because of the large number of new warehouses being constructed. Those units that open in new markets,

moreover, are likely to be an extra drag on earnings. This is because the company does not charge for membership in the first few months because it wants to acquaint businesspeople and shoppers in that region with its low prices and good merchandise. The membership fees, incidentally, are an important part of the company's earnings. One reason that membership is required by Costco is that it helps insure that the customer will continue to do business with its warehouse in order to recoup the cost of membership. What's more, the company's use of a membership fee helps it sell merchandise at lower prices.

■ Insiders, such as officers and board members, have been selling shares of Costco for the past year or so.

Reasons to Buy

■ Costco warehouses generally operate on a seven-day, sixty-eight-hour week, and are open somewhat longer during the holiday season. Generally, warehouses are open between 10 A.M. and 8:30 P.M., with earlier closing hours on the weekend. Because these hours of operation are shorter than those of traditional discount grocery stores and supermarkets, labor costs are lower relative to the volume of sales.

■ In fiscal 2001 Costco plans to open between thirty-six and forty new warehouses, along with eight replacement warehouses. New markets in 2001 include Dallas/Fort Worth, Houston, and Austin, Texas; Minneapolis, Minnesota; Kansas City, Missouri; Durham and Charlotte, North Carolina; Huntsville and Birmingham, Alabama; Charleston, South Carolina; Puebla and San Luis Potosi, Mexico; and Makuhari, Japan (near Tokyo).

What's more, the company plans to continue opening new warehouses at a rate of thirty-five to forty per year for at least three years beyond 2001.

■ The health of Costco's business can be measured not only by the record of sales and profit but also by the record number of new members and membership renewal rates, which remain at the highest level in the company's history. Further, Costco can point to the cleanest inventory levels and best inventory turn rates in its history. In addition, Costco has experienced strong expense control at every level of the company, as well as strong financial and procedural controls that enable the company to achieve the lowest inventory shrinkage (a polite word for theft) numbers of any major retailer in the world. Finally, the company boasts a strong balance sheet.

■ Several factors contributed to the company's recent strong showing. Among them are new store openings and improved margins. What's more, customer traffic and frequency of visits have been climbing thanks to Costco's continued expansion of its ancillary businesses, such as gas stations, food courts, hot dog stands, copy centers, print shops, pharmacies, photo labs, and fresh food departments.

■ Costco has a major alliance with American Express Company to accept American Express cards in all domestic Costco locations. The company says that American Express "has similar customer philosophies to Costco; a great degree of member/customer loyalty; and overall, an upscale consumer and small business focus. We believe that the card acceptance and co-branded card issuance are the first of many unique and strategic business opportunities that will benefit both Costco and American Express, along with the millions of members and cardholders of our two companies."

- Costco's policy generally is to limit advertising and promotional expenses to new warehouse openings and occasional direct-mail marketing to prospective new members. These practices result in lower marketing expenses as compared to typical discount retailers and supermarkets.

  In connection with new warehouse openings, Costco's marketing teams personally contact businesses in the region that are potential wholesale members. These contacts are supported by direct mailings during the period immediately prior to opening.

- Costco knows when a deal is too good to pass up. That's why the company is buying merchandise from Internet retailers. According to Richard Galanti, the firm's chief financial officer, "So many of these e-commerce companies, quite frankly, are using incredible valuations to sell stuff at ridiculous prices. We actually buy some things below cost from some of them."

Total assets: $8,634 million
Current ratio: 1.02
Common shares outstanding: 447 million
Return on 2000 shareholders' equity: 16.2%

	2000	1999	1998	1997	1996	1995	1994	1993
Revenues (millions)	32164	27456	24269	21874	19566	18247	16481	15498
Net income (millions)	631.4	545.3	459.8	350.9	248.8	217.2	190.9	223.2
Earnings per share	1.35	1.18	1.02	.82	.61	.53	.44	.50
Dividends per share	Nil							
Price High	60.5	46.9	38.1	22.6	13.0	9.8	10.8	12.7
Low	25.9	32.7	20.7	11.9	7.3	6.0	6.3	7.5

CONSERVATIVE GROWTH

Delphi Automotive Systems Corporation

5725 Delphi Drive □ Troy, Michigan 48098-2815 □ Investor contact: (877) SEEKDPH □ Dividend reinvestment plan is available: (800) 818-6599 □ Web site: www.delphiauto.com □ Listed: NYSE □ Ticker symbol: DPH □ S&P rating: Not rated □ Value Line financial strength rating: B

Delphi concluded a significant deal with Ericsson Mobil Communications in 2000 to bring "plug-and-play" telematics into the vehicle. Plug-and-play technology makes it possible to cycle in new iterations of computers, phones, and entertainment options as older units grow obsolete.

Electronics will pass through several generations during the typical ten-year life of an automobile. Plug-and-play makes it possible to add new products just by plugging them into existing interfaces. This deal should strengthen Delphi's market-leading position in telematics.

Company Profile

Delphi Automotive Systems is the world's largest and most diversified supplier of components, integrated systems, and modules to the automotive industry. Delphi's primary mission is providing products directly to automotive manufacturers. A wholly owned subsidiary of General Motors prior to February 1999, Delphi was spunoff to GM shareholders in May 1999.

Delphi delivers the broadest range of high-technology solutions worldwide for its customers in the areas of safety, performance, comfort, and aesthetics. It is through the company's approach to new technology and product development that Delphi has established its leadership position while maintaining the tradition of individual product excellence. Today, Delphi's products are organized into three synergistic business sectors, including an aftermarket division (aftermarket refers to products sold for repair and replacement rather than for cars being manufactured):

Electronics and Mobile Communications Sector

As Delphi's fastest growing sector, Electronics & Mobile Communication designs products to enhance safety, comfort, and security, as well as bring entertainment, information, and connectivity to the vehicle.

Mobile multimedia products include telematics, such as wireless phones, but also the OnStar communications system now being expanded beyond Cadillacs into the entire GM fleet. Equally important are rear seat entertainment systems, including video consoles and DVD players. GM says that about half of the 50 million vehicles produced in 2005 will have significant mobile media content, perhaps $1,000 per vehicle. Delphi believes it has a significant "first mover" advantage, thanks to existing technologies (such as OnStar and Delco) as well as its ability to do business throughout the world.

Safety, Thermal, and Electrical Architecture Sector

This sector offers a comprehensive portfolio of vehicle interior, safety, and occupant-protection products; heating and cooling systems to manage vehicle compartment temperatures; and power and signal distribution systems for advanced electronic management of power, signal, and data communications.

The sector coordinates product development in the rapidly expanding cockpit and interior modules market. The sector's Advanced Safety Interior Systems, Gold Dot Connection Systems, and Advanced Thermal Management Systems are just a few of Delphi's high-tech products.

To help improve safety, Delphi has developed its Advanced Safety Interior suite of products. This evolving portfolio of technologies is designed to provide protection in front, side, and rear collisions, as well as when a vehicle rolls over.

Technologies include anticipatory crash, rollover, and occupant-characteristic sensing systems; head and side airbags; variable airbag inflation; adaptive seatbelt restraints; active knee bolster; adaptive force-limiting pedals; and an energy-absorbing steering column.

Gold Dot Connection Systems are flexible printed materials with shaped planar contacts that simplify high-speed, high-density data connections. The technology can be used in a wide variety of applications, including computer instrumentation and emulation, automotive, and military uses. Current applications include telecommunication applications from cellular phones to network switches and routers.

Dynamics and Propulsion Sector

This sector provides technologies for superior ride and handling performance, including advanced suspension, brake, drive line, and steering products. It also offers complete gas and diesel engine management systems to improve fuel efficiency and increase environmental responsiveness, including air and fuel systems, ignition systems, sensors, and exhaust after treatment.

This sector is rapidly transforming its product portfolio from traditional mechanical systems to electronically enhanced systems. The infusion of electronics and the implementation of lean manufacturing principles in this sector provide great opportunities to enhance the company's margins. X-by-Wire Systems, Energen and MagneRide are just three product systems in this sector.

Aftermarket Division

One exciting area that should double in sales in the next five years is Delphi's Aftermarket Operation. Launched in 1999, Delphi's newest division is enhancing its brand and sales in the aftermarket. With aftermarket activities on four continents, Delphi is set to deliver the same quality and technological expertise that go into its original equipment products under the new Delphi Aftermarket brand.

Delphi produces a wide variety of aftermarket products, which fall under five key categories: under car (such as shocks/struts), thermal systems (such as air conditioning systems), energy/engine management systems (such as alternators and batteries), electronics (such as audio and security systems), and remanufactured products.

Shortcomings to Bear in Mind

- You will note in the table at the end of this section that the company's history is difficult to assess because there is no indication what its history of sales and earnings looks like.
- The automotive business is traditionally very cyclical. You can expect years of great prosperity, as well as those when the industry sinks into the doldrums. In this connection, the company can be vulnerable to higher interest rates since people often buy cars on the installment plan. Lenders are quick to raise their rates when interest rates are boosted, as they were in 2000.
- Competition is formidable and includes Bosch, Siemens, Motorola, and Visteon. On the other hand, analysts point out that Delphi's insider position with GM, as well as GM's growing web of relationships

with global OEMs (such as Saab, Suzuki, Isuzu, Subaru, and Fiat) represent a real advantage.

Reasons to Buy

- In 2000 Delphi was recognized as the industry's best electronic supplier by more than 1,300 automotive suppliers and vehicle manufacturers in a poll taken by a leading industry publication.
- Delphi launched its Mobile MultiMedia business less than two years ago and saw its sales jump to $322 million in 2000, an increase of 705 percent over the prior year.
- Delphi joined with Palm, Inc. and the Mayfield Fund to form MobileAria, Inc., a company that in mid-2001 launched a new hands-free mobile Internet service platform for vehicles.
- Delphi's newly developed Passive Occupant Detection System, which is being supplied to Jaguar and four other Ford and Lincoln-Mercury vehicles, enables vehicle manufacturers to improve the effectiveness of air bag protection through smart deployment or suppression of the passenger's air bag.
- The 2000 acquisition of Lucas Diesel Systems, a leading producer of diesel engine management systems for light, medium, and heavy-duty vehicles, enabled Delphi to design a new technology that will make diesel engines cleaner and quieter. This technology gives drivers more acceleration from a standing stop, with reduced noise, lower emissions, and improved fuel consumption.
- Delphi introduced more than 100 new products or processes in 2000, and the company's domestic patent application filings increased by 33 percent. For the industry, these statistics are impressive. Delphi's 16,000 engineers, scientists, and technicians worldwide are a critical part of the company's achievements. More

than a third of them are focused on electronic and high-technology products.

- Delphi is leading the development and integration of multiple X-by-Wire Systems, including steer-, brake-, damp-, roll-, and throttle-by-wire. These advanced systems function through a highly organized network of wires, sensors, and actuators, replacing the traditional system's mechanical hardware connections while improving quality and performance. In the future, X-by-Wire technologies are expected to serve as a foundation for total collision-avoidance systems.

- The Energen family of energy management systems offers solutions to powering vehicles with lower emissions, improved fuel economy, and increased consumer features, such as electric valve trains, satellite communications, on-board computers, and multizoned climate control systems and electric steering.

- MagneRide represents the first vehicle application of a fluid material technically referred to as Magnetic Rheological Fluid. This technology enables a vehicle suspension to adjust instantaneously to road conditions, giving the driver precise handling and an exceptionally good ride. It is activated by an on-board sensor that alerts a controller to apply a magnetic field. This increases the mineral oil consistency of the fluid to a peanut-butter thickness within a few milliseconds. The first systems will be appearing on passenger vehicles in 2003.

- Communiport MMM Systems make drive time more productive, convenient, and enjoyable. Center console "smart" receivers integrate radio and audio controls, navigation, cell phone access, and Internet browser functions through advanced user interfaces such as large full-color flat-panel displays, voice recognition, and text-to-speech technology. Telematics systems combine global positioning satellite functions with cell phone modules. The result: hands-free cell phone use, direct communication with a service center for travel directions, remote vehicle lock/unlock and emergency service. Rear-seat entertainment systems provide video games, TV, and DVD on large rear displays.

Total assets: $18,521 million
Current ratio: 1.34
Common shares outstanding: 560 million
Return on 2000 shareholders' equity: 28.2%

	2000	1999	1998	1997	1996	1995	1994	1993
Revenues (millions)	29139	29192	28479 *					
Net income (millions)	1094	1083						
Earnings per share	1.94	1.91						
Dividends per share	.28	.21						
Price High	21.1	22.3						
Low	10.5	14.0						

*Since Delphi was a recent spinoff from General Motors, the usual information is not available for this table.

The Walt Disney Company

500 South Buena Vista Street □ Burbank, California 91521 □ Investor contact: Winifred Markus Webb (818) 560-5758 □ Fiscal year ends September 30 □ Dividend reinvestment plan is available: (818) 553-7200 □ Web site: www.disney.com □ Listed: NYSE □ Ticker symbol: DIS □ S&P rating: B+ □ Value Line financial strength rating: A

When Disneyland Paris opened a few years ago, it was anything but magical. It had exorbitant prices, bad American-style food, rides still under construction, and groups of bewildered Europeans sheltering their children from the likes of Goofy, Donald Duck, and Pluto.

Since then, all has changed. Instead of going bankrupt, the park is now booming. In fact, Disneyland Paris (as the company now insists on calling the park commonly referred to as EuroDisney) has now overtaken the Eiffel Tower as the number one tourist spot in France, largely because of some key changes. Among them, lower prices, better food, and the addition of some adult amenities, such as wine with dinner.

Company Profile

The Walt Disney Company is a family entertainment company engaged in animated and live-action film and television production, character merchandise licensing, consumer products retailing, book, magazine, and music publishing, television and radio broadcasting, cable television programming, and the operation of theme parks and resorts. It also owns the Disney Cruise Line, a chain of more than 600 Disney retail stores, and ownership interests in two California professional sports teams.

Disney is the world's third largest media conglomerate, outpaced by Time Warner and Viacom. The Walt Disney Company owns the highly successful ABC network, featuring *Who Wants to Be a Millionaire?* It also operates a number of cable channels, including The Disney Channel,

Lifetime TV (50 percent owned), ESPN (with 80 percent ownership), and the A&E Television Networks (38 percent).

Walt Disney Studios produces films under such labels as Touchstone, Hollywood Pictures, and Miramax. The company's theme parks are the most popular in North America and include Walt Disney World, Epcot Center, Magic Kingdom, Animal Kingdom, and Disneyland.

Shortcomings to Bear in Mind

- When the company's newest theme park, Disney's California Adventure, opened in early 2001, it had its share of obstacles to cope with, such as a slowing economy, high gasoline prices, and a crisis with the state's electric utilities. The theme of the new park (which is adjacent to Disney's original Disneyland) is the quintessential California vacation, from the Golden Gate Bridge to the wine country and the beach.

  Despite the adverse comments of the skeptics, Disney's top brass, including CEO Michael Eisner, remain confident that all is well. To prove it, the company is not backing down from its initial attendance goal of seven million annual visitors. In the words of one Disney executive, "As I look at it today, we're excited, and we don't believe there's anything in the economy that should affect us."

- Disney's celebrated family films, especially those that are animated, have been having trouble breaking even of late. Beginning with *The Little Mermaid*, family films were core productions for Disney through the 1990s, creating massive financial profits. More recently, the company has run into problems with high production costs at a time when other studios are beating Disney at its own game. For instance, the blockbuster *How the Grinch Stole Christmas* from Vivendi Universal SA's Universal Pictures sold about $200 million worth of tickets in the United States in 2000.

Disney's films in 2000, such as *Dinosaur, Fantasia 2000*, and the live-action sequel *102 Dalmatians*, had varying degrees of success at the box office. Unfortunately, all failed to be major profit makers, largely because they were too expensive. *Dinosaur* cost at least $130 million to produce, not counting a $70 million production facility the company built specially for the project. Both *Fantasia* and *Dalmatians* cost more than $80 million, and neither had much luck turning a profit.

On a more positive note, Disney was eminently successful in 2000 with a far more modest production, *The Tigger Movie*. This kiddie film required the investment of only $15 million and was a major success at domestic box offices, bringing in $45 million in 2000, along with the sale of five million video and DVD units.

Reasons to Buy

- For more than fifteen years, thousands of business executives have learned Disney's philosophy on leadership, customer loyalty, business creativity, and people management in seminars at Walt Disney World. The list of companies that have taken part includes Delta Air Lines, General Motors, and Goodyear.

"Disney's track record is one of the best in the country as far as dealing with consumers," said Andrew Salmon, a vice president of Ford Credit, a finan-cial and customer-service arm of Ford Motor. "Not everyone will be open enough to share their philosophy."

Disney charges big bucks for its openness: A three-day seminar (which includes admission to the resort's four theme parks) costs $2,800 per person,

- The company unveiled the prototype for a new Disney Store in late 2000. The new Disney Store in Costa Mesa is a prototype that Disney plans to roll out in varying degrees to about 600 of its stores worldwide over the next three years. The cost: more than $300 million. Disney plans to close the remaining 140 stores as their leases expire, which will take several years. Disney officials hope the new store will jump-start a recovery of its ailing consumer products division.

The new store is brighter, contains more merchandise, and has a modular design that can be changed quickly to promote new products, Disney movies, or theme park attractions. What's more, the new outlets are getting a new look that includes interactive kiosks where customers can browse the company's Web site and order products they don't find at the store.

- The company restructured its toy-licensing agreements, allotting its business between Hasbro and Mattel. Analysts believe that the deals, which were forged in the fall of 2000, represent a solid move toward rebuilding the company's struggling consumer products business. For the past dozen years, Disney has dealt mostly with Mattel. Andy Mooney, the president of Disney Consumer Products Worldwide, said the company split the business between the two toy makers to benefit from Mattel's strength in preschool toys and branded toys as well as Hasbro's strength in movie-based programs. Mr. Mooney said that the revamped agreements will enable

Disney "to significantly grow our toy share over the next three to five years."

- Part of the Disney legacy is innovation. Walt Disney pioneered the first cartoon with sound, the first color cartoon, the first feature-length animated film, the first use of the multiplane camera, the first use of stereophonic sound, first 3-D cartoon, the first theme park, and the first use of audio-animatronic entertainment.

- Walt Disney, trying to revive its lagging home video sales, said in 2000 that it would release all future titles on DVD (once known as the digital video disk) at the same time as on videocassette and would revamp the schedule for releasing its animated films into video stores. Slower sales in home video have been one factor behind Disney's slump in earnings.

  Disney has been one of the last Hollywood studios to embrace DVD. But the DVD market is growing faster than even some supporters anticipated, and Disney executives now say that the technology represents an opportunity for the company to resell its animated films to consumers in a new format.

- After Japanese developers signed a deal more than twenty years ago to build a Disney theme park north of Tokyo, they transformed a block of barren coastal land into an important economic engine for the great Tokyo area. That is what Hong Kong officials hope they have signed up for in their agreement with Walt Disney Company to build the company's third overseas theme park on an island near Hong Kong's new airport. With its economy then still in the doldrums as most of Asia had recovered from the prior year's recession, Hong Kong was a city still searching for economic elixirs.

  "This world-class development will mark the beginning of a new era for Hong Kong," chief executive Tung Chee Hwa told reporters after the agreement with Disney was signed in November 1999. Government officials estimate that construction of the Hong Kong Disneyland will create 16,000 jobs and that a further 18,400 jobs will be created once the park opens in 2005. The total cost of the park and related projects is $3.6 billion, of which Disney will contribute only $316 million. For Disney, the park is the first significant beachhead in China, a nation with which it has had a long and occasionally stormy history.

- A $1.4-billion expansion of the Disneyland theme park resort in Anaheim, California, was completed in 2001. The expansion includes a new theme park, called Disney's California Adventure, and a 750-room hotel.

  The theme parks and resorts business are expected to continue to do well. Analysts look for attendance at the Disney theme parks to increase 6 percent in 2001 to sixty million. This is partly due to the addition of the California Adventure. Other favorable factors include higher occupancy at the resorts, increased ticket and room rates, along with increased per-capita spending at the parks.

- Because of the expansion that took place during the past decade, Disney entered the new decade as a substantially different company. It now has 7 theme parks (with more in the works), 27 hotels with 36,888 rooms, 2 cruise ships, 600 Disney Stores, 1 broadcast network, 10 TV stations, 9 international Disney Channels, 42 radio stations, 5 major Internet Web sites, and interests in 9 U.S. cable networks. Further, in the past decade the company has enhanced its library with 17 animated films, 265 live-action films, 1,252 animated television episodes, and 6,505 live-action television episodes.

Total assets: $45,027 million
Current ratio: 1.31
Common shares outstanding: 2,085 million
Return on 2000 shareholders' equity: 4.1%

	2000	1999	1998	1997	1996	1995	1994	1993
Revenues (millions)	25020	23402	22976	22473	21238	12112	10055	8529
Net income (millions)	1879	1383	1871	1886	1533	1344	1110	889
Earnings per share	.91	.66	.90	.92	.74	.84	.68	.54
Dividends per share	.24	.20	.20	.17	.14	.12	.10	.08
Price High	43.9	38.7	42.8	33.4	25.8	21.4	16.2	16.0
Low	26.0	23.4	22.5	22.1	17.8	15.0	12.6	12.0

INCOME

Dominion Resources

Post Office Box 26532 ◻ Richmond, Virginia 23261-6532 ◻ Listed: NYSE ◻ Investor contact: Tom Wohlfarth
(804) 819-2150 ◻ Dividend reinvestment plan is available: (800) 552-4034 ◻ Web site: www.domres.com ◻
Ticker symbol: D ◻ S&P rating: B ◻ Value Line financial strength rating: B++

Investors are sometimes critical of company officials who don't own many shares of their own company. They ask the disturbing question: "How can they expect me to invest in their company when they don't have enough confidence to buy stock themselves?"

If you own Dominion Resources, you won't have this concern. Under voluntary guidelines adopted by the board of directors, Dominion's officers are expected to own company shares in amounts totaling from three to eight times their base salaries. This is a major obligation that required most officers to borrow money.

According to Thomas E. Capps, president and chief executive officer of Dominion, "Loans to purchase these shares come due in five years, and our dividends help pay the interest. We're all personally on the hook if, in the interim, we have not made sound business decisions and grown the company profitably.

"Last year, I purchased an additional ten times my annual salary in shares, making me one of the company's largest individual shareholders. Together, our senior management team also makes up one of the largest shareholder groups, with more than 2.4 million shares valued at year-end 2000 in excess of $161 million.

"Overall, our entire family of employees—executives, management, staff, field or supervision—own about 15.6 million shares. At year's end, our total investment in our business exceeded $1 billion. Employees are Dominion's biggest shareholder as a group, a confidence vote straight from the pocketbook."

Company Profile

Dominion is a holding company headquartered in Richmond, Virginia. Its principal subsidiaries are:

• Virginia Electric and Power Company, a regulated public utility engaged in the generation, transmission, distribution, and sale of electric energy with a 30,000-square-mile region in Virginia and northeastern North Carolina. The company sells electric power to about 2.1 million retail customers (including government agencies) and to wholesale customers such as rural electric cooperatives, municipalities, power marketers and other utilities.

• Consolidated Natural Gas Company (CNG), which was acquired January 28, 2000. CNG operates in all phases of the natural gas industry in the United States, including exploration for and production of oil and natural gas and natural gas transmission, storage, and distribution. Its regulated retail gas distribution subsidiaries serve about 1.7 million residential, commercial, and industrial gas sales and transportation customers in Ohio, Pennsylvania, and West Virginia. Its interstate gas transmission pipeline systems services each of its distribution subsidiaries, non-affiliated utilities and end use customers in the Midwest, the Mid-Atlantic and Northeast. CNG's exploration and production operations are conducted in several of the major gas and oil producing basins in the United States, both onshore and offshore, and in Canada.

The company's other major subsidiaries are:

• Dominion Energy (DEI), which is engaged in the independent power production and the acquisition and production of natural gas and oil reserves. In Canada, DEI has a stake in natural gas exploration, production, and storage.

• Dominion Capital, Inc. (DCI), which is Dominion's financial services subsidiary. DCI's primary business is financial services, which includes commercial lending and residential mortgage lending.

Shortcomings to Bear in Mind

■ The company's acquisitions did not come about without adding some debt. As a consequence, Dominion has a leveraged balance sheet, with long-term debt at the end of 2000 of $10.1 billion compared with shareholders' equity of $7 billion. What's more, coverage of long-term debt interest is only 2.2 times.

In defense of this leverage, Mr. Capps, said, "Last year (2000), Dominion maintained its strong 'High BBB' bond ratings from both Moody's and Standard &

Poor's—ratings considered strong for corporate bonds. We've reduced out debt levels aggressively by selling non-core international, financial services and other assets. At year's end, those moves produced nearly $1.1 billion in net proceeds, with more on the way. We've targeted debt as a percentage of total capitalization to be about 55 percent by the end of 2002. In short, we had to stretch our balance sheet. Our chief financial officer compares it to a rubber band that's tight—nowhere near the snapping point—but now returning to more comfortable levels."

Reasons to Buy

■ Dominion is the largest producer of Btus in the Midwest, Northeast, and Mid-Atlantic regions of the United States, home to 40 percent of the nation's demand for energy. The company will build an even larger position in this region when it completes its $1.3-billion acquisition (in April 2001) of the 1,954 megawatt Millstone Nuclear Power Station, situated in Connecticut on Long Island Sound.

Adding Millstone of the company's growing generation fleet will boost its combined utility and nonutility capacity by 10 percent. According to Mr. Capps, "We should see at least an extra 5 cents in earnings per share each year in the first two years of ownership—and even greater annual contributions beyond that. In 2001, we'll also bring on line nearly 700 megawatts of additional gas-fired generation in Virginia and at our Elwood facility in Illinois, expanding what long-timers call 'iron in the ground.'

"In the years immediately following this, Dominion's power generation team has nearly 3,850 megawatts of new capacity either under construction or on the drawing boards. We've secured turbines and identified site possibilities for another 2,400 megawatts. In total, we hope to have nearly 9,000 new megawatts in service by 2005, most of it gas-fired. Gas from our own production company delivered by our own pipeline will fire four of these facilities in Ohio, Pennsylvania, and West Virginia."

- In 2000 and 2001, natural gas prices reached new and unprecedented high levels. As a consequence, some pundits have called into question the viability of gas as a generation fuel. For its part, Dominion Resources believes that "these high prices cannot be sustained. The laws of supply and demand will work to bring down the market price of natural gas within the new few years."

In fact, gas is firing the economy. Industry forecasts project growth in natural gas consumption of nearly 50 percent in just ten years—half of which will fuel power units. Virtually every major power facility being developed in the United States will use clean-burning natural gas.

- In 2000 the company's trading and marketing groups contributed about $.20 per share to earnings, and the company is looking for a bigger contribution in 2001. At present, Dominion is one of the nation's largest electricity marketers, with about 136 million megawatt-hours traded in 2000. The company ranks in the top twenty-five on the natural gas side, with trading volumes of roughly 1.2 trillion cubic feet. The company's goal is to more than triple its power volumes by 2005 and achieve a fivefold increase in gas volumes during the same period.

- In 2000, just as in past years, *Nucleonics Week* magazine rated Dominion's North Anna and Surry facilities in Virginia as two of the most efficiently run nuclear stations in the United States. For the fifth year in a row, moreover, the magazine ranked North Anna the nation's top performer on a three-year basis, which more accurately reflects the impact of refueling outages on production costs. Surry came in at number four.

- The Consolidated Natural Gas acquisition made Dominion Resources the fourth largest domestic electric and natural gas utility, with over $9 billion in annual revenues. The merger could realize cost savings gains of $150 million to $200 million by 2002.

- Dominion Resources is committed to continuing its $2.58 annual dividend. In the view of management, dividends are an important, if neglected, component of total return. Maintaining the dividend is important to many shareholders who depend on dividends for income.

Some Wall Street pundits say a company intent on share-price growth can't afford to reward its investors with cash. Mr. Capps does not agree. "Unless the laws of gravity change, our share price should rise with rising earnings. And the percentage of earnings we pay as dividends will go down—something Wall Street will view favorably. At year's end, our payout was about 77 percent of total earnings. Over time, we'll work to have earnings growth move that in the neighborhood of 50 to 55 percent."

- In the telecommunications and technology realm, the company is fortunate to have in-house expertise at Dominion Telecom that opens new opportunities. Dominion Telecom plans to invest about $700 million over the next two to three years to expand its fiber-optic network. The company will use this expanded network—planned to span more than 9,000 route miles—to provide Internet, video conferencing, and other broadband services. In the words of Mr. Capps, "Yes, we're looking to be a niche player. We aren't interested in going toe-to-toe with the national telecoms. But we see a real opportunity in offering telecom capacity to Cleveland, Buffalo, Toledo, and other underserved cities in our core energy markets."

Total assets: $ 29,348 million
Current ratio: 0.77
Common shares outstanding: 239 million
Return on 2000 equity: 7.1%

	2000	1999	1998	1997	1996	1995	1994	1993
Revenues (millions)	9260	5520	6086	7678	4842	4652	4491	4434
Net income (millions)	436	639	400	604	515	469	520	559
Earnings per share	1.85	2.99	1.72	3.00	2.65	2.45	2.81	3.12
Dividends per share	2.58	2.58	2.58	2.58	2.58	2.58	2.55	2.48
Price High	67.9	49.4	48.9	42.9	44.4	41.6	45.4	49.4
Low	34.8	36.6	37.8	33.3	36.9	34.9	34.9	38.4

CONSERVATIVE GROWTH

Dover Corporation

280 Park Avenue ◻ New York, New York 10017-1292 ◻ Investor contact: John F. McNiff (212) 922-1640 ◻ Dividend reinvestment plan not available ◻ Web site: www.dovercorporation.com ◻ Listed: NYSE ◻ Ticker symbol: DOV ◻ S&P rating: A ◻ Value Line financial strength rating: A+

Under the management of CEO Thomas L. Reece, the company has tended to pursue more bolt-on acquisitions than stand-alone deals. Generally, Dover's bolt-on acquisitions are smaller and less risky than stand-alone deals, say analysts. Importantly, Dover is more likely to have solid knowledge of the business and the ability to patch up problems with bolt-on deals. For these reasons, it seems likely that the bolt-on route will be pursued in the future.

According to analysts, Dover's disciplined acquisition strategy prevents the company from overpaying, and they are convinced that Dover waits patiently for the right opportunities. Analysts believe than an acquisition should meet most of the these guidelines:

• Strong management that wants to continue to work as part of the Dover family of companies.

• Operates in a niche market.

• High market share, generally number one or two in its sector.

• Manufactures specialty products that are high quality, innovative, and value-adding.

• Makes low-risk/low-technology products that do not require major research investment to maintain market leadership.

• High profit margin.

• Low capital investment needs.

• Financially strong.

In 2000 the company continued to pursue acquisitions, completing twenty-three (a record) for a total investment of $506.3 million. Acquisitions in this span added $84 million in sales and $13 million in operating profit in the fourth quarter of 2000.

Among the acquisitions in 2000 was that of OK International, a company that in the last five years has grown from a small, single product, regional company to a global organization with multiple product lines, primarily focused on the electronic manufacturers workbench. Commenting on the acquisition of OK International in November 2000, John Pomeroy, CEO of Dover Technologies, said, "OK is a great acquisition for us. They have truly become a leader in supplying tools and equipment to electronic manufacturing companies in the last few years."

Company Profile

Dover Corporation is a diversified manufacturer of a wide range of proprietary products and components for industrial and commercial use. The company is comprised of more than fifty independent operating units, most of which are number one in their niche markets. Dover is an enterprise supplying value-added products and services to thousands of customers in more than 100 countries.

Typical of the company's products: printed circuit board assembly equipment, bearings, precision engineered components, pumps, aerospace products, industrial ink-jet printers, garbage trucks, auto service station hydraulic lifts, industrial compressors, and grocery store refrigerator systems.

Over the past forty years, Dover has consistently applied the same strategic themes, including decentralization, specialty markets, market leadership, customer focus, innovation, and diversity. The result has been steady growth in mature end-markets. Dover's businesses are divided into four segments:

• Dover Technologies (the company's largest business, with 2000 revenues of $2,100 million—up 44 percent over the prior year—and an earnings increase of 73 percent to $392 million) concentrates on the manufacture of sophisticated automated assembly equipment for the electronics industry, industrial printers for coding and marking, and, to a lesser degree, specialized electronic components. This segment is made up of nine companies, including Universal Instruments Corporation, Everett Charles Technologies, Inc., and DEK Printing Machines Ltd (U.K.).

These companies have a stake in such products as automated assembly equipment for printed circuit boards, spring probes, high-frequency capacitors, Dow-Key coaxial switches, ferrite transformers, and continuous ink-jet printers.

• Dover Industries (2000 revenues of $1,246 million, a gain of 9 percent, and an earnings increase of 11 percent to $199.7 million) makes products for use in waste handling, bulk transport, automotive service, commercial food service, and machine tool industries. Dover Industries is comprised of twelve companies, including Heil Trailer International, Tipper Tie/Technopack, and Texas Hydraulics.

Dover Industries produces such items as liquid and dry bulk tank trailers, refuse-collection vehicles, packaging systems, automotive lifts, welding torches, car wash equipment, commercial refrigeration, benchtop machine tools, and commercial food service cooking equipment.

• Dover Diversified (2000 revenues were $1,176 million, up 10 percent, with a similar earnings increase to $167.9 million) builds sophisticated assembly and production machines, heat-transfer equipment and specialized compressors, as well as sophisticated products and control systems for use in the defense, aerospace, and commercial building industries. Dover Diversified is made up of twelve companies, including Hill Phoenix, Waukesha Bearings, and A-C Compressor.

Among the products produced are heat exchangers, transformer radiators, rotary compressors, refrigerated display cases, aircraft fasteners, fluid film bearings, high-performance specialty pistons, autoclaves, and machinery for corrugated boxes.

• Dover Resources (revenues in 2000 increased 14 percent to $887 million, making this segment the company's smallest; earnings in 2000 increased 11 percent to $119 million) manufactures products primarily for the automotive, fluid handling, petroleum, and chemical industries. This part of the company comprises nineteen operations, including OPW Fueling Components, Midland Manufacturing, Tulsa Winch, Petroleum Equipment Group, and Duncan Parking Systems.

Some typical products include key card systems, tank monitors, air-operated double-diaphragm pumps, tank car and barge valves, tank monitoring and control systems, loading arms, toggle clamps, EOA robotic and automation components, industrial gas compressors, peristaltic pumps, filtration systems, quartz-based pressure transducers, worm and planetary gear winches, packings for gas compressors, and progressing cavity pumps.

Shortcomings to Bear in Mind

■ Despite its impressive record, Dover might leave some investors cold because few of the individual businesses have spectacular growth prospects or are extravagantly profitable. Also, analysts have difficulty crafting a compelling story about synergies or significant cost-cutting opportunities and are unable to identify a near-term, time-sensitive event that might stimulate investor interest.

Reasons to Buy

■ Dover has a decentralized management structure. Corporate headquarters in New York City consists of about two dozen employees, including president and CEO Thomas Reece and nine other key executives. Dover's fifty operating companies are organized within the four independent subsidiaries, each headed by a CEO who reports to Mr. Reece. Each of the fifty company presidents operates autonomously. Collectively, they manage over 150 factory locations and more than 140 identifiable product/market businesses. The fifty companies are responsible for their own hiring practices. Some 75 percent of these presidents have been promoted from within the organization. On average, about five presidents are

replaced each year. This turnover is the result of poor performance (about one-third fall into this category), retirement (another one-third), and the rest are promoted.

■ Dover has a strong record of earnings increases. In the 1990–2000 period, earnings per share climbed from $.64 to $2.62, a compound annual growth rate of 15.1 percent. In the same span, dividends expanded from $.19 to $.48, a growth rate of 9.7 percent.

■ Dover is a strong cash-flow generator because its companies have above-average operating margins and do not require much additional capital investment. Free cash flow is used to acquire new businesses and for stock repurchases.

■ Dover began 2001 with the acquisition of CPI Products, a global innovator in applications development for automation tooling. CPI designs and manufactures a broad array of end-of-arms, transfer press, and assembly tooling products. The company serves customers in a wide variety of industries that depend on automation tooling to ensure lower costs and more effective production cycles. They include such industries as automotive, appliance, glass, and plastics.

■ In January 2001, Heil Environmental Industries, a Dover subsidiary, acquired Bayne Machine Works. Bayne is a leading manufacturer of hydraulic lift systems used in the waste industry. Bayne's patented rack and pinion rotary actuator is unique in the industry.

According to Heil president, Glenn Chambers, "Bayne's excellent growth record has been the result of new product development, quick delivery, outstanding customer service, after-market support, and high-quality products."

Total assets: $4,132 million
Current ratio: 1.21
Common shares outstanding: 205 million
Return on 2000 shareholders' equity: 22%

	2000	1999	1998	1997	1996	1995	1994	1993
Revenues (millions)	5401	4446	3978	4548	4076	3746	3085	2484
Net income (millions)	531	395	379	393	340	278	202	158
Earnings per share	2.61	1.92	1.69	1.74	1.51	1.23	.89	.69
Dividends per share	.48	.44	.40	.36	.32	.28	.25	.23
Price High	54.4	47.9	39.9	36.7	27.6	20.8	16.7	15.5
Low	34.1	29.3	25.5	24.1	18.3	12.9	12.4	11.3

GROWTH AND INCOME

Duke Energy Corporation

526 South Church Street □ Charlotte, North Carolina 28202-1803 □ Listed: NYSE □ Investor contact: John R. Arensdorf (704) 382-5087 □ Dividend reinvestment plan is available: (800) 488-3853 □ Web site: www.duke-energy.com □ Ticker symbol: DUK □ S&P rating: A- □ Value Line financial strength rating: A+

By 2010, domestic demand for natural gas is expected to expand from 22 trillion to 30 trillion cubic feet per year—mostly to fuel electric generation. The Department of Energy estimates $1.5 trillion will be invested in new pipelines and gas infrastructure over the next fifteen years. Duke Energy is increasing its share of that business by developing new gas projects in high-growth markets in the eastern United States.

In the Southeast, natural gas usage is growing at an annual rate of more than 4 percent, twice the national average. To open the region to natural gas supplies from the Gulf Coast, Duke Energy Gas Transmission (DEGT) purchased the East Tennessee Natural Gas Company and connected its pipelines to Duke Energy's own Texas Eastern system. Further expansion is planned via the Patriot Extension, which will bring natural gas to southwest Virginia for the first time and will introduce a competitive gas supply to North Carolina.

In New England, Duke Energy is a partner in the Maritimes & Northeast Pipeline that was completed in 1999. Originating offshore of Nova Scotia, the pipeline is fueling new merchant plants

and expanding its reach into the Boston area with the current Hubline project.

Company Profile

Duke Energy Corporation is an integrated energy and energy-services provider with the ability to offer physical delivery and management of both electricity and natural gas throughout the United States and abroad. Duke Energy provides these and other services through seven business segments:

• Franchised Electric generates, transmits, distributes, and sells electric energy in central and western North Carolina and the western portion of South Carolina (doing business as Duke Power or Nantahala Power and Light). Revenues in 2000 for this segment were $4,946 million.

• Natural Gas Transmission, through its Northeast Pipelines, provides interstate transportation and storage of natural gas for customers primarily in the Mid-Atlantic and New England states. In 2000, this segment had revenues of $1,131 million.

• Field Services gathers, processes, transports, and markets natural gas and produces and markets natural gas liquids

(NGL). Its operations are conducted primarily through Duke Energy Field Services, LLC (DEFS), a limited liability company that is about 30 percent owned by Phillips Petroleum. Field Services operates gathering systems in eleven states that serve major gas-producing regions in the Rocky Mountains, Permian Basin, Mid-Continent, and Gulf Coast regions. Revenues in 2000 were $9,060 million.

• North American Wholesale Energy's (NAWE's) activities include asset development, operation, and management, primarily through Duke Energy North America, LLC (DETM). DETM is a limited liability company that is about 40 percent owned by ExxonMobil Corporation. NAWE also includes Duke Energy Merchants, which develops new business lines in the evolving energy commodity markets. NAWE conducts its business throughout the United States and Canada. In 2000, NAWE had revenues of $33,874 million.

• International Energy conducts its operations through Duke Energy International, LLC. Its activities include asset development, operation, and management of natural gas and power facilities and energy trading and marketing of natural gas and electric power. This activity is confined to the Latin American, Asia-Pacific, and European regions. Revenues for International Energy in 2000 were $1,067 million.

• Other Energy Services provides engineering, consulting, construction, and integrated energy solutions worldwide, primarily through Duke Engineering & Service, Inc., Duke/Fluor Daniel, and Duke Solutions. In 2000, its revenues were $695 million.

• Duke Ventures is comprised of other diverse businesses, primarily operating through Crescent Resources, Inc., DukeNet Communications, LLC, and Duke Capital Partners (DCP). Crescent develops high-quality commercial, residential, and multifamily real estate projects and manages land holdings primarily in southeastern

U.S. DukeNet provides fiber-optic networks for industrial, commercial, and residential customers. DCP, a newly formed, wholly owned merchant finance company, provides financing, investment banking, and asset management services to wholesale and commercial energy markets. In 2000, this segment was responsible for revenues of $642 million.

Highlights of 2000

■ Duke Energy surpassed its pledge to expand earnings at an annual rate of 8 to 10 percent, achieving an earnings per share gain of 17 percent in 2000. Revenue, moreover, shot up 127 percent to $49.3 billion, and earnings before interest and taxes (EBIT) increased 29 percent to $3.7 billion.

■ Total shareholder return exceeded 75 percent in 2000, and Duke Energy outperformed its peers in the Dow Jones Utilities Index by 67 percent.

■ Duke Partners was created to provide debt and equity capital and financial services to high-growth energy businesses.

■ The company's Energy Services businesses delivered combined EBIT of $688 million in 2000, a 338 percent increase. These strong results were driven by aggressive expansion and management of the company's merchant plant portfolio, as well as gains in energy trading and risk management.

■ In the United States, Duke Energy expanded its regional energy businesses, delivering a record four new power plants and 2,300 megawatts in time for the summer's peak demand. What's more, the company broke ground on six new facilities that added 3,400 megawatts by the summer of 2001. And Duke remains on target with the development of an additional 20,000 megawatts by 2004.

■ Duke Energy merged its Field Services unit with Phillips Petroleum gas gathering, processing, and marketing business.

This move contributed to a 106 percent increase in EBIT for Field Services.

- Internationally, Duke Energy continued to tap the extraordinary potential of Latin American markets. In Brazil, the company increased ownership in one of the country's largest generating companies to 95 percent. Duke also made leadership gains in Peru and El Salvador, and expanded its asset bases in Argentina and Bolivia.

- In Asia Pacific, the company delivered a first-time competitive natural gas supply to Australia and began preconstruction efforts on a pipeline for the state of Tasmania.

Shortcomings to Bear in Mind

- Public utilities are sensitive to changes in interest rates. This is partly because they often borrow money to finance new plants. Higher interest rates shove up the cost of these funds. High interest rates can also cause investors to sell their shares in order to invest their money where the return is greater.

- Duke is particularly strong in its Energy Services businesses, which generated EBIT growth of 374 percent in 2000 compared with the prior year. This segment, which includes trading and marketing of power, now accounts for about 20 percent of Duke's EBIT and is increasingly subject to volatile markets. While open wholesale electricity markets have been the source of strong profits, "we are increasingly concerned that price weakness in the wholesale market would translate into a reduced growth rate, possibly triggering an earnings shortfall," according to a report issued by Argus Research Corporation in 2001.

Reasons to Buy

- Duke Energy posted a 51 percent profit increase in the first quarter of 2001, as demand for natural gas and power surged nationwide. Duke's gains were powered by its power trading and marketing unit, which showed a 324 percent rise in earnings, before interest and taxes. In the same quarter, earnings for the company's natural gas gathering and processing operations climbed 71 percent.

- Duke Energy entered into a major transaction with Phillips Petroleum in 2000. The companies are the nation's two top producers of natural gas liquids (NGL), such as propane and butane. Duke and Phillips combined their gas-gathering and processing operations. Duke owns 70 percent of the new company. Duke says the combination enables the company to release more value from its natural gas operations, which it believes have been undervalued by the market. "It will be more highly valued (in a separate company) than it was as part of our consolidated business," said Richard Priory, chairman of Duke Energy. Duke said the new venture should help the company meet its goal to increase earnings per share by 8 percent to 10 percent a year.

For their part, analysts said the natural gas operations of both companies are considered well-run and solid performers that will only increase in value when combined. Those assets include fifteen gas-processing plants, owned by Phillips in Texas, New Mexico, and Oklahoma, and fifty-two plants owned by Duke in Wyoming, Colorado, Kansas, Oklahoma, New Mexico, Texas, and Canada.

- Duke Power is uniquely positioned to capitalize on its expertise in designing, building, and operating generating facilities. Duke is one of only a few domestic utilities that has historically designed, built, and operated its own power plants. The expertise Duke gained in those areas over the years has been retained through Duke Engineering

& Services, Inc. and Duke/Fluor Daniel (DE&S).

- Duke Power meets its customers' needs for electricity primarily through a combination of nuclear-fueled, fossil-fueled, and hydroelectric generating stations.

Over the past twenty years, Duke's fossil-fueled generating system has consistently been cited by *Electric Light & Power* magazine as the country's most efficient fossil system as measured by heat rate. Heat rate is a measure of efficiency in converting the energy contained in a fossil fuel such as oil, natural gas, or coal, into electricity. A low heat rate means Duke burns less coal to generate a given quantity of electricity, lowering operating costs and helping keep rates competitive.

- Duke Power offers attractive incentive rates for businesses to relocate and expand within its service territory. Duke's Economic Development Rate awards an initial 20 percent discount during the first year for industrial customers who expand their electricity consumption by one megawatt and either hire a minimum of seventy-five new employees or invest at least $400,000 in capital upgrades. Several dozen companies have qualified for the program.

- In the spring of 2001, Duke Energy made a pact with California's Department of Water Resources to sell about $4 billion worth of electricity to the power-starved state over a nine-year period. Duke Energy said deliveries totaling 550 megawatts would begin January 1, 2002, increasing to 800 megawatts on January 1, 2003 and lasting through December 31, 2010. One megawatt powers about 1,000 homes.

- Duke Energy made an agreement to supply natural gas to Ivanhoe's iron-pellet plant at Port Latta, Tasmania, in the spring of 2001. The agreement enables Ivanhoe to convert its pellet plant furnaces from oil to cleaner burning natural gas. For Duke, the deal secures an underpinning load for the company's Tasmanian Gas Pipeline, which expects to begin converting the pellet plant to natural gas in 2002.

Total assets: $ 58,176 million
Current ratio: 0.96
Common shares outstanding: 739 million
Return on 2000 shareholders' equity: 14.5%

	2000	1999	1998	1997	1996	1995	1994	1993
Revenues (millions)	49318	21742	17610	16309	4758	4677	4279	4282
Net income (millions)	1495	1383	1260	974	730	715	639	626
Earnings per share	2.01	1.80	1.72	1.26	1.69	1.63	1.44	1.40
Dividends per share	1.10	1.10	1.10	1.08	1.04	1.00	.96	.92
Price High	45.2	32.7	35.5	28.3	26.5	23.9	21.5	22.4
Low	22.9	23.4	26.6	20.9	21.7	18.7	16.4	17.7

E. I. DuPont de Nemours and Company

1007 Market Street ☐ Wilmington, Delaware 19898 ☐ Investor Contact: Ann K. M. Gualtieri (302) 774-4994 ☐ Dividend reinvestment plan is available: (888) 98-DUPONT ☐ Web site: www.dupont.com ☐ Listed: NYSE ☐ Ticker symbol: DD ☐ S&P rating: B+ ☐ Value Line financial strength rating: A++

DuPont launched a fuel cell business in 2001 to pursue growth in the emerging proton exchange membrane fuel cell market. The company intends to apply its integrated expertise in polymer, coatings, and electro-chemicals technology.

DuPont's goal is to become the leading supplier of materials and components to the emerging worldwide fuel cell market. What's more, DuPont is seeking a strong presence in what it believes will be a $10-billion market for fuel cells by the year 2010.

A fuel cell is a device that converts chemical energy to electrical energy. It does this by using a fuel and an oxidizer (a substance that removes electrons in a chemical reaction). Compared with a battery, a fuel cell's electrodes remain largely unchanged during its operation, whereas a battery's electrodes are gradually used up. Fuel cells are more efficient than conventional electric generators, which cannot convert all the heat that is sent to them. Fuel cells produce less waste heat. On the other hand, fuel cells are extremely expensive and are used only where price is not a factor, such as in a space shuttle.

DuPont opened a multimillion-dollar fuel cell technology center in 2000 near its headquarters in Wilmington, Delaware. The company is also working in partnership with others in the industry to improve capabilities, availability, and economic feasibility of fuel cell technology.

"Increasing global energy requirements and the desire for alternative energy sources in many markets make fuel cells an exciting new growth opportunity for DuPont," said Richard J. Angiullo, vice president and general manager of DuPont Fluoroproducts. "We intend to be a leader in applying integrated materials science and expertise to develop new, cleaner, and more convenient energy sources for people around the world."

Company Profile

DuPont is much more than the largest domestic chemical company. With annual revenues of $28 billion, DuPont links its fortunes to a host of business sectors, including agricultural chemicals, industrial and specialty chemicals, titanium dioxide, fluorocarbons, nylon, polyester, aramid and other fibers, polymer intermediates, films, resins, adhesives, electronic products, automotive paints, coatings, and pharmaceuticals. In mid-2001, DuPont sold the drug business to Bristol-Myers for $7.8 billion in cash. The company operates 200 manufacturing and processing facilities in forty countries.

In its fibers segment, DuPont has a diversified mix of specialty fibers produced to serve end uses such as high-strength composites in aerospace, active sportswear, and packaging. Polymers consists of engineering polymers, elastomers, and fluoropolymers. DuPont's diversified businesses include agricultural products, coal, electronics, films and imaging systems.

In its chemical operations, DD is primarily focused on brand-name downstream materials rather than commodity items. They include Stainmaster carpet; Lycra, Spandex, and Dacron polyester fiber;

Teflon and Silverstone nonstick systems; as well as DuPont automotive paints.

DuPont is also the largest agrochemical producer in the United States and Asia.

Shortcomings to Bear in Mind

- Charles O. Holliday Jr. has been struggling ever since he became CEO of DuPont in early 1998. Soon after he took the reins of the chemical giant, he assured stockholders that he would revamp DuPont and transform it from a producer of cyclical commodity chemicals into a company in tune with the future. To make this transformation, Mr. Holliday pushed DuPont into ag-biotech and pharmaceuticals. This strategy, however, has backfired. Among other things, the backlash against genetically modified crops has put a crimp on new product introductions. Then too, the company's failure to achieve a pharmaceutical alliance has left it with an undersized drug operation—in an era when large size is the only path to success because of the high cost of developing new drugs. And to top off the company's woes, DuPont's traditional businesses are getting brutalized by high oil and gas prices and a weak euro. Add it all up and 2000 did not make anyone happy to own shares in DuPont.
- High costs for oil, natural gas, and other raw materials have been dragging down the company's earnings. A weakening economy is also have a negative impact.
- At the beginning of 2001, the company warned Wall Street that there were steep losses ahead for its pharmaceutical business. However, the company expects this operation to return to profitability in the second half of 2001.

Reasons to Buy

- DuPont and Sabanci Holding announced in early 2001 the completion of an agreement to further expand their multiregional alliance for industrial nylon. The new 50-50 venture, DUSA International, is the world's leading global supplier of heavy decitex nylon industrial yarn and tire cord fabric.

"DUSA International will operate as one global business dedicated to meeting the needs of its customers in tires, mechanical rubber goods, cordage, and webbing better than any other nylon supplier," said Peter Hemken, chief executive of the new company. "This combination offers many benefits, among them the scale and resources to invest, renew, and add value to our offerings for customers."

- In 2000, DuPont and Chemdex Corporation announced the formation of Industria Solutions, Inc., a new business-to-business e-commerce company that will streamline the procurement of materials for the $75-billion worldwide fluid processing market. The fluid processing market includes companies that have a broad range of industries, such as chemical, oil and gas, pulp and paper, power generation, and pharmaceuticals. Products that are used in this vertical market are complex and technical in nature, such as pipes, valves, pumps, motors, compressors, and other materials and equipment required for processing fluid for industrial use.

Industria will leverage the assets and expertise of its founding companies to address supply chain efficiencies in this market. Chemdex brings to the new company its scalable e-commerce technology and expertise in building and operating vertical marketplaces. DuPont, one of the largest purchasers of maintenance and engineering materials in the United States, will contribute substantial buying power to Industria by shifting procurement of these materials to Industria over time.

- Achieving sustained, profitable growth in today's global marketplace requires a clear competitive advantage. DuPont defines that advantage as being number one or two in both market position and technology in its chemicals and specialty businesses that are global in scope. About two-thirds of the company's businesses are already positioned as global leaders by this measure. Among them are Lycra, titanium dioxide, agricultural products, fluoroproducts, nonwovens, aramids, and photopolymers. DuPont has some others, such as polyester, finishes, and ethylene copolymers that are very strong regionally. For these, the company is pursuing creative ways to achieve a strong global position.
- Research and development is essential to DuPont's growth strategy, and the company continues to use its technological strength to add superior competitiveness. DD expects R & D to revolutionize the productivity of its manufacturing assets. A third of DuPont's revenue growth is targeted to come from new products. Research programs balance near- and long-term opportunities. The company's agricultural products pipeline includes fourteen new crop protection chemicals.
- Fluorine chemistry is a core DuPont technology. The company buys flurospar, a naturally occurring mineral, and converts it into fluorochemicals, which can also be further upgraded into fluoropolymers. Fluoroproducts are particularly valuable because of their unique inertness, lubricity, and heat-transfer properties.

The largest and fastest-growing segment is Teflon wire and cable jacketing polymers. They provide flame- and smoke-resistance that allows low-cost plenum installations for the rapidly growing LAN (local area network) market. Teflon, however, is more expensive than polyvinylidine polymers. On the other hand, Teflon can be high-speed melt extruded as a coating. This eliminates the need for an overlay wrap.

- DuPont has paid dividends annually since 1904.
- A new generation of herbicides is contributing to increased earnings at DuPont's agricultural chemicals division.
- DuPont is the world market-share leader in most of its businesses, including nylon, polyester, specialty fibers, titanium dioxide (which serves to make certain substances opaque, such as paint, paper, and plastic), thermoplastics, and other products.
- The company has more than forty research and development and customer service labs in the United States and more than thirty-five labs in eleven other countries.
- DuPont is different from most other chemical companies in two ways: its strong brand franchises (such as Stainmaster, Lycra, and Teflon) and its ownership of Conoco, which is 40 percent of overall sales. Thus, DuPont can differentiate itself from the commodity-type chemical companies because most of the company's chemical products are downstream specialties, with 50 percent of sales abroad.

In addition, the company's business mix has only a tiny portion that can be deemed primary ethylene derivatives, and only about 16 percent of total sales are to construction and automotive markets—with only about half of that being in the more cyclical United States.

What's more, even within the automotive segment, the largest business is refinish paint, which is fairly insensitive to the OEM auto cycle. In elastomers, DuPont expects 20 percent growth over the next five years from its new joint venture with Dow Chemical. And within the construction market, analysts believe market share gains are being made by the new Stainmaster

carpet products, as well as by Corian and Tyvek. DuPont has number one or two positions in virtually every business it is in.

Total assets: $39,426 million
Current ratio: 1.20
Common shares outstanding: 1,039 million
Return on 2000 shareholders' equity: 17.4%

	2000	1999	1998	1997	1996	1995	1994	1993
Revenues (millions)	28268	26918	24767	45079	43810	42163	39333	37098
Net income (millions)	2314	7690	2860	4087	3636	3293	2777	1667
Earnings per share	2.73	2.58	2.54	3.61	3.24	2.91	2.04	1.23
Dividends per share	1.40	1.40	1.37	1.23	1.12	1.02	.91	.88
Price High	74.0	75.2	84.4	69.8	49.7	36.5	31.2	26.9
Low	38.2	50.1	51.7	46.4	34.8	26.3	24.1	22.3

CONSERVATIVE GROWTH

Emerson (formerly Emerson Electric Company)

8000 W. Florissant Avenue ▫ Post Office Box 4100, Station 2197 ▫ St. Louis, Missouri 63136-8506 ▫ Investor relations: Robert T. Sharp (314) 553-2197 ▫ Dividend reinvestment plan is available: (888) 213-0970 ▫ Web site: www.emersonelectric.com ▫ Listed: NYSE ▫ Ticker symbol: EMR ▫ Fiscal year ends September 30 ▫ S&P rating: A+ ▫ Value Line financial strength rating: A++

Emerson—better known for selling electric motors, refrigeration components, and industrial tools—now appears to be positioning itself to cash in on the booming demand for reliable backup power systems for computer networks.

With the country's power grid quickly reaching its capacity, outages are no longer a rare occurrence. And when power goes out, Emerson components kick in, switching the power from one source to another and regulating voltage. Emerson also provides diesel generators and fuel cells that generate temporary electricity. These products have become must-buys for any corporation that uses the Internet for conducting business. "The potential for Emerson is huge," said Edward Whitacre, CEO of SBC Communications and an Emerson board member.

One of the key ways that Emerson is entering more and faster-growing markets is through technology investment. The

company's leading areas of technology spending are now electronics, communications, and software.

In the words of Chairman Charles F. Knight, "I view this as an important shift, given the opportunities for product differentiation and the increased value proposition for customers that these technologies provide. Customers are responding enthusiastically to the intelligence embedded in our products, as well as to our new software and service offerings."

Company Profile

Emerson is a leading manufacturer of a broad list of intermediate products such as electrical motors and drives, appliance components, and process-control devices. The company also produces hand and power tools, as well as accessories.

Founded 108 years ago, Emerson is not a typical high-tech capital goods producer.

Rather, the company makes such prosaic things as refrigerator compressors, pressure gauges, and In-Sink Erator garbage disposals—basic products that are essential to industry.

Without question, Emerson is one of the nation's finest companies and should be a core holding in any portfolio devoted to growth of capital. Let's next glance at the company's five segments:

• Emerson Industrial Automation provides integral horsepower motors, alternators, electronic and mechanical drives, industrial valves, electrical equipment, specialty heating, lighting, testing, and ultrasonic welding and cleaning products for industrial applications. Key growth drivers for the segment include the embedding of electronics into motors and other equipment to enable self-diagnosis and preventative maintenance functionality, as well as alternators for diesel and natural gas generator sets to create reliable distributed power solutions. The Industrial Automation segment is the company's largest, with revenues over $3.4 billion in fiscal 2000, or close to 22 percent of the company's overall revenues of $15.6 billion.

• Emerson Process Automation offers control systems and software, analytical instrumentation, measurement devices, and valves and other control equipment for customers in oil and gas, chemical, power, water and wastewater, food and beverage, pharmaceutical, and other industries. Key growth drivers include Emerson's innovative PlantWeb technology, which redefines plant architecture, and new solution and service opportunities created by Emerson's unique ability to apply its technology to specific customer needs. In 2000, this segment was responsible for a bit over $3 billion in company revenue.

• Emerson Heating, Ventilating and Air Conditioning (HVAC) offers compressors, thermostats, temperature controls, hermetic terminals, and valves for HVAC and refrigeration systems. A key driver of this business is the Copeland Scroll compressor, a revolutionary technology that is more energy efficient, reliable, and quiet than competing traditional technologies. Scroll also has created entirely new compression markets outside of HVAC, such as micro turbine gas boosters for distributed power generation. HVAC is the smallest segment of Emerson, with 2000 revenues of $2.5 billion.

• Electronics and Telecommunications, through Emerson Network Power, delivers comprehensive solutions for highly reliable power. Offerings include AC UPS Systems, DC power systems, precision air-conditioning systems, embedded and power supplies, transfer switches, and site monitoring systems and services for the fast-growing communications and Internet infrastructure markets. Additionally, fiber-optic conduit and connectivity products support the global expansion of broadband communications. Key drivers include the rapid build-out of wireless, broadband, and other data and voice services, and the increasing need for dependable backup power to support the utility grid. In 2000, Electronics and Telecommunications contributed $3.3 billion of the company's overall revenues.

• Appliance and Tools includes the Emerson Storage Solutions, Emerson Tools, Emerson Appliance Solutions, and Emerson Motors brand platforms. Customer offerings feature an extensive range of consumer, commercial, and industrial storage products; market-leading tools; electrical components and systems for appliances; and the world's largest offering of fractional horsepower motors. Key growth drivers include professional-grade tools serving the fast-growing home center market, as well as advanced electrical motors, which create entirely new market opportunities for Emerson. The part of the company was responsible for more than $3.3 billion in revenues in 2000 and was the company's largest contributor to earnings, with a net of $562 million or 26.3 percent of total company profits of $2.1 billion.

Shortcomings to Bear in Mind

- Long celebrated as a model of stable, consistent earnings growth, Emerson has lost some of its luster on Wall Street. While the company's profits have continued their long-running climb, some critics have complained that the company's risk-averse strategy—the same conservative management style that has allowed Emerson to report higher earnings in each of the past forty-three years—has limited growth opportunities.

- After twenty-seven years at the helm of Emerson, Charles F. Knight stepped down as CEO in the fall of 2000. Knight was renown for keeping alive the company's remarkable record of forty-three straight years of record earnings. He was also known for his explosive temper. "If someone's not well prepared, he'll get torn apart," said Albert E. Suter, an Emerson official. That's a trait employees won't have to worry about with the new CEO, forty-six-year-old David N. Farr, the company's former chief operating officer. Knight hasn't vacated his duties entirely—he's still Emerson's chairman. On the other hand, there may be some nervous investors who wonder whether Mr. Farr can duplicate the record of his predecessor.

Reasons to Buy

- In fiscal 2001 Emerson launched a new brand identity to better reflect the company's technology leadership, successful growth strategies, and customer focus. The 110-year-old company shortened its name to "Emerson" and introduced a new corporate logo in recognition of its position as a global technology and engineering leader in process automation, network power, and other fast-growth markets.

- The company has been active on the acquisition front. For instance, in fiscal 2000 Emerson, moving to rev up its growth prospects, agreed to acquire Jordan Industries Inc.'s telecommunications equipment business. At that time, Jordan Industries was a privately owned holding company. Jordan makes products used in deploying fiber-optics wires, cable TV components, and a host of products used in the wireless and data-communications infrastructure. At the time of the acquisition, Jordan had annual sales of $381 million, up a hefty 21 percent in the prior twelve months.

- Emerson has one of the great growth records of all time. For forty-three consecutive years, earnings per share have increased at a compound annual pace of 11 percent. Dividends have done slightly better, with a forty-four-year record, coupled with a compound growth rate of twelve percent.

- In 2000 the company opened its ninth Copeland Scroll compressor plant, this one in Suzhou, China, to meet the growing demand for this technology in Asian markets. Emerson can now produce over five million scroll compressors a year, making the company far and away the market leader. Scroll sales approached $800 million in 2000, representing a 22 percent compound annual growth rate over the prior five years.

- PlantWeb is being selected by an increasing number of large, global customers for their most demanding applications. Emerson's investment in this sector has uniquely positioned the company to lead the transition of the process automation world to a field-based architecture that leverages intelligent devices with new industry-standard communications technology, an inflection point that will dramatically improve the efficiency of customers' operations. Sales in this operation expanded better than 30 percent in 2000.

- Technology is fundamental to Emerson's sales growth. As a consequence, the company has been increasing its investment in engineering and development, notably in such sectors as communications, software, and electronics. E&D investment, moreover, has risen every year since 1973, reaching $600 million in 2000.
- Relative to fixed capital, Emerson is optimizing assets by outsourcing production where the company can identify a more efficient supplier. While Emerson's return on total capital is off modestly from recent highs because of the impact of major acquisitions, the 16.1 percent return in 2000 is impressive when compared with competitors, as well as other industries. What's more, EMR believes that it can boost return on total capital to even higher levels in the years ahead.

- The company has been divesting laggard businesses and placing greater emphasis on its core operations—those with better prospects for growth and profitability. What's more, Emerson has continued its focus on lean manufacturing. It is reducing the time between raw material and finished product. These measures are expediting delivery to customers and enhancing the use of factory space. In sum, these moves are expected to free up an additional $1 billion of operating capital over the next five years.
- Over the years, Emerson has enjoyed its share of recognition. *Business Week*, for instance, named Emerson's Knight (chairman) and Farr (CEO) among the top managers of 2000. *Fortune's Investor's Guide* included Emerson among its "Seven Stocks that are Ready to Run."

Total assets: $15,164 million
Current ratio: 1.05
Common shares outstanding: 427 million
Return on 2000 shareholders' equity: 22.6%

	2000	1999	1998	1997	1996	1995	1994	1993
Revenues (millions)	15545	14270	13447	12299	11150	10013	8607	8174
Net income (millions)	1422	1314	1229	1122	1018	908	789	708
Earnings per share	3.30	3.00	2.77	2.52	2.28	2.03	1.76	1.58
Dividends per share	1.43	1.31	1.18	1.08	.98	.89	.78	.72
Price High	79.8	71.4	67.4	60.4	51.8	40.8	33.0	31.2
Low	40.5	51.4	54.5	45.0	38.8	30.8	28.2	52.8

GROWTH AND INCOME

Energen Corporation

605 Richard Arrington Jr. Boulevard North □ Birmingham, Alabama 35203-2707 □ Investor contact: Julie S. Ryland (800) 654-3206 □ Dividend reinvestment plan is available: (800) 654-3206 or on the Web at www.netstockdirect.com □ Web site: www.energen.com □ Fiscal year ends September 30 □ Listed: NYSE □ Ticker symbol: EGN □ S&P rating: A □ Value Line financial strength rating: B++

When you invest in the shares of a public utility you normally expect modest growth, along with above-average dividends that are increased at a pace in excess of inflation. Rarely do you look for substantial capital gains.

In the past five years, Energen Corporation has *not* been that type of utility.

Here's why. As fiscal 1996 got underway, Energen implemented an aggressive growth strategy that focused on enhancing shareholder value by increasing earnings per share at an average compound growth rate of 10 percent a year over the next five years. The major component of growth under this strategy was to be Energen Resources Corporation, the company's small oil and gas exploration and production operation. Up until that point, this part of Energen had achieved success in the niche play of coal bed methane development in Alabama in the mid- to late 1980s. The company's strategy was to look to Alabama Gas Corporation (Alagasco), its single-state natural gas utility, to provide the solid foundation from which it could confidently pursue diversified growth.

At the time, Alagasco was responsible for about 80 percent of the company's consolidated net income. Based on the slow-growth nature of the utility's mature service territory, the company's management determined that Alagasco was unlikely to generate long-term earnings growth sufficient to enhance shareholder value at a level that would set the company apart from the typical utility. To offset this projected slow growth, the company set out to focus on its small but burgeoning nonregulated oil and gas operations.

The results posted by Energen over the next five years have far exceeded expectations. Energen has generated compound EPS growth of 14.7 percent a year. In all but one of those years, annual earnings per share growth exceeded 10 percent. The largest single-year increase was realized in fiscal 2000, when EPS climbed 27 percent. Fiscal 2000 marked the fourth consecutive year of record earnings for Energen and Energen Resources, and the tenth year in a row for record earnings by Alagasco.

Viewed on a stand-alone basis, Energen Resources's net income mushroomed at a compound rate of 50.9 percent over this five-year span. What's more, Alagasco's net income surpassed expectations by generating a compound growth rate of nearly 11 percent. Today, moreover, Energen Resources produces some 50 percent of consolidated net income—a far cry from its contribution a mere five years earlier.

Company Profile

Based in Birmingham, Alabama, Energen Corporation is a diversified energy holding company with a stake in two main lines of business: the distribution of natural gas and the exploration and production of oil and natural gas.

The holding company dates back to 1978 with the reorganization of its natural gas utility and largest subsidiary, Alagasco. This natural gas utility was launched in 1948 with the merger of Alabama Gas Company and Birmingham Gas Company. Energen's principal subsidiaries were Alagasco and Taurus Exploration (now called Energen Resources).

Alagasco

Alagasco is the largest natural gas distributor in Alabama. The utility serves 456,000 homes and businesses in central and northern Alabama. The service territory covers 22,000 square miles and 175 communities in thirty counties, including Birmingham and Montgomery, with an estimated combined population of 2.4 million. The distribution system includes 9,180 miles of mains and more than 10,650 miles of service lines. In addition, two liquefied natural gas facilities are used to meet peak demand.

Alagasco's distribution system is connected to two major interstate pipeline systems: Southern and Transcontinental Gas Pipe Line Corporation.

Alagasco serves about 70 percent of the potential customers along its gas mains. In addition, about 95 percent of the new homes constructed in its service region during 2000 selected natural gas for space and water heating.

Energen Resources Corporation

Energen Resources Corporation focuses on increasing its production and proved reserves through the acquisition and exploitation of producing oil and gas properties with development potential in North America. (Exploitation is the optimal development of an oil and gas reservoir to extract its hydrocarbons.)

Energen Resources is involved in the exploration and production of natural gas and oil in the Gulf of Mexico, and through coal bed methane projects in Alabama's Black Warrior Coal Basin. The company has recoverable reserves primarily in Alabama, New Mexico, Texas, Mississippi, Louisiana, and the Gulf of Mexico. Natural gas accounts for 73 percent of reserves, oil for 14 percent, and natural gas liquids for 13 percent. (Natural gas liquids [NGL] are liquid hydrocarbons that are extracted and separated from the natural gas stream. NGL products include ethane, propane, butane, and natural gasoline.)

Shortcomings to Bear in Mind

- Natural gas utilities are hostage to the weather. If the winter is mild, utilities sell less gas. The summer weather, on the other hand, is not very important as only a small amount of gas is used in air conditioning—even though that sector holds considerable promise for the future. An electric utility, in contrast, can be hurt by a mild summer because air conditioning can generate huge revenues during a torrid June, July, and August.
- Public utilities are subject to the vagaries of interest rates. There are two reasons for this. First, investors are often on the lookout for a better return. If interest rates rise, income-oriented investors may be tempted to sell their utility shares and invest elsewhere, which

depresses the price of utility shares. Second, utilities tend to be major borrowers, since they have to invest in new distribution facilities. By the same token, when interest rates fall, it augurs well for public utilities.

- Alagasco's cost of gas is expected to be higher in fiscal 2001. The expected increase has been placed into rates through the utility's Gas Supply Adjustment (GSA) rider. Unlike Energen Resources, Alagasco does not profit from the current environment of high natural gas prices. Changes in the utility's gas supply costs, up or down, are passed through to the customer without markup under the terms of the GSA rider.

Reasons to Buy

- Through the company's successful acquisition and exploitation efforts, Energen Resources's total proved reserves have risen from 95.2 billion cubic feet equivalent (Bcfe) at the end of fiscal 1995 to 1.1 trillion cubic feet equivalent (Tcfe) today. The company's production, too, has increased dramatically, from 10.1 Bcfe five years ago to over 70 Bcfe today.
- For the twelve months ended September 30, 2000, Energen achieved record net income of $53 million, or $1.75 per diluted share. This compares with net income of $41.4 million, or $1.38 per diluted share, in fiscal 1999. Energen Resources contributed $27.4 million to consolidated net income, as compared to $17.3 million the prior year. Alagasco, for its part, also performed well, as net income of $26.3 million exceeded results the prior year of $23.3 million.
- Alagasco operates under a progressive rate-setting mechanism that provides the utility the opportunity to earn a return on average equity (ROE) between 12.15 percent and 13.65 percent. Alagasco's

ROE in fiscal 2000 was 13.4 percent. As the utility has made capital investments in its facilities, its average equity level has increased, leading to higher earnings.

■ Alagasco's financial stability, in part, is due to Alabama's progressive regulatory environment. The company's ratepayers and shareholders both benefit from the utility's unique rate-setting mechanism, Rate Stabilization and Equalization (RSE), the prime example of this environment.

■ Natural gas utilities have some advantages over electric utilities. For one thing, they are not as concerned about competition. Natural gas is a preferred fuel, compared with coal, oil, and electricity. It is plentiful and burns clean. Thus, it is not a target of antipollution activists. It can be burned in vehicles instead of gasoline and has some advantages. It is less expensive than gasoline and does less harm to the engine. Of course, it is unlikely to dislodge gasoline

anytime soon except as a fuel for interurban vehicles such as buses, delivery vans, and taxis.

■ Many natural gas utilities are entirely dependent on their revenues from their utility function. This has some disadvantages. For one thing, utilities are regulated and are unlikely to experience high growth. And if the state regulators are tough to deal with—and most state regulators are consumer-oriented—the utility may languish.

On the other hand, when the company is active in exploration, there is the opportunity to increase earnings without the fear of regulation. For its part, Energen derives a hefty portion of its earnings from its oil and gas exploration. What's more, exploration is not tied to weather or season. However, if natural gas prices are weak, this segment of the company will be hurt. Of late, of course, natural gas prices have been historically high.

Total assets: $1,203 million
Current ratio: 0.58
Common shares outstanding: 30.4 million
Return on 2000 shareholders' equity: 13.7%

	2000	1999	1998	1997	1996	1995	1994	1993
Revenues (millions)	556	498	503	448	399	321	377	357
Net income (millions)	53	41	36	29	21	19	22	18
Earnings per share	1.75	1.38	1.23	1.16	.98	.89	1.01	.89
Dividends per share	.68	.66	.63	.61	.59	.57	.55	.53
Price High	33.6	21.2	22.5	20.6	15.6	12.6	11.9	13.4
Low	14.7	13.1	15.1	29.0	21.8	20.1	19.3	18.1

INCOME

Equity Office Properties Trust

Two North Riverside Plaza ▫ Suite 2100 ▫ Chicago, Illinois 60606 ▫ Listed: NYSE ▫ Investor Contact: Diane Morefield (312) 466-3286 ▫ Dividend reinvestment plan is available: (312) 466-3508 ▫ Web site: www.equityoffice.com ▫ Ticker symbol: EOP ▫ S&P rating: Not rated ▫ Value Line financial strength rating: Not rated

Equity Office Properties, a leading REIT that invests in office buildings, bought Spieker Properties Inc. in the summer of 2001. Spieker is the largest commercial real estate owner on the West Coast. It added 25 million square feet to EOP's 124 million square feet across the country. At $7.2 billion, the purchase—for cash, stock and assumed debt—was the biggest domestic transaction in real estate history.

According to Credit Suisse First Boston Corporation, "the Spieker merger improves EOP's all-important return on invested capital." What's more, said the Credit Suisse analyst, the merger will "increase the amount of free cash flow and improve overall balance sheet ratios." In this same report, the analyst also pointed out that Equity Office Properties can now "lay claim to being the number one office player in Boston, Chicago, San Francisco, Silicon Valley, Seattle, Portland, and Atlanta."

Company Profile

Equity Office Properties Trust is the nation's largest publicly held owner and manager of office properties. With a total market capitalization of about $20.8 billion, Equity Office owns and manages 98.9 million square feet of primary Class A office space in 381 buildings in 37 major metropolitan areas in 24 states and the District of Columbia. The company serves more than 6,800 businesses, including many of the most recognized companies in America. The company's buildings are situated in such cities as Boston (55 buildings), Chicago (30), San Francisco (28), New York (6), Seattle (21), Washington, D. C. (25), Atlanta (45), San Jose/Silicon Valley (37), Los Angeles (13) and Denver (15). All told, these top 10 markets are responsible for 77.6 percent of the company's operating income.

The company's origins date back to 1976 when an integrated real estate management and acquisition organization was founded by Samuel Zell, now chairman of EOP. The company's portfolio was consolidated and taken public in July 1997. Since its initial public offering (IPO), the company has more than tripled in size, growing from 32.2 million square feet to 98.9 million

square feet, through strategic acquisitions, including the $4.3 billion Beacon Properties, Inc. merger in December 1997 and the $4.5 billion Cornerstone Properties merger in June 2000.

Office buildings are structures used primarily for the conduct of business, such as administration, clerical services, and consultation with clients and associates. Class A office buildings are generally considered those that have excellent locations and access, attract high-quality tenants, are well maintained and professionally managed. They also achieve the highest rent, occupancy and tenant retention rates within their markets.

Acquisitions

Acquisitions have played an integral part in the company's growth. Equity Office Properties Trust significantly expanded its operations in late 1997 with the acquisition of Beacon Properties for $4.3 billion, adding 130 properties and 21 million square feet to its holdings. In 1999, the Trust completed six acquisitions, investing $393 million and acquiring 10 office properties that contained 589 spaces. In mid-2000, it completed the acquisition of Cornerstone Properties for $2.7 billion. Cornerstone is an office REIT that owns 86 office properties in the United States, totaling over 18.5 million square feet. Finally, its largest acquisition, as note above, was Spieker Spieker Properties.

What is an Equity REIT?

Equity REITs make their money by owning properties, as opposed to mortgage REITs, which lend money to property owners. Equity REITs allow you to invest in a diversified collection of apartment buildings, hospitals, shopping centers, hotels, warehouses and office buildings.

Like mutual funds, REITs are not taxed themselves, providing they pay out at least 95 percent of their taxable income.

That translates into fat dividends for shareholders, as REITs pass along the rents and other income they collect. Dividend yields are typically 6 percent or more. "Put it all together, and you are looking at a double-digit total return. Over the long haul, the return should be lower than traditional stocks, but higher than bonds," says Chris Mayer, a real estate professor at the University of Pennsylvania's Wharton School.

Kevin Bernzott, an investment adviser in Camarillo, California, views REITs as a stock-bond hybrid. "If you select quality REITs, they kick off a highly predictable stream of income, and eventually you may get some price appreciation. We plug them into the bond portion of the portfolio. They're almost like a bond with an equity kicker."

Highlights of 2000

- Announced the $4.5-billion merger with Cornerstone Properties, further establishing Equity Office as the preeminent national office company.
- Completed development of Sunset North Corporate Campus, a three-building, 465,000 square-foot joint venture project in Bellevue, WA.
- Completed the sale of three properties totaling 234,000 square feet in Ventura, CA: Agoura Hills Business Park and Westlake Spectrum Center I and II.
- Acquired equity and debt interest in 1301 Avenue of the Americas, a 1.8-million-square-foot office building in Midtown Manhattan, New York.
- Recognized by *Chicago Magazine* as one of the twenty-five "Best Places to Work" in Chicago.
- Acquired World Trade Center East, a 187,000-square-foot, newly completed office development in Seattle, WA.
- Completed sale of 500 Marquette, a 230,000-square-foot office building in Albuquerque, NM.

- Entered into a joint venture agreement with New York State Common Retirement Fund. New York Common purchased a 49.9 percent interest in Bank of America Tower in Seattle, WA.
- Completed sale of Park Plaza, an 87,000-square-foot office building in Pleasanton, CA.
- Acquired remaining 30 percent interest in Metropoint II, a 150,000-square-foot office building in Denver, CO, originally developed as a joint venture with Miller Global Properties.
- Acquired Two Lafayette Centre, a 131,000-square-foot office building in Washington, D.C.'s central business district.

Shortcomings to Bear in Mind

- The leasing of real estate is highly competitive. Equity Office's properties compete for tenants with similar properties situated in its markets, primarily on the basis of location, rent charged, services provided and the design and condition of improvements.

  The company also experiences competition when attempting to acquire interests in desirable real estate, including competition from domestic and foreign financial institutions, other REITs, life insurance companies, pension trusts, trust funds, partnerships and individual investors.
- Many investors buy shares in real estate investment trusts to achieve high income. In this regard, they may be disappointed with Equity Office Properties Trust, since its dividend yield is below the REIT industry average. "Nevertheless," said Standard & Poor's, "EOP is a well-run REIT and can be considered one of the blue chips of the industry. The trust's chairman, Sam Zell, is one of the most successful U.S. real estate investors. EOP's geographically diversified portfolio insulates it from regional

recessions and overbuilding, and provides it with certain economies of scale. The REIT is also conservatively capitalized, with a high interest coverage ratio and a solid debt-to-total capitalization ratio."

Reasons to Buy

- In June 2000, Equity Office Properties closed a $4.5-billion merger with Cornerstone Properties, Inc. The transaction enhanced EOP's presence in twelve key markets and brought the company's total national portfolio of nearly 100 million square feet of office space.
- Since the company's IPO in 1997, it has met or exceeded analyst projections every quarter. Funds from operations (FFO) is the earnings equivalent by which REITs are evaluated. Equity Office's FFO, on a fully diluted per-share basis has increased 70 percent since the IPO. In 2000 alone, the company's revenues increased 16.6 percent, and net operating income increased 16.5 percent. As a result, EOP's FFO increased by 11.3 percent
- The strength of the company's earnings and cash flow allowed it to increase its dividend for the third consecutive year as a public company. Since mid-1997, the company's dividend has increased by 50 percent.

- Equity Office Properties is well-positioned to sustain this growth, according Timothy H. Callahan, the company's CEO. "We believe that on average, our existing rents are more than 30 percent below current market rents. We expect to realize this embedded growth as new leases are signed at current market-level rents. Over the next five years, approximately 11 percent to 13 percent of our leases expire annually, giving us strong growth potential. The nature of this primary revenue stream—long-term leases with over 6,800 businesses across all industries—helps insulate Equity Office from economic downturns. Finally, our geographic diversity also mitigates our exposure to regional downturns."
- According to Mr. Callahan, "commercial real estate has never been better positioned to head into a slowing economy. Property market fundamentals remain strong—with low-to-moderate vacancy rates across the country, moderate new supply coming on line, and continued, though slowing, growth in the number of jobs being created.
- In 2001, Equity Office Properties Trust was named in *Fortune* magazine's Most Admired list as the number one company in the real estate sector. EOP also scored among the top 5 percent among companies in all industries.

Total assets: $ 18,794 million
Current ratio: NA
Return on 2000 equity: 5.84%
Common shares outstanding: 307 million

	2000	1999	1998	1997	1996	1995	1994	1993
Revenues (millions)	2264	1942	1680	752*				
Net income (millions)	473	442	357	282				
Earnings per share	1.53	1.52	1.24	1.11				
Funds from operations	2.86	2.57	2.33	0.89				
Dividends per share	1.74	1.58	1.38	0.56				
Price High	33.5	29.4	32.0	34.7				
Low	22.9	20.8	20.2	21.0				

* Statistical information only available since the company went public in 1997.

Ethan Allen Interiors, Inc.

Ethan Allen Drive □ Danbury, Connecticut 06811 □ Investor contact: Margaret (Peg) W. Lupton (203) 743-8234 □ Web site: www.ethanallen.com □ Dividend reinvestment plan is not available □ Fiscal year ends June 30 □ Listed: NYSE □ Ticker symbol: ETH □ S&P rating: Not rated □ Value Line financial strength rating: B+

Ethan Allan is now selling its wares over the Internet. In an effort to extend its reach and supplement traditional marketing efforts, the company has expanded and redesigned its Web site to allow for the direct sale of more than 5,000 home-furnishing products.

Analysts believe the company is uniquely positioned to leverage its widely recognized brand name and favorable reputation to swiftly develop a valuable e-commerce endeavor. What's more, Ethan Allen's extensive distribution network and integrated retail structure provides it with a competitive advantage in servicing online customers.

Most other furniture producers have been reluctant to establish an Internet retail presence—such a move would alienate its retail and wholesale customers. For its part, Ethan Allen has no such fears; its furniture is marketed exclusively through its own network of captive stores.

Company Profile

Ethan Allen, one of the ten largest manufacturers of household furniture in the United States, sells a full range of furniture products and decorative accessories through a network of 309 retail stores, of which eighty-two are company-owned. Retail stores are located in the United States, Canada, and Mexico, with more than twenty located overseas. The company has twenty manufacturing facilities and three saw mills located throughout the United States.

The company's stores are scattered across the country, with outlets in nearly every state. However, there are more than a dozen outlets in such states as California,

Texas, and Florida. There is a also a concentrated cluster of Ethan Allen stores along the Eastern seaboard in such states as New Jersey, Connecticut, and Massachusetts.

Within this fragmented industry, the company has the largest domestic furniture retail network utilizing the gallery concept. Comparable-store sales have benefited from a repositioning of the product mix to appeal to a broader consumer base, a program to renovate or relocate existing stores, plus more frequent advertising and promotional campaigns.

Ethan Allen is pursuing an aggressive growth strategy, including investments in technology, employee training, and new stores. Margins have been enhanced by manufacturing efficiencies, lower interest expense, and a strengthening of the upholstery and accessory lines.

With an efficient and flexible vertically integrated structure, a strong, dedicated retail network, an impressive 95 percent brand-name recognition, and a sixty-eight-year reputation for exceptional quality and service, Ethan Allen is uniquely positioned as a dominant force in the home furnishings industry.

As Ethan Allen enters the new millennium, the company's philosophy of design remains the same as it was when it was founded sixty-eight years ago. Styles may have changed from colonial to eclectic, but the company's commitment to exceptional quality, classical design elements, innovative style, and functionality will continue to position Ethan Allen as a preferred brand for years to come.

In keeping with the way consumers live today, the company has organized its product programs into two broad style categories. "Classic" encompasses more historically inspired styles, from early European and French influences to designs from the eighteenth- and nineteenth-century masters. "Casual," on the other hand, captures a clean, contemporary line and an updated country aesthetic.

Shortcomings to Bear in Mind

- This stock is labeled aggressive growth because it has a high beta coefficient of 1.50. A beta of 1 indicates a stock that fluctuates with the market. High betas are indicative of stocks that can be volatile.
- The stock of Ethan Allen can be sensitive to the cyclical whims of furniture demand. For instance, when interest rates rise, housing starts are hurt, as is the furniture industry.

Reasons to Buy

- The company has been reducing its debt in recent years. In 1995, debt as a percentage of capitalization was 40 percent. In the years since, this figure has declined to 28 percent, 20 percent, and 4 percent (at the end of 2000).
- Ethan Allen benefits from vertical integration. Because the company controls many aspects of its operations, it is self-sufficient, efficient, and cost-effective. Business decisions regarding everything from sales events to manufacturing locations are made by Ethan Allen management. That way, the company can position its strategies based on what works best. In other words, the company has eliminated the middle man and the waste, and it is able to avoid bottlenecks. This translates into productivity, increased efficiency, satisfied customers, and steadily climbing profits.
- These efforts are paying off. In fiscal 2000, sales increased an impressive 12.3 percent. Earnings per share advanced 14.6 percent. After paying

$61.3 million in taxes, the company generated an impressive $104.9 million in cash flow, of which $54.7 million was used for capital expenditures to strengthen the company's manufacturing and retail operations. What's more, $49.6 million was spent to repurchase ETH shares in the open market. At the end of 2000, Ethan Allen remained virtually free of debt.

- In 2000, the company's retail network was strengthened with the opening of fifteen new stores in important markets. This continues Ethan Allen's strategy of opening new stores or relocating existing ones to the right trading areas. Today, virtually all of the company's store facades reflect Ethan Allen's fresh, new exterior look. The company has also updated seventy-eight stores with an easy-to-shop interior format.

  The company's new stores are situated in high-traffic shopping areas for customer convenience. Many existing stores have been relocated to better-traveled retail routes. For example, in June 2000, management relocated its Akron, Ohio store less than one mile from its previous location. The company expanded the square footage to take advantage of the more accessible location. By making these changes, the store increased traffic by an impressive 66 percent. In just a few months, moreover, sales were up 50 percent.
- In the realm of advertising, the company allocated over $70 million in a multimedia campaign using a combination of TV, radio, direct mail, e-mail, and print advertising that breaks through the clutter and establishes a strong preference for the Ethan Allen brand. In fact, in 1999 the company was awarded its fourth award for effectiveness in advertising.

  The company's message is being conveyed to the public in a variety of ways. Its television campaign spans twenty-seven weeks of the year, much of which is during prime time. Ethan Allen boasts the largest direct mail campaign in its industry, with more than seventy million direct-mail pieces each year.

Once inside the store, the customer is offered a complimentary copy of *The Treasury of American Home Interiors*, which contains the company's complete product line, enabling the customer to continue shopping at home. Finally, the company's Web site now allows customers to shop and learn about the Ethan Allen brand on the Internet twenty-four hours a day.

- The company's new Simple Finance Plan is an impressive consumer payment program. Now, even consumers on a budget can enjoy their furnishings while they pay for them. With this plan, customers can choose a payment plan that they can afford. First, a line of credit is approved, then the customer selects a payment term and a fixed monthly payment is calculated. It is similar in principle to an auto loan but gives the customer the ability to add on additional purchases.

The plan holds some unique benefits over traditional financing. The company's current low annual percentage rate of 9.99 percent in the United States (11.99 percent in Canada) is very competitive and is much lower than most credit card and bank loan rates.

- Operating a store in today's environment is a complicated business if management doesn't have the right structure in place. Ethan Allen is convinced that "You need to be able to keep the store beautiful and inspiring, help customers select the right products, train and motivate the sales staff, grow a complicated custom business, make accessory house calls, and anticipate customer service requests—all at the same time."

To respond to these demands, Ethan Allen began testing new ways to staff its stores. For example, at its corporate headquarters in Danbury, Connecticut, management looked at its needs—especially on high-traffic weekends—and created an environment to better support the designers who were working on the front lines.

First, the company established the right sales management structure so that designers were able to obtain the training and direction they needed to build their businesses. Then Ethan Allen added specialists in the soft goods and accessories areas to help designers sell more of the complicated product programs. In addition, the company also added a merchandise manager to keep the store beautiful and a customer service specialist to address delivery and service issues. Since this structure has been in place, traffic in the Danbury store increased about 19 percent. During that same period, the store's written business jumped up 35 percent.

- Running a custom business that offers hundred of frames, thousands of fabrics, and endless combinations is a challenge in itself. Running it profitably is even harder. At Ethan Allen, the company does it by marrying state-of-the-art technology with smart work processes and trained processionals.

For instance, new technology like the fabric-cutting machine in operation at the company's Maiden, North Carolina facility is changing the way Ethan Allen does business. Using a computerized mapping system and automated cutting mechanism, the machine can cut perfectly matched pieces on a very complicated fabric pattern with precision and accuracy. In addition to eliminating the cost of human error, the machine allows the company to triple its output using fewer people. Plans are underway to install this technology in Ethan Allen's other upholstery plants.

Total assets: $544 million
Current ratio: 2.18
Common shares outstanding: 41.2 million
Return on 2000 shareholders' equity: 24.4%

	2000	1999	1998	1997	1996	1995	1994	1993
Revenues (millions)	856	762	693	572	510	476	437	384
Net income (millions)	91	81	72	49	28	23	23	deficit
Earnings per share	2.20	1.92	1.63	1.11	.65	.52	.51	deficit
Dividends per share	.16	.12	.09	.06	.01	nil	nil	nil
Price High	33.8	37.8	44.4	28.6	13.0	8.3	10.7	10.5
Low	20.5	24.7	15.7	12.3	6.5	5.7	6.5	5.4

GROWTH AND INCOME

ExxonMobil Corporation

5959 Las Colinas Boulevard ▢ Irving, Texas 75039-2298 ▢ Investor contact: Peter Townsend (972) 444-1000 ▢ Dividend reinvestment program is available: (800) 252-1800 ▢ Web site: www.exxonmobil.com ▢ Listed: NYSE ▢ Ticker symbol: XOM ▢ S&P rating: A- ▢ Value Line financial strength rating: A++

The use of petroleum and other forms of fossil fuels is not likely to become obsolete, despite the burgeoning growth of the Internet and high technology. For its part, ExxonMobil is convinced that the energy savings on the manufacturing and production side will be offset by "energy consuming purchases" made by workers with more money to spend.

"That means more houses, bigger houses, more cars, faster cars," according to Kathleen B. Cooper, chief economist with ExxonMobil. "All you have to do is look around North Dallas—and a lot of other cities around the United States—and you can see that that's going on. And obviously, this means more energy use."

To be sure, online buying may cut down on trips to the local mall, a potential energy saving. "But what it will also require is a lot more of those UPS trucks driving around the neighborhood delivering goods."

Ms. Cooper admitted that the use of solar and wind power will grow rapidly over the next two decades. Even so, those forms of energy will remain minuscule as a percentage of the total energy supply in the United States and throughout the world, less than one-half of one percent.

Finally, the ExxonMobil economist says that world oil demand, which expanded from just over 60 million barrels a day in 1980 to about 77 million barrels in 2000, will have a further increase of 36 million barrels a day by 2020.

Company Profile

Mobil Corporation ceased to exist at the end of November 1999 after government regulators approved the company's $81-billion acquisition by Exxon, reuniting the two largest pieces of the Standard Oil monopoly nearly ninety years after trustbusters split them apart. As a result of this merger, ExxonMobil has passed Royal Dutch Petroleum as the world's largest petroleum company in terms of oil and gas reserves.

The Federal Trade Commission, following an eleven-month review, overcame its initial skepticism about the deal and blessed it, having forced the companies to shed as much as $2 billion in service stations and other assets. Commenting on the decision, Exxon's CEO, Lee R. Raymond, said the two companies were creating "the world's premier petroleum and petrochemical company" and estimated that savings from the merger would exceed the $2.8 billion over three years that the companies had originally anticipated.

Merger Requirements of
the Federal Trade Commission

The companies' chemicals and technology businesses were not affected. The bulk of the divestitures came in the refining and marketing sectors. In the United States, ExxonMobil was required to sell one refinery; this represented about 2 percent of the company's refining capacity. The remaining worldwide refining networks leads the industry, with 50 refineries and total capacity of 6.4 million barrels a day.

In addition, XOM (prior to the merger, the symbol was XON) was required to divest some 770 company-owned or leased service stations in the United States and to assign contracts to new suppliers. These changes affected more than 1,600 stations owned by branded distributors and others. In Europe, Mobil was required to sell its 30 percent interest in the BP/Mobil joint-venture fuels business and its 28 percent interest in the German joint-venture marketing company Aral.

These divestitures should be viewed in the context of the more than 45,000 remaining Exxon, Mobil, and Esso stations worldwide. Here at home, despite the refinery and service station divestitures, XOM's combined refining and marketing business is far stronger than either one of the companies had before.

Shortcomings to Bear in Mind

■ Analysts said the robust results of 2000 might be hard to beat in 2001 because oil prices may not match 2000, when oil stayed above $30 a barrel for much of the year. According to Fadel Gheit, an analyst with Fahnestock & Company,

"It really will require a lot of stars lining up right for them to have as good a year as 2000."

■ Exxon has one of the worst reputations among multinationals, according to a survey of 10,830 people in 1999 by Harris Interactive Inc. and the Reputation Institute, a New York research group. Survey respondents, citing leftover ill will from the Valdez spill and a perception of corporate arrogance, rated Exxon (prior to the merger with Mobil) not much better than Philip Morris, a tobacco company held in contempt by a large part of the public.

While other CEOs court Wall Street, Exxon's Lee Raymond meets with analysts only rarely and routinely castigates at least one analyst per meeting. Contrast Mr. Raymond's reclusiveness, enmity, and lack of charm with the more cordial and affable personalities of the CEOs of Exxon's major rivals: BP Amoco and Royal Dutch Petroleum. As their companies have undergone dramatic changes, BP's Sir John Browne and Shell's Mark Moody-Stuart often have spoken on issues such as the environment and corporate responsibility and have not been reluctant to present their respective corporate financial pictures to the investment community.

■ The 1989 Exxon Valdez oil spill may be a distant memory, but the courts are still working on it. In the fall of 2000, the Supreme Court refused to consider the company's argument about irregularities during jury deliberations. The court let stand the $5 billion in damages that ExxonMobil has to pay stemming from the tanker spill that polluted more than 1,000 miles of shoreline, killing tens of thousands of birds and marine mammals and disrupting fishing. However, the company has other appeals pending. Thus, the court's action doesn't require payment of punitive damages to fishermen and others affected by the spill—the second-largest such award in a U.S. commercial lawsuit. "This decision does not affect the major appeals," said ExxonMobil spokesman Tom Cirigliano. "We continue to believe the $5-billion award was unwarranted and excessive." ExxonMobil said that it has paid $300 million to compensate fishing boat operators, native Alaskans, and others, $2.2 billion to clean up the pollution, and $1 billion for conservation and education programs.

Reasons to Buy

- Originally, management felt that the merger would produce pre-tax synergies (cost savings and profit-improvement items) of some $2.8 billion per year three years after the merger. After a year of merger planning, the company concluded that near-term merger synergies would be considerably higher. Exxon Mobil expects synergies directly attributable to the merger itself to amount to $3.8 billion annually on a pre-tax basis. In addition, management expects cost and margin improvements from its traditional efficiency programs.

- In the important "upstream sector," Mr. Raymond believes that "our exploration and production portfolio of complementary assets is the best in the industry. We are the world's largest private-sector producer of oil and gas combined, and we continue to expand our excellent position in many of the world's most exciting and rapidly emerging oil and gas areas."

- With 17 billion cubic feet of sales a day, ExxonMobil is the world's largest non-government marketer of natural gas. These sales, many of which are underpinned by long-term contracts, produce a strong positive cash flow and provide a solid platform for growth. The company markets gas in North and South America, Europe, the Middle East, and Asia Pacific, with pipeline and LNG (liquid natural gas) sales in more than twenty-five countries—in some regions for more than seventy-five years.

ExxonMobil has access to a diverse portfolio of both mature gas fields and new gas development totaling 57 trillion cubic feet of proved gas reserves and more than 180 trillion cubic feet of discovered resources, providing a solid base for profitable growth. The company is actively pursuing opportunities to develop and bring to market very large resources in areas such as the Middle East, Africa, Russia, Asia, Alaska, eastern Canada, Bolivia, and Europe. The company's proprietary (LNG), gas-to-liquids, gas pipeline, and power generation technologies, coupled with gas marketing expertise, are key to commercializing large remote gas resources in many areas around the world.

- ExxonMobil has an ownership interest in fifty refineries in twenty-seven countries, with 6.4 million barrels of distillation capacity a day. Seventeen of these refineries have lube base-stock manufacturing facilities with a capacity of 156,000 barrels a day. XOM operates thirty-four refineries, with the balance operated under joint-venture agreements.

- ExxonMobil markets gasoline and other fuel products at more than 45,000 branded service stations in 118 countries. Its affiliates serve aviation customers at 700 airports in eighty countries, marine customers at 150 ports in sixty countries, and some one million industrial and wholesale customers in fifty countries. The company markets under three of the best-known brands in the world: Exxon, Mobil, and Esso.

- ExxonMobil had a banner year in 2000 as it benefited from sharply rising oil and gas prices. However, XOM was better-positioned than any other oil giant to capitalize on the price increase, and that was largely the doing of Mr. Raymond.

Under Mr. Raymond, a Ph.D. chemical engineer named chairman in 1994, the company has set new standards of capital and cost efficiency in an industry that has been careening from boom to bust for the past hundred years. "Exxon is the Rolls Royce engine of the oil business—extremely efficient," said Fadel Gheit, an analyst with Fahnestock & Company.

■ ExxonMobil announced the success of two wells drilled in 2000 in the Crazy Horse Exploration Unit, situated in the Gulf of Mexico some 125 miles southeast of New Orleans. The wells confirmed Crazy Horse to be a world-class discovery. Exxon Mobil owns a 25 percent interest in the Crazy Horse Unit, with BP, the operator, owning 75 percent.

The Crazy Horse appraisal well, drilled in Mississippi Canyon Block 822, added new oil pay reservoirs to those encountered in the Crazy Horse discovery. The results confirm that Crazy Horse is at least a billion-barrel discovery, making Crazy Horse the largest oil field discovered in the U.S. Gulf of Mexico. Initial production is expected by 2005 from a floating production facility that will be capable of producing 250,000 barrels of oil per day when it reaches its peak.

■ In 2001, ExxonMobil said it had completed an expansion at the Yanpet joint venture petrochemical complex at Yanbu, Saudi Arabia. Included in the expansion is a second 800,000-ton-per-year cracker, a new 535,000-ton-per-year polyethylene plant, and a new 410,000-ton-per-year ethylene glycol plant. Yanpet is a 50-50 joint venture between Mobil Yanbu Petrochemical Company, a subsidiary of ExxonMobil, and Saudi Basic Industries Corporation.

Total assets: $144,521 million
Current ratio: 0.99
Common shares outstanding: 1,738 million
Return on 2000 shareholders' equity: 24.8%

	2000	1999	1998	1997	1996	1995	1994	1993
Revenues (billions)	233	185	106	120	117	108	101	100
Net income (millions)	16910	8380	6440	8155	6975	6380	4611	5280
Earnings per share	2.41	1.19	1.31	1.62	1.40	1.28	.92	1.06
Dividends per share	.88	.84	.82	.82	.78	.75	.73	.72
Price High	48.2	43.7	38.7	33.7	25.6	21.5	16.8	17.3
Low	35.0	32.2	28.3	24.2	19.4	15.1	14.1	14.5

AGGRESSIVE GROWTH

FedEx Corporation

942 South Shady Grove Road □ Memphis, Tennessee 38120 □ Investor contact: Jeff Smith (901) 818-7037 □ Web site: www.fdxcorp.com □ Direct purchase only, no dividend paid: (800) 446-2617 □ Fiscal year ends May 31 □ Listed: NYSE □ Ticker symbol: FDX □ S&P rating: B □ Value Line financial strength rating: B++

The U.S. Postal Service said in early 2001 that it had struck a seven-year, $6.3-billion alliance with FedEx for air delivery of priority, express, and first-class mail. The service began in August 2001. With the Postal Service expected to lose more than $1 billion in 2001, Postmaster General William J. Henderson said tapping FedEx's fleet of more than 600 planes will give consumers better service at lower cost.

The United States Postal Service had been searching for a company to handle its express and priority mail. That job had previously been handled primarily by Emery Worldwide Airlines. But postal officials said that the deal with Emery had been too costly and inefficient.

Under the new pact, FedEx carries up to 3.5 million pounds of Postal Service mail a day, or the capacity of about thirty wide-body DC-10 airplanes. To meet the demand, FedEx had to hire some 500 new pilots and about 1,000 new mechanics and cargo handlers.

Company Profile

Launched in 1973, FedEx Corporation (formerly FDX Corp.) is the world's leading provider of guaranteed express delivery services. The company offers a wide range of express delivery services for the time-definite transportation of documents, packages, and freight. Commercial and military charter services are also offered by FedEx. The company operates in the United States, France, England, Canada, and Japan. During fiscal 2000, the company acquired Tower Group International & World Tariff Limited. Transportation and logistics services accounted for 83 percent of revenues in fiscal 2000; ground small-package carrier services 11 percent; and other carrier and logistics services 6 percent.

FedEx reported sales of $18.26 billion in the fiscal year ended May 31, 2000. This represented an increase of 8.8 percent over the previous year. Sales at FedEx have increased during each of the prior five years (and since 1995 sales have climbed a total of 94 percent).

Shortcomings to Bear in Mind

- According to management, "We are a very capital-intensive business. To do what we do takes big wide-bodied planes—and lots of them. It takes trucks and vans and large, costly operating hubs, both across America and abroad. It takes a lot of information and telecommunications devices, whether it be scanners and radios in the trucks or what-have-you."

On the other hand, FedEx's global network is now more or less complete, and that will make a big difference, not least because investors can expect the pace of capital spending to decline sharply.

- FedEx is more vulnerable than UPS to a downturn in the economy. That's because it has far too much overhead and unused capacity. It's not surprising that FedEx nets (before interest and taxes) only 7 cents on the revenue dollar, compared with fifteen cents for UPS, which has a work force that is much more unionized. "There is no question that our margins are not high enough, and we need to them get them into double-digit range," said Alan B. Graf Jr., the company's chief financial officer.

Reasons to Buy

- FedEx became the official worldwide delivery service sponsor of the National Football League beginning in the fall of 2000. The three-year agreement gave FedEx NFL marketing rights domestically and worldwide. FedEx also is now an official sponsor of the thirty-two NFL teams, Super Bowl, and Pro Bowl. The company also sponsors:
  - FedEx Field, the home of the NFL's Washington Redskins.
  - The FedEx Orange Bowl, host of the 2000 college football national championship game.
  - The FedEx St. Jude Classic PGA tournament, which raises money for the St. Jude's Children's Research Hospital.
  - The FedEx Championship Series, the country's premier open-wheel racing circuit (CART—Championship Auto Racing Teams).

- USA Basketball—America's men's and women's Olympic teams.
- The Ferrari Formula One racing team in Europe.

■ Increasingly, businesses are seeking strategic, cost-effective ways to manage their supply chains—the series of transportation and information exchanges required to convert parts and raw materials into finished, delivered products. According to management: "Experience tells us that customers prefer one supplier to meet all of their distribution and logistics needs. And FedEx has what it takes: Our unique global network, operational expertise, and air route authorities cannot be replicated by the competition. With FedEx, our customers have a strategic competitive weapon to squeeze time, mass, and cost from the supply chain."

■ In a deal worth $1.2 billion, FedEx bought American Freightways Corporation in 2000. It extended the reach of the company's less-than-truckload (LTL) freight business to forty-eight states, up from eleven states (through Viking Freight, mostly on the West Coast). At the time of the acquisition, American Freightways was the fourth-largest less-than-truckload carrier in the United States. By combining its operations with Viking Freight, FedEx now has the nation's second largest less-than-truckload carrier. "By joining forces, this new FedEx LTL freight group can sell a more complete package of multiregional services and capture business that previously went to the competitors," said Douglas G. Duncan who became president and CEO of the new FedEx freight group overseeing American and Viking.

■ In an effort to make it easier to return merchandise using the Internet, FedEx significantly expanded the capabilities of its system that enables customers and merchants to process package returns electronically. In the fall of 2000, the company announced that its NetReturn system (then three years old) would let customers print a shipping label generated on a PC.

The system also provides the customer with nearby drop-off locations for the return package. Up until then the return service required parcel pickup by FedEx, which often made the system inconvenient. FedEx made this move in hopes that the enhancements would make its system more appealing to current users such as Apple Computer and Hewlett-Packard, as well as to fend off UPS when that company rolled out its online returns system in the early part of 2001. This move by FedEx is an indication that shipping companies and retailers are trying to find ways to avoid repeating the problems of the prior Christmas, when many online retailers were unable to cope with the avalanche of gift returns.

■ FedEx, the world's largest express transportation company, and Tianjin-based Datian W. Air Service Corporation announced in mid-2000 the formation of a joint venture in Beijing. According to the company, this is a "joint venture dedicated to providing unparalleled international express services for customers with shipping requirements to and from China. Federal Express-DTW Co. Ltd. represents the first joint venture in FedEx's global network, bringing together two powerhouses in the express transportation industry. With a strong network and a proven track record in the Chinese marketplace, Datian is an ideal partner for FedEx."

■ When a large corporation decentralizes shipping, it's like a computer's circuitry firing at random: interesting pyrotechnics but not very productive. That's why Unisys chose to harness the buying power of hundreds of sales offices, service locations, and manufacturing sites by utilizing the transportation management services of FDX. Unisys employees simply call a toll-free number staffed by Caliber Logistics. Caliber distribution experts rely on FedEx to ship everything from critical replacement parts to Unisys enterprise servers directly to the customer site. Each shipping decision reflects the most appropriate and cost-effective delivery solution.

- What the stock market seems to be overlooking right now is that for all the books and computers and corduroy britches consumers buy from today's Internet retailers, someone has to deliver the goods. In millions of instances, that someone is FedEx. This helps explain how FedEx has been able to keep growing.

- FedEx has invested heavily in recent years to develop an international infrastructure. It presently can reach locations accounting for 90 percent of world GDP, with twenty-four- or forty-eight-hour service. International delivery services for documents and freight have been growing faster than domestic business in recent years.

- Federal Express, which shut down much of its loss-plagued European delivery business in the early 1990s, began a major expansion in the region. Buoyed by improving global economic conditions and the success of its transatlantic delivery service, FedEx rolled out an expanded schedule of intra-European cargo flights in 2000, offering a new intra-European overnight delivery service called EuroOne. At the same time, the company opened a long-awaited $200-million regional air hub in Paris and continued to add flights and bigger airplanes over the following year.

- FedEx is making a concerted effort to augment its home-delivery business. In February 2001 the company said it was opening delivery offices in eighty-five additional cities, a move that boosted its coverage of the nation to 70 percent—compared with 100 percent for its competitors. This latest move brings it closer to its goal of having delivery in 98 percent of the United States by 2002—one year earlier than when it started the business in March 2000.

Total assets: $11,527 million
Current ratio: 1.20
Common shares outstanding: 285 million
Return on 2000 shareholders' equity: 14.6%

	2000	1999	1998	1997	1996	1995	1994	1993
Revenues (millions)	18257	16773	15703	11520	10274	9392	8480	7808
Net income (millions)	688	531	526	348	308	282	204	110
Earnings per share	2.32	2.10	1.75	1.51	1.35	1.25	.92	.51
Dividends per share	Nil							
Price　High	49.8	61.9	46.6	42.3	22.5	21.5	20.2	18.2
Low	30.6	34.9	21.8	21.0	16.7	14.7	13.4	11.1

CONSERVATIVE GROWTH

Gannett Company, Inc.

1100 Wilson Blvd. □ Arlington, Virginia 22234 □ Investor contact: Gracia Martore (703) 284-6918 □ Dividend reinvestment plan is available: (800) 778-3299 □ Web site: www.gannett.com □ Listed: NYSE □ Ticker symbol: GCI □ S&P rating: A □ Value Line financial strength rating: A++

As the Internet continues to be a growing part of people's lives, more Gannett newspapers are jumping into the World Wide Web. What's more, the online pioneers continue to enhance content and add new products, including those stemming from Gannett's participation in Classified Ventures and CareerPath.com.

As leading information providers for their communities, the company's newspapers are aware that fresh information is essential to success online. Florida Today's Space Online (*www.spaceonline.com*), for instance, covers space shuttle launches—literally—as they blast off. Reporters with laptop computers file stories from the beach at Cape Canaveral, supplying live news online within moments of a launch.

Company Profile

Gannett is an international news and information company that publishes ninety-nine daily newspapers in the United States, including *USA Today*, the nation's largest-selling daily newspaper.

The company also owns more than 300 nondaily publications in the United States and *USA Weekend*, a weekly newspaper magazine. In the United Kingdom, Gannett subsidiary Newsquest PLC (acquired in mid-1999) publishes nearly 300 titles, including fifteen daily newspapers with a combined circulation of about 600,000. Gannett also operates twenty-two television stations in the United States.

Operations Worldwide

Gannett is an international company with headquarters in Arlington, Virginia, and operations in forty-three states, the District of Columbia, Guam, the United Kingdom, Germany, and Hong Kong.

Newspapers

Gannett is the largest domestic newspaper group, in terms of circulation. The company's ninety-nine daily newspapers in the United States have a combined daily paid circulation of 7.8 million. They include *USA Today*, with a circulation of about 2.3 million. *USA Today* is available in sixty countries.

In addition, Gannett owns a variety of nondaily publications and *USA Weekend*, a weekly newspaper magazine with a circulation of 21.8 million, delivered on Sundays in 563 Gannett and non-Gannett newspapers.

Newsquest PLC, the wholly owned Gannett subsidiary also publishes a variety of nondaily publications, including *Berrow's Worcester Journal*, the oldest continuously published newspaper in the world.

Broadcasting

The company owns and operates twenty-two television stations covering 17.5 percent of the United States.

On the Internet

Gannett has more than 100 Web sites in the United States and the United Kingdom, including *USATODAY.com*, the number one newspaper site on the Internet.

Other Ventures

Other company operations include Gannett News Service; Gannett Retail

Advertising Group; Gannett TeleMarketing, Inc.; Gannett New Business and Product Development; Gannett Direct Marketing Services; Gannett Offset, a commercial printing operation; and Gannett Media Technologies International.

Shortcomings to Bear in Mind

- The NBC television network and Gannett Broadcasting signed a new arrangement early in 2000, cutting the amount of money NBC will pay Gannett to carry its shows. The move underscores a mounting struggle over the traditional financial relationship between broadcast networks and local television stations.

    Those familiar with the five-year pact between the two companies said it dramatically reduces the more than $25 million payment of so-called affiliate compensation that NBC annually pays the broadcaster. By the end of the deal, the network's payments to Gannett are expected to sink to the $10-million level.

    For decades the big networks have paid local stations to carry their programming—a practice they are now looking to eliminate. The networks argue that they should end, or at least dramatically reduce, affiliate compensation; longer term, they want the affiliates to pay them. For their part, affiliates counter that the networks are risking their strong distribution, and the stage is being set for some tough negotiations in the future.

- Douglas H. McCorkindale, president and CEO of Gannett, said at the end of 2000 that "2001 promises to be another record year for the company. But, it will be a more challenging one with the absence of Olympics, and election and millennium ad spending and much tougher newsprint comparisons, particularly in the first half of the year."

- Some people consider newspapers a dying medium. In 1990, for instance, 113 million Americans read dailies; today, only 76.6 million do. Classifieds, which account for 27 percent of Gannett's annual revenues, seem destined to move to the Web.

Reasons to Buy

- In mid-2000, Gannett invested $2.6 billion with the purchase of Central Newspapers Inc., owner of the *Arizona Republic* and the *Indianapolis Star*. A month earlier, the company acquired twenty-one newspapers from Thompson Newspapers for just over $1.1 billion.

    The *Arizona Republic* in Phoenix has a weekday circulation of more than 400,000, making it Gannett's second largest paper (*USA Today*, with a circulation of 2.2 million, is the largest). With the Central Newspaper acquisition, Gannett obtains two flagship papers. Notably, the company now has a strong presence in Phoenix where it owns both the *Arizona Republic* and the market's NBC affiliate, KPNX television. The federal government frowns on anyone owning a TV station and a newspaper in the same market. However, the Federal Communications Commission (FCC) is not likely to crack down on Gannett until 2006 when the station's license comes up for renewal. Gannett is banking on the FCC relaxing its rule against this practice by that time.

- Convergence became a reality at Gannett in July 2000 when USA Today Live debuted to cover the Concorde crash near Paris, according to Tom Curley, president and publisher of *USA Today*. Mr. Curley said that USA Today Live takes *USA Today*'s content and makes it available to Gannett televison stations. Reporters from *USA Today* can now provide coverage in the nation's largest newspaper, on one of the most popular news Web sites, and by the largest local affiliate station group. "Nobody else in media can make that claim," Mr. Curley said.

- Gannett has ninety-five domestic newspaper Web sites, including *USATODAY.com*, the number one newspaper site and a leading general news site on the Internet. The company also has Web sites in all of its nineteen television markets. In addition, all of Newsquest's newspapers have an Internet presence. For 2000, the company generated about $63 million in revenue from Internet activities.

- In 1999, Gannett bought the British regional newspaper group, Newsquest PLC, for about $1.7 billion in cash. Newsquest's publications include such major regional newspapers as the *Northern Echo*, based in Darlington, north England, the *Oxford Mail*, the *Evening Argus* in Brighton, south England, and *Westmoreland Gazette* in the Lake District in north England. Newsquest had a pre-tax profit of $204.3 million in 1998 on sales of $483.5 million.

About one-third of Newsquest's newspapers are more than 100 years old. *Berrow's Worcester Journal*, established in 1690, is the oldest continuously published newspaper in the world. While maintaining this fine tradition, Newsquest has been a leader in expanding into new lines of Web-based products and technology. In 1995

Newsquest was the first regional newspaper group in the United Kingdom to launch a Web site. Since then, it has continued to build its Web-based strategy, skill base, and knowledge, with every Newsquest newspaper having an Internet presence. In 1999 it pioneered a new e-commerce service called Shoppers World.

Newsquest also publishes lifestyle and business magazines, local information guides, and seasonal publications. New launches in 1999 included *Limited Edition*, a glossy, high-quality lifestyle magazine, local business news magazines, and a guide to local Web sites.

- In 1999 Gannett elected to get out of cable television, selling all of its properties to Cox Communications of Atlanta for $2.7 billion in cash. Gannett President Douglas H. McCorkindale said the company didn't make a strategic decision to get out of the cable business but decided to sell because "someone just offered us a lot of money." The price of cable franchises has been rising rapidly recently, and Gannett was able to get one of the highest per-household price ever paid—$4,500 to $5,100, depending on how the value is calculated—for its 525,000 subscribers. McCorkindale said the sale would have a "positive" effect on Gannett's earnings. Gannett had owned the cable TV operations for only three-and-a-half years.

Total assets: $12,980 million
Current ratio: 1.12
Common shares outstanding: 264 million
Return on 2000 shareholders' equity: 20.0

	2000	1999	1998	1997	1996	1995	1994	1993
Revenues (millions)	6222	5260	5121	4730	4421	4007	3824	3642
Net income (millions)	972	919	816	713	531	477	465	398
Earnings per share	3.63	3.26	2.86	2.50	1.89	1.71	1.62	1.36
Dividends per share	.86	.82	.78	.74	.71	.68	.67	.64
Price High	81.6	83.6	75.1	61.8	39.4	32.4	29.5	29.1
Low	48.4	60.6	47.6	35.7	29.5	24.8	23.1	23.4

AGGRESSIVE GROWTH

General Dynamics Corporation

3190 Fairview Park Drive □ Falls Church, Virginia 22042-4523 □ Investor contact: W. Raymond Lewis (703) 876-3195 □ Dividend reinvestment plan is not available □ Web site: www.generaldynamics.com □ Listed: NYSE □ Ticker symbol: GD □ S&P rating: B+ □ Value Line financial strength rating: A+

Late in 2000 the U.S. Army selected General Dynamics and General Motors of Canada to supply the Interim Armored Vehicle for a set of new Interim Brigade Combat Teams that can be deployed quickly. The total contract ($4 billion over eight years) is for 2,131 eight-wheeled, nineteen-ton LAV III vehicles that will equip up to six new brigades. The contract includes the Infantry Carrier Vehicle and the Mobile Gun System.

Initially, there had been speculation that the contract would not be awarded to one bidder. "The award is a significant event for General Dynamics," according to a report issued by Credit Suisse First Boston, "because it reaffirms the company's position as the U.S. Army's premier supplier, and it also gives General Dynamics a breadth of products—from the M1A2 tank for the Army's heavy forces down to the LAV III for its lighter forces. It also means that General Dynamics will be evolving along with the Army's attempt to create more mobile, rapidly deployable forces better suited for the post-Cold War environment of peacekeeping and humanitarian missions."

Company Profile

With headquarters in Falls Church, Virginia, General Dynamics has leading market positions in shipbuilding and marine systems, business aviation, information systems, and land and amphibious combat systems. The company has four primary business groups:

Marine Systems

General Dynamics Marine Systems has the broadest range of integration, design, engineering, and production skills in naval shipbuilding. Marine Systems is the U.S. Navy's leading supplier of combat vessels—including nuclear submarines, surface combatants, and auxiliary ships. The group also manages ready-reserve and prepositioning ships and builds commercial vessels.

Aerospace

Gulfstream Aerospace Corporation is the world's leading designer, developer, manufacturer, and marketer of technologically advanced intercontinental business jet aircraft. Gulfstream has produced more than 1,200 aircraft for customers around the world. It offers a full range of aircraft products and services, including the Gulfstream IV-SP, the ultra-long-range Gulfstream V, and the new Gulfstream V-SP. A new company, General Dynamics Aviation Services, has been formed to pursue the worldwide market for aircraft maintenance and refurbishment.

Information Systems and Technology

General Dynamics Information Systems group provides defense and select commercial customers with the infrastructure and systems-integration skills they need to process, communicate, and manage information effectively. It has established a global presence in specialized data acquisition and processing, in advanced electronics, and in the total battlespace information management systems that are key to military superiority in the twenty-first century. It also provides telecommunications solutions and data management services for the commercial market.

Combat Systems

General Dynamics Combat Systems is becoming the world's preferred supplier of land and amphibious combat system development, production, and support. Its product line includes a full spectrum of armored vehicles, light-wheeled reconnaissance vehicles, suspensions, engines, transmissions, guns and ammunition-handling systems, turret and turret-drive systems, and reactive armor and ordnance.

Shortcomings to Bear in Mind

- Although General Dynamics is the largest domestic maker of naval vessels and tanks, end markets for these weapon systems lack growth—or may be shrinking. According to Standard & Poor's, a major statistical and advisory firm, "We're not sanguine about short- or long-term growth prospects of GD's military weapons businesses. Tight global defense budgets, as fundamental changes in global warfare, should temper outsized demand for traditional military hardware, such as GD's tanks, destroyers, and submarines."

- Value Line Survey, a major advisory service, is concerned with the company's aircraft operation. In a report dated March 30, 2001, it said, "Although the Gulfstream unit has been doing well, its recent inventory buildup is troubling."

Reasons to Buy

- Despite the problems experienced by the economy in 2000, General Dynamics fared well. Revenues

advanced 16 percent to $10.4 billion, the highest in the company's history. Net earnings increased 13 percent to $811 million, and per-share earnings expended by 14 percent to $4.03. Free cash flow from operations (after capital expenditures but before corporate and discretionary items) totaled $917 million, outpacing net earnings. Productivity, as measured by sales per employee, improve by 5 percent. Return on shareholders' equity was a very healthy 26 percent, and return on invested capital was also an impressive 24 percent.

- For the second time in two years, General Dynamics made an effort to acquire Newport News Shipbuilding. In 1999, the company offered $1.5 billion, but was rebuffed by Newport News. In late April 2001, it upped the ante to $2.6 billion, and the deal was accepted by both boards.

"Newport News is a solid, well-run company with sustainable revenues and earnings and strong cash flow," said Mr. Chabraja. The merger "provides a wonderful opportunity to save significant amounts of money for the U.S. Navy while retaining both nuclear shipyards."

The combination will make General Dynamics a shipbuilding powerhouse, with control over all the nuclear-powered ships built in the U.S., as well as strong positions making Navy destroyers and auxiliary ships and commercial oil tankers. Finally, the deal strengthens the company's position in competing against Northrop Grumman, which spent $5.1 billion a month earlier to purchase the only other domestic shipmaker, Litton Industries.

- Over the past five years (to the end of 2000), the company's revenues more than tripled, a compound annual growth rate of 28 percent. In the same span, earnings per share more than doubled, with a compound annual growth rate of 17 percent. This growth benefited from the addition of revenues and earnings from businesses GD acquired during the period, along with organic growth (growth that does not include acquisitions) in core businesses that outpaced the rate of growth of the markets in which General Dynamics participates.

Including the acquisition of Primex Technologies late in 2000, the company made a total of eighteen acquisitions during the past five years for a total outlay of $8.1 billion, of which $3.3 billion was in cash.

- Primex Technologies (now called Ordnance and Tactical Systems) is a leading manufacturer of large- and medium-caliber munitions and ball-powder propellant. Ordnance and Tactical Systems contributes components to every NASA Space Shuttle and interplanetary mission and is also a prime contractor for the development of the Army's next-generation tactical weapon, the Objective Crew-Served Weapon.
- Clearly, the past five years have been ones of dramatic growth. Despite significant outlays for acquisitions, moreover, the company ended the period with the strongest balance sheet in the industry, with only minimal debt of $325 million at the end of 2000. In contrast, shareholders' equities was over $3.8 billion. With a strong balance sheet, General Dynamics is well positioned to make additional acquisitions.
- Gulfstream had the most successful year in its history in 2000, producing and delivering more than seventy aircraft. Record North American and international orders totaled eighty-two

aircraft, including twenty to Executive Jet, the world's largest operator of private business jets in the rapidly growing fractional ownership market. This record pace resulted in a backlog of $4.4 billion.

- Gulfstream produces the Gulfstream V and Gulfstream V-SP. The Gulfstream V, the world's first ultra-long-range, large-cabin business jet, is capable of flying 6,500 miles—nonstop from New York to Tokyo—at speeds of up to Mach .885, cruising at altitudes up to 51,000 feet.

The Gulfstream IV-SP is the most popular large-cabin business jet ever manufactured. It has a range of 4,220 nautical miles and can cruise at speeds of up to Mach .85; it has a dispatch reliability rate of 99.7 percent. Like the Gulfstream V, the IV-SP is used in a variety of business, government, and special missions throughout the world.

- In the realm of naval vessels, according to CEO Nicholas D. Chabraja, "I am confident that today's General Dynamics is well positioned to play a central role in virtually any military recapitalization that would ultimately be proposed by the administration and approved by Congress.

"For example, due to well-documented budget constraints, the U.S. Navy's plans call for initiating the construction of an average of only six ships per year for the foreseeable future. The Navy's fleet currently stands at 316 ships, the lowest level since the early 1930s. At a build rate of only six ships per year, the fleet would ultimately fall to about 200 ships. It is hard to believe that any administration could construct a strategy that would bring the fleet below 300 active ships for the first time since World War I, when America first established itself as a true world power.

"Clearly, the case for strengthening the Navy's shipbuilding accounts is strong. And, with three of the nation's six major shipyards, General Dynamics is well positioned to meet any increased demand."

■ The Information Systems and Technology group provides defense and select commercial customers with the infrastructure and systems integration skills they need to process, communicate, and manage information effectively. This group has market-leading positions in the design, deployment, and maintenance of wireline and wireless voice and data networks; command, control, and communications systems; telecommunications system security; encryption; fiber optics; intelligence systems; computing hardware; and life-cycle management and support.

During 2000, Information Systems and Technology companies won significant new work with several key customers. For example, General Dynamics began Army-wide fielding of the Integrated System Control network management system and was awarded a U.S. Army contract for a system that will allow commanders to use electronic messaging on the battlefield.

Another key program for GD is the Pentagon Renovation project, in which a state-of-the-art integrated telecommunications backbone is being installed to meet all of the telecommunications needs of the Pentagon's 25,000 occupants.

■ In a report issued by Credit Suisse First Boston Corporation, the analyst said, "The company has extremely high-quality earnings, an under-leveraged balance sheet, an excellent management team, and relatively low risk related to its defense business."

Total assets: $7,987 million
Current ratio: 1.12
Common shares outstanding: 199 million
Return on 2000 shareholders' equity: 26%

	2000	1999	1998	1997	1996	1995	1994	1993
Revenues (millions)	10359	8959	4970	4062	3581	3067	3058	3143
Net income (millions)	900	715	364	316	270	247	223	207
Earnings per share	4.48	3.54	2.86	2.50	2.14	1.96	1.76	1.65
Dividends per share	1.02	.96	.87	.82	.82	.75	.70	.50
Price High	79.0	75.4	62.0	45.8	37.8	31.5	23.8	30.0
Low	36.3	46.2	40.3	31.6	28.5	21.2	19.0	20.1

General Electric Company

3135 Easton Turnpike □ Fairfield, Connecticut 06431 □ Investor contact: Mark L. Vachon (203) 373-2468 □ Dividend reinvestment plan is available: (800) 786-2543 □ Web site: www.ge.com □ Ticker symbol: GE □ S&P rating: A+ □ Value Line financial strength rating: A++

While the rest of the country sat transfixed in late November 2000 trying to determine who would become the next president of the United States, General Electric made known who would become the next president of that company to succeed the legendary Jack Welch, who will retire at the end of 2001.

As November 2000 drew to a close, three candidates remained in the running: Robert L. Nardelli, president and CEO of GE Power Systems, and W. James McNerney, head of GE Aircraft Engines. In anticipation of their leaving the company, CEO Jack Welch immediately promoted executives to take over their duties.

The winner was Jeffrey R. Immelt, then forty-four, president and chief executive of GE Medical Systems, a $7-billion segment of General Electric. The division, based in Waukesha, Wisconsin, is a world leader in medical diagnostic technology and information systems. Mr. Immelt took over that division in 1997 and has increased profits by 20 percent a year.

Effective at the end of November 2000, Mr. Immelt became president and chairman-elect. In announcing the GE board's decision, Mr. Welch described Immelt as "a natural leader, and ideally suited to lead GE for many years."

Immelt joined GE in 1982 and after a brief stint in corporate marketing held a series of jobs in the company's plastics division. He moved to appliances in 1989, became vice president of consumer service in 1991, and then was made vice president for marketing and product management.

The transition to the top spot was enhanced by Robert Wright and Dennis Dammerman, two GE vice chairmen with extensive experience with the company's broadcasting and finance operations, assuring investors that Mr. Immelt would have qualified tutors to indoctrinate the new CEO with the GE operations he knows least.

Company Profile

General Electric, a superbly managed company, provides a broad range of industrial products and services. Under the stewardship of CEO Jack Welch, GE has transformed itself from operating as a maker of diverse industrial equipment to being a provider of a broad range of commercial and consumer services.

In 1980, manufacturing operations generated about 85 percent of operating profits; currently, services operations generate 70 percent of total operating profits. GE Capital (the company's enormous financing arm and the world's largest non-bank financial operation) alone generates nearly 30 percent of operating profits.

General Electric is one of the world's largest corporations, with 2000 revenues of more than $129 billion. Although GE can trace its origins back to Thomas Edison, who invented the light bulb in 1879, the company was actually founded in 1892.

The company's broad diversification is clearly evident if you examine its components. Operations are divided into two groups: product, service, and media businesses and GE Capital Services (GECS).

Product, service, and media includes eleven businesses: aircraft engines, appliances, lighting, medical systems, NBC, plastics, power systems, electrical distribution and control, information services, motors and industrial systems, and transportation systems.

GECS operates twenty-seven financial businesses clustered in equipment management, specialty insurance, consumer services, specialized financing, and mid-market financing.

Highlights of 2000

- Revenues climbed 16 percent to $129.9 billion, a record.
- Net income rose 19 percent to a record $12.7 billion with fifteen of GE's major businesses posting double-digit earnings gains.
- Operating margin, a key metric of business performance, rose to nearly 19 percent. By contrast, the company struggled for over 100 years to reach the 10 percent level.
- The company made over 100 acquisitions for the fourth consecutive year and moved quickly to acquire Honeywell, whose businesses are, in the words of Mr. Welch, "a perfect complementary fit with our Aircraft Engines, Industrial Systems, and Plastics businesses."
- In 2000, GE continued its share repurchase program, raised the dividend 17 percent, and split the stock 3 for 1.
- GE stock was down 7 percent but outperformed the S&P 500, which was down 10 percent. Share owners who have held GE stock for five years, including 2000, have been rewarded with an average 34 percent total annual return on their investment. Those who held it for a decade, 29 percent; two decades, 23 percent total annual return.

- GE continued to be the world's most honored company—awarded for the fourth straight year *Fortune's* "Most Admired Company in America," as well as, for the third time, "The World's Most Respected Company," by the *Financial Times*.

Shortcomings to Bear in Mind

- In one of the biggest acquisitions in history, General Electric paid $45 billion in the fall of 2000 to acquire Honeywell International Inc., one of the thirty stocks in the Dow Jones Industrial Average. The deal followed an abortive attempt by United Technologies, also a Dow component, to acquire Honeywell. In order to pull the deal off, GE's CEO, Jack Welch, agreed to delay his retirement till the end of 2001 rather than in April of that year.

  In June of 2001, however, the deal fell apart because GE refused to agree to the many demands made by regulators in Europe. In order to appease the European Commission, GE offered a package of remedies, including aerospace divestments with revenues with revenues of $2.2 billion and a commitment to "ring-fence" Gecas, its aircraft leasing arm. But the Commission wanted GE to sell a minority stake in Gecas without giving up control of the subsidiary.

  As negotiations hit a snag, Jeffrey Immelt said, "There will be no more negotiation on the side of GE. We are very far apart as we sit here today, and fundamentally, we are planning our future without Honeywell."

- For nearly two decades under Jack Welch, General Electric has dominated businesses through innovation, efficiency, and toughness. In a host of supposedly mature industries, from aircraft engines to power systems, GE has boosted profits, grabbed market share, and nurtured new products. But this success has not been translated to the business that makes the company a household word—appliances. For years, the division that makes refrigerators, ovens, and dishwashers has suffered from one wrenching problem after another: sagging retail prices, lackluster innovation, prickly relations with union workers, and intense competition with rivals that have sometimes beaten GE to market with innovative products.

In one sense, GE Appliances is such a small part of the GE empire that its disappointing fortunes haven't hurt the company overall. The reason? The appliance operation accounts for less than 3 percent of the company's total revenue. Even so, it remains important to GE's brand identity with consumers. People are much more likely to associate GE with ovens, dishwashers, and refrigerators than with aircraft engines, TV programs, or turbine generators.

Reasons to Buy

- The key to GE's business plan is the requirement that businesses be first or second in market share in their industries. Those that fail to achieve this status are divested.
- General Electric—even before the advent of Honeywell—was one of the major manufacturers of passenger jet engines, and its finance division leases hundreds of airplanes to the world's airlines.
- Jack Welch has developed a defect-reduction program called Six Sigma. Six Sigma contributes mightily to GE's earning growth. Think of sigma as a mark on a bell curve that measures standard deviation. Most companies have between 35,000 and 50,000 defects per million operations, or about 3 sigma. For GE, a defect could be anything from the misbilling of an NBC advertiser to faulty wiring in locomotives. Four years ago, engineers determined that

the company was averaging 35,000 defects per million operations—or about 3.5 sigma. (The higher the sigma, the fewer the errors.) That was a better than average showing, but not enough for Welch's restless mind. He's now maniacal about hitting his goal of reducing defects to the point where errors would be almost nonexistent: 3.4 defects per million, or 6 sigma.

- Despite its huge size, the company continues to demonstrate growth. In the 1990–2000 period, earnings per share climbed from $.40 to $1.27, a compound annual growth rate of 12.2 percent. (The company, moreover, has had twenty-four consecutive annual earnings increases.) In the same ten-year span, dividends per share advanced from $.16 a share to $.57, a growth rate of 13.5 percent.
- NBC has moved aggressively to expand into cable television. The network has stakes in seventeen cable networks, including CNBC, Court TV, and the History Channel. NBC has also moved swiftly in recent years to introduce new entertainment and new channels in Europe, Asia, and Latin America.
- General Electric unveiled two digital imaging systems that it says will transform care in two high-profile medical fields: breast-cancer screening and heart disease. The new products, both thirteen years in development, are intended to replace conventional film-based X-ray equipment with digital technology that provides sharper pictures of breast tissue and coronary arteries. But the price of the new machines could temper their acceptance in the market. The mammography machine, called Senographe 2000D, costs between $400,000 and $500,000, compared with about $100,000 for traditional film-based machines. The cardiovascular system, called GE Innova 2000, is priced at $1 million to $1.3 million and is being introduced into a much larger and more profitable market. GE spent $150

million developing the digital X-ray technology that is at the core of both systems.

■ In early 2001 Jay Leno agreed to a new contract with NBC that will extend his tenure as host of the network's *Tonight* show for another five years. Mr. Leno succeeded Johnny Carson in 1992. After a period when he trailed his late-night rival, David Letterman, Jay Leno has been the consistent leader in late-night shows, and his ratings in 2001 are better than the prior year.

Total assets: $437 billion
Current ratio: 0.76
Common shares outstanding: 9,855 million
Return on 2000 shareholders' equity: 27.5%

	2000	1999	1998	1997	1996	1995	1994	1993
Revenues (millions)	129853	111630	100469	54515	46119	43013	60109	55701
Net income (millions)	12735	10717	9296	8203	7280	6573	5915	4184
Earnings per share	1.27	1.07	.93	.83	.73	.65	.58	.51
Dividends per share	.57	.48	.42	.36	.32	.28	.25	.22
Price High	60.5	53.2	34.6	25.5	17.7	12.2	9.1	8.9
Low	41.6	31.4	23.0	16.0	11.6	8.3	7.5	6.7

GROWTH AND INCOME

General Motors Corporation

100 Renaissance Center □ Detroit, Michigan 48243 □ Investor contact: (313) 556-2044 □ Dividend reinvestment plan is available: (800) 331-9922 □ Web site: www.gm.com □ Listed: NYSE □ Ticker symbol: GM □ S&P rating: B □ Value Line financial strength rating: B++

In a bold move to add some luster and sex appeal to its vehicles, General Motors crossed the Atlantic to find a new car stylist. Anne Asensio, age thirty-nine, joined General Motors in the fall of 2000. She was hired away from French carmaker Renault to help bring a bit of elan to GM's products, which many consumers and industry analysts insist range from merely dull to downright ugly.

One of the top five top designers at Renault, Ms. Asensio was in charge of styling for the company's small and mid-size cars. Asensio had frequent run-ins with engineers at Renault: "They just wanted the car to run properly. I wanted to make sure it looked different." Asensio is tough to match when it comes to drive and determination. With Renault, her grit paid off—she piled up one hit design after another and helped to revive the then-struggling Renault with designs of the popular Megane Scenic minivan and the equally successful Clio subcompact and Twingo minicar.

Company Profile

General Motors Corporation, founded in 1908, is the world's largest vehicle manufacturer. GM designs, manufactures, and markets cars, trucks, automotive systems, heavy-duty transmissions, and locomotives worldwide.

Other substantial business interests include Hughes Electronics Corporation and General Motors Acceptance Corporation.

GM cars and trucks are sold in close to 190 countries, and the company has manufacturing, assembly, or component operations in more than fifty countries.

General Motors' Operations

General Motors North American Operation manufactures vehicles for the following nameplates: Chevrolet, Pontiac, Oldsmobile (to be discontinued), Buick, Cadillac, GMC, and Saturn.

General Motors International Operations meet the demands of customers outside North America, with vehicles designed and manufactured for the following nameplates: Opel, Vauxhall, Holden, Isuzu, and Saab.

General Motors Acceptance Corporation provides a broad range of financial services, including consumer vehicle financing, full-service leasing and fleet leasing, dealer financing, car and truck extended-service contracts, residential and commercial mortgage services, and vehicle and homeowners insurance. GMAC's business spans thirty-three markets around the world.

Hughes Electronics Corporation manufactures advanced technology electronic systems, products, and services for the telecommunications and space, automotive electronics, and aerospace and defense industries on a global scale.

General Motors Locomotive Group manufactures diesel-electric locomotives, medium-speed diesel engines, locomotive components, locomotive services, and light-armored vehicles to a global customer base.

Allison Transmission Division is the world's largest producer of heavy-duty automatic transmissions for commercial-duty trucks and buses, off-highway equipment, and military vehicles.

Shortcomings to Bear in Mind

■ In recent years, General Motors cut back its spending on small vehicles and concentrated on high-profit pickups and sport-utility vehicles (SUVs). This strategy was not exactly a big success, since it drove younger buyers to the showrooms of its competitors. Because of this move, GM's share of the small car market has skidded to 22.7 percent. Even so, the company remains the largest seller of small cars in the United States. However, that's lower than GM's overall market share of 28.2 percent.

Not to worry, says management, the company is gearing up to shore up this neglected realm. In late 2000, General Motors said it would endeavor to revive its fortunes in the small vehicles market in the United States by 2004 with a combination of cars and trucks.

"Some people believe we've given up on the entry-level market because of the financial and competitive challenges," said Ronald Zarrella, president of GM North America. "It's a tough environment, but over the next four years, we will attack this segment with the same discipline and dedication we applied to the truck market."

Zarrella said the company plan to revamp four current models—the Saturn S-series sedan and coupe, the Chevrolet Cavalier, and the Chevrolet S-10 pickup—as well as three other models: Saturn's sport-utility vehicle, which came out in 2001, and two new "crossover" vehicles from Chevrolet and Pontiac that combine aspects of cars and SUVs.

Reasons to Buy

■ A few years ago, domestic automakers thundered in lockstep that they didn't have the technology to improve the fuel economy of their vehicles. Now they are thrashing around in a mad scramble to build cars that consume less gas.

For its part, General Motors announced in mid-2000 that it will begin producing so-called hybrid versions of its full-size pickup trucks and buses. The hybrids will use an electric motor to augment the traditional internal combustion engine, improving the vehicle's fuel economy with no reduction in power.

Fuel economy for the new vehicles, versions of the current Chevrolet Silverado and GMC's Sierra, will be 15 percent better than today's models, GM officials said. The company also said it would improve economy of its diesel-powered buses by as much as 50 percent by 2005, thereby saving an estimated 40 million gallons of diesel fuel annually.

General Motors has seen its market share plummet from 44 percent in the early 1980s to 29 percent today. In order to reverse this trend, the company is now building cars that people want. At an auto show in 2000, for instance, the company displayed such concept cars as its Buick Rendezvous, a luxury-car-based sport-utility vehicle aimed at buyers of Toyota's hot-selling Lexus RX300. It went on sale in early 2001.

For the first time in years, GM cars ranked among the best seen at the year's big auto show, according to a survey of 900 people done by CNW Marketing/Research in 2000.

■ With a new design and marketing wisdom gleaned from the L-series blunders (a car that didn't sell well), Saturn officials were undaunted and set out to bring out another new vehicle—this one a small sport-utility vehicle that was unveiled late in 2000. However, the new car won't go on the market until late 2001. Saturn started out a decade ago as an experiment to prove that a domestic automaker could compete with Japanese rivals in the small-car realm. The new SUV is part of a $1.5-billion investment GM is making to expand Saturn into a full-line brand. The company also has in mind a pickup truck or a minivan based on the SUV. Saturn, obviously, is among the latecomers to the market. "It's a good news-bad news situation for us," said Roland Daniels, president of Saturn. The good news is that the SUV is coming. "The bad news is we're going to have to wait for production until the end of next year (2001)."

■ Just a few years ago, Cadillac was the number one luxury car. By 1997, it had lost that distinction to Lincoln. Three years later, moreover, it had sagged even further to the number three slot. General Motors, for its part, is determined to reverse the slide and has pledged to invest $4.3 billion over the next three or four years to get back into the winner's circle. That amounts to 15 percent of GM's capital budget, aimed at a division that brings in a paltry 4 percent of GM's revenues.

By 2004, there will be as many as nine Cadillac models, up from five. Among them a car-based sport-utility in 2002 as well as the 2001 Cadillac version of the Chevy Avalanche SUV, and the all-new Catera sport-utility sedan. While the old Catera was modeled on the stodgy European Opel Omega, the new Catera is being completely redesigned. The new Cadillacs will not only be sportier, but they will be equipped with more powerful engines, better handling, and the edgy styling of the Evoq concept car, Cadillac's new two-seat roadster that will be in the showrooms in 2002 under a yet-to-be-determined name. "This is the best strategy Cadillac has had in two decades," said Christopher W. Cedergren, an analyst at marketing firm Nextrend Inc.

■ A new CEO took the helm at General Motors in 2000, G. Richard Wagoner Jr., age forty-eight, previously the president and chief operating officer of the company. He moved into his new office on June 1, 2000. Wall Street applauded the move. "It is good to have younger people moving into positions of importance," commented one analyst. Auto industry veterans echoed the sentiment. "In an organization as traditional and hidebound as General Motors, having a person who doesn't know all the reasons that things *can't* be done can be a benefit," said Robert A. Lutz, former president and vice chairman of Chrysler and now the chief executive of the Exide Corporation, the battery maker.

■ Trying to capture the spirit of the times, General Motors occasionally brings out a new brand. A decade ago, for instance, it introduced Saturns and Geos to tap a national desire for affordable, sporty, fuel-efficient cars.

Its latest venture is the Hummer, a brand it acquired a year or so ago. GM is convinced that the decade-long trend toward ever larger and more aggressive looking sport-utility vehicles will continue.

Like a Jeep but far bigger, the Hummer is fashioned after a military vehicle, the Humvee, which was used in the Persian Gulf War. With the cold war ended, the Humvee's manufacturer is looking for civilian buyers. Until now, it has sold only 1,000 a year at a steep price of $100,000.

While cars tend to be five or six feet wide, the Hummer is over seven feet wide. General Motors says the unusual width of Hummers is part of their brand identity. Although Hummers are a bit hard to park, the wide stance should reduce the risk of rolling over.

GM says its research shows that many prosperous baby boomers cannot afford the current model but still love its military look. As a consequence, the company will rely mostly on new models to increase Hummer sales while continuing to sell the original model, now called the Hummer H1. It plans to introduce a scaled down model in 2002, the Hummer H2, to retail for $45,000. The Hummer H3, an even smaller version, will go on sale the following year for under $25,000.

With a national network of Hummer dealerships the company expects to make Hummers as common as BMWs, with sales approaching 150,000 a year.

Total assets: $303,100 million
Current ratio: 1.19
Common shares outstanding: 665 million
Return on 2000 shareholders' equity: 17.1%

	2000	1999	1998	1997	1996	1995	1994	1993
Revenues (millions)	175332	176558	161315	153782	164069	168829	154951	138220
Net income (millions)	4452	6002	2956	6698	4668	6932	5659	2466
Earnings per share	6.68	8.53	5.21	8.70	5.72	7.28	6.20	2.13
Dividends per share	2.00	2.00	2.00	2.00	1.60	1.10	.80	.80
Price High	94.6	94.9	76.7	72.4	59.4	53.1	65.4	57.1
Low	48.4	59.8	47.1	52.3	45.8	37.4	36.1	32.1

AGGRESSIVE GROWTH

Gentex Corporation

600 North Centennial Street □ Zeeland, Michigan 49464 □ Investor contact: Connie Hamblin (616) 772-1800 □ Dividend reinvestment plan is not available □ Web site: www.gentex.com □ Listed: Nasdaq □ Ticker symbol: GNTX □ S&P rating: B+ □ Value Line financial strength rating: A

Recent tire recalls and the belief that under-inflated ties can lead to accidents have the National Highway Traffic Safety Administration mandating that automotive manufacturers introduce low-tire-pressure warning systems over the next several years.

But that's not as simple as it sounds. Redesigning, retooling, and manufacturing instrument panels and/or overhead consoles to accommodate new features and displays requires a costly, time-consuming process that can often take up to three to five years.

Gentex, a company that produces mirrors that dim automatically, has helped the industry simplify the technology by offering a low-tire-pressure warning system in an automatic-dimming rearview mirror. It can simply inform the driver that a tire is underinflated, or it can display the exact pressure of each individual tire.

Company Profile

Gentex is the recognized leader in the manufacture of electrochromic, automatic-dimming mirrors for the auto industry, selling to nearly every automotive manufacturer worldwide.

Gentex Night Vision Safety (NVS) automatic-dimming mirrors are based on the science of electrochromics, which is the process of reversibly darkening materials by applying electricity. During night-time driving, the mirrors use a combination of sophisticated sensors and electronic circuitry to detect glare from vehicles approaching from the rear. The mirror darkens instantly to eliminate the glare and protect the driver's vision.

Although Gentex has earned a dominant market share, the industry still has incredible room for growth. Gentex mirrors are found on the majority of vehicles offering auto-dimming mirrors, yet this represents only 7 percent of the light vehicles produced in the world (about 15 percent in North America).

Today, Gentex is making auto-dimming mirrors even smarter, helping them eliminate blind spots, display the compass heading and outside temperature, turn on your headlights, and unlock your doors. They're rapidly becoming the preferred location as the driver interface for advanced electronic features and displays.

Gentex Night Vision Safety mirrors are offered as standard or optional equipment on over 120 model-year 2000 vehicles around the world.

Gentex was the first company in the world to successfully develop and produce a commercial electrochromic mirror for the motor vehicle industry. As a result, the company is the leading supplier of interior and exterior auto-dimming mirrors to the worldwide automotive market.

Gentex also maintains an extensive line of commercial fire-protection products for the North American market, including smoke detectors and audible/visual signaling devices. Gentex's photoelectric method of smoke detection is preferred by hotels, hospitals, and office buildings because they are less prone to false alarms. Even so, they are quick to detect slow smoldering fires.

Founded in 1974, Gentex operates out of four facilities in Zeeland, Michigan; an automotive sales office in Livonia, Michigan; automotive sales and engineering subsidiaries in Germany, Japan, and the United Kingdom; and four regional domestic sales offices for the Fire Protection Group.

Shortcomings to Bear in Mind

■ Since Gentex sells most of its output to the automotive industry, it can suffer when that industry is struggling, which happens periodically. However, domestic shipments have been steady of late, despite the softening in the North American light vehicle market. The company's CEO, Fred T. Bauer, said, "There currently is a relatively low application rate for our mirrors worldwide, and they are optional (versus standard) equipment on many vehicle models. When automakers reduce production on light vehicles, we are affected to the extent that they reduce production on vehicle models that offer our mirror. To date, our mirrors have been offered on the more popular vehicles, and we haven't been as severely impacted by reductions in vehicle production."

Reasons to Buy

■ In 2000 the company posted record net income of $70.5 million, or $.93 per share, on a 13 percent increase in revenues to $297.4 million. Total Night Vision Safety Mirror shipments to automotive customers in 2000 increased to a record 6.8 million units, up from 6 million the prior year.

■ Gentex has significant new automotive mirror programs that have been awarded and will come into fruition over the next several years, beginning in August 2001. One major area of emphasis is in the midsize, midpriced segment of the vehicle market. In addition, the company is progressing on the development of products that utilized the Photobit

Corporation "camera-on-a-chip" image-sensing technology.

■ Telematics is the fastest growing segment of the automotive industry. It delivers various information systems to vehicles via telecommunications, essentially linking the driver to the burgeoning digital world. Features such as e-mail messaging, global positioning system navigation, and emergency roadside assistance are all made possible by telematics.

■ One of the most significant new products announced in 2000 was the auto-dimming "telematics" mirrors used by the General Motors OnStar global communications/navigation system. That project represents the first time a rearview mirror has served as the driver interface for an in-vehicle safety and security information service. Gentex's electronics expertise, agility, and speed to market were the primary reason GM chose Gentex as its lead development partner in the project.

Based on the initial success of that project, Gentex is now developing similar products for other customers and is working to integrate portions of the telematics system into the mirror—items that currently are part of the complete system but are located elsewhere in the vehicle, and also are supplied by other companies. A good example is the new line of microphones that Gentex has developed that will first be available in mirrors in the 2002 model year.

■ Adding content to the company's mirrors is the primary reason that Gentex has maintained its excellent profit margins in the highly competitive automotive arena. Automakers, according to the 2000 annual report, "are clamoring for features to differentiate their products from those of their competitors. Placing electronic features in an auto-dimming rearview mirror has proven to be a very efficient way for them to accomplish that goal, offering speed to market that could not otherwise be achieved if the features were offered in the vehicle's instrument panel or overhead console—each of which would require significant time and costs for retooling."

In 2000, over 40 percent of all Gentex interior mirrors included at least one added electronic feature. Those products with added features, especially the telematics-type mirrors, have given the company reason to examine its capacity requirements for the next several years. The company completed construction and started manufacturing interior mirrors in its new Riley Street production facility in April 2000. That facility effectively doubled the company's capacity for manufacturing auto-dimming mirrors to a theoretical 14 million units.

- With the recent trends toward telematics mirrors, which add significant electronic content to mirrors, Gentex is closely monitoring its capacity requirements for the 2004 model year and beyond. According to Mr. Bauer, "We see this as a positive development in the company's history, since several automakers have indicated they plan to put telematics mirrors across many of their vehicle lines, and they believe that the mirror is the best place for the driver interface for those systems. And, while we may not be able to produce as many mirrors with our existing building capacity, the telematics units are higher-priced units and have the potential to add revenues and earnings when they utilize Gentex-developed content."
- Gentex is making substantial progress in the development of products based on the Photobit "camera-on-a-chip" image-sensing technology. While the exact applications have not been

revealed, the first product that will go into production in the 2002 model year will enhance the performance/cost structure of the company's existing products. The first revenue-producing product that is being developed is an automotive safety product that currently is not available in any vehicle in the world. "Automakers are impressed with the products' performance to date, and are interested in implementing it in vehicles as early as the 2004 or 2005 model year," said Mr. Bauer.

- The company's line of fire-protection products, which made up 7.3 percent of net sales in 2000, consists of more than sixty different models of smoke alarms and smoke detectors, and more than 160 models of signaling appliances.

Years ago, Gentex revolutionized the fire-protection industry by developing a new type of smoke detector that quickly became the standard technology for use in virtually all commercial applications. Today, the company is developing new sensing technologies to create hybrid detectors that would better detect different types of fires. Smoke, flame, and heat can be detected in a variety of ways, and Gentex continues to advance and simplify these technologies in order to develop new fire-protection products.

- At the end of 2000, Gentex owned seven trademarks and seventy-six domestic and foreign patents that expire at various times between 2002 and 2019. The company also had in process 135 U.S. patent applications, 109 foreign patent applications, and 6 trademark applications. Technologies the company is working on include its white light, high-output light-emitting diodes for automotive and nonautomotive applications, as well as electrochromatic windows for automotive and architectural markets, sun roofs, and sunglasses.

Total assets: $428 million
Current ratio: 9.68
Common shares outstanding: 74 million
Return on 2000 shareholders' equity: 19.6%

	2000	1999	1998	1997	1996	1995	1994	1993
Revenues (millions)	297	262	222	186	149	112	90	64
Net income (millions)	70	65	50	35	24	19	16	10
Earnings per share	.93	.86	.68	.49	.34	.28	.24	.15
Dividends per share	Nil							
Price High	39.9	34.9	22.0	14.1	13.4	6.9	8.8	8.8
Low	16.2	16.0	10.8	8.1	5.2	3.9	4.5	2.5

AGGRESSIVE GROWTH

Harley-Davidson, Inc.

3700 West Juneau Avenue □ Milwaukee, Wisconsin 53208 □ Listed: NYSE □ Investor contact: Patrick Davidson (414) 343-8002 □ Dividend reinvestment plan is available: (877) HDS-TOCK □ Web site: www.harley-davidson.com □ Ticker symbol: HDI □ S&P rating: A- □ Value Line financial strength rating: B++

Although extremely successful today, Harley-Davidson has endured its share of lean times, with red ink splashed on its income statement in years past.

Founded in 1903, the company survived while a host of domestic competitors went belly-up. By the 1950s, HDI was the nation's only major heavy motorcycle maker.

Then, in the 1960s, it began a tough stretch when it tried to stave off Japanese competition. In 1969 Harley was acquired by AMF, a manufacturer of recreational products. However, by 1981 AMF gave up trying patch up the struggling unit and resorted to a management-led buyout.

Beset by inefficient production methods and quality-control problems that blemished its reputation, Harley teetered close to bankruptcy. At this point, the federal government agreed to grant temporary motorcycle-import tariffs. This move gave Harley's new management breathing room to adopt progressive management techniques. These measures made Harley competitive again, and the company returned to public ownership through an initial public offering.

Company Profile

Harley-Davidson, the only major domestic motorcycle manufacturer, is a leading supplier of premium quality, heavyweight motorcycles to the global market. The company benefits from having one of the world's most recognized and respected brand names.

Harley primarily makes twenty-four models of heavyweight (engine displacement 651 cc or more) touring and custom motorcycles, along with a broad range of related products. These include motorcycle parts, accessories, riding apparel, and collectibles.

The company's legendary high-powered motorcycles include the Electra Glide, the Sportster, and the Fat Boy. Many of Harley-Davidson's biking brethren are members of the Harley Owners Group, cruising along with a half-million devotees.

The company sells twenty-four models of touring and custom heavyweight motorcycles, with suggested domestic retail prices ranging from about $5,200 to $19,300. Distribution is handled by more than 1,000 dealerships, including some 600 in the United States.

The touring segment of the heavyweight market includes motorcycles equipped for long-distance riding. They include fairings, windshields, and saddle-bags. Custom motorcycles are differentiated through the use of trim and accessories.

Harley-Davidson competes with such companies as Honda, Suzuki, Kawasaki, and Yamaha.

Despite continuous production increases, domestic consumers often have to wait to purchase a new Harley-Davidson bike at list price.

Studies conducted by Harley-Davidson indicate that a typical U.S. customer is a male in his mid-forties. He has a household income of about $68,000. He uses the bike for recreational purposes and is an experienced motorcycle rider.

In February 1998, the company acquired Buell Motorcycle Company, a business in which HDI held a 49 percent interest since 1993. Buell makes sport and sport-touring motorcycles.

Financial Services

This segment consists of the company's wholly owned subsidiary, Harley-Davidson Financial Services (HDFS). HDFS finances and services wholesale inventory receivables and consumer retail installment sales contracts. HDFS is also an agency for certain unaffiliated insurance carriers, providing property/casualty insurance and extended service contracts to motorcycle owners. The finance unit conducts its business in Canada and Europe, as well as in the United States.

Highlights of 2000

- Total Harley-Davidson motorcycle shipments were 204,592, compared with 177,187 units in 1999, a 15.5 percent increase.
- The company's revenues climbed to $2.25 billion, an impressive gain of 18.8 percent.
- Total Buell motorcycle shipments were 10,189, up a stunning 31.2 percent. However, Buell motorcycle revenue was

only $58.1 million, a decline of 8.5 percent. The decline was caused by a shift in production of lower-priced Buell Blast motorcycles, which target new riders.

- Parts and accessories revenue totaled $447.8 million, a 23.5 percent increase. General merchandise revenue totaled $151.4 million, up 14.1 percent over 1999.
- Full-year operating revenue for HDFS— the financial arm— expanded to $37.2 million, an increase of 34.3 percent.
- Diluted earnings per share soared 31.1 percent to $1.13.

Shortcomings to Bear in Mind

- In the 1990–2000 period, earnings per share climbed from $.15 to $1.13, a compound annual growth rate of 22.4 percent. To be sure, this is an exceptional growth rate. As you might expect, the price of the stock reflects this exemplary record and is rarely cheap. You might want to delay your investment in HDI until it P/E ratio sags a bit.
- New competition is entering Harley-Davidson's core market. A host of new motorcycles are hitting the streets, seeking some of Harley's dominant market share. For instance, Excelsior-Henderson, Polaris, BMW, and others target the heavyweight motorcycle market. Analysts are concerned that some HDI customers may not have the patience to wait for a Harley and may be tempted to buy a bike made by one of these competitors.

Reasons to Buy

- Most companies run advertisements to build sales, but Harley doesn't. In fact, it rakes in millions of dollars each year by licensing its logo for use on everything from Harley-brand coffee to Harley-motif Christmas tree ornaments.
- The Harley cult is so strong that even though the company has been building bikes as fast as it can for the past several years, customers often have to wait a

year or longer before they can take delivery. The company has periodically boosted its production capacity. Even so, Harley apparently likes to keep the supply of its products limited in order to avoid diluting the prestige of ownership.

"The worst thing in the world they could do is satisfy demand," said brand-development expert Al Ries, a spokesman for the marketing firm, Ries & Ries. "The minute you do that, you kill the mystique."

■ One key to running a successful company involves amicable labor relations. All too often there is hostility and antagonism between workers and management. Companies without labor unions often perform better than those with unions. However, some industries, such as automakers, don't have a choice. On the one hand, Ford Motor has a reputation for settling labor disputes effectively, while General Motors has taken an adversarial approach and has often suffered crippling strikes.

For its part, Harley-Davidson has been able to overcome the disadvantages of having to deal with its labor unions, the International Association of Machinists and the United Paper Workers International Union. In a book about the company (*More Than a Motorcycle*), Rich Teerlink (a former CEO) and Lee Ozley (a consultant who worked with Mr. Teerlink) describe how they transformed the company from one that had struggled against fierce Japanese competition into the successful enterprise it is today.

Under Mr. Teerlink's leadership, the unions were invited into the process of change—and on equal footing with management. At one point the parties negotiated a contract largely by achieving consensus, in contrast with the usual adversarial approach.

When Harley was desperate for greater capacity, the company and its unions cooperated in designing and locating a new plant. Harley's management gave up the thought of building it in a state hostile to unions, eventually selecting Kansas City, Missouri. In return, the unions accepted plant design and work force changes to give management substantial productivity gains. Corporate officials, in still another move toward labor-management harmony, agreed to a no-layoff policy. This give-and-take strategy has had yet another dividend: The turnover rate among employees at Harley-Davidson is far below the national average for manufacturing companies.

■ In mid-2000, Ford Motor Company and Harley-Davidson unveiled the 2001 Harley-Davidson F-150 SuperCrew four-door pickup, the second in their lineup of limited-edition trucks. The all-black truck, with distinctive Harley-Davidson features, including orange and gray pin-striping and chrome accessories, is a restyled and customized version of Ford's new F-150 SuperCrew truck.

■ Harley-Davidson announced in 2000 that federal regulators had approved the strategic alliance with U.S. Bancorp. In this arrangement, U.S. Bancorp will acquire and manage Harley-Davidson's Financial Services affinity card program, the Harley-Davidson Chrome Visa. The alliance allows Harley-Davidson Financial Services, Inc., a wholly owned subsidiary of the company, to further develop its core products while providing Harley-Davidson Chroma Visa cardholders card programs and full access to U.S. Bancorp's network of financial resources and services.

■ For more than a decade, Aprilia motorcycles, made by an Italian manufacturer, have triumphed in races around the globe. Now, Aprilia is expanding into the United States, Latin America, and Asia. In part, it is a defensive move. The European market's recent buoyant growth is expected to stabilize in the next few years. What's more, Aprilia is now facing competition on its home turf

from Harley-Davidson. In October 2000, HDI bought out its Italian distributor and has been setting up a dealer network in Italy under more direct Harley-Davidson management.

Total assets: $ 2,436 million
Current ratio: 2.61
Return on 2000 equity: 24.8%
Common shares outstanding: 303 million

		2000	1999	1998	1997	1996	1995	1994	1993
Revenues (millions)		2906	2064	1763	1531	1350	1542	1217	1105
Net income (millions)		348	267	214	174	143	111	104	78
Earnings per share		1.13	.87	.69	.57	.48	.37	.34	.24
Dividends per share		.10	.09	.08	.07	.06	.05	.04	.02
Price	High	50.6	32.0	23.8	15.6	12.4	7.5	7.5	5.9
	Low	29.5	21.4	12.5	8.3	6.6	5.5	5.4	4.0

CONSERVATIVE GROWTH

Hershey Foods Corporation

100 Crystal A Drive ▢ Post Office Box 810 ▢ Hershey, Pennsylvania 17033-0810 ▢ Investor contact: James A. Edris (717) 534-7556 ▢ Dividend reinvestment plan is available: (800) 851-4216 ▢ Listed: NYSE ▢ Web site: www.hersheys.com ▢ Ticker symbol: HSY ▢ S&P rating: A ▢ Value Line financial strength rating: A+

Hershey Foods Corporation introduced several new products in 2001, which are giving a lift to revenue growth. Indeed, Hershey has a good record whenever it introduces new products, including Hershey Bites in 2000, with sales of $92.4 million. According to William F. Christ, Hershey's chief operating officer, "Our new product development and introductions during the last decade have been unsurpassed in our industry. We fully intend to continue our success, but we must have a new dimension. New products require a heightened emphasis on marketing support beyond the introductory years. We've been negligent, in that our support in years two and three have not kept pace with our goals. We intend to increase our advertising support significantly, some of which will be applied in this particular area."

Company Profile

Hershey Foods manufactures consumer food products. The company produces a broad line of chocolate and nonchocolate confectionery and grocery products. Hershey is the domestic leader in chocolate confectionery.

Hershey's principal product groups include confectionery products and grocery products.

Confectionery Products

In North America, the company manufactures chocolate and nonchocolate confectionery products in a variety of packaged forms and markets them under more than fifty brands. The different packaged forms include various arrangements of the same bar products, such as boxes, trays, and bags, as well as a variety of different sizes and weights of the same bar products, such as snack size, standard, king size, large, and giant bars.

Principal products in the United States are Hershey's, Hershey's with Almonds, and Cookies 'N' Mint bars; Hugs and Kisses (both also with almonds) chocolates; Kit Kat wafer bars; Mr. Goodbar chocolate bars; Reese's Pieces candies; Rolo caramels in milk chocolate; Skor toffee bars; and Amazin' Fruit gummy bears fruit candy, just to name a few.

Principal products in Canada include Chipits chocolate chips; Glosette chocolate covered raisins, peanuts, and almonds; Oh Henry! candy bar; Pot of Gold boxed chocolates; Reese's Peanut Butter Cups candy; and Twizzlers candy. The company manufactures, imports, markets, and distributes chocolate products in Mexico under the Hershey's brand name.

Grocery Products

Hershey manufactures a line of grocery products in the baking, beverage, peanut butter, and toppings categories. Principal products in the United States include Hershey's, Reese's and Heath baking pieces, Hershey's drink boxes, Hershey's chocolate milk mix, Hershey's cocoa, Hershey's Chocolate Shoppe ice cream toppings, Hershey's Hot Cocoa Collection hot cocoa mix, Hershey's syrup, and Reese's peanut butter.

Hershey's chocolate milk is produced and sold under license by certain independent dairies throughout the United States using a chocolate milk mix manufactured by the company. Baking and various other products are produced under the Hershey's and Reese's brand names by third parties that have been granted licenses by Hershey.

The company's products are sold primarily to grocery wholesalers, chain grocery stores, candy distributors, mass merchandisers, chain drug stores, vending companies, wholesale clubs, and convenience stores throughout the United

States, Canada, and Mexico. In Japan, the Philippines, Korea, and China, Hershey imports and/or markets selected confectionery products. It also markets chocolate and nonchocolate confectionery products in over ninety countries.

Shortcomings to Bear in Mind

- Hershey Foods does not have an impressive record of growth. In the 1990–2000 period, earnings per share advanced from $1.09 to $2.39, a growth rate of 8.2 percent.
- Although the cost of such raw materials as cocoa and milk are helping margins, the company has had to withstand increases in other expenses, such as freight, distribution, as well as warehouse and promotional outlays.

Reasons to Buy

- In a move that stunned many in the food industry, Rick H. Lenny, age forty-nine, left a senior post at Kraft Foods (part of Philip Morris) to become CEO of Hershey in the spring of 2001. "This is a once-in-a-lifetime opportunity to lead a company with such a story as Hershey," Mr. Lenny said. After an eighteen-year marketing run at Kraft, Mr. Lenny was named president of specialty brands at Pillsbury in 1995. He later became that company's president for North American operations.
- In 2000, the company outperformed the chocolate sector of its industry. Volume for the industry advanced by 3.7 percent in 2000, compared with 5.5 percent for Hershey Foods.
- In August 2000 the company raised its dividend by 7.7 percent; it was the twenty-sixth consecutive annual increase. In the past ten years (1990–2000), dividends expanded from $.42 to $1.08, a compound annual growth rate of 9.9 percent, or well ahead of inflation.

- Like other chocolate companies, Hershey maintains absolute secrecy about its commodity purchases and hedging strategies. In early 2001, cocoa futures prices were below $900 per ton. At one point, moreover, cocoa prices were as low as they had been since the early 1970s. An analyst with Argus Research Corporation remained optimistic on cocoa prices. In early 2001 he said, "The primary harvesting season has already begun, and is well gauged by now, so prices should remain depressed for some time. Cocoa makes up about 17 percent of Hershey's cost of goods sold, and even though the company does not reveal any details on its commodities purchasing, we believe it stands to save over $100 million on cocoa beans in the next year, versus costs in 1999."

  The Argus analyst went on to say, "Milk futures are also very low, and will not return to levels experienced in the late 1990s for quite a while. Again, we believe Hershey must have purchased advantageous futures contracts, and expect savings of another $34 million."

- Hershey's is a solid holding for a conservative investor because it does not fluctuate widely. Value Line gives it a "one" rating for safety, its best rating. The stock's beta coefficient is only .60, according to Value Line. That means that when the market declines, Hershey will only decline 60 percent of that amount. Of course, in a rising market, it will only advance 60 percent of the market.

- The company purchased the breath-freshener mints and gum businesses of Nabisco in late 2000 for $135 million. The acquired brands include Breath Savers mints, and Ice Breakers, Carefree, Stick*Free, Bubble Yum, and Fruit Stripe gums. Annual revenues from this acquisition are about $270 million. This move provides Hershey with a broader line of gum. What's more, it gives HSY a foothold in the fast-growing breath-freshener mints business.

  Commenting on the acquired brands, Mr. Christ said, "Carefree and Stick*Free target the adult enjoyment segment. As one of the first sugar-free brands in this category at its launch in 1968, Carefree has been a consistently strong player and is currently the number four adult enjoyment gum. Stick*Free is a six-year-old brand targeted at denture wearers.

  "Competing in the kid/teen segment, Bubble Yum is the number two player. It is the first bubble gum to be offered in chunk form and is credited with increasing the breadth and penetration of kid/teen gum in the chunk form.

  "A very important aspect of this acquisition is what it adds to our already strong number one position in the front-end of the food store, the convenience store positioning, and, of course, vending. The front-end of the store and counter sales is impulse-driven and about $1.3 billion in total sales value. We were number one prior to the acquisition, so we've significantly improved our overall position, but more importantly, filled a glaring gap in the mint and gum portion of these racks."

- The company is now benefiting from a new computer system. Initially, however, the new information management system led to weaker earnings in 1999 and early 2000. The company also moved to a new warehouse in Pennsylvania, which went smoothly.

- In late 2000, Hershey Foods and ConAgra, a major food processor, announced that they had developed a new ready-to-eat gelatin snack with the Jolly Rancher fruit flavors: Watermelon, Green Apple, Cherry, Strawberry, and Sugar-Free Raspberry. The new product is called Jolly Rancher Gel Snacks.

- Hershey Foods is making a concerted effort to improve its cost structure. In early 2001, Mr. Christ commented on this problem, "Our customers are continually demanding lower costs throughout their supply channels, but also more convenience. Generally, what makes their supply chain more efficient adds costs or inefficiencies to ours. While we have placed a great deal of emphasis on our supply chain costs, I believe we've only scratched the surface." He outlined steps that the company is taking in this realm:
  - Eliminating underperforming items.
  - Reducing the number of "touches" encountered from manufacturing to final delivery to the customer.

- Working hand-in-hand with customers to eliminate escalating costs by having and encouraging closer collaboration through sharing of information that helps reduce costs from the manufacturer to the consumer— the entire supply chain.
- Hershey has a few other trump cards up its sleeve that should keep revenues climbing in 2001, including the repurchase of two million shares of its common stock. What's more, the company boosted prices on a select group of products. Until recently, Hershey had not raised prices on a broad front since December of 1995.

Total assets: $3,448 million
Current ratio: 1.69
Common shares outstanding: 136 million
Return on 2000 shareholders' equity: 28.1%

	2000	1999	1998	1997	1996	1995	1994	1993
Revenues (millions)	4221	3971	4436	4302	3989	3691	3606	3488
Net income (millions)	330	295	333	336	308	280	264	257
Earnings per share	2.39	2.09	2.29	2.23	2.00	1.69	1.52	1.43
Dividends per share	1.08	1.00	.92	.84	.76	.69	.63	.57
Price High	66.4	64.9	76.4	63.9	51.8	33.9	26.8	27.9
Low	37.8	45.8	59.7	42.1	31.9	24.0	20.6	21.8

AGGRESSIVE GROWTH

Hewlett-Packard Company

3000 Hanover Street □ Palo Alto, California 94304 □ Investor contact: Steve Pavlovich (415) 857-2387 □ Dividend reinvestment plan is available: (800) 286-5977 □ Web site: www.hp.com □ Fiscal year ends October 31 □ Ticker symbol: HWP □ S&P rating: A+ □ Value Line financial strength rating: A++

In an unusual alliance between two rivals in the digital-imaging field, Eastman Kodak and Hewlett-Packard formed a joint venture in 2000 to manufacture digital photo-processing machines for use by retailers. The machines, which the companies likened to digital versions of minilabs found at drug stores and photo shops, will use high-end inkjet printers made by Hewlett-Packard and paper made by Kodak.

The machines are expected to cost less than the $70,000 to $100,000 price tag for traditional minilabs. That lower price should prompt more retailers to offer on-site processing. The company will be owned equally by EK and HWP and could generate as much as $1 billion in annual sales by 2005.

Company Profile

Since the spinoff of Hewlett-Packard's test and measurement business (Agilent Technologies, which made up about 15 percent of Hewlett-Packard's revenues) in 1999, the company is now comprised of its computing and imaging businesses. These operations include personal computers (PCs), servers, workstations, and printers, including service and support. The company's servers and workstations run HP's version of the UNIX operating system and Windows NT.

Hewlett-Packard's computer lines include workstations (including its Kayak line) and multiuser systems for both technical and commercial users, the HP Vectra and Brio series of corporate PCs, and the Pavilion PC line for consumers.

The company's 9000 family of workstations and servers run the 64-bit PA-8000 Precision Architecture reduced instruction set computing (PA-RISC) chips. Hewlett-Packard is also developing Intel's next generation 64-bit Merced chip.

Hewlett-Packard is well known for its position in the printer market with its popular HP LaserJet and DeskJet families. There has been aggressive pricing from Lexmark in the printer market, but Hewlett-Packard still dominates and has launched a series of new products.

Hewlett-Packard's PC products include the checkbook-size 200LX palmtop PC with built-in Pocket Quicken, and the HP OmniBook family of notebook PCs for mobile professionals.

Hewlett-Packard's products are used by people in industry, business, engineering, science, medicine, and education.

HWP is one of the nineteen largest industrial companies in the United States and one of the world's largest computer companies. The company had revenues of $48.8 billion in its fiscal 2000 year (ended October 31, 2000).

Nearly 60 percent of Hewlett-Packard's business is generated abroad; two-thirds of that is in Europe. Other principal markets include Japan, Canada, Australia, the Far East, and Latin America. HP is one of the top eight U.S. exporters.

Hewlett-Packard's domestic manufacturing plants are situated in twenty-eight cities, mostly in California, Colorado, the Northeast, and the Pacific Northwest. The company also has research and manufacturing plants in Europe, Asia-Pacific, Latin America, and Canada.

HWP sells its products and services through some 600 sales and support offices and distributorships in more than 130 countries.

Shortcomings to Bear in Mind

■ Analysts believe that Hewlett-Packard's competition has increased in recent years. More companies are selling low-cost printers, while Sun Microsystems competes fiercely in the market for Unix-based computers. HWP is a leader in computers that use the Unix operating systems.

According to some observers, Hewlett-Packard suffers from turf battles, complacency, and slow growth. The company also seems to analyze decisions endlessly and sends no clear message to a fast-moving market.

■ Most of Hewlett-Packard's growth depends heavily on low-margin consumer businesses that no longer have much zip. What's more, a small fraction of it emanates from the lucrative Net-related markets the company covets, such as servers, storage, e-business software, and services. According to a leading analyst, sales of printers and PCs account for about 73 percent of the company's revenue. Servers, storage, and other sophisticated products make up a mere 13 percent.

■ Hewlett-Packard sells inkjet printers, but the real revenue producer is not the printer—it's the cartridge full of ink that needs to be replaced on a regular basis. However, the company's competitors are gnashing their teeth and accusing HWP of restraint of trade. In February 2001, the state Superior Court in San Francisco has certified a class action suit involving plaintiffs in nineteen states who allege that Hewlett-Packard has violated California's Cartwright Antitrust Act and conspired to restrain trade in the market for cartridges of ink to keep the printers running. The suit claims that Hewlett-Packard is "tying" components of the inkjet head to the ink chamber in such a way that competitors can't enter the ink supply business. The suit seeks a consumer rebate for everyone who purchased a Hewlett-Packard inkjet cartridge since 1995, or a total of about $1 billion, plus costs. The design of the printer and patent protection surrounding it permits Hewlett-Packard to charge more than $30 for ink cartridges that would cost less than $10 if the market were open to competition, according to competitors. For its part, HWP said it would prevail but made no further comments.

Reasons to Buy

- On a more positive note, the company has staked its future on a new CEO, forty-five-year-old Carleton S. Fiorina (a former Lucent Technologies executive hired in 1999). Known usually as "Carly," Ms. Fiorina (who is the first woman ever to head one of the thirty companies that make up the Dow Jones Industrial Average) is intent on shaking up Silicon Valley's largest company. Nor does she pull any punches as to what kind of company she has inherited. "Take a deeper look at HP," she says, "and you will see something sick and endangered."

   The star executive, who spent nineteen years with AT&T and Lucent Technologies, appears to be just the person to bring out the best at Hewlett-Packard.

Just as the computer giant needs to shed its lumbering ways, so too did Lucent—AT&T's slow-moving communications-equipment business. Carly Fiorina managed the highly successful spinoff of Lucent in 1996. She then launched a bold $90-million brand-building campaign that helped transform the company from a humdrum maker of phone equipment into an Internet player supplying the gear for the New Economy. And in 1998, after being promoted to president of Lucent's $19-billion global service-provider business, she helped to reinvigorate product development by the long-coddled Bell Labs engineers. "She has it all," said Vodafone AirTouch PLC Chairman Sam Ginn, an HP director who headed the search committee. Incredible as it may seem, the search committee looked at 300 potential candidates before settling on Carly Fiorina.

- Joining a recent invasion of the Internet by some of its major competitors, Hewlett-Packard began overhauling its software business in early 2001, moving it to the Web. Initially, it released two new suites of Internet-based business software containing twenty-five applications designed to assist companies do everything from route incoming phone calls to handle online billing. In the past, the company has been a bit late in entering the software realm. It now gets only about 5 percent of its $49 billion in annual sales from software, though Ms. Fiorina has vowed to change that in the face of sluggish sales of personal computers.

- Carly Fiorina was named to the additional post of chairman in the fall of 2000, becoming the first woman to hold all three top posts at a major computer company. Fiorina's new position marks a nod of approval for the work she's done since July 1999 when she took the helm of Hewlett-Packard. Under her leadership, HP has seen soaring consumer sales of personal computers and printers. It also has secured significant partnerships, including a deal to provide the computer infrastructure for Amazon.com.

- Hewlett-Packard released a new line of Internet-enabled laser printers in the spring of 2001. The four new models, priced at $399 to $1,099, allow users to beam documents for printing from wireless devices, check the paper and toner levels of individual printers from a Web page, and scan documents directly onto the Internet. "We think this is going to generate a lot of interest in displacing those 50 million LaserJet printers already out there, said Vyomesh Joshi, a HP president. "HP is reinventing imaging and printing again."

- Hewlett-Packard has a line of midrange servers, plugging a gap in its product line and putting it back into competition with Sun Microsystems and IBM. Analysts said that the company's N-Class servers, priced starting at $48,000, should help Hewlett-Packard catch up to its competitors in the market for servers—powerful computers that increasingly run everything from corporate networks to Internet-based electronic commerce. The new machines are designed to pick up the slack from the company's aging K-Class line, whose sales started to wane in 1998.

- The company's HP LaserJet 4000 printers produce 1,200 dots per inch print equivalent at full engine speed—an important innovation over competitors who must cut engine speed by half to achieve the highest quality output possible on their printers. The HP LaserJet 4000 is the first product to incorporate HP's new JetSend technology, which allows printers, scanners, and other devices to exchange information directly without a PC.

- In 2000, Hewlett-Packard became a prime provider of computer equipment to Amazon.com in a major deal that made the online retailer one of HP's top five customers. Under the deal, the company will provide 90 percent of Amazon's computer infrastructure, including servers, storage equipment, personal computers, printers and related software. Those close to the deal said the agreement could be valued in the hundreds of millions of dollars.

- Hewlett-Packard is positioning itself to post solid earnings in the next two or three years. A new family of high-end servers that will round out that product line should bolster revenues. A shift to color printing in offices is helping sales of the company's color laser printers. Another plus factor is the move to digital photography, which is fueling demand for the company's color inkjet printers. Also important is the growth of the installed base of printers; it stimulates sales of high-margined supplies, such as replaceable cartridges. Finally, analysts look for Hewlett-Packard's emphasis on the fast-growing Internet infrastructure market to lead to better demand for its servers, storage products, as well as consulting and services.

- Hewlett-Packard announced the acquisition of Bluestone Software in early 2001. Bluestone is a leading provider of business-to-business, business-to-consumer, and wireless open platform solutions.

  Bluestone Software will become the point of integration for the company's current Internet software offerings, which include integrated service management software, security software, Internet service tracking and billing, and e-services integration software. "This is a dynamic new direction for HP software and will change the future for many of our customers," said Bill Russell, vice president and general manager, HP Software Solutions Organization. "The integrated organization will be nimble, limber, and quick to respond to marketplace conditions."

Total assets: $34,009 million
Current ratio: 1.61
Common shares outstanding: 1,994 million
Return on 2000 shareholders' equity: 25.1%

	2000	1999	1998	1997	1996	1995	1994	1993
Revenues (millions)	48782	42370	47061	42895	38420	31519	24991	20317
Net income (millions)	3561	3126	3065	3119	2675	2433	1599	1177
Earnings per share	1.73	1.50	1.44	1.48	1.27	1.16	.77	.58
Dividends per share	.32	.32	.30	.26	.21	.18	.13	.11
Price High	77.8	59.2	41.2	36.5	28.8	24.2	12.8	11.2
Low	29.1	31.7	23.5	24.1	18.4	12.3	9.0	8.0

CONSERVATIVE GROWTH

Illinois Tool Works Inc.

3600 West Lake Avenue ◻ Glenview, Illinois 60025-5811 ◻ Investor contact: John L. Brooklier (847) 657-4104 ◻ Dividend reinvestment plan is available: (888) 829-7424 ◻ Web site: www.itwinc.com ◻ Listed: NYSE ◻ Ticker symbol: ITW ◻ S&P rating: A+ ◻ Value Line financial strength rating: A

How Illinois Tool Works Began

Founded in 1912, Illinois Tool Works' earliest products included milling cutters and hobs used to cut gears. Today ITW is a multinational manufacturer of highly engineered components and systems.

In 1923, the company developed the Shakeproof fastener, a patented twisted tooth lock washer. This product's success enabled ITW to become the leader in a new industry segment—engineered metal fasteners.

Illinois Tool soon expanded the Shakeproof line to include thread-cutting screws, preassembled screws, and other metal fasteners.

By the late 1940s the line grew to include plastic and metal/plastic combination fasteners. Today, ITW units produce fasteners for appliance, automotive, construction, general industrial, and other applications.

After World War II the company also expanded into electrical controls and instruments, culminating in the formation of the Licon division in the late 1950s. Today, ITW units provide a wide range of switch components and panel assemblies used in appliance, electronic, and industrial markets.

In the early 1960s the newly formed Hi-Cone operating unit developed the plastic multipack carrier that revolutionized the packaging industry. Hi-Cone multipacks today are used to package beverage and food products as well as a variety of other products.

Also in the 1960s, the company formed Buildex to market existing Shakeproof fasteners as well as a line of masonry fasteners to the construction industry. Buildex today manufactures fasteners for drywall, general construction, and roofing applications.

In the mid-1980s ITW acquired Ramset, Phillips Drill (Red Head), and SPIT, manufacturers of concrete anchoring, epoxy anchoring, and powder actuated systems; and Paslode, maker of pneumatic and cordless nailers, staplers, and systems for wood construction applications. Today, the construction industry is the largest market served by Illinois Tool Works.

In the 1970s ITW purchased Devcon Corporation, a producer of adhesives, sealants, and related specialty chemicals. Today the company's engineered polymers businesses offer a variety of products with home, construction, and industrial applications.

In 1986 Illinois Tool acquired Signode Packaging Systems, a multinational manufacturer of metal and plastic strapping stretch film, industrial tape, application equipment and related products. Today ITW offers a wide range of industrial packaging systems, including Dynatec hot-melt adhesive application equipment.

In 1989 Illinois Tool Works acquired Ransburg Corporation, a leading producer of finishing equipment.

ITW expanded its capabilities in industrial finishing with the purchase of DeVilbiss Industrial/Commercial division in 1990. Today, DeVilbiss and Ransburg manufacture conventional and liquid electrostatic equipment, while Gema Volstatic (acquired with the Ransburg and DeVilbiss purchases) produces electrostatic powder coating systems.

The company acquired the Miller Group in 1993. Miller is a leading manufacturer of arc welding equipment and related systems. Miller's emphasis on new product development and innovative design fits well with ITW's engineering and manufacturing strategies.

Premark International Inc.

In the latter part of 1999 the company made its biggest purchase yet— Premark International Inc.—a $2.7-billion conglomerate making everything from industrial food equipment to gym equipment to residential flooring and appliances.

The Street did not take kindly to this huge acquisition. The day after the announcement, the stock dropped 8 percent, closing at $73.69 on September 10, 1999. More than a year later the stock was still under siege, as it sagged below $50. No one seemed to notice that 90 percent of Premark's revenue came from nonconsumer goods, making it, at least in management's view, a good fit for ITW.

In the beginning, Premark modestly diluted company earnings—about $.02 a share. But this is not unusual in a major acquisition. However, analysts believe that Premark will add modestly to earnings in 2001, perhaps $.20 a share. What's more, if Illinois Tool Works is able to improve Premark's operating margins to 18 percent, they believe that Premark could contribute $.53 to EPS by 2004.

Company Profile

Illinois Tool Works is a multinational manufacturer of highly engineered fasteners, components, assemblies, and systems. ITW's businesses are small and focused, so they can work more effectively in a decentralized structure to add value to customers' products.

The company has subsidiaries and affiliates in forty countries on six continents. More than 500 ITW operating units are divided into six business segments:

Engineered Products—North America

Businesses in this segment are located in North America and manufacture short-lead-time components and fasteners and specialty products such as adhesives, resealable packaging, and electronic component packaging.

In 2000, revenues from this segment grew 7 percent, and operating income advanced 9 percent, helped by contributions from the construction, automotive, consumer durable, and fluid products businesses. Despite slower revenue growth in the fourth quarter, moreover, full-year operating margins of

19.2 percent were 30 basis points higher than 1999.

Engineered Products—International

Businesses in this segment are located outside North America and manufacture short-lead-time components and fasteners and specialty products such as electronic component packaging and adhesives.

In 2000, revenues from this segment advanced 15 percent, and operating income grew 16 percent, largely because of strength in the construction and automotive businesses. Full-year operating margins of 10.1 percent were up only modestly from the prior year.

Specialty Systems—North America

Businesses in this segment operate in North America and produce longer-lead-time machinery and related consumables and specialty equipment for applications such as industrial spray coating, quality measurement, and static control.

In 2000, revenues from this ITW operation were up 6 percent, while operating income gained a more modest 4 percent. Fourth quarter restructuring charges and slow revenue growth hurt operating margins slightly, as they ebbed 20 basis points to 16.8 percent.

Specialty Systems—International

Operations in this segment do business outside North America. They have stakes in longer-lead-time machinery and related consumables and specialty equipment for industrial spray coating and other applications.

In 2000, revenues and operating income increased 8 percent and 10 percent, respectively, thanks to strength in the industrial packaging and food equipment businesses. Full-year operating mar-

gins improved 20 basis points, to 9.8 percent, compared with 1999.

Consumer Products

Businesses in this segment are located primarily in North America and manufacture household products which are used by consumers, including small electric appliances, physical fitness equipment, and ceramic tile.

In 2000, revenues declined 4 percent and operating income dropped substantially.

Leasing and Investments

This segment makes investments in mortgage-related assets, leveraged and direct-financing leases of equipment, properties, and property developments, and affordable housing. In 2000, operating income declined a modest 1 percent.

Shortcomings to Bear in Mind

- The stock has historically traded at a premium to the market, but based on its exceptional performance over the years it would appear to be warranted. With some 500 businesses, Illinois Tool offers investors wide diversification by product line, geographic region, and industry. This helps insulate the company from weakness in any one sector. Over the years this has resulted in consistent performance despite the cyclicality of the automotive and construction sectors.

Reasons to Buy

- Acquisitions are likely to remain a key component of the company's growth strategy. ITW has grown steadily over the years largely by taking underperforming businesses and turning them into solid performers. This strategy was again employed in 2000.

Specifically, the company completed thirty-one "bottom-up" acquisitions—companies that are directly related to or integrated into an existing product line or market. These transactions, representing more than $1 billion in combined revenues, are typically initiated by operating management for both North American and international businesses. According to management, "Looking ahead, our pipeline of potential acquisitions remains full."

A second type of acquisition, which the company undertakes far less frequently, is a major, or "top-down," proposition. These transactions are identified by senior management and represent entirely new businesses for ITW. Illinois Tool completed the largest transaction of this type in its history when ITW merged with Premark in late 1999.

This merger brings the company nearly eighty decentralized businesses with products marketed in more than 100 countries. Two principal lines of business—commercial food equipment and laminate product used in construction—represent about $2.5 billion in revenues. Their products have strong

brand names such as Hobart, Wilsonart, Traulsen, Vulcan, and Wittco, established market positions, good distribution channels, and benefit from value-added engineering—all the things ITW looks for in a successful acquisition.

■ Illinois Tools's record of sustained quality earnings is the result of a very practical view of the world. The company relies on market penetration—rather than price increases—to fuel operating income growth. What's more, the company's conservative accounting practices serve as a reliable yardstick of financial performance. These results then generate the cash needed to fund ITW's growth through both investing in core businesses and acquisitions.

■ Illinois Tool Works has an exceptional record of growth. In the 1990–2000 period, earnings per share climbed from $.84 to $3.15, an annual compound growth rate of 14.1 percent. In the same ten-year stretch, dividends advanced from $.17 to $.76 for a growth rate of 16.2 percent.

Total assets: $9,603 million
Current ratio: 1.83
Common shares outstanding: 302 million
Return on 2000 shareholders' equity: 17.7%

	2000	1999	1998	1997	1996	1995	1994	1993
Revenues (millions)	9984	9333	5648	5220	4997	4152	3461	3159
Net income (millions)	958	841	810	587	486	388	278	207
Earnings per share	3.15	2.99	2.67	2.33	1.97	1.65	1.23	.92
Dividends per share	.76	.63	.54	.46	.36	.31	.28	.25
Price High	69.0	82.0	73.2	60.1	48.7	32.8	22.8	20.3
Low	49.5	58.0	45.2	37.4	26.0	19.9	18.5	16.3

Intel Corporation

2200 Mission College Boulevard ❑ Santa Clara, California 95052-8119 ❑ Investor contact: Alex Lenke (408)
765-1480 ❑ Dividend reinvestment plan is available: (800) 298-0146 ❑ Web site: www.intc.com ❑ Listed:
Nasdaq ❑ Ticker symbol: INTC ❑ S&P rating: A ❑ Value Line financial strength rating: A++

You may be convinced that you already have enough power in your PC to handle the most demanding tasks. Intel, the semiconductor giant, is ready to convince you otherwise. In 2000, Intel revealed the features of its newest family of microprocessors, called the Pentium 4 line.

These processors perform at speeds of 1.4 gigahertz and higher and contain a staggering forty-two million transistors—twice as many as 1995's Pentium Pro. By contrast, most computers sold before the advent of the Pentium 4 run much slower, at 700 megahertz or less.

The Pentium 4 also has a much faster connection to the memory chips that store software programs. All that extra capability boosts the processor's handling of power-hungry applications such as 3-D graphics, multimedia audio and video, and data encryption. As you might expect, Pentium 4 PCs are faster than Pentium III models. But they don't come cheap—about $2,500 for the first PCs equipped with the new chips.

Company Profile

It has been about three decades since Intel introduced the world's first microprocessor, making technology history. The computer revolution that this technology spawned has changed the world. Today, Intel supplies the computing industry with the chips, boards, systems, and software that are the "ingredients" of computer architecture. These products are used by industry members to create advanced computing systems.

Intel Architecture Platform Products

Microprocessors, also called central processing units (CPUs) or chips, are frequently described as the "brains" of a computer because they control the central processing of data in personal computers (PCs), servers, workstations, and other computers. Intel offers microprocessors optimized for each segment of the computing market. Chipsets perform essential logic functions surrounding the CPU in computers and support and extend the graphics, video, and other capabilities of many Intel processor-based systems. Motherboards combine Intel microprocessors and chipsets to form the basic subsystem of a PC or server.

Wireless Communications
and Computing Products

These products are component-level hardware and software focusing on digital cellular communications and other applications needing both low-power processing and reprogrammable, retained memory capability (flash memory). These products are used in mobile phones, handheld devices, two-way pagers, and many other products.

Networking and Communications Products

System-level products consist of hardware, software, and support services for e-business data centers and building blocks for communications access solutions. These products include e-commerce infrastructure appliances; hubs, switches, and routers for Ethernet networks; and computer telephony components. Component-level products include communications silicon components and embedded control chips designed to perform specific functions in networking and communications applications, such as telecommunications, hubs, routers, and wide area networking. Embedded control chips are also used in laser printers, imaging, storage media, automotive systems, and other applications.

Solutions and Services

These products and services include e-commerce data center services as well as connected peripherals and security access software.

Major Customers

• Original equipment manufacturers of computer systems and peripherals.

• PC users who buy Intel's PC enhancements, business communications products, and networking products through reseller, retail, and OEM channels.

• Other manufacturers, including makers of a wide range of industrial and telecommunications equipment.

Shortcomings to Bear in Mind

■ Intel, adding to a string of embarrassing product delays and revenue shortfall that beset the company in 2000, said it canceled plans for a new low-cost computer chip. The company also delayed the introduction of its next-generation processor, the Pentium 4. Intel is a technology-industry bellwether that, until recently, was lauded for its impeccable manufacturing and rigid adherence to testing and quality control. However, in 2000 Intel delayed several chip rollouts and had to recall others because of design flaws and problems in the group of semiconductors called the "chipset" that surrounds the processor.

The latest two setbacks show "their internal system has broken down," said analyst Rick Whittington of Banc-

America Securities. "They are now going for total quality control. They aren't taking any chances."

■ Intel's long-awaited Pentium 4 microprocessor went on sale in late 2000, giving the company bragging rights over its rival, Advanced Micro Devices. The two new Pentium 4 versions run at 1.4 and 1.5 gigahertz, compared with ADM's Athlon chip at 1.2 gigahertz. In the third quarter of 2001, the Pentium 4 reached 2 gigahertz. On the other hand, the Pentium 4 is very large, making it expensive to produce, thus putting pressure on gross profit margins in 2001.

■ Intel gets almost all of its revenue and profit from chips for personal computers. And demand for PCs is growing at about 15 percent a year, a lackluster pace by high-tech standards. On the other hand, Intel is well aware of the problem. It has acquired companies and revamped divisions to augment its presence in the much faster growing networking, wireless, and telecom markets. On a more negative note, Ken Pearlman, research director for Firsthand Funds, says Intel will remain primarily a PC-chip company for the foreseeable future. In 2000, PC and server hardware accounted for 84 percent of Intel's sales—and all of profits. What's more, 2001 is shaping up as a tough one for Intel; marketing costs for the new Pentium 4 chip are eating into profit margins. In the words of Joseph Osha, an analyst with Merrill Lynch, "To expect Intel to dominate in communication chips the way it did in PC chips is unreasonable."

■ Though Intel's profits have held up well so far, many analysts believe that the rise of the Internet will inevitably erode its margins. Consumers are increasingly expected to use simpler, lower-cost devices—from hand-held machines to television set-top boxes—to access the Internet. The proliferation of these so-called Internet appliances, they note, will not replace personal computers by any means. But the Internet will fuel more diverse computing technologies and other access devices.

Reasons to Buy

- There seems to be no end to how fast or how small transistors can be. At the end of 2000, for instance, Intel revealed new semiconductor technologies and manufacturing procedures that will produce chips ten times faster than those now available. In order to increase power and slash costs, the industry seeks to cram more and more transistors onto ever smaller silicon chips.

  For its part, Intel has developed a transistor that is a mere 0.03 microns wide. This advanced technology enables the company to build microprocessors that have more than 400 million transistors and run at 10 gigahertz. Such lightning-fast transistors could complete 400 million calculations while you're turning a page in this book. Intel said that it plans to have the product available commercially by 2005. In addition, these chips will actually use less electricity than today's processors, making them suitable for smaller battery-powered devices.

- In the fall of 2000, Intel introduced the world's fastest computer chip, running at 1.5 gigahertz, in its latest bet that consumers and businesses increasingly will feel the need for speed. Intel has been locked in a race with its main rival, Advanced Micro Devices, to produce the fastest chip. The new chip, code-named "Willamette," far outpaces the processing power of AMD's latest product, the Athlon chip, running at 1.2 gigahertz, or one billion bits of information per second.

- In April of 2001, Intel introduced an even faster microprocessor. The 1.7 gigahertz Pentium 4 microprocessor sells for $352 in volume purchases by PC makers, or less than half the price for the one launched only five months earlier. That 1.5 gigahertz model introduced in November 2000 at $637 was reduced to $256 in the spring of 2001.

  In still another advance, Intel announced in May 2001 that its engineers had made a chip that combines the central functions of wireless devices into one piece of silicon, a device that will lead to smaller and faster consumer products. The new chip, according to the company, will enable consumer devices to be much smaller—cell phones that could fit in a lapel pin or wristwatch-size computers, for instance. Currently, makers of cell phones and other wireless devices use multiple chips for computing and communications chores, making it difficult to shrink those products beyond a certain point.

  Analysts said no other company appears to have developed anything similar yet. "I wouldn't call it a breakthrough product, but it is moving in the right direction," said Sean Badding, senior analyst at The Carmel Group, a market research firm. "Intel knows the market better than anyone, in my mind. They are now fulfilling a market that they believe will be on the upward trend in the next couple of years."

- Intel's processors provide brainpower for about 90 percent of the world's computers. But critics say the company's newest chips have far more processing power than the average consumer needs for popular computer uses, such as word processing, using spreadsheets, and playing games. While developers are likely to write software that demands more powerful chips, doubts persist over how many customers will bite.

  For its part, Intel says that the increasing popularity of the Internet—for everything from video streaming to electronic commerce to ever more realistic 3-D games—will require greater computing power.

- In 2001, Intel signed an agreement to supply Germany's Siemens AG with $2 billion in chips for mobile phones during the next three years. Intel is now Siemens's primary flash-memory chip supplier. Flash-memory chips are an essential component of advanced mobile phones because they retain stored data even when the phone is turned off.

    The deal allowed Intel to lock in a good price for flash-memory chips—then in short supply—before supply caught up with demand and prices fell. In 2000, major flash-memory chip producers couldn't meet the demands of mobile phone producers.

- Intel landed a contract in 2000 to supply Sweden's Telefon AB L. M. Ericsson with $1.5 billion in flash-memory chips over a three-year period. The contract was one of the first major deals in the company's effort to tap into the fast growing market for cellular phones. It ensures a steady supply of chips for Ericsson at a time when flash-memory use is rising at a swift pace. Once used primarily in computers, flash-memory is becoming an increasingly important component of mobile phones, hand-held organizers, digital cameras, and music players that download songs from the Internet.

- Intel acquired Danish chipmaker Giga AS in 2000 for $1.25 billion in a recent foray into the fast growing market for high-speed communications chips. Giga makes semiconductors that route vast streams of data traffic through the core of heavy-duty optical networks. Mark Christensen, general manager of Intel's network-communications group, said Giga's customers include many of the world's largest communications-gear providers, including Cisco Systems, Nortel Networks, and Alcatel SA of France. Giga's newest 10 gigabit-per-second chips are just beginning to appear in routers and switches, he said.

Total assets: $47,945 million
Current ratio: 2.52
Common shares outstanding: 6,730 million
Return on 2000 shareholders equity: 28.2%

		2000	1999	1998	1997	1996	1995	1994	1993
Revenues (millions)		33726	29389	26273	25070	20847	16202	11521	8782
Net income (millions)		10535	7314	6178	6945	5157	3491	2562	2277
Earnings per share		1.51	1.17	.89	.97	.73	.50	.37	.33
Dividends per share		.07	.05	.04	.03	.03	.02	.02	.02
Price	High	75.8	44.8	31.6	15.5	17.7	9.8	4.6	4.7
	Low	29.8	25.1	16.4	15.7	6.3	4.0	3.5	2.7

International Business Machines Corporation

New Orchard Road □ Armonk, New York 10504 □ Investor contact: Hervey C. Parke (914) 499-5008 □
Dividend reinvestment plan is available: (888) IBM-6700 □ Web site: www.ibm.com/investor □ Listed: NYSE □
Ticker symbol: IBM □ S&P rating: B □ Value Line financial strength rating: A++

In a joint effort with a German company, Infineon Technologies AG, IBM plans to make semiconductor chips that will extend battery life in hand-held instruments. By using the new chips, a laptop computer could be left in standby mode for months—or even years—without running down the battery. Today's batteries, by contrast, give up the ghost within eight or ten hours.

According to analysts, IBM could be among the first in the race to develop this innovative technology, known as Magnetic Random Access Memory, or MRAM. It uses magnetic, rather than electronic, charges to store bits of data. MRAM has the promise of storing more information and using less battery power than traditional Dynamic Random Access Memory, or DRAM, used in most computer devices.

Company Profile

Big Blue is the world's leading provider of computer hardware. IBM makes a broad range of computers, including PCs, notebooks, mainframes, and network servers. The company also develops software (it's number two, behind Microsoft) and peripherals. IBM derives about one-third of its revenues from an ever expanding service arm that is the largest in the world. IBM owns Lotus Development, the software pioneer that makes the Lotus Notes messaging system.

The company's subsidiary, Tivoli Systems, develops tools that manage corporate computer networks. Finally, in an effort to keep up with the times, IBM has been making a concerted effort to obtain a slice of Internet business.

Shortcomings to Bear in Mind

- IBM ranked fourth in the worldwide PC market in 2000 with a 6.8 percent share of units sold, down from 7.9 percent the prior year, when it was still in the retail PC business, according to market researcher Gartner Dataquest. In the United States, where it ranks fifth, its unit market share fell to 5.4 percent, down from 7.3 percent in 1999.

  Some analysts are convinced that IBM's PC unit wastes the company's resources on a commodity business. They maintain that it is tangential to its main thrust of providing hardware and services to users of large-computer systems, such as banks and airlines.

- In 2000, IBM's hardware sales were hurt by lackluster demand for mainframes and servers coupled with the company's exit from the PC retail market. This weakness also hurt IBM's services and software revenues in 2000.

Reasons to Buy

- Sony Corporation hired IBM in the spring of 2001 to develop and produce a high-performance microprocessor for Sony's next generation of consumer electronics, including PlayStation 3. This deal was a major win for IBM's semiconductor business, which had sales of $3.5 billion to external customers in 2000. The Sony pact could bring IBM revenue of between $2 and $4 billion over three years, beginning in 2004.

- IBM introduced a new family of microchips in April of 2001. They are intended to reduce sharply the size, power requirements, and cost components in Internet appliances and portable consumer electronic devices. The company said the new chips would enable its customers to design Internet devices using, on average, one-tenth the number of microchips in current products.
- Although IBM is well-known as the titan of computer hardware, it is the Global Services division that is proving to be the company's star performer. While sales for the rest of Big Blue are barely inching ahead, the Global Services division is averaging more than 10 percent sales growth a year. That has helped pull up overall growth at IBM to about 5 percent per year. In 2000, the division accounted for 37.6 percent of the company's revenues. With revenues of $33.2 billion in 2000, the group is the largest tech-services company in the world. Now, IBM services chief Douglas T. Elix has even bigger plans: He expects to double the division's sales in the next five years. That would make it IBM's largest unit, with 46 percent of Big Blue's revenues by 2005. By designing computer systems for major corporate clients, IBM believes it can maintain a tighter grip on all the technology its customers buy. According to analysts, IBM is better than its competitors at linking hardware sales to lucrative services. Big Blue generates more than $4 in software services revenues for every $1 in big hardware sales. This compares with a mere $.24 for Sun Microsystems and $.47 for Compaq.
- In 2001, IBM invested $1 billion in the Linux operating systems because it's the best answer to competing private standards and increasing demands on the Internet. With predictions of a thousandfold increase in Internet traffic in the next few years, the networked world will be "several orders of magnitude more complicated than anything we know today," said IBM's CEO, Louis Gerstner. He went on to say that the proliferation of wireless devices as well as demands on Web servers amount to a prescription for meltdowns. "We're headed for a wall," he said. This means more viruses, hacker attacks, and security problems at a time when voice, data, dial tone, and switching are converging, he said. Mr. Gerstner said IBM decided to invest in Linux because it's growing faster than the mainstay operating system, Microsoft's Windows NT.
- In the fall of 2000, IBM introduced software, hardware, and services for companies selling wireless connections to the Internet. The products and services are designed to serve millions of customers who want wireless Web access but use different kinds of devices. Potential customers include telephone companies and wireless-services start-ups, as well as corporations that want to let employees have wireless access to company databases. "In the next two to three years, I think we are talking about a $100-billion market to enable the Internet to be fully wireless, and we think IBM can address half that market," said Michel Mayer, general manager of IBM's Pervasive Computing Division.
- The company announced in the fall of 2000 that it would invest $5 billion— the largest investment in IBM's history—into building the world's most advanced chip-making plant at East Fishkill, New York, as well as expanding existing semiconductor plants.

With the East Fishkill investment, IBM is joining the parade of semiconductor manufacturers making the expensive transition from manufacturing chips on wafers that are 200 millimeters in diameter to 300 millimeters. The larger wafers enable manufacturers to produce two and a half times more chips per wafer. However, obtaining that benefit requires them to invest in larger, vastly more complicated production equipment.

The East Fishkill factory is not likely to be ready until 2003, putting IBM somewhat behind Intel and NEC in the transition to making chips on larger silicon wafers. In its defense, IBM says it is willing to lag behind a bit—so that its competitors can cope with any glitches in new machinery being designed for handling the new wafers.

- IBM said it will be a prime supplier of advanced chips and components to the main builder of China's Internet system, Huawei Technologies Company. Huawei, founded in 1988, is China's primary maker of routers and optical data-transmission systems used by telecommunications companies. The multiyear agreement, made in late 2000, could enhance IBM's chances of selling a broader range of computer products, including server computers, in China, as the nation increases its use of the Internet. "We view Huawei as a very significant customer, and this establishes a stronghold for our technology in the Asia-Pacific region," said Steve Longoria, IBM's director of marketing for network processing.
- In 2000, IBM and Compaq Computer agreed to sell each others' key data-storage products. They said they would spend $1 billion over three years making sure their systems work well together. The alliance is a bid to gain ground against leader EMC Corp. in the fast growing market for storage systems used by major computer users. In the past, the incompatibility of storage products has been a major headache for customers. Under the arrangement, IBM and Compaq plan "to make it a heck of a lot easier" for customers to put together storage-systems components made by each, said Nicholas Donofrio, senior vice president for technology at IBM.
- IBM, i2 Technologies, and Ariba agreed to form an alliance in 2000 to service the hot business-to-business sector. The companies will sell an integrated technology to meet the needs of businesses that seek to capture a part of the B2B e-commerce marketplace, which is estimated to total $1.3 trillion to $1.4 trillion by 2003.

IBM Global Services, IBM's consulting arm, brings its existing e-business technology to the table, while i2 provides its TradeMatrix software, which links suppliers and manufacturers. For its part, Ariba provides software that processes orders on the Internet.

- In a move to expand its ability to manage Web sites and software applications for corporate customers, IBM in 2000 formed a multibillion-dollar deal with Qwest Communications International Inc. The pact calls for IBM to build and help operate Internet data centers for Qwest across North America.

One of the fastest growing segments of the electronic economy is the so-called hosting business, in which information technology companies manage computer systems that run Web sites or internal software programs for corporate customers. The idea is that by allowing an outside concern to act as host for those computers, rather than managing them internally, companies can focus on their core business while receiving expert technical support.

- Competing against everyone from Electronic Data Systems to Big Four accounting firms to boutique shops offering only Web services, IBM has emerged as the world's largest purveyor of technology services, according to *BusinessWeek*. It counsels customers on technology strategy, helps them prepare for mishaps, runs all their computer operations, develops their applications, procures their supplies, trains their employees, and even gets them into the dot-com realm.

■ IBM launched a security system that it expects will set the industry standard for protecting confidential documents such as those used in the growing sector of electronic commerce. Unlike previous security measures that rely on software "firewalls" that filter out unauthorized users of information, IBM has developed a security chip embedded within the computer hardware, which adds additional levels of security. "People from outside your organization can get at your software," said Anne Gardner, general manager of desktop systems for IBM. "People from the outside can't get to your hardware."

■ IBM scientists intend to spend the next five years building the fastest computer in the world, 500 times faster than anything in existence today. The machine,

dubbed Blue Gene, will be turned loose on a single problem. The computer will try to model the way a human protein folds into a particular shape that gives its unique biological properties so as to understand the nature of consciousness, the origins of sex, the causes of disease, and many other mysteries.

The company is paying for it, as it does many ambitious pure-science ventures, in hopes of being able to spin off new knowledge into products for the fast growing market in biological computing. What's more, research scientists at the company relish the opportunity to sink their teeth into a daunting problem such as how proteins fold up into working molecular machines. "Nature does this day in and day out, second by second, and has done it for billions of years," said Sharon Nunes, a senior manager in computational biology at IBM. "We really want to understand the fundamental why and how."

Total assets: $88,349 million
Current ratio: 1.22
Common shares outstanding: 1,763 million
Return on 2000 shareholders' equity: 39.2%

	2000	1999	1998	1997	1996	1995	1994	1993
Revenues (millions)	88396	87548	81667	78508	75947	71940	64052	62716
Net income (millions)	8093	7712	6328	6093	5429	6334	2965	13
Earnings per share	4.44	4.12	3.29	3.01	2.76	2.76	1.23	deficit
Dividends per share	.51	.47	.44	.39	.33	.25	.25	.40
Price High	134.9	139.2	95.0	56.8	41.5	28.7	19.1	15.0
Low	80.1	80.9	47.8	31.8	20.8	17.6	12.8	10.2

International Paper Company

400 Atlantic Street ▭ Stamford, Connecticut 06921 ▭ Investor contact: Carol Tutundgy (914) 397-1632 ▭ Dividend reinvestment plan is available: (800) 678-8715 ▭ Web site: www.internationalpaper.com ▭ Listed: NYSE ▭ Ticker symbol: IP ▭ S&P rating: B- ▭ Value Line financial strength rating: B++

Svetogorsk, Russia, is a world away from the Adirondack Mountains of New York where International Paper was founded more than a century ago. When IP bought the Svetogorsk Mill about three years ago, it had not seen a profit since its privatization six years earlier. But International paper found an eager and highly educated work force, world class assets, and a vast Russian market rich with opportunity.

To bring the plant out of its sea of red ink, International Paper sent in an experienced team, one that had worked on the transition of the company's mill in Kwidzyn, Poland. They were convinced they could work similar magic in Russia.

Drawing on IP's technology resources and knowledge of European markets, the team quickly brought the paper machines at Svetogorsk up to Western standards. Within a year, the mill started to set records and became profitable. Today, the Svetogorsk Mill is the market leader in Russia for photocopy paper and is exporting substantial quantities of paper to Western Europe.

The rewards of this success are shared by the employees and people of Svetogorsk. With regular paychecks for the workers and a steady tax base for the community, the town has come to life. New roads and parks are just a few of the signs of progress.

For one member of the team, IP's success in Svetogorsk is simple, "We know how to operate paper mills and bring value to customers. With the right

people—whether in the U.S. or Russia— we can succeed."

Company Profile

International Paper is a global forest products, paper, and packaging company that is complemented by an extensive distribution system, with primary markets and manufacturing operations in the United States, Europe, and the Pacific Rim.

A Glance at International Paper's Operations

• International Paper manufactures the broadest line of office papers for advanced digital imaging printers as well as more traditional office equipment. In addition, IP offers printing papers for offset printing and opaques for books, direct mail, and advertising materials. Hammermill and Springhill brands are produced in the United States. In Europe, the company is the leading supplier of office papers, with its EverRey, Duo, Presentation and Tecnis brands. In New Zealand, Carter Holt Harvey produces fine papers at the Mataura mill.

• The company's converting and specialty group provides papers for specialized applications, such as envelopes, tablets, security papers, and release backings. This business group has had extensive success in developing new products with higher returns, using its diverse technical and product-development capabilities.

• International Paper manufactures coated papers and bristols in the United States and Germany. The company's improved Miraweb II and new Accolade coated papers target high-end magazines and catalogs. Publication Gloss and Hudson Web are also used for catalogs, magazines, and newspaper coupon inserts. Zanders Ikono remains the preferred coated freesheet paper for premium printing applications.

• The company's Springhill and Carolina coated bristols are used for book covers and commercial printing. Its uncoated Springhill bristols are used for commercial printing and converting applications, such as file folders, tags, tickets, and index cards.

• International Paper is a major producer of market pulp in the United States, France, Poland, and New Zealand. Its grades range from high-purity pulp for acetate and fabrics to fluff pulp for hygiene products and paper pulp for the production of paper and paperboard.

• The company manufactures three million tons of containerboard annually at seven manufacturing facilities in the United States, Europe, and New Zealand. Its facilities are among the most efficient in the world. What's more, aggressive cost-management efforts are targeted at continuously improving the company's competitive cost position. In addition, International Paper manufactures one of the industry's widest product ranges, including visual-appeal grades such as ColorBrite and WhiteTop linerboard.

• In specialty panels, the company designs and produces engineered products based on wood and paper. Its Masonite subsidiary molds wood fiber into a broad line of door facings with many different designs and sizes. The company's customers fabricate these facings into doors that bring style, functionality, durability, and economy to both new construction and remodeling. Today, Masonite is the world leader with its CraftMaster brand. It also manufactures a line of hardboard exterior siding and industrial hardboard and softboard.

• International Paper owns or manages about 12 million acres of forest lands in the United States, mostly in the South, where loblolly pine trees thrive. The company's forest lands are managed to strike a balance between the public's need for forest products, the sustainability of the forests, and the health and well-being of the forest environment. In the United States, the company has developed advanced land-management techniques that enable it to harvest trees while providing watershed protection, wildlife habitat preservation, and recreational opportunities.

Shortcomings to Bear in Mind

■ The CEO of International Paper, John T. Dillon, has a plan to break the paper cycle. As chief executive officer for the past five years, and an IP employee for thirty-five years, Mr. Dillon has watched the industry's fortunes ebb and flow as predictably as the tides. As demand climbs, paper companies build new capacity. Ultimately, this overbuilding leads to a glut of paper on the market, which depresses prices and saps profit margins. When demand catches up with supply and prices become stronger, the cycle begins again.

Mr. Dillon has a cure for the feast-or-famine fortunes of the industry. He's abandoning the old ways, cutting back on production, and throwing vast sums of money into acquisitions to give IP enough bulk to better control prices. However, in 2001 prices are slumping. Analysts are concerned that the debt Dillon has taken on might be a burden, since money is needed to pay interest on the debt. And they are not convinced that IP's acquisitions will give the company enough clout to dictate prices.

However, John Dillon is not buying the arguments of the doomsayers. He points out that a similar strategy was eminently successful for another Dow Industrial stock, Alcoa. For its part, Alcoa gobbled up competitors and now accounts for about 17 percent of the world market for aluminum, as well as nearly 50 percent in North America. Despite an industrywide slump in 2000, coupled with crippling energy costs, Alcoa posted record earnings in the fourth quarter of 2000.

Reasons to Buy

- Mr. Dillon is not shy about defending IP's strategy of making acquisitions. In his view, "Successful acquisitions during the past few years have provided the platform for focusing on our core businesses. As a consequence of acquiring Federal Paper Board in 1996, we were able to build a world-class consumer packaging business. With the addition of Union Camp in 1999, we gained world-class assets and a very strong position in uncoated papers and industrial packaging. The Champion International acquisition in mid-2000 significantly strengthened our coated papers position, while also giving us a strategically important printing papers business in Brazil, low-cost U.S. uncoated assets, and the Weldwood business in Canada. Both Union Camp and Champion strengthened xpedx— our distribution business. And all three companies brought major timberlands and important wood products operations."

  Mr. Dillon went on to say, "In terms of results, the Union Camp integration continues to progress very well, is ahead of our plan, and is considered a real home run. Our merger with Champion International is also doing very well. This move allowed us to take major actions to bring our cost structure down and significantly sharpen our focus on core businesses. There is a lot more to do, and we have a plan to get the results this year (2001). In fact, the Champion merger synergies target has been increased by nearly 20 percent, from $425 million to $500 million."

- Although acquisitions are a key part of International Paper's strategy, it has taken other actions as well. In the words of Mr. Dillon, "In October (of 2000), we took aggressive and bold steps to improve our returns through a rationalization and realignment program, which addresses our commitment to improved competitiveness. We not only proceeded with a $3-billion divestiture program, we increased the target to $5 billion, including timberland sales."

  In the fourth quarter of 2000, for instance, International Paper announced that it was taking 1.2 million tons of capacity out of the IP systems. The company's actions removed 18 percent of its domestic uncoated papers capacity and 7 percent of its U.S. market pulp capacity. This was accomplished through an indefinite shutdown of IP's Mobile, Alabama, mill; the staged closure of its Lock Haven, Pennsylvania, facility; and the downsizing of the Courtland, Alabama, mill. Finally, by closing the company's Camden, Arkansas, facility and realigning its Kraft papers production, International Paper reduced its domestic containerboard system by 5 percent.

- The art and science of papermaking is advancing at a rapid rate, and International Paper is in the forefront of that progress. At the same time, it is critical to keep all of the company's employees abreast of the latest technical advances. Advanced training at the company's new Manufacturing Technology Center

(MTC) in Cincinnati, Ohio, is ensuring that IP's pulp and paper mill process area employees have an in-depth understanding of new problem-solving techniques. The MTC offers management skills courses for both hourly operators and supervisors. Stu-dents are taught by a faculty made up of seasoned technical employees from across the company. To make the course interactive, students are required to bring a specific problem from their mill to discuss in class and then return home with solutions.

Total assets: $42,109 million
Current ratio: 1.41
Common shares outstanding: 481 million
Return on 2000 shareholders' equity: 8.1%

	2000	1999	1998	1997	1996	1995	1994	1993
Revenues (millions)	28180	24573	19541	20096	20143	19797	14966	13685
Net income (millions)	969	551	308	310	434	1153	432	314
Earnings per share	2.16	1.33	1.00	1.03	1.49	4.50	1.73	1.27
Dividends per share	1.00	1.00	1.00	1.00	1.00	.92	.84	.84
Price High	60.0	59.5	61.8	61.0	44.6	45.7	40.3	34.9
Low	26.3	39.5	35.5	38.6	35.6	34.1	30.3	28.3

CONSERVATIVE GROWTH

The Interpublic Group of Companies, Inc.

1271 Avenue of the Americas ▫ New York, New York 10020 ▫ Investor contact: Susan V. Watson (212) 399-8208 ▫ Dividend reinvestment plan is available: (201) 324-0498 ▫ Web site: www.interpublic.com ▫ Ticker symbol: IPG ▫ S&P rating: A+ ▫ Value Line financial strength rating: A+

Interpublic, one of the world's largest advertising giants, became even larger in March 2001 when it bought True North Communications, Inc. in a stock-for-stock pooling of interests transaction, valuing True North at $2.1 billion.

The merger created a company with offices in more than 130 countries and combined 2000 revenues of $7.2 billion. The merger also propelled Interpublic into first place among the world's advertising behemoths, ahead of the previous leaders: Britain's WPP Group and Omnicom Group Inc. of New York.

Chicago-based True North is parent to the agencies Foote Cone & Belding, known for its "Raid Kills Bug Dead" campaign for S. C. Johnson and the dancing raisins ads for the California Raisin Advisory Board, and the Bozell Group, known for the "milk mustache" ads for the dairy industry featuring celebrities.

The deal came at a propitious time when advertisers, hurt by a slowdown in the world economy, are seeking to shave costs, particularly in advertising. Interpublic, now able to offer a lower over all cost for advertising, media services, and marketing, stands to benefit from its merger with True North Communications.

"Big is good," said Brendan Ryan, CEO of FCB Worldwide, True North's lucrative ad agency, which is number four in the country. "It's absolutely a can't-miss deal." FCB Worldwide and its clients, which include Coors Brewing Company, Kraft Foods Inc., and Quaker Oats Company, were said to be the key factor in IPG's willingness to swing the deal.

Company Profile

The Interpublic Group of Companies is the largest advertising and marketing services management company in the world. It includes McCann-Erickson World-Group, The Lowe Group, Draft Worldwide, Initiative Media Worldwide, Octagon sports marketing, the Public Relations Group, ten independent advertising agencies, and the specialized marketing services companies of the Allied Communications Group. Interpublic pioneered the concept of the advertising agency holding company with its formation in 1961.

Interpublic's agencies and allied companies operate in more than 125 countries around the world and employ more than 37,000 people. The company serves more than 4,000 multinational, regional, and local clients, representing many of the best-known corporations and names.

How an Advertising Agency Works

The principal functions of an advertising agency are to plan and create advertising programs for its clients and to place advertising in various media such as television, cinema, radio, magazines, newspapers, direct mail, outdoor, and interactive electronic media.

The planning function involves analysis of the market for the particular product or service, evaluation of alternative methods of distribution, and choice of the appropriate media to reach the desired market most efficiently.

The advertising agency develops a communications strategy and then creates an advertising program, within the limits imposed by the client's advertising budget, and places orders for space or time with the media that have been selected.

The company generates income from planning, creating, and placing advertising in various media as well as from planning and executing other communications or marketing programs. Historically, the commission customary in the industry was 15 percent of the gross charge (billings) for advertising space or time. More recently, lower commissions have been negotiated, but often with additional incentives for better performance.

Interpublic, the Corporate Parent

Interpublic, the corporate parent, is based in New York City. It sets company-wide financial objectives, establishes fiscal management and operational controls, provides strategic direction, guides personnel policy, plans top management succession, coordinates global investor relations and initiatives, and manages and approves mergers and acquisitions. In addition, Interpublic provides centralized functional services that offer its companies operational efficiencies, including accounting, finance, marketing information retrieval and analysis, legal counsel, real estate expertise, recruitment aid, employee benefits, and executive compensation management.

The parent company does not get involved with advertising campaigns or other client-specific marketing programs, which are planned, developed, and executed separately and confidentially within each agency. The individual companies are so autonomous that they often compete with each other for business. This extraordinarily high level of operational independence and autonomy was pioneered by Interpublic in the 1960s and remains central to the Interpublic business concept today.

Shortcomings to Bear in Mind

■ It's no secret that Interpublic is doing well. In the period 1990–2000, earnings per share advanced from $.40 a share to $1.51, a compound annual growth rate of 14.2 percent. Dividends in this same period also climbed at a good clip, expanding from $.12 to $.37, a growth rate of 11.9 percent. That's why the price-earnings ratio may be on the high side when you decide to examine this company.

- The acquisition of True North Communications did not impress all analysts. At the time of the deal, Interpublic had already been hit by soft results at its Lowe Lintas Group, which has been feeling the effect of merger-related client losses. And with the growth of FCB expected to be limited in 2001, it would give Interpublic another agency that was not performing that well, said Lauren Fine, who covers the advertising industry for Merrill Lynch. "It's a doubling down, as far as I can tell," she said.

On the other hand, there were analysts who applauded the acquisition. "This is a good strategic fit," said Karen Ficker, an analyst with ING Barings. She said that she expected minimal client conflict from the deal, now that True North no longer has Daimler-Chrysler's Chrysler Group account.

- In 2001, growth in advertising expenditures is expected to moderate from recent record rates in the fact of slower economic activity and the absence of political, dot-com, and Olympic-related promotions. In particular, revenue comparisons for advertising agencies are expected to be sluggish in the first half of 2001.

However, demand for marketing services is expected to remain relatively robust as clients continue to disperse their promotional activities across an array of communications channels. Despite the slowdown in advertising expenditures, Interpublic is looking for double-digit earnings growth in 2001.

Reasons to Buy

- The long-term outlook for the advertising industry is positive because of new markets, new advertisers, and new product introductions. A growing number of media outlets, increasing market segmentation, and other factors should guarantee expanding business opportunities.

- In the fourth quarter of 2000, Interpublic's agency system gained net new business of $484 million, up 64 percent over the same period of 1999. Major new accounts won during the quarter included Verizon, Deutsche Bank, Princess Cruises, and Tommy Hilfiger. In addition, the company expanded its long-term relationship with Coca-Cola.

During all of 2000, moreover, net new business totaled $2,560 million (compared with $1,839 million the prior year), including assignments from Microsoft, Pfizer, 3Com, the United States Navy, H&R Block, Merrill Lynch/HSBC, Kohl's, and H&M. In early 2001 the trend accelerated, with Interpublic agencies gaining several new accounts, including Virgin Mobile, Bestfoods, Mass Mutual, Revlon, and Marriott.

- Acquisitions are nothing new to Interpublic. In November 2000, the company acquired Deutsch, Inc., a domestic advertising and marketing communications agency with 1999 billings of $1.2 billion. At that time, Deutsch was America's largest independent agency and by far the fastest growing among the top twenty-five. Both *Adweek* and *Advertising Age* magazines named Deutsch Agency of the Year in 1998, and *Adweek* repeated that recognition in 1999 as well.

"Deutsch is the model in our industry of how excellence in creativity and business solutions can drive continuing expansion," said John J. Dooner, chairman and CEO of Interpublic. "But what makes Deutsch stand out is not just its creative awards and overall growth, but Donny Deutsch's and his management team's vision and drive that has transformed the company from a leading creative ad agency into a leading creative marketing communications firm, as well."

Deutsch, which is headquartered in New York, also has offices in Chicago, Los Angeles, and Boston. Its accounts include Bank One, DirecTV, Domino's Lenscrafters, Microsoft's Expedia.com, Mitsubishi Motors, Pfizer, Snapple, Sun America, and Tommy Hilfiger.

- Hill, Holliday, Connors, Cosmopulos, owned by Interpublic, expanded its integrated capabilities in 2001 by acquiring SF Interactive, an interactive marketing agency. SF Interactive brings digital and CRM capabilities to Hill, Holliday's San Francisco office and expands the agency's footprint on the East Coast to include Washington, D.C.

- In still another deal consummated in 2001, Interpublic's Jack Morton Worldwide, a brand communications agency, acquired Planet Interactive, a Boston-based multimedia developer of Web sites, CD-ROMs, and digital installations. Planet Interactive is expected to significantly expand Jack Morton's digital media capabilities, allowing it to offer full-service digital media design and production services to clients on the East Coast.

- According to Value Line Survey, "IPG has done an admirable job filling out its business portfolio in some high-growth, nontraditional areas (like market research, direct marketing, and public relations) that are less likely to be hurt by the poor economy. It also has significant exposure internationally. As long as the recent domestic softness does not spread abroad (assuming that a severe recession does not materialize at home), the group should see decent earnings growth in 2001."

Total assets: $8,727 million
Current ratio: 1.03
Common shares outstanding: 307 million
Return on 2000 shareholders' equity: 23.5%

	2000	1999	1998	1997	1996	1995	1994	1993
Revenues (millions)	5626	4978	3969	3126	2538	2180	1984	1794
Net income (millions)	473	373	310	239	205	168	152	125
Earnings per share	1.51	1.24	1.11	.95	.85	.72	.67	.56
Dividends per share	.37	.33	.29	.25	.22	.20	.18	.16
Price High	55.9	58.4	40.3	26.5	16.8	14.5	12.0	11.9
Low	32.7	34.4	22.6	15.7	13.2	10.6	9.2	8.0

Jefferson-Pilot Corporation

P. O. Box 21008 ❑ Greensboro, North Carolina 27420 ❑ Investor contact: John T. Still, III (336) 691-3382 ❑
Dividend reinvestment plan is available: (800) 829-8432 ❑ Web site: www.jpfinancial.com ❑ Listed: NYSE ❑
Ticker symbol: JP ❑ S&P rating: A+ ❑ Value Line financial strength rating: A+

Jefferson-Pilot launched a new advertising campaign in March of 2001 that represents a significant departure from the company's previous advertising. For the first time, Jefferson Pilot is appearing on such prime-time network TV shows as *Frasier*, *West Wing*, *Law & Order*, *Dateline*, and *60 Minutes*. The campaign was developed to bolster Jefferson Pilot's national name recognition.

Built around the theme, "Financial Freedom, It Has Its Advantages," the advertisements are designed to capture viewers' attention through humor. The first commercial to appear, for example, featured a man shattering his alarm clock with a golf club, suggesting that Jefferson-Pilot has helped provide the financial freedom that allows him to sleep in.

Company Profile

Jefferson-Pilot has two business segments: insurance and communications. Within the insurance segment, JP offers individual life insurance products, annuity and investment products, and group insurance products through these principal subsidiaries: Jefferson Pilot LifeAmerica Insurance Company, Jefferson Pilot Securities Corporation, Jefferson Pilot Financial Insurance Company, Benefit Partners, and Jefferson Pilot Life Insurance Company.

Major products in the life insurance sector are universal life insurance, variable life insurance, and term life insurance. In the annuity and investment sector, Jefferson-Pilot markets single-premium and flexible-premium deferred annuities, immediate annuities, equity indexed annuities, variable annuities, mutual funds, and asset management programs. Finally, in the group operation (Benefit Partners), the principal products are group term life insurance, group disability income insurance, and group dental insurance.

Within the communications segment, JP operates three television broadcasting stations and seventeen radio broadcasting stations, and provides sports and entertainment programming. These operations are conducted through Jefferson Pilot Communications Company.

Revenues by Segment (in millions)

	2000	1999	1998
Individual products	$1,684	$1,468	$1,424
Annuity and investment products	629	511	506
Benefit partners	537	164	313
Communications	206	200	195
Corporate and other	182	218	172
Totals	$3,238	$2,561	$2,610

Shortcomings to Bear in Mind

- According to Value Line Survey, a leading statistical and advisory service, "the aging of annuity policies in force, particularly among recently acquired business, has contributed to higher surrender rates. Indeed, fixed annuity surrenders as a percentage of beginning fund balances reached 25 percent in the third quarter of 2000, up from 17 percent in the prior-year period."

- If the economy continues to weaken, the advertising business of the communications group is likely to feel the impact. One of the first ways to cut expenses during a recession is to reduce advertising expenses.

Reasons to Buy

- Jefferson-Pilot enjoyed another year of excellent results in 2000. Earnings per share, before realized investment gains, expanded by 13 percent to $2.85, while total earnings per share increased 12 percent to $3.29. Return on equity was a strong 16.8 percent. Cash dividends climbed another 12 percent.

- Over the past five years, the company's operating earnings per share grew at an annual rate of 16 percent. Total earnings, including realized investment gains, grew at a 14 percent annual pace. JP's cash dividend has been raised every year at an annual rate of nearly 12 percent. The share price, moreover, has increased at a compound rate of 19 percent per year in that five-year span.

- The company's annuity and investment products enjoyed excellent marketing results in 2000, with total annuity sales advancing 42 percent to almost $1.4 billion. JP also successfully completed the purchase and integration of Polaris Financial Services and Polaris Advisory Services into the company's broker/dealer, Jefferson Pilot Securities Corporation.

Through Jefferson Pilot Securities, the company sold $3.7 billion of investment products in 2000, a gain of 56 percent over the prior year.

- Jefferson Pilot Communications, one of the premier broadcast media operations in the nation, produced broadcast cash flow of nearly $90 million in 2000. The company's seventeen radio stations are all located in markets that grow faster than the industry as a whole, enabling Jefferson-Pilot to enjoy 22 percent compounded cash flow growth from radio over the last five years.

The company's three network-affiliated VHF television stations also operate in excellent markets. In both radio and TV, the company's stations operate at cash flow margins that rank well in the industry. JP Sports syndicates and produces some of the best college sports products in the nation, and profitably builds name recognition, particularly in the Southeast, for the company's financial products.

- Jefferson-Pilot has exhibited strong financial quality, stability, and reliability, as well as prudent balance sheet management. The average credit quality of the company's $16-billion bond portfolio is A1, and the portfolio is 94 percent investment grade.

- Today, Jefferson-Pilot is a focused provider of financial products and services to increasingly upscale markets. JP creates and administers a portfolio of competitive financial products in centralized, very efficient operations, and distributes them via diversified sales channels.

- Jefferson-Pilot is focused on the high end of the financial services market. The company is using its capability in variable universal life, as well as its broker/dealer, Jefferson Pilot Securities Corporation, to service agents and clients in the estate planning and wealth-preservation market. This is reflected in the average size of JP's life sale, which ranks the company among the top-tier life companies serving the affluent market. Demographic projections indicate strong growth over the next two decades in both the over-sixty-five population and the forty-five-to-fifty-four age cohort, providing tremendous potential for retirement-planning and wealth-preservation products and services in that target market.

- Jefferson-Pilot's annuity management has capitalized on the favorable market conditions by adding new products, including popular multiyear rate guaranteed contracts; by responding quickly and aggressively to changing interest rates; and by focusing more effectively on all of the elements necessary to be a performance leader in the dynamic annuity marketplace.

- The company's life insurance sales have performed well in recent years. In the words of Ken Mlekush, President—Life Companies, "Jefferson-Pilot's growth has been tremendous—our life sales last year (2000) were more than six times our sales in 1992. We've achieved this by building and acquiring distribution and by pursuing new ventures, such as our investment in Highland Capital, our marketing tie with RSM McGladrey, and our alliance with Allstate.

  "Now we're implementing a new plan to keep us at the forefront of the industry. Premier Partnering grew out of an intensive, fact-based research process that told us what we need to do to be the Partner of Choice for top producers, and it's changing the way we do business. We're focusing intensively on the individual top-producing agent. We're focusing on targeted markets using strong marketing packages, such as our CPA Security and LifeComp programs. We're aggressively recruiting new top-performing producers. And we're dramatically re-engineering our service operations. We're excited about Premier Partnering's potential, and our whole organization is energized to make it happen."

- Jefferson-Pilot views the Internet as a very substantial opportunity. With a surging percentage of domestic households now possessing Internet connections, and with online banking established as a viable consumer product, there is no question as to its potential as a medium.

  According to management, "Certain of our product may achieve direct distribution via the Internet, but the real opportunity, we believe, is to upgrade our service levels and strengthen our relationship with our clients."

- The company had an enviable record of growth in the 1990–2000 period. Earnings per share advanced from $1.31 to $4.93, a compound annual growth rate of 14.2 percent. What's more, the record was consistent, with no dips along the way. In the same ten-year stretch, the per-share dividend climbed from $.44 to $1.44, a compound growth rate of 12.6 percent.

- The company has capitalized on a consolidation trend underway in the life insurance business to add to its core life insurance business. In 1995, JP acquired the life insurance and annuity business of Kentucky Central Life and Health Insurance Company. Also in 1995, the company acquired Alexander Hamilton Life Insurance Company of America from Household International. In 1997, Jefferson-Pilot purchased the life insurance unit of Chubb Corporation. At the end of 1999, the company acquired The Guarantee Life Companies Inc.

- Benefit Partners, the company's group nonmedical products business, was formed when JP acquired Guarantee Life Insurance Company in 1999 and merged its existing small group nonmedical operations into Guarantee's. This business is headquartered in Omaha, Nebraska, and headed by Bob Bates, former CEO of Guarantee, and is proving to be a highly synergistic combination. According to David A. Stonecipher, CEO of Jefferson-Pilot, "The consolidation of Guarantee with Jefferson-Pilot during 2000 was the smoothest and most efficient integration that we have experienced in any acquisition. Most important, this acquisition has met all financial expectations we established for it."

Total assets: $27,321 million
Common shares outstanding: 154 million
Return on 2000 shareholders' equity: 16.8%

	2000	1999	1998	1997	1996	1995	1994	1993
Revenues (millions)	3238	2460	2610	2578	2125	1569	1334	1247
Net income (millions)	512	470	418	370	291	255	230	219
Earnings per share	3.29	2.95	2.61	2.32	1.82	1.58	1.40	1.29
Dividends per share	.96	.86	.77	.69	.62	.56	.50	.46
Price High	50.6	53.1	52.3	38.6	26.5	21.4	16.3	17.1
Low	33.3	40.8	32.4	22.9	20.1	15.0	12.9	13.5

CONSERVATIVE GROWTH

Johnson & Johnson

One Johnson & Johnson Plaza ◻ New Brunswick, New Jersey 08933 ◻ Investor contact: Helen E. Short (732) 524-6492 ◻ Dividend reinvestment plan is available: (800) 328-9033 ◻ Web site: www.jnj.com ◻ Listed: NYSE ◻ Ticker symbol: JNJ ◻ S&P rating: A+ ◻ Value Line financial strength rating: A++

Stents, the tiny metal scaffolds that transformed the care of heart patients in the 1990s, are on the threshold of a major advance that may put an end to one of cardiology's most baffling enigmas.

Each year, about 700,000 patients in the United States undergo angioplasty, in which a balloon is used to clear an obstruction in a coronary artery and a stent is deployed to keep it open. Unfortunately, a high percentage of procedures—some 15 to 20 percent—develop serious problems within six months as the stent develops restenosis (arterial scarring).

Now, heart researchers and stent makers are developing a new generation of stents that not only prop open the artery but deliver drugs to the site of the blockage in an effort to keep the vessel open. Research studies suggest that stents coated with a drug called rapamycin put a stop to restenosis. Rapamycin is an immune system suppressant drug marketed by American Home Products. JNJ has licensed the drug, which it calls Sirolimus, for use with stents. It halts the replication of certain cells that, as part of the body's response to injury, are involved in the proliferation of scar tissue.

Johnson & Johnson is well along in the development of its "pharma stent," which is coated with rapamycin. The company is widely regarded as being well ahead of competitors in a race to bring similar coated devices to market.

In 1994 JNJ initiated a new era in heart treatment with its first stent, which dominated the market for three years. But its days of glory were short-lived when rivals invaded its domain with better technology.

Now, however, the company is poised to make a comeback. Analysts and physicians are convinced that JNJ's Cordis unit is about to reclaim much of its former market share for angioplasty devices. Among other recent accomplishments, Cordis received FDA approval for the Checkmate System for gamma radiation of in-stent restenosis, coupled with its acquisition of Atrionix, which brings JNJ a company with promising technology for treating atrial fibrillation—a condition for which until now there has been no effective treatment.

"We're predicting that J&J is going to be the leader in this field for a few years," said William O'Neill, director of cardiology at William Beaumont Hospital, Royal Oak, Michigan.

Company Profile

Johnson & Johnson is the largest and most comprehensive health care company in the world, with 2000 sales of $29.1 billion.

JNJ offers a broad line of consumer products, ethical and over-the-counter drugs, as well as various other medical devices and diagnostic equipment.

The company has a stake in a wide variety of endeavors: anti-infectives, biotechnology, cardiology and circulatory diseases, the central nervous system, diagnostics, gastrointestinals, minimally invasive therapies, nutraceuticals, orthopaedics, pain management, skin care, vision care, women's health, and wound care.

Johnson & Johnson has 194 operating companies in fifty-one countries, selling some 50,000 products in more than 175 countries.

One of Johnson & Johnson's premier assets is its well-entrenched brand names, which are widely known in the United States as well as abroad. As a marketer, moreover, JNJ's reputation for quality has enabled it to build strong ties to health care providers.

Its international presence includes not only marketing but also production and distribution capability in a vast array of regions outside the United States.

One advantage of JNJ's worldwide organization: Markets such as China, Latin America, and Africa offer growth potential for mature product lines.

The company's well-known trade names include Band-Aid adhesive bandages, Tylenol, Stayfree, Carefree and Sure & Natural feminine hygiene products, Mylanta, Pepcid AC, Neutrogena, Johnson's baby powder, shampoo and oil, and Reach toothbrushes.

The company's professional items include ligatures and sutures, mechanical wound closure products, diagnostic products, medical equipment, surgical dressings, surgical apparel and accessories, and disposable contact lenses.

Shortcomings to Bear in Mind

- In 2000 the Food and Drug Administration (FDA) strengthened its warnings for JNJ's popular heartburn drug, Propulsid. The FDA said seventy deaths and 200 other episodes of irregular heartbeats have been linked to the drug since it was approved for marketing in 1993. However, about 85 percent of the events occurred in patients with conditions known to put them at risk if they took the drug, according to the FDA.

The fatalities and other events have continued to occur even though the FDA has ordered changes in the product's labeling four previous times since 1993. Propulsid already carries a so-called black-box warning—used in instances where approved medicines can be especially risky for some patients—highlighting its association with potentially fatal heart arrhythmia.

"Propulsid has been a major source of growth for J&J's pharmaceutical business," said one analyst. "There's no question there is going to be a negative effect."

In the spring of 2000, JNJ said it would cease marketing Propulsid in the United States. However, there are no plans to curtail marketing in Europe and other international markets where the drug generally is prescribed for other digestive afflictions at lower doses and where the incidence of life-threatening heart problems is much lower.

Reasons to Buy

- The company's largest and fastest growing segment is pharmaceuticals. Despite the severe decline in Propulsid sales, the pharmaceutical unit had a sales increase of 15.2 percent in 2000. Excluding Propulsid from the picture, the pharmaceutical business grew by an impressive 23.1 percent.

JNJ's strong growth in pharmaceutical sales came from a wide range of products, including Procrit/Eprex for treating anemia; Risperdal, an antipsychotic medication; Levaquin, an anti-infective; Duragesic, a transdermal patch for chronic pain; Remicade, a treatment for rheumatoid arthritis and Crohn's disease; Ultram, an analgesic for moderate to severe pain; Topamax, to treat epilepsy; and Aciphex/Pariet, a proton pump inhibitor for gastrointestinal disorders. Also worth noting is that each of these products has substantial opportunity for further growth, and each has considerable patent life remaining.

- Johnson & Johnson acquired Alza Corporation in March 2001 for $10.5 billion. The deal will add about $700 million to the company's pharmaceutical business. Alza developed the bestselling time-release delivery of the NicoDerm anti-smoking patch, which is sold by GlaxoSmithKline p.l.c.

Alza also makes time-release capsules that enable patients to take pills less frequently, as well as systems that use electricity to push drugs through the skin. In addition, Alza will contribute to JNJ's line with such products as Concerta, a once-a-day remedy for an attention-deficit-hyperactivity disorder drug; Ditropan XL for urinary incontinence; and the cancer drug Doxil.

The Alza products are expected to immediately benefit from JNJ's deep pockets and worldwide marketing reach, which will help produce more revenue than if Alza sold them on its own.

- The FDA approved JNJ's new drug for Alzheimer's disease in 2001. Reminyl, which became available in May 2001, was approved to treat mild to moderate Alzheimer's cases. The Alzheimer's Association estimates four million Americans

suffer from progressive neurological disease. The association believes that if no cure is found, as many as 14 million will develop Alzheimer's by the middle of the century. Reminyl was shown to be effective in improving or helping to stabilize patients' ability to think and perform daily tasks in studies involving more than 2,650 subjects.

Initially, the company launched the sale of Reminyl in the United States, the United Kingdom, Denmark, and Sweden. Approval has also been granted by fourteen other countries, where market introduction is in the works.

- Taking advantage of the Internet, JNJ is determined to become the best-connected health care company in the world. In the words of CEO Ralph S. Larsen, "We anticipate the Internet will enable us to change the ways we conduct business within and among our 194 companies, helping us to capture economies of scale while maintaining our decentralized management structure."

The company is pursuing strategies based on three principles:

- Using the Internet to create new ways of connecting with its customers, including physicians, hospitals, consumers, and retail partners.
- Transforming JNJ's core business processes—redesigning the ways the company works—in order to take full advantage of the Internet technology to save time, money, and improve quality.
- Creating a Web-savvy culture throughout "our entire employee base around the world, recognizing that the Internet is an important tool in everything we do—at work and at home."

- A new contact lens made by Johnson & Johnson promises to clear the fuzzy vision of aging Americans who would rather squint that be caught wearing bifocals. The Acuvue Bifocal disposable contact lenses are being heavily marketed by the company to the 80 million people who have presbyopia, a vision problem that usually begins shortly after the fortieth birthday. Caused by a loss of flexibility in the eye, presbyopia makes it hard to thread a needle, read a newspaper, or focus on a computer screen. The lenses are paper-thin and can be worn continuously for seven days or during waking hours for two weeks. Designed with five invisible concentric rings that bring distant and near objects into focus, they allow wearers to shift back and forth easily. They cost about $13 to $14 a pair.

- The company can boast of impressive world leadership:
  - It is the largest medical-device company.
  - It is the eighth largest pharmaceutical company.

- JNJ has the largest:
  - Over-the-counter pharmaceutical business.
  - Disposable contact lens business.
  - Minimally invasive surgical equipment business.
  - Surgical suture business.
  - Blood glucose monitoring business.
- Skin care is the largest consumer market in which Johnson & Johnson participates—some $47 billion at retail. What's more, JNJ believes that it has the fastest growing skin portfolio in the world. Its presence extends from its well-known heritage in baby products to consumer toiletries to prescription pharmaceuticals. Four of the company's five key skin care brands—Neutrogena, RoC, Clean & Clear, and Johnson's pH5.5—have been growing at double-digit rates.

Total assets: $31,321 million
Current ratio: 2.16
Common shares outstanding: 2,780 million
Return on 2000 shareholders' equity: 27.4%

	2000	1999	1998	1997	1996	1995	1994	1993
Revenues (millions)	29139	27471	23657	22629	21620	18842	15734	14138
Net income (millions)	4800	4167	3669	3303	2887	2403	2006	1787
Earnings per share	1.70	1.47	1.34	1.21	1.09	.93	.78	.69
Dividends per share	.62	.55	.49	.43	.37	.32	.29	.26
Price High	53.0	53.5	44.9	33.7	27.0	23.1	14.2	12.6
Low	33.1	38.5	31.7	24.3	20.8	13.4	9.0	8.9

CONSERVATIVE GROWTH

Johnson Controls, Inc.

Post Office Box 591 ◻ Milwaukee, Wisconsin 53201 ◻ Investor contact: Denise M. Zutz (414) 524-1200 ◻ Dividend reinvestment plan is available: (800) 828-1489 ◻ Fiscal year ends September 30 ◻ Web site: www.johnsoncontrols.com ◻ Ticker symbol: JCI ◻ S&P rating: A+ ◻ Value Line financial strength rating: A

Johnson Controls strengthened its position as the battery industry's technology leader with the 2000 acquisition of Gylling Optima, the maker of spiral-wound lead-acid batteries sold globally under the Optima brand name.

The Optima battery has more energy and power per pound than any traditional lead-acid batteries. In addition to being the battery of choice for many automotive and marine applications today, it will be an excellent technology for the 42-volt electrical systems now being developed by automakers for new vehicles.

Although the company's automotive segment brings in 75 percent of annual revenues, JCI has a substantial stake in electronic systems that control such factors as heating, lighting, and security in buildings. Less than 25 percent of the world's nonresidential buildings have digital automated building controls, and fewer than 3 percent outsource facility management responsibilities. Existing buildings represent, according to management, "A huge untapped market for Johnson Controls, and remain the main target for our growth strategies."

Company Profile

Johnson Controls, Inc. is a global market leader in automotive systems and facility management and control. In the automotive market, it is a major supplier of seating and interior systems and batteries. For nonresidential facilities, Johnson Controls provides building control systems and services, energy management, and integrated facility management.

Automotive Systems Group
- Global market leader in seating and interior systems for light vehicles, including passenger cars and light trucks.
- Systems supplied include seating, overhead, door, instrument panels, storage, electronics, and batteries.
- All systems are sold to the original equipment automotive market. However, the automotive replacement market is the major course of sales for batteries.
- Major customers include AutoZone, Costco, DaimlerChrysler, Fiat, Ford, General Motors, Honda, Interstate Battery Systems of America, John Deere, Mazda, Mitsubishi, Nissan, NUMMI, Peugeot, Renault, Sears, Toyota, Volkswagen, and Wal-Mart.
- 275 locations worldwide.

Controls Group
- The Controls business is a leader in supplying systems to control heating, ventilating, air conditioning (HVAC), lighting, security, and fire management for buildings. Services include complete mechanical and electrical maintenance.
- World leader in integrated facility management, providing facility management and consulting services for many *Fortune* 500 companies. The company manages more than one billion square feet worldwide.
- Customers worldwide include education, health care, industrial, government, and office buildings.
- 300 locations worldwide.

Shortcomings to Bear in Mind

- The company's large exposure to the automotive industry often worries investors. While it is difficult to argue that such concerns are unfounded, some analysts are convinced that they are overemphasized. For one thing, during periods of economic weakness Johnson Controls's earnings have typically held up considerably better than those of most auto suppliers. On the other hand, there is no doubt that car sales are subject to sharp ups and downs.

Reasons to Buy

- Over the past ten years, 1991–2000, the company's earnings per share increased without interruption, climbing from $1.03 to $5.09, an impressive annual compound growth rate of 17.3 percent. In the same ten-year span, dividends advanced from $.60 to $1.12, a more modest growth rate of 6.4 percent. However, the dividend payout ratio is extremely favorable at only 22 percent. A low payout ratio is characteristic of a company with solid growth prospects.

- Integration of electronics into vehicle interiors is one of the company's specialties, ranging from global positioning systems to digital compasses and Homelink. The company, moreover, is continuously developing new products and holds more patents than any other automotive interior supplier.

- The company's automotive business is expected to expand in the years ahead as automakers continue outsourcing seating and interior systems in North America and Europe as well as in emerging global markets. What's more, the company's development of innovative features and application of new technologies for the automotive interior will strengthen the company's leadership position, as Johnson Controls makes its customers' vehicles more comfortable, convenient, and safe.

- In the company's automotive business, its strategy is to supply larger modules and, over time, deliver complete interiors to its automotive customers. Johnson Controls is well on the way toward achieving this goal, having received its initial orders in 2000 to provide complete interiors for future vehicle models.

- Nearly every automotive system the company makes today includes electronics. New products such as the company's AutoVision, an in-vehicle video system and PSI tire pressure-sensing system, are electronics based. What's more, electronics are a part of its seats and other interior systems as well. An innovative use of electronics creates new features and functions for car interiors, as well as new way for the company's automaker customers to differentiate their vehicles. More than one-third of all vehicles made in North America in 2000 had Johnson Controls's on board, and, says CEO James H. Keyes, "there's a lot more to come."

- In August 2000, Johnson Controls announced the acquisition of Ikeda Bussan, the main supplier of seats to Nissan globally. In addition to strengthening its relationship with Nissan, Ikeda builds on and expands the company's existing technical resources in Japan, furthering its ability to exceed "the expectation of our global automotive customers and supporting future growth in Asia," according to Mr. Keyes.

- By incorporating electronics into its batteries, Johnson Controls has created industry-first antitheft and power-management features. In addition, a new spiral-wound battery technology, the result of an acquisition in 2000, gives the company new growth opportunities in specialty applications and for the 42-volt automotive electrical systems under development.

- Industry studies estimate that 75 percent of all tires are improperly inflated. The company's PSI system uses a radio-frequency transmitter in each tire, which sends air pressure information to an in-vehicle electronic display.

- The annual market for automotive electronics in North America will reach a total of $28 billion by 2004. To help meet this demand, according to management, "We're expanding and accelerating our electronics capabilities and creating new partnering programs with leading electronics firms."

- According to a spokesman for the company, "With more than 110 years of experience in the controls industry, Johnson Controls understands buildings better than anyone else. That's why tens of thousands of commercial, institutional, and government building owners and managers around the world turn to Johnson Controls to improve the quality of buildings' indoor environments by maximizing comfort, productivity, safety, and energy efficiency."

- The company engineers, manufactures, and installs control systems that automate a building's heating, ventilating, and air conditioning, as well as its lighting and fire safety equipment. Its Metasys Facility Management System automates a building's mechanical systems for optimal comfort levels while using the least amount of energy. In addition, it monitors fire sensors and building access, controls lights, tracks equipment maintenance, and helps building managers make better decisions.
- Building systems at some companies are critical to achieving their corporate missions. In the pharmaceutical industry, for example, the failure of a building's equipment or staff to maintain the proper laboratory conditions could mean the loss of years of new drug research and development. In a bank's data center, moreover, the failure of cooling equipment could shut down computer systems, delaying millions of dollars in transactions every minute.
- The company's Metasys facility management system monitors and controls heating, ventilating, and air conditioning systems in buildings to ensure maximum occupant comfort with a minimum of energy costs. Hundreds of Metasys systems were installed in 1998, including new projects at the Pentagon, the Kremlin, and the new Beijing International Airport.

Metasys technology has been improved and expanded since its introduction to create new benefits for customers. Metasys leads the industry in its ability to integrate with other building systems such as lighting, access, and fire/safety systems. Today, Metasys can also integrate controllers made by other companies for power monitoring equipment, refrigeration systems, laboratory fume hoods, manufacturing process controls, and more.

- The company's Controls Group does business with more than 7,000 school districts, colleges, and universities as well as over 2,000 health care organizations. These customers benefit from performance contracting, a solution that lets them implement needed facility repairs and updates without up-front capital costs. Performance contracting uses a project's energy and operational cost savings to pay its costs over time. For instance, using a performance contract, Grady Health System in Atlanta was able to complete energy efficiency upgrades that will generate $20 million in savings over the next ten years.

Total assets: $9,428 million
Current ratio: 0.95
Common shares outstanding: 86 million
Return on 2000 shareholders' equity: 20.2%

	2000	1999	1998	1997	1996	1995	1994	1993
Revenues (millions)	17155	16139	12587	11145	10009	8330	6870	6182
Net income (millions)	472	387	303	265	235	196	165	138
Earnings per share	5.09	4.13	3.25	2.85	2.14	1.80	1.49	1.37
Dividends per share	1.12	1.00	.92	.86	.82	.78	.72	.68
Price High	65.1	76.7	61.9	51.0	42.7	34.9	30.9	29.6
Low	45.8	49.0	40.5	35.4	31.3	22.9	22.4	21.5

GROWTH AND INCOME

Kimberly-Clark Corporation

P. O. Box 619100 ◻ Dallas, Texas 75261-9100 ◻ Investor contact: Michael D. Masseth (972) 281-1478 ◻ Dividend reinvestment plan is available: (800) 730-4001 ◻ Web site: www.Kimberly-Clark.com ◻ Ticker symbol: KMB ◻ S&P rating: A- ◻ Value Line financial strength rating: A++

Diapers are big business for Kimberly-Clark and its archrival Procter & Gamble. In early 2001, Kimberly-Clark launched a redesigned line of Huggies diapers across its European markets, demonstrating the company's intention to bolster its position in the $4.6-billion European diaper market.

Research conducted by Kimberly-Clark in Europe convinced the company that a new approach was needed. It now divides diaper-age children into three groups: "Beginnings" (0 to 3 months), "Freedom" (4 months or more), and "Adventurers" (12 months or more). Early indications from market research show that this will be a winner with the European consumer.

"Our new products are drier than our competitors' and are clinically proven to protect against diaper rash," said James Meyer, president of Infant & Child Care for Kimberly-Clark Europe. "More importantly, however, we believe that our new range of products and positioning now matches the way parents see the growth and development of their baby."

Product improvements in the new Huggies diaper range include a softer outer cover and leak guards for the "Beginnings" stage, greater absorbency and dryness for the "Freedom" stage, and a new super-premium, better fitting diaper for the "Adventurers" stage.

"Since 1996, our diaper sales in Europe have more than doubled," said Mr. Meyer. "And we are confident that the new Huggies product and positioning will continue this volume and market share growth. In fact, Huggies is the fastest growing of the top 50 non-food grocery brands in the UK."

Kimberly-Clark ended 2000 with a 25 percent volume share in its European markets, up 3 percentage points from the prior year. The company, moreover, increased its annual share in the United Kingdom to nearly 31 percent, compared with 24 percent in 1999.

Company Profile

Kimberly-Clark is a worldwide manufacturer of a wide range of products for personal, business, and industrial uses. Most of the products are made from natural and synthetic fibers using advanced technologies in absorbency, fibers, and nonwovens.

The company has manufacturing facilities in forty countries and sales in more than 150. Kimberly-Clark has been one of *Fortune* magazine's "Most Admired" corporations since 1983.

The company's well-known brands include Kleenex facial and bathroom tissue, Huggies diapers and baby-wipes, Pull-Ups training pants, GoodNites underpants, Kotex and New Freedom feminine care products, Depend and Poise incontinence care products, Hi-Dri household towels, Kimguard sterile wrap, Kimwipes industrial wipers, and Classic premium business and correspondence papers.

Shortcomings to Bear in Mind

- If Kimberly-Clark is to succeed, it must continually battle against the relentless, determined Procter & Gamble, one of the most innovative and skillful companies in the world.
- Growth in earnings has been rather pedestrian of late. In the 1991–2000

period, earnings per share advanced from $1.49 to $3.31, a compound annual growth rate of 8.3 percent. In the same ten-year stretch, dividends expanded from $.68 a share to $1.07, a growth rate of 4.6 percent.

However, the all-important payout ratio is indicative of a growth company. The company pays out less than a third of its earnings in the form of dividends, thus a generous portion is available to invest in expansion.

Reasons to Buy

- Kimberly-Clark launched the revolutionary Cottonelle Fresh Rollwipes in the summer of 2001, America's first and only dispensable, pre-moistened wipe on a roll. This breakthrough product delivers the cleaning and freshening of pre-moistened wipes with the convenience and disposability of toilet paper. It is the most significant category innovation since toilet paper first appeared in roll form in 1890.

The company says the compelling case for the product is that it comes on a roll with a dispenser that fits most bathroom toilet-paper holders. The dispenser holds a semi-sealed roll of moist wipes and also has a spindle for traditional toilet paper. The retail price of the Cottonelle Fresh Rollwipes starter pack (dispenser along with four rolls) is $8.99, and a refill pack of four rolls is $3.99.

In its first twelve months, retail sails of Cottonelle Fresh Rollwipes are estimated to reach $150 million. Over the next six years, retail sales of this category could exceed $500 million. "In addition," says a company spokesman, "because usage of the product is almost entirely incremental to dry toilet paper, it should result in a significant increase in the $4.8-billion domestic toilet paper market."

Research conducted by Kimberly-Clark shows that consumers agree that moist methods clean and freshen better than dry toilet paper alone. The results of a recent Kimberly-Clark survey showed that 63 percent of respondents have used moist cleansing, and one out of four use a moist cleansing method on a daily basis.

- The cornerstone of Kimberly-Clark, according to management, is "brands and technology. Let's take our successful relaunch of Kleenex Cottonelle bathroom tissue. It's a great example of how we're now applying to tissue the same formula that's worked so well for us in personal care and health care—that is, employing technology to deliver superior-performing products that win in the marketplace."

Using a patented process first commercialized at the company's mill in Villey-Saint-Etienne, France, KMB has produced a tissue with superior bulk, strength, softness, and absorbency—while reducing manufacturing costs. As a result, Kleenex Cottonelle has achieved record profits for the company's premium bathroom tissue business in North America. What's more, the company has begun applying this and other patented tissue technologies to improve the quality and reduce the manufacturing cost of many other Kimberly-Clark products.

These include a significantly improved Kleenex Scottfold towel for commercial users introduced in late 1998 and a new Scott household towel that became available in domestic stores in 1999. Still another introduction in 1999 was an even better Andrex bathroom tissue, which is already one of the best-selling nonfood grocery brands in the United Kingdom.

- As the world's foremost producer of nonwoven fabrics, Kimberly-Clark also brings sophisticated technology and cost advantages to bear on its health care products, which include sterile wrap, surgical drapes and gowns, and other protective apparel. In fact, the company holds an impressive 25 percent of the hundreds of patents granted in the nonwoven field since 1995.

In the opinion of KMB management, "health care is a business that continues to exceed expectations and offers enormous potential for further growth."

- In the realm of professional health care products, the company has been achieving impressive results, much of it emanating from innovative surgical gowns, drapes, and wraps. The same is true of the performance of KMB's nonwoven materials segment, which supplies versatile fabrics to its consumer-products operations and other businesses at a cost advantage compared with its competition.

- One of Kimberly-Clark's strengths stems from the leadership position it holds in three core technologies—fibers, absorbency, and nonwovens. It also comes from the company's capacity in high-speed manufacturing and from its constant emphasis on innovation, productivity, and cost reduction.

- Kimberly-Clark, as it is now constituted, is a balanced company. Before the Scott Paper merger and other acquisitions, the company derived almost half of its revenues from diapers and other personal care products. That portion is now a third. Consumer tissue also accounts for about a third of revenues, with the balance coming from a combination of away-from-home and other products.

- In Central and Eastern Europe, Kimberly-Clark extended its line of consumer products in Russia with the introduction of economy-priced diapers and feminine care products. The company also acquired Zisoft-Bobi, a Czech diaper and incontinence care products manufacturer, making Kimberly-Clark the largest personal care products company in that country. This presence provides a platform for offering products throughout Central and Eastern Europe. KMB has already introduced Kleenex and Scottex tissue products throughout the region and markets Huggies diapers in Russia, Romania, Croatia, Slovenia, and the Baltic states.

- Kimberly-Clark has dominance in many of its brands throughout the world. In country after country, the company's position in its product is either number one or two. In Australia, for instance, its Snugglers diapers and Thick & Thirsty paper towels fall into this group. The same holds true in such countries as Bolivia with Bebito diapers, Intima feminine pads, Sanex paper towels, and a host of other products. Similarly, in Brazil this distinction includes Monica diapers, Chiffon paper towels, and Neve bathroom tissue; in China, it's Comfort & Beauty feminine pads; in the Netherlands, Page bathroom tissue and paper towels; in Mexico, Kleen Bebe diapers and Petalo bathroom tissue; in Spain, Monbebe diapers; in Germany, Camelia feminine pads and Tampona tampons; in Israel, Titulim diapers, Lily feminine pads, Molett bathroom tissue and paper towels, and Iris paper napkins. The list goes on and on.

Total assets: $14,480 million
Current ratio: 0.86
Common shares outstanding: 534 million
Return on 2000 shareholders' equity: 33.2%

	2000	1999	1998	1997	1996	1995	1994	1993
Revenues (millions)	13982	13007	12298	12547	13149	13789	7364	6973
Net income (millions)	1801	1609	1353	1403	1404	1104	535	511
Earnings per share	3.31	2.98	2.45	2.44	2.49	1.98	1.67	1.59
Dividends per share	1.07	1.03	.99	.95	.92	.90	.88	.85
Price High	73.3	69.6	59.4	56.9	49.8	41.5	30.0	31.0
Low	42.0	44.8	35.9	43.3	34.3	23.6	23.5	22.3

Kimco Realty Corporation

3333 New Hyde Park Road ◻ Suite 100 ◻ Post Office Box 5020 ◻ New Hyde Park, New York 11042-0020 ◻ Investor contact: Scott G. Onufrey (516) 869-7190 ◻ Dividend reinvestment plan is available: (877) 453-1506 ◻ Web site: www.kimcorealty.com ◻ Listed: NYSE ◻ Ticker symbol: KIM ◻ S&P rating: Not rated ◻ Value Line financial strength rating: B++

Milton Cooper, Kimco's chairman, calls the REIT Modernization Act the Emancipation Proclamation of the REIT sector. He believes the act will give REITs the ability to retain a greater percentage of their earnings as the taxable subsidiaries will be treated as separate businesses with the ability to retain cash flow. In addition, he noted that this act should give REITs the ability to compete more effectively with other real estate companies and be more entrepreneurial and aggressive in their expansion and operating strategies.

The law, which became effective January 1, 2001, now enables REITs to own a taxable REIT subsidiary (TRS). The law permits a REIT to own up to 100 percent of the stock of a TRS that can provide services to tenants and others without jeopardizing a REIT's ability to avoid paying federal income taxes at the corporate level. To ensure that a REIT remains focused on core real estate operations, the bill contains a size limit on TRSs. Specifically, TRS securities may not exceed 20 percent of a REIT's assets, and income received from a TRS may not exceed 75 percent of a REIT's gross revenues.

Anticipating new opportunities when the REIT Modernization Act became effective on January 1, 2001, Kimco formed a subsidiary that operates as a merchant developer. The new legislation allows the subsidiary to immediately sell properties it develops, instead of holding the assets for at least four years, and receive after-tax profits.

Company Profile

Kimco Realty Corporation is the largest publicly traded real estate investment trust (REIT) that owns and operates a portfolio of neighborhood and community shopping centers (measured by gross leasable area). It has interests in 498 properties: 432 shopping centers, 2 regional malls, 55 retail store leases, and other projects totaling 66 million square feet of leasable area in 41 states.

Since incorporating in 1966, Kimco has specialized in the acquisition, development, and management of well-located centers with strong growth potential. Self-administered and self-managed, the company's focus is to increase the cash flow and enhance the value of its shopping center properties through strategic retenanting, redevelopment, renovation, and expansion, and to make selective acquisitions of neighborhood and community shopping centers that have below market-rate leases or other cash flow growth potential.

A substantial portion of KIM's income consists of rent received under long-term leases, most of which provide for the payment of fixed-base rents and a pro rata share of various expenses. Many of the leases also provide for the payment of additional rent as a percentage of gross sales.

KIM's neighborhood and community shopping center properties are designed to attract local area customers and typically are anchored by a supermarket, discount department store, or drugstore, offering day-to-day necessities rather than high-priced luxury items. Among the company's major tenants are Kmart, Wal-Mart, Kohl's, and TJX Companies.

Kimco's core strategy is to acquire older shopping centers carrying below-market rents. This space is then released at much higher rates.

Funds From Operations

REITs are not valued by earnings per share (EPS) but rather by funds from operations (FFO) per share. FFO is calculated by adding net income and depreciation expense and then subtracting profits from the sale of assets. If a REIT pays out 90 percent or more of its taxable income in dividends, it is exempt from paying federal income taxes. FFO per share is in excess of net income because depreciation is added in. This means that a REIT such as Kimco pays out only about 66 percent of its FFO in dividends, with the balance of 34 percent available for acquisitions and improving existing properties.

Shortcomings to Bear in Mind

- Real estate, like many industries, is cyclical. KIM's performance will be, to some degree, dependent on the health of the economy in its markets. Kimco's prospects will also be dependent upon the balance between supply and demand for shopping center space in each of its markets.

  In the fourth quarter of 2000, for instance, Kimco experienced its first single-digit FFO growth in three years. Management attributed the slowdown to the lower-than-expected pace of acquisitions for both Kimco Classic and its more recently formed Income REIT (KIR). According to a report issued by Credit Suisse First Boston in February 2001, "The pace of acquisitions in 2000 decelerated in 2000 from 1999 levels due to higher interest rates, which narrowed the spread between cap rates for

buying new properties and Kimco's cost of funding. The company stated that spreads have since improved."

Later in the same report, the analyst said, "Kimco retains a seasoned and highly regarded management team that is at times opportunistic, but most importantly, keenly focused on generating value for shareholders. Kimco also maintains a conservative balance sheet with a debt-to-market capitalization of 30 percent and fixed charge of 3.0 times. We believe the company should remain a leader among the shopping center REITs."

Reasons to Buy

- In the spring of 2001, Milton Cooper, age seventy-two, announced that he would step down as CEO of Kimco, a company he cofounded forty years ago. However, he will be replaced by an experienced executive, David B. Henry, who resigned his post at General Electric. He was chief investment officer and senior vice president at GE Capital Real Estate, as well as chairman of GE Capital Investment Advisors. David Henry, age fifty-one, joined Kimco as chief investment officer with the expectation that he will become Kimco's CEO in one year.

  Mr. Cooper, who has known Mr. Henry for more than fifteen years, said, "Finding a person to entrust the future of my life's work was not easy, but I believe he is perfectly suited to lead Kimco. His impressive background and vast industry relationships will help Kimco expand its business platform and operating capabilities. He will lead our company to the next level." Although Mr. Cooper will no longer be CEO when Mr. Henry takes the reigns, he will remain with Kimco as chairman.

- Kimco's customers include some of the strongest and most rapidly growing chains in the United States, such as Costco, Home Depot, Circuit City, Best Buy, Ames, Wal-Mart, Value City, Target, Kohl's, and Kmart.

- Nearly all of the company's revenue is contractual. This means that even when a retailer's sales slump, it does not change the rent they must pay to Kimco under the lease agreement or the value of the company's real estate.

- The Kimco Income REIT (KIR), a strategic joint venture with institutional investors launched in 1999, has a portfolio of $850 million in gross real estate assets comprising high-quality, well-leased properties financed primarily through nonrecourse mortgages. During 2000, KIR acquired fifteen neighborhood and community shopping centers from Philips International Realty Corporation. The Kimco Income REIT also acquired six properties from Center Trust, Inc. The acquired properties are 98 percent leased to a diverse tenant base, including Kohl's, Kmart, Marshall's, and others.

- During 2000, Kimco recorded a total return on investments of 39 percent for shareholders.

- Knowledge of local markets and trends is crucial to success in the real estate sector. Kimco's decentralized asset management staff—situated in such cities as New York, Los Angeles, Chicago, Philadelphia, Dallas, Phoenix, Tampa, Charlotte, and Dayton, provides knowledge of real estate developments that are analyzed by professionals on the scene.

- Kimco's success comes not by accident but as the careful product of business principles that have remained firmly in place since the company was founded in the 1950s. The company invests in properties that are undervalued assets, where management knows it will be able to capitalize on the margin between the price at which it can buy the property

and the price at which it can lease it. The average rent on properties in Kimco's portfolio remains below the market, providing the company with significant upside potential.

- Management is clearly aligned with shareholders as indicated by their collective 21.2 percent ownership stake in the company.

- Kimco has had a knack for opportunistic buys. In 1998 it did a sale-leaseback to take control of some 10 million square feet of space of Venture Stores real estate. It seemed like a risky move because Venture Stores was tottering. When the retailer eventually went belly-up, Kimco quickly leased the Venture units to new tenants at even higher rates.

In a more recent move into the bankruptcy realm, Kimco was awarded asset designation rights for thirty-four former Hechinger Stores and Builders Square locations at the end of 1999. The rights enable Kimco to direct the disposition of the positions held by the bankrupt estate. Separately, Kimco acquired fee title to seven Hechinger locations and one ground lease position.

- Kimco Realty, in a joint venture in the spring of 2001 with Simon Property Group and the Schottenstein Group, was awarded asset designation rights for all of the real estate property interests of the bankrupt estate of Montgomery Ward LLC and its affiliates. These property interests consist of 250 former Montgomery Ward department stores and other operating real estate assets. All told, the designation rights include 315 separate fee simple and leasehold property interests. These designation rights enable the venture to auction off the properties held by the bankrupt estate. According to Lorraine Mirabella, a writer for the *Baltimore Sun*, "Kimco has apparently lined up deals with retailers such as Target Corp., Kohl's, May Department Stores Co., and Federated Department Stores Inc. to take over the sites—many at desirable locations—said David M. Fick, managing director of Legg Mason Wood Walker in Baltimore.

Fick said he believes Kimco already has deals for at least half the Wards stores. Fick estimated that the average rents of the Wards stores ranged from $2 to $4 per square foot and could be released in the $6-to-$12-per-square-foot range."

Total assets: $ 3,112 million
Current ratio: NA
Return on 2000 equity: 12%
Common shares outstanding: 62 million

	2000	1999	1998	1997	1996	1995	1994	1993
Rental income (millions)	459	434	339	199	168	143	125	99
Net income (millions)	205	177	122	86	74	52	41	32
Earnings per share	2.86	2.46	1.93	1.78	1.61	1.33	1.17	1.05
Funds from operations	4.03	3.61	3.03	2.63	2.37	2.16	1.98	1.77
Dividends per share	2.88	2.43	1.97	1.72	1.56	1.44	1.33	1.25
Price　High	44.8	40.8	41.6	36.2	34.9	28.1	25.9	26.2
Low	32.8	30.9	33.4	30.3	25.3	23.6	22.1	20.3

CONSERVATIVE GROWTH

Leggett & Platt, Incorporated

No. 1 Leggett Road □ Carthage, Missouri 64836 □ Investor contact: David M. DeSonier (417) 358-8131 □ Dividend reinvestment plan is not available □ Web site: www.leggett.com □ Listed: NYSE □ Ticker symbol: LEG □ S&P rating: A- □ Value Line financial strength rating: A

According to a U.S. Department of Labor Study, the age group that spends the most amount on furniture is the forty-five-to-fifty-four-year-old bracket. The second highest amount is spent by those thirty-five to forty-four. The Census Bureau says the number of consumers in the forty-five-to-fifty-four age group expanded 14.1 percent in a recent five-year period. The thirty-five to forty-four age group advanced 7.3 percent. At the same time, the general population increased only 4.7 percent.

There are a number of reasons why middle-aged people spend more money on furniture:

a) Their income is high during this span of their lives.

b) They are more likely to be home-owners than are younger people.

c) These more mature couples have sold their starter homes. Their new homes, moreover, are larger and may need a whole new set of more expensive furniture. In 1993, the average home had 2,100 square feet of living space, up 5 percent from 1988. According to surveys, the average home has now increased to 2,200 square feet. Larger homes require much more furniture than smaller ones. For instance, a home with 3,000 square feet needs 2.5 times as much as one with 2,000 square feet.

Company Profile

Founded in 1883, Leggett & Platt is a leading manufacturer of engineered products serving several major markets, including residential furnishings, commercial furnishings, aluminum products, industrial materials, and specialized products. Products include components for bedding and furniture, retail store fixtures, displays, die castings, custom tooling and dies, drawn steel wire, welded steel tubing, control cable systems, and automotive seating suspension.

Standard & Poor's added Leggett & Platt to the S&P 500 Index in October 1999. The S&P 500 is widely regarded as one of the most important standards for measuring U.S. stock market performance. The index includes a cross section of large-capitalization companies in a host of industries. As a component of the S&P 500, Leggett should gain increasing recognition throughout the investment community.

Here is a glimpse of LEG's businesses:

Residential Furnishings

Leggett & Platt is the world's leading supplier of a broad line of components, many of which are proprietary, for bedding and residential furniture. Manufacturers of mattresses and box springs can buy almost all of their component requirements from Leggett. Product lines have been expanded to include a wide range of components for stationary and motion upholstered furniture as well.

In addition, the company designs and produces select lines of finished home furnishings and consumer products. Customers include manufacturers, retailers, distributors, and institutions.

Residential Furnishings is by far the company's largest segment. In 2000, its sales increased 9.2 percent totaling $2.1 billion.

Commercial Furnishings

Leggett's rapidly expanding lines of commercial furnishings include creative store fixtures, point-of-purchase displays, and storage and material handling systems. A multitude of retailers, brand-name packagers of consumer products, as well as companies in the food service, health care, and other industries are increasingly looking to Leggett as a one-stop one-shop resource. Manufacturers of office and institutional furnishings and additional commercial products also can buy Leggett components designed and produced to meet their requirements. The company's components add significant value, comfort, and distinctive features to chairs and other office furniture.

Commercial Furnishings, Leggett's second largest segment, had a revenue increase in 2000 of 26.7 percent to $983.5 million. A number of acquisitions were largely responsible for this large increase.

Aluminum Products

The Leggett companies in its aluminum group are North America's leading independent suppliers of aluminum die castings, primarily for nonaluminum applications. Major customers include manufacturers of consumer products, telecommunications and electrical equipment, plus other industrial products that incorporate aluminum and zinc die cast components. Leggett's aluminum smelting and refining operations produce raw materials for internal use in die casting plants and for sale to other manufacturers of aluminum products.

Aluminum Products didn't fare well in 2000 as total sales decreased by 0.5 percent to $529 million. Hurting this operation were such factors as higher natural gas costs, smelting losses, plant underutilization, and plant closure costs.

Industrial Materials

Several Leggett companies produce industrial materials for a wide range of customers, including other Leggett operations. Drawn steel wire and welded steel tubing are produced in various strategic locations. Additional operations produce specialty wire products, such as rolled, flattened, and shaped wire, proprietary bale ties, tying heads, and other parts for automatic baling equipment.

Industrial Materials, also enhanced by acquisitions, had a revenue growth in 2000 of 8.4 percent to $317.8 million. However, without the acquisitions sales would have risen only 2.5 percent.

Specialized Products

Two smaller units are engaged in manufacturing specialized products. One concentrates on manufacturing components primarily for automotive applications. The other business unit designs, builds, and sells specialized machinery and equipment. In the automotive segment, LEG manufactures seating suspension, lumbar support, and control cable systems. In the machinery sector, the company manufactures highly automated quilting machines for fabrics used to cover mattresses and other home furnishings. It also has a stake in implements used to fabricate springs of various types, industrial sewing machines, and other equipment designed primarily for the assembly of bedding.

Specialized Products turned in good results in 2000, with revenues climbing 32.2 percent. Here again, acquisitions played a prominent role. Without them, sales would have been flat with a modest decline of 0.3 percent.

Shortcomings to Bear in Mind

- The market is concerned about a slowdown in the economy and the potential impact on the furniture business. To an extent, Leggett's business is tied to home-buying and new housing starts. The two years after a home is purchased are normally years of heavy furniture purchases.
- Demand was weak in 2000 in part because of reduced housing activity as interest rates began to climb in late 1999. The impact was made worse by the widespread effects of higher energy prices

that were not fully offset by improved operating efficiencies, cost cutting, and price increases in some business units.

On a more positive note, the company set out to put in place strategies to cope with the EPS decline in 2000. Management announced a four-point plan:

- Correcting problems in underperforming businesses, including the aluminum and commercial fixtures segments.
- Closing, consolidating, or selling those operations that cannot be fixed.
- Reducing acquisition activity and capital expenditures.
- Using free cash flow and modest proceeds from divestitures to repurchase stock.

Reasons to Buy

- Leggett & Platt boasts a remarkable record of growth. In the 1990–2000 period—despite a dip in EPS in 2000—earnings per share climbed from $.31 to $1.32, a compound annual rate of 15.6 percent. In the same ten-year stretch, dividends per share expanded from $.11 to $.42, a growth rate of 14.3 percent. What's more, Leggett & Platt has increased its dividend for thirty consecutive years.
- Since 1967, acquisitions have been a key part of Leggett's growth strategy. The company traditionally pursues friendly acquisitions—those that fit with existing operations either in marketing, technology, or both.

Normally, Leggett's acquisitions broaden the company's product lines, providing entry into additional markets or secure sources of select raw materials. The company uses cash, stock, or combinations of the two in making acquisitions. In the past ten years, Leggett & Platt made more than 136 acquisitions.

On average, each acquired company accounted for $21 million in annual revenue. As a result of the relatively small size of each individual acquisition, the company lessens its exposure to blunders. This strategy, while difficult to execute, has been and will continue to be the backbone of Leggett & Platt's future growth.

- Leggett's commitment to research and development has kept pace with company growth. LEG has R & D facilities at both centralized and divisional locations. At those locations, engineers and technicians design and build new and improved products in all major lines and machinery. They also perform extensive tests for durability and function. Leggett's experience and accumulation of data in this highly specialized area of R & D is unmatched.

- Participation in such diverse furnishings categories as bedding and residential, office, and contract furniture gives Leggett & Platt the opportunity to spread new product developments into several sectors at all price points while limiting its exposure to any one sector.

- Since 1998, Leggett & Platt has been ranked in the top 20 percent of *Fortune* magazine's top 500 companies, based on performance measures, including growth of revenue, profits, and dividends, as well as total shareholder return and return on assets.

Total assets: $3,373 million
Current ratio: 2.95
Common shares outstanding: 196 million
Return on 2000 shareholders' equity: 14.7%

		2000	1999	1998	1997	1996	1995	1994	1993
Revenues (millions)		4276	3779	3370	2909	2466	2110	1858	1527
Net income (millions)		264	290	248	208	153	135	115	86
Earnings per share		1.32	1.45	1.24	1.08	.93	.80	.70	.52
Dividends per share		.42	.35	.32	.27	.23	.19	.155	.135
Price	High	22.6	28.3	28.8	23.9	17.4	13.4	12.4	12.5
	Low	14.2	18.6	16.9	15.8	10.3	8.5	8.3	8.2

AGGRESSIVE GROWTH

Eli Lilly and Company

Lilly Corporate Center ◻ Indianapolis, Indiana 46285 ◻ Investor contact: Patricia A. Martin (317) 276-2506 ◻ Dividend reinvestment plan is available: (800) 451-2134 ◻ Web site: www.lilly.com ◻ Listed: NYSE ◻ Ticker symbol: LLY ◻ S&P rating: A- ◻ Value Line financial strength rating: A++

Eli Lilly may have found its next blockbuster drug in a surprising medical advance: a little-noticed experimental drug called Zovant that is able to reduce deaths from septic infections. The commercial introduction of Zovant is scheduled for the second half of 2001.

The company said research shows that Zovant is so effective at fighting sepsis that an independent research-monitoring committee brought an abrupt early end to the drug's clinical trial. Stopping a trial early—because a drug works so well—is a most unusual step undertaken only when the independent group concludes that it would be unethical to continue giving some patients a placebo, an inert substance.

Sepsis, an infection in the bloodstream, normally carries a death rate of 30 percent to 50 percent. It has been devastating, too, for a variety of biotechnology companies that have tried and failed to produce drugs to treat it.

Investors have been concerned about Lilly's dependence on Prozac. However, other drugs are beginning to play important roles. In 2000 and 2001, for instance, results were helped by such drugs as Zyprexa, Gemzar, Evista, and ReoPro.

"As our product line continues to become more diversified, we have become less dependent on Prozac's performance," said Sidney Taurel, Lilly's CEO.

Mr. Taurel went on to say, "The addition of innovative products from our pipeline and from our partnerships, combined with continuing strong sales growth from newer products, will help drive improved top-line performance and overall strong earnings growth in the coming years."

Company Profile

Eli Lilly is one of the world's foremost health care companies. With a solid dedication to R & D, Lilly is a leader in the development of ethical drugs—those available on prescription.

It is well-known for such drugs as Prozac (to treat depression); a number of antibiotics such as Ceclor, Vancocin, Keflex, and Lorabid; and insulin and other diabetic care items. Some of its other important drugs include Gemzar (to treat cancer of the lung and pancreas), Evista (to treat and prevent osteoporosis), ReoPro (a drug used to prevent adverse side effects from angioplasty procedures), Zyprexa (a breakthrough treatment for schizophrenia and bipolar disorder), Dobutrex (for congestive heart failure); Axid (a medication that reduces excess stomach acid), and Sarafem (for the treatment of Premenstrual Dysphoric Disorder). Lilly also has a stake in animal health and agricultural products.

Like most drug companies, Lilly is active abroad and does business in 120 countries.

Shortcomings to Bear in Mind

■ In August 2000, a federal appeals court cleared the way for the sale of a generic version of Prozac, the world's top-selling antidepressant, as early as the summer of 2001, about two years earlier than expected. In 2001, however, the FDA approved the application of a pediatric extension for Prozac, thereby granting Lilly an additional six months of marketing exclusivity. Unless there are new developments, it would appear that Lilly's Prozac patent will expire at the end of August 2001.

■ Some critics are concerned that Premenstrual Dysphoric Disorder (PMDD) is a mental illness. Some drug companies, including Eli Lilly, are treating it as one. For its part, Lilly is promoting Sarafem for PMDD. However, this drug is nothing new; it is simply Prozac, the popular antidepressant, packaged under a different name. The medical community is skeptical about this use of the drug. In the view of some critics, it seems odd that women suffering from problems associated with menstrual cycles should be looked upon as mentally ill.

The various drug companies, on the other hand, are doing nothing illegal or unethical, as Sarafem has been approved by the Food & Drug Administration for the treatment of Premenstrual Dysphoric Disorder. What's more, the American Psychiatric Association included PMDD in the appendix of its current *Diagnostic and Statistical Manual of Mental Disorders*. This is the part of the publication set aside for issues needing further research before being officially accepted as a mental ailment.

Meanwhile, Sarafem can help take the sting out of the expiration of Prozac's patent at the end of August 2001. With Sarafem, Lilly has a separate patent to use the drug for PMDD through 2007.

Reasons to Buy

- The company's leading drugs did well in 2000. Prozac and Sarafem had combined sales of $2.6 billion (down 2 percent from the prior year); Zyprexa, $2.4 billion (up 27 percent). In the fourth quarter of 2000, Zyprexa's sales passed Prozac, making it the company's leading product; Humulin (a form of insulin), $1.1 billion (up 2 percent); Gemzar, $559 million (up 23 percent); Evista, $522 million (up 60 percent); ReoPro, $418 million (down 7 percent); Humalog (a form of insulin), $350 million (up 56 percent).

- Lilly is making an effort to increase its marketing and scientific staffs. Sidney Taurel, Lilly's CEO, says the company has increased its sales force, but it has doubled the number of biologists on its payroll. "We have the highest research and development to sales ratio in the U.S. and by far the lowest ratio of marketing to sales," he said. The productivity of sales representatives who call on physicians and keep them posted on Lilly's pharmaceuticals has traditionally been the company's focus, rather than the size of its sales force. "It was sort of a religion at Lilly for many years," said Mr. Taurel. Now the company's marketing expenditures are rising at 14 percent a year, while sales are advancing at a 10 percent pace. At the end of 1999, Lilly had 2,300 salespeople in the United States. By the end of 2000, the number had mushroomed by 60 percent to 3,700.

- In January 2001, the FDA granted approval for a new form of Prozac (Prozac Weekly), a 90 milligram formulation. No other antidepressant offers patients on long-term treatment the convenience of taking just one pill once a week.

- Although Pfizer has the lead in the erectile dysfunction realm with its Viagra, Eli Lilly has its own drug nearly ready to join the fray. Erectile dysfunction affects 30 million men in the United States alone.

The company has joined forces with Icos Corporation whose pill, Cialis, has been successfully tested on 212 men. Research demonstrated that Cialis enhanced erections for 88 percent of men, compared with 28 percent for those taking a placebo. Lilly plans to request FDA approval for Cialis in the latter part of 2001.

Alex Zisson, a pharmaceutical analyst with Chase H&Q, said, "Cialis looks very, very similar to Viagra. There is no market, especially a billion-dollar market, that is fully satisfied by one drug. The second and third drugs usually expand the market."

- Diabetes, within the endocrine category, is a good example. As the developer of the first insulin product and one of the world's major suppliers of insulin, Lilly has long been a global leader in the field. But diabetes, which affects more than 100 million people worldwide, continues to cause severe long-term complications, suffering, lost productivity, and death.

For many patients with this disease, diabetes is also inconvenient. Diabetics have to check their blood glucose several times a day. They may have to give themselves one or more shots of insulin. And they must take insulin at least thirty minutes before a meal or risk severe complications.

Lilly believes that it has an answer that gives patients with diabetes a better quality of life—and a good deal more convenience. Humalog acts faster than traditional insulin to control blood glucose levels. Patients take it right before a meal, compared with thirty to forty-five minutes before with current products. Humalog provides them with more freedom, better health, and fewer complications.

- Diabetics look forward to the day when they can take insulin in pill form rather than by injection. In the fall of 2000, Lilly said that it would work with the Generex Biotechnology Corporation to try to develop a form of insulin that can be taken orally. Lilly made initial payments to Generex and will pay the company royalties if the drug makes it to the market. Lilly received worldwide rights to the compound and will be responsible for continuing studies.

- The Food and Drug Administration (FDA) gave Lilly approval to sell Zyprexa for the treatment of manic depression, also known as bipolar disorder. In the past, Zyprexa was used primarily to treat schizophrenia. "The market for mania is almost as big as the market for schizophrenia," said Dr. John M. Davis, a psychiatry professor at the University of Illinois at Chicago. Prior to the new FDA ruling in late 1999, Zyprexa was already generating sales at an annual rate of about $2 billion a year. In the past, lithium and older antipsychotic drugs were the leading medicines used in bipolar disease.

- Evista is the company's fastest-growing drug. More than one million women in more than fifty countries have already used the product for the prevention or treatment of osteoporosis. And more good news might be on the horizon. Early data suggest Evista many reduce the incidence of breast cancer and benefit the heart in postmenopausal women.

- Diabetes is the leading cause of adult blindness, a condition for which no satisfactory treatments are currently available. Lilly is conducting studies of Protein Kinase C-beta inhibitor, a promising compound being investigated for the prevention of diabetes-related blindness and other complications of chronic diabetes.

- Among hard to treat diseases is an affliction called attention-deficit disorder, or ADD for short. ADD is often characterized by an inability to concentrate and may also include aggression and hyperactivity. Up until recently, the drug used most often was Ritalin (produced by Novartis AG), which has its share of side effects, notably its tendency to be a stimulant. The drug is also available in generic form, methylphenidate. Because of Ritalin's side effects, researchers have been trying to find a treatment for ADD that doesn't involve the use of stimulants. Now it appears that Lilly has come up with such a drug—it's called tomoxetine. Researchers say that tomoxetine doesn't trigger sleeplessness and has relatively little tendency to suppress appetites.

"This will open windows for patients who would otherwise not be medicated," said Joseph Biederman, the chief of pediatric psychopharmacology at Massachusetts General Hospital in Boston, who ran a study on tomoxetine in 2000.

"The market could easily exceed $1 billion for a product like tomoxetine," said Hemant K. Shah, an independent medical-industry analyst. "Ritalin has such a bad name that it would not be that difficult to convert people to a nonstimulant."

- The antibiotic Oritavancin was moved into Phase III trials, giving the company ten late-stage pipeline candidates in 2001.

Total assets: $14,691 million
Current ratio: 1.87
Common shares outstanding: 1,127 million
Return on 2000 shareholders' equity: 55.3%

		2000	1999	1998	1997	1996	1995	1994	1993
Revenues (millions)		10953	10003	9237	8518	7346	6764	5712	6452
Net income (millions)		2905	2721	2098	1774	1524	1307	1269	1347
Earnings per share		2.65	2.28	1.94	1.57	1.33	1.15	1.09	1.15
Dividends per share		1.04	.92	.80	.74	.69	.66	.63	.61
Price	High	109.0	97.8	91.3	70.4	40.2	28.5	16.6	15.5
	Low	54.0	60.6	57.7	35.6	24.7	15.6	11.8	10.9

Lowe's Companies, Incorporated

1605 Curtis Bridge Road ◻ Post Office Box 1111 ◻ Wilkesboro, North Carolina 28656 ◻ Investor contact: Robert A. Niblock (336) 658-4000 ◻ Dividend reinvestment plan is available: (877) 282-1174 ◻ Web site: www.lowes.com ◻ Fiscal year ends Friday closest to January 31 of following year ◻ Listed: NYSE ◻ Ticker symbol: LOW ◻ S&P rating: A+ ◻ Value Line financial strength rating: A+

How Lowe's Got Started

In 1946 a young veteran of World War II, H. Carl Buchan, returned home to the town of North Wilkesboro to resume a role as half owner of a hardware store his wife's father incorporated in 1921. Besides miscellaneous hardware and some building materials, North Wilkesboro Hardware stocked produce and groceries, snuff, dry goods, notions, and harnesses and horse collars.

Ten years later, Buchan bought the North Wilkesboro Hardware Company from brother-in-law James Lowe, with a vision of creating a chain of hardware stores. Buchan sold out all the inventory except heavy hardware and building materials. During the postwar building boom, he established a reputation for Lowe's low prices by cutting out wholesalers and dealing directly with manufacturers.

Lowe's soon grew into a regional chain of stores selling building supplies and big-ticket consumer durables. Although the company did have some retail customers, the majority of business came from professional contractors who built homes. The typical Lowe's store was a free-standing building situated near railroad tracks at the edge of a southern town.

With the growth of the do-it-yourself, home-improvement and repair industry, it occurred to the company that every homeowner was a potential Lowe's customer if "we could bring ourselves up to speed as retailers. Throughout the eighties, we nurtured the growth of our homeowner customer franchise, enlarging our sales floors and expanding our merchandise offering.

Consumers responded enthusiastically, and by the end of the decade, Lowe's was gaining a reputation as a home-center retailer, with a wide variety of products, friendly service, and unbeatable prices."

In the late 1980s, Lowe's began transforming from a chain of conventionally sized units into its current 150,000-square-foot prototype, which is the largest in the industry. Lowe's continues its most aggressive expansion plan ever, thriving in metropolitan markets with superstores in half of the nation's top twenty-five most populated cities.

Company Profile

Lowe's Companies, Inc. is the second largest domestic retailer of home-improvement products serving the do-it-yourself and commercial business customers. (Home Depot is number one.) Capitalizing on a growing number of U.S. households (about 100 million), the company has expanded from fifteen stores in 1962 and now operates more than 650 stores in forty states. Lowe's competes in the highly fragmented, $300-billion home-improvement industry.

The company sells more than 40,000 home-improvement products, including plumbing and electrical products, tools, building materials, hardware, outdoor hard lines, appliances, lumber, nursery and gardening products, millwork, paint, sundries, cabinets, and furniture. Lowe's has often been listed as one of the 100 best companies to work for in America.

The company obtains its products from about 6,500 merchandise vendors from around the globe. In most instances, Lowe's deals directly with foreign manufacturers rather than third-party importers.

In order to maintain appropriate inventory levels in stores and to enhance efficiency and distribution, Lowe's operates seven highly automated, efficient, state-of-the-art regional distribution centers (RDCs). RDCs are strategically situated in North Carolina, Georgia, Ohio, Indiana, Pennsylvania, Washington, and Texas.

Late in 2000, the company broke ground in Findlay, Ohio on an $80-million regional distribution center. Completed in October 2001, the 1.25-million-square-foot facility employs 500 people and supplies products to some 100 stores throughout the lower Great Lakes region.

Lowe's serves both retail and commercial business customers. Retail customers are primarily do-it-yourself homeowners and others buying for personal and family use. Commercial business customers include building contractors, repair and remodeling contractors, electricians, landscapers, painters, plumbers, and commercial building maintenance professionals.

During 1999 Lowe's acquired Eagle Hardware & Garden, a thirty-six-store chain of home-improvement and garden centers in the West. The acquisition accelerated Lowe's' West Coast expansion and provided a stepping stone for the company into ten new states and a number of key metropolitan markets.

In recent years, the company has been transforming its store base from a chain of small stores into a chain of home-improvement warehouses. The current prototype store (the largest in the industry) has 150,000 square feet of sales floor and another 35,000 square feet dedicated to lawn and garden products. The company is in the midst of its most aggressive expansion in company history. Lowe's is investing $2 billion a year and opening more than one store each week.

Shortcomings to Bear in Mind

- In the final quarter of fiscal 2000, Lowe's reported its first quarterly earnings decline in five years. EPS fell to $.37, compared with $.39 in the same quarter of the prior year. The disappointing results were no surprise to analysts, since the company had given them ample warning by telling them earlier that lumber prices had hit a nine-year low and that customer spending was weak.

- Despite owning 650 stores in forty states, Lowe's is still struggling to expand beyond its Southeastern roots and build a national brand. One problem is its name. Unlike Home Depot, the name does not make you think of home improvement. In fact, it might make you think of a theater chain—Loews Cineplex Entertainment Corporation of New York. The company's name, moreover, might also bring to mind Loews Corporation, a diversified concern with a stake in insurance, Lorillard cigarettes, Bulova watches, hotels, and offshore drilling.

In 2001, Lowe's decided it was time to overcome these misconceptions, launching its first network advertising campaign. In January 2001 it began running commercials on four major networks during such prime-time shows as *Law & Order*, *Who Wants to Be a Millionaire?*, and *Everybody Loves Raymond*.

Without naming its competitor, the ads portray Lowe's as a well-lit, organized alternative to cluttered warehouse stores that frustrate shoppers. For instance, one thirty-second spot shows a woman wandering aimlessly and begins, "Yesterday, finding anything at a home-improvement store meant searching for hours. Getting dirty and lost. People accepted this. Today, there's Lowe's."

Reasons to Buy

- To enhance its extensive line of national brands, such as DeWalt, Armstrong, American Standard, Olympic, Owens Corning, Sylvania, Harbor Breeze, and Delta, the company is teaming up with vendors to offer preferred brands exclusive to Lowe's. These include Laura Ashley, Sta-Green, Troy-Bilt, and Alexander Julian among others.

  In categories where preferred brands are not available, Lowe's has created its own brands, including Kobalt tools, Reliabilt doors and windows, and Top Choice lumber.

- Lowe's advanced to the number two spot in domestic appliance sales in mid-2000. However, the company is the number one seller of appliances among home-improvement centers. In its stores, Lowe's features such leading brands as Whirlpool, KitchenAid, Frigidaire, Maytag, Jenn-Air, and General Electric.

- During the 1991–2000 period, Lowe's racked up an explosive record of growth as its earnings per share shot up from $.12 to $1.06, a compound annual growth rate of 24.3 percent. In the same ten-year span, dividends, although very modest, advanced from $.035 to $.07 for a much less impressive growth rate of 7.2 percent. Obviously, you would not buy this stock for current income, since the yield is a tiny fraction of one percent.

- In 2000, the company opened 100 new retail stores, including twenty relocations. Seven units were closed during the year. At the end of 2000, Lowe's operated 650 stores in forty states representing 67.8 million square feet, an increase of 19 percent over the prior year.

  At the beginning of 2001, Lowe's listed these objectives for 2001:

- To open 115 to 120 stores, reflecting square-footage growth of 18 to 20 percent.
- Total sales are expected to increase about 17 to 19 percent in the fifty-two weeks of fiscal 2001 versus the fifty-three weeks in 2000.
- The company expects to report a same-store sales increase of 2 to 4 percent.
- Gross margin is expected to improve by 20 to 30 basis points. There are 100 basis points in one percent.
- Operating margin is expected to increase by 20 to 30 basis points.
- Diluted earnings per share of $2.45 to $2.50 is expected for the year to end February 1, 2002.

- In an effort to expand beyond its traditional Southeast base, the company announced a major commitment to Northeast growth in 2001, with plans to build more than seventy-five stores from Philadelphia to Maine over the next five years. This represents an estimated $1.3 billion investment in the region. Demonstrating this commitment was the February opening of Lowe's in Danvers, Massachusetts. This marked the first of a twenty-five-store, $430-million commitment to the Boston area. A second store in Brockton was opened late in 2001. In the spring of 2001 the company opened its first unit in the New York City market (North Bergen, New Jersey).

- Formica Corporation announced that it had created a strategic alliance with Lowe's in late 2000. Lowe's now carries Formica brand laminate sheets, as well as countertops clad with Formica brand laminate, Formica brand adhesives, beveled edges, sealants, and caulk. In addition, Lowe's also offers Formica Tile, a tile-design surfacing, as well as Surell and Fountainhead solid surfacing material.

Total assets: $11,376 million
Current ratio: 1.43
Common shares outstanding: 766 million
Return on 2000 shareholders' equity: 14.7%

	2000	1999	1998	1997	1996	1995	1994	1993
Revenues (millions)	18779	15905	12245	10137	8600	7075	6110	4538
Net income (millions)	810	673	482	357	292	226	224	132
Earnings per share	1.06	.90	.68	.52	.43	.34	.35	.23
Dividends per share	.07	.06	.06	.06	.06	.05	.05	.04
Price High	33.7	33.2	26.1	12.3	10.9	9.7	10.4	7.5
Low	17.2	21.5	10.8	7.9	7.2	6.5	6.7	3.0

INCOME

The Lubrizol Corporation

29400 Lakeland Boulevard □ Wickliffe, Ohio 44092-2298 □ Investor contact: Joanne Wanstreet (440) 347-1252 □ Dividend reinvestment plan is available: (877) 573-3998 □ Web site: www.lubrizol.com □ Listed: NYSE □ Ticker symbol: LZ □ S&P rating: B+ □ Value Line financial strength rating: B+

Lubrizol leads the industry in developing solutions to complex environmental and lubrication questions. The company's PuriNOx Performance Systems, for instance, is among the latest in a long line of products designed to make the world a cleaner, healthier place.

PuriNOx is a low-emission water-blend fuel product combining additive chemistry with a specialized blend unit. This clean-air technology makes it easier to reduce particulate matter and nitrogen oxide emissions. By substituting this unique low-emission fuel technology for commercial diesel fuel, both old and new equipment and vehicles can immediately begin improving air quality. Field trials underway in 2001 in areas like Hong Kong and the Houston ship channel will help advance this technology.

In the spring of 2001, Lubrizol and Laketran, a mass transit provider in northeast Ohio, announced air-emissions reductions achieved during a six-month market demonstration in which ten Laketran buses ran on Lubrizol's PuriNOx fuel in regular service on area highways. The buses demonstrated up to 32 percent reductions in nitrogen oxide emissions and between 26 percent and 55 percent reductions in particulate emissions compared with conventional diesel fuel.

PuriNOx is a stable blend of conventional diesel fuel, purified water, and a proprietary Lubrizol additive package. The company designed the new fuel in conjunction with Caterpillar, Inc., as an alternative to conventional diesel fuel for vehicle fleets and stationary equipment.

PuriNOx is a revolutionary system, but it represents just one of the company's fluid technologies for a better world. Lubrizol's interests range from defoamers, which improve performances of coatings, metalworking fluids, and lubricants, to alternative fuel technologies to reduce or eliminate harmful emissions or greenhouse gases.

Company Profile

Lubrizol was founded by six men with an idea that set the stage for every Lubrizol product that followed. From the beginning, the company recognized a problem, used technology to solve it, and developed a product that was better than anything else available.

Next, Lubrizol found a way to make it easy for its customers to use the product.

The result of that first idea was a product called Lubri-Graph. Designed to eliminate the squeak caused by the leaf springs in early model cars, it was sold with a ten-gallon pressurized drum dispenser that made it easy to apply.

Lubrizol is a fluid technology company concentrating on high-performance chemicals, systems, and services for transportation and industry. LZ develops, produces, and sells specialty additive packages and related equipment used in transportation and industrial finished lubricants. The company creates its products through the application of advanced chemical and mechanical technologies to enhance the performance, quality, and value of the customer products in which they are used.

Lubrizol groups its product lines into two operating segments: chemicals for transportation and chemicals for industry. Chemicals for transportation made up about 82 percent of consolidated revenues and 85 percent of segment pre-tax operating profit in 2000.

Lubrizol products can be found in a variety of markets, including coatings, inks, compressor lubricants, and metalworking fluids. The company is also combining the expertise of its equipment-related businesses with chemicals for transportation and industry to provide integrated solutions for lubrication or environmental problems.

Highlights of 2000

- The company settled its long-standing patent litigation with Imperial Oil Limited, a Canadian affiliate of ExxonMobil Corporation. It resulted in a special gain of $19 million, as well as a ten-year agreement for Lubrizol to supply lubricating and fuel additives to Imperial Oil. This agreement is expected to add an incremental $490 million (in Canadian dollars) to Lubrizol's revenues during the period.

- Lubrizol expanded its joint venture with PetroChina in Lanzhou, China, and is now consolidating all of the revenues from this joint venture.
- The company increased its equity ownership from 40 to 50 percent in Lubrizol India Limited and assumed responsibility for managing the venture.
- Lubrizol formed a joint venture with GE Transportation Systems to provide remote fluid management equipment and services to the railroad and mining industries.
- The company acquired the Alox Metalworking Additives Business in 2000 and is now integrating it into its Painesville, Ohio, plant.
- In January 2001, Lubrizol acquired ROSS Chem, Inc., which specializes in antifoam and defoaming agents for the coatings, inks, textile, food, and metalworking industries.
- The company completed its second manufacturing rationalization program, which produced savings of $7 million in 2000, with another $13 million expected in 2001.
- In 2000, Lubrizol bolstered revenues from its heavy-duty diesel engine oil additives through new technology and is now marketing its higher-performing GF-3 engine oil additives for passenger car motor oils.

Shortcomings to Bear in Mind

- In the 1990–2000 period, earnings per share made no progress. Rather, EPS declined from 2.67 to $2.22—hardly a record that would lead you to regard Lubrizol as a growth company. In the same ten-year period, dividends per share inched ahead from $.73 to $1.04, a very modest growth rate of 3.6 percent. However, the dividend yield is far above most other stocks, which leads me to think this stock should be considered suitable for investors seeking dependable income.

- Management believes that the global growth rate for lubricant additives is about 1 percent per year. Due to changing industry market forces, such as improved engine design and longer drain intervals, the company does not expect the annual growth rate to exceed 1 percent in the future.
- In the fourth quarter of 2000, profits were essentially flat with the same quarter of the prior year. William G. Bares, the company's CEO, said that financial performance was hurt by "difficult economic and competitive conditions," including raw material costs, higher energy expenses, and the effect of a stronger U.S. dollar on exports—which are continuing into 2001.

Reasons to Buy

- Lubrizol chemical products all have one thing in common: They do their work in the molecular world wherever surfaces interact. It doesn't matter whether the surfaces are the parts of a diesel engine or paint on a wall. Lubrizol chemicals are designed to slip between them, helping things to work better. Lubrizol chemicals enhance performance. They improve the operating efficiency of equipment and extend its useful life. For the company's customers, that means lower maintenance costs and a reduction in scheduled downtime.
- Improving performance and extending equipment life is one part of the equation. The other is the increased demand placed on chemical manufacturers by environmental regulations and worker health and safety. These are top priorities in all of the company's markets, so they are top priorities for Lubrizol. In addition to improving operating efficiency, Lubrizol chemicals also reduce harmful emissions. They extend the useful life of performance fluids, which results in less waste fluid for disposal.

The company's antimist technologies, with applications in metalworking, coatings, and inks, and the transportation industry, help keep work environments cleaner and safer and save energy and maintenance costs.

- Joint ventures offers Lubrizol an entry to emerging geographic regions and new product markets. In 2000 the company expanded its existing joint venture with PetroChina, which is now the largest integrated lubricant additive manufacturing and marketing company in China.

  Another joint venture, GE Lubrizol, which produces patented real-time oil condition monitoring and regeneration systems for locomotive and mining equipment, has signed a letter of intent with Detroit Diesel Corporation to jointly develop remote monitoring and diagnostic services for Detroit Diesel engines used in mining applications.

- Lubrizol anticipates that e-business will play a significant role in its future. In 2000 the company joined Envera, a business-to-business network for the petroleum and chemical industry. As a member of Envera, Lubrizol can take advantage of state-of-the-art e-business solutions without having to develop them itself.

- In 2000 Lubrizol announced that it had purchased Alox Metalworking Additive Business from RPM, Inc. Alox Corporation is a leading supplier of additives for corrosion prevention in metalworking products. The acquisition further supports Lubrizol's growth strategy for metalworking additives; it follows two previous metalworking acquisitions in 1997 and 1998.

- Italy's third largest fuel and lubricant marketer, Kuwait Petroleum Italia SpA (KPIT), is introducing to the Italian market Lubrizol's PuriNOx under the brand Q White. During 2001, KPIT leased and installed three of Lubrizol's patented blending units required to mix the finished, low-emission fuel. With no need for hardware add-ons, engine modifications, or replacements, the technology helps protect the environment by reducing smog-forming nitrogen oxides and particulate matter. "Needless to say, Lubrizol is extremely enthusiastic about this new development, which will enable us to make our low-emission diesel alternative available to the Italian market," said Alex Psaila, European PuriNOx Business Manager for Lubrizol. "The fact that KPIT is such a major marketer devoting substantial resources to marketing the technology bodes well for Europeans who are putting forth the effort to improve air quality. It will be a large-scale initiative."

■ Through an exclusive agreement with Clean Diesel Technologies, Inc. (CDTI), Lubrizol became a licensed distributor and blender of CDTI's patented Platinum Plus fuel additive technology in the spring of 2001. Platinum Plus is a platinum and cerium catalyst that, when mixed with diesel fuel, facilitates the combustion of carbon-rich particulate (soot) into carbon dioxide, thus removing particulate from the filter. Typically, particulate will combust on its own, but only at temperatures higher than those generally found in diesel exhaust systems. Platinum Plus, however, lowers the temperature of particulate combustion, allowing soot to be "burned off" at normal exhaust temperatures.

Total assets: $1,660 million
Current ratio: 2.58
Common shares outstanding: 51 million
Return on 2000 shareholders equity: 13%

		2000	1999	1998	1997	1996	1995	1994	1993
Revenues (millions)		1776	1780	1615	1669	1593	1658	1593	1518
Net income (millions)		118	123	87	155	135	133	149	114
Earnings per share		2.22	2.25	1.55	2.68	2.23	2.08	2.26	1.67
Dividends per share		1.04	1.04	1.04	1.01	.97	.93	.89	.85
Price	High	33.9	31.4	40.2	46.9	32.4	37.4	38.6	36.4
	Low	18.2	18.0	22.4	30.4	26.5	25.5	28.5	26.6

CONSERVATIVE GROWTH

McCormick & Company, Incorporated

18 Loveton Circle □ Post Office Box 6000 □ Sparks, Maryland 21152-6000 □ Investor contact: Joyce L. Brooks (410) 771-7244 □ Web site: www.mccormick.com □ Dividend reinvestment plan is available: (800) 424-5855 □ Fiscal year ends November 30 □ Listed: NYSE □ Ticker symbol: MKC □ S&P rating: A- □ Value Line financial strength rating: B++

The company made a strategic acquisition in mid-2000 with the purchase of the Ducros business from Eridania Beghin-Say for $379 million. With annual sales of about $250 million, Ducros has two basic businesses: spices and herbs, and dessert aid products. Headquartered in France, the Ducros business has five

manufacturing plants in France, Portugal, and Albania.

Ducros has achieved sales growth of more than 7 percent compounded annually during the last three years. Consumer products comprise 88 percent of sales, while industrial products sold to the food industry and other food processors are 12 percent of sales. In France, the Ducros name has a 96 percent brand recognition among consumers.

Robert J. Lawless, CEO of McCormick said, "One of the company's goals is to expand by acquiring leading brands in key markets. Ducros is a business that clearly meets this strategic goal. Ducros is an ideal fit, both geographically and operationally. Together, Ducros and McCormick will hold the number one share positions in France, Spain, Portugal, Belgium, the U.K., Ireland, and Switzerland and number two positions in several other key European markets."

Company Profile

McCormick, the world's foremost maker of spices and seasonings, is committed to the development of tasty, easy-to-use new products to satisfy consumer demand.

When investors hear the name McCormick, they think of the spices they use every day. Indeed, McCormick is the world's largest spice company. Yet the company is also the leader in the manufacture, marketing, and distribution of such products as seasonings and flavors to the entire food industry. These customers include foodservice and food-processing businesses as well as retail outlets.

McCormick also has a stake in packaging. This group manufactures specialty plastic bottles and tubes for food, personal care, and other industries. Founded in 1889, McCormick distributes its products in about 100 countries.

McCormick's U.S. Consumer business, its oldest and largest, is dedicated to the manufacture and sale of consumer spices, herbs, extracts, proprietary seasoning blends, sauces, and marinades. They are sold under such brand names as McCormick, Schilling, Produce Partners, Golden Dipt, Old Bay, and Mojave.

Many of the spices and herbs purchased by the company are imported into the United States from the company of origin. However, significant quantities of some materials, such as paprika, dehydrated vegetables, onion and garlic, and food ingredients other than spices and herbs originate in the United States.

McCormick is a direct importer of certain raw materials, mainly black pepper, vanilla beans, cinnamon, herbs, and seeds from the countries of origin.

The raw materials most important to the company are onion, garlic, and capsicums (paprika and chili peppers), which are produced in the United States; black pepper, most of which originates in India, Indonesia, Malaysia, and Brazil; and vanilla beans, a large portion of which the company obtains from the Malagasy Republic and Indonesia.

Shortcomings to Bear in Mind

- The company purchases certain raw materials that are subject to price volatility caused by weather and other unpredictable factors. While future movements of raw material costs are uncertain, a variety of programs, including periodic raw material purchases and customer price adjustments, help McCormick address this risk. Generally, the company does not use derivatives to manage the volatility related to this risk.
- Trying to find the one you want can be daunting. This may not be a shortcoming, except for people who are overwhelmed when they look at the hundreds of different spices in the supermarket—until someone tells you they are arranged alphabetically. I didn't realize this until recently. Whenever my wife puts spices on the list, I hunt and hunt trying to locate the product she insists I buy. No more hunting since an obliging clerk tipped me off about the alphabetical arrangement. What a relief!
- The company does not have a strong balance sheet; only 69 percent of capitalization is in common equity. However,

coverage of bond interest is more than adequate at 10.2 times.

Reasons to Buy

- The market for McCormick's consumer products—spices, herbs, extracts, propriety seasoning blends, sauces and marinades—varies worldwide. In the United States, for instance, usage is up, and consumers are seeking new and bolder tastes.

  Although many people use prepared foods and eat out, a *Parade Magazine* survey reports that 75 percent of families polled eat dinner together at least four nights a week. A study indicates that 70 percent of all meals are prepared at home, and a Canned Food Association survey reports that 51 percent of women eighteen to sixty-four actually "scratch-cook" meals six times a week.

- In the company's industrial business, said Mr. Lawless, "Our customers are constantly seeking new flavors for their products. In this environment, the ability to identify, develop, and market winning flavors is essential. We flavor all kinds of products—spaghetti sauce, snack chips, frozen entrees, yogurt, a pack of chewing gum. In restaurants, we provide seasonings for a gourmet meal, salad dressings at a casual dining chain, and coating and sauce for a quick-service chicken sandwich.

  "To anticipate and respond to changing tastes in markets worldwide, we are investing in research and development staff, equipment, instrumentation, and facilities. These investments enable us not only to create innovative products but also to use sensory skills to make sure that the flavors we deliver are winners in the marketplace."

- McCormick has paid dividends every year since 1925. In the 1990–2000 period, dividends climbed from $.23 to $.76, a compound annual growth rate of 12.7 percent. In the same ten-year stretch, earnings per share advanced from $.76 to $1.99, a growth rate of 10.1 percent.

- Worldwide, the retail grocery industry continues to consolidate, creating larger customers. What's more, in many of McCormick's markets, the company has multiyear contracts with customers to secure the shelf space for its products. McCormick's capabilities in category management and electronic data interchange, along with its high-quality products and service, also forge a link to its increasingly larger customers.

- The company's past successes and future potential are rooted in the strength of the McCormick name. As a consequence, the company is now experiencing a 95 percent brand awareness rating in the United States. This leadership role in the food industry ensures that consumers will enjoy a McCormick product at nearly every eating occasion. Grocery store aisles present more than 700 well-known products from major processors that rely on McCormick for seasoning or flavor.

- In the United States, McCormick continues to roll out the Quest program (which was launched in 1997). Quest seeks to increase volume by encouraging retailers to reduce their prices on McCormick items. Quest prices most of the company's best-selling spice items and all of its seasoning mixes to the customer, net of discounts and allowances. The objective is to increase consumer sales. Using McCormick's category-management capabilities, the company is working with its customers to provide a wide variety of products at attractive prices. This benefits its customers with higher volumes sold and gives the consumer a better value as well.

- McCormick is bent on improving its profit margins. After approaching 40 percent in the early 1990s, the company's gross profit margin declined to 34.5 percent in 1998 but bounced back to 37.9 percent in 2000. According to Mr. Lawless, "With the addition of the higher-margin Ducros business, we expect to reach a gross profit margin of 42 percent in 2003."

McCormick's cost-reduction initiatives focus on supply chain management, from procurement of materials through distribution of the manufactured product. In 2000, the company created a platform to consolidate its worldwide sourcing of spices, herbs, and certain other agricultural products to be used by its operations around the globe.

The company has also improved plant efficiencies and reduced working capital in the domestic spice-processing facility by significantly reducing the number of distinct items carried in inventory and working with customers to accept alternative product or pack size. In distribution, moreover, McCormick is joining forces with other food processors to obtain freight efficiencies.

Total assets: $1,660 million
Current ratio: 0.60
Common shares outstanding: 8 million voting, 60 million nonvoting
Return on 2000 shareholders' equity: 37.1%

	2000	1999	1998	1997	1996	1995	1994	1993
Revenues (millions)	2124	2007	1881	1801	1732	1859	1695	1557
Net income (millions)	138	122	106	998	83	98	108	100
Earnings per share	1.99	1.69	1.43	1.30	1.03	1.20	1.32	1.22
Dividends per share	.76	.68	.64	.60	.56	.52	.48	.44
Price High	37.8	34.6	36.4	28.4	25.4	26.6	24.8	29.8
Low	23.8	26.6	27.1	22.6	18.9	18.1	17.8	20.0

CONSERVATIVE GROWTH

McDonald's Corporation

One McDonald's Plaza □ Oak Brook, Illinois 60523 □ Investor contact: Lynn Irwin Camp (630) 623-8432 □ Dividend reinvestment plan is available: (800) 228-9623 □ Web site: www.mcdonalds.com □ Ticker symbol: MCD □ S&P rating: A+ □ Value Line financial strength rating: A++

In a bold move into a new realm, McDonald's opened two hotels in Switzerland in the spring of 2001. The Golden Arch Hotels cater to business travelers during the week and families on the weekend. If the venture works out, you may see more McDonald's hotels around the world.

When Jack Greenberg, the company CEO, announced the new concept in late 2000, he said that clients will be attracted by the things they have come to expect from McDonald's: quality, service, cleanliness, and value. At a Swiss Golden Arch hotel, a room costs between 169 Swiss francs and 189 francs ($95 to $106).

To be sure, sceptics abound. In the words of one, "It will be a challenge to make McDonald's hotels work." On a more positive note, the company met with the same skepticism in 1976 when it opened its first restaurant in Switzerland. Today, McDonald's has 120 restaurants in that mountain paradise. What's more, these outlets serve 70 million customers every year in a country with a population of 7.4 million. According to Urs Hammer, a company official, if one Big Mac customer in a thousand checks in at a Golden Arch hotel, the project will be prove the head-shakers wrong again.

Company Profile

McDonald's, which boasts one of the world's most valuable brand names, is the world's number one fast-food chain. The company operates more than 28,000 restaurants worldwide, and its more than 12,800 domestic outlets command a 42 percent share of the nation's fast-food hamburger business.

Most McDonald's outlets are the familiar freestanding variety, with a heavy emphasis on playgrounds to attract its devoted audience: kids.

McDonald's is building mini-units with simplified menus at such alternative locations as Wal-Marts. About 80 percent of the company's restaurants are franchised. Restaurants abroad accounted for 63 percent of the company's sales in 2000. Every day, McDonald's serves more than 40 million people in 118 countries around the world. Annually, that's nearly 15 billion people served. Yet, on any given day, that amounts to less than 1 percent of the world's population. Obviously, the proliferation of McDonald's outlets is far from saturation.

The company develops, operates, franchises, and services a worldwide system of restaurants that prepare, assemble, package, and sell a limited menu of value-priced foods. These restaurants are operated by McDonald's or under the terms of franchise arrangements by franchisees who are independent third parties, or by affiliates operating under joint-venture agreements between the company and local businesspeople.

The company's franchising program is designed to assure consistency and quality. What's more, McDonald's is selective in granting franchises and is not in the practice of franchising to investor groups or passive investors.

McDonald's restaurants offer a substantially uniform menu consisting of hamburgers and cheeseburgers, including the Big Mac and Quarter Pounder with Cheese, the Filet-O-Fish, several chicken sandwiches, French fries, Chicken McNuggets, salads, milk shakes, McFlurries, sundaes and cones, pies, cookies, and soft drinks and other beverages.

McDonald's restaurants operating in the United States and certain international markets are open during breakfast hours and offer a full or limited breakfast menu, including the Egg McMuffin and the Sausage McMuffin with Egg sandwiches, hotcakes and sausages, three varieties of biscuit sandwiches, and Apple-Bran muffins. The company believes in testing new products and introducing those that pass muster.

The company, its franchisees, and affiliates purchase food products and packaging from numerous independent suppliers. Quality specifications for both raw and cooked food products are established and strictly enforced.

Diversified Operations

Although McDonald's operates primarily in the quick-service restaurant business, it also has a stake in other ventures: Aroma Cafe, Boston Market, Chipotle Mexican Grill, and Donatos Pizza. Collectively, these four businesses are referred to as "Other Brands."

In the first quarter of 2001, the company bought a 33 percent stake in Pret a Manger, a closely held United Kingdom-based chain, which offers cold sandwiches, sushi, and salads and has limited seating in its units. The fifteen-year-old takeout chain—which caters to "healthy eaters"—has about 100 restaurants in the U.K. Andrew Rolfe, CEO of Pret a Manger, said the company plans to open twenty new restaurants in the United Kingdom and seven in New York City in 2001, with possible expansion into Asia in 2002.

The latest addition to its roster of restaurants was announced in the spring of 2001. It is called "McDonald's with the Diner

Inside." The new restaurant combines a traditional McDonald's outlet with a full-sized diner. Customers can order from a menu of 122 breakfast, lunch, and dinner items.

Highlights of 2000

- McDonald's served nearly one billion more customers in 2000 than the prior year. Earnings per share expanded by 10 percent. Despite a number of operating challenges, worldwide comparable sales were positive, and systemwide sales increased 7 percent in constant currencies (before being translated into U.S. dollars).
- During 2000 the company added 1,606 restaurants, 103 McDonald's dessert-only kiosks, and 792 restaurants operated by the company's Other Brands, 707 of which were the result of McDonald's acquisition of Boston Markets. McDonald's also introduced the Golden Arches into two new countries in 2000: American Samoa and French Guiana.
- Europe's constant currency sales increased 9 percent in 2000. During the year the company added 517 restaurants and posted slightly positive comparable sales in Europe. These results were tempered by a decline in consumer confidence in Europe's beef supply. However, by educating customers about McDonald's strict product specifications that assure the safety of its beef from disease, the company partially offset the negative impact.
- Asia Pacific sales increased 9 percent in 2000 in constant currencies, despite weak consumer spending in many markets. McDonald's increased its market presence by adding 606 restaurants in Asia Pacific.

Shortcomings to Bear in Mind

- The company reported a 16 percent drop in earnings in the first quarter of 2001. Sales of hamburgers in Europe continued to slide following outbreaks of animal diseases. Results were also hurt by weak economies in some markets. What's more, comparisons were made tougher by strong results a year earlier. It was the second consecutive quarterly drop.

  McDonald's has struggled with waning European sales since late in 2000, when mad cow disease, a fatal, brain-wasting disorder, was found in herds in several countries. The company has also had to endure outbreaks of the highly contagious foot-and-mouth disease there, as farmers have been forced to destroy beef herds.
- In 2000, Latin America's performance continued to be hurt by difficult economic conditions, stemming from the major devaluation of currency in Brazil in January 1999.
- McDonald's has never been an income stock, since its dividend yield is below 1 percent. However, like most public companies, McDonald's has traditionally paid a quarterly dividend—but no more. Beginning in 2000, its dividend is now paid only once a year. The last quarterly dividend was $.04875, paid in December 1999. The new annual dividend is $.215. Thus, if you own 100 shares, you will receive $21.50 every December—unless, of course, the dividend is increased, which is likely.

Reasons to Buy

- The company replaced the Big Xtra burger on its nationwide menu in early 2001. The new item is another quarter-pounder called the Big N' Tasty. Before introduction, the Big N' Tasty had been successfully tried at 2,000 restaurants around the country. The Big N' Tasty is similar to the Big Xtra—a quarter-pound beef patty on a bun with lettuce, tomato, ketchup, onions, and pickles. However, the new product has a somewhat different taste and bun. What's more, it is cheaper because of lower food and paper costs.
- A behind-the-scenes transformation is underway at McDonald's. The com-

pany's relatively new chief executive, Jack M. Greenberg, is leading an overhaul of the long-insular restaurant company that has made both franchisees and investors more optimistic than they have been in years. In a break with tradition, Mr. Greenberg has turned to outsiders to fill key posts. The result: McDonald's has found modest success with new products, including a bagel breakfast sandwich and the McFlurry sundae, coupled with regional discounts.

- McDonald's has long been popular with children because of its elaborate playground facilities and the frequent promotional tie-ins with major motion picture characters.
- Seeking to add a new dimension to its offerings, McDonald's embarked on one of its most ambitious menu expansions in early 2001. Its called "New Tastes Menu" and was introduced in all of its domestic restaurants. It offers up to forty new food items—including new sandwiches, drinks, and breakfast items—that will rotate four at a time for several weeks in different parts of the country.

The idea behind the strategy, backed by a $30- to $40-million national advertising campaign, is to try to win back customers who have switched to rival restaurants in a brutally competitive fast-food arena.

"New Tastes" is the result of an ambitious plan—ordered up by Mr. Greenberg—to dramatically improve the menu. For years, McDonald's has been criticized for both the quality of its food and the size of its menu—limited mainly by the company's long reliance on a system to premake sandwiches. That changed in 2000 when the company equipped all of its domestic restaurants with the expensive "Made For You" kitchen systems that allow customers to customize sandwiches more conveniently.

Total assets: $21,684 million
Current ratio: 0.70
Common shares outstanding: 1,311 million
Return on 2000 shareholders' equity: 21.5%

	2000	1999	1998	1997	1996	1995	1994	1993
Revenues (millions)	14243	13259	12421	11409	10687	9794	8321	7408
Net income (millions)	1977	1948	1769	1642	1573	1427	1224	1082
Earnings per share	1.46	1.39	1.26	1.15	1.11	.99	.84	.73
Dividends per share	.22	.20	.18	.16	.15	.13	.12	.11
Price High	43.6	49.6	39.8	27.4	27.1	24.0	15.8	14.8
Low	26.4	35.9	22.3	21.1	20.5	14.3	12.8	11.4

CONSERVATIVE GROWTH

The McGraw-Hill Companies, Inc.

1221 Avenue of the Americas ▢ New York, New York 10020-1095 ▢ Investor contact: Donald S. Rubin (212) 512-4321 ▢ Dividend reinvestment program is available: (888) 201-5538 ▢ Web site: www.mcgraw-hill.com ▢ Listed: NYSE ▢ Ticker symbol: MHP ▢ S&P rating: not rated ▢ Value Line financial strength rating: A+

In 2001, Stephen B. Shepard, editor-in-chief of McGraw-Hill's *BusinessWeek*, received the highest honor awarded by the magazine industry, the Henry Johnson Fisher Award. Under Mr. Shepard's leadership, *BusinessWeek* helped set the national agenda for business and economic issues, pioneered coverage of the New Economy, exposed the Mob on Wall Street, and broke the story of prison labor in China. What's more, circulation expanded by 40 percent since Mr. Shepard became editor-in-chief of McGraw-Hill's flagship business publication in 1984.

During those years, moreover, *Business-Week* has been a National Magazine Award finalist eighteen times, winning four times. The publication also won numerous Overseas Press Club awards, and three Gerald Loeb Awards for distinguished business and financial journalism among others.

Company Profile

The McGraw-Hill Companies is a multimedia information provider. The company publishes textbooks, technical and popular books, and periodicals (*BusinessWeek, Aviation Week, ENR,* and others) and also maintains Standard & Poor's as one of its divisions. McGraw-Hill holds leadership positions in each of the markets it serves.

Financial Services
- Standard & Poor's Ratings Services is the number one rating service in the world and is applying its leadership to rating and evaluating a growing array of nontraditional financial instruments.
- Standard & Poor's Indexes, led by the S&P 500, are the world's benchmark measures of equity market performance.
- Standard & Poor's *Compustat* is the leading source of financial databases and advanced PC-based software for financial analysis.
- Standard & Poor's MMS supplies the world with real-time fundamental and technical analysis in the global money, bond, foreign exchange, and equity markets.
- Standard & Poor's *Platt's* is the key provider of price assessments with the petroleum, petrochemical, and power markets.

- Standard & Poor's *J. J. Kenny* produces the most comprehensive evaluating pricing information for the fixed-income investment community.
- Standard & Poor's *DRI* is the leading supplier of economics-driven information to corporate and government clients.

Educational and Professional Publishing
- The McGraw-Hill School Division stands number one in providing educational materials to elementary schools.
- Glencoe/McGraw-Hill tops the grade 6–12 segment.
- CTB/McGraw-Hill is the preeminent publisher of nationally standardized tests for the K–12 market in the United States.
- Irwin/McGraw-Hill is the premier publisher of higher educational materials in business, economics, and information technology.
- The Professional Book Group is the leading publisher of business, computing, and reference books serving the needs of professionals and consumer worldwide.

Information and Media Services
- *BusinessWeek* is the world's most widely read business publication, with a global audience of 6.3 million.
- F. W. Dodge is the leading provider of information to construction professionals.
- Sweet's Group is the premier supplier of building products information, in print and electronically.
- *Architectural Record* stands atop its industry as the official publication of the American Institute of Architects.
- *Aviation Week & Space Technology* is the world's most authoritative aerospace magazine.
- Tower Group International is the leading provider of customs brokerage and freight forwarding services.

Shortcomings to Bear in Mind

- In 2000, the Professional Book Group's operations were hampered by a lack of major new software releases. This hurt the computer book market, as well as the scientific, technical, medical, and business and general reference lines. As a result, revenue in 2000 showed only a modest gain. However, the company's professional titles sold well abroad, as International Publishing registered solid growth in Latin American and Asia/Pacific markets. But these gains were offset by softness in Canada and Europe.

Reasons to Buy

- Every business day, Standard & Poor's indexes are cited as key benchmarks of stock market performance. The worldwide reputation of the S&P 500 has nurtured a growing international family of indexes.

- S&P indexes are the foundation for a growing array of investment funds and exchange-traded products that continue to generate new revenue. The company receives fees based on assets and trading activity. In addition, the recent volatility of the stock market has increased the revenue stream. Currently, more than $700 billion is invested in mutual funds tied to the S&P indexes.

- SPDRs (S&P depository receipts), linked to and directly tracking S&P indexes, consistently top the American Stock Exchange's most active list. Similarly, trading volume on the Chicago Mercantile Exchange of futures and options linked to S&P indexes is also high. Both exchanges introduced new trading instruments in 1998 tied to S&P indexes.

- Europe contributes almost half of McGraw-Hill's international revenue, growing at a double-digit rate. With a push from the new Monetary Union, the European market will be a springboard for growth in many of the company's key businesses. Here are some expectations:

- European companies that once financed their growth mainly by borrowing from banks are shifting to the issuance of corporate bonds instead, while nontraditional financial instruments also boom. Those are both large opportunities for Standard & Poor's Rating Services, which has built the world's largest network of ratings professionals.

- Increases in investments by Europeans building retirement funds—the result of a transition to privately funded pension plans—will accelerate demand for global financial information. These are pluses for Standard & Poor's Financial Information Services.

- The continued growth of English in business communications and as a second language in everyday use widens. These will benefit the company's educational products and the European edition of *BusinessWeek*.

- The promise of the global economy depends on educational training. This is a plus for McGraw-Hill's global publishing activities—most notably the company's business, finance, engineering, information technology, and English instruction products.

- In Asia, economic problems have slowed growth but have not seriously affected the company's operations or diminished the region's long-term opportunities. McGraw-Hill's brands are strong in Asia. In a survey of 6,000 executives representing eleven Asian countries, MHP was chosen as one of Asia's 200 leading companies.

- In the construction industry, the McGraw-Hill Construction Information Group (MH-CIG) is the foremost source of information crucial to new construction projects and planning. MH-CIG has increasingly turned to the Internet and other electronic tools to gather and distribute information. By the end of 2000, nearly half of its revenue derived from electronic products.

Dodge Plans is the latest of several MH-CIG electronic products stemming from print media. It provides access— online or by CD-ROM twice weekly—to the plans, specifications, and bidding requirements for more than 60,000 new construction and renovation projects.

- Growing enrollments are a worldwide phenomenon and will keep the education market growing here and abroad for the next several years. In the United States, the combination of more students, the best funding picture in a generation, and a robust adoption schedule is expected to produce steady growth in the education market for the foreseeable future.

- The digital economy and e-commerce have the capacity to transform McGraw-Hill, adding a completely new dimension to its products and services. More than 90 percent of the company's information is already in digital form, and in each of the company's major business units there are major efforts to create and deliver a host of new electronic services.

- The McGraw-Hill Professional Book Group publishes nearly 800 titles per year in computing, business, science, technical, medical, and reference markets. The group continues to expand by creating publishing alliances with partners such as Oracle and Global Knowledge, transforming key reference titles into Internet-based services. In addition, the Professional Book Group offers electronic products, ranging from Internet subscription services to CD-ROMs, and is building its capabilities in on-demand publishing.

- The company launched an education Web site in early 2001 that is sold to schools, teachers, and parents who have children in kindergarten through the twelfth grade. The part-free, part-pay site, called the McGraw-Hill Learning Network, offers interactive textbooks, learning exercises, and teacher tips. It also sells school supplies, including flash cards, maps, globes, and workbooks.

Parents can log on, with the aid of password protection, to see their children's assignments, grades, and progress. McGraw-Hill expects that parents will buy electronic textbooks so their kids can leave the print books at school. Parents seeking access to the entire site have to buy one electronic book priced at $4.95 per year.

The site is a centerpiece of McGraw-Hill's digital and Internet strategy. It is also the company's first big bet on the kindergarten through twelfth grade market, which has been slower to adopt electronic learning than the professional and college markets.

- Tribune Education, acquired by McGraw-Hill in the fall of 2000 for $634.7 million, is a leading publisher of supplementary educational materials for the K–12, higher education, professional education, and consumer markets, with strength in language arts, math, foreign language, social studies, health, English, reading, educational software, and teacher training.

"The Tribune Education acquisition solidifies McGraw-Hill's Education position as the nation's largest provider of K-12 educational materials," said Harold McGraw III, CEO of the company.

- Mayfield Publishing Company, acquired by McGraw-Hill early in 2001, is a highly regarded educational publisher based in California. It published eighty-five titles in 2000 and expects to publish ninety-two new and revised titles in 2001. "As global enrollments continue to rise, our acquisition of the Mayfield Publishing Company, along with our recent acquisition of Tribune Education, further enables us to capitalize on the world's growing education market," said Harold McGraw III.

Total assets: $4,089 million
Current ratio: 1.23
Common shares outstanding: 195 million
Return on 2000 shareholders' equity: 20%

	2000	1999	1998	1997	1996	1995	1994	1993
Revenues (millions)	4308	3992	3729	3534	3075	2935	2761	2196
Net income (millions)	481	402	342	291	250	227	203	172
Earnings per share	2.40	2.02	1.71	1.46	1.25	1.14	1.03	.88
Dividends per share	.94	.86	.78	.72	.66	.60	.58	.57
Price High	67.7	63.1	51.7	37.7	24.6	21.9	19.3	18.8
Low	41.9	47.1	34.3	22.4	18.6	15.9	15.6	13.8

INCOME

MDU Resources Group, Inc.

Post Office Box 5650 □ Bismarck, North Dakota 58506-5650 □ Investor contact: Arlene Stillwell (800) 437-8000, ext. 7621 □ Dividend reinvestment plan is available: (800) 813-3324 □ Web site: www.mdu.com □ Listed: NYSE □ Ticker symbol: MDU □ S&P rating: A- □ Value Line financial strength rating: A

After serving MDU Resources for twenty-five years, John A. (Jack) Schuchart retired as the company's chairman in early 2001. It's unlikely that his distinguished service will soon be forgotten, since MDU's headquarters is situated in the Schuchart Building in Bismarck, North Dakota.

During the past quarter century, MDU has not only grown but has transformed itself and no longer relies primarily on revenues from its public utilities, as Jack Schuchart explains:

"Essentially, we were in one line of business 25 years ago. The company was known as Montana-Dakota Utilities Company. It was a combination electric and natural gas utility. We also had a coal company and some income from our oil interests, but they were viewed as incidental to the utility business. We employed about 1,800 people in our operations in five states.

"From a financial point of view, we had 2.4 million shares outstanding in 1975. Today we have 65 million shares. Reported revenues in 1975 were $86.5 million. Our revenues in 2000 were nearly $2 billion, and our earnings exceeded the 1975 revenues!"

Company Profile

MDU Resources Group, Inc. is a natural resource company. The company's diversified operations, such as oil and gas and construction materials, should help MDU Resources grow at a better rate than electric utilities that depend entirely on their electric business. MDU Resources Group has a number of operations:

Electric Distribution

Montana-Dakota Utilities Company generates, transmits, and distributes electricity and provides related value-added products and services in the northern Great Plains. In 2000, this operation had earnings of $17.7 million, or 16 percent of total corporate earnings.

Natural Gas Distribution

Montana-Dakota Utilities Company and Great Plains Natural Gas Company distribute natural gas and provide related value-added products and services in the northern Great Plains. In 2000, earnings from natural gas distribution was $4.8 million, or 4 percent of MDU's total corporate earnings.

Utility Services

Operating throughout most of the United States, Utility Services, Inc. is a diversified infrastructure construction company specializing in electric, natural gas, and telecommunication utility construction, as well as interior industrial electrical, exterior lighting, and traffic stabilization. In 2000, Utility Services was responsible for earnings of $8.6 million, or 8 percent of corporate total.

Pipeline and Energy Services

WBI Holdings, Inc. provides natural gas transportation, underground storage, and gathering services through regulated and nonregulated pipeline systems and provides energy marketing and management throughout the United States. Operations are situated primarily in the Rocky Mountain, Midwest, southern, and central regions of the United States. In 2000, WBI Holdings had earnings of $10.5 million, or 10 percent of the MDU total.

Oil and Natural Gas Production

Fidelity Exploration & Production Company is engaged in oil and natural gas acquisition, exploration, and production throughout the United States and in the Gulf of Mexico. This business was responsible for 2000 earnings of $38.6 million, or 35 percent of the corporate total.

Construction Materials and Mining

Knife River Corporation mines and markets aggregates and related value-added construction materials products and services in the western United States, including Alaska and Hawaii. It also operates lignite and coal mines in Montana and North Dakota. In 2000, this business brought in earnings of $30.1 million, representing 27 percent of MDU Resources's total.

Highlights of 2000

- The company achieved an exceptional 68 percent annual total return on its common stock in 2000. That was better than the Standard & Poor's Electric Utility Index, as well as the S&P 500 Index. For the past five years, moreover, MDU Resources produced a 24 percent compound annual total return on its common stock. This compares favorably to the 17 percent for the Standard & Poor's Electric Utility Index and 18 percent for the S&P 500 Index.

- The MDU Resources Board of Directors recognized this growth by increasing the dividend by 5 percent in August of 2000. This was the tenth consecutive annual increase and continues MDU's unbroken record of consecutive quarterly dividends dating back to 1937.

- Total corporate revenues reached $1.9 billion, up 46 percent from the preceding year. Earnings were $110.3 million, up 32 percent over 1999. Diluted earnings per share, moreover, climbed to $1.80 compared with $1.52 the prior year.

Shortcomings to Bear in Mind

- MDU's construction materials and mining segment enjoyed a 48 percent growth in 2000 as a result of high-volume sales of cement and ready-mix concrete. Even so, there may be some disappointments ahead, according to Argus Research Corporation. "The growth is, however, exaggerated because of acquisitions made during 2000. In the fourth quarter of 2000, the segment actually saw a 12 percent decline in earnings. We are encouraged by the dynamics of the business, but are concerned that operating margins and sales may come under more pressure as energy costs rise and demand for building materials declines in the weakening economy."

Reasons to Buy

- MDU Resources has an established position in the coal bed natural gas fields in the Powder River Basin of Wyoming and Montana. This provides the company's natural gas and oil production segment with additional reserve potential of low-cost coal bed natural gas.

    In addition, MDU continues enhancing production from its existing gas fields in Colorado and Montana. The company's strong reserve position, both onshore and offshore in the Gulf of Mexico, provides this group a large geographic base upon which to expand.

- In 2000, the company's natural gas and oil production reached an all-time high of 40.5 billion cubic feet equivalent (Bcfe). What's more, year-end proved reserves of over 400 Bcfe set the stage for MDU's natural gas and oil production segment to continue making major contributions to the company's earnings.

    WBI Holdings—which includes both the pipeline and energy services and the natural gas and oil production businesses—reached earnings of $49.1 million in 2000. This amount exceeds MDU Resources's total earnings of just four years earlier.

- Since 1992, the company's construction materials and mining business has continued to expand. This segment's revenues reached $631.4 million in 2000, a 34 percent increase. At the same time, earnings from this operation surged 47 percent to $30.1 million.

    A number of factors augur well for this business:
    - The federal government's commitment to improve the nation's highway system.
    - The economic and geographic diversity of MDU's markets.
    - The segment's strong position in those markets.
    - Its 895 tons of strategically located aggregate reserves.

- Utility services had an excellent year in 2000, as earnings climbed 32 percent, while expanding its market position and becoming a national player in this industry. The company's utility services growth strategy is built on:
    - The continued outsourcing of services in the utility industry.
    - The replacement of transmission and distribution lines.
    - The demand for fiber-optic cable installation.

- Unlike most public utilities, MDU Resources is active in the acquisition realm. The company made these moves in the past couple years:
    - In 1999 the company acquired MTN Utility Construction and Design, a full-service electric, natural gas, and telecommunications contractor headquartered in Montana.
    - During the same year, the company acquired Loy Clark Pipeline Company of Beaverton, Oregon.
    - The company acquired a pipeline gathering system that connects its existing pipeline system to developing coal bed methane production in Wyoming's Power River Basin. Coal bed methane holds promise to be a valuable new natural gas supply source for the company's pipeline system.
    - During 1999 the company completed the acquisition of 80 percent of American Resources Offshore, Inc.'s offshore properties, thus increasing both oil and natural gas reserves and production.
    - In 2000, the company continued this aggressive trend with the acquisition of the Connolly-Pacific Company, a southern California aggregate mining and marine construction company. As is often the case with MDU's

acquisitions, the existing management team remained in place after the completion of the acquisition. Connolly-Pacific is vertically integrated and specializes in furnishing and placing rock to construct multilift dikes, enclose new landfills, and repair existing breakwaters and levees.

- The addition of the Wagner-Smith companies, based in Ohio, increased the services availability to the company's growing customer base. In early 2001, MDU acquired the Capital Electric companies. This move further broadened the company's geographic scope and complements existing utility services companies. These companies also provide refurbishing and new wiring services to power plants. This is an important addition to utility services, given that the need for new generation in America is estimated to be 10,000 megawatts per year until 2008.

- In 2000, MDU's public utility operation continued its strong performance by providing natural gas and electricity to customers in the northern Great Plains. The acquisition of Great Plains Natural Gas Company, moreover, added some 22,000 new customers in southeastern North Dakota and western Minnesota.

Total assets: $2,313 million
Current ratio: 1.69
Common shares outstanding: 61 million
Return on 2000 shareholders' equity: 14.3%

		2000	1999	1998	1997	1996	1995	1994	1993
Revenues (millions)		1874	1280	897	608	515	464	450	440
Net income (millions)		110	83	74	55	46	42	40	39
Earnings per share		1.80	1.52	1.44	1.24	1.05	.95	.91	.89
Dividends per share		.86	.82	.78	.75	.73	.72	.70	.67
Price	High	33.0	27.2	28.9	22.3	15.7	15.4	14.3	14.7
	Low	17.6	18.8	18.8	14.0	13.3	11.5	11.3	11.5

AGGRESSIVE GROWTH

Medtronic, Inc.

7000 Central Avenue NE ❑ Minneapolis, Minnesota 55432-3576 ❑ Listed: NYSE ❑ Investor contact: Rachael Scherer (763) 505-2694 ❑ Dividend reinvestment plan is available: (888) 648-8154 ❑ Web site: www.medtronic.com ❑ Ticker symbol: MDT ❑ Fiscal year ends April 30 ❑ S&P rating: A ❑ Value Line financial strength rating: A+

Sid Sanders knew all about open-heart surgery using cardiopulmonary bypass—and he wanted no more of it. Suffering from coronary artery disease since the late 1970s, Sid underwent a quintuple bypass in 1982. Recovery was slow and painful. He struggled with depression and memory loss. Over the years his disease grew steadily worse. In 1999 he was told that he needed a second open-heart procedure, this time for a one-vessel bypass.

"What about minimally invasive surgery? And using the Octopus tissue stabilizer from Medtronic?" inquired Sid after conducting research on the Internet. This procedure is often referred to as beating-heart surgery—it avoids cardiopulmonary bypass and may allow a smaller incision. The Octopus2 device makes such surgery possible.

Sid recuperated quickly. No memory loss or depression. "An incredible difference!" he exclaimed.

Strong and vital all his adult life, suddenly at sixty-two Heinrich Hajduga of Germany found climbing stairs difficult and could barely keep up with normal daily activities. The symptoms of heart failure were severely limiting his life. Over the next several years he was in and out of the hospital repeatedly. Ultimately, as a last desperate measure, he was placed on a heart-transplant list.

Later he was referred to the Bad Oeynhausen Heart Center where he was identified as an ideal candidate for a new Medtronic InSync ICD, which provides biventricular pacing and defibrillation. Within one week of his implant, Mr. Hajduga had regained much of his quality of life, and his witty and energetic old self re-emerged. Now, at sixty-eight, he can once again enjoy long walks and an active family life. "This new therapy has given me a second life."

Company Profile
Medtronic is the world's leading medical-technology company. Over the past half century, Medtronic has pioneered in the development of sophisticated instruments that help restore health, extend life, and alleviate pain.

Medtronic's devices help regulate erratic heartbeats, tremors, and incontinence. About half of the company's revenues come from the sale of defibrillators and pacing devices, including products for slow, irregular, and rapid heartbeats.

Medtronic also has a stake in spinal implant devices, mechanical and tissue heart valves, as well as implantable neurostimulation and drug-delivery systems, catheters, stents, and guide wires used in angioplasties.

Shortcomings to Bear in Mind
- Like most great growth companies, Medtronic typically sells at a lofty price-earnings ratio. So far, however, this has not been a problem since the stock continues to climb.

Reasons to Buy
- The year 2000 marked the company's fifteenth consecutive year of strong, steady increases in revenues and earnings. Over this period, Medtronic achieved a compound annual growth rate of 19.0 percent for revenues and 23.2 percent for earnings per share.

  Revenues in 2000 were just over $5 billion, a 19 percent increase over the $4.23 billion recorded the previous year. Earnings per share set an all-time record, up 20 percent. The company also completed its sixth stock split in a decade. In the past fifteen years, moreover, the stock price has advanced at a compound annual rate of 37.5 percent.
- It is not surprising then that Medtronic was selected by *Fortune* magazine in 2000 as one of America's most admired companies, ranking number one in the medical products and equipment industry.
- Building on Medtronic's strong historic base of cardiac rhythm management and neurological therapy, the company has continue to expand, helped by a number of strategic mergers involving several major companies—all with leading product lines worldwide:
  - In mid-2001, the company continued to broaden its portfolio of medical devices, moving into the diabetic realm with the acquisition of MiniMed, Inc., a maker of insulin pumps and wearable glucose monitors, along with its affiliate, Medical Research Group, Inc., which is developing both an implantable insulin pump and a fully implanted glucose sensor. The purchase price was $3.7 billion.

MiniMed is the leading insulin-pump manufacturer, with an estimated 80 percent domestic market share. The main product of MiniMed is an external pump, worn at the patient's belt. It administers insulin continuously to people with Type I diabetes, those who develop the disease early in life and are insulin-dependent. Type II diabetics, by contrast, are typically diagnosed in the middle age or older and may be able to control their blood sugar with diet, weight reduction, exercise, and one of the non-insulin oral products. Approximately 16 million Americans have diabetes, with 2,500 more learning of their affliction each day.

- Sofamor Danek, of Memphis, Tennessee, is a global leader in spinal and cranial surgery and an innovator in the new frontier of surgical navigation.
- Arterial Vascular Engineering (AVE), based in Santa Rosa, California, is a prominent player in the world's coronary stent business because of innovation and commitment to customer responsiveness.
- Physio-Control, of Redmond, Washington, leads in external defibrillators, the crucial devices that give more people a chance of surviving sudden cardiac arrest.
- Avecor, of Minneapolis, Minnesota, produces the world's best operating room oxygenator and other products used for blood circulation during heart surgery.
- Midas Rex, of Fort Worth, Texas, makes the world's leading high-speed drills essential to neurological surgery.

■ Major product introductions during Medtronic's fiftieth year underscored its research and development vitality. Brand new products designed to treat life-threatening heart rhythm disorders include:

- The Medtronic.Kappa 700 pacemaker series that constantly monitors a patient's heart and automatically adapts to precisely what the patient needs at any moment.
- The Gem platform of implantable defibrillators featuring the GEM II DR—the smallest, most powerful dual-chamber defibrillator available today. It has twice the number of transistors as a Pentium II computer chip, is no bigger than a small pager, and protects a patient from unnecessary shocks.
- The InSync stimulator for the most effective, life-restoring treatment of heart failure available today.

■ To maintain this ambitious product development pace, Medtronic invested nearly $500 million in R & D during fiscal 2000, and nearly $3.6 billion over the past five years. This investment is borne out in performance: the U.S. Patent and Trademark Office ranks Medtronic first in the world for the number of patents issued for medical devices from 1969 through 1998.

■ Since its origin, Medtronic has held a clear market leadership in cardiac pacing, chiefly with pacemakers designed to treat bradycardia (hearts that beat irregularly or too slow) and more recently, tachyarrhythmia (hearts that beat too fast or quiver uncontrollably, called tachycardia and fibrillation). Today, more than half the cardiac rhythm devices and leads implanted throughout the world come from Medtronic.

■ The worldwide coronary vascular market is estimated at $4 billion and is expected to grow because it serves significant, unmet medical needs. Medtronic's coronary vascular products include several types of catheters used to unblock coronary arteries, stents that support the walls of an artery and prevent more blockage, and products used in minimally invasive vascular procedures for coronary heart disease, the chief cause of heart attack and angina.

Medtronic merged with Arterial Vascular Engineering (AVE) in 1999. AVE, founded through a collaboration of engineers and cardiologists in 1991, is a leader in the $2-billion worldwide coronary stent market. Medtronic's recent acquisition of USCI/Bard significantly expands its balloon catheter, guide catheter, guide wire, and stent graft product lines.

- Medtronic's cardiac surgery group offers superior products to support cardiac surgeons, including tissue heart valves that are best represented by the Freestyle stentless valve, the Mosaic stented tissue valve, and the Hall mechanical valve. In addition, the company is expanding its leadership in cardiac cannulae used to connect a patient's circulatory system to external perfusion systems used in conventional and minimally invasive surgeries.

The acquisition of Avecor adds to Medtronic's well-established line of perfusion systems designed to sustain patients during open-heart surgery. These systems include market-leading oxygenators, blood pumps, arterial filters, and autotransfusion and monitoring products that are used to circulate and oxygenate the blood and regulate body temperature during procedures when the heart must be stopped while repairs are made.

Finally, Medtronic is leading the way in developing products to make cardiac surgery less invasive and, ultimately, reduce pain, patient recovery time, and medical costs. One new product that addresses these needs is the Octopus2 tissue-stabilization system that allows the cardiac surgeon to repair blocked blood vessels while the heart is still beating.

- In fiscal 2000, 70 percent of the company's revenues were generated from sales of products introduced within the past two years. This measurement is a key indicator of Medtronic's ability to lead global advances in medical technology.

- Medtronic today enjoys about a 52 percent worldwide market share for cardiac rhythm management products. In fact, Medtronic is the leader in every major market segment the company serves, demonstrating strength and long-term sustainable growth.

- The company's Gem and Gem II implantable cardioverter defibrillator (ICD) systems accounted for a major portion of that growth. Their proprietary software, PR Logic software, has been the key. With PR Logic, Medtronic ICDs can increase accuracy to sense the onset of an arrhythmia, then differentiate between a life-threatening ventricular arrhythmia, which may require high current response, or a less intense arrhythmia, which could be terminated by pacing.

In the United States alone, only one in five who need the protection of a device currently has one. Over 350,000 people die from tachyarrhythmia-related diseases every year. With the introduction of the enhanced Gem III system in fiscal 2001, the company believes it is in an even better position to reach more patients.

In addition, the Jewel AF ICD system, introduced in the United States in mid-2000, is the world's first ICD to offer new therapeutic capabilities for detecting and treating arrhythmias of the atria (upper chambers), in addition to the ventricles (lower chambers).

- Medtronic's market share gains have been driven by best-in-class products such as the Kappa, Sigma, and Vitatron pacing systems, the CapSure Z and CapSureFix lines of pacing leads and, advanced programmers and programming software. Today's Kappa pacemaker systems adapt to patients' specific needs while providing physicians intuitive, easy-to-use diagnostic information and patient-management tools as never before.

- Vitatron—Medtronic's second leading brand—became the world's fastest-growing brand in 2000 thanks to patient-focused therapies such as the Collection II, Selection 900AF, and 9000AF devices, which have worldwide growth in excess of 20 percent. In the United States, Vitatron grew over 40 percent in 2000.

Total assets: $5,669 million
Current ratio: 3.24
Common shares outstanding: 1,200 million
Return on 2000 shareholders' equity: 24.7%

	2000	1999	1998	1997	1996	1995	1994	1993
Revenues (millions)	5015	4134	2605	2438	2169	1742	1391	1328
Net income (millions)	1111	905	595	530	438	294	232	198
Earnings per share	.82	.76	.63	.56	.47	.32	.25	.21
Dividends per share	.16	.12	.11	.10	.07	.05	.04	.04
Price High	62.0	44.6	38.4	26.4	17.5	15.0	7.0	6.0
Low	32.8	29.9	22.7	14.4	11.1	6.5	4.3	3.2

CONSERVATIVE GROWTH

Merck & Co., Inc.

One Merck Drive □ P. O. Box 100 □ Whitehouse Station, New Jersey 08889-0100 □ Investor contact: Laura Jordan (908) 423-5185 □ Dividend reinvestment plan is available: (800) 831-8248 □ Web site: www.merck.com □ Listed: NYSE □ Ticker symbol: MRK □ S&P rating: A+ □ Value Line financial strength rating: A++

Merck named a leading biologist, Peter S. Kim, a professor at MIT, to take over its celebrated research department at the end of 2000. Only forty-three, Dr. Kim is universally regarded as a leader in his field. He is a member of the National Academy of Sciences, an investigator supported by the Howard Hughes Medical Institute, and a member of the AIDS Vaccines Research Committee of the National Institute of Health.

Selecting Dr. Kim gives the company a charismatic leader who can convince even more distinguished scientists to leave academia to join Merck. In addition, Merck is building a new laboratory in Cambridge, which is likely to enhance recruiting in a region noted for its academic excellence. What's more, Merck recently bought a lab in La Jolla, California to make it easier to attract scientists on the West Coast.

Finally, by hiring Dr. Kim, Merck may be betting that deciphering the structure of recently discovered human proteins will yield the next generation of powerful pharmaceuticals. Dr. Kim's experiments showing that drugs can block the AIDS virus make him uniquely qualified to move from the university realm to the drug industry.

Company Profile

Merck is a leading research-driven pharmaceutical products and services company. Directly and through its joint ventures, the company discovers, develops, manufactures, and markets a broad range of innovative products to improve human and animal health. Merck also provides pharmaceutical and benefit services through Merck-Medco Managed Care.

Human Health Products

Human health products include therapeutic and preventative drugs, generally sold by prescription, for the treatment of human disorders. Among these are elevated cholesterol products, which include Zocor and Mevacor; hypertensive/heart failure products include Vasotec, the largest-selling product among this group, Cozaar, Hyzaar, Prinivil and Vaseretic; anti-ulcerants, of which Pepcid is the largest selling; antibiotics, of which Primaxin and Noroxin are the largest selling; ophthalmologicals, of which Timoptic, Timoptic-XE, and Trusopt are the largest selling; vaccines/biologicals, of which Recombivax HB (hepatitis B vaccine recombinant), M-M-R II, a pediatric vaccine for measles, mumps, and rubella, and Varivax, a live virus vaccine for the prevention of chickenpox, are the largest selling; HIV, comprised of Crixivan, a protease inhibitor for the treatment of human immunodeficiency viral infection in adults, which was launched in the United States in 1996; and osteoporosis, which includes Fosamax for treatment and prevention in postmenopausal women.

Animal Health Products

Animal health products include medicinals used to control and alleviate disease in livestock, small animals, and poultry. Crop protection includes products for the control of crop pests and fungal disease.

Merck-Medco

Merck-Medco primarily includes Merck-Medco sales of non-Merck products and Merck-Medco pharmaceutical benefit services, primarily managed prescription drug programs and programs to manage health and drug utilization.

Highlights of 2000

CEO Raymond V. Gilmartin said in early 2001, "Our five key products, Vioxx, Zocor, Cozaar/Hyzaar, Fosamax, and Singulair, drove Merck's performance for the year and created a powerful platform for growth." These five products accounted for 57 percent of Merck's worldwide human health sales in 2000.

"Each of the five medicines offers unique competitive advantages," said Mr. Gilmartin. Vioxx, a once-a-day medicine, is the only Cox-2 drug approved in the United States for both osteoarthritis and acute pain. Since its extraordinarily successful launch in 1999, Vioxx has become the world's fastest growing branded prescription arthritis drug. It is already Merck's second-largest selling medicine. In the United States Vioxx now accounts for about 50 percent of new prescriptions in the Cox-2 class, despite being the second drug to be marketed in this class in the United States. Sales of Vioxx reached the $2.2 billion level in 2000.

Zocor, Merck's cholesterol modifying drug, is showing continued strong growth based on the product's demonstrated ability to act favorably on all major lipid parameters—HDL, LDL, and triglycerides. In the United States, the market for "statin" medicines is expanding nearly 20 percent a year, primarily from products such as Zocor that can significantly affect cholesterol levels from its initial dose.

Cozaar and Hyzaar maintain strong leadership in a class of highly effective and well-tolerated high blood pressure medicines called angiotensin II antagonists. Physicians continue to gain confidence in these products, prescribing them for more than 7 million patients worldwide. This broad acceptance makes Cozaar and Hyzaar the world's most widely prescribed drugs in their class.

Fosamax, the leading product worldwide for the treatment and prevention of postmenopausal osteoporosis, has been outperforming the competition because it is the only osteoporosis medicine indicated and consistently proven to reduce the incidence of fractures of the hip as well as the spine. Merck has strengthened the competitive advantage of Fosamax through its recent introduction of a unique form that is effective, even when taken only once a week.

Singulair, Merck's once-a-day leukotriene antagonist, is one of the world's top selling asthma drugs. Singulair is gaining market leadership in the United States for several reasons: It can be used in children as young as two, it is not a steroid, and it has better compliance because patients can take it orally. Typically, drugs used to treat asthma are inhaled.

Merck-Medco continued its strong performance in 2000, bolstering its position as the nation's most successful pharmacy benefit manager. The addition of the United-Healthcare Group contract, with 10 million clients, and the acquisition of ProVantage with its 5 million lives, helped fuel Merck-Medco's growth in 2000. For the year, the volume of prescriptions handled increased 22 percent to more than 450 million.

Shortcomings to Bear in Mind

- Product patents for Vasotec, Vaseretic, Mevacor, Prinivil, Prinzide, Pepcid, and Prilosec (which Merck manufactures and supplies to Astra for the U.S. market) went off-patent in 2000 and 2001. On the other hand, Merck contends that its newer products "will keep us competitive." Increasingly greater percentages of the company's overall sales derive from the fourteen new drugs and vaccines it has introduced since 1995.
- The markets in which the company's business is conducted are highly competitive and, in many ways, highly regulated. Global efforts toward health care cost containment continue to exert pressure on product pricing.

  In the United States, government efforts to slow the increase of health care costs and the demand for price discounts from managed care groups have limited the company's ability to mitigate the effect of inflation on costs and expenses through pricing.

  Outside of the United States, government mandated cost-containment programs have required the company to similarly limit selling prices. Additionally, government actions have significantly reduced the sales growth of certain products by decreasing the patient reimbursement cost of the drug, restricting the volume of drugs that physicians can prescribe, and increasing the use of generic products. It is anticipated that the worldwide trend for cost containment and competitive pricing will continue and result in continued pricing pressures.

Reasons to Buy

- Vioxx was given to 8,000 patients to determine whether it produced adverse stomach irritation. In a study published in the *New England Journal of Medicine*, it was found that Vioxx reduced the risk of serious gastrointestinal complications by one-half when compared with naproxen, a leading drug used to treat pain. Still another study (published in November 2000) showed that Vioxx significantly reduced moderate-to-severe acute pain after dental surgery to a greater degree than codeine when combined with acetaminophen (the chemical name for Tylenol).
- Fosamax, with annual sales of more than $1 billion, is used primarily for the treatment of osteoporosis in women, but it is also effective in the enhancement of bone density in men according to a 2000 study in the *New England Journal of Medicine*. Osteoporosis, a disease in which bones become fragile and prone to fractures, is often regarded as a women's disease. C. Anthony Butler, an analyst with Lehman Brothers, predicts the male market will have little effect on sales in the short run, given the need to convince men and their doctors that osteoporosis is not merely a female affliction. Even so, he believes the addition of men could increase the drug's annual sales to $3 billion in 2007, up from his earlier forecast of $2.5 billion.
- Long known for its impressive research capability, Merck says the most promising drug in its pipeline is the aspirin-like pain killer, etoricoxib. It is the next generation of Vioxx and will face competition from a similar compound being developed by Pharmacia Corporation that will be sold in cooperation with Pfizer, the nation's leading drug company, and its superior sales force.

Also important is a cholesterol-lowering preparation that is combined with Merck's Zocor, along with a drug under development by Schering-Plough called ezetimibe. Since the two drugs act by different mechanisms, tests have shown that a combination tablet of very low doses reduces cholesterol by 47 percent.

This is much better than drugs currently on the market. "Zocor-ezetimibe will be a unique treatment paradigm and will dominate the field," according to Dr. Edward Scolnick, who was president of Merck's research laboratories up until recently. He is also a member of the company's board of directors.

Total assets: $39,910 million
Current ratio: 1.38
Common shares outstanding: 2,353 million
Return on 2000 equity: 46.0

	2000	1999	1998	1997	1996	1995	1994	1993
Revenues (millions)	40363	32714	26898	23637	19829	16681	14970	10498
Net income (millions)	6822	5890	5248	4614	3881	3335	2997	2687
Earnings per share	2.90	2.45	2.15	1.92	1.60	1.35	1.19	1.17
Dividends per share	1.21	1.10	.95	.85	.71	.62	.57	.52
Price High	79.0	87.4	80.9	54.1	42.1	33.6	19.8	22.1
Low	52.0	60.9	50.7	39.0	28.3	18.2	14.1	14.3

AGGRESSIVE GROWTH

Microsoft Corporation

One Microsoft Way □ Redmond, Washington 98052-6399 □ Investor contact: Carla Lewis (425) 936-3703 □ Dividend reinvestment plan is not available □ Web site: www.microsoft.com □ Fiscal year ends June 30 □ Listed: Nasdaq □ Ticker symbol: MSFT □ S&P rating: A- □ Value Line financial strength rating: A++

Aided by a new Web search engine that looks for offers to sell counterfeit or illegally copied software, Microsoft has been on the prowl to eradicate the culprits that are responsible. In 2000, the company announced actions against 7,500 Internet listings for allegedly pirated products in thirty-three countries.

Microsoft said it is responding to a surge in illegal activity on the Web, which continues to present software pirates with novel ways to distribute unauthorized copies. The new piracy tools range from the sort of file-sharing technology used by the Napster music service to Web auctions, where Microsoft found that many people have been selling bogus software to the highest bidder. Some consumers received counterfeit software, while others received nothing at all.

In Europe, the Middle East, and Africa, the company said it has taken action in 2,274 instances of suspected piracy, sending notices to Web site owners asking them to remove products listed for sale. It filed a number of lawsuits and took part in scores of raids with law-enforcement officials in that region. In Croatia alone, police during one month simultaneously raided the premises of fifty-two suspected pirates.

After a long and acrimonious trial, the Justice Department and seventeen states proposed the most sweeping antitrust action in a quarter century against one of history's most successful enterprises. In late April 2000, U.S. District Judge Thomas Penfield Jackson ordered the breakup of Microsoft into two separate entities, with one company devoted to Office software applications and other built around its core Windows operating systems business.

In a subsequent court filing, Microsoft said that if the government's breakup plan were adopted, its employees might "leave the company in droves."

In the weeks that followed, the stock plummeted from a high of just under $120 to about half that value.

In late June of 2001, the U.S. District Court of Appeals for the District of Columbia threw out two of the government's three antitrust claims against Microsoft and excoriated U.S. District Judge Thomas Penfield Jackson for his handling of the historic case. The ruling, which sends the case back to a lower court and prevents Judge Jackson from hearing it again, all but ends the risk of a court-ordered breakup of the software giant.

On the other hand, it falls far short of a complete victory for Microsoft. The seven-judge panel upheld the finding that Microsoft holds monopoly power and declared it repeatedly and ruthlessly used its dominance to protect its Windows monopoly from competition. As a result, Microsoft still faces the prospect of lawsuits from both states and individual customers, not to mention restraints on its conduct that could haunt the company for years to come.

Company Profile

Microsoft is the dominant player in the PC software market. It climbed to prominence on the popularity of its operating systems software and now rules the business-applications software market. Microsoft, moreover, has set its sights on becoming the leading provider of software services for the Internet.

By virtue of it size, market positioning, and financial strength, Microsoft is a formidable competitor in any market it seeks to enter. Earnings have shown explosive growth in recent years, enhanced by a strong PC market in general, along with new product introductions and market-share gains.

Microsoft is best known for its operating-systems software programs, which run on close to 90 percent of the PCs currently in use. Its original DOS operating system, of course, gave way to Windows, a graphical user interface program run in conjunction with DOS, which made using a PC easier.

The company entered the business-applications market in the early 1990s via a lineup of strong offerings combined with aggressive and innovative marketing and sales strategies. The company's Office suite, which includes the popular Word (word processing), Excel (spreadsheet), Power-Point (graphics), and Outlook (e-mail) software programs, is now by far the best-selling applications software package.

Shortcomings to Bear in Mind

- Not long ago, Microsoft set up a stealth team of crack engineers to dream up a brand new version of its software suite, Office, while continuing to crank out the old standby. It's a tough, two-track strategy that pitted a "today" development team against a "tomorrow" team, as one person close to the teams put it. It's unclear, he says, "how today and tomorrow will meet."

  For Microsoft, the stakes are high: Office, contributes about a third of the company's overall revenue ($9.2 billion in the fiscal year ended June 20, 2000). What's more, Office's growth rate is sinking as the company finds it harder to find new users for the software. According to one analyst, Drew Brosseau of SG Cowen, Office sales will grow at just 4 percent in fiscal 2001 compared with 17 percent in fiscal 2000. "Without a new user community, it's a pretty tough business," he says.

- In 2000, a group of key Linux software developers and major computer manufacturers said they would—for the first time—compete with Microsoft's Office suite of applications for the personal computer. Until mid-2000, the Linux operating system (which is free) had its greatest impact in the computer server market where many Internet service providers and Web applications and service companies routinely use the program.

- For as long as there have been personal computers, software publishers have tried to stop people from making unauthorized copies of programs. A variety of methods, such as copy-proof floppy disks, have been tried, but most have failed. The industry estimates that piracy costs it some $12 billion a year worldwide. In the fall of 2000, Microsoft said it had found a way to put a sharp crimp in piracy. Unless you are a hacker, you will no longer be able to lend your copy of Office to a friend or relative.

  Although the new feature should cut down on some unauthorized copying, it won't have much impact on professional counterfeiters, who are especially prevalent in China and some other Asian countries. Nor will it stop dedicated hackers.

- Even mighty Microsoft is not immune to hackers. With carefree abandon, hackers wormed their way into the company's private domain in October 2000. What's more, the intrepid knaves were able to set up twenty-five unauthorized accounts and were able to rummage through Microsoft's internal computer network. To be sure, no corporate network is entirely safe from invasion by today's artful computer miscreants. However, Microsoft's inability to defend its own turf raises some questions about security. According to one observer, the company fell prey to the vulnerability of its own design. "Shame on Microsoft for letting this happen," said David J. Brumley, a Stanford University computer security officer who works with the FBI to put the cuffs on computer thugs.

Reasons to Buy

- In the fall of 2000, Microsoft put on sale its most powerful operating system ever, hailing the product as an important piece in the company's strategy to shift its focus to the Internet. Windows 2000 Datacenter Server is the top-of-the-line version of Microsoft's family of operating systems for corporate computer networks. Capable of powering computers with up to thirty-two processors, Datacenter targets the biggest and most demanding networks, such as those found in financial establishments or scientific research institutions that need to crunch huge amounts of information.

- Microsoft unveiled a new line of high-end computer server systems in the fall of 2000 that run Windows 2000, the latest business version of Windows. The servers are the first set of products in the company's "Dot-Net" initiative to bridge personal computing technology with the Internet. According to CEO Steve Ballmer, the new server software—years in the making—is one of Microsoft's most important product launches. "For twelve years, we've been banging our head on this," he said, adding that software sales to enterprises will become an increasingly important revenue source. The launch is a direct attack on the company's chief competitors, Sun Microsystem and Oracle Corporation. Sun's Unix-based computer systems run some of the busiest Web sites. For its part, Oracle's database software manages the reams of data at many Fortune 100 companies.

- The Supreme Court decided against an early review of the Microsoft antitrust case in the fall of 2000, delaying a final judgment for as long as two years and freeing the company to march into new markets unshackled by the courts. The Supreme Court's eight-to-one ruling was a setback for the Justice Department and nineteen states. They argued that the case was important to the nation's economy and should be resolved quickly.

As a result of the ruling, Microsoft first makes its case before the D.C. Circuit Court of Appeals, a respected legal panel that has taken Microsoft's side in earlier skirmishes. Once the lower court has ruled, Microsoft or the government can appeal to the Supreme Court. "This is a serious setback for the government," said William Kovacic, a George Washington University law professor and antitrust expert. "Their strategy was to speed this case to resolution as quickly as possible. I think the government gambled and failed. At this point, I think the possibility of breakup is next to zero."

■ Microsoft kicked off a major effort to enter the lucrative world of high-end, big-ticket computing in the fall of 2000. While the company has locked up the market for software for personal computers and more powerful servers capable of crunching large amounts of data, it has yet to penetrate the most powerful echelons of computing. Steve Ballmer, CEO of Microsoft, said his company was ready to enter the field with an arsenal of software, including a high-end operating system called Windows 2000 Datacenter Server, and a suite of business applications such as Exchange 2000 Server, a messaging program, and SQL Server 2000, a database program. "This is the broadest product launch in Microsoft history," said Mr. Ballmer.

■ More than 150 software developers have signed up to make games for the company's Xbox, its video-game console. These developers bolster Microsoft's bid to compete with Sony's PlayStation2 and the Nintendo Game Cube. Among the 150 third-party developers are some of the biggest names in gaming, including Activision, Bandai, Capcom, Eidos, Hudson Soft, Infogames, Konami, Midway Home Entertainment, Namco, Sierra, and THQ. "The games are what people want," said J. Allard, general manager of Xbox. "The games are what's going to make or break us."

Total assets: $52,150 million
Current ratio: 3.64
Common shares outstanding: 5,335 million
Return on 2000 shareholders' equity: 22.8%

	2000	1999	1998	1997	1996	1995	1994	1993
Revenues (millions)	22956	19747	14484	11358	8671	5937	4649	3753
Net income (millions)	9421	7625	4786	3454	2176	1453	1210	953
Earnings per share	1.70	1.39	.89	.66	.43	.29	.25	.20
Dividends per share	Nil							
Price High	117.1	119.9	72.0	37.7	21.5	13.7	8.1	6.1
Low	40.3	68.0	31.1	20.2	10.0	7.3	4.9	4.4

GROWTH AND INCOME

Minnesota Mining and Manufacturing Company

3M Center, 225-1S-15 ◻ St. Paul, Minnesota 55144-1000 ◻ Investor contact: Matt Ginter (651) 733-8206 ◻ Web site: www.3M.com ◻ Dividend reinvestment plan is available: (800) 401-1952 ◻ Listed: NYSE ◻ Ticker symbol: MMM ◻ S&P rating: A ◻ Value Line financial strength rating: A++

When GE selected a new chief executive to replace the legendary Jack Welch, the two runners-up for the post were immediately courted by companies looking for their own CEO replacements. Among them was Minnesota Mining and Manufacturing, as its chairman, Livio D. DeSimone, was slated to retire January 1, 2001. W. James McNerney Jr., who headed GE's aircraft-engines division, was fifty-one years old when he took the reins of 3M in December 2000.

Mr. McNerney said that a notably bright spot is 3M's technology business, which he described as "far broader and deeper than most people understand." One of the company's strongest performers in this realm is the segment that makes fiber-optic cabling systems and tiny, flexible circuits used in ink-jet printers.

Within the first three weeks on the job, Mr. McNerney outlined a cost-cutting strategy that focused on four key factors, one of which was the implementation of six sigma—a strategy he brought with him from General Electric. To be sure, Minnesota Mining is relatively inexperienced when dealing with these new programs and strategies. However, "there can be no doubt regarding their effectiveness," according to an analyst at Argus.

Company Profile

Minnesota Mining and Manufacturing Company is an international manufacturer with a vast array of products (more than 50,000). The company has a stake in such items as tapes, adhesives, electronic components, sealants, coatings, fasteners, floor coverings, cleaning agents, roofing granules, fire-fighting agents, graphic arts, dental products, medical products, specialty chemicals, and reflective sheeting.

The company's Industrial and Consumer Sector is the world's largest supplier of tapes, producing more than 900 varieties. It is also a leader in coated abrasives, specialty chemicals, repositionable notes, home cleaning sponges and pads, electronic circuits, and other important products.

The Life Sciences Sector is a global leader in reflective materials for transportation safety, respirators for worker safety, closures for disposable diapers, and high-quality graphics used indoors and out. This sector also holds leading positions in medical and surgical supplies, drug-delivery systems, and dental products.

3M has a decentralized organization with a large number of relatively small profit centers aimed at creating an entrepreneurial atmosphere.

Minnesota Mining is a highly diversified manufacturer of industrial, commercial, consumer, and health care products that share similar technological, manufacturing, and marketing resources. Its business initially developed from its research and technology in coating and bonding.

Shortcomings to Bear in Mind

- 3M operates on the philosophy that if you throw enough money at enough scientists they will come up with something interesting. They have—the $1.2 billion annual research budget yielded such innovations as a drug to treat genital warts, transparent tape, and skin patches to deliver drug therapy. On the other hand, the strategy is something of a dud in the profit column. Over the past decade, earnings per share have inched ahead 5 percent a year, barely keeping up with inflation. In a bull market for technology, this tech company sells at a lower multiple than the S&P 500.
- Over the past ten years, the company's growth, although steady, has not been dynamic. In the 1990–2000 period, earnings per share increased from $2.96 to $4.68, an annual compound growth rate of only 4.7 percent. In the same ten-year stretch, dividends expanded in similar fashion, from $1.46 to $2.32, a growth rate of 4.7 percent.

Reasons to Buy

- MMM has many strengths:
  - Leading market positions. Minnesota Mining is a leader in most of its businesses, often number one or number

two in market share. In fact, 3M has created many markets, frequently by developing products that people didn't even realize they needed.

- Strong technology base. The company draws on more than thirty core technologies—from adhesives and nonwovens to specialty chemicals and microreplication.
- Healthy mix of businesses. 3M serves an extremely broad array of markets— from automotive and health care to office supply and telecommunications. This diversity gives the company many avenues for growth while also cushioning the company from disruption in any single market.
- Flexible, self-reliant business units. 3M's success in developing a steady stream of new products and entering new markets stems from its deep-rooted corporate structure. It's an environment in which 3M people listen to customers, act on their own initiative, and share technologies and other expertise widely and freely.
- Worldwide presence. Minnesota Mining has companies in more than sixty countries around the world. It sells its products in nearly 200 countries.
- Efficient manufacturing and distribution. 3M is a low-cost supplier in many of its product lines. This is increasingly important in today's value-conscious and competitive world.
- Strong financial position. 3M is one of a small number of domestic companies whose debt carries the highest rating for credit quality.
- To sustain a strong flow of new product, 3M continues to make substantial investments—about $1 billion a year—in research and development.
- Minnesota Mining is a global leader in industrial, consumer, office, health care, safety, and other markets. The company draws on many strengths, including a rich pool of technology, innovative products, strong customer service, and efficient manufacturing.
- The unrelenting drive toward smaller, lighter, more powerful, and more economical electronic products creates strong demand for leading-edge 3M Microflex Circuits. Minnesota Mining is the world's number one supplier of adhesiveless flexible circuitry. 3M Microflex Circuits connect components in many of the world's ink-jet printers. They also link integrated circuits to printed circuit boards efficiently and reliably, making it possible to develop even smaller cellular phones, portable computers, pagers, and other electronic devices.
- 3M supplies a wide variety of products to the automotive market, including high-performance tape attachment systems; structural adhesives; catalytic converter mounts; decorative, functional, and protective films; and trim and identification products.
- The Life Sciences Sector produces innovative products that improve health and safety for people around the world. In consumer and professional health care, 3M has captured a significant share of the first-aid market with a superior line of bandages. 3M Active Strips Flexible Foam Bandages adhere better to skin—even when wet—and 3M Comfort Strips Ultra Comfortable Bandages set new standards for wearing comfort. Under development are tapes, specialty dressings, and skin treatments that will reinforce and broaden the company's leading market positions and accelerate sales growth.
- In pharmaceuticals, 3M is a global leader in technologies for delivering medications that are inhaled or absorbed through the skin, and the company is expanding its horizons in new molecule discovery.
- Hostile conditions lie under any vehicle's hood, but 3M's Dyneon Fluoropolymers withstand the heat. Found in seals, gaskets, O-rings, and hoses in

automotive and airplane engines, the company's fluoropolymers outperform the competition when high temperatures and chemicals cross paths. And 3M technology isn't merely under the hood. Minnesota Mining also makes products for the vehicle's body and cabin that identify, insulate, protect, and bond, such as dimensional graphics, Thinsulate Acoustic Insulation, cabin filters, and super-strong adhesives and tapes that replace screws and rivets. The company is also developing window films that help keep the cabin cool by absorbing ultraviolet light and reflecting infrared light.

- Post-it Notes were named one of the twentieth century's best products by *Fortune* magazine, and Scotch Tape was listed among the century's one hundred best innovations by *Business Week* magazine. Also, 3M ranked as the world's most respected consumer-goods company and fifteenth overall in a survey published by the *Financial Times of London*. Finally, 3M achieved Vendor of the Year status from four leaders in the office-supply industry.

Total assets: $14,404 million
Current ratio: 1.35
Common shares outstanding: 396 million
Return on 2000 shareholder's equity: 28.6%

	2000	1999	1998	1997	1996	1995	1994	1993
Revenues (millions)	16724	15659	15021	15070	14236	13460	15079	14020
Net income (millions)	1872	1711	1526	1626	1516	1359	1345	1263
Earnings per share	4.68	4.21	3.74	3.88	3.63	3.23	3.18	2.91
Dividends per share	2.32	2.24	2.20	2.12	1.92	1.88	1.76	1.66
Price High	122.9	103.4	97.9	105.5	85.9	69.9	57.1	58.5
Low	78.2	69.3	65.6	80.0	61.3	50.8	46.4	48.6

GROWTH AND INCOME

J. P. Morgan Chase & Company

270 Park Avenue ☐ New York, New York 10017-2070 ☐ Investor contact: John Borden (212) 270-7318 ☐ Dividend reinvestment plan is available: (800) 758-4651 ☐ Web site: www.jpmorganchase.com ☐ Listed: NYSE ☐ Ticker symbol: JPM ☐ S&P rating: B+ ☐ Value Line financial strength rating: A

The merger of J. P. Morgan and Chase Manhattan at the end of 2000 created the nation's largest bank, with assets of $715 billion. It is not surprising that JPM might want to brag a little in its first annual report. J. P. Morgan Chase can boast that it is:

- The world's largest corporate debt house.
- The world's largest provider of risk-management products, including foreign exchange and derivatives.

- One of the world's largest global equity research coverage lists.
- In the top four among global advisors in mergers and acquisitions.
- A leading brokerage house in Asia.
- A leading equity derivatives house worldwide.
- The third largest equity underwriter in Latin America.
- One of the largest global private equity funds, with $24 billion under management.

• Winner of the "European Leveraged Loan House of the Year."

• The largest global custodian, with $2.3 trillion in assets under custody.

• The provider of operating services that are provided to 50 percent of *Fortune* 1000 companies and 80 percent of the top 100 global banks.

Company Profile

Rather than describe all the nuts and bolts of this huge institution, I thought it might be easier to understand J. P. Morgan Chase with a few brief facts concerning the bank's many accomplishments:

• Advisor on more than 500 mergers and acquisitions worldwide, valued at more than $888 billion.

• Largest book manager of corporate debt and equity in the United States, with over $545 billion raised.

• The world leader in global syndicated loans.

• Rated the world's best overall derivatives dealer—equity, interest rates, and credit.

• A sales and trading powerhouse, serving clients from more than thirty trading rooms around the world.

• Closed more than 1,800 direct equity and mezzanine transactions since inception in 1984.

• Second largest private bank in the world.

• More than $320 billion in private banking client assets under management, including brokerage, trust, and custody services.

• Leading funds transfer agent, moving $1.2 trillion in funds daily.

• Serves more than 30 million customers, small businesses, and middle-market companies across the United states.

• Number one full-service bank for consumers and small businesses in the New York tristate area.

• Number one in market penetration and lead share for middle-market companies in the New York tri-state area.

• Number two originator of residential mortgage loans in the United States, with more than $76 billion originated in 2000.

• One of the largest originators of auto loans and leases in the United States, with $25 billion in managed assets.

• Fifth largest domestic credit card issuer.

Shortcomings to Bear in Mind

Despite the bank's many fine accomplishments, they didn't shield it from the economic problems that hurt the nation in 2000:

■ Total operating revenue of $32.8 billion for J. P. Morgan Chase was 3 percent higher than in 1999, despite a difficult market environment in the second half of 2000.

■ Operating results of the bank in 2000 were hurt by market-to-market declines in the values of investments held by JPMorgan Partners (the firm's principal vehicle for private equity investing). However, during its seventeen-year history, JPMorgan Partners has consistently produced a record of superior financial returns over multiple business cycles and widely varying conditions in the capital markets. It is recognized as one of the most successful private equity organizations in the world.

■ Operating earnings in 2000 were $5.93 billion, compared with $7.43 billion in 1999, and diluted operating EPS declined to $2.96 in 2000, down from $3.65 the prior year.

■ On a reported basis, which includes merger and restructuring costs and special items, net income in 2000 was $5.73 billion, compared with $7.50 billion in 1999. Diluted net income per share (assuming conversion of convertible securities) was $2.86 in 2000, down from $3.69 the year before.

Reasons to Buy

- J. P. Morgan Chase has in excess of $42 billion in equity capital. The firm has relationships with more than 5,000 primary corporate clients with a balanced footprint across North America, Europe, Asia, and Latin America.
- With total assets of $715 billion and stockholders' equity of $42 billion, the firm's financial position is strong, as reflected in a tier 1 capital ratio of 8.5 percent and double A credit ratings. Moreover, operating results are broadly diversified by business and region.
- The company's philosophy through the succession of mergers over the past ten years has been that leadership positions drive growth and shareholder value. According to William B. Harrison Jr., JPM's CEO, "Leadership positions enable us to serve clients better, attract partners and intellectual capital, and lead to meaningful economies of scale that benefit all shareholders.

  "Today, J. P. Morgan Chase holds top-tier positions in mergers and acquisition advisory, derivatives and risk management, investment management and private banking, private equity, and operating services. We are also known as the leading provider of corporate debt products in the world, driven by both our bond and loan origination and syndication capabilities."
- In addition to the strength and diversification in the merger wholesale business, J. P. Morgan Chase has a solid retail and middle-market financial services franchise that is the leading bank in the New York metropolitan area, the largest U.S. mortgage company, and a top-ranked credit card and auto finance company.

Mr. Harrison said, "These retail businesses are embarking on a path toward greater efficiency, less bureaucracy, focused investments, and higher growth. Both Six Sigma and technological innovation will play a significant role in enhancing distribution, service quality, and client intimacy."

- The merger of J. P. Morgan and Chase Manhattan created pre-tax synergies of $3 billion—$2 billion of cost savings and $1 billion of incremental net revenue. "Our experience in past mergers," said Mr. Harrison, "has helped us to develop a detailed process of tracking accountability for business execution. The best evidence of our success to date is the fact that we were able to close on the formation of our new firm in less than four months, an important accomplishment for both client coverage and employee retention."
- The momentum of strong revenue from advisory activities continued throughout 2000, as revenues increased 49 percent from 1999 to $1.5 billion. Robert Fleming Holdings Limited, with its broad network in Europe and Asia, extended the geographic reach of the firm's advisory practice. Likewise, the acquisition of the Beacon Group, LLC (a privately held investment-banking firm) augmented the advisory capabilities of the Investment Bank.
- Equity underwriting revenues nearly tripled in 2000, primarily as a result of the acquisition of Hambrecht & Quist, which extended J. P. Morgan Chase's underwriting practice into the fast growing fields of health care and technology-related industries.
- Cardmember Services is the fifth largest credit card issuer in the nation, servicing more than 20 million accounts. The business unit has cobranded relationships with significant partners, including

Continental Airlines, Shell Oil, Toys 'Я' Us, and Wal-Mart. Its joint venture with First Data Corporation is the largest merchant processor, with annual servicing volume in excess of $170 billion. In 2000, Cardmember Services focused on enhancing its relationships with cardholders and expanding its customer base. It opened a record 3 million new accounts during 2000 and ended the year with managed receivables exceeding $36 billion. Cardmember Services provides both consumer and commercial products.

- Home Finance provides mortgages and related home finance products to almost 4 million consumers across the United States. HF is a market leader (top three ranking) in mortgage loan origination and servicing, home equity-loan and equity-line origination and manufactured home loan originations. Total loans originated in 2000 were $76 billion, and the total mortgage servicing portfolio at the end of 2000 was $362 billion, for an increase of 16 percent over the prior year.

- In the bank's 2000 annual report, it lists a host of distinctions and accomplishments:

  - One of the top five asset managers worldwide, with $638 billion in global assets under management.

  - One of the top five global managers of corporate cash and equivalents, with more than $135 billion under management.

  - U.S. mutual funds business with over $320 billion in client assets.

  - Relationships with an estimated 35 percent of the individuals listed in the *Forbes* 400.

  - Private banking relationship clients in thirty-six countries.

  - Number one global custodian.

  - Number one domestic dollar clearer.

  - Number one trustee for all domestic taxable debt offerings.

  - Number one in orders of merit from *Global Investor* client satisfaction survey.

  - Number one in custody and transaction services in *Euromoney* annual survey.

  - Number one in issuing and paying agent services for domestic commercial paper.

  - Best trustee for Europe and Asia Pacific; runner up for North America (International Securitization Report).

  - Number one bank lender to small businesses in the company's Texas markets.

Total assets: $715 billion
Common shares outstanding: 1,929 million
Return on 2000 shareholders' equity: 13.5%

	2000	1999	1998	1997	1996	1995	1994	1993
Net interest income (millions)	9512	8744	8566	8158	8340	8202	8312*	
Net income (millions)	5727	5394	4016	3708	2461	2970	2486	
Earnings per share	2.86	4.18	2.82	1.65	2.02	1.66	2.08	
Dividends per share	1.28	1.09	.96	.83	.75	.65	.55	
Price High	67.2	60.8	51.7	42.2	32.0			
Low	32.4	43.9	23.7	28.2	21.4			

*Because of the merger of J. P. Morgan and Chase Manhattan at the end of 2000, a more complete table is not available.

National City Corporation

P. O. Box 5756, Dept. 2101 ◻ Cleveland, Ohio 44101-0756 ◻ Investor contact: Derek Green (216) 222-9849 ◻ Dividend reinvestment plan is available: (800) 622-6757 ◻ Web site: www.national-city.com ◻ Listed: NYSE ◻ Ticker symbol: NCC ◻ S&P rating: A ◻ Value Line financial strength rating: A

National City, a major Midwestern bank based in Cleveland, is finding that fee-based businesses are growing at a healthy clip compared with more conventional banking operations. National Processing, for example, is enjoying a substantial momentum as a leading processor of merchant card transactions as it continues to expand from its strong base of national accounts into midsize and smaller merchants.

This growth has been the direct result of restructuring efforts that took place at National Processing in 1999. Over the 1999–2000 period, moreover, earnings doubled at National Processing, and the company's 87 percent position tripled in value.

Company Profile

National City provides broad-based banking and financial services to about 8.5 million consumers in Ohio, Pennsylvania, Kentucky, Michigan, Illinois, and Indiana. Services are delivered through more than 1,200 branch offices and more than 1,600 ATMs. A growing number of customers choose the convenience of National City's online banking service at *www.national-city.com*. Enhancements completed in 2000 have increased the Web site's versatility, functionality, ease of use, and interconnectivity.

Since David A. Daberko was named chairman and chief executive officer of National City Corporation in mid-1995, the company, once known only to Ohioans, has more than doubled in size through acquisitions.

National City subsidiaries provide financial services that meet a wide range of customer needs, including commercial and retail banking, trust and investment services, item processing, mortgage banking, and credit card processing.

Retail Banking

The retail banking business includes the deposit-gathering branch franchise, along with lending to individuals and small businesses. Lending activities include residential mortgages, indirect and direct consumer installment loans, leasing, credit cards, and student lending.

Fee-Based Businesses

The fee-based businesses include institutional trust, mortgage banking, and item processing.

● Institutional trust includes employee benefit administration, mutual fund management, charitable and endowment services, and custodial services.

● Mortgage banking includes the origination of mortgages through retail offices and broker networks and mortgage servicing.

● Item processing is conducted by National City's majority-owned subsidiary, National Processing, Inc. (NYSE: NAP), and includes merchant credit card processing, airline ticket processing, check guarantee services, and receivables and payables processing services.

Customer Needs and Preferences

To gain insight into customer preferences, National City has been making substantial investments in data warehouse technology to more effectively capture and manage customer information. This capability has already resulted in more effective cross-selling and has given the bank tools to better understand and predict customer needs and preferences.

The bank is well aware that customer demand for financial services transcends traditional time and place limitations. To that end, the company initiated a multi-year plan to reconfigure its branch delivery system—reducing traditional full-service branches while expanding nontraditional alternatives. This includes in-store locations, limited-service facilities, and off-site ATMs—which, along with better call-center capability, makes it easier and more convenient for customers to do business with National City.

Shortcomings to Bear in Mind

- The weakness in the economy that began in late 2000 and has continued into 2001 is hurting corporations of nearly every stripe. Nor are banks immune. A weak economy, for instance, virtually assures an increase in problem assets and loan losses. However, CEO David A. Daberko says "We expect the problems to be manageable and of a lesser scope for National City than for the industry as a whole."
- National City has a lackluster record of growth. In the 1990–2000 period, earnings per share expanded from $.97 to $2.13, a compound annual growth rate of 8.2 percent. In the same ten-year span, however, dividends per share outperformed EPS growth, climbing from $.47 to $1.14, a growth rate of 9.3 percent.
- In recent years, banks have been finding it increasingly difficult to expand revenues. Those with the broadest product mix are more likely to have an easier time registering top-line growth. In addition, savings from cost-cutting efforts, which have propelled earnings for many large banks in recent years, are

becoming more difficult to come by, placing greater emphasis on top-line growth. Loan growth also remains a regional phenomenon, with strength in areas of the Southeast and Midwest where economies continue to grow at a rate above the national average.

Reasons to Buy

- During 2000, NCC's Internet offerings "began to come of age," said Mr. Daberko in early 2001. "With the rollout of a new online banking product, participation has risen sharply, and we are adding thousands of new customers each month. We also introduced significant new Web-based cash management capabilities for corporate customers and a dedicated small business banking Web site."
- In corporate banking, National City's second largest business, the bank has worked hard to retain its position as the number one middle-market lender in its region. The bank's markets have been economically vibrant, as evidenced by low rates of unemployment and significant growth in small and medium-size businesses over the past several years. The bank's decentralized system of credit approval permits quick responsiveness to customer needs. At the same time, the company's product capability is second to none. For example, NCC introduced an innovative lending product, Corporate Select, that utilizes built-in interest rate protection options inside a conventional loan. This helps companies manage risk in a seamless, straightforward manner. Corporate Select offers a competitive advantage in winning and strengthening customer relationships. There is no comparable product current available in the market. Through initiatives such as these and a strong team of relationship managers, National City has been able to maintain or increase market share in virtually all

of its markets. What's more, the company has been particularly successful in western Pennsylvania, which it entered through the merger with Integra Financial Corporation.

- National City is one of the five top originators of federally guaranteed student loans in the country. What's more, in dealer finance, the company is ranked as the fifth largest noncaptive originator of retail loans and leases. National City offers competitive credit card products and indirect consumer installment loans and leases for automotive, marine, recreational vehicle, heavy equipment, and property improvement.

- National City provides professional investment services to individuals, families, and businesses. Through an integrated structure encompassing personal trust, investment management, private banking, and brokerage, National City offers a single-source solution for clients to manage their personal and family wealth. Clients maintain relationships with skilled financial professionals, and state-of-the-art technology enables efficient access to trust, investment, and brokerage services.

National City's primary objective is to produce sustainable, above-average investment performance. Offering thirty-nine mutual funds, National City covers the full spectrum of investment styles. In 1999, seven mutual funds in the Armada and Parkstone fund families earned impressive four-star or five-star ratings (the two best ratings) from Morningstar, an industry rating service, for their relative performance over the previous five-year period.

National City also provides professional investment services for businesses. The PlanWorks online reporting service allows 401(k) participants to check their balances, fund performance, and elections in a secure, Internet-based environment. In a survey of stock transfer clients conducted by Group Five, Inc., National City's stock transfer service was recognized as the industry leader in customer service and satisfaction in each of the last two years.

- The bank undertook a number of restructuring actions in 2000 to improve business mix and long-term growth prospects. NCC sold or securitized (taken off the balance sheet and transformed into a hybrid security that can be sold in the open market) several billion dollars of low-yielding assets to reduce reliance on purchased funds, raise capital ratios, and reduce exposure to future interest rate volatility. In addition, National City closed sixty-nine underperforming Loan Zone consumer finance stores and announced its intention to exit the low-return automobile leasing business.

These restructuring moves made room on the balance sheet for higher-return assets, such as the nonperforming mortgage loans generated by the company's First Franklin subsidiary. These loans are readily salable to third parties at premium to origination costs but have greater lifetime value when held on the balance sheet.

- National City has been very successful in originating large volumes of high-quality assets, with average loan growth of 12 percent during 2000 (adjusted for loan sales and securitizations). What's more, corporate loan growth was particularly strong. An emphasis on syndications and commercial finance, along with initiatives to increase market share in Chicago and Detroit, were factors that contributed to this favorable trend.

- Based on the changing preferences of consumers, National City is changing the way it delivers financial products and services. More than a third of traditional branches were converted by the end of 2000 to the "Bank Express" model, improving the customer service environment and efficiency of National City's 13,000 retail professionals. Many

consumers also like the convenient hours and locations of some 100 branches in grocery stores and other retail sites.

Total assets: $88,535 million
Return on assets in 2000: 1.52%
Common shares outstanding: 608 million
Return on 2000 shareholders' equity: 21.3%

	2000	1999	1998	1997	1996	1995	1994	1993
Loans (millions)	65604	60204	58011	39573	35830	25732	22566	20843
Net income (millions)	1302	1404	1333	807	733	465	429	404
Earnings per share	2.13	2.22	2.00	1.83	1.64	1.48	1.32	1.21
Dividends per share	1.14	1.09	.97	.86	.94	.65	.59	.53
Price High	29.8	37.8	38.8	33.8	23.6	16.9	14.5	14.0
Low	16.0	22.1	28.5	21.3	15.3	12.6	11.9	11.6

CONSERVATIVE GROWTH

The New York Times Company

229 West 43rd Street □ New York, New York 10036 □ Investor contact: Catherine Mathis (212) 556-1981 □ Dividend reinvestment plan is available: (800) 414-6280 □ Web site: www.nytco.com □ Listed: NYSE □ Ticker symbol: NYT □ S&P rating: B+ □ Value Line financial strength rating: B++

In a move to widen its distribution over the Web, the Internet unit of the *New York Times* signed a deal in 2001 to provide some of its articles to Internet media giant Yahoo! Under the pact, the *Times* provides Yahoo!'s News section with articles each day from the national, politics, business, international, technology, and arts sections of the *Times*, as well as local news from newyorktoday.com and Boston.com.

"We're pleased to be working with Yahoo! in this important syndication agreement," said Catherine Levene, vice president of strategy and business development for New York Times Digital. While the *New York Times* has been syndicating its content over the Internet for years, it has been mostly in the form of headlines or abstracts.

According to Robert Hertzberg, an analyst with Jupiter Media Metrix, "You can describe their syndication strategy up to now as a tease. This is really giving away a lot of the goods, and I expect it will be

good for the *Times*, through subscription to print publication and building traffic at the *New York Times* site."

Company Profile

Dating back to 1851, the New York Times Company is a diversified media company. Its segments consist of two groups: newspapers and broadcasting.

In the second quarter of 2001, the company sold its Magazine Group to Advance Publications Inc. for an estimated—according to analysts—$400 million (the amount was not disclosed by the company). It consisted of three golf publications and related activities in the golf field. In 1999 the company and Scholastic Inc. jointly launched a biweekly teen magazine called *The New York Times Upfront*. It is sold in schools or by home delivery.

The Newspaper Group is comprised of the *New York Times* (which is circulated in all fifty states, U.S. territories, and around the world), the *Boston Globe*, and investments in twenty-two regional newspapers. The *Times* has an average daily circulation of 1,149,576. On Sunday, circulation jumps to 1,691,287. About 60 percent of the Monday-through-Friday circulation is sold in thirty-one counties that make up the greater New York City area, which includes New York City, Westchester County, and parts of upstate New York, Connecticut, and New Jersey; 40 percent are sold elsewhere. On Sundays, however, 56 percent of circulation is sold in the greater New York City area and 44 percent elsewhere.

Since 1993, the company has owned the *Boston Globe*, New England's largest newspaper. The *Globe*, which was launched in 1872, has weekday circulation of 477,074, which shoots up to 722,729 on Sundays.

The New York Times Company has a stake in twenty-two regional newspapers with total daily circulation during the week of 736,800, which moves up modestly to 787,600 on Sundays. Among these newspapers are the *Gadsden Times*, the *Tuscaloosa News*, *Times Daily*, *Santa Barbara News-Press*, the *Press Democrat*, and the *Sarasota Herald-Tribune*.

The company also owns newspaper distributors, a news service, a features syndicate, and microfilm and Internet-related operations.

The Broadcast Group consists of eight network-affiliated television stations and two radio stations. The TV stations serve Wilkes-Barre/Scranton, Pennsylvania; the Quad Cities area of Illinois and Iowa; Fort Smith, Arkansas; Huntsville, Alabama; Oklahoma City, Oklahoma; Des Moines, Iowa; Memphis, Tennessee; and Norfolk, Virginia. The two radio stations are situated in New York City.

The company's Internet sites are consolidated under a separate division, New York Times Digital. The sites include NYTimes.com, Boston.com, NYToday.com, WineToday.com, GolfDigest.com, and Abuzz.com. In 2000, the company created a new class of common stock to track the performance of New York Times Digital.

The company has interests in a Canadian newsprint mill, Donohue Malbaie, which manufactures newsprint. The company also has a 40 percent interest in a partnership operating a supercalendered paper mill in Maine. Supercalendered paper is higher quality than newsprint and is used in the paper's Sunday magazine section.

Finally, the New York Times Company has a 50 percent interest in the *International Herald Tribune*.

Results in 2000

In 2000, the Newspaper Group was by far the largest part of the company, with revenues of $3.16 billion and operating profit of $677.64 million. The Broadcast Group was a distant second, with 2000 revenues of $160.3 million and an operating profit of $48.8 million. Magazines brought in revenues of $115.4 million in 2000, with an operating profit of $19.3 million. The smallest operation, New York Times Digital, had revenues of $66.6 million but was in the red for the year.

Shortcomings to Bear in Mind

■ Newspapers are not immune to the vagaries of the economy. Advertising is always a place that companies can retrench when they are having trouble coping with a slump in revenues.

The vulnerability to a dip in advertising can be seen if you examine the company's revenue sources. The Newspaper Group's major source of revenues is advertising, not circulation. The *New York Times*, for example, had advertising revenues in 2000 of $1,295 million, compared with $468 million for circulation. Similarly, the *Boston Globe* brought in $488 million in advertising revenues and only $134 million from circulation. What it amounts to is this: subscribers are not likely to stop reading the paper, but advertisers may cut back when they are searching for ways to rein in expenses.

- There is always the threat of fewer readers as younger people view the news on television or the Internet.
- In 2001 there was fear that newsprint costs would be increased.

Reasons to Buy

- In 2000 the company was ranked number one in the publishing industry in *Fortune*'s survey of the Global Most Admired Companies. What's more, the *New York Times* was ranked first among all companies in the survey for the quality of its products and services.
- In 2000 the company's diluted earnings climbed 18 percent over the prior year. That marked the sixth consecutive year that the New York Times Company exceeded its goal of growing EPS by at least 10 to 15 percent. The gain in 2000, moreover, was even more impressive since it was net of the company's investment in NYTD (the company's digital unit), which amounted to about $62 million, excluding a year-end write-down of intangible assets.

  As 2001 got underway, the company was confident that the year would be the seventh consecutive year that earnings would meet this same goal. According to a company spokesman, to make certain it is able to meet its 2001 goal, "We recently announced a home delivery price increase at the *Times*, which will result in adding approximately $14 to $16 million to the bottom line this year. Now, that's in addition to the home delivery increase at the *Boston Globe*, which took place last October (of 2000) and we'll still get much of the benefit of that in 2001. So the total of those two actions would be approximately $18 to $20 million total for the bottom line in 2001."

- Also enhancing results in 2001 and beyond is the *Times*'s continuing transformation of the *Times* from a New York City newspaper into a national newspaper. According the an official of the company, "Our ad revenue base at the *Times* is now broader and more diverse than that of any other newspaper in the country. That makes us less vulnerable to a softening in any particular category. At the same time, our ongoing national expansion effort supports the aggressive advertising rate increase that we're made in such areas as color premiums."

- Janet Robinson, president and general manager of the New York Times Newspaper Group, said to a group of analysts in early 2001, "In regard to the year ahead, we are going to continue to concentrate on our national expansion and really concentrate on the two levers that we talk about so often with all of you: advertising and circulation. We will be opening four print sites and one Sunday print site, in fact, this year. In the second quarter, we'll be opening Gastonia, North Carolina. Dayton, which is our Sunday plant, will be opening in the second quarter, as well. A Minneapolis site and an Ann Arbor site in the third quarter, and Columbia, Missouri, in the fourth quarter. So with that expanded availability, we expect to have strong circulation growth in the year."

  Ms. Robinson went on to say, "In regard to the advertising side, as I outlined earlier, we feel quite confident, particularly because of the strong breadth of categories that we have. We are not dependent on classified and retail the way many of the other newspapers are."

- The *New York Times* benefits from the increased use of color in advertisements.

In the words of Ms. Robinson, "We have been very aggressive with our color premiums this year (2001), which of course will add to our revenues quite dramatically this year. We went up 40 percent with color premiums. Last year (2000), about 12 percent of all of the ads that appeared in the paper were color ads. That was up from 9 percent the prior year. We're expecting anywhere from between 11 and 18 percent of our ads this year to be color ads.

"We have benefited by the great work of our production facilities and our outside print sites in regard to color quality. Advertisers have praised us for the kind of color reproduction that we indeed display every day. We're won two awards that really underscore the quality performance that we have in that area, so we are able to command these premiums quite easily."

Ms. Robinson also told analysts, "We are finding that many advertisers are asking for positions within the paper as well, which also relates to color, primarily because these are franchise positions (premium positions, which are often noticed by readers, such as the back page or an upper right-hand corner) that we can demand even more premiums for, as well, because we demand not only a color premium, we also demand a franchise premium, as well."

Total assets: $3,607 million
Current ratio: 1.12
Common shares outstanding: 163 million
Return on 2000 shareholders' equity: 27%

	2000	1999	1998	1997	1996	1995	1994	1993
Revenues (millions)	3489	3131	2937	2866	2615	2409	2358	2020
Net income (millions)	398	310	287	262	84	136	213	6
Earnings per share	2.32	1.73	1.49	1.33	.43	.70	1.02	.04
Dividends per share	.45	.41	.37	.32	.28	.28	.28	.28
Price High	49.9	49.8	40.6	33.2	20.0	15.5	14.8	15.6
Low	32.6	26.5	20.5	18.2	12.8	10.1	10.6	11.2

CONSERVATIVE GROWTH

Nordson Corporation

28601 Clemens Road ◻ Westlake, Ohio 44145-4551 ◻ Investor contact: Barbara T. Price (440) 414-5344 ◻ Dividend reinvestment plan is available: (800) 622-6757 ◻ Web site: www.nordson.com ◻ Fiscal year ends Sunday closest to October 31 ◻ Listed: Nasdaq ◻ Ticker symbol: NDSN ◻ S&P rating: A- ◻ Value Line financial strength rating: B++

Acquisitions are a key component of Nordson's growth strategy. Over the past five years, they have spurred Nordson's entry into the realm of systems for advanced semiconductor packaging as well as the manufacture of telecommunications equipment and medical devices.

In late 2000, for instance, Nordson completed the acquisition of EFD, Inc., the world's leading producer of low-pressure precision dispensing systems. Headquartered in Rhode Island, the company's valve applicators are used to dispense fluids such as solder pastes, fluxes, coatings, adhesives, inks, paints, sealants, and solvents. The addition of EFD complements Nordson's fast-growing businesses that produce equipment for high-performance materials used in the electronics and medical markets.

EFD's record of rapid growth, high profitability, and leadership in the company's targeted growth markets will further accelerate Nordson's performance in this key sector of the company. Both Nordson and EFD have technologies and market positions that will improve one another's performance. The acquisition of EFD will add nearly $70 million to sales in 2001 and will produce cash flow well above most acquisitions of its size.

Company Profile

Nordson Corporation designs, manufactures, and markets systems that apply adhesives, sealants, and coatings to a broad range of consumer and industrial products during manufacturing operations.

Nordson's high value-added product line includes customized electronic-control technology for the precise application of materials to meet customers' productivity, quality, and environmental management targets.

Nordson products are used around the world in the appliance, automotive, construction, container, converting, electronics, food and beverage, furniture, graphic arts, metal finishing, nonwovens, packaging, and other diverse industries.

Nordson markets its products through its international sales divisions in North America, Europe, Japan, and the South Pacific. These organizations are supported by a network of direct operations in thirty-one countries. Consistent with this strategy, more than 50 percent of the company's revenues are generated outside the United States.

Nordson has manufacturing facilities in Ohio, Georgia, Alabama, California, Connecticut, Germany, the Netherlands, Sweden, and the United Kingdom.

The U.S. Automatic Company, the parent of Nordson, was founded in Amherst, Ohio in 1909. Initially, the company specialized in high-volume, low-cost screw machine parts for the burgeoning automotive industry.

In the years following World War II, Walter Nord, along with sons Eric and Evan, searched for a proprietary product to serve as a basis for future growth. This resulted in the acquisition of patents covering the "hot airless" method of spraying paint and other coating materials. The company later expanded its product line to include air-spray equipment and incorporated the highly efficient electrostatic process in both airless and air-spray painting systems.

Beginning in the late 1960s, Nordson pioneered the technology and equipment for applying powder coatings with the development of the compact and efficient cartridge-type recovery/recycle systems. Nordson has steadily refined its cartridge-booth technology and is an innovator in all aspects of the powder coating process for both organic and porcelain enamel applications. Today, Nordson is the acknowledged industry leader in powder coatings systems.

Each year, the worldwide appliance industry transforms millions of square feet of prefinished sheet steel into consumer durables, including refrigerators, ranges, washers, and dryers. Before appliances are assembled, manufacturers use Nordson flatline powder coating systems to apply flexible porcelain enamel "powder paint" that quickly turns steel into gleaming panels of white, almond, and black metal that can be bent and wrapped to achieve new model designs. The benefit to manufacturers is increased line speed, higher quality, and lower operating costs. Consumers benefit, too: these uniformly coated appliances are more attractive and less prone to corrosion.

Shortcomings to Bear in Mind

- The company's record of growth leaves something to be desired. In the 1990–2000 period, earnings per share advanced from $.76 to $1.85, which amounts to a compound annual growth rate of 9.3 percent. In the same ten-year span, dividends performed much better, climbing from $.18 in 1990 to $.52 in 2000, a growth rate of 11.2 percent. The company has increased its dividend for thirty-seven consecutive years. Even so, the all-important payout ratio is still a conservative 28 percent, indicating the company is plowing back earnings in order to enhance growth.

- Nordson has not been a stock that has benefited investors in recent years. In the 1994–2000 period, the stock traded in a narrow, lackluster range, typically fluctuating between $18 and $33 and lacking an upward trend.

Reasons to Buy

- Worldwide revenues expanded to a record $741 million in 2000, more than 50 percent of which was derived from the company's operations abroad. This reflects volume growth of 8 percent, which was reduced by 2 percent because of the impact of a stronger dollar.

  For adhesive dispensing systems, Nordson's largest business segment, sales volume grew by 7 percent, with strong performance in each geographic region. Sales volume in the advanced technology segment was particularly strong in 2000, increasing 28 percent over the prior year. This excellent volume growth, coupled with the cost reductions associated with the company's Action 2000 initiatives, led to strong earnings. Earnings per share before nonrecurring charges grew 25 percent to a record $1.85.

  The Action 2000 program is a project that seeks to improve performance, reduce costs, and accelerate growth. The goal of achieving annual manufacturing and procurement cost savings of $10 million by the end of 2001 is well on its way to being realized.

- The production of long-lasting batteries—expected to represent 50 percent of the total battery market within the next five years—is already a strong growth area for Nordson. Battery manufacturers use Nordson's high-speed equipment to coat battery linings with a conductive coating of carbon. The company's MEG compact spray gun is the only product available that applies a consistent carbon film while reducing overall material usage. Nordson is the market leader in coating AA and AAA batteries. What's more, new product offerings for coating C and D varieties were introduced in 2001.

- Nordson's finishing businesses have always set a high priority on new product developments that enhance customer productivity. As industry continues to demand increased efficiencies and cost controls, these developments are paying off handsomely for the powder coating, liquid finishing, and container businesses.

  While powder coating offers distinct advantages over liquid finishing in applying paint to many types of products, liquid technologies have held the lead in quick color change. Now, Nordson's newest powder coating system introduces a technology that makes color changes possible in as little as fifteen minutes. "Fast color changes makes Nordson a market winner in powder coating," says Mark Gacka, vice president. "These new offerings allow manufacturers to change colors faster than ever before. And it makes powder coating economical for a wider range of industrial uses."

- "Finishers of consumer and industrial products come to Nordson for the most efficient methods to apply liquid paints and powder coatings," says Sam Dawson, vice president of Nordson. "Spraying coating materials is the easy part . . . our ability to control their precise application is where we deliver real value to our customers."

Nordson markets complete material application systems that help manufacturers improve product quality while lowering material usage. "Today, finishers want to reduce the environmental impact of their operations," says Dawson. "That's why Nordson focuses on providing systems that apply solvent-free powder coatings and low-solvent liquid paints. Finishers who convert to these finishes can meet environmental goals and reduce waste-disposal costs without sacrificing quality.

"Proactive involvement in the industries we serve, through memberships in professional associations and relationships with coatings suppliers, is key to understanding our customers' needs," Dawson adds. "This involvement, combined with our experience base, gives Nordson two competitive advantages—the best equipment available and the fastest new-product cycle time."

- Nordson technology delivers precise applications of both hot and melt adhesive and cold glue, simultaneously, to tightly seal cases of agricultural products, beverages, and consumer packaged goods. The hot-melt adhesive delivers an instant bond to seal the cases. At the same time, the slower-setting cold glue permeates the paper fiber to ensure that packages remain intact regardless of the environmental conditions. This dual-gluing process ensures that shipments won't be rejected due to carton failure during transit—a substantial customer benefit.

- Nordson's strategy is to participate in the higher-growth segments of the global economy by expanding its expertise to electronic assembly and printed circuit board coating. In the future as electronic parts become smaller, labor rates continue to increase in emerging countries, and electronics assembly become more complex, we will continue to see more highly automated electronic assembly processes. Management is convinced that Nordson will be a major participant in the market for electronics assembly equipment with internally developed products and acquired businesses.

- Nordson made a strong commitment to e-commerce during 2000 with the creation of a new Web site, *www.enordson.com*. It enables customers to place orders directly over the Internet as well as track the status of their orders and use other value-added features of Nordson's commercial Web sites.

Total assets: $610 million
Current ratio: 1.46
Common shares outstanding: 16 million
Return on 2000 shareholders' equity: 27%

	2000	1999	1998	1997	1996	1995	1994	1993
Revenues (millions)	741	700	661	637	609	581	507	462
Net income (millions)	55	50	47	50	53	53	47	41
Earnings per share	1.85	1.48	1.43	1.43	1.46	1.42	1.23	1.07
Dividends per share	.52	.48	.44	.40	.36	.32	.28	.24
Price High	33.0	33.0	26.2	32.5	32.5	30.5	31.5	27.4
Low	18.1	21.5	21.1	22.2	22.8	26.9	26.0	19.1

Orthodontic Centers of America, Inc.

13000 Sawgrass Village Circle, Suite 30 ◻ Ponte Vedra Beach, Florida 32082 ◻ Investor contact: John Glover (904) 280-6285 ◻ Dividend reinvestment plan not available ◻ Web site: www.ocai.com ◻ Listed: NYSE ◻ Ticker symbol: OCA ◻ S&P rating: Not rated ◻ Value Line financial strength rating: B+

The stocks of physician practice management companies (PPMCs) have fallen on hard times in recent years. PPMCs, also known as medical practice consolidators, typically affiliate with physicians and provide, for a fee, various business and financial services. The services provided by a PPMC give a physician or dentist more time to treat patients instead of doing bookkeeping, paying bills, or hiring janitors.

Although the concept seemed sound when they were first created, these PPMCs took their lumps when Medicare and Medicaid saw fit to reduce the amount they would pay for treatments. These reduced reimbursements took their toll on PPMC profits and alienated physicians who suffered as their incomes eroded.

Orthodontic Centers of America, by contrast, has largely avoided these pitfalls and has an enviable record of growth in the years since it became a public company in 1994. The reason OCA has not been hurt by the antics of Medicare and Medicaid is because most of the cost of straightening teeth is paid largely by the patient's parents. Only 20 percent is paid for by a third party, such as an indemnity insurer.

What Is an Orthodontist?

Orthodontists are dentists with specialized training in the branch of dentistry that prevents and corrects irregularly positioned teeth. Orthodontics has been practiced since the days of the ancient Egyptians, but methods of treatment involving the use of bands and removable appliances have become prominent only since the beginning of the twentieth century.

In addition to causing poor personal appearance, irregularly positioned teeth are difficult to clean, are more likely to decay, and may lead to gum diseases. Finally, teeth that need the services of an orthodontist can also cause chewing and speech problems and may even damage the jaw.

In order to deal with these abnormalities, orthodontists cement metal or plastic braces around each tooth, then connect the braces with wires. By gradually tightening the wires, the teeth eventually move into proper position. In some instance, a tooth is extracted so that other teeth can be moved into its space.

Orthodontic treatment is ordinarily initiated when patients are between the ages of ten and sixteen and usually lasts about two years. Adults, too, may seek treatment from an orthodontist. However, treatment time is often longer than for youngsters.

Company Profile

Orthodontic Centers of America is the leading provider of practice management services to orthodontic practices in the United States based on annual net revenue, annual net income, number of affiliated orthodontists, and the number of orthodontic centers.

The company develops orthodontic centers and manages the business operations and marketing aspects of the affiliated orthodontists' practices, thereby enabling affiliated orthodontists to focus on delivering quality patient care.

Orthodontic Centers of America was founded in 1985. As of the end of 2000, the company managed 592 centers in the

United States, Canada, Puerto Rico, Japan, and Mexico.

Orthodontic centers are generally situated either in shopping centers or in professional office buildings. Nearly all include private treatment rooms and large patient waiting areas. The centers normally include up to six treatment rooms and range in size from about 2,000 square feet to 2,500 square feet.

According to the company, the average cost of developing a new orthodontic center is about $255,000, including the cost of equipment, leasehold improvements, working capital, and funding for losses with the initial operation of the orthodontic center.

OCA has an agreement with BriteSmile, Inc., a developer and manufacturer of light activated teeth whitening technology and related products, whereby BriteSmile's teeth whitening systems are being installed at some of the company's orthodontic centers.

Shortcomings to Bear in Mind

- No company is perfect. In the words of Gasper Lazzara Jr., DDS, chairman of Orthodontic Centers of America, "Because we insist on affiliating with top-flight orthodontists—those focused on quality service and expanding their practices in their communities—it remains a challenge to recruit enough of them to enable us to take advantage of all the opportunities we see.

  "You might say we're still in the infant stage of demonstrating our worth to the profession. We offer a compelling, proven alternative for practitioners who are interested in growing high-quality practices. But our success in helping to grow practices has yet to be fully appreciated by the orthodontic community in general. This is changing, however, as the word about our achievements spreads."

- The shares of OCA dropped precipitously in early 2001, reflecting some concerns regarding the company's revenue recognition practices. On the other hand, analysts don't fret over this matter. They believe that the company's recording of 24 percent of a new contract's value in the first month of a contract's life is one that properly reflects the economic realities of the orthodontics business. They point out that an estimated 30 percent of the costs of treatment are typically recognized during the initial patient visit. To be sure, many patients do not have enough ready cash to make a large upfront payment. However, analysts say that OCA's accounting closely matches revenues with expenses over the course of treatment, making these concerns more an issue of timing rather than fraudulent revenue booking.

Reasons to Buy

- Orthodontic Centers of America had another banner year in 2000 as net revenue increased 30.4 percent to $295.1 million. Similarly, net income totaled $63 million, a gain of 35.4 percent ahead of 1999. Net income per share increased to $1.27, a gain of 32.3 percent over the prior year.

- In the 1995–2000 period, earnings per share climbed impressively from $.24 to $1.27, a compound annual growth rate of 39.5 percent. In the same five-year span, revenues expanded from $41.6 million to $295.1 million, a growth rate of 48 percent. What's more, both earnings and revenues increased every year during that stretch.

- Over the past few years, the company has opened or acquired hundreds of centers. As these units mature, the company's operating profits are likely to climb, enhanced by efficiency and capacity utilization. One way to augment utilization is by extending the interval between patient visits. Over the past six years or so, this has grown from thirty days to forty-five days. This allows orthodontists to treat more patients. More recently, the company has been adding licensed assistants (general dentists) to take over routine procedures, thereby freeing up more of the orthodontist's time.

- The company has an aggressive advertising program, including an 800-number phone line and an Internet site, www.4braces.com. According to the company's annual report, "Our television and radio advertising promotes the names of individual affiliates as well as that of Orthodontic Centers of America. Our nationwide 800 number, featured in many of those ads, enables each affiliate to benefit from our growing national reputation."

- OCA adds value to its affiliates' practices by delivering tangible services. The company contributes expertise in financing, marketing, real estate, and office design. It cuts the affiliates' costs through supply-purchasing services and skillful application of technology. Importantly, OCA provides business management services and expertise so that orthodontists can do what they do best—deliver quality care. As a result, the company's orthodontists boast a 95 percent patient satisfaction rate, while charging below-average fees and enjoying above-average profits.

- About 200 new orthodontists graduate each year in the United States, and OCA's recruiting efforts are continuing to make strong inroads at residency programs around the country.

- Some 1.8 million new patients begin treatment each year in the United States. OCA believes that more than half of U.S. children could benefit from treatment, but a mere 20 percent actually receive it.

- The company's centers treat an average of seventy-eight patients a day, compared with forty-five in a traditional practice. OCA's seasoned orthodontists on average initiate treatment for 513 new patients each year, compared with 200; bring in $6,600 in daily gross revenues, compared with $3,000; and earn $421,000 in cash compensation, compared with $300,000 for orthodontists in a traditional practice.

- New technologies and marketing strategies are fueling growth in the adult market, especially for cosmetic treatment.

- In 2000, the company's bad-debt experience as a percentage of net revenue declined to 0.7 percent, compared with 0.8 percent the year before. What's more, this bad-debt experience is better than that of traditional practitioners.

- International markets, such as Japan and Mexico, are vastly underserved and represent a significant growth opportunity.

- OCA has the necessary infrastructure in place to support efficient growth. The company's centers now operate at just a third of capacity on average, and it is continuing to develop information systems and methods that will enhance center productivity and fuel robust internal growth.

- Studies show that an orthodontist's time typically is consumed by tasks that don't necessarily leverage the orthodontist's expertise. OCA has been exploring innovative methods to optimize and leverage the value of that time.

- Building on successful pilots, OCA is moving toward wider deployment of BriteSmile, Inc.'s proprietary teeth-whitening process. BriteSmile's revolutionary method makes teeth seven to ten times whiter in a single treatment, compared with the two- to eight-week series of treatments required by the traditional gel/tray whitening process.

- To capitalize on the growing interest in cosmetic dentistry, OCA opened its first Cosmetic Dental Center in Jacksonville in 1999. Modeled on upscale spas and beauty boutiques, the center does not look like the traditional dental office. It offers only cosmetic treatments, including BriteSmile whitening, noninvasive porcelain laminates, and the new Invisalign technology, a no-braces orthodontic procedure for adults that uses unobtrusive, clear, removable appliances.
- Internationally, OCA is rapidly becoming a notable presence in Japan, which represents a $4-billion potential market that is essentially untapped.

Japan's orthodontic industry today is small and fragmented, with only about 700 certified practitioners generating only about $320 million annually in an affluent nation with an enormous potential market. The company entered Japan in mid-1998 and had opened twenty-four centers by the end of 1999.
- The company entered Mexico in 1999, opening two centers in Mexico City and another two in 2000. With a population of 20 million, the city has a potential market of 6.5 million. In addition, OCA is exploring promising future opportunities in Europe in such markets as the United Kingdom, Italy, Portugal, and Spain.

Total assets: $368 million
Current ratio: 2.82
Common shares outstanding: 49 million
Return on 2000 shareholders' equity: 22%

	2000	1999	1998	1997	1996	1995	1994	1993
Revenues (millions)	295	226	171	117	71	42	25	19
Net income (millions)	63	47	34	23	14	9	4	6
Earnings per share	1.27	.96	.70	.50	.34	.24		
Dividends per share	Nil							
Price High	35.3	20.1	24.1	20.3	22.6	12.1	3.1	
Low	11.1	10.8	11.8	11.0	10.4	2.9	2.8	

Note that the table is incomplete because the company did not go public until 1994.

CONSERVATIVE GROWTH

PepsiCo, Incorporated

700 Anderson Hill Road ▫ Purchase, New York 10577-1444 ▫ Investor contact: Susan Watson, CFA (914) 253-2711 ▫ Dividend reinvestment plan is available: (800) 226-0083 ▫ Web site: www.pepsico.com ▫ Listed: NYSE ▫ Ticker symbol: PEP ▫ S&P rating: A ▫ Value Line financial strength rating: A+

PepsiCo added some major brands to its lineup of products in the final month of 2000 with the $13.4-billion acquisition of Quaker Oats. The big prize was Gatorade, a leading sports drink, growing at 11 percent a year. This made PepsiCo the dominant company in the $2.5-billion-a-year sports drink category. "Gatorade would do even better under PepsiCo than it has

under Quaker Oats because of better marketing and distribution," said John Sicher, publisher of Beverage Digest.

The deal pushed Pepsi to the forefront of the noncarbonated business, the most dynamic segment of the soft drink industry, and gave Pepsi control of such well-known foods as Life Cereal, Rice-A-Roni, and Aunt Jemima pancake syrup.

Mr. Sicher said the deal could help Frito-Lay. "Quaker Oats's grain-based snacks could show real growth within the Frito-Lay marketing and distribution system." Quaker officials said Frito-Lay's marketing muscle could grab more shelf space for Quaker cereals and put its granola bars in more vending machines.

Company Profile

PepsiCo is among the most successful consumer products companies in the world with 2000 revenues of $20.4 billion. PepsiCo brands are among the best-known in the world and are available in about 190 countries and territories. The company consists of:

- Frito-Lay Company, the largest manufacturer and distributor of snack chips.
- Pepsi-Cola Company, the second largest soft drink business.
- Tropicana Products, the largest marketer and producer of branded juice.

Some of PepsiCo's brand names are 100 year old, but the corporation is relatively young. It was founded in 1965 through the merger of Pepsi-Cola and Frito-Lay. Tropicana was acquired in 1998.

Frito-Lay Company

Major Frito-Lay products include Ruffles, Lay's, and Doritos brands snack chips. Other major brands include Cheetos cheeseflavored snacks, Tostitos tortilla chips, Santitas tortilla chips, Rold Gold pretzels, SunChips multigrain snacks, and Wow! fatfree snacks. Frito-Lay also sells a variety of snack dips, cookies, nuts, and crackers. Today, Frito-Lay brands account for 58 percent of the domestic snack chip industry.

Frito-Lay products are often known by local names, such as Matutano in Spain, Sabritas and Gamesa in Mexico, Elma Chips in Brazil, and Walkers in the United Kingdom. The company markets Frito-Lay brands on a global level and introduces products for local tastes.

Frito-Lay's Results in 2000

Frito-Lay North America gained nearly two market-share points in 2000, bringing its share to over 58 percent. Revenues grew 7 percent to $8.4 billion, and operating profit for the year expanded 10 percent to $1.8 billion. Finally, profit margins improved by over half a point, reflecting higher volume, higher effective net pricing, and reduced commodity costs.

In its operation abroad (Frito-Lay International), revenues accelerated a solid 14 percent to $4.3 billion, led by double-digit increases at Sabritas and Gamesa. Full-year operating profits grew an impressive 19 percent to $483 million, despite a 2 percent point squeeze on net sales and operating profits caused by weaker foreign currencies.

Pepsi-Cola Company

PepsiCo's beverage business was founded at the turn of the last century by Caleb Bradham, a New Bern, North Carolina druggist who first formulated Pepsi-Cola. Today, consumers spend about $32 billion on Pepsi-Cola beverages. Brand Pepsi and other Pepsi-Cola—including Diet Pepsi, Pepsi One, Mountain Dew, Slice, and Mug brands—account for nearly one-third of total soft drink sales in the United States, a consumer market totaling about $58 billion.

In 1992, Pepsi-Cola formed a partnership with Thomas J. Lipton Company. Today, Lipton is the biggest selling ready-to-drink brand in the United States.

Abroad, Pepsi-Cola Company's soft drink operations include the business of Seven-Up International. Pepsi-Cola beverages are available in about 160 countries.

Pepsi-Cola's Results in 2000

As a result of the year's steady and profitable finish, Pepsi-Cola of North America's net sales grew more than 8 percent, and profits climbed a strong 9 percent.

Pepsi-Cola International's results were consistently healthy. Bottler case sales were up 5 percent, and the division expanded market share in most of its top twenty-five markets. Net sales rose 3 percent to $1.8 billion on volume gains and better pricing.

Tropicana Products, Inc.

Tropicana was founded in 1947 by Anthony Rossi as a Florida fruit packaging business. The company entered the concentrate orange juice business in 1949. In 1954 Rossi pioneered a pasteurization process for orange juice. For the first time, consumers could enjoy the fresh taste of pure, not-from-concentrate, 100 percent Florida orange juice in a ready-to-serve package. Today, Tropicana is the world's largest marketer and producer of branded juices with products available in fifty countries.

Principal brands in North America are Tropicana Pure Premium, Tropicana Season's Best, Dole juices, and Tropicana Twister. Overseas, principal brands include Tropicana Pure Premium and Dole juices, along with Fruvita, Hitchcock, Looza, and Copella. Today, Tropicana Pure Premium is the fourth largest brand of all food products sold in grocery stores in the United States.

Tropicana's Results in 2000

Tropicana's volume expanded to a robust 8 percent, more than double the growth rate of the prior year. Its domestic market share rose to 35 percent. Net sales increased 6 percent, and operating profit rose a dramatic 30 percent, helped by large volume gains, favorable fruit costs, supply chain productivity, and accelerated profit growth abroad. For the full year, operating profits would have been four points higher but were hurt by unfavorable foreign currency exchange rates. Combined with operating profit growth of over 55 percent in 1999, Tropicana's operating profits doubled in the two years since the PepsiCo acquisition.

Shortcomings to Bear in Mind

■ The acquisition of Quaker Oats has its negative aspects. Acquiring Quaker's food business comes at a time when consumers are becoming increasingly impatient with sit-down meals. About 11 percent of Pepsi's business is now in an ailing food business, ranging from pasta to cereal that grows at a snail's pace of 2 percent a year. On the other hand, there is some speculation that the company may sell the food business in the next year or two. Under current accounting rules, the company must wait two years following an acquisition. In any event, Steven S. Reinemund, PepsiCo's new CEO, says there are no immediate plans to shed this line. "We haven't bought a collection of cats and dogs here," said Mr. Reinemund. "These are great brands. We intend to grow all of it."

Reasons to Buy

■ The company's growth record is solid, if not spectacular. In the 1990–2000 period, earnings per share advanced from $.66 to $1.45, a compound annual growth rate of 8.2 percent. In the same ten-year span, dividends per share expanded at an even greater clip, rising from $.19 to $.56 for a growth rate of 11.4 percent, far ahead of inflation.

■ PepsiCo is no longer a soft drink bottler, since it sold its bottling operations in 1999. This is a negative blow to soft drink sales, which are now lower than in the past. However, the remaining business is likely to be much more profitable than the bottling operation.

■ To be sure, the sports drink Gatorade was the big prize in the company's late-2000 purchase of Quaker Oats. However, management is salivating over the possibilities that Quaker brings for boosting its sales of snacks and fruit drinks. According to Roger A. Enrico, vice chairman of PepsiCo, Quaker's clout in the noncarbonated beverage aisle could also pay dividends by getting retailers to provide shelf space for it Tropicana division's growing line of fruit drinks, such as Tropicana Twisters. The market for noncarbonated drinks is about $16 billion, compared with $58 billion for carbonated drinks, but is growing much faster according to the industry trade publication *Beverage Digest*. Enrico also says that Quaker's granola bars, rice cakes, and fruit bars are complementary to the Frito-Lay division's industry-leading lineup of salty snacks such as Tostitos corn chips and Lay's potato chips.

- Carbonated drinks, such as Pepsi and Mountain Dew, are still the mainstay of the company's business. However, sales of noncarbonated beverages, such as Aquafina bottled water and SoBe drinks, are expanding at a rapid pace as consumer's tastes become more diverse.

- With the acquisition of Quaker Oats, Pepsi now has an immense stable of strong brands, thus boosting its clout among retailers and providing the company with greater advantage in the tussle among beverage companies for hard-to-get space in convenience-store coolers. "When the PepsiCo guy walks into 7-Eleven, they're going to have to pay a lot more attention to him than they do to Coke," one Pepsi bottler said. "He'll have Pepsi, Gatorade, SoBe, and Tropicana. He owns the refrigerator door."

- The Pepsi-Cola Division introduced Dole single-serve juices into vending machines, coolers, and other retail outlets throughout the United States in early 2001. The new Dole products are being distributed by Pepsi bottlers in 16-ounce plastic bottles and 11.5-ounce cans. The noncarbonated, caffeine-free, single-serve Dole line includes nine natural fruit flavors: Apple, Orange, Pineapple-Citrus, Ruby Red Grapefruit, Cranberry Juice Cocktail, Paradise Blend, Cranberry-Grape, Orange-Strawberry-Banana, and Strawberry-Kiwi.

Total assets: $17,551 million
Current ratio: 1.16
Common shares outstanding: 1,444 million
Return on 2000 shareholders' equity: 30%

	2000	1999	1998	1997	1996	1995	1994	1993
Revenues (millions)	20438	20367	22348	20917	31645	30421	28472	25021
Net income (millions)	2014	1845	1760	1730	1865	1990	1784	1588
Earnings per share	1.45	1.23	1.16	1.10	1.17	1.24	1.11	.98
Dividends per share	.56	.54	.52	.49	.45	.39	.35	.31
Price High	49.9	42.6	44.8	41.3	35.9	29.4	20.6	21.8
Low	29.7	30.1	27.6	28.3	27.3	16.9	14.6	17.3

AGGRESSIVE GROWTH

Pfizer Inc.

235 East 42nd Street □ New York, New York 10017-5755 □ Investor contact: Ronald C. Aldridge (212) 573-3685 □ Dividend reinvestment plan is available: (800) 733-9393 □ Web site: www.pfizer.com □ Listed: NYSE □ Ticker symbol: PFE □ S&P rating: A+ □ Value Line financial strength rating: A++

When Pfizer acquired the Warner-Lambert Company in the spring of 2000, analysts focused primarily on how much Lipitor, the cholesterol-lowering drug, would bolster Pfizer's profit margins. However, Wall Street may have overlooked an equally impressive part of the deal—Warner-Lambert's biotechnology unit, Agouron Pharmaceuticals, a leader in computer-aided drug design. Instead of tediously screening thousands of substances to discover a new drug, Agouron scientists employ 3-D computer visualization techniques to create molecules that precisely knock out invaders bent on inflicting damage to the human body.

Today, Agouron's pipeline is well stocked with potential wonder drugs that Pfizer can now latch onto to maintain its growth rate. For instance, the once obscure Agouron is among the leaders developing a prescription drug targeted specifically against the virus that causes the common cold. It also has two promising AIDS drugs in development.

In mid-2000, Pfizer put the finishing touches on its acquisition of Warner-Lambert. By year-end the company had completed the cross-training of sales forces from Pfizer and the former Warner-Lambert to sell each others' drugs. That field force, numbering nearly 8,000 representatives, is the largest in the industry. Initially, only Lipitor, the blockbuster cholesterol drug developed by Warner-Lambert, was being promoted by salespeople from both companies under a co-marketing arrangement that preceded the merger.

Company Profile

Pfizer traces its history back to 1849 when it was founded by Charles Pfizer and Charles Erhart. In those early days, Pfizer was a chemical firm. Today it is a leading global pharmaceutical manufacturer, creating and marketing a wide range of prescription drugs.

PFE also has an important stake in hospital products, animal health items, and consumer products.

Pfizer's growth over the past half century was paced by strategic acquisitions, new drug discoveries, and vigorous foreign expansion. Its most recent move involved the giant acquisition of Warner-Lambert in 2000, making the new firm the largest pharmaceutical company in the world.

Shortcomings to Bear in Mind

- In mid-2000, Pfizer halted two large-scale trials of an experimental cancer treatment for a late-stage form of prostate cancer and an advanced form of lung cancer because the drug wasn't effective. The failure of prinomastat is a setback for Pfizer because the drug is at the forefront of a new strategy to combat cancers by starving them of a blood supply instead of poisoning them, as conventional chemotherapy does. Such so-called antiangiogenesis drugs promise to contain cancers and sidestep the side effects of drugs that aim to destroy the cells outright. However, Pfizer said it will continue tests of prinomastat as a treatment for other kinds of tumors and with less advanced cancers.

  Because the growth of new blood vessels, called angiogenesis, is particularly important in early tumor growth, Pfizer said it now believes the drug may be more effective in early-stage cancer than the latter stages of diseases studied in the discontinued trials.

- With the acquisition of Warner-Lambert in 2000, the company now has a sprawling $4.7 billion research and development operation—the largest of its kind in the industry. That might seem like a big plus factor, but some analysts are not so sure. There's a risk that this complex operation could turn bureaucratic and, in the process, stifle innovation rather than enhancing it. In the drug industry, there's scant evidence that bigger research programs are better—least of all when they are the product of mergers.

- Criticism of Pfizer's marketing tactics is growing. For instance, the Food and Drug Administration (FDA) requested a meeting with William C. Steere Jr., the company's former CEO, in order to discuss the repeated warning letters it had sent to Pfizer. The letters insisted that the company had failed to follow federal drug-marketing regulations by making claims about certain drugs that could not be substantiated. Pfizer has received about a dozen warnings since the end of 1996, including one ordering it to stop creating brochures that the FDA contends improperly implied that Zithromax was more effective than Augmentin, an antibiotic made by SmithKline Beecham.

- Like most stocks with bright prospects, Pfizer often sells at an elevated price-earnings ratio.
- As most diabetics are aware, they have to be wary of developing such life-threatening complications as high blood pressure, strokes, heart attacks, cataracts, blindness, kidney disease, and amputations. One of the most difficult of these complications to treat is nerve damage, which affects up to 50 percent of diabetics. So far, despite nearly two decades of research, no company has developed a drug to prevent nerve damage.

For its part, Pfizer has been testing a compound called zenarestat, which is part of a class of compounds called aldose reductase inhibitors. At first it appeared that the drug was helping. Unfortunately, too many of the 2,700 patients who tried zenarestat suffered toxicity to their kidneys when the drug was taken at the maximum tested dosage. Pfizer announced late in 2000 that it would halt development of zenarestat.

Reasons to Buy

- Pfizer's domestic prescription business had a banner year in 2000. For instance, Neurontin's Rx volume surged ahead 43 percent; Celebrex: 29 percent; Lipitor: 29 percent; Zyrtec: 26 percent; Viagra: 21 percent; Aricept: 17 percent;

Accupril/Accuretic: 17 percent; Norvasc: 13 percent; and Zoloft: 9 percent.

- Pfizer finally won FDA approval for a schizophrenia drug called ziprasidone, ending months of speculation over the fate of this product. An expert panel recommended ziprasidone for approval in mid-2000, but the FDA delayed its approval until February 2001. The drug was originally to be marketed under the trade name of Zeldox, but the name may be changed to Geodon. Analysts had feared that the drug might not be approved or would be subject to such restricted use that it wouldn't be able to compete with such established medications as Lilly's Zyprexa or J&J's Risperdal. Instead, Pfizer succeeded in getting a label with relatively few restrictions. However, Pfizer tells physicians to bear in mind that ziprasidone is more likely to cause heart-rhythm problems than some other antipsychotic preparations currently available.
- The company invested $4.4 billion in research and development in 2000, while fully supporting its current products, including Lipitor, which had sales exceeding $5 billion, a Pfizer record. Lipitor is now the second-largest selling pharmaceutical product of any kind in the world.

For 2001, Pfizer expects an R & D investment of about $5 billion, supporting 156 projects in nineteen therapeutic areas. Over the next two years, moreover, the company believes its pipeline will yield such important new products as Zeldox (antipsychotic), Vfend (antifungal), valdecoxib (for arthritis), pregabalin (to treat pain), and inhaled insulin (to control diabetes).

- In 2000, Pfizer once again set an industry record with eight products generating revenues in excess of $1 billion: Lipitor (to lower cholesterol), Norvasc (a cardiovascular drug), Zoloft (an antidepressant), Zithromax (a broad-spectrum quinolone antibiotic), Viagra (to treat male erectile dysfunction), Neurontin (anticonvulsant), Celebrex (to treat arthritis), and Diflucan (antifungal). What's more, three of these products had sales of more than $2 billion in 2000: Lipitor, Norvasc, and Zoloft. These $8-billion products, representing 74 percent of the company's human pharmaceutical revenues, grew 23 percent in aggregate in 2000.

- Each day, 20,000 people around the world go to work promoting Pfizer products to the medical profession. They fill their "detail" bags with free samples of popular drugs such as Viagra and Zithromax, and they quote favorable conclusions from scientific studies (often company sponsored) that show how Lipitor is the most potent way to control cholesterol and should be used instead of Merck's Zocor. By nearly all counts, Pfizer is the industry's largest, and most effective, sales force.

  According to Henry A. McKinnell, Ph.D., who became the company's CEO at the beginning of 2001, "Pfizer has never been stronger and today possesses strengths and capabilities unequaled in the pharmaceutical industry. Our U.S. sales force, for example, was recently ranked as best in class in a survey of physicians, the sixth year in a row for this honor."

- Aricept is the world's leading medicine for the symptomatic treatment for Alzheimer's disease. Total third-party product sales in 2000 were over $700 million. In the United States, the United Kingdom, France, Germany, and Japan, Aricept is being copromoted by Pfizer and Eisai Co., Ltd., the company that discovered and developed the compound. Eisai records sales and Pfizer records a portion of the profit.

  About 10 percent of people over age sixty-five suffer from Alzheimer's disease, including 4 million Americans. Americans spend as much as $100 billion a year to treat Alzheimer's disease. Aricept has been taken for more than 314 million patient days by more than one million patients with mild to moderate Alzheimer's disease to enhance or maintain cognition and function by preserving levels of the neurotransmitter acetylcholine in the brain. In controlled clinical trials of up to six months, more than 80 percent of patients taking Aricept experienced improved cognition or no further decline, compared to 58 percent of patients on a placebo.

- Pfizer's Animal Health Group (AHG) in not only one of the largest in the world, but it is also noteworthy for the breadth of its product lines and its geographic coverage. Innovative marketing has become an AHG hallmark in its efforts to succeed in a highly competitive market. An independent survey of U.S. veterinarians, for example, named the Pfizer sales force the best in the industry.

Total assets: $33,510 million
Current ratio: 1.44
Common shares outstanding: 6,314 million
Return on 2000 shareholders' equity: 24.8%

	2000	1999	1998	1997	1996	1995	1994	1993
Revenues (millions)	29574	16204	13544	12504	11306	10021	8281	7478
Net income (millions)	6495	3360	2627	2213	1929	1554	1298	1180
Earnings per share	1.02	.87	.67	.57	.50	.41	.35	.31
Dividends per share	.36	.31	.25	.23	.20	.17	.16	.14
Price High	49.3	50.0	43.0	26.7	15.2	11.1	6.6	6.3
Low	30.0	31.5	23.7	13.4	10.0	6.2	4.4	4.4

Philip Morris Companies Inc.

120 Park Avenue ❑ New York, New York 10017-5592 ❑ Investor contact: Nicholas M. Rolli (917) 663-5000 ❑ Dividend reinvestment plan is available: (800) 442-0077 ❑ Listed: NYSE ❑ Web site: www.philipmorris.com ❑ Ticker symbol: MO ❑ S&P rating: A ❑ Value Line financial strength rating: A

Although Philip Morris is one of the world's largest companies, with 2000 revenues of more than $80 billion, it does not intend to relax. In late 2000 and early 2001 it was busy augmenting its food empire.

In mid-2000, Philip Morris acquired Nabisco Holdings Corporation for $18.9 billion. The company plans to combine Nabisco with its Kraft Foods to create a huge and profitable food company that will help offset its tobacco liabilities. The merger created a mammoth food company that combines such dominant brands as Oreo cookies, Ritz crackers, Planters nuts, and Life Savers candies with the Philip Morris brands of Kraft, Jell-O, Maxwell House, and Oscar Mayer. More than 90 percent of Nabisco's domestic brands are leaders in their respective categories.

In mid-2001, the company completed an initial public offering of 280 million shares (16 percent of the total) of Kraft Foods Inc. at $31/share, or $8.7 billion. It was the second-largest IPO since AT&T Wireless Group raised $10.6 billion in April 2000. The IPO could help Philip Morris pay down some of the $11 billion in debt it acquired when it bought Nabisco Holdings Corporation in 2000.

Acquisitions Abroad

Kraft Foods, a major subsidiary of MO, acquired Societe des Cafes Ennasr in March of 2001. Societe des Cafes Ennasr, a coffee producer based in Casablanca, Morocco, manufactures well-known Moroccan coffee brands. In 2000, it had nearly a 25 percent share of that country's $100-million packaged coffee market.

In early 2001, Kraft Foods announced two separate agreements that will augment its coffee businesses in Bulgaria and Romania. Its company in Bulgaria acquired the producer of Nova Brasilia branded coffee. In another move, Kraft Foods International purchased the coffee brands of Supreme Imex Romania. Under the agreement, Nova Brasilia will continue to manufacture and distribute such products as Nova Brasilia, Classic, Brasiliero, and Prestige. These brands will strengthen Kraft Foods Romania's number two position in coffee.

Company Profile

Operating in nearly 200 countries, Philip Morris is the largest consumer packaged-goods company in the world, the largest domestic cigarette manufacturer, the nation's largest food processor (Kraft), and its Miller Brewing is the nation's second largest brewer.

As noted, Philip Morris is primarily a tobacco company, with such major brands as Marlboro (the top-selling brand in the United States), Merit, Virginia Slims (the bestselling women's cigarette), Benson & Hedges, and Parliament. Philip Morris has a 49.4 percent share of the domestic tobacco market. Outside the United States, the company also has well-known brands such as L & M and Lark.

The company's other large operation is food as a result of prior acquisitions of General Foods (1984) and Kraft (1988). Some well-known names include Jell-O, Shake 'n Bake, Lender's Bagels, Philadelphia Cream Cheese, Post cereals, Velveeta, Kool-Aid,

Miracle Whip, Oscar Mayer, Cracker Barrel cheese, Tang, and Maxwell House coffee.

Ranking third is the company's beer business, featuring such brands as Miller Lite, Miller Genuine Draft, Miller, Icehouse, Red Dog, Lowenbrau, Meister Brau, and Milwaukee's Best. During 1997, Miller sold its equity interest in Molson Breweries in Canada and 49 percent of its ownership of Molson USA, which holds the rights to import, market, and distribute the Molson and Foster's brands in the United States. Currently, Miller holds a 21 percent share of the domestic beer market.

Finally, MO also has a stake in financial services (Philip Morris Capital Corp.).

Shortcomings to Bear in Mind

- Miller Brewing had a difficult year in 2000, as its domestic shipment volume declined 2.6 percent. As a consequence, the company completed a number of strategic actions, such as selling premium brands at premium prices. The company also elected to focus on the five core brands that account for three-quarters of its volume: Miller Lite, Miller Genuine Draft, Miller High Life, Icehouse, and Foster's. Going forward, Miller has demographic trends working in its favor. The legal drinking age population is expected to expand by 1 percent a year, reversing recent negative trends. In addition, the light-beer category is expected to continue its growth of 4 to 5 percent per year—another trend that should help Miller.

- As most investors are aware, Philip Morris is being besieged by the many pressures facing the U.S. tobacco industry: public smoking restrictions, possible excise tax hikes, congressional hearings, negative media coverage, litigation. Still, we should remember that the company's tobacco segment has faced similar threats before and has overcome them. It's important to note that while the tobacco industry has rarely lost or paid to settle a smoking-health product liability case over the past forty years, this seems to be changing. In 1999 a jury in San Francisco awarded $1.5 million in damages to compensate a former smoker with lung cancer, the largest such award against the tobacco industry and the first against Philip Morris. The verdict, following a monthlong superior court trial, served abrupt notice to the tobacco industry that it remains vulnerable to suits brought by individual smokers, despite a $206-billion settlement with states in 1998 that ended their efforts to recoup health outlays linked to smoking-related illnesses.

- The European Union, whose fifteen member nations make up one of the world's biggest tobacco markets, agreed on a law that will significantly enlarge health warnings on cigarette packages and make them much more explicit. Under the law, to take effect in the countries of the EU by October 2002, the warnings must cover at least 30 percent of the pack's surface, up from as little as 4 percent. The law will also require more graphic warnings, such as "Smokers die younger," and could eventually allow individual EU governments to demand that manufacturers place on the pack color photos showing how smoking-related diseases can ravage the body.

Reasons to Buy

- In 2000 the company continued its steady growth:
  - Operating revenues were up 3.2 percent to $80.3 billion.
  - Operating companies income was up 5.9 percent to $16.0 billion, with each of its operating companies contributing to that growth.
  - Excluding the adverse currency impact on pre-tax income of $495 million, operating companies income would have been up 9.2 percent.

- Net earnings were up 6.3 percent to $8.4 billion.
- Diluted earnings per share advanced 12.4 percent, meeting the company's target of $3.71.
- Again, excluding the negative currency impact, EPS would have climbed 16.3 percent.

■ Philip Morris is continuing its strong performance in the tobacco realm abroad. In the company's key Western Europe region—where MO is the leader in the premium-price category with a two-thirds share—volume rose 4.3 percent in 2000. In Asia the company's volume gained 7.3 percent, fueled by the performance of several brands such as Marlboro, L&M, and Parliament. Finally, the company had exceptional growth in some of its Asian markets: in Malaysia volume rose 26 percent; in Korea it climbed 43 percent; and in Thailand, 60 percent.

■ The key to Philip Morris is still its Marlboro brand. The year 2000 marked the twenty-fifth anniversary of Marlboro as the number one brand in the industry. For 2000, Marlboro's retail share was up again by 1.1 percentage points to 37.1 percent. Today, Marlboro's share is larger than the shares of the next seven leading brands combined. What's more, Marlboro is the number one brand in every state in the country, as well as the number one brand among adult men as well as women.

■ In a demographic study sponsored by Sanford C. Bernstein & Co., it was found that young smokers, those between the ages of eighteen and twenty-four, have a strong preference for Marlboro, Camels, and Newport. Among these, Marlboro, the leading brand of MO, was the clear winner with a whopping 78 percent preference. This is a key finding, since smokers typically carry their preferences with them as they mature.

■ Philip Morris's outstanding brands, marketing, and infrastructure have made the company the market leader in tobacco in the United States and in thirty other major markets around the world. They have also won the company first place positions in eighteen of its twenty most profitable food categories in North America and in more than forty of its major coffee, confectionery, cheese, and powdered soft drink businesses.

■ Despite the never ending strife against antismoking forces, Philip Morris has been a most successful company. Unlike many other huge companies, Philip Morris is growing at a consistent and impressive pace. In the 1990–2000 period, earnings per share climbed from $1.28 to $3.71, a compound annual growth rate of 11.2 percent. Similarly, dividends per share expanded from $.52 to $1.97, a growth rate of 14.2 percent.

■ Kraft is one of the largest coffee companies in the United States. Major brands include Maxwell House, Yuban, Sanka, Maxim, and General Foods International Coffees. The company's coffee business has been gaining both volume and market share in a highly competitive environment. This performance was attributable to the success of Kraft's licensing agreement to roll out Starbuck's coffee to grocery customers, as well as the introduction of Maxwell House Slow Roast coffee.

■ Including Nabisco, Philip Morris has ninety-one brands that each generated $100 million or more in revenues in 2000. Of these brands, fifteen generated $1 billion or more, led by Marlboro.

■ In the international sphere, the company is meeting the growing global demand for American-blend and low-tar and low-nicotine cigarettes. In Western Europe, for instance, MO captured more than 90 percent of the growth in the low-tar and low-nicotine segment in the five-year period through 2000.

Total assets: $79,067 million
Current ratio: .66
Common shares outstanding: 2,224 million
Return on 2000 shareholders' equity: 56.7%

	2000	1999	1998	1997	1996	1995	1994	1993
Revenues (millions)	80356	78596	74391	72055	69204	66071	65125	60901
Net income (millions)	8520	7675	5372	6310	6303	5478	4725	3568
Earnings per share	3.71	3.19	2.20	2.58	2.56	2.17	1.82	1.35
Dividends per share	1.97	1.84	1.68	1.60	1.47	1.22	1.01	.87
Price High	45.9	55.6	59.5	48.1	39.7	31.5	21.5	25.9
Low	18.7	21.3	34.8	36.0	28.5	18.6	15.8	15.0

INCOME

Piedmont Natural Gas Company

Post Office Box 33068 ◻ Charlotte, North Carolina 28233 ◻ Investor contact: Headen B. Thomas (704) 364-3483 Ext. 6438 ◻ Dividend reinvestment program is available: (800) 937-5449 ◻ Fiscal year ends October 31 ◻ Listed NYSE ◻ Web site: www.piedmontng.com ◻ Ticker symbol: PNY ◻ S&P rating: A- ◻ Value Line financial strength rating: B++

Piedmont Natural Gas's customer base has increased at a rate of 5.8 percent per year over the last five years, compared with an industry average of about 2 percent. This exceptional growth has largely been a function of new home construction enhanced by a regional economy that is among the fastest growing in the nation.

A key factor in further growth is the low saturation by PNY of its market—it serves only 45 percent of its potential heating market. According to one analyst, "We believe that future customer growth levels will remain well above the industry average for the foreseeable future."

Company Profile

Incorporated in 1950, Piedmont Natural Gas is an energy services company, primarily engaged in the transportation, distribution, and sale of natural gas and the sale of propane to residential, commercial, and industrial customers in North Carolina, South Carolina, and Tennessee.

The company is the second largest natural gas utility in the Southeast, serving over 690,000 natural gas customers. Piedmont Natural Gas and its nonutility subsidiaries and divisions are also engaged in acquiring, marketing, transporting, and storing natural gas for large-volume customers, in retailing residential and commercial gas appliances, and the sale of propane to over 480,000 customers in twenty-eight states.

An unregulated subsidiary of the company is an equity participant in a venture that is marketing natural gas to an additional 476,000 customers in Georgia, the first state in the venture's eight-state southeastern market to open to retail competition for natural gas.

Other business interests in which the company is engaged that are not subject to state utility regulation include the sale of propane and investments in a natural gas pipeline and an interstate LNG (liquefied natural gas) storage facility and marketing natural gas and other energy products and services to deregulated markets.

Highlights of 2000

- Piedmont joined with the propane subsidiaries of Atmos Energy, TECO

Energy, and AGL Resources to form a new propane company, US Propane. Through a series of transactions that closed in August of 2000, US Propane acquired the general partner of Heritage Propane Partners, L.P. The acquisition of Heritage by US Propane created the fourth largest propane distributor in the country. The Heritage/US Propane combination now serves over 480,000 customers in twenty-eight states. Heritage, moreover, is recognized as one of the best-managed propane companies in the United States.

- A major contributor to the nonutility earnings of Piedmont Natural Gas was the performance of the company's 30 percent investment in SouthStar Energy Services. This investment generated $1.7 million in net income in 2000, compared with a start-up loss of $5.3 million the prior year. Doing business in Georgia as Georgia Natural Gas Services, SouthStar is the largest unregulated natural gas marketer there, with a 35 percent market share and over 530,000 customers.

- Other success stories in 2000 were the company's 35 percent and 16.5 percent interests in Pine Needle LNG Company and Cardinal Pipeline Company, respectively. These companies completed their first full year of operation in 2000 and contributed a total of $3.2 million to net income, compared with $1.1 million in 1999. These storage and pipeline facilities are also strategic supply-related assets critical to the company's utility operations.

- In October 2000, Piedmont signed an agreement to purchase the natural gas system serving Gaffney and Cherokee Country, South Carolina from Atmos Energy Corporation. With the completion of this acquisition, Piedmont gained

5,400 customers previously served by Atmos Energy. Cherokee Country is strategically located on the I-85 corridor immediately north of Spartanburg County and complements Piedmont's growth plans in South Carolina.

- In August 2000, the company began the largest single construction project in its history. Gas service was expanded into the North Carolina counties of Mitchell, Avery, and Yancey, a region known as Mayland. The project has now been completed at a cost of $44.5 million, $38.5 million of which was provided from an expansion fund escrowed by the North Carolina Utilities Commission. The project includes eighty-five miles of steel transmission pipeline and over twenty-five miles of plastic distribution piping. With the completion of this project, the company now serves all of its franchised counties in North Carolina.

Shortcomings to Bear in Mind

- The company has benefited from extraordinary growth in its service territory. However, customer growth can be a double-edged sword, as it is expensive to continuously expand an underground pipe system to keep up with new construction. On the other hand, Piedmont has effectively lowered its cost to connect a customer to about $1,800, a significant decline over prior years. Analysts, moreover, expect this cost to continue to decline, which would contribute to future earnings growth.

- The company buys natural gas from a number of different sources, which it then arranges to be transported into its system through one of four interstate pipelines. However, the majority of Piedmont's service territory, situated in North and South Carolina, only connects to one interstate pipeline, the

Transcontinental Gas Pipe Line Corporation (Transco). As Transco is the company's sole vehicle to receive gas into the bulk of its system, the company's capacity options are somewhat more limited than most utilities. Thus, PNY has fewer opportunities to play off one pipeline against another in order to achieve more favorable rates.

On a more positive note, this problem does not exist for the company's operation in Tennessee. In that state, numerous pipelines serve the region.

Reasons to Buy

- During 2000, the company added a record 34,800 new natural gas customers. It also increased its dividend for the twenty-second consecutive year. For the year, the company reported a 10 percent increase in net income over the prior year, from $58.2 million in 1999 to $64 million in 2000. Diluted earnings per share rose 8 percent, from $1.86 in 1999 to $2.01 in 2000. What's more, earnings from nonutility activities contributed $11.5 million to net income, or $.36 per share for the year.

- Piedmont Natural Gas enjoys an economically robust and diverse service area that is among the fastest growing in the nation. The company's three-state service area consists of the Piedmont region of the Carolinas—Charlotte, Salisbury, Greensboro, Winston-Salem, High Point, Burlington, and Hickory in North Carolina and Anderson, Greenville, and Spartanburg in South Carolina—and the metropolitan area of Nashville, Tennessee. Both *Plant Sites and Parks* and *Site Selection* magazines continue to rank the Carolinas and Tennessee among the best in the nation for business relocation and expansion and business climate.

The center of the Piedmont area is the Greater Charlotte urban region—sixth largest in the nation—with over 6 million people within a 100-mile radius. Charlotte is the nation's second largest financial center. It is headquarters city for Bank of America, the nation's largest bank, and for First Union National bank, the sixth largest. Wachovia Corporation, the nation's sixteenth largest bank, is headquartered in Winston-Salem.

Charlotte/Douglas International Airport, with over 500 flights per day and twenty-three million passengers annually, is US Airways' largest hub and the twentieth busiest airport in the world.

The Nashville region is a diverse center of a retail trading area of over two million people, where health care is the largest industry. It is also home to major transportation, publishing, printing, financial, insurance, and communications companies as well as twenty colleges and universities.

- An important factor in analyzing any public utility is the region's regulatory environment. In the Piedmont region, regulators in the different states have generally been supportive of the company's regulatory needs over the past few years. In the opinion of Daniel M. Fidell and Tracey W. McMillin, analysts with A. G. Edwards, "Our conclusion is based on several factors, such as purchased gas and weather normalization mechanisms in rates that serve to smooth the impact of changes in gas prices and abnormal weather conditions. In addition, PNY has benefited from fair and timely rate relief in the past to recover costs associated with extensive system growth, including recovery of more than $14 million in fiscal 2000."

Total assets: $1,445 million
Current ratio: 0.96
Common shares outstanding: 31 million
Return on 2000 shareholders' equity: 12.6%

	2000	1999	1998	1997	1996	1995	1994	1993
Revenues (millions)	830	686	765	776	685	505	575	553
Net income (millions)	64	58	60	55	49	40	36	38
Earnings per share	2.01	1.86	1.96	1.85	1.67	1.45	1.35	1.45
Dividends per share	1.44	1.36	1.28	1.21	1.15	1.09	1.01	.95
Price High	39.4	36.6	36.1	36.4	25.8	24.9	23.4	26.4
Low	23.7	28.6	27.9	22.0	20.5	18.3	18.0	18.8

GROWTH AND INCOME

Pitney Bowes Inc.

1 Elmcroft Road □ Stamford, Connecticut 06926-0700 □ Investor contact: Charles F. McBride (203) 351-6349 □ Dividend reinvestment plan is available: (800) 648-8170 □ Web site: www.pitneybowes.com □ Listed: NYSE □ Ticker symbol: PBI □ S&P rating: A+ □ Value Line financial strength rating: A

In mid-2001, Pitney Bowes acquired Danka Services International (DSI), a wholly owned subsidiary of Danka Business Systems PLC, for $290 million. It is now part of Pitney Bowes Management Services, a leading provider of facilities management services for the business support functions of creating, processing, storage, retrieval, distribution, and tracking of information, messages, documents, and packages.

"Acquiring DSI is in accord with our mission to provide leading-edge, global, integrated mail and document-management solutions," said Michael J. Critelli, CEO of Pitney Bowes. "More than ever, today's corporations see their documents as strategic assets and understand that information sharing, through efficient document imaging, distribution, management can 'unlock' this value and build distinct competitive advantage.

"From outgoing and incoming mail and messaging management, document creation production, to distribution, archiving, and retrieval, Pitney Bowes Management Services provides a variety of ways to input, access, and manage documents, giving customers tools to match their tasks, processes, and their individual work habits," said Critelli. Using the latest available technology, PBMS manages mail centers, copy and reprographic centers, facsimile services, electronic printing and imaging services, and records management services for customers across the United States, as well as in Canada and the United Kingdom.

Beginning operations in 1991 as Kodak Imaging Services (a division of Eastman Kodak), it was acquired by Danka in 1996 and became Danka Services International. Today, DSI has about 330 customer operations and employs about 3,400 people in the United States, Canada, the United Kingdom, Ireland, France, Italy, Denmark, Sweden, Germany, Norway, the Netherlands, and Belgium.

Pitney Bowes Management Services today represents more than 15 percent of Pitney Bowes consolidated revenue and is among the fastest growing components of the business. Combined, Pitney Bowes Management Services and DSI will produce nearly $1 billion in annualized revenue, making it one of the largest players in the market.

"DSI has a solid track record of providing customers with leading-edge technology, process management expertise, and turn-key people-friendly solutions," said Randy Miller, who will remain with the combined companies as president.

Company Profile

A pioneer and world leader in mailing systems, Pitney Bowes is a multinational manufacturing and marketing company that provides mailing, shipping, dictating, copying, and facsimile systems; item identification and tracking systems and supplies; mailroom, reprographics, and related management services; and product financing.

The key to Pitney Bowes will probably continue to be consistency rather than spectacular growth, in view of the maturity of its highly profitable postage meter rental business and the moderate growth of some of its other annuity revenues, such as service.

On the other hand, analysts believe that the stock has limited downside risk; it should appeal largely to long-term investors.

Pitney Bowes is best known as the worldwide leader in mailing systems. It markets a full line of mailing systems, shipping and weighing systems, addressing systems, production mail systems, folding and inserting systems, as well as mailing software.

Pitney Bowes Software Systems, a division of Mailing System located in Illinois, offers a full range of advanced software and services for business communications plus marketing and mailing applications to *Fortune* 1000 companies.

Shipping and Weighing Systems (SWS) provides parcel and freight information and automation systems for the shipping and transportation management functions of the logistics market.

SWS's products are marketed through Mailing Systems's worldwide distribution channels, with particular emphasis on North America. Service is provided by specially trained service representatives and a National Remote Diagnostic Center.

Pitney Bowes Transportation Software, a division of Pitney Bowes located in Minnesota, markets and develops logistics management solutions and provides consulting services.

Other Businesses of Pitney Bowes

The company's other businesses are also important. A brief description of each follows.

Pitney-Bowes Management Services (PBMS) is a leading provider of facilities management services for the business support functions of creating, processing, storage, retrieval, distribution and tracking of information, messages, documents, and packages.

Using the latest available technology, PBMS manages mail centers, copy and reprographic centers, facsimile services, electronic printing and imaging services, and records management services for customers across the United States, as well as in Canada and the United Kingdom.

Pitney Bowes Facsimile Systems is a leading supplier of high-quality facsimile equipment to the business market. It is the only facsimile system supplier in the United States that markets solely through its own direct sales force nationwide.

Pitney Bowes' Copier Systems concentrates on serving larger corporations with multiunit installations of its full line of equipment.

Pitney Bowes Financial Services provides lease financing programs for customers who use products marketed by Pitney Bowes companies.

Shortcomings to Bear in Mind

- Several small newcomers are racing to develop a computer-generated stamp that would replace the old expensive system of stamping inky, eagle-adorned postmarks onto envelopes. The new "stamps" would include a bold, black bar code below the traditional postmark. Instead of going to the post office to purchase postage in bulk, users would save time by simply ordering and downloading stamps off the Internet and printing them onto envelopes.

  On the other hand, Pitney postage meters still dominate the domestic market, despite aggressive competition from digitally savvy companies like Neopost and Francotyp-Postalia AG of Germany. And analysts expect Pitney Bowes to garner 30 percent of the international postage meter market by 2004, up from about 14 percent at present.

Reasons to Buy

- At the end of 2000, the company spun off to shareholders its office-systems business, which sells and services copiers and fax machines. At the time of the spinoff, the operation had revenues of $700 million, representing close to 15 percent of Pitney-Bowes' total. The office-systems unit was experiencing margin pressure and was in need of major new investment to help it improve technology and provide training to support new digital products. By spinning it off, the company will have greater flexibility.
- Some observers are concerned that the volume of mail may be declining, as people rely more on the telephone and their connection with the Internet.

  Pitney's CEO, Michael Critelli, responds to this concern: "Outside experts confirm our internal findings that mail volumes worldwide will continue to increase for the next ten years. Lots of paper-based communication is going away, but it is more than being offset by growth engines."

  According to Mr. Critelli, there is explosive growth in direct-mail marketing. To be sure, individual mailings are falling a couple of percent each year. On the other hand, direct mail is climbing at a far faster pace, between 6 and 8 percent a year. As a result, says the Pitney CEO, the overall volume of mail is going up each year. What's more, the same trend is visible in other developed markets. In the developing world, moreover, the growth of mail is even more explosive. China, for example, is registering increases of 25 percent a year.

- Two companies, Stamps.com and E-Stamp, are trying to cut into the PBI's postage-meter sphere by selling stamps online. In order to avoid locking horns with Pitney Bowes, however, these two upstarts set out to sell their products to small and home office customers who don't use postage meters—a potential annual market of nearly $22 billion. So far the idea has been more of a fizzle than a sizzle. The companies struggled to create products that are easy to use. But the bureaucrats in the U.S. Postal Service have hampered them at every turn. For starters, the USPS insisted on a $500 monthly spending limit per customer. What's more, it spewed out some red tape in the form of a seventy-nine-page rule book of technical requirements such as insisting that stamps printed onto the envelope from the computer be placed precisely one-quarter inch from the top and the side. Finally, the biggest challenge has been trying to convince customers to do these transactions online.

■ Pitney Bowes has a consistent record of earnings growth. In the 1990–2000 period, earnings per share mounted from $.81 to $2.17, an annual compound growth rate of 10.4 percent. In the same ten-year span, dividends per share climbed from $.30 to $1.14, a growth rate of 14.3 percent.

■ As the largest business unit of Pitney Bowes, Mailing Systems is the world leader in helping customers manage their messages through mailing solutions. These systems are marketed to businesses of all sizes—from the smallest office to *Fortune* 500 companies. With over a million customers worldwide, Pitney Bowes Mailing Systems is focused on keeping business messages moving and its customers ahead of the curve.

   With products such as the DocuMatch Integrated Mail System, Paragon II Mail Processor, and the AddressRight System, large mailers have the tools they need to drive their businesses and enhance competitiveness. The Galaxy Mailing System and Series 3 Folder and Inserter address similar needs in midsize organizations. With DirectNet, a hybrid mailing service, the company is able to assist customers of all sizes with value-added capabilities to improve the efficiency and impact of their messaging applications.

■ Pitney Bowes has a number of businesses that lag the economic cycle, but they should also resist a downturn. About two-thirds of total revenues come from annuity sources such as postage meter rentals, rentals of other mailing and business equipment, facilities management, rental, finance, service, and supply revenues.

■ Patents and other intellectual property will be more valuable than ever in the Internet era. Pitney Bowes has been ranked in the top 200 of domestic patents issued for thirteen years in a row. The company holds more than 3,000 active patents worldwide—200 on Internet concepts alone.

Total assets: $7,901 million
Current ratio: 0.91
Common shares outstanding: 259 million
Return on 2000 shareholders' equity: 48.4%

		2000	1999	1998	1997	1996	1995	1994	1993
Revenues (millions)		3881	3812	4221	4100	3859	3555	3271	3543
Net income (millions)		563	533	568	526	469	408	348	369
Earnings per share		2.17	1.96	2.03	1.80	1.56	1.34	1.11	1.16
Dividends per share		1.14	1.02	.90	.80	.69	.60	.52	.45
Price	High	54.1	73.3	66.4	45.8	30.7	24.1	23.2	20.5
	Low	24.0	40.9	42.2	26.8	20.9	15.0	14.6	18.1

Praxair, Inc.

39 Old Ridgebury Road ▢ Danbury, Connecticut 06810-5113 ▢ Investor contact: Scott S. Cunningham (203) 837-2073 ▢ Dividend reinvestment plan is available: (800) 432-0140 ▢ Web site: www.praxair.com ▢ Listed: NYSE ▢ Ticker symbol: PX ▢ S&P rating: A ▢ Value Line financial strength rating: B++

In a January 17, 2001 conference call sponsored by J. P. Morgan Securities, Inc., analysts interviewed John Campbell, a well-respected industrial gases consultant and publisher of the insightful monthly piece, *CryoGas International*.

Mr. Campbell commented on Praxair: "The gases industry has historically performed well relative to the rest of the chemical sector during economic hard landings." To illustrate the point, he went back to 1991, a period of weakness in the economy. He said, "Praxair's U.S. gases operating income actually increased in 1991. We think that the relatively stable nature of pricing in the gases industry is why the industry does well during periods of soft economic growth."

In another part of the interview, Mr. Campbell said, "Praxair had one of the best CEOs in the retired Bill Lichtenberger, but they have a dynamo in the new CEO, Dennis Reilley, who came from DuPont last year (2000). Praxair has a significant focus on shareholder value, growing key end markets with unique offerings, lowering capital intensity with a higher service content, and a focus on generating price improvements. Key market focuses for Praxair include surface technologies, health care, metals technologies, food and beverage, distributor type business."

Company Profile

Praxair serves a diverse group of industries through the production, sale, and distribution of industrial gases and high-performance surface coatings, along with related services, materials, and systems.

Praxair, which was spun off to Union Carbide shareholders in June 1992, is the largest producer of industrial gases in North and South America; it is the third largest company of its kind in the world.

Praxair's major customers include aerospace, chemicals, electronics, food processing, health care, glass, metal fabrication, petroleum, primary metals, as well as pulp and paper companies.

As a pioneer in the industrial gases industry, Praxair has been a leader in developing a wide range of proprietary and patented applications and supply-system technology.

The company's primary industrial gases products are atmospheric gases (oxygen, nitrogen, argon, and rare gases) and process gases (helium, hydrogen, electronics gases, and acetylene). Praxair also designs, engineers, and supervises construction of cryogenic and noncryogenic supply systems.

Praxair Surface Technologies provides metallic and ceramic coatings and powders used on metal surfaces to resist wear, high temperatures, and corrosion. Aircraft engines are its primary market, but it serves others, including the printing, textile, chemical, and primary metals markets, and provides aircraft engine and airframe component overhaul services.

The company was founded in the United States in 1907 as Linde Air Products Company.

Shortcomings to Bear in Mind

■ Analysts are concerned about the electricity problems in California because electricity is the single largest cost component in industrial gas production. It also has an impact on industrial gas customer demand.

- High natural gas prices are also a worry and are hurting margins of industrial gas producers.
- The slowing domestic economy is curtailing industrial gas consumption by such important customers as the steel industry.

Reasons to Buy

- In the past ten years (1990–2000), earnings per share advanced from $.85 to $2.98 (with no dips along the way) at an impressive compound annual growth rate of 13.4 percent. Dividends, which were initiated in 1992, climbed from $.13 to $.62.
- Praxair acquired Interwest Home Medical Inc. in the second quarter of 2001 for $42 million, plus the assumption of debt. The deal enables Praxair to expand its delivery of health care products and services in the Rocky Mountain region. Interwest Home Medical, which rents and sells home oxygen and respiratory equipment and other home medical equipment, has twenty-five branch locations in Utah, Arizona, Idaho, Nevada, Colorado, Alaska, and California.
- In answer to the electricity crisis in California, John Campbell had this to say: "With regard to power, those parts of the country like California that are experiencing high power costs could see plant shutdowns. If this power problem continues, it could result in product shortages and could stimulate cogeneration and private, nonregulated power interest by the gases companies. Utility islands are a potentially very interesting opportunity for gas companies—where you take steam turbines to drive compressors and use the waste saturated steam for a customer process improvement. While the power shortage problem will be difficult on the cost side, it could actually provide some opportunities. For fifty years, rising energy prices have been good for the gases industry, as it opens up new applications."
- Hydrogen is part of a comprehensive portfolio of bulk and specialty gases, technologies, and services Praxair provides refining and chemical customers worldwide. For example, Praxair supplies more than fifty refineries and petrochemical plants from its 280 miles of pipeline along the Texas and Louisiana Gulf Coast. Other Praxair pipeline enclaves serving these industries are situated in Ecorse, Michigan; Edmonton in Alberta, Canada; Salvador, Brazil; Antwerp, Belgium; and Beijing, China.
- In addition to helium for fiber optics, Praxair's $400-million electronics portfolio includes semiconductor materials and services, electronic assembly applications, and specialty materials being developed by Praxair Surface Technologies. One of the fastest growing businesses, Praxair Semiconductor Materials, builds and manages advanced gas systems in Asia, Europe, and North America, helping chip manufacturers lower the cost of ownership, reduce environmental impact, and improve productivity.
- Beyond its long-standing supply of pure oxygen and bulk storage equipment to hospitals and other medical facilities worldwide, Praxair delivers respiratory therapy gases and equipment and a host of on-site gas-management services, including asset, inventory, transaction, and distribution management. Praxair's home oxygen services, moreover, provide respiratory patients with life support, as well as therapies to help with sleep disorders or other illnesses in the home environment.
- Praxair's Surface Technologies develops high-performance coatings and allied technologies that provide resistance to wear, high temperatures, corrosion, and fatigue for metal parts. More recently, it has diversified into materials that

answer the needs of the rapidly evolving electronics industry, adding to the already considerable portfolio of products and services offered by Praxair Semiconductor Materials.

- Praxair Metals Technologies was formed in 2000 to develop and commercialize technologies and services to the global metals industry. The organization may be new, but Praxair has been bringing innovations to the metals industry for most of its ninety-year history. Praxair's argon-oxygen-decarburization technology, for example, is used by the majority of the world's stainless steel producers. Oxy-fuel combustion, post-combustion, hot-oxygen-injection, slag splashing, and tundish inerting technologies are just a few more examples. Praxair holds more than 275 patents for steelmaking technologies.

- The addition of carbon dioxide to Praxair's portfolio opens up new avenues for growth in relatively noncyclical markets: food preservation, beverage carbonation, and water treatment. Looking ahead, increased demand for beverage carbonation and water treatment, particularly in emerging South American and Asian markets, promises to generate continued growth. Supplying global beverage-carbonation customers also leads to opportunities in new markets for other Praxair products and technology. Use of carbon dioxide in new food-preservation markets, such as bakery goods and dairy products, is also on the verge of rapid growth.

- In recent years, Praxair has developed noncryogenic air-separation technology, which allows lower-cost delivery to customers who have smaller volume needs. By sacrificing a small amount of purity, these customers can purchase a gas that meets customer needs at a discount to the cost of traditional supplies of product in cryogenic liquid form. This product is less expensive for Praxair to produce—and thus higher-margined relative to "cryo" liquid. Not least, demand is growing dramatically.

- The company sees opportunities to differentiate its offering in the food and beverage segment, based on the need for higher standards of food safety. Praxair is bringing the potential to save more than fifteen billion gallons of water and $70 million each year to the U.S. poultry processing industry through a water recycling system that helps increase production and reduce water consumption without compromising food safety.

- The sparkle in soft drinks, the freshness of pastries, the crunch in an apple—chances are Praxair carbon dioxide or nitrogen had something to do with it. At Praxair's Food Technology Laboratory—the only one of its kind in the industry—technologies and equipment are developed and tested to assist bakers, meat processors, and specialty foods producers deliver products that retain their taste and freshness.

Total assets: $7,762 million
Current ratio: 0.95
Common shares outstanding: 159 million
Return on 2000 shareholders' equity: 20.4%

	2000	1999	1998	1997	1996	1995	1994	1993
Revenues (millions)	5043	4639	4833	4735	4449	3146	2711	2438
Net income (millions)	480	441	425	416	335	262	203	143
Earnings per share	2.98	2.72	2.60	2.53	2.11	1.82	1.45	1.06
Dividends per share	.62	.56	.50	.44	.38	.32	.28	.25
Price High	54.9	58.1	53.9	58.0	50.1	34.1	24.5	18.6
Low	30.3	32.0	30.7	39.3	31.5	19.8	16.3	14.1

The Procter & Gamble Company

Post Office Box 599 ◻ Cincinnati, Ohio 45201-0599 ◻ Investor contact: Tom Hills (513) 983-2414 ◻ Dividend reinvestment plan is available: (800) 764-7483 ◻ Web site: www.pg.com ◻ Listed: NYSE ◻ Fiscal year ends June 30 ◻ Listed: NYSE ◻ Ticker symbol: PG ◻ S&P rating: A ◻ Value Line financial strength rating: A++

Procter & Gamble (P&G) decided to team up with Coca-Cola in early 2001. The two companies indicated they would combine their juice and snack products in a venture that would pit the new company, to be equally owned by P&G and Coke, squarely against PepsiCo's Frito-Lay.

From the vantage point of Procter & Gamble, the new venture provides lagging Pringles chips with more sales outlets. Coke investors, however, weren't impressed, and the stock immediately plunged 7 percent. They see the deal as one based on weakness, not on strength.

One observer, however, gives thumbs up to the pact. According to John Sicher, publisher of *Beverage Digest*, Coca-Cola is following the lead of PepsiCo in marketing snacks and drinks together, as Pepsi has done with its Frito-Lay subsidiary. "PepsiCo has shown some real benefits in jointly marketing and selling beverages and snack foods. Now, for the first time, Coke will be able to do this on a significant basis around the world."

In terms of global distribution, the Coke bottling system really has no peer. In the United States alone, the deal will result in an increase in Pringles distribution outlets from 150,000 to 1.5 million.

What Coke contributes to the new company is its powerful, global distribution network, which includes 16 million outlets, as well as the brands Minute Maid, Hi-C, Five-Alive, Fruitopia, Cappy, Kapo, Sonfil, and Qoo. For its part, Procter & Gamble brings to the party its reputation for innovation through research and development, along with such brands as Pringles, Sunny Delight, and Punica.

Company Profile

Procter & Gamble is a uniquely diversified consumer-products company with a strong global presence. Established in 1837, P&G today markets its broad line of products to nearly 5 billion consumers in more than 140 countries.

Procter & Gamble is a recognized leader in the development, manufacturing, and marketing of superior quality laundry, cleaning, paper, personal care, food, beverage, and health care products, including prescription pharmaceuticals.

Among the company's more than 300 brands are Tide, Always, Whisper, Didronel, Pro-V, Oil of Olay, Pringles, Ariel, Crest, Pampers, Pantene, Crisco, Vicks, Bold, Dawn, Head & Shoulders, Cascade, Iams, Zest, Bounty, Comet, Scope, Old Spice, Folgers, Charmin, Tampax, Downy, Crisco, Cheer, and Prell.

Based in Cincinnati, the company has operations in more than seventy countries and employs 110,000 people.

Procter & Gamble is a huge company, with 2000 sales of $40 billion. In the same fiscal year (which ended June 30, 2000), earnings per share advanced from $2.85 to $2.95. Dividends also climbed—as they have for many years—from $1.14 to $1.28.

Such outstanding results tend to dispel the notion that large companies are only for widows and orphans. In my estimation, Procter & Gamble is a core holding, a term used by my profession to indicate a stock you must own.

Shortcomings to Bear in Mind

- Even the best of companies fall from favor once in a while. Procter & Gamble took its lumps in 2000, as the stock plummeted from a high of $118 to about $52. In its 2000 annual report, management admitted that "we lost critical balance in several key areas:

- We grew top-line sales more than we had over the past few years, but bottom-line earnings growth came in below historical rates.
- We introduced more new brands than during any other period in our history, but our biggest, most profitable brands didn't grow at acceptable rates.
- We invested for the future—in new businesses and developing markets—but some costs grew faster than revenues.
- We made important leadership changes, placing people into new jobs as part of our organizational restructuring, but we lost continuity in some parts of the business."

- Over a recent five-year period (through 2000), while the rest of the world was growing with great gusto, Procter & Gamble was mired in a slow-growth universe. In that span, the company's sales inched ahead at a lackluster 3.6 percent a year. Nor did its archrival, Unilever, have any sales gains to boast about. Every one of the markets they compete in are barely growing, flat, or declining. Shampoo sales, for instance, expanded a mere 2.4 percent in 2000; deodorant volume was up 1.2 percent; dishwasher liquid sales dipped 0.5 percent; and toothpaste revenues fell 1.5 percent.

Reasons to Buy

- In a major move, Procter & Gamble purchased the Clairol hair care and coloring business from Bristol-Meyers Squibb in May 2001 for $4.95 billion. Clairol is a world leader in hair color and hair care products, with about $1.6 billion in annual sales throughout the world. The deal was P&G's biggest acquisition to date.

In the words of CEO A.G. Lafley, "Clairol's brands are known and loved by millions of consumers around the world. Clairol brings P&G into the fast-growing business of hair colorants and positions us for further growth in one of our core business categories: hair care." Clairol controls 39 percent of the hair coloring market. L'Oreal is the leader, with 50 percent. The global colorant segment alone has generated annual growth in the range of 4 percent to 6 percent over the past five years, about double the growth of shampoo, conditioners, and styling aids.

- The Food & Drug Administration (FDA) gave its approval to Actonel, the latest in a class of drugs that treat osteoporosis, a generative bone disease that often results in a hip or vertebral fractures, especially in post-menopausal women.

Approved by the FDA in April of 2001, Actonel is being sold jointly with Aventis SA. Within a decade, annual volume of Actonel could reach the $1 billion level. Known generically as risendronate, Actonel is well tolerated by patients with gastrointestinal diseases, which can be aggravated by similar drugs. As baby boomers age, treatment of osteoporosis is an increasingly important pharmaceutical front.

- Procter & Gamble has more leading brands than any other consumer products company in the world. P&G's megabrands generate significant sales and hold strong leadership positions. Eight brands, moreover, are global leaders in their categories. Ten brands each generate over a billion dollars in sales a year—far more billion-dollar brands than the company's key competitors. Finally, Procter & Gamble has several other brands already in the market that the company believes have billion-dollar potential.

- In a recent U.S. survey by Cannondale Associates, retailers were asked to rank manufacturers on a number of competencies. P&G was ranked number one in virtually every category:
  - Clearest company strategy.
  - Brands most important to retailers.
  - Best brand marketers overall.
  - Most innovative marketing programs.
- The company is making a concerted effort to woo Hispanic consumers. In one recent twelve-month period, for instance, Procter & Gamble distributed 4.5 million copies of its promotional magazine *Avanzando con tu Familia*, or *Getting Ahead with Your Family*. That amounts to one for every two Latino households. P&G's goal is to build a fire under some brands that are lagging. The company leads in various categories of the Hispanic market, including detergents and shampoos, but some key brands are not up to snuff, including P&G's Cover Girl and Dawn, its dishwashing detergent.

  The company views Hispanics as an underserved market of 32 million people—a market that is growing fast. Over the next fifty years, the Hispanic population will grow by 100 million according to U.S. census estimates, contributing more than half of the country's population increase. What's more, Hispanics are getting more affluent. Mean household income has expanded by 13.4 percent (adjusted for inflation) in the past decade to close to $40,500. Finally, Latinos tend to spend big on the type of products that the company sells, such as diapers and shampoo.

- The company has been selling its minor brands in order to concentrate on such core brands as Tide laundry detergent, Crest toothpaste, Pringles potato chips, and its Olay line of skin-care products.

In October 2000, for instance, Procter & Gamble sold Clearasil, the world's best-selling brand of acne treatment, to Britain's largest drugstore chain, Boots Company PLC, for $340 million. Now available in more than 100 countries, Clearasil is the leading brand in such countries as the United States, the United Kingdom, Germany, and France. It had global sales of $137 million in 1999.

- Procter & Gamble is known for product innovation. More than 8,000 scientists and researchers are accelerating the pace of new products. The company has a global network of eighteen technical centers in nine countries on four continents. What's more, P&G holds more than 27,000 patents and applies for 3,000 more each year. Not surprisingly, the company is among the top ten patent producing companies in the world—well ahead of any other consumer-products manufacturer.

- Today, about half of P&G's sales come from North America, yet 95 percent of the world's population lives outside that region.

  According to recently retired CEO John Pepper, "If we can achieve these levels of success around the world in just our existing businesses, we'll more than double our current sales and profits."

  "This tremendous potential for growth exists in category after category," states Procter & Gamble's annual report. Capitalizing on this potential will not be easy, but the company will pursue it by staying focused on the company's key value and globalization strategies while placing particular emphasis on three fundamental areas:
  - Better products at more competitive prices.
  - Deeper, broader cost control.
  - Faster, more effective globalization.

- In August 1999 the company announced the $2.3-billion acquisition of the Iams Company, a worldwide leader in pet nutrition. Iams is a popular maker of premium pet foods known for its tiny paw-print logo and higher-priced meals for finicky cats and dogs. Founded in 1946 by animal nutritionist Paul Iams, the Dayton, Ohio, company has catered to doting pet owners and has allowed its products to be sold by a select group of veterinarians. Over the years it has groomed legions of faithful customers.

  This was the largest acquisition in P&G's history. Through the purchase of Iams, Procter & Gamble entered the $25 billion global pet nutrition market with two outstanding brands of dog and cat food, Eukanuba and Iams.

  According to CEO Durk I. Jager, "It's a great fit for P&G and Iams. Iams's products are based on superior science, just like our brands. In fact, we see major opportunities to apply our expertise in nutrition, bone and tooth health, hygiene, and hair and skin care. We can leverage our global scale and distribution capability to expand Eukanuba and Iams around the world. Today, only about 30 percent of Iams's sales come from outside the United States."

- Procter & Gamble believes in product quality. One of the reasons given for the company's problems in 2000 is its refusal to get into the lower-quality, lower-cost private-label business. That just goes against the grain.

  P&G believes that the consumer will reward even minor product advantages, and it will not launch a brand if it does not have a competitive advantage. Then, it will continually improve its products and make every effort to maintain that advantage. Tide, for example, has been improved more than seventy times over the years.

Total assets: $34,194 million
Current ratio: 1.00
Common shares outstanding: 1,306 million
Return on 2000 shareholders' equity: 28.8%

		2000	1999	1998	1997	1996	1995	1994	1993
Revenues (millions)		39951	38125	37154	35764	35284	33434	30296	30433
Net income (millions)		4230	4148	3780	3415	3046	2645	2211	2015
Earnings per share		2.95	2.85	2.56	2.28	2.15	1.86	1.55	1.41
Dividends per share		1.28	1.14	1.01	.90	.80	.70	.62	.55
Price	High	118.4	115.6	94.8	83.4	55.5	44.8	32.3	29.4
	Low	52.8	82.0	65.1	51.8	39.7	30.3	25.6	22.6

GROWTH AND INCOME

Royal Dutch Petroleum Company

Carel van Bylandtlaan 30 ◻ 2596 HR The Hague ◻ The Netherlands ◻ In the United States: Shell Oil Company ◻ 630 Fifth Avenue, Suite 1970 ◻ New York, NY 10111 ◻ Investor contact: David A. Sexton (212) 218-3112 ◻ Dividend reinvestment plan is not available ◻ Web site: www.shell.com/investors ◻ Ticker symbol: RD ◻ S&P rating: A- ◻ Value Line financial strength rating: A++

Just a few years ago, oil production wasn't feasible in waters much deeper than 1,500 feet. New technology has changed all that—coupled with the need to replace dwindling reserves. The industry has discovered vast new deposits of oil and natural gas as far down as 3,800 feet below the Gulf's waves and is now able to help tap the precious hydrocarbons profitably.

High on the list of new technologies is three-dimensional seismic imaging, which offers a close-up look at the bedrock and its contents miles below the ocean's bottom. Smarter, nimbler robots can perform complex tasks at depths that would defeat any human diver. New drilling techniques make it possible to maneuver drill bits horizontally to reach elusive reservoirs.

For its part, Royal Dutch Petroleum has a 45 percent interest in the giant Ursa Production Platform that operates in the Gulf of Mexico. "We drill it deeper and cheaper," said a spokesman for the company. Royal Dutch and its floating workplace 100 miles off the coast of Louisiana are at the center of a sea change in the exploration and production strategies of the world's leading oil companies. Ursa, the most sophisticated of the above-water installations, cost a hefty $1.45 billion to develop. Only such major companies as Royal Dutch can come up with that kind of cash. So far, the investment has been worth it. That $1.45-billion price tag translates into a relatively modest investment of $3.62 per barrel to tap the field's enormous oil reserves, estimated at 400 million barrels of oil and gas.

Company Profile

Royal Dutch Petroleum Company is a holding company that, in conjunction with the Shell Transport and Trading Company, p.l.c., an English company, owns—directly or indirectly—investments in the numerous companies of the Royal Dutch/Shell Group. Royal Dutch has an interest of 60 percent in the Shell Group and Shell Transport an interest of 40 percent.

The Royal Dutch/Shell Group operates in more than 135 countries around the world, and its core businesses include Exploration and Production, Oil Products, Chemicals, Downstream Gas and Power, and Renewables.

Exploration and Production

This segment of Royal Dutch is involved with searching for oil and gas fields by means of seismic survey and exploration wells; developing economically viable fields by drilling wells and building the infrastructure of pipelines and treatment facilities necessary for delivering the hydrocarbons to market.

Crude oil prices remain unpredictable. Nevertheless, overall world demand is likely to continue growing, driven by the economic recovery of several Asia-Pacific countries and the continuing strength of the U.S. economy. Technological advances—particularly in drilling—will drive down industry costs.

Actions in 2000: In addition to performing well against financial, production, and reserve targets in 2000, the business has achieved significant success in areas as diverse as the North Sea, Kazakhstan, Brazil, Nigeria, the Philippines, and the Gulf of Mexico. Portfolio management has included increased shareholding in Sakhalin Energy to 55 percent in an asset exchange deal, the acquisition of Fletcher Challenge Energy based in New Zealand, which is nearing completion, as well as groundbreaking agreements in China.

Oil Products

Oil Products concentrates on sales and marketing of transportation fuels, lubricants, specialty products, and technical services. It also takes part in refining, supply, trading, and shipping of crude oil and petroleum products. Oil Products serves over 20 million customers a day through some 46,000 service stations, and more than one million industrial and commercial customers.

Actions in 2000: Availability of locally tailored retail fuels expanded to thirty countries. A range of e-business initiatives were launched. Exceeded cost improvement targets set for the end of 2001. Further refinery rationalization achieved by closure of Sola in Norway and the sale of two refineries in Europe and the United States. Improvements to retail portfolio continued via divestitures and acquisitions in Europe, Africa, and Latin America.

Chemicals

Chemicals has a global stake in producing and selling base chemicals, petrochemical building blocks, and polyolefins. Its products are widely used in plastics, coatings, and detergents.

Actions in 2000: A program creating a stronger business continued during 2000 and was completed in early 2001. The portfolio has now been reduced from over twenty-one business areas to eleven. A program of cost improvements generated results ahead of schedule. In China, a joint venture agreement was concluded for a $4-billion petrochemical complex in Guangdong province. Basell, a 50-50 joint venture with BASF, was also created to form one of the world's largest polyolefins businesses.

Downstream Gas and Power

This segment of Royal Dutch directs its efforts to commercializing natural gas through investments in processing and transportation infrastructure, including liquefied natural gas (LNG), pipelines, and gas-to-liquids operations; marketing and trading of natural gas and electricity to industrial and domestic customers; developing and operating independent power plants.

Actions in 2000: First cargoes of LNG were delivered from Oman and from the second LNG train in Nigeria. The Group's share of LNG capacity from projects in which it has an interest increased by 39 percent over 1999. Progress was made in developing natural gas markets in India, Brazil, and China. Financing was obtained

for six new power plants, including three in Turkey. Feasibility studies are proceeding in four countries to develop gas-to-liquids plants. The gas and electricity marketing business, including e-business activities, has expanded with new ventures launched in Australia and Greece.

Renewables

In this sector, the company has a stake in bringing renewable resources to everyday life by developing viable businesses; manufacturing and marketing solar energy systems; implementing rural electrification projects in developing countries; converting wood fuel into marketable energy; and developing wind energy projects.

Actions in 2000: Delivered the UK's first offshore wind project as part of the Blyth Offshore Wind consortium. In Germany, started a wind farm to supply customers in Hamburg. A joint venture began operating a biomass-fueled, combined-heat-and-power plant in Sweden. Solar centers opened in Germany, Sri Lanka, and India.

Shortcomings to Bear in Mind

- In the 1990–2000 period, earnings per share gains were less than impressive. EPS advanced from $2.07 to $3.67, a compound annual growth rate of only 5.9 percent. In the same ten-year stretch, dividends expanded from $1.06 to $1.45, a compound annual growth rate of 3.2 percent.

- An analyst with Credit Suisse First Boston Corporation is critical of the company's attempt to put its excess cash to work. "Royal Dutch has hit the growth path again and seems willing to reduce the problem of its underleveraged balance sheet (with cash in excess of $5 billion) via the method it has most often used in the past: spending it. We do not believe that this enhances the chances of shareholder returns being maximized at this time. The companies that have the best chance of rewarding shareholders are those which remain capital-disciplined, not periodically going through bouts of being focused on strategic positioning."

Reasons to Buy

■ Royal Dutch has great and growing competitive strength:
  ● In exploration and production—unrivaled operational experience, leadership in deep waters, the largest private gas reserves, and the industry's lowest finding and development costs.
  ● In downstream gas and power—the lowest cost for building and operating liquefied natural gas (LNG) facilities and a leading position, through InterGen, in developing independent power plants.
  ● In oil products—the best-known and most preferred brand, selling to 20 million customers a day through 46,000 service stations in ninety countries.
  ● In chemicals—world-scale chemical plants and leadership in various products.
■ Two energy marketing and trading businesses—one in the United Kingdom and one in the United States—are set to grow on the strength of their relationships with industrial and commercial customers. Shell Gas Direct of the United Kingdom, which is now selling not only natural gas but also electricity, continues to be ranked highly in terms of its customer service in independent market surveys. Coral Energy, based in the United States, is offering its customers both gas and electricity directly from regional trading hubs and, through a robust financial products business, allows them to tailor the cost of their energy to meet specific objectives.

■ After negotiations that dragged on for twelve long years, Royal Dutch finally hammered out a joint venture with China National Offshore Oil Corporation. The $4.05-billion contract signed in late 2000 by Shell Chemicals is the biggest joint venture ever made with a Chinese company.

The first phase of construction on the plant in the southern city of Huizhou, Guangdong province, will enable the complex to produce 800,000 tons of ethylene and 2.3 million tons of petrochemical products a year beginning in 2005. Shell Chemicals, a unit of Royal Dutch, holds a 50 percent stake in the joint venture. The $4.05 billion covers only the first phase of the project, with major construction slated to begin in 2003. A subsequent phase "will involve a huge sum of investment in oil refineries," a Chinese news agency said, but did not give additional details.

Shell, which has more than twenty petroleum and petrochemical projects in China, will incorporate several patented technologies in the project to allow production of lower-end chemical products that China is currently incapable of making.

Total assets: $57,086 million
Current ratio: 1.08
Common shares outstanding: 2,144 million
Return on 2000 shareholders' equity: 20.7%

		2000	1999	1998	1997	1996	1995	1994	1993
Revenues (millions)		149146	105366	93692	128155	128313	109872	96919	93631
Net income (millions)		13094	7534	5146	8031	8126	7492	5440	4434
Earnings per share		3.67	2.11	1.55	2.40	2.48	2.20	1.67	1.63
Dividends per share		1.45	1.59	1.58	1.51	1.45	1.37	1.21	1.18
Price	High	65.7	67.4	60.4	59.4	43.5	35.4	29.2	27.0
	Low	50.4	39.6	39.8	42.0	33.4	26.8	24.2	19.7

AGGRESSIVE GROWTH

Safeway Inc.

Post Office Box 99 □ Pleasanton, California 94566-0009 □ Investor Contact: Melissa C. Plaisance (925) 467-3790 □ Dividend reinvestment plan is not available □ Web site: www.safeway.com □ Listed: NYSE □ Ticker symbol: SWY □ S&P rating: B+ □ Value Line financial strength rating: B++

Safeway was first incorporated in 1926, upon payment of a $960 tax and a $15 recording fee to the state of Maryland. However, the company traces its roots back to 1915 and the small Idaho town of American Falls, where Marion B. Skaggs bought his father's tiny grocery store for $1,088. At only 576 square feet in overall size, Mr. Skaggs's first store was minuscule compared to the company's 55,000 square-foot-prototype superstore today.

Less than eleven years later, with the help of his five brothers and other pioneering grocers, Skaggs built his fledgling organization to 428 grocery stores and meat markets, spanning ten western states. In 1926, these units merged with the 322 former Sam Seelig stores in southern California (which had adopted the name "Safeway" the previous year).

Company Profile

Safeway Inc. is one of the largest food and drug retailers in North America. At the end of 2000, the company operated 1,688 stores in the Western, Southwestern, Rocky Mountain and Mid- Atlantic regions of the United States and Canada. The company's retail operations are situated principally in California, Oregon, Washington, Alaska, Colorado, Arizona, Texas, the Chicago metropolitan area, and the Mid-Atlantic region.

The company's Canadian retail operations are situated principally in British Columbia, Alberta, and Manitoba/Saskatchewan.

Each of Safeway's twelve retail operating areas is served by a regional distribution center consisting of one or more facilities.

The company has sixteen distribution/warehousing centers (thirteen in the United States and three in Canada), which collectively provide the majority of all products to Safeway stores. The principal function of manufacturing operations is to purchase, manufacture and process private label merchandise sold in stores operated by the company.

In early 2001, Safeway acquired Genuardi's Family Markets, Inc., which at the close of the transaction, operated thirty-nine stores in Pennsylvania, Delaware, and New Jersey.

Safeway also holds a 49 percent interest in Casa Ley, S.A. de C.V., which at the end of 2000, operated ninety-seven food and general merchandise stores in western Mexico.

Safeway's average store size is about 44,000 square feet. Safeway's primary new store prototype is 55,000 square feet and is designed both to accommodate changing customer needs and to achieve certain operating efficiencies.

Most stores offer a wide selection of both food and general merchandise and feature a variety of specialty departments such as bakery, delicatessen, floral, and pharmacy.

At the end of 2000, the company owned about one-third of its stores and leased its remaining outlets. In recent years, Safeway has preferred ownership because it provides control and flexibility with respect to financing terms, remodeling, expansions, and closures.

Highlights of 2000

■ Net income increased 12.5 percent, to $1.1 billion ($2.13 per share). Excluding the estimated effects of a strike involving the operator of the company's northern California distribution center, net income in 2000 was up 19.3 percent, to $1.2 billion ($2.26 per share).

- Total sales rose 11 percent, to $32 billion, primarily due to strong store operations, new store openings and the Randall's acquisition completed in the fourth quarter of 1999. On a strike-adjusted basis, comparable-store sales increased 3.3 percent, while identical store sales (which exclude replacement stores) were up 2.7 percent.

- Gross profit, adjusted for the effects of the strike, improved 64 basis points, to 29.93 percent of sales from pro forma results in 1999. This increase reflects continuing improvements in buying practices and product mix.

- On a pro forma basis, operating and administrative expense, excluding the effects of the strike, declined 11 basis points, to 22.49 percent of sales. This was the eighth consecutive year of improvement in the company's O&A expense-to-sales ratio.

- During the fourth quarter of 2000, there was a forty-seven-day strike involving the Teamsters union and Summit Logistics, the company that operates Safeway's Northern California Division's distribution center. Although the strike was settled on favorable terms, it had a one-time adverse effect on sales, product costs and distribution expenses at 246 Safeway stores in northern California, Nevada, and Hawaii. Management estimated the strike reduced fourth-quarter earnings by about $0.13 per share.

- Capital spending increased to $1.8 billion in 2000. During the year, the company opened 75 new stores, expanded or remodeled 275 existing outlets and closed 46 older stores, resulting in a 4 percent net addition to total retail square footage. In 2001, the company

says it will invest more than $2.1 billion and open 90 new stores, while remodeling 250 units. At the end of 2000, about 70 percent of Safeway's store system had been newly rebuilt, enlarged or extensively remodeled during the preceding five years.

- With 1,160 in-store pharmacies at the end of 2000, the company was the eighth-largest drug retailer in North America.

- The company added fuel stations to a number of its stores in 2000 and plan to add more in 2001.

Shortcomings to Bear in Mind

- Safeway has a rather leveraged balance sheet, with less than half of its capitalization in shareholders' equity. However, coverage of debt interest is more than adequate at 6.8 times, despite the additional debt incurred to finance the acquisition of Randall's in September of 1999, and the repurchase of Safeway stock in late 1999.

- The weak sales performance in the fourth quarter of 2000 was caused mostly by the diversion of management's attention as it dealt with the difficult forty-seven-day strike. According to a report issued by Credit Suisse First Boston Corporation, "Management explained that various diversions and disruptions associated with the strike prevented the proper focus on sales and operating initiatives, which contributed to the weak sales results. We certainly understand the issue, but we do find it somewhat troubling that a warehouse strike in one division can materially impact sales trends throughout the entire company."

- Despite this negative observation, the report goes on to point out "Safeway has delivered on all of its objectives over the years, while creating an enormous amount of shareholder value along the way. Management has developed the industry's most efficient and profitable large chain with strong competitive advantages. Safeway also remains a proven consolidator, with many more opportunities that still lie ahead. As we have seen over the years, Safeway is quite capable of undertaking accretive acquisitions at any time, and investors are generally well rewarded. Overall, this company still remains exceptionally well positioned, and long-term investors should look beyond the current quarter with confidence that the peak is still far away."

Reasons to Buy

- Almost 85 percent of the company's sales come from stores situated in areas growing faster than the national average in the U.S. and Canada. By concentrating the majority of its capital spending in attractive, high-growth areas were the company commands strong market positions, CEO Steven A. Burd believes "we enhance our prospects for long-term sales growth and operating margin improvement."

- In early 2001, the company acquired Genuardi's Family Markets, Inc., with thirty-nine stores in Pennsylvania, Delaware, and New Jersey. One of the region's leading supermarket chains, Genuardi's is renowned for superior-quality perishables and great customer service. According to Mr. Burd, "Its operating philosophy and corporate culture should mesh well with Safeway's."

- At about the same time, the company purchased eleven ABCO stores in Arizona to complement Safeway's eighty-nine-store Phoenix Division. Mr. Burd says, "Acquisitions continue to be a key element of our long-term growth strategy."

- Safeway believes its greatest opportunity for meaningful long-term growth revolves around the acquisition of other established supermarket companies that are either the leading or second-leading chains in their respective market regions, or offer room for improvement in operating performance. This strategy proved successful with the 1997 acquisition of Vons Inc., and such acquisitions as Dominick's (acquired in late 1998), Carr-Gottstein Foods (1999) and Randall's in the fall of 1999.

- During the past eight years, Safeway has consistently ranked among the industry's leaders in the following key measures of financial performance: same-store sales growth, cost reduction, working capital management, operating cash flow margin expansion, and earnings-per-share growth.

- Safeway has developed a line of more than 1,100 premium corporate brand products since 1993 under the "Safeway Select" banner. The award-winning Safeway Select line is designed to offer premium quality products that the company believes are equal or superior in quality to comparable best-selling nationally advertised brands, or are unique to the category and not available from national brand manufacturers.

The Safeway Select line of products includes carbonated soft drinks; unique salsas, the Indulgence line of cookies and other sweets, the Verdi line of fresh and frozen pastas, pasta sauces and olive oils, Artisan fresh-baked breads, Twice-the-Fruit yogurt, NutraBalance dog food, Ultra laundry detergents and dish soaps, and Softly paper products.

The Safeway Select line also includes an extensive array of ice creams, frozen yogurts and sorbets, Healthy Advantage items such low-fat ice creams and low-fat cereal bars, and Gourmet Club frozen entrees and hors d'oeuvres. In addition, Safeway has repackaged over 2,500 corporate brand products primarily under the Safeway, Lucerne, and Mrs. Wright's labels.

■ Safeway has an exceptional record of growth. Over the past ten years (1990–2000), earnings per share climbed from $.21 to $2.13, a compound annual growth rate of 26.1 percent. What's more, earnings per share dipped only once in this span.

■ Safeway stores have been able to hold their own in all of the markets in which they operate, including those areas where Wal-Mart and Target have been opening supercenters that sell food and have hurt other grocers.

Total assets: $15,965 million
Current ratio: .85
Common shares outstanding: 498 million
Return on 2000 shareholders' equity: 23.0%

	2000	1999	1998	1997	1996	1995	1994	1993
Revenues (millions)	31977	28860	24484	17269	16398	15627	15215	15152
Net income (millions)	1092	971	807	622	461	326	250	123
Earnings per share	2.13	1.88	1.59	1.25	.97	.68	.51	.26
Dividends per share	Nil							
Price High	62.7	62.4	61.4	31.7	22.7	12.9	8.0	5.7
Low	30.8	29.3	30.5	21.1	11.3	7.7	4.8	2.7

GROWTH AND INCOME

SBC Communications Incorporated

175 East Houston, Room 8-A-60 ◻ San Antonio, Texas 78205 ◻ Investor contact: Jose M. Gutierrez (210) 351-2100 ◻ Dividend reinvestment plan is available: (800) 351-7221 ◻ Web site: www.sbc.com ◻ Listed: NYSE ◻ Ticker symbol: SBC ◻ S&P rating: A- ◻ Value Line financial strength rating: A+

For many decades, American Telephone & Telegraph was the essence of the telephone industry. Although there were many other telephone companies—hundreds, in fact—Ma Bell was what came to mind when you dialed your telephone.

That all ended in 1984 when the federal government decreed that AT&T could keep its Bell Labs and long-distance service but had to divest the Bell companies that provided local telephone service. At the stroke of a pen, this brought forth seven Regional Bell Operating Companies, often known as Baby Bells. The term hardly fits these huge companies, since none had less than $10 billion in annual revenues.

With the passage of time there are no longer seven. In 1997 Southwestern Bell (now SBC Communications) acquired Pacific Bell, with local service in California. In 1998 SBC acquired an independent company, Southern New England Telecommunications, for $4.4 billion in stock. In still another Baby Bell elimination, Bell Atlantic acquired NYNEX, with operations in New York and New England. Of the seven Regional Bell Operating Companies spawned in 1984, only three are left standing: SBC Communications, Bell Atlantic (now Verizon), and BellSouth.

In October 1999, SBC acquired still another Baby Bell, Ameritech, for $62 billion in stock. Based in Chicago, Ameritech provides local phone service in five Midwestern states: Illinois, Michigan, Ohio, Indiana, and Wisconsin. SBC shareholders now own 56 percent of the combined company, while former Ameritech shareholders hold 44 percent.

Company Profile

SBC Communications now ranks first among U.S. telecommunications providers, with 61 million access lines, and second with 16 million domestic wireless subscribers.

As of late 1999, SBC Communications became one of the thirty stocks in the Dow Jones Industrial Average. As you might surmise, SBC is *not* an industrial company; it's clearly a public utility, and might more properly have been included in the Dow Jones Utility Average. Moreover, the same thing could be said of AT&T, which has been a component of the Industrial Average since 1939 when it replaced IBM. To atone for their egregious prewar blunder, some kindly souls let IBM back into the Average in 1979.

As it is now constituted, SBC Communications serves 61.3 access lines in high-growth regions. It also reaches more than 113 million potential domestic wireless customers and has equity stakes in international telecommunications businesses reaching more than 375 million potential customer.

International operations include a 10 percent interest in Telefonos de Mexico, cable and telecommunications operations in the United Kingdom and Chile, and wireless operations in France, South Korea, and South Africa. SBC also has a long-distance alliance and cable television operations in Israel. Additional ventures were formed in 1997 with Switzerland, South Korea, and Taiwan. What's more, the company has joined with thirteen other international companies to build a transpacific fiber-optic cable for long-distance traffic between the United States and China, which was completed in 2000. Finally, in 1998 the company and eleven partners agreed to build an undersea communications pipeline between the United States and Japan for operation in mid-2000.

Shortcomings to Bear in Mind

- Under sharp criticism at an Illinois Commerce Commission hearing in the fall of 2000, Ameritech executives publicly acknowledged that their phone service in the state is "not acceptable" and promised to do better. For more than three hours, Ameritech officials endured criticism from consumers and competitors who said their phone service has deteriorated markedly since SBC Communications took control of Ameritech a year earlier. Customers told of waiting repeatedly for Ameritech technicians who never arrived and of wasting hours waiting on hold to get through to Ameritech service representatives. For its part, the company attributed its sluggish performance to the loss of more skilled technicians than it anticipated. Bad weather in the spring was also a factor, since it caused more outages than usual.

- In mid-2000, SBC Communication quietly placed their cable TV properties on the auction block, effectively marking the end of the company's run at the booming cable television business. The company completed the sale of its cable TV properties in the spring of 2001 for an undisclosed sum. SBC inherited their cache of cable TV properties as a result of mergers. Although the company was interested for a while in developing cable strategies, in recent years it has decided instead to focus on long distance, Internet, and high-speed data services instead.

  SBC Communications was one of the first Bells to aggressively launch plans to take on phone companies outside of its service area by offering competing telephone service over cable TV lines. In the early 1990s, SBC set up a $5-billion cable TV partnership with Cox Communications Inc., the big

Atlanta-based cable TV operator. The deal unwound after SBC decided that new federal rules governing the cable TV business were inhospitable.

Reasons to Buy

- Ever since the Baby Bell local phone companies emerged from the old AT&T in 1984, theirs has been a cozy club. With their mutually exclusive territories, they have reaped the fruits of their dominance as relatively friendly neighbors. Now, however, that truce has come apart at the seams. SBC has invaded the territories of BellSouth, Verizon (which includes what used to be Bell Atlantic and NYNEX), and Qwest Communications (which includes what used to be U.S. West). In so doing, SBC hopes to siphon off $1 billion in annual revenue from its Bell brethren.

- Federal regulators gave the stamp of approval to a joint venture between SBC Communications and BellSouth to create the nation's second largest wireless phone service. The venture, which was sanctioned in the fall of 2000, created a domestic wireless enterprise with more than 19 million customers, second only to Verizon Wireless. The new company will have combined revenue of at least $10 billion, with operations in forty of the nation's fifty largest markets. To obtain the approval of the Federal Communications Commission, the two Bell companies had to divest wireless operations in Louisiana, Indianapolis, and Los Angeles. SBC owns 60 percent of the new company.

  BellSouth and SBC say the joint venture will enable them to better compete by offering customers everything from wireless Internet access and interactive messaging to attractive national rate plans and a host of other services. Analysts believe that wireless penetration in the United States, now about 30 percent, will reach 70 and perhaps 80 percent within ten years.

- The Federal Communications Commission (FCC) cleared the way in the fall of 2000 for SBC to offer high-speed Internet service through remote fiber-optic equipment terminals located in neighborhoods. The company hopes to have 18,000 remote terminals operating by the end of 2002, up from 4,000 at the end of 2000.

  Remote terminals make digital subscriber lines (DSL) available to virtually all their telephone subscribers in certain metropolitan areas. Before the FCC decision, residents had to live within 3.3 miles of one of the company's central offices to be eligible for DSL. By installing fiber-optic lines and remote terminals in neighborhoods, the company reaches customers beyond that limit.

- In the biggest move by a major local phone company into the torrid electronic-commerce business, SBC acquired Sterling Commerce for $3.9 billion in 2000. Based in Dallas, Texas, Sterling provides software that enables businesses to electronically transmit orders, invoices, and payment data to suppliers.

  Sterling, which had revenues of $561 million in fiscal 1999, provides electronic-commerce systems to over 45,000 customers worldwide, including many large corporations such as Wal-Mart, Johnson & Johnson, and Sony. Sterling's revenue growth in 2000 is targeted at 20 percent, with 27 percent forecast for 2001.

  SBC's CEO, Edward E. Whitacre Jr., is betting that the move into high-margin e-biz services will help convince customers and investors that his company is more than a fuddy-duddy Baby Bell stuck in slow-growing traditional telephone markets.

- In the breathless atmosphere of cutting-edge investments and next-generation opportunities, the phone companies don't rate—or at least no one seems to think so. Think again. The Baby Bells are a critical link in the value chain of the enabling technologies necessary for the Internet to be commercially successful.

  And unlike most of the stocks that makeup the Internet realm, their prices are reasonable; their P/E ratios are typically below average. What's more, their earnings are rising, and their survival and growth are not in doubt.

  The Bells are the largest Internet service providers in the country and the largest cellular providers, yet they "are being completely ignored." But Link said he's been buying the stocks because he believes they are still cheap. He noted that their earnings are growing—from 8 to 10 percent annually to 12 to 14 percent.

- Cisco Systems, the data networking company, announced in 2000 that it had entered into a multibillion-dollar alliance with SBC Communications. Under the agreement, SBC will be among the biggest buyers of Cisco's routers and switches that are used to build the Internet's infrastructure. It is one of the first times that Cisco has closely aligned itself with a traditional phone company. It will provide equipment to send information over five different networking platforms, including digital subscriber lines, which are faster than dial-up modems, and other services that can transmit data, voice, and video. The two companies hope to develop products to make it easier for Internet users to switch between different Internet service providers as well as a local area network.

- SBC Communications won federal approval to offer long-distance phone service to consumers in Kansas and Oklahoma, becoming the first local phone company created with the 1984 breakup of AT&T to offer interstate service in multiple states. On March 7, 2001, the company was able to begin selling service in those states. It had been estimated that consumers in Oklahoma had been spending $220 million a year on long distance, while those in Kansas were spending about $175 million prior to the invasion on their turf of SBC Communications. In the summer of 2000, moreover, the company got a similar decision in the state of Texas where it acquired a million new customers after only three months in that state.

Total assets: $97,980 million
Current ratio: 0.52
Common shares outstanding: 3,385 million
Return on 2000 shareholders' equity: 25.4%

	2000	1999	1998	1997	1996	1995	1994	1993
Revenues (millions)	53313	48960	45323	25044	13898	12670	11619	10690
Net income (millions)	7746	7439	7690	3364	2101	1889	1649	1435
Earnings per share	2.26	2.15	2.08	1.84	1.73	1.55	1.37	1.20
Dividends per share	1.01	.97	.94	.89	.86	.83	.79	.76
Price High	59.0	59.9	54.9	38.1	30.1	29.3	22.1	23.5
Low	34.8	44.1	35.0	24.6	23.0	19.8	18.4	17.1

Stryker Corporation

Post Office Box 4085 □ Kalamazoo, Michigan 49003-4085 □ Investor contact: David J. Simpson (616) 385-2600 □ Web site: www.strykercorp.com □ Listed: NYSE □ Dividend reinvestment plan is not available □ Ticker symbol: SYK □ S&P rating: B+ □ Value Line financial strength rating: A

During 2000, Stryker Corporation, a global leader in such orthopedic products as hip implants and powered surgical instruments, launched groundbreaking new products and readied others for introduction in 2001.

The Stryker Navigation System

Stryker's Leibinger division, whose core business is surgery of the head and neck, introduced into a growing market the unique Stryker Navigation System for image-guided surgery. Image-guided surgery has become the standard of care in neurosurgery and is growing for ear, nose, and throat and spinal indications. It employs preoperative magnetic resonance imaging (MRI) or computer tomography imaging (CT) scans to enable the surgeon to identify key anatomical landmarks during surgery. Stryker has the only system on the market with two-way active wireless communications for the tracking of instruments by the camera during surgery. What's more, it is the only system that allows the surgeon control of the imagery from the surgical instrument.

Neptune Waste Management System

At the end of 2000, Stryker Instruments introduced the Neptune Waste Management System, a self-contained device for handling and disposing of fluid and smoke waste from surgical procedures. This innovation is designed to increase the safety of patients and medical staff while facilitating efficient waste disposal and utilization of operating rooms. With billions of pounds of infectious waste generated annually in hospitals and medical facilities—and safety an increasing concern—

the market for Neptune systems shows great promise.

Company Profile

Stryker Corporation was founded in 1941 by Dr. Homer H. Stryker, a leading orthopedic surgeon and the inventor of several orthopedic products. The company now ranks as a dominant player in a $12-billion global orthopedics industry. SYK has a significant market share in such sectors as artificial hips, prosthetic knees, and trauma products.

Stryker develops, manufactures, and markets specialty surgical and medical products worldwide. These products include orthopedic implants, trauma systems, powered surgical instruments, endoscopic systems, and patient care and handling equipment.

Through a network of 258 centers in twenty-five states, Stryker's Physiotherapy Associates division provides physical, occupational, and speech therapy to orthopedic and neurology patients. The physical therapy business represents a solid complementary business for Stryker, in view of the high number of its surgeon customers who prescribe physical therapy following orthopedic surgery.

A major component of Stryker's success is the optimal use of resources in manufacturing and distribution. Taking advantage of both information technology and leading-edge workflow management practices, the company monitors quality and service levels at its sixteen plants throughout North America and Europe for continuous improvement. This attention to operations has resulted in the inclusion of Stryker facilities in the elite *Industry Week* Best Plants list twice in the last three years. The Stryker Instruments plant in Kalamazoo, Michigan, was named one of the best plants in 2000, and the Howmedica Osteonics facility in Allendale, New Jersey, was honored in 1998.

Shortcomings to Bear in Mind

■ At the end of 1998 the company acquired Howmedica, formerly the orthopedic division of Pfizer, so as to become a stronger competitor in the global medical marketplace. In order to do this, Stryker took on considerable additional debt. As a consequence, its balance sheet (which previously had very little debt) is now very leveraged. Common equity is only 44 percent of total capitalization. I generally regard anything less than 75 percent as a negative factor.

Management is well aware of the hazards of debt and is making a concerted effort to whittle it down to the $500-million level by the end of 2002. In contrast, it was $1,181 million at the end of 1999 and $876 million a year later.

Reasons to Buy

■ Throughout the acquisition of Howmedica, Stryker knew that retention of the orthopedic sales force—from both Stryker and Howmedica—would be critical to the success of the merger. Fortunately, all but a fraction of a percent of the members of the combined sales forces worldwide elected to remain with the company. In all likelihood, they were motivated by the comprehensive range of products, the company's rewarding compensation structure, as well as a conviction that Stryker has a bright future.

The newly merged company now has an orthopedic sales force of some 2,200 professionals who are bent on earning the trust of physicians and hospital personnel around the globe.

■ With the acquisition of Howmedica, Stryker seized the opportunity to grow and expand its presence in the global orthopedic marketplace. Propelled by aging populations, increased longevity, rising living standards, and higher patient expectations around the world, this market now stands at close to $12 billion.

At the same time, hospitals and buying groups, spurred on by governments and private payers alike, are demanding higher quality medical products at lower costs. These pressures create challenges that only the largest and most efficient companies can surmount. Since its founding, Stryker has won wide respect for the quality of its products. Now, the company has the capacity to serve the medical marketplace more effectively.

■ The union of Howmedica and Osteonics has made Stryker a formidable competitor in the knee market, with an emphasis on rapid development of global products that are both easier to use and less costly to manufacture. The company's leading knee implants—Duracon from the Howmedica line and Scorpio from the Osteonics line—cover the major areas of surgeon preference in total knee arthroplasty.

The Duracon line, which is entering its tenth year of clinical success with more than 360,000 implanted, was significantly augmented in 1999 with the launch of the Duracon Total Stabilizer. This complete revision system incorporates new technology that offers the potential for knee revisions that are even more reliable.

■ Stryker continues its advancements in reconstruction technologies with the Trident Ceramic Acetabular System. The Trident hip has alumina ceramic bearing surfaces, which in laboratory tests have shown more than 200 times less wear than conventional polyethylene and metal. This unique design was approved by the Food and Drug Administration in 2001, making it the first contemporary ceramic-on-ceramic system available in the United States.

■ Stryker's knee implant line addresses the full spectrum of treatment from early intervention to fusion, and it offers options for both primary and revision surgery. The Duracon Total Stabilizer, launched in late 1999, added a revision option to this leading knee design. In 2000 a revision system was introduced for Stryker's innovative and widely used Scorpio knee. These two revision systems were significant sales growth drivers in 2000.

■ Since its introduction in 1999, the Xia Spinal System has demonstrated excellent growth, enhanced by its best-in-class implants, Reliance instrument technology, and overall ease of use for surgeons and nurses. This rod-and-screw fixation system is designed to help relieve pain by stabilizing the spine. Its performance was a major factor in the doubling of spine product sales in the United States in 2000.

■ In spite of a low-growth market for in-patient hospital beds, Stryker Medical's Zoom Drive finished its first year on the market with strong sales in 2000. This advanced critical-care product is the first and only motorized patient-handling device that increases patient mobility without requiring transfers for specialized medical procedures. What's more, its design helps reduce strain and injury to hospital staff.

■ Analysts believe that industry trends are setting the stage for continued growth for Stryker in the years ahead. Virtually all market dynamics point in that direction. These are the key factors:

● The population as a whole is aging. In fact, the target population for orthopedic implants for knees and hips is expected to increase 68 percent in the next nine years, according to a report issued by Gerard Klauer Mattison & Company, Inc., a brokerage firm headquartered in New York City.

● Mild inflation in average selling prices for orthopedic implants in the United States compares favorably to the declining price environment of the past decade.

● Consolidation among orthopedic implant and device manufacturers over the past few years has greatly decreased the number of competitors in sectors such as orthopedic implants, spinal devices, arthroscopy products, and other orthopedic products. This serves to consolidate market share and mitigates price competition.

● Advances in orthopedic technology—much of which has taken place in the past decade—have markedly decreased operating and recovery times. These advances have decreased the amount of time a surgeon must spend with each patient, thus giving the surgeon more time to perform more operations in a period. Consequently, according to the Gerard Klauer Mattison report, "we believe that procedural volume will increase."

For its part, Stryker has set itself up to benefit from these microeconomic dynamics, according to the Mattison report. "For example, Stryker has strategically used acquisitions over the past few years to broaden and deepen its product portfolio. Furthermore, innovation in orthopedic implants and instrumentation has provided the company with certain competitive advantages that should be important ingredients for gaining market share in the coming years."

Total assets: $2,431 million
Current ratio: 1.66
Common shares outstanding: 196 million
Return on 2000 shareholder's equity: 25.9

	2000	1999	1998	1997	1996	1995	1994	1993
Revenues (millions)	2289	2104	1103	980	910	872	682	557
Net income (millions)	221	161	150	125	101	87	72	60
Earnings per share	1.10	.81	.77	.64	.52	.45	.38	.31
Dividends per share	.07	.07	.06	.06	.05	.02	.02	.02
Price High	57.8	36.6	27.9	22.7	16.1	14.6	9.4	9.9
Low	43.3	22.2	15.5	12.1	9.9	9.0	5.9	5.3

CONSERVATIVE GROWTH

Sysco Corporation

1390 Enclave Parkway □ Houston, Texas 77077-2099 □ Investor contact: Ms. Toni R. Spigelmyer (281) 584-1458 □ Web site: www.sysco.com □ Dividend reinvestment plan is available: (800) 730-4001 □ Fiscal year ends the Saturday closest to June 30 □ Listed: NYSE □ Ticker symbol: SYY □ S&P rating: A+ □ Value Line financial strength rating: A+

Sysco, the nation's leading foodservice marketer and distribution organization, has a clear competitive edge—it can offer discounts as well as extraordinary ser-vice. The posh Hudson River Club in New York City, for example, began buying high-quality beef from Sysco a couple years ago when Sysco undercut a local distributor.

Later, when the club's chef, Matthew Maxwell, discovered that he had to have more pork just hours before an important banquet, the Sysco salesman promptly hopped in his own car and delivered 225 pounds of the urgently needed pork tenderloin.

Company Profile

As they go about their lives, many people encounter the familiar Sysco trucks, bearing giant blue lettering, delivering products to customers. Few are aware, however, of Sysco's far-reaching influence on meals served daily throughout North America. As the continent's largest marketer and distributor of foodservice products, Sysco operates seventy-eight distribution facilities serving more than 356,000 restaurants, hotels,

schools, hospitals, retirement homes, and other locations where food is prepared to be eaten on the premises or taken away and enjoyed in the comfort of the diner's chosen environment.

Sysco is by far the largest company in the foodservice distribution industry. In sales, Sysco dwarfs its two chief competitors, US Foodservice and Performance Food Group.

The company's operations break down as follows: restaurants (65 percent of 2000 sales), hospitals and nursing homes (10 percent), schools and colleges (6 percent), hotels and motels (5 percent), other (14 percent).

With annual sales in 2000 of $19.3 billion, Sysco distributes a wide variety of fresh and frozen meats, seafood, poultry, fruits and vegetables, plus bakery products, canned and dry foods, paper and disposables, sanitation items, dairy foods, beverages, kitchen and tabletop equipment, as well as medical and surgical supplies.

Sysco's innovations in food technology, packaging, and transportation provide customers with quality products, delivered on time, in excellent condition, and at reasonable prices.

Acquisitions

• In 2000, the company acquired FreshPoint Holdings, Inc., one of the largest foodservice and wholesale produce distribution companies in North America. Current annualized sales of FreshPoint Holdings are about $750 million, approaching the $1 billion in produce sales generated by Sysco during 1999. FreshPoint distributes a product mix of 60 percent fresh vegetables, 25 percent fresh fruit, and 15 percent other produce and refrigerated products. Its customer base of more than 20,000 includes foodservice establishments, such as restaurants, hotels, cruise ships, government facilities, and other institutional customers.

Bill M. Lindig, Sysco's chairman of the board at that time, said management was surprised by how little customer duplication exists between the two companies.

• The company's distribution network extends throughout the entire fifty states, as well as portions of Canada. In February 2001 the company bolstered its Canadian operation with the acquisition of HRI Supply Ltd., one of the largest wholesale foodservice distributors in the British Columbia interior. It distributes about 6,000 products to 1,500 customers. Also early in 2001, the company bought the Freedman Companies, a specialty meat supplier based in Houston, Texas. This move enhanced Sysco's ability to provide precision-cut specialty meat products throughout the southern United States.

• Sysco acquired Guest Supply in January 2001. A New Jersey company that supplies personal guest care and housekeeping items to hotels, Guest Supply had sales of $366 million in the fiscal year that ended September 29,

2000. "This merger exemplifies our more recent acquisition strategy of bringing specialty distributors to the Sysco family to better serve our customers," said Charles Cotros, Sysco's CEO. What's more, Guest Supply's product line provides an entree into a new niche of the hospitality market, said Mr. Cotros.

Shortcomings to Bear in Mind

■ I am having trouble finding anything wrong with Sysco. However, the balance sheet is more leveraged than I would like. Common stock as a percentage of capitalization is only 63 percent. I would prefer a figure closer to 75 percent. On the other hand, coverage of bond interest is more than adequate at a healthy 11.4 times.

■ The stock has performed well in recent years and often sells at a lofty PE multiple of 30 or more.

■ During a recession, it's possible that more food will be prepared at home, and restaurants will see some empty tables. In response to this idea, Mark Husson, a food retail analyst with Merrill Lynch, said, "I don't think the economy will take a shuddering downward turn, but if it does, we can't rely on people's collective memory of how to cook. People think it's their God-given right to eat in restaurants."

Reasons to Buy

■ The company's momentum continued into fiscal 2001. In the first half of the year, revenues expanded by 14.4 percent to $10.7 billion, while net earnings climbed 36.5 percent to $283.4 million.

■ In January 2001 Sysco announced the signing of a multiyear contract with the Ross Products Division of Abbott Laboratories, one of the nation's leading pharmaceutical companies. The agreement provided Sysco an exclusive access to Abbott's Nutra-Balance brand name for use in marketing and sales of nutritional products that Sysco distributes to hospitals, nursing homes, and other medical and extended-care facilities.

"Sysco's market share in the food-service long-term health care segment is experiencing continued growth," said Richard J. Schnieders, the company's president and chief operating officer. "This joint marketing strategy will further enhance our 'one-stop-shopping' concept and provide additional efficiencies to our valued health-care customers."

- Unlike some of its competitors, who order all their products from headquarters, Charles Cotros, Sysco's CEO, encourages his seventy-eight branches to reach their own decisions about which products to carry and how to price them. Sysco's 6,500 sales representatives carry laptop computers that can instantly place orders and confirm inventory. In contrast, smaller distributors still take orders with pads and pencils and are often unsure which items are on the warehouse shelf.

- Sysco keeps margins high by selling products under its own label, a strategy it began a year after its founding. It saves on national advertising and passes some of the savings along to its customers. Its private-label business carries an estimated 24 percent gross margin, or 10 percent more than it earns on national brands.

- While Sysco does not manufacture or process any products, the company is dedicated to procuring products of the most consistent quality for America's diners. This ideal is reinforced by a team of more than 180 quality-assurance professionals, unparalleled in the industry. They continually consult with 1,500-plus worldwide growers and manufacturers of Sysco brand products, developing product specifications, monitoring production processes, and enforcing Sysco's stringent standards.

- Sysco has a solid record of growth. In the past ten years (1990–2000), earnings per share advanced from $.18 to $.68 (with no dips along the way), a compound annual growth rate of 14.2 percent. In the same decade, dividends per share climbed from $.025 to $.18, a growth rate of 24.6 percent.

- Although acquisitions played a vital role in establishing geographic footholds in Sysco's early years, the company's sustained growth in market share primarily reflects internally generated sales increases within each market served.

- As the largest distributor of foodservice products in North America, Sysco assists customers in creating a vast array of dining choices. Menus have greatly improved since a French chef named Boulanger offered a choice of soups, or "restoratives," to patrons who paused at his inn to refresh themselves as they traveled during the 1700s. The sign in French read "restaurant," and his establishment may have been the first to offer a menu.

Today's diverse menu choices could not have been imagined then—raspberries from Australia served fresh in Wisconsin in January; gourmet pesto sauce rich with garlic, fresh basil, and pine nuts delivered to a Vancouver chef's doorstep; or artfully prepared hearts of lettuce served in an Arizona college cafeteria each day. Providing choices from soup to nuts, and everything in between, Sysco leads the way in helping chefs in restaurants, schools, business cafeterias, health care locations, lodgings, and other facilities increase the variety and quality of food choices in North America.

- Whether dining in an upscale restaurant or picking up pasta as the entree for a meal at home, people spend less time on food preparation than ever before. They want variety and flavor in the foods they choose to eat, yet their time to prepare meals is constantly in competition with work and leisure activities. More than ever, people are turning to meals prepared away from home for greater convenience, quality, and, most of all, choice.

It is a trend that started in World War II as women began to work outside the home. Business cafeterias, coffee shops, school lunchrooms, and restaurants broadened the range of dining choices for people who were used to much simpler fare. Twenty-five years ago, not many consumers could identify kiwi fruit. During the past three decades, foodservice offerings have moved from fruit cocktail with a cherry on top to kiwi and other exotic fare; from steak and potatoes to fajitas with all the trimmings.

■ Each day, the drivers of Sysco's nearly 5,800 delivery vehicles crisscross the cities and counties of North America to deliver more than two million cases of product. From the back alley door of a small deli in Los Angeles to the loading dock of a major hospital in St. Louis, Sysco distributes a range of 275,000 products systemwide that have been transported by rail, trucked, or flown from points near and far around the globe to Sysco warehouses. That foods are shipped daily so reliably and accurately is possible only because of advances in computer technology, transportation, refrigeration, and warehousing.

In the 1970s, the typical fleet unit was a twelve- to sixteen-foot truck with modest refrigeration capabilities. Frozen and dry goods were the primary commodities of the foodservice industry. Today's twenty-eight- to thirty-six-foot, single-axle trucks typically have three separate food storage compartments with the most reliable mechanical refrigeration systems available.

Total assets: $4,814 million
Current ratio: 1.53
Common shares outstanding: 663 million
Return on 2000 shareholders' equity: 28.5%

	2000	1999	1998	1997	1996	1995	1994	1993
Revenues (millions)	19303	17423	15328	14455	13395	12118	10942	10022
Net income (millions)	454	362	325	302	277	252	217	202
Earnings per share	.68	.54	.48	.43	.38	.34	.30	.27
Dividends per share	.22	.19	.16	.15	.12	.10	.08	.07
Price High	30.4	20.6	14.4	11.8	9.0	8.2	7.3	7.8
Low	13.1	12.5	10.0	7.3	6.9	6.2	5.3	5.6

AGGRESSIVE GROWTH

Texas Instruments Incorporated

Post Office Box 660199 ▫ Dallas, Texas 75266-0199 ▫ Investor contact: Ron Slaymaker (214) 480-6388 ▫ Dividend reinvestment plan not available ▫ Web site: www.ti.com ▫ Listed: NYSE ▫ Ticker symbol: TXN ▫ S&P rating: B+ ▫ Value Line financial strength rating: A+

Digital signal processors (DSPs) are the idiot savants of the semiconductor world. Unlike a microprocessor, which performs many tasks reasonably well, a digital signal processor can be programmed to do a few things extraordinarily well at a fraction of the power consumption and cost of a microprocessor.

DSPs can manipulate sounds, images, and data ten times faster than the most powerful microprocessors and are now used in everything from digital cameras to automobiles to cell phones. DSPs, moreover, are especially good at performing fast real-time calculations. DSPs are an ideal device when you want to compress, decompress, encrypt, or filter signals and images.

Texas Instruments owns about half of the $4-billion-a-year market for digital signal processors. And it is also the number one supplier of analog chips with an eleven percent share of a $21-billion-a-year market. CEO Tom Engibous's TXN strategy revolves around keeping his company number one in DSPs and analog chips as the market for both mushroom. Demand for DSPs is expanding at more than 25 percent a year, in part because they are ideally suited for mobile communications and in part because they are programmable. Thus they appeal to companies developing products for new, fast changing niches.

Company Profile

Texas Instruments is a global semiconductor company and the world's leading designer and supplier of digital signal processors (DSPs) and analog technologies, the engines driving the digitalization of electronics. The company's businesses also include materials and controls, educational and productivity solutions, and digital imaging. Texas Instruments has manufacturing or sales operations in more than twenty-five countries.

Semiconductors

The worldwide leader and pioneer in digital signal processing solutions since 1982, Texas Instruments provides innovative DSP and mixed-signal/analog technologies to more than 30,000 customers in the computer, wireless communications, networking, Internet, consumer, digital motor control, and mass storage markets worldwide. In 2000, the company's semiconductor revenues ($10.3 billion) represented 86.7 percent of total TXN revenues.

To help customers get to market faster, TI offers easy-to-use development tools and extensive software and hardware support, enhanced by its extensive network of third-party DSP solutions providers that produce more than 1,000 products using TI technology.

Materials and Controls

Materials and Controls is a leader in engineering and control devices for the transportation, appliance, HVAC (heating, ventilating and air conditioning), industrial/commercial, and electronic/communication markets. This division also provides innovative custom solutions in materials and controls and sensors, including TIRIS, a radio frequency-based identification technology.

Educational and Productivity Solutions

TI is a recognized leader in hand-held educational technology, with a exceptional strength in the graphing calculator market. By working closely with teachers to develop learning tools and educator programs, TI can develop the best products to meet their needs.

Digital Imaging

Digital Light Processing uses more than 500,000 microscopic mirrors on a chip to reflect images on screen. This Emmy award-winning technology displays information digitally and creates bright, clear, and vivid images.

Shortcomings to Bear in Mind

- Like most stocks with bright prospects, Texas Instruments often sells for a lofty PE ratio—far above the general market.

- The company's growth record has not been a smooth one. In 1990 and 1991, for instance, it recorded red ink. Earnings per share also fell sharply in 1996, to $.19 from $.71 the prior year.

Reasons to Buy

- Texas Instruments introduced new products for the voice-over-Internet Protocol (VoIP) market in early 2001. This new technology allows for the transmission of both voice and data over high-speed Internet, or broadband, communications systems. TI is carving out a niche in this market with customized digital signal processors (DSP), with programmable software from Telogy Networks Inc., a company it acquired in 1999.

  For home use, broadband VoIP offers combined data and voice services through a single connection. This means, for example, that several people in a single household could e-mail or talk to their pals across town all at the same time, eliminating the need for more than one phone. For their part, businesses will benefit by reaping cost savings from the bundling of voice and data services. The market for VoIP gateway equipment, according to some industry analysts, is expected to expand to $10 billion by 2005 from just over $1 billion now.

- When CEO Jerry Junkins was stricken with a fatal heart attack in the spring of 1996, the stock of Texas Instruments plummeted 25 percent. That's when Tom Engibous, then head of the company's semiconductor division, took the reins. Rather than respond to the death of Mr. Junkins with paralysis, Engibous galvanized the company. Accelerating changes that Junkins had set in motion, he transformed Texas Instruments from a large, unfocused colossus with a reputation for arrogance to a linchpin of the digital communications revolution. "This is a company that has completely reinvented itself. It is unlike anything I have ever seen before in the technology arena," said Drew Peck, an analyst with S. G. Cowen Securities.

  At the time of Mr. Junkins's death, the company had been dabbling in everything from military electronics and notebook computers to memory chips and printers. Today, after selling off fourteen businesses and acquiring fifteen others, it is focused on being number one in digital signal processors (DSPs) and analog chips, two of the semiconductor industry's fastest growing segments. Under Tom Engibous, a husky, ruddy-cheeked former hockey player at Purdue University, the company's market capitalization has exploded from $10 billion to more than $70 billion. What's more, TI's digital signal processors now provide the power for two out of three digital cell phones, as well as most high-performance disk drives and a third of all modems.

- Texas Instruments announced in late 2000 that it would develop third-generation software and hardware for Handspring Inc.'s Visor hand-held computers. Third generation, or 3G, is designed for wireless high-speed voice and data transmission. The device, expected to reach the market in 2002, will give users access to voice telephony, high-speed data, streaming multimedia, e-mail, Web browsing, two-way messaging, and Web-based games.

- In the largest acquisition in company history, TXN purchased Burr-Brown Corporation in mid-2000 for $6.1 billion in stock. The acquisition of Burr-Brown is expected to help Texas Instruments increase its 11 percent share of the $22 billion market for analog chips. Burr-Brown's chips amplify a cell phone's signal.

- Texas Instruments has more than 6,000 patents worldwide.
- The company has an 80 percent market share of the graphing calculator market in North America.
- In 1999 the company acquired Unitrode Corporation, a major designer and supplier of power management components, the fastest growing segment of the analog semiconductor market.
- Texas Instruments teamed up with Advanced Micro Devices (AMD) in 2000 to develop an integrated system for the company's DSP-based open multimedia application platform (OMAP) and AMD's flash memory devices. This collaborative effort is expected to yield a product that has longer battery life and is more compact, enabling its customers to include additional features in wireless appliances, such as global positioning systems. OMAP serves as a blueprint for the manufacturing of wireless devices. The OMAP architecture should increase chip sales for TXN, as Sony, Nokia, and Ericsson will adopt the technology for their cell phones.
- In the spring of 1999, a mere 1 percent of American households who were on the Internet used a DSL (digital subscriber line) or cable modem. That rose to 5 percent of connected households by the end of that year, and it had more than doubled to 11 percent by the fall of 2000. DSL and cable modems are the clear choice for broadband to the home, although fixed wireless and satellite are becoming available but are likely to fill niche roles.

Texas Instruments sees DSL and cable modems competing yet coexisting as the preferred methods for delivering broadband to the home. According to Engibous, "For the moment, people are using their broadband connections to speed up their computer link to the Internet. But TI believes broadband will become pervasive in the residence, much as electricity has become an invisible, yet ever-present, part of our homes."

- When the year 2000 got underway, many within the industry expected handset sales growth as high as 70 to 80 percent. As a result, several of the company's major customers built inventory early in the year that they were still absorbing late in 2000. Yet with actual unit growth exceeding 50 percent in 2000, "wireless is still a strong and attractive market," according to Tom Engibous. "No other market this big is growing this fast.

"Even in today's tougher environment, the world will add 200 million new wireless subscribers this year (2000) alone. In-Stat projects that wireless handset sales will surpass 1 billion in 2003, an incremental gain of around 600 million units, compared to their forecast for 2000."

Total assets: $17,720 million
Current ratio: 2.54
Common shares outstanding: 1,640 million
Return on 2000 shareholders' equity: 17.3%

	2000	1999	1998	1997	1996	1995	1994	1993
Revenues (millions)	11861	9468	8460	9750	9940	13128	10315	8523
Net income (millions)	2174	1406	716	809	281	1088	722	460
Earnings per share	1.22	.88	.45	.51	.19	.71	.48	.31
Dividends per share	.09	.09	.07	.09	.09	.08	.06	.05
Price High	99.8	55.8	22.6	17.8	8.6	10.5	5.6	5.3
Low	35.0	21.3	10.1	7.8	5.1	4.3	3.8	2.9

United Parcel Service, Incorporated

55 Glenlake Parkway N. E. □ Atlanta, Georgia 30328 □ Investor contact: Kurt Kuehn (404) 828-6977 □ Dividend reinvestment plan not available □ Web site: www.ups.com □ Listed: NYSE □ Ticker symbol: UPS □ S&P rating: Not rated □ Value Line financial strength rating: A+

Although the company's delivery vans are a familiar sight across the nation, it's two-wheeled vehicles may go unnoticed. These silver mountain bikes pick up urgent next-day shipments in and around Atlanta's high-rise office towers because they are faster than trying to drive vans through the rush-hour gridlock. "Bikes are definitely quicker," said a part-time UPS courier who has been riding bikes since the company began using them in that city in the spring of 2000. "We take shortcuts down alleys and across paths that trucks could never make it through."

Riders carry brown UPS satchels that can hold sixty or more next-day letters. Bicycles enable United Parcel to extend its geographic reach downtown and push back evening cutoff times for premium-priced shipments. Next-day morning deliveries are a key battleground between UPS and FedEx, which holds a larger share of that highly profitable business.

At $600 each, bikes are far less expensive than the $40,000 vans—and bikes don't have to stop for gas. Couriers are paid the same hourly rates whether they deliver packages on foot, riding bikes, or driving, and there is no shortage of bike riders. The UPS bike program launched in Atlanta is destined to expand to other metropolitan cities where "Big Brown" faces similar rush-hour congestion. In fact, UPS managers in other large cities have been calling headquarters to get the low-down on how the program works.

Company Profile

United Parcel, known as Big Brown, is one of the largest employee-owned companies in the nation. With a fleet of 149,000 vehicles and 536 airplanes, UPS delivers 12.5 million packages and documents each day, or more than 3 billion a year.

The company's primary business is the delivery of packages and documents throughout the United States and in over 200 other countries and territories. In addition, UPS provides logistic services, including comprehensive management of supply chains, for major companies worldwide.

United Parcel has built a strong brand equity by being a leader in quality service and product innovation in its industry. UPS has been rated the second strongest business-to-business brand in the United States in a recent Image Power survey and has been *Fortune* magazine's Most Admired Transportation Company in the mail, package and freight, category for sixteen consecutive years.

The UPS shares sold in late 1999 represent about 10 percent of the company's total ownership. The rest is still owned by about 125,000 of its managers, supervisors, hourly workers, retires, foundations, and descendants of the company's early leaders. The company sold only Class B shares to the public. Each share has one vote, as compared with the Class A stock, which has ten votes per share.

Shortcomings to Bear in Mind

■ By going public after all these years, there could be a downside to bear in mind. For one thing, UPS is worried that the new attention will dramatically reshape its culture, built on promoting line workers from within and opening distribution centers in college towns. "It will be a shock to its insular culture," said Benn Konsynki, a professor at Emery University's Goizueta Business School who has served as a consultant to United Parcel.

■ The company was hurt in 2000 by the high price of fuel. Oil prices tripled, to more than $30 a barrel, as OPEC was able to cut down its output while demand was rising.

Reasons to Buy

■ In March 2001, UPS bought Mail Boxes Etc., a retail shipping franchiser, based in San Diego that generates more than $1.5 billion in annual revenues. At the time of the $200-million transaction, Mail Boxes had 4,300 stores, including 900 in twenty-nine countries overseas. "This is another way to broaden our presence on the retail side," said a spokesman for United Parcel. "The growth of e-commerce has made it very clear to us that the residential and small-office, home-office part of the market is going to continue to expand."

■ United Parcel Service signed a two-year contract with eBay, the world's largest online auction site, at the end of 2000. "UPS will make it easier and faster for eBay members to complete their eBay transactions," said Jeff Jordan, eBay senior vice president. The alliance enables buyers and sellers to find drop-off locations, arrange pickups, print labels, and send packages via United Parcel.

More than 10 million people have registered to buy or sell items on eBay, and the auction site has turned thousands of hobbyists into full-time traders. Such customers are coveted by UPS, partly because they don't ask for volume price discounts. "This gives us access to a whole new set of customers," said Alan Amling, the company's director of electronic commerce.

■ UPS emerged as the big winner in a savage lobbying contest against six other domestic cargo and passenger airlines. The company won approval in late 2000 to launch six new weekly roundtrip flights to China. In order to obtain this plum, UPS and the carriers spent months cultivating friendly ties on Capitol Hill and the White House. For its part, UPS got endorsements from more than 350 members of Congress and several state governors, as well as the blessing of the Teamsters union.

For United Parcel Service, the decision handed down by the U.S. Department of Transportation significantly bolsters its position in Asia's burgeoning freight markets. In years past, the company had to rely on partners to deliver its shipments to China. However, those arrangements did not enhance its reliability or its image with customers.

The company's CEO, James P. Kelly, said flying directly to China cuts shipment times, and "We will be able to provide better service and better value." For example, the reduction saves a full day on shipments to Shanghai from the United States—to two days instead of three.

■ Since the company first issued shares to the public in late 1999, UPS has been disseminating detailed information about its financial performance across a range of business units, thus adhering to Securities and Exchange Commission regulations required of a public company. From these reports, it is clear that United Parcel is steadily taking market share away from its competitors, putting intense pressure on such rivals as FedEx and Airborne to match these results.

"FedEx is aggressively doing stock deals and filling holes in its product portfolio," said Greg Burns, transportation analyst at Lazard Freres & Company. "UPS isn't, but part of that is cultural. UPS is a much more conservative company than FedEx. And part of it is market-driven. UPS already has a broad portfolio of products."

■ United Parcel has developed a system that makes it easier to return unwanted or damaged merchandise purchased on the Internet. UPS initially offered it to a limited number of customers in late 2000; it expanded the service in the first quarter of 2001. Online spending is big business and getting bigger; it reached $10 billion in 2000, or double the level of the prior year. Some customers, however, are reluctant to buy online if they are concerned about the difficulty of returning merchandise. The new system is helping to eradicate this fear among those who may prefer to do business with brick-and-mortar merchants.

■ CEO James P. Kelly, age fifty-six, has repositioned the UPS delivery folks as foot soldiers of the dot-com revolution. "We're a ninety-two-year-old company that's reinvented itself several times, and we're doing it again," he said. Kelly has lived through many of these reinventions since he started as a UPS relief driver for the 1963 holiday season. Working his way through night school at Rutgers University, Kelly decided to become a full-time driver when he realized it paid double what he was making as an accountant. From there, he climbed up the management ladder, handling labor relations and other divisions before becoming CEO in 1997.

The recast United Parcel is more than just a cargo hauler. Kelly has organized the company to manage an array of logistics systems for its dot-com customers, from managing inventory to performing customer service functions. Some six years ago, Kelly saw the power of the Internet as a sales channel and made it a key focus. Kelly's big bets are paying off. Already UPS handles 55 percent of all Internet purchases. By contrast, the U.S. Postal Service accounts for 32 percent, with 10 percent left for Federal Express.

■ The company has poured a stunning $11 billion into technology in the last decade—mainframes, PCs, hand-held computers, wireless modems, cellular networks, and 4,000 programmers and technicians. UPS used to be a trucking company with technology. Now it's a technology company with trucks.

■ United Parcel Service, Inc., trying to adapt its rigid culture to the free-wheeling Internet economy, formed a subsidiary, eVentures, in early 2000 that will test and launch new businesses aimed at boosting the company's presence in electronic commerce. Already, eVentures is working on its first incubation project in Atlanta, which would significantly expand the potential reach of UPS's fast growing logistics division by targeting small and medium-size companies.

If the initial test of the logistics project is successful, UPS plans to expand the service gradually across the country. Such a move would increasingly pit UPS against a crowded field of competitors, including Federal Express, who also run warehouses and fill orders for companies that don't want to handle those complicated tasks on their own. One major advantage for UPS, however, is that no logistics rival can match UPS's ubiquitous fleet of chocolate-brown delivery vans.

The eVentures unit plans to eventually work on several different projects at a time, launching and running each new business until it is declared financially sound or liquidated. The new subsidiary also expects to invest in Internet start-up companies working on longer-term ideas that could help UPS further develop its electronic-commerce capabilities.

■ The company acquired Fritz Companies, Inc. in the second quarter of 2001. Fritz is one of the world's leading freight-forwarding, customs-brokerage, and logistics concerns, with $1.6 billion in gross revenues in the most recent fiscal year. The company owns and operates 400 facilities in more than 120 countries.

"This acquisition enhances UPS's strategy by providing comprehensive solutions across the supply chain at any point our customers desire, moving goods of any size, by any mode, anywhere in the world," said Joe Pyne, UPS's senior vice president for corporate development. "This expands our flexibility to offer a broader portfolio of services, including air, ground, and ocean freight, to our global customer base."

Total assets: $21,662 million
Current ratio: 1.58
Common shares outstanding: 164 million
Return on 2000 shareholders' equity: 30.1%

	2000	1999	1998	1997	1996	1995	1994	1993
Revenues (millions)	29771	27052	24788	22458	*			
Net income (millions)	2795	2325	1741	909				
Earnings per share	2.38	2.04	1.57	.82				
Dividends per share	.68	.58	.43	.35				
Price High	69.8	76.9						
Low	49.5	61.0						

* United Parcel was a private company prior to 1999, and thus no additional statistics are available.

CONSERVATIVE GROWTH

United Technologies Corporation

One Financial Plaza ▫ Hartford, Connecticut 06101 ▫ Investor contact: Thomas McEachin (860)-728-7575 ▫ Dividend reinvestment plan is available: (800) 519-3111 ▫ Web site: www.utc.com ▫ Listed: NYSE ▫ Ticker symbol: UTX ▫ S&P rating: B+ ▫ Value Line financial strength rating: A++

International Fuel Cells (IFC), a subsidiary of United Technologies, delivered the world's first gasoline-powered fuel cell demonstrator units to the U.S. Department of Energy and a major manufacturer in 2000. IFC also joined the California Fuel Cell Partnership and successfully powered a vehicle at a Partnership event late in 2000.

Although hype in investment markets has at times driven fuel cell company valuations into outer space, United Technologies's International Fuel Cells remains the proven fuel cell provider in the world, having powered every American manned space flight since 1966 and offering the only commercially available fuel cell power plants.

In 2000, the company's International Fuel Cells business supplied a one-megawatt fuel cell system to the Anchorage, Alaska U.S. Postal Service facility, the first time such a system has been integrated into an electric utility's power grid. IFC expects to produce by 2003 a new line of 150 kilowatt units for commercial use. These new units would apply PEM (proton exchange membrane) technology, the most easily manufactured and scalable (that is, easily expandable) fuel cell technology. At the end of 2000, IFC announced that a 5 kilowatt fuel cell unit could be ready for residential and light commercial use by 2002, with some beta units in place in 2001.

Company Profile

United Technologies provides high-technology products to the aerospace and building systems industries throughout the world. Its companies are industry leaders and include Pratt & Whitney, Carrier, Otis, Sikorsky, International Fuel Cells, and Hamilton Sundstrand. Sikorsky and Hamilton Sundstrand make up the Flight Systems segment.

Pratt & Whitney

Products and services include large and small commercial and military jet engines, spare parts and product support, specialized engine maintenance and overhaul and repair services for airlines, air forces, and corporate fleets; rocket engines and space propulsion systems; industrial gas turbines.

Its primary customers are commercial airlines and aircraft-leasing companies; commercial and corporate aircraft manufacturers; the U.S. government, including NASA and the military services; regional and commuter airlines.

Carrier

Products and services include heating, ventilating, and air conditioning (HVAC) equipment for commercial, industrial, and residential buildings; HVAC replacement parts and services; building controls; and commercial, industrial, and transport refrigeration equipment.

Carrier emphasizes energy-efficient, quiet operation, and environmental stewardship in its new residential and commercial products. The new Weather-Maker residential air conditioner using Puron, a non-ozone-depleting refrigerant, provides the domestic market with low operating costs and sound levels— about the same as a refrigerator's. The Puron unit gives Carrier a healthy lead over competitors, as chlorine-free refrigerants become the standard.

Its primary customers are mechanical and building contractors; homeowners, building owners, developers, and retailers; architects and building consultants; transportation and refrigeration companies; and shipping operations.

Otis

Products and services include elevators, escalators, moving walks and shuttle systems, and related installation, maintenance, and repair services; modernization products and service for elevators and escalators.

Its primary customers are mechanical and building contractors; building owners and developers; homeowners; architects and building consultants.

Flight Systems

Products and services include aircraft electrical and power distribution systems; engine and flight controls; propulsion systems; environmental controls for aircraft, spacecraft, and submarines; auxiliary power units; space life-support systems; industrial products including mechanical power transmissions, compressors, metering devices, and fluid handling equipment; military and commercial helicopters, spare parts, civil helicopter operations; and maintenance services for helicopters and fixed-wing aircraft.

Its primary customers are the U.S. government, including NASA, FAA, and the military services; foreign governments; aerospace and defense prime contractors; commercial airlines; aircraft and jet engine manufacturers; oil and gas exploration companies; mining and water companies; construction companies; and hospitals and charters.

Shortcomings to Bear in Mind

- The company has a somewhat leveraged balance sheet, with only 57 percent of its capitalization in common equity. However, coverage of bond interest is very healthy at 14.1 times.

Reasons to Buy

- United Technologies posted strong revenue and earnings growth in 2000. Diluted earnings per share jumped 18 percent to $3.55; net income increased 18 percent to $1.8 billion; and revenues expanded 10 percent to $16.6 billion. The commercial businesses—Carrier and Otis—generated 54 percent of total segment revenues, and international revenues contributed 55 percent of total revenues.

With seven consecutive years of 18 percent or better earnings growth, the company's cumulative return to shareholders in the period reached 436 percent, compared with 139 percent average for its peer industry group and 213 percent for the Dow Jones Industrial Average.

- UTX has been reaping the benefits of prior actions. For instance, the 1999 restructuring program, when completed, will eliminate $750 million in annual costs. The company has also reduced annual purchasing costs by $900 million in the last three years and is on track to eliminate almost eight million square feet of extra factory space.

- Otis Elevator is taking elevator design to a new level. In early 2000 the company unveiled an innovative model that uses rubber belts to hoist elevator cars. This is notable because for the past century most elevators have been lifted by steel ropes. The Gen2, short for Generation 2, is a gearless machine pulled up and down by a device that resembles a belt for trousers. The product marks Otis's entry into the "machine-room-less" elevator market, so called because the system eliminates the need for a separate machine room above the shaft. The Gen2 also provides a quieter, smoother ride.

Gen2 is designed for buildings with two to twenty floors. That segment, which includes apartment buildings and hotels, is one of the hottest segments of the industry, accounting for about 75 percent of the new elevators sold each year.

Elevators without machine rooms are appealing because they can save developers money and give building owners more rentable space. "An elevator machine room can cost anywhere from $10,000 to $20,000, depending on the type of building," says Ray Moncini, vice president for Otis North America. "The guys who build buildings work on very small margins." He also noted that the system is less expensive to install and is energy-efficient because it uses smaller motors that can be mounted inside the shaft.

- In 2000 Sikorsky launched its S-92 commercial helicopter, its first new helicopter since the Black Hawk and the S-76 in the 1970s.

- Pratt & Whitney's PW6000 engine for narrow-body aircraft is now firmly launched with Airbus's 100-passenger A318, with seven of eight airlines selecting the PW6000 over a competitor's engine. Without a placement on the popular 737, Pratt & Whitney has been at a disadvantage in the higher-volume narrow-body segment; the PW6000 fixes this emphatically.

- Three major acquisitions, a joint venture, and a divestiture changed the company's portfolio of businesses in 1999. The divestiture was of UT Automotive for $2.3 billion in cash, which generated a $650 million capital gain.

  The acquisitions were in the company's core businesses, augmenting UTX's already industry leading positions. Sundstrand joined Hamilton Standard to more than double the size of the company's aerospace systems activities and presence. International Comfort Products brings $750 million of residential product sales to Carrier's North American comfort cooling and heating businesses. LG Industrial Systems's elevator business adds more than $500 million to Otis's sales, mostly in Korea where LG is the leading elevator company. With the completion of a joint venture agreement incorporating Toshiba's air conditioning business, Carrier strengthened its position in Japan and its industry leading range of products.

- Through internal growth and acquisition, Carrier's commercial refrigeration business has become a leader in the highly fragmented $17-billion global industry. Carrier's acquisition of Electrolux Commercial Refrigeration will broaden its offerings to supermarkets, convenience stores, and food and beverage markets, particularly in Europe. A new transport refrigeration unit, the Vector, can cool a trailer from 30° C to minus 20° C twice as fast as a conventional unit can.

- In 2000, Carrier introduced ComfortChoice, a new Web tool that gives utility companies an innovative way to manage energy distribution and consumers a way to save on energy costs. A "smart" thermostat is the core of the system. Utility companies can download instructions remotely over the Internet to the customer's thermostat, curtailing air conditioning and heating at peak demand times; the customer can override such instructions or agree to limit energy use in exchange for a lower energy bill.

  The potential savings are significant: If 30,000 local households had ComfortChoice installed, peak demand could be reduced by as much as 150 megawatts, equal to the power produced by a medium-size generating plant. In addition, Carrier's Comfort-Zone II system now gives more control of power to the consumer, offering up to eight heating and air conditioning zones in the home.

- Sikorsky Aircraft Corporation, one of the world's biggest helicopter makers, said that its Comanche armed helicopter program passed a key milestone in mid-2000 with a $3.1-billion U.S. Army contract. Sikorsky and Boeing have been working on the aircraft, which can fly backward at high speeds and circumvent radar, for about a decade. The U.S. Army has said it views the Comanche as the centerpiece of its plan to modernize its aviation capabilities. Starting in 2006, the army wants to buy 1,200 Comanches spread over twenty years for about $34 billion. The $34 billion would be split by Sikorsky and Boeing.

Total assets: $25,364 million
Current ratio: 1.14
Return on 2000 equity: 24.5%
Common shares outstanding: 468 million

	2000	1999	1998	1997	1996	1995	1994	1993
Revenues (millions)	26583	24127	25715	24713	23512	22802	21197	21081
Net income (millions)	1808	841	1255	1072	906	750	616	487
Earnings per share	3.55	1.65	2.53	2.11	1.73	1.43	1.16	.83
Dividends per share	.83	.76	.70	.62	.55	.52	.48	.45
Price High	79.8	78.0	56.2	44.5	35.2	24.5	18.0	16.6
Low	46.5	51.6	33.5	32.6	22.7	15.6	13.8	11.0

CONSERVATIVE GROWTH

Varian Medical Systems, Inc.

3100 Hansen Way ▫ Palo Alto, California 94304-1038 ▫ Investor contact: Spencer Sias (650) 424-5782 ▫ Dividend reinvestment plan is not available ▫ Web site: www.varian.com ▫ Fiscal year ends on Friday nearest September 30 ▫ Ticker symbol: VAR ▫ S&P rating: B+ ▫ Value Line financial strength rating: B++

When William Reinka discovered he had prostate cancer at age seventy-eight, his local urologist suggested that he wait and see how the disease would progress. "But I didn't want to sit around and wait for the cancer to grow," Mr. Reinka said. So he turned to the Internet, helped by his daughter who has a Ph.D. in public health.

He found that improved diagnostic techniques over the past twenty-five years had shown the disease to be far more common than previously thought. He also learned that prostate cancer patients now have several treatment options, often used in combination: surgical prostate removal, radiation therapy, brachytherapy, hormonal therapy, and even watchful waiting.

"I read about IMRT [intensity modulated radiation therapy], a new method with minimal side effects, and I discovered that Varian had an excellent instrument," said Mr. Reinka. He also discovered Dr. Bradley Kramer, Medical Director of Radiation Oncology at the Midwestern Regional Medical Center in nearby Zion, Illinois. Midwestern is one of the first community clinics to provide SmartBeam IMRT. Until recently, this advanced therapy has only been found in university or large urban hospitals.

Dr. Kramer agreed with Mr. Reinka's treatment choice. He offered Mr. Reinka a regimen of external beam radiation using a combination of SmartBeam IMRT and brachytherapy in which radiation is delivered internally through catheters. Compared to standard external beam radiation treatment, SmartBeam IMRT causes less damage to the surrounding tissue, thus decreasing the risk of impotence and injury to the adjacent bladder, rectum, and intestine.

"IMRT may allow physicians to retreat a patient with radiation using a more focused treatment, whereas this may not have been possible with standard conformal radiation therapy," said Dr. Kramer. He projects an expansive future for IMRT in prostate and other cancer therapy and praises Varian Medical Systems as his partner in therapy. "IMRT is probably the best way currently to deliver conformal photon irradiation, targeting the tumor more precisely."

Company Profile

Varian Medical Systems is the world's leading manufacturer of integrated radiotherapy systems for treating cancer and other diseases. It is also a leading supplier of X-ray tubes for imaging in medical, scientific, and industrial applications. Established in 1948, the company has manufacturing sites in North America and Europe and in forty sales and support offices worldwide.

In the spring of 1999 the company (formerly Varian Associates, Inc.) reorganized itself into three separate publicly traded companies by spinning off two of its businesses to stockholders via a tax-free distribution.

Since then, the company has significantly broadened its product and business offerings, acquired new businesses, and set records for sales and net orders. More importantly, Varian put itself at the forefront of a radiotherapy revolution that is making a dramatic difference in the struggle against cancer.

About three out of every ten people will be afflicted with some form of cancer. The good news is that their chances of surviving, of beating cancer, have greatly improved thanks to recent advances in radiation therapy—many of which have been led by Varian Medical Systems.

The company has three segments:

Varian Oncology Systems

Varian Oncology Systems is the world's leading supplier of radiotherapy systems for treating cancer. Its integrated medical systems include linear accelerators and accessories and a broad range of interconnected software tools for planning and delivering the sophisticated radiation treatments available to cancer patients. Thousands of patients all over the world are treated daily on Varian systems. Oncology Systems works closely with health care professionals in community clinics, hospitals, and universities to improve cancer outcomes. The business unit also supplies linear accelerators for industrial inspection applications.

Varian X-Ray Products

Varian X-Ray Products is the world's premier independent supplier of X-ray tubes, serving manufacturers of radiology equipment and industrial inspection equipment, as well as distributors of replacement tubes. This business provides the industry's broadest selection of X-ray tubes expressly designed for the most advanced diagnostic applications, including CT scanning, radiography, and mammography. These products meet evolving requirements for improved resolution, faster patient throughput, longer tube life, smaller dimensions, and greater cost efficiency. X-Ray Products also supplies a new line of amorphous silicon flat-panel X-ray detectors for medical and industrial applications.

Ginzton Technology Center

The Ginzton Technology Center acts as Varian Medical Systems' research and development facility for breakthrough technologies and operates a growing brachytherapy business for the delivery of internal radiation to treat cancer and cardiovascular disease. In addition to brachytherapy, current efforts are focused on next-generation imaging systems and advanced targeting technologies for radiotherapy. The center is also investigating the combination of radiotherapy with other treatment modalities, such as bioengineered gene delivery systems.

Highlights of 2000

Fiscal 2000 (ending September 30, 2000) was an outstanding year for Varian Medical Systems by almost every measure. The company reported:

• A 28 percent increase in annual earnings per diluted share to $1.64, compared with pro-forma earnings per share of $1.28 in 1999.

• A 17 percent, or $100 million, increase in annual sales, compared with the prior year.

- A 19 percent increase in annual net orders to $762 million.
- An 18 percent increase in the company's year-ending backlog to a record $473 million.

Here are some developments in the company's three operations during 2000:

Oncology Systems

- Oncology Systems again set records for annual net orders, sales, and operating earnings. It launched the Silhouette Edition Clinac, featuring a new compact, patient-friendly design that fits small treatment rooms. It developed the Helios 6.2 inverse treatment planning software for IMRT and began volume shipments of new solid-state Portal Vision imagers for treatment verification.
- The first installations of the fully integrated systems using Varian's Generation 6 architecture were completed, and leading clinics began working with Varian's new Respiratory Gating System for improving treatment precision.
- Varian formed an alliance with GE Medical Systems, offering interfaced imaging equipment and See and Treat Cancer Care to North American radiation oncologists. Oncology Systems also shipped the first new Linatron M for industrial inspection.

X-Ray Products

- X-Ray Products achieved double-digit growth in annual sales and orders. It tripled the operating life and manufacturing volume for its innovative 0.5 second CT scanner tube—the world's most powerful tube for high-speed, high-resolution CT scanning.
- Product development teams completed a unique integral housing design for compact, lightweight, oil-free tubes, putting a mammography unit into preproduction and prototyping a second unit for CT scanning.

- The business expanded its flat panel imaging line with larger, more sensitive receptors for medical applications.
- Consolidation of Arlington Heights manufacturing facility in Salt Lake City led to an improved cost structure in the company's glass tube products business.

Ginzton Technology Center

- The Ginzton Technology Center increased sales of brachytherapy products by more than 200 percent, compared with the prior year. Two new products—the VariSource 200 Afterloader for high-dose rate brachytherapy and the BrachyVision 6.0 software—contributed to the higher sales. Production capacity for the VeriSource product line tripled. Production commenced on a new longer-lasting and more and more flexible source wire for high-dose rate brachytherapy. The business formed an alliance with Cordis, a Johnson & Johnson Company, to supply and service radiation sources for cardiovascular brachytherapy.

Shortcomings to Bear in Mind

- Investors are well aware that Varian Medical has a bright future; they have pushed the price-earnings ratio of VAR to lofty levels. You might want to wait for a sinking spell before you buy shares in this strong growth company.

Reasons to Buy

- A record backlog and continuing growth in net orders point to the potential of another year of strong growth for Oncology Systems. Growth should be driven by demand for IMRT-ready systems, particularly in North America, Western Europe, and Japan. Initiatives to upgrade and modernize cancer care for underserved populations should lead to growth in international markets. Product initiatives will focus on integrating systems to simplify complex treatments.

- Growth for the X-Ray Products business will be focused in the market for high-end CT scanning tubes as manufacturers continue to demand high X-ray tube capability for their next generation of fast CT scanners. Additional growth should come from an emerging business in filmless, flat panel imaging systems for industrial and medical applications. X-Ray Products will continue to expand it product line with new tube designs.
- The global market for brachytherapy products should continue to grow, partly with the help of new cardiovascular applications and the desire for less invasive therapeutic options. Ginzton Technology Centers will compete in this market with a broad line of devices and software, including some new products that should be introduced during 2001. Research will remain focused on advancing targeting technology for radiotherapy as well as the use of biotechnology to enhance outcomes with radiotherapy.

Total assets: $603 million
Current ratio: 1.72
Common shares outstanding: 31 million
Return on 2000 shareholders' equity: 23.3%

	2000	1999	1998	1997	1996	1995	1994	1993
Revenues (millions)	690	590	1422	1426	1599	1576	1552	1311
Net income (millions)	53	8	74	82	122	106	79	46
Earnings per share	1.64	.27	2.43	2.74	3.81	3.01	2.22	1.26
Dividends per share	Nil	.10	.39	.35	.31	.27	.23	.20
Price High	57.8	43.0	58.4	67.0	62.9	57.4	39.3	30.0
Low	28.4	16.3	31.6	45.9	40.5	34.5	28.3	19.0

GROWTH AND INCOME

Vectren Corporation

20 N.W. Fourth Street ◻ Evansville, Indiana 47708 ◻ Investor contact: Steven M. Schein (812) 491-4209 ◻ Dividend reinvestment plan is available: (800) 446-2617 ◻ Web site: www.vectren.com ◻ Listed: NYSE ◻ Ticker symbol: VVC ◻ S&P rating: A- ◻ Value Line financial strength rating: A

Unlike many power companies, Vectren's electric utility (Southern Indiana Gas & Electric Company, or SIGECO) strives to provide low-cost and environmentally sound electric generation. Since 1995, the company has had SO2 scrubbers installed on 85 percent of its coal-fired capacity, far exceeding government standards. In addition, Vectren is participating in an updated State Implementation Plan (SIP) to reduce nitrogen oxide (NOx) emissions from power generating plants as part of an Environmental Protection Agency plan to reduce ozone throughout the United States. Vectren will be committing about $160 million in capital expenditures over four years, including about $40 million in 2001, to bring its plants into compliance with standards set for 2004.

What's more, the company's coal-burning plants are already low producers of nitrogen oxide because of steps that the utility took in recent years to retrofit its plants with pollution-control equipment. Previous expenditures of about $20 million already have cut NOx emissions by 50 percent. Finally, the new program will install additional nitrogen oxide technology on the company's four largest electric generating units that will reduce these emissions by 85 percent as compared with the levels of 1990.

Company Profile

Vectren Corporation was created in March 2000 with the merger of two Indiana public utilities: Indiana Energy, Inc. (a natural gas distributor) and SIGCORP, Inc. (primarily an electric utility). The name "Vectren" was dreamed up by someone who combined the word "vector" (forward direction) and "energy." According to the 2000 annual report, "It connotes a company moving in new directions, consistent with its core energy industry skills, to create growing value for its shareholders." Frankly, I was happy with its old name of Southern Indiana Gas & Electric. But when it teamed up with Indiana Energy, something had to give. Regardless of the name, both parts of the company are excellent utilities, at least in part because the state of Indiana has a commission that treats utilities fairly—most states don't.

Regulated Operations

The company's wholly owned subsidiary, Vectren Utility Holdings (VUHI), has three operating public utilities: Indiana Gas Company, Inc., Southern Indiana Gas and Electric Company (SIGECO), formerly a wholly owned subsidiary of SIGCORP, and Ohio operations.

VUHI's regulated subsidiaries serve about one million customers. Indiana Gas and its subsidiaries provide natural gas and transportation services to a diversified base of customers in 311 communities situated in forty-nine of Indiana's ninety-two counties. SIGECO provides generation, transmission, distribution, and the sale of electric power to Evansville, Indiana, and seventy-four other communities. It also distributes natural gas to Evansville, Indiana, and sixty-four communities in ten counties in southwestern Indiana. Vectren's Ohio operations (formerly the natural gas distribution assets

of Dayton Power & Light, acquired in October 2000) provide natural gas and transportation services to Dayton, Ohio, and sixteen counties in west-central Ohio.

Nonregulated Businesses

Vectren is involved in nonregulated activities through three primary business groups:

• Energy Services trades and markets natural gas and provides energy-performance contracting services.

• Utility Services provides utility products and services, such as underground construction and facilities locating, meter reading, and materials management, as well as the mining and sale of coal.

• Communications provides integrated broadband communications services, including local and long-distance telephone, Internet access, and cable television. In addition, this segment also invests in other energy-related opportunities and provides corporate information technology.

Shortcomings to Bear in Mind

■ Electric and natural gas utilities are both subject to a sharp earnings impact from the weather. If the summer is hot, electric utilities benefit because they sell more power for air conditioning. In the winter, both types of utilities enjoy robust profits when the weather is cold. This is particularly true for natural gas distributors, because the bulk of their sales are for space heating. A mild winter can hurt earnings severely. Unfortunately, the weather is extremely difficult to forecast.

Reasons to Buy

■ Vectren is well on target toward realizing total net savings of $200 million over a ten-year period in merger-related cost reductions and efficiencies. In 2000 the company incurred the majority of up-front costs necessary to achieve those future savings. Vectren believes that the major portion of those benefits will be achieved in the third through sixth years of merged operations. The key factor will be the avoidance of duplicate expenditures for computer systems and other infrastructure requirements.

- From an investor's point of view, Vectren is both an income and a growth story. In the words of CEO Niel Ellerbrook, "Our income strategy is to provide steady income gains and secure dividend increases from our successful and efficient core utility operations.

  "Our growth strategy is straightforward and sensible. We will stay focused and grow earnings from our core regulated utility operations by providing safe, reliable, high-quality service, adding new customers, and controlling costs. We will build nonregulated businesses around our core strengths and customer relationships and create new technology-oriented products and services appropriate to our customer base."

- In October 2000, the company completed the purchase of the natural gas distribution assets of Dayton Power & Light for about $465 million, including working capital. This acquisition, now Vectren Energy Delivery of Ohio, added about 310,000 new natural gas customers in sixteen west-central Ohio counties contiguous to the company's eastern Indiana service area. It raised Vectren's total base of utility customers to the one million level.

- Communications, one of the company's nonregulated segments, represents one of the most promising opportunities for providing new services to the company's customers, as well as enhanced value to shareholders. The company has built a broadband communications network and now is offering telephone service, two-way interactive digital cable television, and high-speed Internet access in Evansville, Indiana, in partnership with Utilicom Networks, LLC. Vectren's investment in broadband communications projects now stands at about $33 million, including the company's minority ownership in its operating partner, Utilicom Networks.

At the end of 2000, the company invested $8 million of its $100-million commitment to help finance the building and operation of similar broadband communications networks in Indianapolis and Dayton, subject to Utilicom Networks raising a total of $600 million of capital to fully fund these ventures.

The networks in Indianapolis and Dayton will consist of about 4,500 miles of cable, passing about 470,000 homes and businesses. Vectren has a 14 percent equity interest in the Evansville project and, upon completion of all new funding and assuming conversion of convertible debt into equity, Vectren also will own up to 31 percent of both the Indianapolis and Dayton ventures and up to 10 percent of Utilicom Networks.

- In October 2000, the company announced the purchase of Miller Pipeline Corporation for $68.3 million by Vectren's 50 percent-owned joint venture, Reliant Services LLC. Miller Pipeline is one of the premier contractors for installing and repairing natural gas, water, and wastewater distribution systems in the United States and is also well positioned to assist Reliant in expanding into fiber-optic and electric facilities installation. Miller Pipeline has averaged double-digit revenue growth in recent years, with more than $80 million in revenue in 2000.

- Vectren is also committed to complete the investment of an additional $20 million in Haddington Energy Partners, L.P., raising the company's total commitment to $30 million. Haddington's portfolio of energy-related development opportunities includes gas storage, gathering, and processing, as well as fuel cell and distributed generation projects.

- In 2000 Vectren's nonregulated businesses continued to perform well. Earnings from these businesses, many of which are barely out of the start-up phase, increased by 64 percent to $.41 per share, before merger and integration costs.

- In contrast to the well-publicized electric energy experience in California, Vectren continues to provide a reliable flow of low-cost electricity to its customers in southern Indiana. Ownership of its own highly efficient coal mines, which will supply about 75 percent of the fuel for the company's electricity generating units, has helped Vectren maintain this enviable position.

- Vectren has allocated substantial future capital expenditures for building new gas-powered, peak-load generating units and meeting newly promulgated emission-control requirements for its coal-fired generating units. These expenditures will assure the company's continued ability to maintain system reliability, meet its environmental responsibilities, and deliver low prices to consumers. The new gas-powered units will assure an adequate reserve margin to meet the growing needs of customers in its service region fr the foreseeable future.

- In October 2000, the board of directors increased the quarterly dividend by 5.2 percent, to $1.02 on an annual basis. This was the forty-first consecutive year that dividends have increased. Few companies can match this exceptional record of annual dividend increases.

- The company's retail electric rates continue to be the lowest in the state of Indiana and about 33 percent below the national average. This is partially a direct result of the utility's strategic initiatives over the years to procure its own coal reserves and mine the coal itself through Vectren's wholly owned subsidiary, Vectren Fuels, Inc.

Total assets: $2,909 million
Current ratio: 0.57
Common shares outstanding: 61 million
Return on 2000 shareholders' equity: 14.9%

		2000	1999	1998	1997	1996	1995	1994	1993
Revenues (millions)		1649	1068	998	972	965	404	475	499
Net income (millions)		109	91	87	68	84	33	34	35
Earnings per share		1.78	1.48	1.41	1.10	1.36	1.09	1.15	1.22
Dividends per share		.98	.94	.90	.88	.85	.80	.77	.75
Price	High	26.5	24.6	26.4	25.8	22.0	18.1	17.5	18.6
	Low	15.0	17.6	19.6	17.1	17.0	13.2	13.1	14.1

GROWTH AND INCOME

Verizon Communications

1095 Avenue of the Americas □ New York, New York 10036 □ Investor contact: John Diercksen (212) 395-1845 □ Dividend reinvestment plan is available: (800) 631-2355 □ Web site: www.verizon.com □ Ticker symbol: VZ □ S&P rating: B+ □ Value Line financial strength rating: A+

Verizon Wireless and Cingular Wireless, two of the country's biggest cellular companies, captured new shares of airwaves in such cities as Boston and New York in a federal government auction that ended in January of 2001.

The auction, which began in December 2000, was a key step in the attempts of wireless phone firms to venture into new territories and expand their services in markets that were previously plagued by overcrowded airwaves. Of the eighty-seven companies that participated in the auction, thirty-five won licenses.

For its part, Verizon paid $8.8 billion for about a quarter of the 422 licenses available in 195 markets across the country, from New York, Boston, and Washington to Seattle and Los Angeles.

Company Profile

Verizon is well positioned to capitalize on the "new economy" growth trends that are shaping communications around the world. Verizon is:

• The nation's largest local exchange carrier, covering one-third of the country.

• The nation's largest wireless company, with 26.3 million customers.

• The world's largest print and Internet directory business.

• A major competitor in high-growth international markets, with a presence extending to forty countries in the Americas, Europe, Asia, and the Pacific.

Verizon Communications, formed by the merger of Bell Atlantic and GTE, is one the world's leading providers of high-growth communications services. Verizon companies are the largest providers of wireless communications in the United States, with more than 108 million access line equivalents and more than 27 million wireless customers. Verizon is also the world's largest provider of print and on-line directory information. A Fortune 10 company with more than 263,000 employees and about $65 billion in revenues, Verizon's global presence extends to forty-four countries in the Americas, Europe, Asia, and the Pacific.

In April 2000, the company and Vodafone Group Plc completed its agreement to combine U.S. wireless assets, including cellular, PCS, and paging operations. For its part, Vodafone Group Plc contributed its U.S. wireless operations to an existing Bell Atlantic partnership in exchange for a 65.1 percent interest in the partnership. Bell Atlantic retained a 34.9 percent interest.

On June 30, 2000, Bell Atlantic and GTE completed a merger. With the closing of the merger, the combined company began doing business as Verizon.

Here is a brief description of Verizon's operations:

Domestic Telecom

With more than 64 million access lines in 67 of the top 100 domestic markets, and nine of the top ten, Verizon reaches one-third of the nation's households, more than one-third of *Fortune* 500 companies, as well as the federal government.

Domestic Wireless

Verizon Wireless is the nation's largest wireless communications voice and data provider. The company's footprint covers more than 90 percent of the population, 49 of the top 50, and 96 of the top 100 U.S. markets.

International

Verizon has wireline and wireless operations in the Americas, Europe, Asia, and the Pacific, and a global presence, including FLAG, the world's longest undersea fiber-optic cable, which extends to forty countries.

Information Services

Verizon is the world's largest directory publisher, providing sales, publishing, and related services for nearly 2,500 directory titles in forty-seven states and eighteen countries. The company also develops and markets SuperPages.com and BigYellow.com.

Shortcomings to Bear in Mind

■ More than three years after introducing the nation's first all-in-one phone plans, a unit of Verizon Communications pulled the plug on the offering, forcing 370,000 customers nationwide to switch their local and long-distance service to less attractive options.

The plans, which offered local and long-distance phone service for a flat monthly fee, were originally touted as a groundbreaking effort to simplify phone service and spur competition in local markets. But after losing $100 million a year on the effort and making little headway in drawing customers away from local powerhouses such as Pacific Bell and BellSouth, Verizon decided to throw in the towel on the plan, known as Verizon OneSource.

- In the past ten years (1990–2000) the company's growth was lackluster. In that span, earnings per share advanced from $1.69 to $2.91, an annual compound growth rate of only 5.6 percent. In the same period, dividends expanded at a snail's pace, from $1.18 to $1.54, a growth rate of 2.7 percent.
- In early 2001, Verizon said it was adding 3,500 DSL customers (digital subscriber lines) each working day and indicated that rate is expected to hold throughout the year. At that pace, the company would add about 900,000 DSL customers in 2001.

However, Fred Salerno, Verizon's chief financial officer, cautioned that the actual number of new subscribers for the year could end up substantially lower because of factors such as customer turnover, economic conditions, and the company's approach to pricing and discounts.

- Handset sales have been disappointing of late. In the spring of 2001, Argus Research Corporation said, "This may be partly due to consumer belt-tightening in the face of a slowing economy. But it is also a function of consumer perception that there is really no compelling reason to upgrade their handsets, as most consumers have yet to find a service or application available on the new handsets that is useful or cool enough to justify the expense of an upgrade."

However, the trend is likely to reverse once third-generation services are rolled out and content becomes available that can take advantage of the new phones and services capabilities. However, said Argus, "a year could pass before the arrival of 3G services and content is acknowledged and recognized in the market place. And it could take as long as three to four years before these high-speed, high-value services become ubiquitous."

Reasons to Buy

- In early 2001 the company announced that it would create a multinational network to serve large businesses, pitting itself more directly against global long-distance companies such as AT&T, British Telecommunications, France Telecom SA, and WorldCom.

Prior to making this move, Verizon had been hampered in its ability to offer full service to global corporations because it was not able to reach some business hubs directly. As a consequence, rather than hand off phone and data communications bound for Europe, Asia, or Latin America to other carriers as it was doing previously, Verizon decided to invest $1 billion over five years, installing its own transmission equipment and buying capacity on undersea and underground cables, enabling the company to keep that business for itself.

The new communications network will use cables owned by Telecom Holdings Ltd. and Metromedia Fiber Network Inc., companies in which Verizon holds an ownership stake. Once the network is up and running, the company expects to save at least $300 million over five years because it won't have to lease lines to carry traffic outside the United States.

- Through synergies resulting from the Bell Atlantic-GTE merger and the formation of Verizon Wireless, Verizon achieved $535 million in annual merger-related expense savings in 2000. Its goal is to bring savings to $2 billion a year by the end of 2003.

- Verizon's long-distance unit continued its strong growth in 2000. The year ended with 4.9 million customers nationwide, or 44 percent more than the prior year, making Verizon the nation's fourth-largest provider of long-distance.

- Verizon added 190,000 DSL (digital subscriber lines) in the fourth quarter of 2000, or 46 percent more than the prior quarter. The 540,000 lines in service at the end of 2000 represent an increase of more than 500 percent over the number in service at the end of 1999. Verizon equipped about 500 central offices for DSL in 2000 and ended the year with 1,850 equipped offices, or 30 percent more than a year earlier.

- Verizon ended 2000 with data circuits in service equivalent to 45.9 million voice-grade lines, or 60 percent more than at the end of 1999. Combined with 62.9 million voice-grade lines, Verizon ended the year with 108.8 million total access equivalents in service, or 20 percent more than at the end of the prior year.

- A ruling by the Federal Communications Commission (FCC) in March 2001 granted Verizon permission to charge market-driven prices for some special services it offers to customers. This ruling, moreover, gave VZ the same flexibility that its competitors already had. What's more, the FCC ruling affected dedicated point-to-point services purchased by large business customers and long-distance carriers for telecommunications services between states.

For example, these services include dedicated high-speed lines that customers were using to connect to multiple locations across the country. Before the action by the FCC, the company's prices for these services were controlled by price regulations. Finally, the ruling affected the company's offerings in such metropolitan areas as New York, Washington, Philadelphia, Tampa, Dallas–Fort Worth, and Los Angeles.

Total Assets: 165 billion
Current ratio: 0.52
Common shares outstanding: 2,699 million
Return on 2000 shareholders' equity: 31.1%

	2000	1999	1998	1997	1996	1995	1994	1993
Revenues (millions)	64707	33174	31566	30457	13081	13430	13791	12990
Net income (millions)	8000	4621	4228	3710	1739	1700	1543	1482
Earnings per share	2.91	3.01	2.72	2.48	1.98	1.94	1.77	1.70
Dividends per share	1.54	1.54	1.54	1.49	1.43	1.40	1.38	1.34
Price High	66.0	69.5	61.2	45.9	37.4	34.4	29.8	34.5
Low	39.1	50.6	40.4	28.4	27.6	24.2	24.2	24.8

GROWTH AND INCOME

Vulcan Materials Company

1200 Urban Center Drive □ Birmingham, Alabama 35242 □ Investor Contact: Charles R. Brown II (205) 298-3220 □ Dividend reinvestment plan is available: (800) 519-3111 □ Web site: www.vulcanmaterials.com □ Listed: NYSE □ Ticker symbol: VMC □ S&P rating: A □ Value Line financial strength rating: A

The largest capital expansion project in the history of Vulcan's chemicals segment was completed with the start-up of the Mitsui joint venture, situated at Geismar, Louisiana. The 600-ton-per-day chloralkali plant began operations in August 2000, adding 210,000 tons of chlorine and 230,000 tons of caustic capacity per year.

The Geismar ethylene dichloride (EDC) plant was commissioned at the end of 2000. Mitsui will purchase the entire output of EDC—270,000 tons per year—to sell in Asian markets. This facility's state-of-the-art technology includes automatic chemical analyzers and a highly efficient distribution-control system for pipeline customers. These advancements improve cost efficiency, product quality, and environmental stewardship.

The company expects its joint venture with Mitsui will take some of the volatility out of its chloralkali business unit. The project is structured to provide attractive and relatively stable returns and will add to Vulcan's earnings in 2001.

Vulcan's chemicals are vital to products that help improve people's health, safety, and standard of living. For instance, chlorine products purify 98 percent of the nation's public water supply and are used to make 85 percent of all medicines. Look into your refrigerator and you'll see an increasing number of products made possible by Vulcan. This list includes cake mixes, milk cartons, vegetable juice, water, gelatin, and sodas. Even the refrigerator itself may contain refrigerant, insulation, and other components using Vulcan products.

Company Profile

Vulcan Materials is the largest domestic producer of construction aggregates (a product category that includes crushed stone, sand, and gravel). The company does not materially depend upon sales to any one customer or group of customers. Typically, its products are sold to private industry. However, most of VMC's construction materials are ultimately used in public projects.

From 330 aggregates plants and other production and distribution facilities, Vulcan provides a diversified line of aggregates, other construction materials and related services to all parts of the construction industry in twenty-one states, plus the District of Columbia and Mexico. Vulcan's principal product, crushed stone, is used in virtually all forms of construction. Controlling the largest quantity of reserves in the industry contributes to Vulcan's long-term success. Vulcan now has 10 billion tons of proven and permitted aggregates reserves. Wise stewardship of these resources preserves their availability for many years to come and ensures a steady supply of raw material.

Vulcan's Chemicals segment is a significant producer of basic industrial and specialty chemicals. Through its Chloralkali Business Unit, it produces chlorine, caustic soda, hydrochloric acid, potassium chemicals, and chlorinated organic chemicals. The food and pharmaceutical markets provide stable demand for several of chloralkali's chemical products.

Through its Performance Systems Business Unit, it provides process aids for the pulp and paper and textile industries, chemicals and services to the municipal, industrial and environmental water-management markets. It also has a stake in the custom manufacture of a variety of specialty chemicals.

A Look at the Industry

Aggregates account for about 95 percent of the weight of each ton of asphalt that is used to pave highways and parking lots and for 85 percent of the weight of ready-mix concrete used for such projects as dams, highways, and foundations.

Vulcan quarries and processes the stone to various sizes, so that it conforms to specific engineering standards. Independent truckers or customer trucks haul the stone to the construction site—rarely more than twenty or thirty miles away.

There are two major exceptions to this rule. The first exception is the Reed quarry, which ships a large portion of its production great distances, mainly by barge on the Mississippi River system. A much smaller portion is shipped by rail.

The company's so-called Crescent Market Project is the second exception to the local-market rule of thumb. Because aggregates deposits along the Gulf Coast are limited, most aggregates are supplied from inland sources seventy or more miles away. Consequently, transportation costs increase the product's delivery prices substantially.

Vulcan participates in a venture that produces crushed limestone at a quarry near Cancun, Mexico, ships the product to the U.S. Gulf Coast and markets the stone in a number of cities, including Houston, Galveston, New Orleans, Mobile, and Tampa.

The economics of the project work because ocean shipping costs much less than truck or rail transportation, even though the distance is much greater.

The largest end-use for aggregates is highway construction and maintenance. Crushed stone is used as a highway base material, and as the major portion of the asphaltic concrete and ready-mixed concrete used as a surface material.

Shortcomings to Bear in Mind

- The company's chloralkali unit is part of its commodity chemicals business. A commodity differs from a proprietary product, in that it is not differentiated from the products of its competitors. In order to survive in a commodity business, you should be a low-cost producer or offer a unique service, such as quick delivery.
- Caustic soda prices tend to be volatile. For instance, prices peaked in April 1991 at nearly $300 per ton; and then they plummeted to $61 in March 1994.

  In 2000, sales of the chemicals segment reached $605.8 million, up 11 percent from 1999, due primarily to second-half production from the new chloralkali joint venture with Mitsui at Geismar, Louisiana. Record earnings, improved pricing, and higher volumes for key products more than offset significantly higher costs for natural gas and hydrocarbon-based raw materials, which rose $31 million over the prior year. In addition, reorganization expenses for the Performance Chemicals business unit totaled $32 million in 2000. As a result, Chemicals lost $20.1 million in 2000, compared to the prior year's earnings of $25.8 million.

Reasons to Buy

- In June of 1998, the Transportation Equity Act for the 21st Century (TEA-21) was signed into law. This $216 billion, six-year transportation authorization is expected to increase demand significantly. Most of this impact still lies ahead due to long lead times for large projects.
- In 2000, for the eighth consecutive year, Vulcan's Construction Materials segment reported record sales numbers. Annual sales reached $1.9 billion, up 4 percent over the prior year. Aggregates

shipments increased 1 percent, to 222.3 million tons (for the ninth consecutive record year), and aggregates pricing improved 4 percent. Earnings of $375.7 million were up 2 percent despite the negative effect of higher fuel and liquid asphalt costs, weak construction markets in some areas, and early winter weather.

- Historically, the Construction Materials segment enjoys good results when housing starts are strong. Conversely, Chemicals enjoys its best results when caustic soda prices are high. The inverse relationship between changes in housing starts and caustic prices has been almost perfect for the last twenty-five years.

The relationship occurs because the demand for chlorine is heavily dependent upon economic activity, especially construction. Demand for caustic is much less cyclical because of the diverse nature of its end-use markets. Hence, when economic activity is strong, chlorine demand increases sharply, putting caustic in an oversupply situation.

However, when the economy is slack, chlorine production is curtailed, thus reducing caustic production and creating a shortage of caustic.

- Vulcan manufactures sodium chlorite at a world class facility at the company's Wichita, Kansas chemical complex. Vulcan is the largest North American producer of sodium chlorite and the world's second-largest. Sodium chlorite is used in a variety of applications, including drinking and industrial water treatment, air scrubbing and paper, textile, and electronics manufacturing.

- In 2000, Vulcan Materials acquired the assets of Garves W. Yates & Sons, Inc. of Abilene, Texas. These assets include six quarry sites, four portable aggregate production plants, a portable asphalt plant and a fleet of trucks used to transport stone and asphalt products. Commenting on the acquisition, CEO Donald M. James said, "This acquisition will expand significantly the reach, scope and flexibility of our operations in Texas, particularly in the Abilene and Brownwood areas, along the Interstate 10 corridor west of San Antonio and along the Interstate 20 corridor west of Fort Worth. Moreover, the Yates business represents a valuable addition to Vulcan's limestone reserves in Texas, especially in Abilene. The state of Texas is receiving approximately a 61 percent increase in transportation funding under the TEA 21 legislation, and the Yates Acquisition positions Vulcan to participate more fully in the increased highway construction in Texas expected over the next five years."

- In late 2000, Vulcan Materials acquired eleven aggregates production sites and the associated transportation and distribution assets formerly owned by Tarmac in Maryland, Pennsylvania, South Carolina, and Virginia. These facilities significantly extend the geographic scope of the company's operations in the eastern United States. In the last five years, the company's long-term acquisition strategy has added almost 100 aggregates plants, bringing the total to 236.

- Vulcan produces more of the crushed stone needed to build and maintain the nation's highways and streets than any other company. While construction is a sign of a booming economy, roadwork is necessary at all times. Over half of Vulcan's crushed stone, sand, and grave was used in highways and other public works projects in 2000. Funding these public projects is less interest-rate-sensitive than private-sector funding.

The Stevenson Expressway in Chicago is Illinois's largest construction project ever undertaken. Made possible by federal funding, the expressway required 700,000 tons of Vulcan aggregates to complete the northbound lanes in 2000.

- Over the last five, twenty, and forty years, Vulcan delivered an average return of more than 15 percent per year to shareholders.

- In 2000, for the fourth year in a row, *Industry Week* magazine named Vulcan one of the 100 best-managed industrial companies in the world.

Total assets: $3,229 million
Current ratio: 1.21
Common shares outstanding: 101 million
Return on 2000 shareholders' equity: 14.9%

	2000	1999	1998	1997	1996	1995	1994	1993
Revenues (millions)	2492	2356	1776	1679	1569	1461	1253	1134
Net Income (millions)	220	240	248	209	189	166	98	88
Earnings per share	2.29	2.35	2.44	2.03	1.79	1.54	.89	.80
Dividends per share	.84	.78	.69	.63	.56	.49	.44	.42
Price High	48.9	51.3	44.7	34.6	22.2	20.1	18.8	18.7
Low	36.5	34.3	31.3	18.4	17.7	16.0	14.7	13.4

AGGRESSIVE GROWTH

Walgreen Company

200 Wilmot Road ▫ Mail Stop #2261 ▫ Deerfield, Illinois 60015 ▫ Investor contact: Rick J. Hans (847) 914-2385 ▫ Dividend reinvestment program is available: (888) 290-7264 ▫ Fiscal year ends August 31 ▫ Web site: www.walgreens.com ▫ Ticker symbol: WAG ▫ S&P rating: A+ ▫ Value Line financial strength rating: A+

A *Wall Street Journal* reporter recently told Walgreen's management, "We don't write about Walgreens much because you're so boringly consistent." To this statement, an official of the company replied, "Well, if twenty-six years of consecutive earnings growth—and twelve straight years of increased store openings—equal 'boring,' we'll take that adjective any day."

The year 2000 was another positive one for Walgreen Company. Despite opening 462 new stores, earnings increased 21.2 percent on sales growth of 19 percent.

On November 20, 2000, L. Daniel Jorndt, CEO of the company, said, "Opening 462 stores definitely impacts earnings. New stores take two to three years to reach profitability. So, short term—sure, we could pump up earnings by slowing growth. But long term, few shareholders would thank us. Right now, more than 1,000 of our stores are less than three

years old. That puts us in excellent position as these stores become profitable."

Nor is growth likely to ebb in fiscal 2001, said the president of Walgreen, David W. Bernauer, when asked how many stores would be added in 2001. "Approximately 500—a new store every seventeen hours. And we plan to stay at that level for the foreseeable future. Our goal is 6,000 stores by 2010, and research shows there's room for more than 10,000 Walgreens across America. We've established a beachhead in every new market where we must be to meet our goals, including Atlanta, Los Angeles, and San Diego. That's why, at this time, we've put international expansion on the back burner. We just see so much opportunity in the U.S."

Company Profile

Walgreen, one of the fastest growing retailers in the United States, leads the chain drugstore industry in sales and profits. Sales for 2000 reached $21.2 billion, produced by 3,165 stores in forty-three states and Puerto Rico.

Founded in 1901, Walgreen today has 115,000 employees and 88,000 shareholders of record. The company's drugstores serve 2.8 million customers daily and average $6.4 million in annual sales per unit. That's $610 per square foot, among the highest in the industry. In 2000 the company filled 288 million prescriptions, or nearly 10 percent of the retail market—and more per store than all major competitors. With a market capitalization of $33.2 billion at the end of fiscal 2000, Walgreen ranks third among U.S. retailers and fifth in the world. Walgreen has paid dividends in every quarter since 1933 and has raised the dividend in each of the past twenty-four years.

Stand-Alone Stores

Competition from the supermarkets has convinced Walgreen that the best strategy is to build stand-alone stores. Since the rise of managed care, many pharmacy customers now make only minimal copayments for prescriptions. That leaves convenience as the major factor in choosing a pharmacy. The freestanding format makes room for drive-thru windows, which provide a speedy way for drugstore customers to pick up or drop off prescriptions.

On the other hand, the company's stand-alone strategy is more expensive. Walgreen insists on building its units on corner lots near an intersection with a traffic light. Such leases normally cost more than a site in a strip mall.

More Than a Pharmacy

Home meal replacement has become a $100-billion business industrywide. In the company's food section, Walgreens carries staples as well as frozen dinners, desserts, and pizzas. In some stores, expanded food sections carry such items as fruit and ready-to-eat salads.

In the photo department, the company builds loyalty through a wide selection of products and the service of trained technicians. Walgreens experimented with one-hour photo service as early as 1982, but it was in the mid-1990s before, according to Dan Jorndt, "We really figured it out." Since 1998, one-hour processing has been available chainwide, made profitable by "our high volume of business. We've introduced several digital photo products that are selling well and are evaluating the long-term impact of digital on the mass market."

Highlights of Fiscal 2000

- Fiscal 2000 was the twenty-sixth consecutive year of record sales and earnings. Net earnings were $776.9 million, or $.76 per share (diluted), an increase of 24.5 percent over the prior year. Excluding a nonrecurring charge, the earnings rose 21.2 percent to $756.3 million, or $.74 per share (diluted).
- Total net sales increased by 18.9 percent to $21.2 billion. Comparable drugstore (those open at least one year) sales were up 11.7 percent in 2000, 11.2 percent in 1999, and 9.4 percent in 1998. New store openings amounted to 10.6 percent of sales gains in 2000, 10.0 percent in 1999 and 10.4 percent in 1998. The company operated 3,165 drugstores as of August 31, 2000, compared with 2,821 a year earlier.
- Prescription sales increased 25.3 percent in 2000, 23.3 percent in 1999, and 20.6 percent in 1998. Comparable drugstore prescription sales were up 19.0 percent in 2000, 19.4 percent in 1999, and 15.6 percent in 1998.

Prescription sales were 55.2 percent of total sales for fiscal 2000 compared with 52.4 percent in 1999 and 49.6 percent in 1998.

Pharmacy sales trends are expected to continue, primarily because of expansion into new markets, increased penetration in existing markets, availability of new drugs, and demographic changes such as the aging population.

Shortcomings to Bear in Mind

- Walgreen often chooses a freestanding location on the site of an existing strip center—for instance, a piece of the mall parking lot. For the property's owners, this usually means an opportunity to charge more for the stand-alone space while renting out the old strip center space. Increasingly, however, supermarkets and other big retailers are starting to put exclusionary provisions in their leases prohibiting a drugstore from occupying free-standing space on shopping center properties they anchor. Walgreen management says it has encountered such provisions but insists that they aren't yet "a real problem."

- According to one analyst, "gross margins are likely to narrow as Walgreen becomes more aggressive on pricing in order to continue to gain market share from other drug, supermarket, and mass merchandise retailers. Gross margins could also come under pressure as an increase in third-party prescription sales as a percentage of total pharmacy sales drives pharmacy sales to nearly 58 percent of total sales." On the other hand, says the analyst, "operating margins should widen, aided by improved expense control and greater sales leverage."

- One problem with rapid growth is the current shortage of pharmacists. Management concedes that "it is the most challenging part of growth. However, while we have spot shortages, we expect to recruit the pharmacists we need to cover our 500 planned new stores in fiscal 2001."

- The stock has performed so well in recent years that its P/E multiple is extremely high.

Reasons to Buy

- Some investors are concerned that the company is diluting sales by putting stores so close together, "just cannibalizing yourself." To that concern, Mr. Bernauer replied, "I haven't gone to a party in two years where that question hasn't come up. The answer is yes—when we open a store very near another one, the old store usually sees a drop in sales. But in virtually every case, it builds back to its original volume and beyond. Here's the scenario: as you add stores, overall sales in the market increase, while expenses are spread over a larger base. Bottom line, profitability increases. Our most profitable markets are the ones where we've built the strongest market share."

- Investors are also wondering about e-commerce. They ask, "Is there a long-term future?" To this concern Mr. Bernauer said, "Though there's a lot of carnage on the early e-commerce road, we definitely see a future for *walgreens.com*. That's not, however, in 'delivered-to-your-door' merchandise. Frankly, we never thought there would be a big demand for prescriptions by mail, and we were correct—well over 90 percent of prescription orders placed through our Web site are for store pickup. It's not convenient, when you need a prescription or a few drugstore items to wait three days for it to show up.

  "What *does* excite us is using the Internet to provide better service and information. We're already communicating by e-mail with nearly 20,000 prescription customers per day."

- The company's new pharmacy system, Intercom Plus, is now up and running in all Walgreens stores across the country. This system, which cost over

$150 million, has raised Walgreen's service and productivity to a new level. While providing increased patient access to Walgreen's pharmacists, it also substantially raises the number of prescriptions each store can efficiently dispense.

- Walgreen's management is heartened by the increase in prescription usage in the United States due to the dramatic aging of the population. Between 1995 and 2005, the demographics of people age fifty-five or older in the United States will grow at a compound rate of 3.8 percent—double the rate of the rest of the population. The good news for Walgreen is that these graying Americans need twice as many prescriptions per year as the rest of the population.

- Every corner of Walgreen's strategy is focused on convenience: how fast people get into the store or are served in the drive-thru pharmacy, how fast they get out, how easily they find what they came to buy, and how well Walgreens' clerks remind them of what they forgot to buy.

- Food departments are another example. Recently, a major grocery chain cited drugstores as a reason behind disappointing sales gains: "Fill-in shopping needs," said the grocery CEO, "are increasingly being satisfied in convenience and drug stores." Walgreen, with highly convenient, on-the-way-home locations, is on the receiving end of this trend.

Total assets: $7,104 million
Current ratio: 1.54
Common shares outstanding: 1013 million
Return on 2000 shareholders' equity: 20.1%

	2000	1999	1998	1997	1996	1995	1994	1993
Revenues (millions)	21207	17839	15307	13363	11778	10395	9235	8295
Net income (millions)	756	624	514	436	372	321	282	245
Earnings per share	.74	.62	.51	.44	.38	.33	.29	.25
Dividends per share	.14	.13	.13	.12	.11	.10	.09	.08
Price High	45.8	33.9	30.2	16.8	10.9	7.8	5.7	5.6
Low	22.1	22.7	14.8	9.6	7.3	5.4	4.2	4.4

AGGRESSIVE GROWTH

Washington Mutual, Incorporated

1201 Third Avenue ▫ Seattle, Washington 98101 ▫ Investor contact: JoAnn DeGrande (206) 461-3186 ▫ Dividend reinvestment plan is available: (800) 234-5835 ▫ Web site: www.wamu.com ▫ Listed: NYSE ▫ Ticker symbol: WM ▫ S&P rating: B+ ▫ Value Line financial strength rating: A

In a move that enhances its position as a national leader in mortgage originations—and increases by more than 40 percent the residential mortgages it services—Washington Mutual acquired Fleet Mortgage Corporation in the spring of 2001. Fleet Mortgage, which was purchased for $660 million in cash, was a unit of FleetBoston Financial Corporation.

The transaction, along with the August 2000 acquisition of Bank United Corporation and the mortgage operations of the PNC Financial Services Group (February 2001), increased Washington Mutual's residential mortgage servicing portfolio to $451.5 billion, making the nation's largest thrift institution the nation's second largest mortgage-servicing company.

"This acquisition solidifies Washington Mutual's position as one of the nation's leading mortgage lenders," said Kerry Killinger, the company's chief executive officer. "This one move adds substantial scale to our mortgage-servicing business in an industry where economies of scale are increasingly important. The acquisition further diversifies our revenue base, strengthening our sources of recurring, noninterest income."

Company Profile

Washington Mutual, the nation's largest thrift institution, is a *Fortune* 500 company dating back to 1889. Washington Mutual provides a diversified line of products and services to consumers and small to midsize businesses. At the end of 2000, Washington Mutual and its subsidiaries had consolidated assets of $194.7 billion. The company operates 2,000 offices throughout the nation.

The company has a stake in consumer banking, financial services, mortgage banking, commercial banking, and consumer finance. Although the company operates principally in California, Washington, Oregon, Florida, Texas, and Utah, it has physical operations in forty states. Washington Mutual is:

• The eighth largest banking company and the largest domestic savings institution.

• Ranked number fifty-four among the *Fortune* 500 U.S. corporations, based on profit, in 2000.

• Holds the number one mortgage-market share position in California, Connecticut, Illinois, Massachusetts, Oregon, Washington, and Utah. With the recent acquisition of PNC Mortgage, the company is also the leading residential lender in the state of Pennsylvania.

• Ranked number four in a national survey of the Top 25 Companies for Executive Women in *Working Woman* magazine's December/January 2001 issue.

• Named one of the best companies to work for by *Washington CEO* magazine in the June 2000 issue.

• Received Employer of the Year award at the National Business Leadership Summit 2000 for its success in promoting the hiring of people with disabilities.

• Ranked twenty-second in America's fifty best companies for minorities by *Fortune* magazine in the July 10, 2000, issue. Of the company's nearly 30,000 employees, more than 11,000 are employees of color—representing 37 percent of the company's total work force.

• Named one of *Fortune* magazine's most-admired companies in the mortgage finance category in the February 19, 2001, issue.

Highlights of 2000

■ The company produced record earnings of $1.90 billion, or $2.36 per share, an increase of 12 percent, despite a tough interest rate environment most of the year.

■ WM achieved a 21.15 return on average common equity, comfortably exceeding the company's long-term target of 20 percent.

■ The bank's operating efficiency was 47.97 percent in 2000, compared with 47.16 percent in 1999, mainly due to the impact of interest rates and strategic balance sheet restructuring in the first half of 2000.

■ The ratio of nonperforming assets to total assets was a solid 0.53 percent at the end of 2000, compared with 0.55 percent a year earlier.

■ Washington Mutual's five-year total shareholder return through the end of 2000 (assuming the reinvestment of dividends) averaged 25.61 percent per year. This performance ranked in the top 25 percent of the nation's largest banks and outpaced the Standard & Poor's 500 and Standard & Poor's Financial Indices.

- Generated record loan volume of $66.01 billion, an increase of 12 percent over the prior year.
- Added more than 514,000 net new retail checking accounts, reaching a total of 4.8 billion accounts at the end of 2000.
- Announced the signing of an agreement to acquire Houston-based United Corporation, a move that will expand the company's consumer and business banking and speciality finance businesses. It gives Washington Mutual a top-tier presence in Texas, the third largest economy in the United States.
- Launched project Occasio, the bank's revolutionary concept stores in Las Vegas, and announced the extension of this concept into Phoenix, Arizona. The bank's competitors think it costs too much money to give people personal service. However, Washington Mutual has come up with a different approach, which it dubs Occasio, which is Latin for "favorable opportunity." According to the company, "By implementing this new retail banking strategy that combines new and efficient tools with friendly service, we're created a place that customers are excited to visit.

"This retail banking strategy was eighteen months in the making. We started by dismantling the traditional banking experience and starting anew—from the customer's prospective: Since we're all about serving people, we placed a concierge at the front entry to help direct them and answer their questions."

Shortcomings to Bear in Mind

- Interest rates are a major concern of financial institutions. Although interest rates fell in 2001, there could come a day when that trend will be reversed.

- The economy clearly slowed as 2001 got underway, and that trend, said management in the 2000 annual report, "suggests even greater diligence will be required to maintain credit quality. We adhere to underwriting standards that help place the company among the industry leaders in overall credit quality."

Reasons to Buy

- Interest rate cuts made by the Federal Reserve in 2001 will help Washington Mutual, according to R. Jay Tejera, director of research at Seattle's Ragen MacKenzie brokerage. "That's because the most important thing is the Fed cuts. That will just open up the margin." The margin Tejera referred to is the net interest margin, the difference between what a financial concern pays for funds what it earns from these funds. The greater the margin, the more money is made. At the end of 2000, Washington Mutual's margin was 2.42 percent. "That's the single biggest driver of profit, and I expect to see the margin close to 3 percent before year's end," Tejera said in early 2001.
- Washington Mutual added more than a half million checking accounts during 2000. Income from the checking-account base, plus mortgage activity, enabled the thrift's noninterest income to skyrocket to 30 percent, to $549 million, from $423 million in 1999.
- For years Washington Mutual has relied on a compensation program that offers tangible incentives to its employees and rewards its highest performers. Broad-based stock option plans give everyone in the company an opportunity to share in its success. Senior management bonuses, moreover, are tied to specific financial targets and the company's performance.
- In 2000 the bank invested in the expansion of Washington Mutual's presence online. In June the company

launched an innovative suite of financial-services Web sites at the URL *www.invest1to1.com*. The sites provide online financial planning, stock trading and research, and investment information for the company's mutual fund family with WM Group of Funds, as well as educational tools, online applications, and instant quotes for the bank's insurance subsidiary.

Washington Mutual also upgraded its mortgage lending site, *wamumortgage.com*, which experienced a 300 percent increase in traffic soon afterward. All of the sites can be reached through their individual addresses or through Washington Mutual's corporate Web site, *www.wamu.com*.

- Late in 2000 the bank launched a pilot stage of its state-of-the-art Optis automated mortgage origination platform, which puts the best of today's technology in the hands of consumers, Realtors and brokers. The Optis technology automates 80 percent of the steps in the mortgage process, making it easy and fast for the bank's customers to work with it.

- Noninterest income primarily includes depositor and other retail banking fees, securities and insurance fees and commissions, loan servicing and loan-related income, and gains on the sale of loans and mortgage-backed securities. In 2000, noninterest income increased 31 percent to $1.98 billion, compared with $1.51 billion in 1999. This increase was driven mostly by a 28 percent increase in depositor and other retail banking fees and ongoing gains on the sale of loans.

Importantly, noninterest income represented 32 percent of total income in 2000, up from 25 percent the prior year. This is clear evidence of the bank's success in reducing its reliance on net interest income. Equally important, noninterest income growth far exceeded increases in noninterest expenses, which totaled $3.13 billion in 2000, up 7 percent from the $2.91 billion of 1999.

Total assets: $194,716 million
Return on assets in 2000: 1.01%
Common shares outstanding: 877 million
Return on 2000 shareholders' equity: 21.2%

	2000	1999	1998	1997	1996	1995	1994	1993
Gross income (millions)	15767	13571	12457	7524	3408	1626	1316	1180
Net income (millions)	1899	1877	1643	823	114	191	172	175
Earnings per share	2.36	2.18	1.89	1.43	38	1.15	1.09	1.16
Dividends per share	.76	.65	.55	.47	.40	.34	.31	.22
Price High	37.3	30.5	34.4	32.3	20.4	13.1	11.1	12.6
Low	14.4	16.5	17.8	18.8	11.6	7.4	7.0	8.0

INCOME

Washington Real Estate Investment Trust

6110 Executive Boulevard ❑ Rockville, Maryland 20852-3927 ❑ Investor contact: Larry E. Finger (301) 255-0820 ❑ Dividend reinvestment plan is available: (800) 278-4353 ❑ Web site: www.writ.com ❑ Listed: NYSE ❑ Ticker symbol: WRE ❑ S&P rating: Not rated ❑ Value Line financial strength rating: B++

Washington Real Estate Investment Trust (WRIT) has had an enviable record. Over the past twenty-eight years, WRIT shareholders earned a compound annual rate of return of 18.5 percent. This compares favorably to the total returns (stock appreciation plus dividends) of 13.0 percent for the Standard & Poor's 500 and 12.6 percent for the real estate investment trust industry over the same period.

What's more, the company's record is consistent: WRIT has produced positive earnings every year since its inception. The company's streak of thirty-five consecutive years of increased earnings per share (EPS) is matched by only ten other publicly traded companies in the United States. The dividend has also been raised for thirty straight years. Finally, its streak of twenty-eight consecutive years of increased Funds From Operations (FFO) per share is nearly three times as long as any other in the real estate investment trust industry. FFO is often used by the REIT industry instead of earnings per share.

Company Profile

Washington Real Estate Investment Trust, founded in 1960, invests in a diversified range of income-producing properties. Management's purpose is to acquire and manage real estate investments in markets it knows well and to protect the company's assets from the risk of owning a single property type, such as apartments, office buildings, industrial parks, or shopping centers.

WRIT achieves its objectives by owning properties in four different categories. The trust's properties are primarily situated within a two-hour radius of Washington, D.C., that stretches from Philadelphia in the north to Richmond, Virginia, in the south. Its diversified portfolio at the end of 2000 consisted of 23 office buildings, 10 shopping centers, 9 apartment complexes, and 15 industrial distribution centers.

Highlights of 2000

Total revenues for 2000 increased $15.8 million, or 13 percent, to $134.7 million.

The percentage increase in real estate rental revenue from 1999 to 2000 by property type was office buildings, 15 percent; retail centers, 1 percent; multifamily, 14 percent; and industrial, 19 percent.

Office Buildings

During 2000, WRIT's office building revenues and operating income increased by 15 percent and 17 percent, respectively. These increases were primarily due to increased rental rates, acquisitions of Wayne Plaza and Courthouse Square in 2000, and acquisitions of 600 Jefferson Plaza, 1700 Research Boulevard, and Parklawn Plaza in 1999. However, there were offsetting factors, including the 1999 sales of Arlington Financial Center and 444 North Frederick Road, and a slight decline in occupancy rates.

Retail Centers

During 2000, the company's retail center revenues and operating income increased 1 percent and 2 percent, respectively. The increases were due to the 2000 acquisition of 833 S. Washington Street, combined with increased rental rates and occupancy levels, but offset in part by the 2000 sales of Prince William Plaza and Clairmont Center.

Multifamily

WRIT's multifamily revenues and operating income increased by 14 percent and 19 percent, respectively, in 2000. These increases were primarily due to the 1999 acquisition of Avondale Apartments, combined with increased rental rates and occupancy levels.

Industrial

The company's industrial revenues and operating income increased 19 percent and 21 percent, respectively, in 2000. These increases were primarily due to the 1999 acquisitions of Dulles South IV,

Amvax, and Sully Square. Other factors included increased rental rates and occupancy levels, notably at Northern Virginia Industrial Park, but were offset to some degree by the loss of revenues from the 1999 sales of the Department of Commerce Industrial Center and V Street Distribution Center.

Shortcomings to Bear in Mind

- Investors may be concerned that the economy's weakness in 2001 will have a negative impact on Washington Real Estate Trust. According to CEO Edmund B. Cronin Jr., "Historically, the Greater Washington-Baltimore has outperformed the national economy in all economic cycles. I see no reason today why history will not repeat itself. Greater Washington's economic engines in a softening economy as well as during growth periods are the federal government and the technology industry. The latter has a risk profile substantially lower than many of those on the West Coast and in New England.

  "One aspect of this lower risk profile is that the greater Washington-Baltimore technology sector achieves 38 percent of its sales to the federal government, as compared to 5 percent in Silicon Valley. That, along with the fact that federal government spending will continue to grow, provides a platform for a soft landing in this region."

Reasons to Buy

- The Greater Washington, D.C., economy is a unique blend of "old economy" service companies and "new economy" high-technology growth companies, anchored by the very significant federal government presence. On the growth side:
  - Washington Dulles International Airport and Baltimore-Washington International Airport were ranked number one and two in passenger growth in 1999, the most recent year for which data are available.
  - The Greater Washington region ranks first in the United States in high-tech and bio-tech employment.
  - George Mason University Center for Regional Analysis (GMU) projects economic growth in the region of 4.1 percent in 2001, which is substantially higher than is projected for the nation as a whole.
  - Federal spending in this region has increased every year for twenty consecutive years, even in years when federal spending has decreased nationally. GMU projects federal spending in the region will grow by 3 percent in 2001.

    While growth is very important, from an investment perspective, economic stability is equally important. In this context, no other region in the country can compete with the Greater Washington region:
  - Federal government spending accounts for 31 percent of the area's gross regional product.
  - The Greater Washington region is not exposed to new or old economy manufacturing fluctuations.
  - Greater Washington is home to thirty-two colleges and universities, several of which have world-class reputations at both the undergraduate and graduate levels.

- MAE East, situated in Tysons Corner, Virginia, is one of only two Internet convergence centers in the United States. The presence of MAE East and the thousands of high-tech firms in the area has spawned a concentration of data centers in the region where large Internet and other high-tech firms process tremendous amounts of data. As a result, it is estimated that up to 60 percent of the world's Internet traffic flows through northern Virginia.

This concentration of high-tech companies has served to attract even more high-tech firms. Amazon.com, Cisco Systems, and Global Crossing have all set up shop in the Washington-Baltimore market.

The region's real estate markets are the beneficiary of this growth. Vacancies are extremely low, and rental rate growth is very strong.

- Prior to acquiring a property, WRIT performs extensive inspections, tests, and financial analyses to gain confidence about the property's future operating performance, as well as any required near-term improvements and long-term capital expenditures. Upon completion of this evaluation, the company develops well-informed operating projections for the property. Accordingly, when the company announces an acquisition and its anticipated return on investment, it is confident that the property will meet or exceed its projections.
- Washington Real Estate Investment Trust has always recognized the value of capital improvements to remain competitive, increase revenues, reduce operating costs, and maintain and increase the value of its properties.
- FFO per share growth is the most widely recognized earnings performance measure in the REIT industry. WRIT has outperformed industry average FFO per share growth by over 400 basis points over the last three years. (One percent equals 100 basis points.) The extent of WRIT's outperformance, moreover, has increased in each of the last three years. The company's average 13.5 per share growth over the past three years is one of the highest in the industry.

- Another common REIT industry performance measure is core portfolio net operating income (NOI) growth or same store NOI growth. NOI represents real estate portfolio income before interest expense, depreciation, and corporate general and administrative expenses.

Core portfolio NOI growth excludes income attributable to new acquisitions and developments and is therefore a good measure of how a company's existing portfolio performed in the most recent period as compared to the prior period. WRIT's core portfolio NOI growth is among the highest in the industry and dramatically higher than the REIT industry overall. Using this measure, Washington Real Estate had average annual growth of 8.5 percent in the past three years, compared with the industry's 5.6 percent.

Total assets: $632 million
Current ratio: not relevant
Return on 2000 equity: 17.4%
Common shares outstanding: 36 million

		2000	1999	1998	1997	1996	1995	1994	1993
Revenues (millions)		135	119	104	79	66	53	46	39
Net income (millions)		45	44	41	30	28	26	23	22
Funds from operations		1.79	1.57	1.39	1.23	1.13	1.05	.96	.93
Earnings per share		1.16	1.02	.96	.90	.88	.88	.82	.80
Dividends per share		1.23	1.16	1.11	1.07	1.03	.99	.92	.89
Price	High	25.0	18.8	18.8	19.6	17.5	16.6	21.1	24.8
	Low	14.3	13.8	15.1	15.5	15.3	13.9	14.9	18.6

Weyerhaeuser Company

Post Office Box 9777 □ Federal Way, Washington 98063-9777 □ Investor contact: Kathryn F. McAuley (253) 924-2058 □ Dividend reinvestment plan is available: (800) 561-4405 □ Web site: www.weyerhaeuser.com □ Listed: NYSE □ Ticker symbol: WY □ S&P rating: B+ □ Value Line financial strength rating: B++

A century ago, Weyerhaeuser was a fledgling enterprise in the woods of Washington. When the company was founded on January 18, 1900, few could have foreseen how the industry would develop. The concept of timber as a renewable resource, for instance, was unthinkable in 1900. Today, it is the guiding principle of the industry.

Or, who would have guessed that wood would eventually be used in everything from aspirin to apparel, in addition to lumber and paper? And who would have thought that Weyerhaeuser would be making engineered wood products that have the benefits of wood and the strength of steel?

Finally, could Frederick Weyerhaeuser and the company's other founders have envisioned what their company would become in the year 2000? Here is how it looks today:

• The world's largest owner of softwood timber and the world's largest producer of softwood market pulp and softwood lumber.

• One of the largest producers of containerboard packaging and fine paper.

• The world's second largest producer of oriented strand board (OSB).

• The world's largest producer and distributor of engineered wood products.

• One of the largest producers of hardwood lumber.

• A company that serves customers in more than sixty countries.

Company Profile

Weyerhaeuser is primarily engaged in the growing and harvesting of timber and the manufacture, distribution, and sale of forest products. It is also in real estate development and construction.

The company's wood products businesses produce and sell softwood lumber, plywood, and veneer; composite panels; oriented strand board; hardboard; hardwood lumber and plywood; doors; treated products; logs; chips and timber.

These products are sold primarily through the company's own sales organizations. Building materials are sold to wholesalers, retailers, and industrial users.

Weyerhaeuser's pulp, paper, and packaging businesses include:

• Pulp—manufactures chemical wood pulp for world markets.

• Newsprint—manufactures newsprint at the company's North Pacific Paper Corporation mill and markets it to West Coast and Japanese newspaper publishers.

• Paper—manufactures and markets a range of both coated and uncoated fine papers through paper merchants and printers.

• Containerboard Packaging—manufactures linerboard and corrugating medium, which is primarily used in the production of corrugated shipping containers, and manufactures and markets corrugated shipping containers for industrial and agricultural packaging.

• Paperboard—manufactures bleached paperboard that is used for production of liquid containers and is marketed to West Coast and Pacific Rim customers.

• Recycling—operates an extensive wastepaper collection system and markets it to company mills and worldwide customers.

• Chemicals—produces chlorine, caustic, and tall oil, which is used principally by the company's pulp, paper, and packaging operations.

Highlights of 2000

- Net earnings were $840 million, or $3.72 per share. This compares with $527 million, or $2.56 per share, in 1999. The company's improvement reflects the additional earnings from the MacMillan Bloedel and Trus Joist acquisitions, stronger pulp and paper markets, another strong performance from the real estate segment, and continued focus on operating more efficiently. The company's net earnings in 2000 include the costs of $56 million associated with the integration of acquisitions.
- Net sales were a record $16 billion, or well above the $12.8 billion of the prior year.
- Cash flow provided by operations before working capital changes was $1.7 billion, compared with $1.4 billion in 1999.
- Integration of the MacMillan Bloedel and Trus Joist acquisitions currently is producing $141 million in annual synergies, ahead of projections. Management expects to achieve its goal of $200 million before the end of 2002.

Shortcomings to Bear in Mind

- The major markets, both domestic and foreign, in which the company sells its products are highly competitive, with numerous strong sellers competing in each realm.

  Many of Weyerhaeuser's products compete with substitutes for wood and wood fiber products. The real estate and financial services subsidiaries, moreover, also compete in highly competitive markets with numerous regional and national firms in real estate development and construction and in financial services.

Reasons to Buy

- Weyerhaeuser made a hostile, $7-billion bid for Willamette Industries in late 2000. Willamette is a leading forest-products company based in Portland, Oregon. By early 2001, Willamette was still resisting, but Weyerhaeuser's new CEO, Steven R. Rogel (who began in December 1997), had not given up the chase. "There is no better fit for us than Willamette," he said. "All of our focus is to bring that transaction to a close as rapidly as we can."
- Weyerhaeuser is uniquely positioned in its industry. It manages more privately owned timber than any other company. Likewise, Weyerhaeuser leads the industry in private forestry, having launched—nearly a generation ago—a program to maximize timber yield on every acre of planted forest land.
- To build on the timber asset and increase shareholder value, Weyerhaeuser is following a strategy that contains five elements:
  - Sell or dispose of nonstrategic assets.
  - Work assiduously to upgrade the company's portfolio of land, mills, and other facilities.
  - Ally strategically with domestic and international partners.
  - Emphasize value-added products.
  - Continually improve product quality and the cost efficiency of production.
- The company is improving its returns on its pulp, paper, and packaging sector by reducing its exposure to commodity grades, improving process reliability, and maintaining tight controls on capital spending.
- As a leader in the use of advanced silviculture practices, Weyerhaeuser is getting the most out of the trees on the millions of acres of land the company owns or manages. Because of these practices, the

company will greatly increase how much timber it harvests over the next ten years. This increased harvest level comes at a time when privately managed woodlands such as Weyerhaeuser's are being called upon to play an even bigger role in meeting society's demand for softwood sawtimber. The company has also selectively pruned many of its trees to produce knot-free lumber and other higher-value products that command higher market values and maximize the value the company gets from its timber harvest.

- The company believes that it has good prospects in the Southern Hemisphere—especially New Zealand and South America. Weyerhaeuser owns a 51 percent interest in 193,000 acres of managed forest land and related assets in New Zealand. As the majority owner, the company is responsible for the management and marketing activities of the joint venture.

  In 1998 the company also made additional investments through its partnership with institutional investors known as the World Timberfund. This partnership currently holds a 97 percent interest in a venture that has acquired 234,000 acres of private agricultural land in Uruguay that is being converted into plantation forests.

- Weyerhaeuser has been narrowing its business focus since 1990. The company divested its milk carton, personal care products, insurance, nursery products, and gypsum wallboard businesses. What's more, WY reduced its investments by selling selected real estate assets.

  Extensive restructuring was carried out by former CEO John W. Creighton Jr. when he took the reins in 1991. He helped transform Weyerhaeuser—a one-time laggard—into one of the industry's most profitable players. In years past, investors scorned Weyerhaeuser as unwieldy and paternalistic. It was loaded down with outdated mills. What's more, it was hobbled by a host of noncore subsidiaries making everything from milk cartons to disposable diapers. Besides jettisoning these business, Creighton led his managers through an eighteen-month reengineering in which each mill and tree farm had to redesign the way it worked. Creighton planned to add $700 million to operating earnings by 1995—a goal he achieved a year earlier than anticipated.

- Weyerhaeuser owns or manages an enormous expanse of highly productive forest land in North America. Thirty years ago, the company had the foresight to pioneer the High Yield Forestry program. As a result, the company will see a dramatic increase in its timber harvest over the next twenty years. By the year 2020, the timber harvest from the land WY owns and manages in the United States will increase by about 70 percent from 1995 levels and significantly enhance cash flow from this source. Meanwhile, Weyerhaeuser's manufacturing facilities are operating more efficiently and producing higher quality products than ever before.

- The company is also differentiating other parts of its product line. For instance, Weyerhaeuser's Containerboard Packaging business began exploring new packaging solutions for customers. What's more, its Pulp operation is working on new absorbency fibers. Both efforts will help the company develop higher-value products capable of producing new growth opportunities and higher margins. New absorbency fibers, for instance, improve product function and provide manufacturers with greater flexibility and speed in commercializing their product upgrades. Management is convinced this will allow providers to develop a greater range of products and increase demand for its own products.

■ The company's last two acquisitions—MacMillan Bloedel and Trus Joist—changed the face of Weyerhaeuser. MacMillan Bloedel, for instance, significantly increased the company's Canadian presence. Weyerhaeuser made its first Canadian investment in 1965, and then steadily increased is presence north of the border.

But it was the purchase of MacMillan Bloedel in 1999 that made Weyerhaeuser one of Canada's largest forest products company. Today, WY's Canadian operations employs 12,500 people who produce 39 percent of the company's lumber, 59 percent of its oriented strand board, 42 percent of its pulp, and 40 percent of its fine paper.

Total assets: $18,195 million
Current ratio: 1.24
Common shares outstanding: 213 million
Return on 2000 shareholders' equity: 12.0%

	2000	1999	1998	1997	1996	1995	1994	1993
Revenues (millions)	15980	12262	10766	11210	11114	11788	10398	9545
Net income (millions)	840	527	339	351	463	983	589	463
Earnings per share	3.72	2.56	1.70	1.76	2.34	4.83	2.86	2.26
Dividends per share	1.60	1.60	1.60	1.60	1.60	1.50	1.20	1.20
Price High	74.5	73.9	62.0	63.9	49.9	50.4	51.3	46.5
Low	36.1	49.6	36.8	42.6	39.5	36.9	35.8	36.3

INCOME

WGL Holdings, Inc.
(formerly Washington Gas Light Company)

1100 H Street, N.W. ▢ Washington, D.C. 20080 ▢ Investor contact: Melissa Bockelman (202) 624-6410 ▢ Dividend reinvestment program is available: (888) 269-8845 ▢ Fiscal year ends September 30 ▢ Listed NYSE ▢ Web site: www.washgas.com ▢ Ticker symbol: WGL ▢ S&P rating: A- ▢ Value Line financial strength rating: A

Washington Gas Light (the principal subsidiary of WGL Holdings, Inc.) provides natural gas to an area that is blessed with a number of advantages over most other geographic regions:

● The Washington area has more high-technology workers than Silicon Valley.

● More than half of households in the region include two or more wage earners.

● The metropolitan area's residents are the most educated in the nation.

● Washington, the nation's most affluent metropolitan area, has an average after-tax household income of nearly $57,000 (29 percent above the U.S. average).

● $12.8 billion in new and expanded infrastructure projects are planned for the region over the next twenty-five years.

Company Profile
As of November 2000, WGL Holdings, Inc. became the parent company for Washington Gas Light Company and other subsidiaries that operated under Washington Gas prior to this restructuring. The new company holds Washington Gas and a well-balanced group of growing and successful energy-related, retail businesses that includes natural gas and power marketing; consumer financing; and commercial and residential

heating, ventilating, and air conditioning services.

• Washington Gas Light Company is the local natural gas distribution company that provides natural gas service to more than 875,000 residential, commercial, and industrial customers throughout metropolitan D.C. and the surrounding region, including parts of Maryland, Virginia, and West Virginia. The company, which serves an area of 6,648 square miles, has been providing natural gas to the D.C. region for 152 years.

• Hampshire Gas Company is the regulated natural gas storage business that serves Washington Gas.

• American Combustion Industries, Inc. (ACI) is a full-service mechanical and electrical contractor involved in the installation and service of HVAC systems. ACI specializes in large-scale commercial and federal installations, including power plants and cogeneration systems.

• Washington Gas Energy Systems, Inc. is in the business of providing turnkey design/build renovation projects to the commercial and federal markets. Washington Gas Energy Systems specializes in the innovative engineering and design of cost-saving energy systems.

• Washington Gas Energy Services, Inc. is a retail energy marketing company that serves the greater Washington, D.C., area and beyond to Baltimore, Maryland, and Richmond, Virginia. The company markets natural gas and electricity to consumers at competitive prices.

• Brandywood Estates, Inc. is a partner, along with a major developer, in a venture designed to develop land for sale or lease in Prince George's County, Maryland.

• WG Maritime Plaza I, Inc. holds a partnership interest in the first phase of the development of a twelve-acre parcel of land in Washington, D.C.

• Washington Gas Consumer Services, Inc. evaluates and performs unregulated functions. None are being performed at present.

• Crab Run Gas Company is an exploration and production subsidiary whose assets are being managed by an Oklahoma-based limited partnership.

• Primary Investors, LLC, operating as Primary MultiCraft, currently provides essential residential and light commercial HVAC and plumbing services. The company also engages in the installation, retrofit, and service of equipment related to those services.

Highlights of 2000

■ For the third consecutive winter, the average temperature in the company's service region was five degrees warmer than normal. Even so, WGL Holdings performed well with record earnings per share of $1.79, an increase of 22 percent.

■ Return on common equity improved to 11.9 percent, compared with 10.4 percent in 1999.

■ The annual dividend per share was raised by $.02, while the payout ratio remained below 70 percent, which is considered good for a public utility.

■ Diversified, energy-related operations contributed $.06 to per-share earnings.

■ The company added 29,436 new customers, the most ever in a single fiscal year. This amounted to an increase of 3.5 percent. In northern Virginia, moreover, meter growth topped 4 percent, more than twice the industry average.

■ The company has one of the industry's highest credit ratings and has a strong balance sheet.

Shortcomings to Bear in Mind

■ In 1999 the company was joined by Thayer Capital Partners in committing $25 million each as co-investors in Primary Investors. Primary then acquired nine companies, most of which are residential HVAC firms and all of which are situated in the Washington, D.C., metropolitan area. However, Primary has not had smooth sailing in integrating the nine companies, and no additional acquisitions are planned at this time. Although WGL is disappointed by this first-year performance, management is committed to Primary's business strategy. According to CEO James H. DeGraffenreidt Jr., "We believe that our recent steps to strengthen the leadership team and its plans to achieve better execution will lead to stronger performance in the upcoming year."

- Washington Gas Light has been in the consumer financing business for many years. However, in 2000 that operation produced net income of only $800,000, down substantially from $1.7 million the prior year. The problem stemmed from higher interest costs and fewer loans with deferred payment terms. To correct the problem, the company has been adding seasoned professionals, refining sales efforts, and implementing new information systems.

Reasons to Buy

- WGL's 22 percent increase in earnings in 2000 came about because of some strategic decisions made by the company in recent years to enhance long-term value by transforming the company. WGL has improved the way it manages, expands, repairs, and maintains its pipes, plants, and facilities; the way it prepares and deploys its people; and the way it serves its customers. These decisions resulted in 12 percent lower operation and maintenance expenses in 2000. What's more, these lower expenses are expected to produce even greater success in the future.

- WGL has been steadily expanding its energy-related retail business sector. The company's commercial heating,

ventilating, and air conditioning (HVAC) businesses have continued to grow since the acquisition of American Combustion Industries, Inc. (ACI) in 1998 and are delivering solid results. These businesses, moreover, increased revenues by 52 percent in fiscal 2000 to $47 million. Net income climbed from $1.2 million to $3.2 million in 2000.

- The company's franchise area possesses a significant number of conversion opportunities for Washington Gas Light to pursue. Conversion takes place when owners of older homes that use some other energy source (typically electricity or fuel oil) for their space heating are persuaded to convert to natural gas. The company now has about two-thirds of the business in existing structures in its service territory.

The conversion potential is a legacy of events that took place during the 1970s. This was when natural gas was perceived to be in short supply. To "cure" the problem, WGL's regulators imposed a moratorium on new gas hook-ups. This ruling prohibited Washington Gas from investing in facilities to serve new customers. With natural gas denied to them, homeowners turned to electricity. Electric heat pumps became a popular alternative for heating new homes built during the mid- to late-1970s. As a consequence, a thick ring, composed of thousands of electrically heated homes, sprung up around the company's service territory. Washington Gas calls this an "electric doughnut."

When the moratorium was lifted in 1980, WGL had to make large capital investments to extend its gas line beyond the doughnut so that it could provide service to new customers in the growing parts of its franchise area. Meanwhile, the electric heat pumps are now nearing the end of their useful lives. Consequently, with the favorable economics and greater effectiveness of natural gas heating, coupled with the presence of natural gas mains crossing through the area, the aging electric doughnut provides Washington Gas with a significant opportunity to tap into these lines to recapture this business from the electric company.

■ Washington Gas enjoys the stability of a customer base that is made up of 92 percent of residential customers, with 95 percent of these using natural gas for space heating. Of the remaining 8 percent, most are small commercial accounts that also use natural gas for space heating. Lacking are the industrial customers that can make the territory sensitive to the ups and downs of the economy.

On the other hand, since WGL sells most of its gas for space heating, it is particularly sensitive to changes in the weather. To offset this weather sensitivity

the company features declining rate blocks. Translated, this means that successively higher levels of usage each month are charged lower incremental rates. In addition, there are other temperature-shielding rate mechanisms. Even so, the weather still makes earnings quite volatile.

To be sure, the vagaries of the weather also help or hurt other natural gas companies. Some of them have found a way to mitigate this volatility by making a deal with the regulators to set up a weather normalization scheme. Under this arrangement, the utility adds an extra charge during a warm winter and gives back a little when the heating season is abnormally cold. However, Washington Gas Light has rejected this idea, fearing that the various state commissions would lower their allowed rate of return as an offset.

Total assets: $1,940 million
Current ratio: 0.96
Common shares outstanding: 46 million
Return on 2000 shareholders' equity: 11.9%

	2000	1999	1998	1997	1996	1995	1994	1993
Revenues (millions)	1249	972	1040	1056	970	829	915	894
Net income (millions)	83	67	69	82	82	63	60	55
Earnings per share	1.79	1.47	1.54	1.85	1.85	1.45	1.42	1.31
Dividends per share	1.24	1.22	1.20	1.17	1.14	1.12	1.11	1.09
Price High	31.5	29.4	30.8	31.4	25.0	22.4	21.3	22.9
Low	21.8	21.0	23.1	20.9	19.1	16.1	16.0	18.1

AGGRESSIVE GROWTH

Zebra Technologies Corporation

333 Corporate Woods Parkway □ Vernon Hills, Illinois 60061-3109 □ Investor contact: Douglas A. Fox (847) 793-6735 □ Dividend reinvestment plan not available □ Web site: www.zebra.com □ Listed: Nasdaq □ Ticker symbol: ZBRA □ S&P rating: B+ □ Value Line financial strength rating: B+

For nearly thirty years, Zebra Technologies has focused on a single idea: take bar code printing to its fullest potential. Zebra is the world's leading manufacturer of bar code label printing systems. Zebra's printers,

supplies, and software are hard at work in all types of companies, big and small. Today, more than 60 percent of the Fortune 500 companies in over ninety countries use Zebra products to become more productive, more efficient, and more profitable.

Zebra's technology can benefit its customers in a host of ways. For instance, Wal-Mart uses lightweight Zebra mobile printing systems for several in-store printing functions, such as shelf labeling and merchandise re-ticketing. In another sector, new compliance labeling, such as the General Motors GM1724-A standard, uses high-density, two-dimensional bar codes to pack large amounts of information onto a shipping label. Clear and accurate scanning of these labels is assured with the use of Zebra printers and supplies. Far to the north, Alaska Marine Lines keeps costs low and productivity high in delivering essential food, clothing, and building materials to the people of southeast Alaska. Using Zebra printers and PolyPro synthetic labels, Alaska Marine Lines's automatic data-capture system speeds goods from port to port, while customers track their orders on the Web.

Bar code printers, supplies and related products represent an $8-billion industry that continues growing as businesses in more and more countries adopt the technology. And if analysts's projection are on the mark, sales could climb at a 15 percent to 20 percent annual clip, putting the industry at the $18-billion level by 2004.

Bar codes have become ubiquitous, showing up on parcels, food packages and practically every retail product consumers purchase. Zebra Technologies believes the advantage afforded by thermal transfer printing, including the ability to print high-resolution images on a wide variety of label materials at a lower cost than that of competing technologies, make it the technology of choice in Zebra's target market for the foreseeable future.

One of the fastest-growing sectors in the bar code labeling industry is plastic card printers, which have the ability to produce on-site, full-color, photographic quality plastic cards. The company believes personalized card applications, such as driver's licenses, loyalty cards, school and work identification cards, and financial transaction cards, are well suited to benefit from plastic printer card technology. Plastic card printers range in price from $2,495 to $9,995.

Company Profile

Zebra Technologies designs, manufactures, and supports a broad range of direct thermal and thermal transfer bar code label printers, receipt printers, instant-issuance plastic card printers, and secure identification printing systems, as well as related accessories and support software.

The company markets its products worldwide, principally to manufacturing and service organizations for use in automatic identification, data collection, and personal identification systems.

The company's equipment is designed to operate at the user's location or on a mobile basis to produce and dispense high-quality bar code labels and plastic cards in time-sensitive applications and under a variety of environmental conditions. Applications for Zebra's products are diverse. They include applications where bar-coding is used to identify or track objects or information, particularly in situations that require high levels of data accuracy and where speed and reliability are critical. Plastic cards are used where secure, reliable identification is required on-demand.

Applications for the company's technology cut across all industries and geographic locations. They include inventory control, small-package delivery, baggage handling, automated warehousing, just-in-time manufacturing, employee time and attendance records, file-management systems, hospital information systems, shop floor control, and library systems, among others. At the end of 2000, some two million Zebra printers were installed in more than ninety countries.

The company believes the growth of its label and receipt printers will be enhanced by the proliferation of bar code label standardization programs. These programs are driven by competitive forces on businesses worldwide to reduce costs, improve quality and increase productivity.

The company offers forty bar code printer models. At the high end of the label printer market, Zebra produced printers targeted at applications requiring continuous operations in high-output, mission-critical settings. These units provide a wide variety of option configurations, features, print widths, speeds and dot densities, including standard 600-dpi printer. The company offers five Zebra models, with list prices ranging from $4,295 to $7,495.

The company also offers ten printer models designed for less demanding applications. These units offer fewer option configurations and features, and are priced from $1,395 to $3,295.

Highlights of 2000

In April of 2000, Zebra acquired Comtec Information Systems for $88.5 million in cash. Situated in Warwick, Rhode Island, Comtec is an industry leader in the design, manufacture and support of portable wireless thermal printing solutions. Comtec also offers a comprehensive line of specialty labeling supplies, wireless radio and infrared communication integration expertise, and professional services. Comtec has leading market positions in the retail, transportation, warehousing and distribution, hospitality and gaming, and healthcare industries. Comtec's products are used by more than 60 percent of the top 100 retailers in the nation.

Zebra's net sales increased 19.7 percent in 2000 to a record $481.6 million. A significant portion of this sales growth was due to the addition of sales derived from the Comtec acquisition. Hardware sales increased 17.6 percent, to $377.8 million. Sales of supplies increased 16.8 percent, to $80.7 million.

Because of the higher proportion of service revenue in the printer business from the Comtec acquisition, service and software revenue advanced 113.7 percent, to $17.3 million.

Geographically, North American sales increased 25 percent, to a record $301.6 million. The high concentration of Comtec sales in North America contributed to the sales growth in the region.

International sales for 2000 were $180 million, up 11.9 percent and accounted for 37.4 percent of Zebra's net sales. All international regions experienced sales increases to record levels, with strong sales growth posted in Asia Pacific and Latin America.

Shortcomings to Bear in Mind

- The company derives about 37 percent of its net sales from abroad. Like all companies with substantial foreign business, Zebra can suffer when adverse movements in exchange rates drag down otherwise strong results from its overseas operations. The company says it is most vulnerable to dips in the value of the euro, the Deutsche mark, the pound sterling, and the yen.
- Another concern is the proliferation of alternative bar code and automatic identification technologies. Depending on their needs, businesses can choose from among ink jet, laser, impact dot matrix, and laser etching technologies. For its part, Zebra Technologies points out that its products generally provide the best low-cost, high-quality printing solutions for its target markets. However, a competitor's technological breakthrough with any one of these alterna-